Praise for
The Origins of the Grand Alliance:
Anglo-American Military Collaboration from the Panay Incident to Pearl Harbor

"In *The Origins of the Grand Alliance* William T. Johnsen provides a uniquely empathetic description and analysis of the stresses and strains that characterized Anglo-American relations in the years leading up to World War II. Johnsen's grip on the strategic, political, and cultural contexts is thoroughly persuasive. This is a work on the experience of cooperation, including military planning, in a time of approaching hostilities. It is a very, very good book!"

—Colin S. Gray, author of
Strategy and Defence Planning: Meeting the Challenge of Uncertainty

"The World War II Anglo-American 'special relationship' constitutes one of the closest alliances in history. Contrary to popular opinion, however, that was not inevitable, and creating the alliance was not an easy process. Nor was it a process that began only after Pearl Harbor. To the contrary, by the time the United States officially entered the war in December 1941, the two nations already possessed a combined global strategy and a series of military accords that their representatives had reached in the preceding four years. Making excellent use of a wide variety of unpublished document and manuscript collections in Great Britain and the United States as well as available published sources, William Johnsen explains just how and why these military components of the alliance originated and developed before the official U.S. entry into the war. In doing so he analyzes and offers key insights into the events, individuals, and early agreements that enabled the two nations to establish such close military bonds and operate so effectively from 1942–1945."

—Mark A. Stoler, author of
Allies in War: Britain and America against the Axis Powers, 1940–1945

"In this significant work, Johnsen describes and analyzes the initial steps in building the coalition that defeated the Axis Powers. His thorough, balanced use of archival sources and his masterful consideration of the vast array of secondary sources touching on his subject result in clear images of key personalities, institutions, and processes. This book will guide twenty-first-century strategists while earning accolades from historians."

—Brigadier General Harold Nelson, USA (Ret.),
former U.S. Army chief of military history

"This is an important contribution to the historical understanding of the military history of World War II and represents the most authoritative account of the military dimensions of the Anglo-American relationship to date."

—Theodore A. Wilson, author of
Coalition Warfare: A Guide to the Issues

"Johnsen makes a singular contribution to the literature by not only synthesizing the findings of other scholars, but also bringing his own research and analysis to bear on an array of critical issues."

—Colonel Paul L. Miles, USA (Ret.)

The Origins of the Grand Alliance

BATTLES AND CAMPAIGNS

The Battles and Campaigns series examines the military and strategic results of particular combat techniques, strategies, and methods used by soldiers, sailors, and airmen throughout history. Focusing on different nations and branches of the armed services, this series aims to educate readers by detailed analysis of military engagements.

SERIES EDITOR: Roger Cirillo

An AUSA Book

THE ORIGINS OF THE GRAND ALLIANCE

ANGLO-AMERICAN
MILITARY COLLABORATION
FROM THE PANAY INCIDENT
TO PEARL HARBOR

WILLIAM T. JOHNSEN

Copyright © 2016 by The University Press of Kentucky

Scholarly publisher for the Commonwealth,
serving Bellarmine University, Berea College, Centre College of Kentucky, Eastern
Kentucky University, The Filson Historical Society, Georgetown College, Kentucky
Historical Society, Kentucky State University, Morehead State University, Murray
State University, Northern Kentucky University, Transylvania University, University
of Kentucky, University of Louisville,
and Western Kentucky University.
All rights reserved.

Editorial and Sales Offices: The University Press of Kentucky
663 South Limestone Street, Lexington, Kentucky 40508-4008
www.kentuckypress.com

The views expressed in this book are those of the author and do not necessarily reflect
the official policy or position of the U.S. Army War College, the Department of the
Army, the Department of Defense, or the U.S. Government.

Library of Congress Cataloging-in-Publication Data

Names: Johnsen, William Thomas, 1952– author.
Title: The origins of the grand alliance : Anglo-American military
  collaboration from the Panay incident to Pearl Harbor / William T. Johnsen.
Description: Lexington, Kentucky : The University Press of Kentucky, 2016. |
  Series: Battles and campaigns | Includes bibliographical references and
  index.
Identifiers: LCCN 2016018515| ISBN 9780813168333 (hardcover : alk. paper) |
  ISBN 9780813168357 (pdf) | ISBN 9780813168364 (epub)
Subjects: LCSH: United States—Military relations—Great Britain. | Great
  Britain—Military relations—United States. | United States—Foreign
  relations—1933–1945. | Military planning—United States—History—20th
  century. | Military planning—Great Britain—History—20th century. |
  World War, 1939–1945—Diplomatic history. | Alliances—History—20th
  century.
Classification: LCC E183.8.G7 J636 2016 | DDC 327.73009/04—dc23
LC record available at https://lccn.loc.gov/201601851

This book is printed on acid-free paper meeting
the requirements of the American National Standard
for Permanence in Paper for Printed Library Materials.

Manufactured in the United States of America.

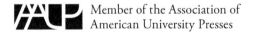 Member of the Association of
American University Presses

For Kathy, my best friend,
to whom I owe it all

Contents

List of Illustrations   viii

Preface and Acknowledgments   ix

Dramatis Personae   xiii

List of Abbreviations   xviii

Prologue   xix

Introduction   1

1. Lessons Lived, Learned, Lost: Episodic Progress in U.S. and British Experiences in Coalition Warfare, 1900–1918   11
2. Neither Friend nor Foe: U.S.-British Relations in the Interwar Years   33
3. Groping in the Dark: U.S.-British Coalition Encounters, 1936–1939   49
4. Ties That Bind: The Effects of Supply Negotiations on Anglo-American Cooperation, 1938–1940   65
5. The Americans Come to Listen, August–September 1940   81
6. Two Steps Forward, One Step Back: Inching toward Collaboration, Autumn 1940   105
7. Full-Dress Talks: The American-British Conversations-1 Conference, January–March 1941   131
8. Easier Said Than Done: Implementing the American-British Conversations-1 Report, April–July 1941   161
9. Muddy Waters: Reexamining the Coalition's Grand Strategy, June–October 1941   189
10. Racing an Unseen Clock: More Problems Than Solutions   217

Conclusion   235

Chronology   257

Notes   261

Selected Bibliography   343

Index   387

Photographs follow page 188

Illustrations

Maps

1. Areas of Strategic Responsibility in the Atlantic under ABC-1   154
2. Areas of Strategic Responsibility in the Pacific and Far East under ABC-1   156
3. Areas of Strategic Responsibility, 1 December 1941   249

Figures

1. U.S. Military Mission under ABC-1   153
2. British Military Mission under ABC-1   153
3. U.S. Special Observer Group, London, May 1941   168
4. British Joint Staff Mission, Washington, D.C., May 1941   169
5. British Army Staff, British Joint Staff Mission, May 1941   170
6. British Admiralty Delegation, British Joint Staff Mission, June 1941   170

Preface and Acknowledgments

As this is a work that attempts to address questions, it seems legitimate to begin with the fundamental question, Why—seventy-five years on and thousands of books later—another book on World War II? On one level, despite the number of books on the subject, the reading public—whether longtime readers or neophytes—retains a considerable appetite for the conflict, its titanic clash of ideologies, and the conduct of massive campaigns in the air, on land, and at sea on a scale likely never again to be replicated. Nowhere is this truer than in Great Britain and the United States, the two main partners in this narrative. More importantly, studies of World War II still have much to offer in general as well as in specific areas where historians have not yet exhausted either sources or analyses of those materials. As a firm adherent to the idea that the past informs the future, I believe that the conduct of coalition warfare in World War II is one of those areas where history and historians still have much to tell.

A more personal reason for writing this book is that almost four decades ago Professor Morton J. "Jay" Luvaas, the inaugural Distinguished Visiting Professor of History at the U.S. Military Academy at West Point, introduced a small group of cadets to the complexities, intricacies, and nuances of coalition warfare, in particular those inherent in World War II. Despite the warm, stuffy classroom of early-autumn afternoons, Jay kindled in me a fascination with the topic that has lasted my entire adult life, whether as a student of history or as a military practitioner. I have learned much during this journey and hope to offer insights into what remains a critical aspect of modern warfare.

This book has taken far longer to complete than it should have, but a number of military reassignments, career changes, and increased responsibilities precluded the attention the project deserved. Such are the vagaries of life. However, this prolonged period also gave me contact with many people who cheerfully helped with the project. As a result, I have many to recognize. First, I owe a tremendous debt to the U.S. Army and the U.S. Military Academy, which made possible my attendance at Duke University. I am also indebted to the Military Academy for providing me a research fellowship during academic year 1983–1984 that allowed me to perform the bulk of archival research to support this book. The Association of Graduates of the U.S. Military Academy provided funds to underwrite the costs of that research.

Numerous scholars have encouraged and supported this work. I owe a special debt to the faculty of the Department of History at Duke University for what was truly a life-changing experience. Professor Theodore Ropp altered the way I think about history specifically and about life generally. Professor I. B. "Bill" Holley showed me how to be a critical thinker and taught me the writer's craft. His teaching, coaching, and mentoring skills have served as a model that I have tried to emulate, but with much less success. Colonel (ret.) Paul L. Miles, now of Princeton University, originally suggested the general subject, and his probing questions caused me to refine my thoughts.

Several colleagues lent their expertise to this effort. I thank Michael Neiberg for offering his considerable expertise and review of chapter 1. Kevin Weddle also reviewed several chapters. Kevin Dixon provided comments on the logic of the introductory chapter. Colonel (ret.) Gregory Fontenot applied his rigorous eye and analytical skills to an earlier version of the entire manuscript. My wife, Kathy, proofread the entire manuscript. Each of these individuals gave freely of their valuable time, and I am grateful for their support. In addition, I am indebted to three anonymous reviewers. Collectively, all of these individuals have saved me from numerous blunders. I alone am responsible for any remaining faults or for not heeding their cogent advice.

In the course of gathering the research to support this project, I received valuable assistance from a number of institutions. I am grateful to Her Majesty's Government for the use of Crown Copyright material contained in the National Archives of the United Kingdom, Public Records Office, London. I also thank the trustees of the Liddell Hart Centre for Military Archives, Kings College, London, for access to material in their collection. I was able to obtain photographs from the George C. Marshall Foundation, the Naval History and Heritage Command, and the U.S. Army Military History Institute of the U.S. Army Heritage and Education Center, U.S. Army War College. I am grateful to each of these three institutions for allowing me access to their photograph collections.

Wherever I carried out research, I received able assistance from archivists who guided me through their collections. I thank in particular Martha Crowley of the Operational Naval Archives, Naval History and Heritage Command; Charles Shaughnnessy of the Navy and Old Army Branch, National Archives; and Richard Summers and David Keough of the incomparable U.S. Army Military History Institute. The staff of the U.S. Army War College Library represent the epitome of customer service. Research librarians Greta Andrusyszyn and Jeannette Moyer were most helpful. Kathy Hindman and especially Dianne Baumgartner responded cheerfully and quickly to literally scores of interlibrary loan requests.

The leadership of the U.S. Army War College allowed me to relinquish my duties as the dean of academics and return to the teaching faculty. I am also thankful for a sabbatical leave during academic year 2012–2013 that allowed me the time to complete this project.

Throughout the decades surrounding this project, my family has remained my anchor. Our daughters, Amanda and Lindsey, were a preschooler and an infant, respectively, when this project started. They endured my prolonged absences and the household's enforced periods of quiet but never once complained when this project claimed the few spare moments available to me. Through it all, they provided the laughter, happiness, and love that kept me grounded. However, from start to finish over many years, my wife, Kathy, has been the rock that kept it all together. This book would not have been possible without her patience, organizational skills, and ability to handle the realities of life while I got to play. For this and much, much more, I am and will remain eternally grateful.

Dramatis Personae

(1937–1941)

Great Britain

Aiken, William A. "Max," Lord Beaverbrook. Canadian business tycoon; British newspaper mogul. Close confidant of Churchill. Minister of aircraft production, May 1940–May 1941. Minister of supply, June 1941–February 1942.

Bailey, Admiral Sir Sidney. Retired in 1939. Recalled to active duty to chair the Bailey Committee, which examined the level of cooperation to be sought with the United States (June–July 1940).

Beaumont-Nesbitt, Brigadier General (later Major General) Frederick. Chief, British Military Intelligence, 1939–1940. Served with the British Joint Staff Mission, 1941–1942.

Bellairs, Rear Admiral Sir Roger M. Recalled to active duty to head the British delegation of the first American-British Conversations, January–March 1941.

Brooke-Popham, Air Chief Marshal Robert. Commander in chief, Far East Command, November 1940–December 1941.

Cadogan, Sir Alexander. Diplomat. Permanent under secretary of foreign affairs, 1938–1946.

Chamberlain, Neville. Chancellor of the Exchequer, November 1931–May 1937. Prime minister, May 1937–May 1940. Died November 1940.

Chatfield, Admiral Lord (Alfred) Ernle. First sea lord, 1933–1938. Minister for coordination of defense, September 1939–May 1940.

Churchill, Sir Winston Spencer. Chancellor of the Exchequer, November 1924–June 1929. First lord of the Admiralty, September 1939–May 1940. Prime minister, May 1940–July 1945.

Danckwerts, Rear Admiral (later Vice Admiral) Victor H., Royal Navy. Delegate to the first American-British Conversations, January–March 1941. Died of natural causes January 1944.

Dill, Field Marshal Sir John. Chief of the Imperial General Staff, May 1940–December 1941. Head of the British Joint Staff Mission and personal representative of the minister of defence (Churchill), January 1942 until his death in November 1944 from aplastic anemia.

Dykes, Lieutenant Colonel (later Brigadier General) Vivian. Director of plans, War Office. Secretariat, Combined Chiefs of Staff. Killed in an air accident, 30 January 1943.

Eden, Anthony, Lord Avon. Secretary of state for foreign affairs, December 1935–February 1938. Secretary of state for war, May–December 1940.

Freeman, Air Vice Marshal Wilfrid. Vice chief of Air Staff, 1940–1942. Attendee of the Riviera Conference, Placentia Bay, August 1941.

Hampton, Commander (later Captain) T. C. Admiralty Plans Section. Representative, secret talks in Washington, D.C., June 1939. Killed commanding H.M.S. *Carlisle* off Crete, May 1941.

Harris, Air Vice Marshal (later Marshal of the Royal Air Force) Arthur T. "Bomber," Royal Air Force. British Joint Staff Mission, June 1941. Commander in chief, Bomber Command, February 1942–September 1946.

Ismay, Major General (later General) Lord Hastings. Deputy secretary and then secretary, Committee of Imperial Defense, 1936–1940. Chief staff officer for the minister of defence from May 1940. Member, British Chiefs of Staff Committee from May 1940. Deputy secretary to the War Cabinet from May 1940. Secretary general of the North Atlantic Treaty Organization, 1952–1957.

Lindsay, Sir Ronald. His Majesty's ambassador to the United States, 1930–1939.

Kerr, Philip, Lord Lothian. His Majesty's ambassador to the United States, June 1939 until his death in December 1941.

Morris, Major General (later General) Edwin L. British army representative at the first American-British Conversations, January–March 1941.

Pakenham-Walsh, Major General (later Lieutenant General) Ridley. Supply/materiel mission to the United States, 1940.

Phillips, Captain (later Admiral) Thomas V. Director, Naval War Plans, Admiralty, 1935–1939. Deputy chief and vice chief of Naval Staff, June 1939–October 1941. Commander, British Eastern Fleet, from October 1941 until killed on 10 December 1941 aboard H.M.S. *Prince of Wales*.

Portal, Air Chief Marshal Charles, Lord Portal of Hungerford. Commander in chief, Bomber Command, April 1940. Chief of Air Staff, October 1940–February 1946.

Pound, Admiral Sir Dudley. First sea lord, June 1939 until his death from a brain tumor in October 1943.

Purvis, Arthur. Canadian businessman. Head, British Purchasing Commission. Killed in an air accident en route to the Riviera Conference, Placentia Bay, August 1941.

Slessor, Air Commodore (later Marshal of the Royal Air Force) Sir John. Deputy director and director of plans from December 1937. Air Staff member, British Purchasing Commission, 1940. Royal Air Force representative to the first American-British Conversations, January–March 1941.

Wood, Edward F. L., Lord Halifax. Foreign secretary, February 1938–December 1940. His Majesty's ambassador to the United States, January 1941–May 1946.

United States

Arnold, Major General (later General of the Air Force) Henry H. "Hap." Chief, U.S. Army Air Corps/Army Air Force, September 1938–June 1946.

Chaney, Major General (later Lieutenant General) James E. Chief, U.S. Army Special Observer Group, May 1941–January 1942. Commander, U.S. Army Forces in the British Isles, January–June 1942.

Embick, Major General (later Lieutenant General) Stanley D. Recalled to active duty to lead U.S. delegation to the first American-British Conversations. Key strategic adviser to General George Marshall throughout World War II. Served as chief of the Joint Strategic Survey Committee and concurrently as chairman of the Inter-American Defense Board.

Emmons, Major General (later Lieutenant General) Delos C. Member U.S. delegation, Anglo-American Standardization of Arms Conference, August–September 1940.

Gerow, Brigadier General (later General) Leonard T. Member, War Plans Division, Army Staff, 1935–1942. Chief of the War Plans Division, October 1940–February 1942.

Ghormley, Rear Admiral (later Vice Admiral) Robert L. Chief, Navy War Plans Division, and assistant chief of naval operations, 1938–1940. Anglo-American Standardization of Arms Conference (August–September 1940). Special naval observer, London, 1940–1942. Attended first American-British Conversations.

Harriman, E. Averell. U.S. business magnate. Special representative of President Franklin D. Roosevelt. Lend-Lease program "expediter," March 1941–October 1943.

Hart, Admiral Thomas C. Commander in chief, U.S. Asiatic Fleet, July 1939–June 1942.

Hopkins, Harry L. U.S. secretary of commerce, December 1938–September 1943. Lend-Lease administrator, 1941–1945. Roosevelt's alter ego and "fixer."

Hull, Cordell. U.S. secretary of state, March 1933–November 1944.

Ickes, Harold. U.S. secretary of the interior, March 1933–February 1946. Close Roosevelt adviser. Strong proponent of aid to Great Britain.

Ingersoll, Captain (later Admiral) Royal E. Member and chief, War Plans Division, 1935–1938. Participant in initial naval talks in Britain, January 1938. Assistant to the chief of naval operations, 1940–1942.

Johnson, Louis. Assistant secretary of war, 1937–1940. Secretary of defense, 1949–1950.

King, Admiral (later Fleet Admiral) Ernest J. Commander in chief, Atlantic Fleet, February–December 1941. Commander in chief, U.S. Fleet, December 1941–December 1945, and concurrently chief of naval operations, March 1942–November 1945.

Kirk, Captain (later Vice Admiral) Alan G. U.S. naval attaché to the United Kingdom, 1939–1941. Chief of naval intelligence, March–October 1941. Commanded amphibious landings at Sicily, Italy, and Normandy. Later U.S. ambassador to Belgium (1946–1949), Soviet Union (1949–1951), and Taiwan (1962–1963).

Knox, Frank. Secretary of the navy, July 1940 until his death in April 1944. Strong Republican proponent for intervention.

Leahy, Admiral (later Fleet Admiral) William D. Chief of naval operations, 1937–1939. U.S. ambassador to Vichy France, 1940–1942. Recalled to duty in 1942 as chief of staff to the president, July 1942–March 1949.

Lee, Lieutenant Colonel (later Major General) Raymond E. U.S. Army attaché to Britain, 1935–1939 and June 1940–December 1941. Acting assistant chief of staff, army intelligence, December 1941–June 1942.

Marshall, General (later General of the Army) George C. Chief of staff of the army, September 1939–November 1945. President Truman's mediator for the Chinese Civil War, December 1945–January 1947. Secretary of state, January 1947–January 1949. President, American Red Cross, September 1949–September 1950. Secretary of defense, September 1950–September 1951. Nobel Peace Prize recipient, 1953.

McNarney, Colonel (later General) Joseph T. On the staff of the U.S. Army War Plans Division, 1939–1941. U.S. Air Corps representative to the first American-British Conversations, January–March 1941. Member, U.S. Army Special Observer Group, London, June–December 1941.

Morgenthau, Henry, Jr. U.S. secretary of the Treasury, January 1934–July 1945. Key adviser to Roosevelt and a strong proponent of aid to Great Britain and intervention.

Purnell, Captain (later Rear Admiral) William D. Chief of staff, U.S. Asiatic Fleet, December 1939–April 1942.

Stark, Admiral Harold R. Chief of naval operations, August 1939–March 1942. Commanded U.S. Naval Forces Europe, March 1942–August 1945.

Stimson, Henry L. Secretary of war, May 1911–March 1913. Secretary of state, March 1929–March 1933. Secretary of war, July 1940–September 1945. Republican. Protégé of Elihu Root. Successful Wall Street businessman. Strong proponent of U.S. intervention.

Strong, Brigadier General (later Major General) George V. Assistant chief of staff, U.S. Army. Chief, War Plans Division, War Department, 1938–1940. Member of the U.S. delegation to the Anglo-American Standardization of Arms Conference, August–September 1940.

Turner, Captain (later Admiral) Richmond Kelly "Terrible." Director, Navy War Plans Division, October 1940–July 1942.

Welles, Sumner. Under secretary of state, May 1937–August 1943. Strong personal relationship with Roosevelt. Welles often sidestepped his boss, Secretary of State Cordell Hull.

Willson, Captain (later Vice Admiral) Russell. U.S. naval attaché to Britain, January 1937–January 1939.

Woodring, Henry H. U.S. secretary of war, September 1936–July 1940. A strong anti-interventionist.

Abbreviations

ABC	American-British Conversations
ADB	American-Dutch-British
AEF	American Expeditionary Force
BEF	British Expeditionary Force
BJSM	British Joint Staff Mission, Washington, D.C.
CINC	commander in chief
CNO	chief of naval operations
RAF	Royal Air Force
SPENAVO	special naval observer
SPOBS	Special Army Observer Group in London
SWC	Supreme War Council
USSOG	U.S. Special Observer Group
WPD	War Plans Division

Prologue

At 2:41 a.m. on the morning of 7 May 1945 in Reims, France, Lieutenant General Walter B. Smith, U.S. chief of staff of the Supreme Headquarters Expeditionary Force, accepted from General Alfred Jodl the German High Command's unconditional surrender of German land, sea, and air forces. Accompanying Smith and signing the instrument of surrender were representatives of key Allied forces in the coalition that defeated Fascist Italy and Nazi Germany.[1] To accommodate Soviet demands and ensure that the Germans did not fight on against the Red Army, a second formal surrender ceremony occurred in Berlin on 9 May. This ceremony culminated a series of surrenders that began in Italy on 29 April and marked the end of the supposed thousand-year German Reich.[2]

Almost four months later, on 2 September 1945 (Far East time), exactly six years to the day from the German invasion of Poland, official hostilities against Japan ended with the formal signing of the instrument of surrender. General of the Army Douglas MacArthur, supreme commander of the Allied Powers, presided over the ceremony on board the U.S.S. *Missouri* anchored in Tokyo Bay. With him were the representatives of the coalition that had defeated Japan: Australia, China, Canada, France, Netherlands, New Zealand, and the Soviet Union.[3]

By the time of these ceremonies, forces of the Anglo-American coalition within the Grand Alliance had fought a global war on three continents and in a dozen major theaters of operation. Anglo-American armies had battled across Africa and the Mediterranean to the Middle East; from Norway to Italy and the Balkans; from the western tip of France's Brittany Peninsula to Prague. In the Far East, Allied forces fought in China, Burma, and India and island-hopped from New Guinea to the Netherlands East Indies to the Philippines. Predominantly U.S. forces seized island chain after island chain across the central Pacific, encircling the Japanese home islands. Coalition naval operations swept the seven seas and conducted amphibious assaults on a scale never seen before or since. From the Arctic Ocean to the Cape of Good Hope, from the Gulf of Mexico to the Mediterranean, across the length and breadth of the Pacific Ocean, and throughout the Far East from Pearl Harbor to India to Australia to the Aleutians, Anglo-American naval forces conquered the seas. Royal Air Force and U.S. Army Air Force units supported the land and sea campaigns, and, with sustained bombing campaigns, took the war to the heart of Germany, Italy, and Japan. Millions of men along with tens of thousands of aircraft and thousands of ships engaged in a veritable death struggle with Axis forces. Americans and British would fight in multinational units, oftentimes incorporating units of additional nations. In the end, the armed forces of the coalition led by the United Kingdom and the United States, at great cost (nearly one million dead or missing, millions wounded and displaced, and trillions of dollars spent), achieved victory in what is arguably the most successful military coalition the world has yet known.

Battles and campaigns alone, although vitally important, are never enough to secure victory. Within a coalition, national interests and policies must meld to create grand strategy, which then guides the coalition's strategy that balances ends, ways, and means to place battles and campaigns in their proper context. The conception, planning, development, and execution of policy and strategy require command-and-control and liaison organizations, processes, and communication channels to coordinate these activities. In a global war, where strategic requirements always exceeded available resources, there had to be mechanisms for ensuring the appropriate allocation of materiel and resources necessary to support strategy.

By 1945, the Anglo-American military coalition, the core of the Grand Alliance, had created, modified, and adapted all the organizations, processes, and systems necessary to fight the war together. Nonetheless, these accomplishments did not occur overnight. They had to be initiated, nurtured, and occasionally fought over. The story told in this book is an effort to explain the origins of the Anglo-American coalition, outline its early development, and clarify how this early collaboration set the conditions that led to the Allied victory in 1945.

Introduction

The questions surrounding coalitions, the nations that compose them, and their strategies are timeless. Indeed, in the twenty-five hundred years since Thucydides first described the complexities posed in achieving close cooperation among allies in his account of the Peloponnesian War, understanding of the issues inherent in coalition warfare has assumed increasing importance for historian and practitioner alike.[1] Extensive U.S. experience in twentieth- and early-twenty-first-century warfare reinforces this conclusion.[2] Moreover, it is difficult to foresee the United States involved in a future major conflict without partners. A better understanding of the past, therefore, may offer insights useful for future coalition efforts.

Examining the military aspects of coalitions is particularly important. As Gordon Craig cogently noted at the U.S. Air Force Academy during the Harmon Memorial Lecture of 1965, the detailed investigation of the military aspects of coalition cooperation commenced only after World War I.[3] Fifty years after Craig's lecture, the study of the military elements of coalition warfare remains relatively undeveloped. For example, there is no adequate official or agreed upon definition of the term *coalition warfare*.[4] A definition would superficially appear simple: warfare conducted by a coalition, which is "an ad hoc arrangement between two or more nations for common action" or "warfare conducted by an alliance of states."[5] However, such constructs reinforce Karl von Clausewitz's dictum of nearly two centuries ago that "everything in war is simple, but the simplest thing is difficult."[6] Because of the gaps in our understanding, the study of the military elements of multinational cooperation affords fertile and relatively unfurrowed ground for historians and practitioners to investigate, examine, and analyze.

Nowhere is this opportunity more profitable than in the origins of the Anglo-American coalition of 1941–1945. At first glance, it would seem a poor choice, for in the past seven decades the U.S.-British coalition of World War II has undergone intense scrutiny. However, although historians have written much about the period after the United States became an active belligerent, the discussion initially tended to focus on the "special relationship" between the two powers and accented the close cooperation in political, diplomatic, and economic arenas once the United States entered the ongoing war.[7] Historians generally have paid less attention to the period prior to formal U.S. entry into the war, in particular the military aspects of the coalition. Indeed, many excellent works completely overlook the extensive pre–Pearl Harbor military interactions or quickly gloss over them to get to the heart of the action of World War II. That said, some first-rate works do in part address elements of the military coalition during the period: *Strategic Planning for Coalition Warfare, 1941–1942, United States Army in World War II* by Maurice Matloff and Edwin M. Snell; *Bargaining for Supremacy: Anglo-American Naval Collaboration, 1937–1941* by James Leutze; *Allies of a Kind: The United States, Britain, and the War against Japan* by Christopher Thorne; *The Creation of the Anglo-American Alliance: A Study of Competitive Collaboration* by David Reynolds; *Fool-Proof Relations: The Search for Anglo-American Naval Cooperation during the Chamberlain Years, 1937–1940* by Malcolm Murfett; *Leadership and Indecision: American War Planning and Policy Process, 1937–1942* by Mark Lowenthal; and *Dominion or Decline: Anglo-American Naval Relations in the Pacific, 1937–1941* by Ian Cowman, to name only some of the best.[8]

Although each of these works is valuable in its own right and collectively they fill in many of the gaps in the information on the early, informal cooperation between the United States and Great Britain, no one treatment offers a comprehensive picture of the military elements of the early Anglo-American collaborative process. As official historians, Matloff and Snell focus appropriately on the equities of the U.S. Army. Leutze scrutinizes naval aspects of the discussions but touches on army and air issues only when they affect the naval story. His analysis also effectively ends with the American-British Conversations of January–March 1941, almost a full year before the United States entered the ongoing conflict. Reynolds's superb treatment concentrates on the political-diplomatic-economic origins of the de facto alliance, occasionally treating military aspects. Thorne addresses the Pacific side of the war and mostly the period after Pearl Harbor. Murfett and Cowman likewise offer excellent analyses of coalition planning and preparations in the Far East but do not address the remainder of the globe. Lowenthal uses the coalition's efforts as a vehicle to examine U.S. planning processes and mechanisms, in particular the role played by Franklin D. Roosevelt. Several of these works accent the competitive nature of the early negotiations and the ensuing frictions that bedeviled the partners, sometimes at the expense of recognizing the coalition's significant successes.

Many analyses examine the upper reaches of coalition leadership, paying less attention to subordinate leaders and planners. There is no doubt that Franklin Roosevelt and Winston Churchill set the overall conditions for Anglo-American cooperation, but these titans were not the only key actors in this story. Mid- to upper-level military officers and key defense civilians performed the hard pick-and-shovel work of translating key decisions into strategy and plans. Most importantly, they carried out the actions necessary to turn decisions into success on future battlefields.

This account, therefore, offers a comprehensive assessment of the extent and importance of the considerable informal military cooperation that took place before the United States officially entered World War II. The narrative that follows examines the creation of the military strategic framework of the coalition and assesses how that foundation contributed to the eventual defeat of Germany, Italy, and Japan. Although many factors manifestly contributed to the ultimate victory, not least the Soviet Union's joining of the coalition, the coalition partners' ability to orchestrate their efforts and coordinate the many elements of modern warfare successfully must rank high in any assessment. Specifically, this work addresses the question of whether the informal Anglo-American collaborative efforts prior to Pearl Harbor made a vital difference that paid off in terms of substantially more effective cooperation after the United States joined the war against Germany and Japan.

Despite historian Greg Kennedy's contention that "there is little to be gained from studying, as is often done, the development of Anglo-American relations in that region [the Far East] from 1937–1941,"[9] late 1937 seems a most appropriate starting point for this assessment. As developed later in this book, several key events occurred in close temporal proximity. Japan's expanded war in China and threats of further aggression in the Far East led British prime minister Neville Chamberlain to the dual decisions to appease the dictators in Europe while pursuing U.S. assistance in meeting Japanese aggression in the Far East. Franklin Roosevelt, believing the United States to be out of the worst of the Great Depression and concerned about the dictators' aggressive behavior, delivered his Quarantine Speech in Chicago in October 1937, calling for the diplomatic equivalent of a medical quarantine. About the same time, Roosevelt approached Sir Ronald Lindsay, the British ambassador to the United States, about the possibility of bilateral naval staff talks to deal with Japan. Pearl Harbor offers a suitable end for the analysis because a major contention of this work is that the Anglo-American coalition had forged by December 1941 the foundations for eventual victory.

The primary theme of the story told here concerns the military collaboration that led to the success of the wartime coalition. Without question, military planning took place within a political, diplomatic, informational, and economic context. This work, however, addresses those aspects only to the extent necessary to provide sufficient background, pulling together the many threads for a fuller, more comprehensive account of the coalition's military aspects.

In addition, a number of secondary themes thread their way through the narrative. The first concerns whether the "special relationship" between President Franklin D. Roosevelt and Prime Minister Winston Churchill translated into a special relationship between the United States and Great Britain. Over the years, this relationship has spawned a veritable cottage industry of historical and political inquiry, which Alex Danchev categorizes into three essential schools of thought: evangelists, functionalists, and terminalists.[10] Winston Churchill laid out the first school in his magisterial six-volume history *The Second World War*.[11] Indeed, Danchev labels Churchill "the evangelist-in-chief."[12] However, as David Reynolds points out, Churchill's magnificent account is flawed. Many of the early treatments of the coalition based on Churchill's work were overly sentimental or framed by the emerging Cold War and the desire among Churchill and others on both sides of the Atlantic to sustain the "special relationship" in the face of the Communist threat.[13]

Over time, the pendulum swung back as historical revisionists added balance to the debates. As "functionalists" emerged, the inquiry and analysis shifted to focus on common fate and interests, not sentimental attachments such as language and shared culture.[14] Other observers focus on the competitive nature of the coalition, where two great nations pursued their sometimes divergent national interests in a common cause. Still more analysts emphasize the trials and tribulations sustained within the coalition and stress points of friction. The terminalists argue that the "special relationship" was over before the end of World War II. Indeed, for many in this school of thought, it had never existed. Instead, Churchill and subsequent British leaders used the myth of a special relationship to "punch above their weight" and wield influence within a unique geostrategic context that ended with the war.[15] In the end, although each school offers elements of truth, no one school adequately explains this incredibly complex collaborative relationship. As historians obtain further distance from the personalities, gain access to more records, and benefit from competing analyses, a richer picture of events can emerge. This work intends to add to that picture.

Another thread traces Roosevelt's thinking about the nature and timing of an ultimate U.S. contribution to the war against the Axis Powers. Was Roosevelt isolationist or noninterventionist, hesitant or cautious, reluctant or duplicitous? Because of the importance of the topic and a lack of definitive insights into Roosevelt's thinking and motivations, the historiography of this issue is extensive, starting even before war's end and continuing up to today. The sides staked out in this debate range from Roosevelt as the lead conspirator to Roosevelt as Churchill's unwitting dupe or an indecisive proponent of "ad hocery" or a "reluctant belligerent."[16] Seeking a middle ground, the narrative offered here examines this contentious topic.

Churchill's role as a grand strategist, in particular his efforts to bring the United States into the war, offers another analytical thread. An apparently inexhaustible supply of historical evaluations of Churchill as grand strategist runs the full range from success to failure. Not least is Churchill's own account in *The Second World War*, where he made good his promise, often stated throughout the war, to "leave it to history, but remember that I shall be one of the historians," seized the initiative (and the market), laid out the base narrative, and set the conditions for subsequent analysis.[17] By placing Churchill within the context of events, readers may obtain a clearer understanding of Churchill's performance as grand strategist.

Despite the importance of these two giants of the twentieth century, this work does not focus on Roosevelt, Churchill, or their special relationship. Although that relationship was a necessary element of a victorious coalition effort, it is insufficient to explain the overall success of the military partnership. Nevertheless, because of their individual and collective influence on the course of collaboration between their militaries, the narrative, perforce, addresses the nature and evolution of their respective roles, but only insofar as they inform the examination of military collaboration within the coalition.

In examining the origins of the coalition, this work invokes David Hackett Fischer's "idea of contingency . . . not in the sense of chance," but rather in the sense of "something that may or may not happen. This is not to raise again ill-framed counter-factual questions about what might have happened in the past. It is rather to understand historical events as a series of real choices that people actually made."[18] Such an approach is necessary because observers, like statisticians using a scatter-plot graph, can over time reduce what occurred as a series of fits and starts, successes and failures into a recognizable trend. However, although some trends or their origins might have been apparent to the participants in events at the time, most remained shrouded in secrecy, doubt, risk, miscalculation, and an opponent's decisions. Leaders and planners lived in an uncertain and dangerous environment and faced choices with potentially dire consequences. Thus, if today it appears that they took small, halting steps or missed opportunities, such outcomes are more apparent in retrospect.

Avoiding twenty-twenty hindsight is another goal. Because readers know how World War II ended, what appears obvious in retrospect may not have been apparent to the individuals at the time, who, tugged and pulled by the vagaries of the moment, did not know how it all might turn out. Hindsight also allows modern observers to see a much more orderly trace of events than appeared to contemporaries. Thus, one must guard against artificially establishing a narrative of events more linear and ordered than was apparent to the actors of the day or leaping to a conclusion simply because one knows what in fact happened. Rather, one must carefully follow the path of this story through the participants' experiences, not one's much fuller picture of the past. Thus, the narrative seeks to examine and judge events in as contextual light as possible.

To these several ends, this work analyzes the early informal military collaboration between the United States and Great Britain along the lines suggested in Gordon Craig's Harmon Lecture: the coalition's formulation of policy and grand strategy; its development of the military strategy necessary to achieve the ends of that policy; its crafting of effective operational planning on an international scale; and its creation of an effective command structure and liaison organization with its all-important channels of communication.[19] In addition, the narrative examines the vitally important logistical and materiel issues, in particular the allocation of war production, that either enabled or constrained the ways to achieve the coalition's ends.

The story begins with a brief excursion into British and American coalition experiences in the Great War, followed by an overview of the political, economic, and diplomatic issues of the interwar era. These two chapters establish the context and tone that set the stage for and influenced the initial collaborative efforts. Chapter 3 outlines the first tentative Anglo-American military conversations. The subsequent chapter introduces key aspects of supply negotiations and the allocation of war materiel that intertwined the two countries and their militaries before the fall of France. Chapter 5 examines initial U.S. efforts to ascertain if Britain would survive in the wake of the French collapse and the coordination that occurred after that critical determination. Chapter 6 focuses on the first true cooperation that occurred in London and the Far East in autumn 1940. The next chapter examines the American-British Conversations, known as ABC-1, the full-fledged staff talks held in utmost secrecy in Washington, D.C., from January to March 1941 that established the blueprint for global coalition collaboration. Chapters 8 and 9 review vexing problems that beset the more detailed subordinate planning necessary to turn grand strategy into practical military plans as well as the successes and failures in implementing the provisions agreed at ABC-1. Chapter 10 outlines the state of cooperation at the time of Pearl Harbor. The narrative closes with conclusions and observations.

Although the definition of terms risks applying false or anachronistic labels, a common understanding of several major concepts and terms utilized in this study will be helpful. Many of the terms defined herein have occasionally complex derivations, but those complexities need not detain the reader. More important is establishing a common understanding and using terms consistently. For example, strategy formulation ideally but rarely follows a simple flow: national or coalition interests dictate policy—the overall objectives necessary to protect or further those interests. Policy, in turn, drives strategy—the dynamic equilibrium of ends (objectives, aims), ways (options, courses of action), and means (resources) needed to achieve policy goals and objectives. Although not all scholars agree on this point, one may subdivide strategy into several categories that help formulate and implement strategy. At the top is *grand strategy*, or the synchronization of political, economic, diplomatic, informational, and military elements of national or coalition power to achieve desired goals.[20] Subsidiary levels of strategy might include security strategy, defense strategy, military strategy, and theater strategy.[21] The focus here is on coalition policy, grand strategy, military strategy, and theater strategy. Subordinate to strategy is *operational art*—the synchronization of battles and campaigns to achieve strategic ends and tactics, the employment of troops in battles and engagements.[22] Operational-level planning and operational art occasionally arise in the narrative; tactical issues do not.

Grand strategy, especially at coalition level, is about big ideas: competing national values, interests, needs, and desires. In practice, it is also about making hard choices, for at this level requirements always outstrip available resources. Moreover, choices at this level usually will be the most difficult ones because easier decisions normally will have been resolved at lower levels. However, strategy, in particular military strategy, must be more than ideas and choices. Someone must turn those decisions into concrete actions. Otherwise, strategy will be little more than an exercise in mental gymnastics.[23]

Once political leaders have agreed on grand strategy, they must provide coherent guidance to their military commanders. Unity of strategic direction focuses on the political direction given to military commanders.

Unity of command within coalitions is a more complex issue meriting a brief elaboration. As Napoleon noted long ago, "Nothing is more important in war than unity of command."[24] However, translating this principle of war into reality is oftentimes a trying task, nowhere more so than in coalitions. An indication of the difficulty encountered in achieving this seemingly simple maxim is the fact that the U.S. Army and U.S. Navy did not hammer out an initial agreement on unity of command until 1938, and debates on how best to achieve such unity continue to this day.[25] Obtaining unity of command within a coalition is even harder. Even a coalition united against a common foe often finds itself divided by conflicts over national sovereignty, differing political objectives, divergent military goals, competing economic issues, internal political problems, or scarce resources.[26] Finally, rarely do nations willingly place their forces under another power's command.[27] In short, a coalition commander rarely commands at all but strives to achieve unity of effort through personal influence and exhortation of peers, a method not always known to produce desired results.

In the period 1938–1941, British and U.S. militaries tended to use the term *joint* to refer to plans and operations of multiple services within their respective military establishments as well as to describe plans and operations with allies and partners. This practice led to confusion that plagued the early staff conversations. At the Arcadia Conference in December 1941–January 1942, the partners agreed that the term *combined* would refer to plans or operations involving forces or agencies of more than one country and the term *joint* would apply to the plans or operations of multiple services or agencies from within a single country.[28] Where possible, the narrative uses the terms *combined* and *joint* in these senses, but when citing documents from the period the text adheres to the usage contained in the original.

At the time in question, the U.S. military establishment consisted of the Department of the Navy and the War Department. The U.S. Navy and a very small U.S. Marine Corps composed the service elements of the Department of the Navy. During the initial period of this story, the U.S. Fleet consisted of the Battle Force, principally based on San Diego; the Scouting Force, largely stationed at Norfolk, Virginia; and the U.S. Asiatic Fleet in Manila. On 1 February 1941, the Navy Department reorganized the U.S. Fleet into the U.S. Atlantic Fleet, the U.S. Pacific Fleet, and the U.S. Asiatic Fleet. At the time, the service portions of the War Department included the U.S. Army and the U.S. Army Air Corps, which was a subordinate element of the army. The army also included the Organized Reserves and, when federalized, the Army National Guard of the United States.

The U.S. Chiefs of Staff at the time included the chief of naval operations (CNO), Admiral Harold R. Stark, and the chief of staff of the U.S. Army (CSA), General George C. Marshall. The chief of the U.S. Army Air Corps, Major General Henry H. "Hap" Arnold, was subordinate to the CSA. On 20 June 1941, although still technically subordinate to the CSA, the U.S. Army Air Corps became the U.S. Army Air Force. Thereafter, Marshall treated Arnold as a peer within the U.S. Chiefs of Staff. The naval members, in particular Admiral Ernest J. King when he became the CNO, did not always do so, especially early in the war.

During this period, the individual chiefs who composed the U.S. Chiefs of Staff represented only their respective services. Not until January 1942 did they become an informal corporate body, and only with the National Defense Act of 1947 would a formal structure emerge. Thus, throughout this narrative, the U.S. Chiefs of Staff were individual advisers to the president and only an informal collective body when dealing with their British counterparts.[29] This configuration allowed Roosevelt to keep all of the threads of power running through his hands, a situation most to his liking and consistent with his methods of operation.[30] Nevertheless, this account refers to the U.S. Chiefs of Staff when they met as a body to negotiate or provide a collective position to the British.

The British Chiefs of Staff Committee—composed of the first sea lord, the chief of the Imperial General Staff, and the chief of the Royal Air Force (RAF), was a long-standing collective body that provided consolidated recommendations coordinated among all services to Churchill, who was both prime minister and minister of defence.[31] Like Roosevelt, Churchill kept the reins firmly in his hands.

1

Lessons Lived, Learned, Lost

Episodic Progress in U.S. and British Experiences in Coalition Warfare, 1900–1918

> We have learned a lot from the last war in these [coalition] matters—it is good we should so rapidly apply that knowledge and plunk for the right thing from the very beginning.
> —Sir Henry Pownall, Chief of General Staff, British Expeditionary Force (1939), *Chief of Staff*

> Dealing with the enemy is a simple and straightforward matter when contrasted with securing close cooperation with an ally.
> —Major General Fox Conner, Chief of Operations, American Expeditionary Force (1918), "The Allied High Command and Allied Unity of Direction," speech to the Army War College, 1940

Before examining Anglo-American military cooperation during the period 1937–1941, some understanding of the previous experiences in coalition warfare, the so-called intellectual baggage that each power brought to the discussions, is essential. In this instance, the respective British and U.S. experiences leading up to and during World War I offer a suitable starting point.

Throughout the nineteenth century, the United States adhered to George Washington's admonition to avoid foreign entanglements because exploration and consolidation of the continental hinterland absorbed American energies. After defeating Spain in 1898, however, the United States acquired substantial overseas territories for the first time and emerged on the international scene as a nascent global power. Many Americans, even if not totally isolationist, nonetheless remained suspicious of overseas involvement. However, with an increased military presence in the Pacific and the Caribbean as well as the special attitude of the United States toward China, elements of the American public began advocating a more active foreign policy, particularly in the Pacific.[1] President Theodore Roosevelt's brokering an end to the Russo-Japanese War, for which he received the Nobel Peace Prize of 1906, creation of a modern "blue water" navy, and the circumnavigation of the globe by the Great White Fleet in 1907–1909 manifested the emergence of the United States as a major power.[2]

At the same time, impediments to extensive collaboration abroad remained. The U.S. military establishment was not prepared for large-scale collaborative efforts. The army constituted little more than a constabulary force, and weaknesses in its organization and structure discovered during the Spanish-American War would take more than a decade to resolve. The U.S. Navy—preeminent U.S. naval theorist Rear Admiral Alfred Thayer Mahan, and Roosevelt's Great White Fleet notwithstanding—was not yet a modern navy equal to European standards. As a result, the armed services remained preoccupied with the demands of the defense of the Western Hemisphere.[3] Moreover, U.S. political leaders after Roosevelt sought to preserve U.S. neutrality in world affairs. For example, in his biography of Newton D. Baker, U.S. secretary of war during World War I, Frederick Palmer notes that in 1915 President Woodrow Wilson saw an article in the *Baltimore Sun* indicating that the army's General Staff was preparing contingency plans for a possible war against Germany. The president ordered Henry S. Breckinridge, the acting secretary of war, to investigate the claim "and, if it proved true, to relieve at once every officer of the General Staff and order him out of Washington."[4] Wilson's temper cooled after Secretary Baker informed him that it was the General Staff's duty to prepare such plans, "but, Mr. Breckinridge directed me to caution the War College to 'camouflage' its work. It [the order] resulted in practically no further additional studies."[5]

Great Britain, in contrast, began the twentieth century in the midst of the Boer War, 1899–1902, the last of the great wars to consolidate its empire.[6] Even before that conflict, Britain had begun to reassess its level of global engagement and emerge from self-imposed "splendid isolation" as it attempted to reduce the potential for conflicts. For example, after resolving a confrontation with the United States over Venezuela (1895–1896), British leaders sought rapprochement with the United States that would help secure U.S. interests in Asia as a quid pro quo for U.S. protection of British interests in the Western Hemisphere.[7] A more pressing issue stemmed from Anglo-German competition after German unification that accelerated into rising tensions after Wilhelm II discarded Chancellor Otto von Bismarck in 1890 and seized control of German foreign policy. Faced with an increasingly menacing Wilhelmine Germany, Britain once more focused its attentions on the European balance of power and in particular on Britain's role in maintaining that delicate equilibrium. The threat from Germany subsequently led to the Anglo-French Entente Cordiale of 1904, the Anglo-Russian Entente of 1907, and British efforts to broker diplomatic solutions to the Balkan wars, all of which culminated in the outbreak of World War I and the commitment of British land forces to the Continent for the first time in almost sixty years.[8]

In the midst of the First Moroccan Crisis of March 1905–May 1906 between France and Germany over Moroccan independence, Britain and France began exploring the possibilities of military cooperation. The relationship started in December 1905 when Major Victor Huguet, the French military attaché in London, approached Major General James Grierson, director of military operations on the Imperial General Staff, and inquired about British intentions on the Continent. Grierson replied that the British had been examining the possible deployment of a 100,000- to 150,000-man force to northwestern Europe in the event of a general European war and that the British preferred to plan for operations in Belgium, but, if necessary, they could shift their focus to supporting the French left flank.[9] A few days later, Huguet contacted his friend, Lieutenant Colonel (ret.) Charles à Court Repington, the influential military correspondent of the *Times* (London), and queried him about British plans. Repington contacted British officials, who agreed to use Repington as an informal conduit and posed several questions that Repington relayed to Huguet. Shortly thereafter, the British government decided to enter into direct staff talks and terminated Repington's role.[10]

Staff talks proceeded at a desultory pace during 1906–1910 as tension over Morocco cooled and Anglo-German relations warmed. Anglo-French planners designated ports of debarkation for what would become the British Expeditionary Force (BEF), specified initial assembly areas, and began plans for the forward rail transport of British forces. The fact that as early as 1908 the French decided to locate the BEF near Cambrai and Arras on the Belgian border but neglected to inform their British partners offers a revealing indication of the level of coalition cooperation.[11]

Major General Henry Wilson's accession to the post of director of military operations rejuvenated the staff conversations. Convinced that little practical work had been accomplished, Wilson, a close friend of General Ferdinand Foch and described by historian Roy Prete as "French speaking, ardently Francophile, and a convert to offensive doctrine," immediately set about altering what he perceived to be a disgraceful state of unpreparedness.[12] By August 1911, Wilson's energetic efforts resulted in the planned deployment of a BEF of approximately 150,000 men on the French left flank.[13] From this position, they would fall upon an anticipated open German right flank south of the Meuse River. Only later would Anglo-French commanders find out how badly they had underestimated the scope of the sweeping envelopment of the Schlieffen Plan, the German plan to quickly conquer France. Now that they were already engaged in battle, it would be too late to draw up new plans. The BEF would have to execute the only plan it had—with near disastrous short-term results for the BEF as well as long-lasting strains within the coalition.[14]

Throughout 1912–1914, coalition planners concentrated on refining the general terms agreed upon in 1911. From the available evidence, Wilson appears to have been the principal, if not the sole, negotiator between the British and French staffs. It is clear that he was coordinating Anglo-French activities, not planning for combined operations of the two armies.[15] There also are indications that Wilson may have made commitments he had not cleared with his civilian masters in the War Office, an omission that would have significant consequences in August 1914 when His Majesty's Government did not immediately enter the war. British indecision not only delayed mobilization and movement of the BEF to France but also upset French mobilization and concentration timetables because the French had to wait for the British to move forward on their left flank. The delay also sowed seeds of French suspicions over ultimate British intent.[16] Contemporary French documents and Marshal Joseph Joffre's memoirs indicate that when Joffre presented Plan XVII in April 1913, he noted, "I was conscious . . . that since the agreement was problematical and subject to political considerations, it was impossible to base *a priori*, a strategic offensive upon eventualities which might very well never materialize."[17] In this statement lies a key issue in coalition planning, especially prewar planning: key decisions about going to war rest ultimately in the hands of politicians, not soldiers.

British and French naval authorities also carried out staff discussions during this period, albeit less extensive than those of their army colleagues. In the first meeting in January 1906, Admiral Sir John "Jacky" Fisher, the first sea lord, apparently lectured Captain Mercier de Lostende, the French naval attaché, about current British strategy and expressed the opinion that the Royal Navy could take care of itself.[18] By November 1908, when the French resurrected naval conversations, the German Imperial Navy had evolved into a major threat. Fisher proposed that the Royal Navy would take responsibility for the North Sea, while the French Navy would defend the Mediterranean. Naval conversations lapsed shortly thereafter when de Lostende informed Fisher that although the French government agreed in principle, the French did not have sufficient strength to control the entire Mediterranean.[19] The French reopened discussions in July 1911 during the second Franco-German crisis over Morocco.[20] Over the next year, Anglo-French naval authorities negotiated an agreed division of labor: the British would patrol the North Sea, the Dover–Calais straits, and the Mediterranean Sea east of Malta, while the French would defend the lower English Channel and the Mediterranean west of Malta.[21] These provisions stood when war broke out and remained in effect throughout the course of the war.

According to historian Samuel R. Williamson, despite the staff talks, "the new Anglo-French intimacy did not mean there was genuine joint strategic planning. There was joint consultation and some joint discussion," but there were no plans for closely interlocking Allied operations.[22] Moreover, absent significant political changes, there could be no wartime unity of strategic direction or command of their two armies. The BEF would fight alongside the French army as an independent force, and the two fleets would loosely coordinate their individual actions.[23] At the outset of war in 1914, the British and French clearly relied instead upon the traditional concept of cooperation between national forces rather than on true unity of strategic direction or command. One should not judge them too harshly, however. Each nation had differing strategic interests that occasionally led them to diverging paths, and neither power had engaged with allies since the Crimean War sixty years earlier. Moreover, as a close student of coalition warfare has observed, "the opening of the First World War occurred while strategists . . . were emphasizing the national aspects of war to the exclusion of alliance considerations."[24]

The failure to achieve unity of strategic direction and command would plague coalition efforts throughout the ensuing war. As planned, British and French forces initially operated independently within their delineated zones of operations.[25] The German envelopment through Belgium during the initial Battle of the Frontier (20–24 August 1914) quickly unhinged the Anglo-French plan. As British and French forces reeled under heavy German pressure, the failure of General Sir John French, BEF commander, to coordinate with the French Fifth Army under General Charles Lanrezac led to a significant gap that risked the entire French defense in Belgium and northern France. Only a direct order to Sir John French from Field Marshal Lord Horatio Kitchener, Britain's secretary of state for war, to conform to Joffre's directions restored adequate inter-Allied coordination that allowed the British and French armies eventually to halt the German advance along the Marne River. In doing so, however, French and Joffre suffered multiple episodes of strategic disappointment and distrust that fostered friction between the two armies for the remainder of their respective tenures of command. Differing national interests and objectives during the "race to the sea" that followed the "miracle of the Marne" further exacerbated the sense of distrust and animosity.[26]

Although Belgian and British forces briefly operated under Foch's direction during the First Battle of Ypres in October–November 1914, a lack of common strategic direction continued throughout 1915 and 1916. Debates between proponents of the Western Front and advocates for an emphasis in the eastern Mediterranean, arguments over offensive versus defensive strategies, conflicts over where offensive operations should take place in northwest Europe, and sensitivities over respective casualty levels further heightened tensions.[27] Despite defeats and stalemate as well as an Allied agreement at Chantilly on 6 December 1915 that the armies would better synchronize their plans for 1916, each army reverted to national planning in strictly national zones of operation.[28]

The German offensive at Verdun that began in February 1916 and ground down the French army for the remainder of the year in a massive battle of attrition and the abortive British offensive on the Somme from July to November 1916 failed to lead to a more coordinated Allied approach to the higher strategic direction of the war.[29] Only a long train of Allied disasters—the continuing meat grinder of Verdun, mutinies in the French army, the massive bloodletting of British Commonwealth forces at Paschendale that cost 350,000–500,000 casualties for a few square miles of mud, increasing shipping losses, the rout of the Italian army at Caporetto, and, most important, the Bolshevik Revolution and Russia's exit from the war—finally convinced the Allied governments of the need for a centralized organization to coordinate the war.[30] Meeting at Rapollo, Italy, leaders of the British, French, and Italian, but not U.S., governments established the Supreme War Council (SWC) on 7 November 1917. The council consisted of the prime minister and one additional member of government of each power, making it a political rather than military body. Indeed, Prime Minister David Lloyd George saw the SWC as a way to enhance British authority, wrest control of strategy from the military, and reduce rising American influence.[31] Georges Clemenceau, named premier of France ten days after Rapollo—famous for his rebuke "War! this is something too serious to entrust to the military"—also used the SWC to exert his political will over his generals as well as over coalition policy and strategy.[32]

Each nation also provided a military adviser as a member of the Military Council, a subordinate body of the SWC that oversaw day-to-day operations.[33] The initial military members included General Sir William Robertson, chief of the Imperial General Staff. Even though the French government initially named General Ferdinand Foch, Clemenceau, upon assuming the premiership, refused to release Foch from his duties as chief of the General Staff and named instead the recently promoted Major General Maxime Weygand,

Foch's chief of staff and alter ego. General Luigi Cadorna, recently routed at Caporetto, served as the Italian representative. President Wilson later named General Tasker H. Bliss, former army chief of staff, as the U.S. representative.[34]

Initially at least, the SWC may have created as many tensions as it resolved. The rapid turnover of early personnel assignments and overall immaturity of political and military staff processes hobbled early efforts. For example, Lloyd George distrusted Robertson and quickly replaced him with the more malleable Lieutenant General Sir Henry Wilson (who had been promoted by this time), though frictions remained. Weygand had only recently received his promotion to major general and was significantly junior to the other military representatives. The disaster at Caporetto had badly tainted Cadorna. Bliss was well respected and trusted, but President Wilson's absence from the full SWC meant Bliss had no immediate political backing. Not least, Field Marshal Sir Douglas Haig, commander of the BEF, and General Henri-Philippe Pétain, commander in chief (CINC) of the French army, intensely resented the new arrangements, which they perceived as political interference in their operations. Worse, Haig and Pétain quickly recognized that by working together outside the Military Council, they could circumvent the SWC.[35] As historian William Philpott observes, the result was that "the SWC functioned less as a forum for deciding Allied policy than as a 'military debating society,' where Allied differences and resentments could be aired and discussed at length" and issues were frequently left unresolved.[36] More critical, Elizabeth Greenhalgh concludes that "not only was Versailles [home of the Military Council] a talking shop. It was a trilingual talking shop. . . . It was also an uneven talking shop."[37]

Despite its many shortcomings, the SWC was a step, albeit belated and small, in the right direction. As Greenhalgh concludes, "The SWC marked the transition from political coordination of military policy by conference to coordination by committee."[38] This transition was more important than it may sound. Heretofore, the heads of state had met only episodically and usually only when German successes drove them to assemble. Under the new organization, the permanent military representatives met routinely, sorted through the many competing requirements, resolved what they could, and set the negotiating table for any political decisions.

Hand in hand with the matter of unity of strategic direction, the prickly issue of unity of command of coalition forces dogged the Allies. Despite the logic of subordinating the much smaller BEF to Joffre's direction or command, the idea of placing British troops under foreign command was alien to prior British experience.[39] Instructions from Secretary of War Kitchener to Sir John French in August 1914 exemplified the strong British attitudes: "I wish you distinctly to understand that your command is entirely an independent one, and that you will in no case come in any sense under the orders of any Allied General."[40] Strikingly, it appears neither Kitchener nor French communicated these terms to Joffre, nominally the overall coalition commander.[41] Indeed, when Sir Douglas Haig assumed command of the BEF in December 1915, his instructions from Lord Kitchener were virtually identical to those Sir John French received.[42] The trauma of a year and a half of war had apparently done little to shake the attitudes of 1914. Even during several conferences in 1916, the Allies only loosely coordinated their efforts.[43]

Early 1917 saw the first Allied attempt to gain true unity of command. Enamored of General Robert Nivelle, who had replaced Joffre as CINC of the French army, and distrustful of his own commanders, Lloyd George subordinated the British army to Nivelle's direction for the duration of the spring 1917 offensive. British commanders, aware no doubt of Lloyd George's political machinations to oust Robertson and Haig, strongly resented the new arrangements.[44] Moreover, British and French staffs planned separately, with only minimal coordination of plans in independent areas of operation.[45] The Allies only informed one another of their intended actions, in effect providing liaison not unity of command. Although the two armies did cooperate more closely, Lloyd George's machinations, Nivelle's personal and professional arrogance, and the dismal failure of the offensive further jaundiced the idea of unified command.[46]

As a result, the Allies shelved the question of unified command until the collapse of Russia and the Italian debacle at Caporetto once again forced them to address the issue. Facing a likely and massive German attack somewhere on the Western Front in spring 1918, Foch called for establishing a General Allied Reserve, positioned to counter a German offensive in either the British or French sector.[47] Although the rationale for such a reserve made sense, implementation faced substantial obstacles. First, the British and French were convinced that the German attack would fall most heavily on their respective sector and were reluctant to provide forces to the General Reserve. Second, all parties realized that a General Reserve would require a single CINC to control its movements and operation. At this juncture, however, diverging national interests and strategies meant that national commanders placed insufficient trust in each other to submit their forces to a coalition commander or to contribute the forces necessary to compose the reserve.[48]

The SWC attempted to skirt the issue of unified command of the General Reserve by establishing an Executive War Board chaired by Foch. Foch proposed that the body, composed of the permanent military representatives of the SWC, with him as president, have responsibility for determining the size of the reserve; the extent of each nation's contribution; the location of the reserve; the time, place, and period of its employment for the defensive; and, should a counterattack be appropriate, the time, employment, and direction of attack. The SWC ratified Foch's proposals on 2 February 1918, and by 6 February he had designated each nation's contribution.[49]

At this point, however, support for the General Reserve began to erode. National commanders naturally hesitated to give up any forces to it. Nevertheless, by the end of February Foch had hammered out agreements with the French and the Italians, and it appeared that the problem might be resolved.[50] However, the British reply to Foch's entreaties dealt the General Reserve its deathblow. Haig, having made separate arrangements with Pétain for French support in the event of an attack in the British sector, indicated that he would not provide forces for the General Reserve. His Majesty's Government affirmed his stand. Foch, in turn, referred the issue back to the SWC for resolution, where it died during the SWC meeting of 14–15 March.[51]

The question of the General Reserve would not stay buried, however. Only a week later, on 21 March 1918, the long-anticipated German offensive shattered the Western Front near the juncture of the British and French armies. In accordance with their informal agreement, Haig quickly called upon Pétain for support. An increasing gap between the two armies and French fear of the loss of Paris, however, led Pétain to refuse.[52] Faced with looming catastrophe, Haig proposed during a meeting of British and French representatives at Doullens, France, on 26 March 1918 that Foch *"should coordinate the actions of the Allied Armies on the Western Front."*[53] The British and French governments quickly approved Foch's appointment. Foch's power to coordinate the Anglo-French armies did not provide, however, for control of all Allied forces, for the Doullens agreement included neither the Belgian nor the Italian nor the American army. In addition, national commanders retained the right to appeal any decisions to home governments.[54]

Continued German successes and uncoordinated Allied efforts eventually forced the realization that Foch's powers under the Doullens agreement were insufficient and more dynamic action was necessary. Accordingly, General John J. Pershing, commander of the American Expeditionary Force (AEF), subordinated American forces to Foch's strategic direction on 28 March 1918.[55] Pershing's offer is a strong indication of the depth of the Allies' peril. Like his British counterparts, Pershing had strict instructions from Secretary of War Newton D. Baker that "the President directs me to communicate to you the following . . . the underlying idea must be kept in view that the forces of the

United States are a separate and distinct component of the combined forces, the identity of which must be preserved."[56]

Pershing's prior experience served him well in carrying out this guidance. The president and first captain of the West Point Class of 1886, Pershing had served on the frontier for more than a decade. His actions at San Juan Hill in the Spanish-American War earned him the admiration of Theodore Roosevelt. In 1905, Pershing married Helen Frances Warren, daughter of the chairman of the Senate Military Affairs Committee. Successful tours in the Philippines burnished Pershing's reputation and, combined with his marital connection and friendship with Theodore Roosevelt, led to his promotion in 1905 from captain to brigadier general over the heads of 862 more senior officers. In 1916, President Woodrow Wilson placed Pershing in command of the Punitive Expedition pursuing the marauding Pancho Villa, who had been attacking American border towns along the Rio Grande. After having led one of the largest U.S. forces since the Civil War, Pershing was the natural choice to command the AEF upon U.S. entry into World War I in 1917.[57]

Despite Pershing's subordination of U.S. forces to Foch's strategic direction, the situation continued to deteriorate. On 3 April, the SWC met at Beauvais and quickly agreed that a single commander of Allied forces was essential to avert defeat. The British, French, and American governments therefore charged General Foch "with the coordination of the action of the Allied armies on the Western Front. To this end, all powers necessary to secure effective realization are conferred on him. The British, French, and American Governments for this purpose entrust to General Foch the strategic direction of military operations."[58] The Beauvais agreement set the conditions for Allied unity of direction and command for the remainder of World War I.

Yet, although later named CINC of the Allied armies in France, Foch never attained supreme command in the strictest sense.[59] Rather, he directed execution of military strategy. Grand strategy remained the purview of political leaders, and national military leaders controlled operations. National commanders retained the right to appeal Foch's decisions to their governments, a significant constraint on his command authority. As a result, as General Tasker Bliss later pointed out, Foch "was given no power of command. He could only consult and advise. The result was as one might expect. He had to waste precious time in traveling from one headquarters and the other, persuading commanders to do what he should have been empowered to order."[60] Thus, unable to give orders to the armies under his direction, Foch depended largely on the confidence and personal relationships between him and the various national commanders.[61]

Fortunately, as Allied successes accumulated over the summer of 1918, so, too, did Foch's informal authority. In the final analysis, Foch received the responsibility and authority to provide unity of effort, which is probably the maximum power that any coalition commander can reasonably expect. As General Bliss cogently pointed out, "Unified command came in 1918 at the first moment it could possibly come. Opposition gave way only when it was manifest that every other course had failed. Unified command was accepted, not for the purpose of winning victory but to prevent irretrievable defeat."[62]

Concomitant with the struggles over a unified Allied command, sharp differences arose concerning the amalgamation of Allied and especially U.S. units late in the war. At the time, the term *amalgamation* had a rather broad meaning, varying from the assignment of low-level units—such as army battalions, brigades, and divisions or destroyer squadrons—of one nation to serve under the direction of another nation's commander. As indicated earlier, with the rare exception of the First Battle of Ypres in October–November 1914, British and French armies operated separately.[63] Once the United States entered the war, however, the seemingly endless pool of American manpower brought amalgamation to the forefront.

The integration of U.S. naval forces with the Royal Navy represents the pinnacle of amalgamation and inter-Allied cooperation during World War I. This success was due to a variety of circumstances. Limited U.S. naval forces were available for service with British allies as early as 24 April 1917, less than three weeks after the United States declared war against Germany. Because naval ships and units normally operate as discrete entities within specified areas of operation, the combined command and control of British and U.S. naval forces was relatively simple. Lastly, because the Royal Navy dwarfed the initial U.S. contribution, it made good sense to subordinate U.S. naval forces to British control.

The assignment of Rear Admiral William S. Sims as the U.S. Navy representative in London may have been the most fortuitous circumstance that facilitated rapid amalgamation of U.S. and British naval forces. As U.S.-German tensions escalated over German unrestricted submarine warfare, Sims, recently assigned president of the Naval War College, was summoned secretly to Washington near the end of March 1917. There, he received instructions to proceed clandestinely to London, in his words, "to get in touch with the British Admiralty and learn how we could best and most quickly cooperate in the naval war."[64] Sims was an excellent, if somewhat controversial, choice. On the one hand, born in Canada to American parents, Sims had a well-established reputation as an Anglophile. In fact, President William Howard Taft personally reprimanded Sims in 1910 after Sims delivered a speech in London essentially calling for an Anglo-American union in the event of war with Germany. This attitude also made Sims unpopular with many U.S. naval officers and supporters of U.S. navalism, who, in the words of historian David Trask, "ordinarily viewed the Royal Navy as their principal rival and potential enemy."[65] On the other hand, Sims was a noted naval reformer and gunnery expert and brought strong professional credentials to the mission. He had served as naval aide to President Theodore Roosevelt and had been the naval attaché in Paris, where he had mastered French. His strong pro-British views and connections in London made it likely, at least in the eyes of CNO Admiral William S. Benson, that Sims would quickly gain British cooperation. That did not stop Benson from admonishing Sims: "Don't let the British pull the wool over your eyes. It is none of our business pulling their chestnuts out of the fire. We would as soon fight the British as the Germans."[66]

Benson's attitude was not unique. Since its inception, the U.S. Navy naturally had seen the Royal Navy as its principal rival. A common hangover from the Revolutionary War, a growing trade and financial rivalry, and a general low-level Anglophobia among significant elements of the U.S. population, especially among ethnic Irish and Germans, added to the mix. There had been some recent thawing of relations, leading historian Bradley F. Smith to conclude that "by the eve of World War I, a substantial portion of the American population had come around to perceiving Britain as a strong, but aging and generally benevolent lion."[67] The aging lion still occasionally flexed its muscles, however, and the British blockade policy against Germany and perceived British violations of U.S. neutral rights generated significant anger against Britain.[68]

By the time Sims arrived in London, President Woodrow Wilson had requested a declaration of war against Germany, and Sims immediately began full discussions with members of the British Admiralty. Although the British initially were reluctant to share information, Sims argued that neither he nor the United States could be effective partners without such access. The British soon included him in all their naval planning, and as Sims later noted, "sitting in conference with them every morning, I became, for all practical purposes, a member of their organization."[69] Sims worked so closely with his British counterparts that he operated out of an office in the Admiralty rather than following U.S. naval tradition of maintaining his headquarters afloat. Indeed, the degree of cooperation between Sims and the Royal Navy was such that David Trask concludes, "The United States never developed a distinctly independent naval strategy or set of tactics during 1917–1918. Sims helped bring about the acceptance of British ideas."[70]

Although Sims generally enjoyed smooth sailing in London, he faced much rougher waters in his dealings with Washington. His arrival in Britain coincided with the height of the German U-boat campaign that had Britain on the brink of disaster. The British needed antisubmarine vessels—destroyers, frigates, subchasers—and they needed them at once. Quickly grasping the severity of the situation, Sims urged the immediate dispatch of all available American antisubmarine forces to Europe.[71] The first U.S. destroyers reached Queenstown (now Cobh), Ireland, on 4 May 1917, less than a month after Sims's arrival in London, and Anglo-American planners quickly integrated the destroyers into the Royal Navy's operations.[72]

Nonetheless, the German U-boat campaign picked up momentum. In response, Sims recommended dispatching all available destroyers to the United Kingdom and shifting the U.S. shipbuilding program to the production of merchant marine and antisubmarine craft. Sims's advice ran into considerable resistance. First, the general unpreparedness of U.S. ships and trained crews to operate them delayed deployment of additional antisubmarine assets. Second, the undeveloped U.S. industrial base would take months to begin producing antisubmarine craft and merchant ships in the quantities desperately needed. Third, no plans existed on a national or coalition basis for the employment of these forces, and British and American naval leaders disagreed on the efficacy of convoy operations. Fourth, U.S. naval leaders were dissatisfied with British naval strategy, believing that reliance on blockade, peripheral operations, and antisubmarine operations was too defensive in nature. Wedded to the theories propounded by the U.S. Navy's own rear admiral Alfred Thayer Mahan, U.S. Navy leaders wanted a more offensive strategy that would seek a large-scale fleet action with the German High Seas Fleet.[73] Although not overtly voiced, the immediate dispatch of all destroyers would have stripped the U.S. Fleet of its escort screen. Absent the destroyer screen, the U.S. Fleet could not sortie against the High Seas Fleet. Although the probability of such an engagement had become increasingly unlikely since the Battle of Jutland in June 1916, many American admirals, their thinking deeply rooted in Mahan's ideas, undoubtedly resented that their battleships would be largely useless. Last, sending only destroyers almost guaranteed their employment under overall British command, leaving the bulk of the U.S. Navy leadership on the sidelines.

These latter two points were not simply narrow questions of military ego. President Wilson was concerned that denying the U.S. Navy a major role in the defeat of Germany would weaken U.S. influence at the postwar peace table. Most importantly, a shift to building antisubmarine craft meant deferring the Naval Act of 1916, which focused on building battleships and a "navy second to none." This last point especially endeared Sims to no one. His recommendation upset most of the leadership of the U.S. Navy. Congressional proponents who favored capital-ship construction and President Woodrow Wilson feared that any delay in the building program of 1916 would permit the Royal Navy to retain its dominance in capital ships in the postwar era.[74]

After President Wilson and Admiral Benson dispatched Admiral Henry T. Mayo, CINC, U.S. Atlantic Fleet, to Europe for a firsthand review of the situation, Washington eventually agreed with Sims's proposal. Disagreements still erupted, however, over how best to conduct the antisubmarine campaign. The British, increasingly strangled by the U-boat offensive, naturally wished to concentrate on protecting merchant ships and their precious cargoes of foodstuffs and war materiel. The United States, however, wanted to concentrate on protecting U.S. troop convoys. Because there were few such U.S. troop convoys in 1917, U.S. arguments initially did not prevail. By January 1918, however, naval leaders could no longer defer a decision. The British ultimately acceded to U.S. demands to the point of diverting Royal Navy escorts and supplying troopships at the expense of British commerce.[75]

Although subsequent events vindicated Sims's recommendations, his championing of antisubmarine warfare over the battle fleet earned him few friends in the U.S. Navy. Sims also remained suspect in the eyes of his superiors in Washington, who believed him to be too cooperative with the British. Many fellow American officers resented his relationships with the British and feared that he had gone native. This attitude was so widespread that President Wilson commented at the Versailles Peace Conference that Sims ought to be wearing a British, not American, uniform.[76] Moreover, the deferral of capital-ship construction to build antisubmarine craft, coupled with the limits imposed later under the Washington Naval Treaty of 1922, meant that the U.S. Navy would continue to lag behind the Royal Navy throughout the interwar era.[77]

The operational command and control of U.S. naval forces operating in Europe offers an example of smoother inter-Allied cooperation. In the first instance, Sims, as commander of U.S. Naval Forces in European Waters, maintained ultimate command of U.S. vessels scattered around the British Isles. Because of the decentralized nature of U.S. dispositions, however, the Admiralty dispatched all operational orders after consultation and approval by Sims or his staff. Once approved, the British admiral commanding an area where U.S. vessels operated would pass the orders to the senior American naval officer. Depending on circumstances, U.S. ships would operate independently under American command or, if part of a larger force, under control of a British admiral.[78] These procedures allowed close integration with the Royal Navy, while high command and operational command remained firmly in American hands. This system, established immediately upon the arrival of U.S. naval forces, remained in effect throughout the course of the war.

This successful integration was due in large part to Sims's dedication to the principle of Allied cooperation, his rapid and strong support of British strategic concepts and operating methods, and local British and American naval officers maintenance of close working relationships with their counterparts. Two examples highlight the level of Anglo-American cooperation at the operational and tactical levels. In the first instance, when Admiral Rosslyn Wemyss assumed duties as first sea lord, he reorganized the Admiralty to include an American Planning Section within the British Plans Division. This inclusion greatly facilitated development of overall Anglo-American naval strategy and plans, with the Americans frequently providing the impetus behind new initiatives.[79]

The second instance concerned whether Admiral Sir Lewis Bayly, CINC, Irish Coast, should retain control of U.S. naval forces personnel then assigned to his command. Bayly had a well-earned reputation as an irascible and demanding commander, and there was some question in British minds about Bayly retaining his command. However, when the Admiralty queried then U.S. assistant secretary of the navy Franklin D. Roosevelt, Roosevelt recorded in his diary, "I told him frankly that our people from Sims down to the youngest destroyer officer felt that [Bayly] was the ideal man to command this station."[80] The fact that Bayly appointed Captain Joel Pringle of the U.S. Navy as his chief of staff contributed to this sense of satisfaction with Bayly's style of command. So dedicated was Bayly to coalition cooperation that when he went on leave, he insisted that Sims assume command of all operations, one of the few times in history that Royal Navy forces served under the flag of an American admiral.[81]

Historians have largely agreed with the participants about the successful amalgamation and unity of command within Anglo-American naval forces. British historian Arthur Marder, the leading authority on the Royal Navy of this period, concludes that "the general harmony of Anglo-American naval effort is a rare exception in the annals of wartime relations among allies."[82] American historian David R. Woodward opines, "Eventually, Anglo-American naval cooperation saw a level of amalgamation never achieved by land forces with the British and the French," although he adds the caveat, "but not without serious disagreements over priorities and strategy."[83] At the operational level, in particular the nexus between Bayly and Sims, great credit must go to Sims, who early on set the tone for his relationships with his British counterparts: "I believe there is no case on record where allies have cooperated together for any considerable time without more or less serious friction. I am out to make an exception in this mater [*sic*]."⁸⁴

The amalgamation of U.S. ground forces into British or French armies proceeded on an entirely different course. Although there were several good reasons for these differing paths, without a doubt, national and personal pride were involved. In addition, some key leaders, such as General Tasker Bliss, thought that amalgamation would lead to too great a loss of inadequately trained American lives. However, only one key consideration really mattered: the AEF's role in securing a coalition victory would determine the level of influence that the United States could wield at the peace table.⁸⁵ As David Trask observes, "This elemental decision was consistent with the president's intention to avoid political commitments that might compromise his peace plans while making an essential contribution to victory over the Central Powers."⁸⁶ Thus, the president's guidance circumscribed American policies on amalgamation. It also meant the mobilization of a large army that would sail to France to fight independently under its own commanders, using its own doctrine, in its own sector, "to strike the decisive blow against the German army."⁸⁷ These essential principles would guide Wilson's principal agent, General John J. Pershing, throughout the course of the war.

Adhering to these principles was not easy. Even before U.S. entry into the war, British military leaders argued for enlisting U.S. personnel directly into the British, Canadian, or French armies, thereby eliminating the prolonged time required to create an independent American army. Once the United States formally entered into war, Lieutenant General Sir Tom Bridges, British army representative on the Balfour Mission in the United States to coordinate military and supply efforts, suggested to U.S. Army chief of staff General Hugh Scott that the United States forgo creating its own army and instead send 500,000 men immediately to Britain to undergo training and employment by the British army. Once aware of Bridges's proposal, however, President Wilson quickly quashed the idea, though it would continue to resurface over the next year and a half.⁸⁸

Marshal Joffre, also in the United States on an initial coordination mission, likewise argued for the rapid transportation of individual U.S. replacements for training and employment in French units.⁸⁹ Joffre got no further than Bridges. Contrary to his British counterpart, however, Joffre quickly recognized that the Americans would never tolerate such a proposition and accepted the early arrival of a single American division as a means to boost French morale.⁹⁰ This initial recognition of American sensitivities also laid the groundwork for U.S.-French cooperation that would grow considerably over time. Coincidentally,

President Wilson decided that because the U.S. Navy already was cooperating with the Royal Navy, the bulk of the AEF would cooperate with the French army. Whether there was a direct cause and effect is unknown, however, in the wake of the failed Nivelle Offensive, pairing the AEF with the French army made sense. Regardless of reason, the vast majority of the AEF would train with the French army, would receive the bulk of its heavy weapons, equipment, and artillery support from French sources, and would fight predominantly alongside French forces—but as independent American units.[91]

Even with President Wilson's decisions, Pershing continuously had to fend off rising Allied pressure for more extensive amalgamation.[92] Although the Allies initially agreed to employ U.S. ground forces in divisional or larger units under their own commanders, Allied reverses throughout 1917 made it seem that only the immediate use of American manpower spelled the difference between victory and defeat.[93] With the British and French armies nearing exhaustion in December 1917, Pétain approached Pershing about integrating U.S. forces into French divisions at the regimental or even battalion level. Irrevocably devoted to the principle of an independent American command, Pershing adamantly rejected the proposal but did offer the entire First Infantry Division should an emergency require early employment of U.S. forces.[94]

To reduce manpower deficiencies, in January 1918 the British proposed using their shipping assets to transport 150 independent U.S. infantry battalions to France for training and service with the BEF. Pershing tentatively agreed with the plan, but only after expressing strong reservations.[95] In his memoirs, however, he remarked that he did not seriously object to Haig's plan because he saw it as a way to get additional shipping assets for faster transport of American units to France and that "it was not my intention at any time to agree to amalgamation in any permanent sense with either of the Allies."[96] Problems later developed over the implementation of the plan, not least President Wilson's objections, and the Allies shelved it in favor of the Six Division Plan, where the British agreed to ship six complete U.S. divisions to France to train under British supervision prior to assimilation into the AEF. Pershing recommended acceptance of the plan to the War Department. Although President Wilson eventually agreed to it, he admonished: "[Only] a 'sudden and manifest emergency' should be allowed to 'interfere with the building up of a great distinct American force at the front, acting under its own flag and its own officers.'"[97] After working out the details, U.S. regiments or divisions trained and went into the trenches to gain combat experience under command of British or French division or corps commanders.

When the Germans launched their climactic offensive in March 1918, it soon became apparent that the Allies needed more American units brought on line. Although steadfastly refusing wholesale incorporation of American forces, Pershing grudgingly acknowledged that prompt attachment of certain American forces to the British and French armies would be necessary to stop the Germans. He accordingly placed elements of the AEF at Foch's disposal on 28 March. Pershing nonetheless specified that amalgamation would be temporary and occur at no lower than division level, so that the American divisions would retain unit integrity and the ability quickly to transfer back to an eventual independent American army.[98] Foch immediately began to reposition U.S. divisions—starting with the transfer of the First Infantry Division into the British zone—usually to quiet sectors where they relieved more veteran Allied units for active campaigning. Over the next eight months, twenty-five U.S. divisions, thirty infantry brigades, nine field artillery brigades, and numerous smaller, specialized detachments would serve with the French. Nine U.S. divisions served with the British army.[99]

Pershing's concession did not end matters as German advances throughout April brought the British and French armies to the brink of collapse. British and French political leaders once again pressured Wilson for wholesale amalgamation of individual U.S. soldiers as well as units. In doing so, they failed to reckon with Wilson's dedication to an independent American army. The British especially grossly miscalculated when Lloyd George instructed Rufus Isaacs, marquess of Reading, the British ambassador to the United States, to convey to Wilson: "We can do no more than what we have done. It rests with America to win or lose the decisive battle of the war."[100] Wilson, so irate that he refused to see the ambassador, later commented in a cabinet meeting, "[I] fear that I will come out of the war hating [the] British."[101] After his temper cooled, his eventual response superficially supported amalgamation but contained caveats that fully preserved U.S. freedom of action. Colonel E. M. House, Wilson's trusted adviser, also informed Reading that this was Wilson's "last word on the subject." Reading, acknowledging defeat, cabled London that "the American position should be accepted, not only without raising any objection, but also without having any in mind."[102]

Nor did the British and French fare any better with Pershing. Despite intense pressure, the AEF commander obdurately refused to consider any further initiatives that might jeopardize an independent American army. These arguments raged throughout May and into June. Only one account of a highly acrimonious exchange at the Allied conference at Versailles during 1–2 June 1918 is necessary to convey the levels of frustration on both sides.

Foch (to Pershing): You are willing to risk our being driven back to the Loire [River]?
Pershing: Yes, I am willing to take that risk.
Lloyd George: Well, we will refer it to your President.
Pershing: Refer it to the President and be damned. I know what the President will do. He will simply refer it back to me for recommendation and I will make the same recommendation as I have made here today.[103]

Despite Pershing's outburst, the Allies did not relent. Even after Pershing placed the Second and Third Infantry Divisions in active operations under French corps commanders and was preparing to introduce even more divisions into combat under higher-level British and French commanders, the Allies continued to press Wilson and Pershing throughout June and July. Only when the last offensive planned by General Erich Ludendorff, de facto leader of the German army, stalled in mid-July and the Allies moved to the counteroffensive did calls for amalgamation finally subside—but not disappear.[104]

The mixing of forces affected not only American forces but French and British units as well. During the final Allied offensive of 1918, French contingents (division and higher) were attached to the American command for combat operations.[105] The assignment of British units with American forces occurred on a less-extensive basis. Except for artillery and transportation, only small, specialized elements of the British army served under U.S. command during the final battles because the British refused to place any of their fighting divisions under a U.S. corps commander.[106] A snub not forgotten that would color future Anglo-American collaboration for years to come.

On the eleventh hour of the eleventh day of the eleventh month of 1918, the guns finally fell silent on the Western Front. The Great War was over. Yet keen observers reckoned that this peace would be temporary. Foch remarked at the signing of the Versailles Peace Treaty, "This is not a peace. It is an armistice of twenty years."[107] From the other side of the hill, German diplomat Count Harry Kessler noted in his diary, "Today the Peace Treaty was ratified in Paris; the War is over. A terrible era begins for Europe, like the gathering of clouds before a storm, and it will end in an explosion probably still more terrible than that of the World War."[108]

Given the likelihood of such an outcome, what lessons or insights could or should have British and U.S. military leaders garnered? The coalition experience reinforced Clausewitz's dictum that "war is a continuation of politics by other means."[109] Each partner fought for its national interests and guarded those interests dearly, sometimes at the expense of coalition cohesion. Such conditions made difficult the design of coherent coalition policies and grand strategy and argued for a political decision-making body to oversee the higher direction of the war effort. Unfortunately, it took more than three years of fighting, the loss of hundreds of thousands of lives, and the virtual exhaustion of the British and French armies before the looming German offensives of 1918 finally forced the Allies to form the Supreme War Council.

Despite its many warts, the SWC nonetheless provided an advantage over the previous ad hoc conferences called to deal with the crisis of the moment. Moreover, political leaders recognized that effective strategic oversight by the SWC required a permanent military body to provide advice. Although political machinations reduced the effectiveness of the Military Council, it still represented a dramatic improvement in military advice relative to the vacuum that had previously existed. Similarly, exigencies, not foresight, eventually drove the coalition to appoint Foch as generalissimo. In practice, however, the most Foch could do was convince, cajole, and sometimes browbeat national commanders into complying with his guidance. Fortunately for the coalition, Foch adeptly managed the national commanders and their egos. In his role, Foch had what all high-level coalition commanders must have: the confidence of respective national political leaders and the trust of the military leaders of national contingents. In sum, people and personalities matter, especially in coalitions.

Reflections from a participant in this drama echo these conclusions. From 1934 to 1940, Major General Fox Conner, the G3 operations officer of the AEF, delivered an annual lecture at the U.S. Army War College entitled "The Allied High Command and Allied Unity of Direction." His preface, emphasizing that "dealing with the enemy is a simple and straight-forward matter when contrasted with securing close cooperation with an ally," set the tone for his address.[110] At the end of his presentation, he summarized what he believed to be the lessons in coalition warfare derived from the experiences of World War I. These insights, which would influence future U.S.-British military collaboration, bear recounting in detail:

1. National Pride plays some, though a small, part in preventing or postponing Unity of Direction and Unity of Command.
2. The ulterior motives of the several members of a Coalition form the principal obstacle to securing either Unity of Direction or Unity of Command.
3. With the exception of America and possibly Belgium, all Nations, or rather the Politicians of all Nations, in the World War were

filled with ulterior motives, and with grandiose ideas of the "Compensations" they would obtain at the peace table. It is likely to be so again.
4. With the exceptions noted, all Nations were "jockeying" for postwar "positions."
5. "Open Covenants, openly arrived" is beyond the realities of European statesmanship or politics. One is constantly reminded of Captain Peter Wright's tribute to the Americans at the Supreme War Council:—"They were all quite untouched by the taint of bad faith and personal calculation that seems to load the air where the great are."
6. As between Allies so opposed in racial characteristics, as well as National interests, as the British, the French, the Italians, and Americans, only an actual or a threatened catastrophe is likely to bring about anything approaching either Unity of Direction or Unity of Command.
7. In spite of the assertion just made, America should, if she ever indulges in the doubtful luxury of entering another Coalition, advocate, coincident with entering a war with Allies, the establishment of a Supreme War Council. Such an institution is primarily necessary to provide decent interment for "Fool Schemes."
8. Unity of Command should be sought, at least between Allies of equal standing, in matters of strategy only. It is quite hopeless to expect a worth-while Nation, unless it reaches the state of Austria in 1916 and 1917, to surrender the tactical command of its troops.[111]

Like its individual parts, the overall record of British and American experiences in coalition partnerships before and during World War I reveals mixed progress. The evidence suggests that the level of cooperation within the coalition varied considerably, as the partners hesitantly groped toward a semblance of coalition unity. Although oftentimes the journey was uncoordinated, disjointed, and replete with multiple fits and starts, by the end of the war the Allies had achieved modest progress, however episodic. Whether these many lessons were lessons lived and learned or lived and lost is explored more fully in the examination of Anglo-American coalition experiences in the interwar period.

2

Neither Friend nor Foe

U.S.-British Relations in the Interwar Years

If the British and Americans achieved any understanding of the complexities in coalition warfare from their experiences in World War I, that wisdom quickly faded from memory. This occurred not out of any conscious decision to avoid the subject but because of preoccupation with more pressing problems and a general revulsion against war. In Britain, public reaction against war was strong; as British historian Norman Gibbs points out, "It is essential . . . to realize that the war of 1914–1918 was regarded as justifiable in Britain only if it could genuinely be regarded as a war to end war. . . . War had involved commitment and war had been horrible. Therefore, the commitment itself had been wrong."[1] In a similar vein, historian Michael Howard notes that British intervention with land forces in World War I "was regarded (not least by the soldiers themselves) as an atypical and disagreeable experience under no circumstances to be repeated."[2] Indeed, not until 1932 did an official committee meet to study the lessons of the war.[3] Perhaps the most famous of many examples of the tenacity and endurance of antiwar sentiment was the Oxford Union Debate of 9 February 1933, which "resolved by a large majority: 'That this House will in no circumstances fight for its [Britain's] King or country.'"[4]

These reactions took place within the context of Britain's new geostrategic conditions. In the summer 1919, Britain seemed to be in a strong position. The country had played a critical role in the Allied victory over the Central Powers, and no other country posed an immediate threat. Shared sacrifices and victory contributed to a cohesive populace and empire. Even if Britain owed some short-term debt to the United States, the country's economic position appeared strong. Indeed, as part of the peace settlements, Britain garnered even more imperial possessions or protectorates as well as their accompanying resources.[5]

Historian Anne Orde argues that Britain followed three sometimes competing approaches in the interwar era to maintain international peace while sustaining its global position. The first she describes as "Atlanticism," or close cooperation, perhaps even alliance, with the United States. The second is imperial isolationism, or a strong focus on developing the empire while avoiding any commitments outside the empire—that is, to Europe. The last thread was to remain active in global, especially European, affairs. Unfortunately for Britain, these three approaches failed. Atlanticism quickly collapsed when the United States failed to ratify the Versailles Treaty, refused to join the League of Nations, and withdrew into diplomatic isolation, although some optimists in Britain clung to the belief that the United States would eventually come around. International leadership rapidly faded away as Britain's increasing economic decline eroded its ability to sustain its political, military, and diplomatic roles.[6] As a result, Britain settled on the middle path: promote a permanent peace and work through the League of Nations while allowing laissez-faire business and commercial interests to sustain the empire.[7]

The United States took a similar if more complex path. As historian George Herring notes, for the United States "the era of the 1920s in fact defies simple explanation. . . . United States foreign policy derived from numerous, conflicting pressures, producing a bundle of seeming contradictions."[8] With no immediate threat to the United States, two broad oceans, and a potent navy, successive Republican administrations retreated into selective diplomatic isolation but did not withdraw entirely from world affairs. For example, in 1928 Secretary of State Frank Kellogg and French foreign minister Aristide Briand negotiated the Kellogg-Briand Pact, in which the United States, France, and other signatories, including Germany, renounced war as an instrument of national policy and pledged to resolve international disputes by peaceful means. The United States committed to extensive international disarmament, as evidenced by U.S. leadership of multiple disarmament conferences, particularly in naval ships and armaments. American financiers, with government support, negotiated numerous, extensive, and successful efforts to resolve German reparations problems and European debt crises—for instance, the Dawes Plan of 1924 and the Young Plan of 1929–1930. Finally, the United States followed aggressive financial and trade policies referred to as the "diplomacy of the dollar."[9]

These policies enjoyed widespread internal support as the American public recoiled from World War I and subsequent peace treaties. The United States had entered the war with a wave of optimism to create a peaceful and democratic world. By the end of the bruising political campaign over the Versailles Treaty, many Americans concluded that "little or nothing had been gained and the foreign nations were as venal and self-centered as ever."[10] Thus, for the twenty years following 1918, the United States sought protection through nonmilitary means: geographic barriers, disarmament conferences and treaties, diplomatic and economic sanctions, and legislation to keep the United States out of foreign wars.[11]

Strong anti-British feelings, going back to the American War of Independence, reinforced the backlash to war. U.S. demographic trends were a key aspect of anti-British sentiment. In 1914, for instance, the United States had more than 8 million people who had been born in Germany or had at least one parent born in Germany and approximately 4.5 million Americans of Irish descent.[12] Both groups were potent anti-British voting blocks in key states. For example, Senator Henry Cabot Lodge (R–Mass.), with a substantial Irish electorate, opposed the Versailles Treaty because it failed to address the question of Irish independence. Lodge also co-opted key Progressive senators opposed to British imperialism, especially in Ireland and India, which he combined with a strong thread of Anglophobia in the Senate as a weapon to defeat the Versailles Treaty and U.S. membership in the League of Nations.[13] In addition, British violations of U.S. neutral rights prior to American entry into the war came to a head in the early 1920s with more than 2,000 claims against Britain over ships or cargoes seized during 1914–1917. Antipathy to things British was so strong that throughout the 1920s several states passed initiatives requiring the teaching of "American" as opposed to "English" as the official written and spoken language.[14]

The British harbored a substantial set of frustrations regarding their American cousins as well. Political leaders resented that the United States stood by until April 1917 while Britain and France bore the brunt of the casualties and grievous economic costs of the war. That it took more than a year for the AEF to become a viable fighting force while Britain took considerable casualties added further frustrations. The British public as well as political elites took umbrage when Americans took credit for "saving" the Allies and "winning" the war. Wilson's leveraging of the limited U.S. military role into a major role at the peace table as well as his moralizing tone and diktats rankled. His failure to deliver ratification of the Versailles Treaty, to bring the United States into the League of Nations, and to ensure security guarantees to Britain and France only aggravated hard feelings.[15]

Economic competition in the 1920s and 1930s created further friction between the two powers. During the war, Britain lost between 10 and 15 percent of its overseas assets, and the United States deeply penetrated British markets, especially in Latin America.[16] As a result, by 1919 the dollar had replaced the pound sterling as the dominant world currency.[17] At the same time, New York City began supplanting London as the global financial capital. U.S. business interests were increasingly buying British firms, oftentimes in hostile acquisitions. British adoption of American business practices resulted in a backlash against the "Americanization" of British business, manufacturing, and culture.[18]

To make up some of these losses, Britain resorted to trade practices that alienated not only U.S. businessmen but also, significantly, the U.S. Congress. Britain's so-called Stevenson Plan of 1922 offers but one example of this trend. In the immediate postwar period, the price of rubber dropped precipitously. To shore up rubber prices and stabilize the pound–dollar exchange rate, the British, who controlled approximately 75 percent of global rubber production at the time, curtailed sales. At the time, the United States was consuming approximately 75 percent of all rubber production, mostly for tires for the booming auto industry. Thus, whereas increased rubber prices would mean more dollars for Britain, thereby easing its currency-exchange issues, these higher costs drove up the price of automobiles, violating the maxim to never get between Americans and their cars. Increased rubber production in the Netherlands East Indies and the introduction of rubber plantations in Liberia drove down costs to the point where Britain was compelled to end the plan in 1928; however, a bitter aftertaste remained on both sides.[19]

On a macroscale, overarching British trade policies fostered friction. The introduction of the system of British Imperial Preference provides but one key example. At a conference in Ottawa in 1932, leaders of the British Empire reduced tariffs and trade barriers within the empire as a means of stimulating economies hurt by the Great Depression. Unfortunately, these measures also penalized countries not within the empire, such as the United States, which saw the protectionist system as violating free-trade principles. By the mid-1930s, few issues would bedevil Anglo-American relations more than this one. Indeed, "it became a State Department axiom that there could be no cooperation on other matters until a trade agreement had been reached."[20] Tensions over Imperial Preference eventually led career diplomat J. Pierpont Moffat to declare in 1936, "[Britain] thinks she can count on our help politically, yet hit us below the belt commercially all over the world."[21]

Nowhere would economic issues have larger consequences for overall British-U.S. relations in the 1930s than the World Economic Conference held in London in June and July 1933. Originally called by President Herbert Hoover, the conference sought to identify ways to reduce tariffs, increase prices, and stabilize currencies to mitigate the Great Depression. The recently inaugurated U.S. president, Franklin Roosevelt, initially supported the conference, gave British prime minister Ramsay MacDonald and French president Édouard

Herriot indications that he would return the United States to the gold standard, and sent messages to fifty-four heads of state supporting currency stabilization. On 3 July 1933, however, Roosevelt effectively scuttled the conference when he unexpectedly repudiated a U.S. return to the gold standard and withdrew support for any international currency stabilization schemes.[22]

Roosevelt's reversal had several critical consequences. First, it collapsed the conference and ended all likelihood of an internationally coordinated route out of the Great Depression. Two, it soured many of the most prominent British leaders on Franklin Roosevelt.[23] Most importantly, Roosevelt earned the lasting enmity of Neville Chamberlain. Then chancellor of the Exchequer, Chamberlain was the son of Joseph Chamberlain and half-brother of Austin Chamberlain, both distinguished statesmen. After a successful career in business in Birmingham, he entered local politics, serving on the city council and as lord mayor. Chamberlain entered Parliament in 1918 at the age of fifty, and by 1932 he was head of the Conservative Party and chancellor of the Exchequer. In 1937, he would rise to prime minister.[24] As historian Greg Kennedy has observed, Chamberlain "was convinced that the Americans deliberately misled and duped him in discussions about their aims . . . and attitudes toward his proposals."[25] Chamberlain's disdain for U.S. economic policies expanded into a personal distaste for Franklin Roosevelt that would further taint relations not only between the two men but also between their respective countries until Chamberlain's fall from power in May 1940.[26]

The repayment of British war debts to the United States was the final economic irritant to Anglo-American cooperation. By the early 1930s, many countries, including Britain, had either stopped making payments or were well in arrears. The view on the eastern side of the Atlantic was that Europe had shouldered most of the costs—whether in blood or treasure—for defeating Germany, while the United States took full advantage of Europe's predicament to improve its economic position. The United States, therefore, should forgive all war debts, thereby easing Europe, but especially Britain, out of the depression. From an American perspective, however, these debts were fairly owed. Indeed, President Hoover and his secretary of state, Henry L. Stimson, felt betrayed when the debtor powers sought renegotiation or forgiveness of their debts.[27] By 1934, France had defaulted three years in a row, and Britain offered a lump sum payment of $60 million as full settlement of an $8 billion debt. In reaction, Senator Hiram Johnson (D–Calif.) introduced, Congress passed, and in April 1934 Roosevelt signed the Johnson Debt Default Act, which prohibited private or U.S. government loans to any country that defaulted on its war debts. Although popular in the United States, this act would effectively tie

Franklin Roosevelt's hands when war broke out in 1939, much to the ultimate detriment of the United Kingdom.[28]

Concomitant with these matters was the issue of Anglo-American naval rivalry. Because the at times intense rivalry influenced future cooperation between the two navies, the story deserves elaboration. Despite a meteoric rise under President Theodore Roosevelt, by 1914 the U.S. Navy lagged far behind the Royal Navy. British interference with U.S. neutral rights during World War I aggravated U.S. sensitivities, culminating in Wilson's Naval Program of 1916, which sought to build a "navy second to none." Although temporarily sidetracked by the urgent need to divert U.S. shipbuilding to antisubmarine craft and merchant ships during the war, the U.S. naval program of 1919 called for an additional ten battleships and six battle cruisers, resulting in a U.S. Fleet that would surpass the Royal Navy.[29] British actions at the Paris Peace Conference, in particular efforts to secure the Royal Navy's superiority by destroying rather than redistributing interned German ships, annoyed all powers. British reliance on blockade conflicted with American ideas of freedom of the seas and neutral rights, placing the Americans and the British at loggerheads.[30] Only a U.S. Navy capable of challenging the Royal Navy could secure freedom of the seas and neutral rights as envisaged by the Americans. Although the U.S. Senate's failure to ratify the Treaty of Versailles ultimately mooted the issue, neutral rights remained a matter of bilateral contention nonetheless.

The Royal Navy also contributed to the naval rivalry. Although Great Britain was still the world's predominant naval power, World War I had tremendously strained it navy. The Royal Navy had to rely on the United States to help defeat the German U-boat threat and had required Japanese assistance in the Pacific and Indian Oceans to cope with German U-boats and surface raiders. It had not defeated the Germans in a major fleet action; ultimately, armies had decided the war. These points called into question the need for a capital fleet and boded poorly for the Royal Navy in the budget battles that followed the end of the war.[31]

Financial stringencies drove nations, including the United States, Britain, and other naval powers, to the negotiating table at the Washington Naval Conference of 1921–1922. Although the conference was a very important military and diplomatic event, the details of the negotiations do not require elaboration.[32] For this narrative, the critical issue is that the British, recognizing they could not sustain a naval race with the United States and that the likelihood of an armed conflict with the United States was extremely low and diminishing, scrapped their long-held two-power standard and agreed to parity of capital ships with the United States.[33]

The Washington Naval Treaty of 1922 left unresolved the issue of cruiser limitations, which distinctly favored Britain and would continue to nettle many in the U.S. naval establishment.[34] To resolve this sticking point, in 1927 President Calvin Coolidge called for the signatories of the Five Powers Treaty from the Washington Conference to convene in Geneva.[35] On a purely military level, the issue boiled down to the number of cruisers that Britain and the United States could possess. In short, differing geostrategic circumstances and naval doctrines led to an impasse among the military negotiators.[36]

Political factors exacerbated the tensions. On the British side, there was intense political support led by Winston Churchill, then chancellor of the Exchequer, for the Admiralty's obdurate position that Britain could not have fewer than seventy cruisers.[37] Prime Minister Stanley Baldwin likewise was unwilling to compromise and recalled his chief delegate from Geneva for three days of consultations. At the same time, the U.S position hardened. Congressional navalists and their allies within the Navy Department had been pressing for a significant increase in the size and composition of the U.S. Fleet. President Coolidge, who wanted to tamp down naval spending, took personal offense at perceived British duplicity, called for a massive shipbuilding program that would result in U.S. domination in the cruiser category, and refused to budge from his position.[38] Amid mutual acrimony, the talks collapsed. The rancor on both sides of the Atlantic became so severe that the two and a half years after the Geneva Conference were, according to historian B. J. C. McKercher, a time when "relations between Britain and the United States fell to one of their twentieth century nadirs."[39]

Eventually, however, British and U.S. political leaders recognized that for economic reasons they had to avert a naval race. Both sides also realized, in retrospect, that their uniformed leaders' fixation on narrow technical details had obstructed a broader overarching diplomatic solution.[40] In an act of conciliation, Prime Minister Ramsay MacDonald traveled to Washington to meet with President Hoover in October 1929 to agree on the policy issues for the upcoming London Naval Conference. The two leaders worked out a compromise at their level and expended considerable effort bending their respective naval establishments to their will so that political, not naval, leaders controlled negotiating positions at the conference.[41]

Once the conference convened, personalities made a tremendous difference. MacDonald was not as politically invested as had been Baldwin, and Hoover was much more conciliatory than was Coolidge. Moreover, Churchill's departure from the Exchequer and gradual banishment to the "political wilderness" removed a considerable impediment to compromise.[42] Nor were political leaders solely responsible for the change of tenor. British historian Stephen Roskill notes, "Much of the credit for that accomplishment [Anglo-American teamwork] is attributed to the broad-mindedness of Admiral W. V. Pratt, which contrasted markedly with the Anglophobia of Admiral H. P. Jones, his predecessor as chief American naval 'expert.'"[43]

In the end, there was a remarkable degree of Anglo-American cooperation at the conference, especially relative to the discord less than three years earlier at Geneva.[44] Although the technical details of the agreement are important, they need not detain the reader. In short, a compromise focusing on overall tonnage limits gave each side the flexibility to build the types of cruisers it desired.[45] More important than the technical success of the conferences was the outcome that the U.S. Navy got the parity it had craved for more than twenty years and recognized that it was never going to fight the Royal Navy. Equally, Britain acknowledged that it would not fight the United States and accepted that it could not afford to engage in a naval arms race with America. The agreement did not end competition between the two navies, but, as historian Phillips O'Brien observes, "the American navy was starved of crucial anti-British oxygen," and "by settling most of the outstanding Anglo-American naval issues at London, both were allowed to concentrate on legitimate issues of national or imperial security."[46] Nonetheless, as Roskill notes, some chilliness remained on the British side as they continued to look down upon their parvenu "cousins."[47] No doubt, residual envy and irritation remained on the U.S. side as well.

If by the end of the London Naval Conference the United States and Britain no longer saw each other as potential adversaries, neither did they see each other as a potential ally. At this point, both countries essentially had returned to a policy of avoiding military commitments. To understand why, it is necessary to return to the immediate post–World War I period and trace the development of the broad strategic context on both sides of the Atlantic.

In August 1919, the Cabinet of the United Kingdom met to determine guidance to the military services in preparing its upcoming budget estimates. Two key assumptions in that guidance would have crucial consequences for future British planning for coalitions. First, the Cabinet directed, "it should be assumed . . . for framing future estimates that the British Empire will not be engaged in any great war during the next ten years and that no Expeditionary Force is required for this purpose." In the second case, the Cabinet noted, "the principle function of the Military and Air Forces is to provide garrisons for India, Egypt, the new mandated territory, and all territory (other than self-governing) under British control, as well as to provide the necessary support to the civil power at home."[48]

The general public recoil from war and the so-called Ten-Year Rule effectively meant, as Norman Gibbs points out, that "strategic doctrine in Britain between the two World Wars was largely based upon a return to the concept of independence or isolation."[49] Moreover, because the Ten-Year Rule ruled out a BEF, there was no need to plan for one. The practical effects were such that Chief of the Imperial General Staff "Sir George Milne [noted] in 1926 that the Army was now completely out of date, added that the war against Germany in 1914 was 'abnormal,' and that although retaining fees were being paid to reservists for another Continental war it was very unlikely that they would ever be required."[50] As a consequence of these conditions, the military services planned for three separate and uncoordinated tasks: the navy for the threat from the Japanese Fleet in the Pacific, the RAF for strategic bombing in Europe, and the army for the defense of the far-flung overseas empire.[51] Finally, in the era of financial stringency that quickly followed World War I, there were insufficient funds available for the adequate subsistence of the three services. As Gibbs concludes, "for [the British government], concentration upon the air and sea was both enough to absorb the major part of Britain's resources and a political as well as military justification for her [sic] refusal to contemplate a large army for major continental war."[52]

Avoiding another major commitment of land forces on the Continent echoed outside government circles as well. Sir Basil Liddell Hart, the preeminent military theorist of the interwar era, concluded that Britain had committed a fundamental error in its strategic approach to World War I. He urged that any future British participation in a conflict be based on the traditional British way of war—blockade and concentration on economic objectives, but with two new twists to this traditional approach. First, air power would augment naval power to hasten economic collapse of the opponent. Then, once the enemy was on its knees, Britain would unleash a small armored force to finish off the last resistance.[53] These ideas caught the imagination of influential elements of the civil and military communities; thus, much of the debate on land warfare during the interwar era centered on mechanization and questions of tactics, doctrine, logistical support, and firepower, among others.[54] Preoccupied with the problems of modern war as applied to their national forces, the British military largely overlooked the problems of coalition warfare during the era between the two world wars.[55]

Similarly, the U.S. retreat into political and military isolation obviously had tremendous effect on the armed services, the army in particular. As Russell Weigley concludes, "The [U.S.] Army during the 1920s and early 1930s may have been less ready to function as a fighting force than at any time in its history."⁵⁶ Like the British, American plans developed along individual service lines, not on joint, much less multinational planning. The army was concerned primarily with the defense of the United States and its overseas territories. Any form of offensive action relied on infantry forces, but with no proposed theater of operations. The U.S. Army Air Corps was preoccupied with strategic bombing, but only in defense of the United States and its territories. The navy remained focused on capital ships and an offensive in the Pacific.⁵⁷ As a result, much of the limited strategic planning between the wars before 1939 was meaningless. General Thomas T. Handy, a longtime member of the Army War Plans Division (WPD) during the 1930s, noted that as late as 1936 there were only eleven officers assigned to the WPD. He pointed out that these officers were responsible not only for strategic planning but also for planning for all staff divisions within the War Department as well as for preparation of the budget. With these numerous responsibilities and demands, the officers had little time for realistic planning, and so, in the words of historian Maurice Matloff, U.S. strategic planning in the interwar era "represented little more than abstract academic exercises."⁵⁸

Despite the best intentions of both the U.K. and the U.S. leadership to remain aloof from alliances and their reluctance to prepare for war of any kind, coalition warfare in particular, the two great democracies gradually awoke to the dangers posed by Germany, Italy, and Japan in the 1930s. Japan's seizure of Manchuria in 1931 and continued aggression against central China; Germany's resignation from the World Disarmament Conference in 1933, departure from the League of Nations, and covert then overt rearmament; and Italian encroachments on Ethiopia caused the British to reassess their strategy and defense planning to include their level of engagement in Europe and the Far East.⁵⁹

Throughout this period, Neville Chamberlain, chancellor of the Exchequer, was a key adviser to Prime Ministers Ramsay MacDonald and Stanley Baldwin on strategy, defense, and rearmament. Although the government relied throughout most of the 1930s on a strategy of deterrence based primarily on the Royal Navy, Chamberlain opposed the Admiralty's efforts to maintain or increase its budget. Recognizing the increasing role of air power, the British placed greater emphasis on the RAF. These priorities left little money available for the British army, but few in government saw this as a major problem.⁶⁰ By 1934, British grand strategy in Europe meant forsaking any coalition action with Belgium, France, Holland, or Italy and relying on a larger RAF to deter a German attack on Belgium or the British Isles. In the Far East, Britain would "show teeth" and work with, rather than confront, Japan and avoid any overtures to the United States.⁶¹

By early 1935, the balance of power in Europe was shifting dramatically. On 16 March, Adolf Hitler renounced the arms-limitations provisions of the Versailles Treaty and embarked on a massive rearmament program, particularly with the German air force (Luftwaffe). In June, Germany manipulated Britain into signing the Anglo-German Naval Treaty and began building a small but potent fleet. Italy was a rising military competitor in the Mediterranean and had invaded Ethiopia. On 7 March 1936, Nazi Germany reoccupied the demilitarized Rhineland, precipitating a major crisis in which France and Britain ultimately offered only weak protests.[62] Throughout the remainder of 1936 and early 1937, the international situation continued to deteriorate. In Europe, the Spanish Civil War erupted in June 1936, with Germany and Italy providing military support to Franco's fascist Nationalist forces and the Soviet Union supporting the Republican side. Italy annexed Ethiopia and joined with Germany to create the Rome–Berlin Axis. In the Far East, the British were discovering that their reliance on deterrence and traditional offshore balance-of-power strategy was not working. Japanese withdrawal from all treaties concerning naval limitations and accelerated naval construction allowed Japan to reach de facto naval parity with the United States, which had deferred much ship construction because of the Great Depression.[63] The Japanese invasion of central China, coercion of British interests in Shanghai and Hong Kong, and perceived threats to Australia and New Zealand called into question the strategy of appeasing Japan.

Amid these tumultuous events, Chamberlain assumed the office of the prime minister in May 1937 and undertook a comprehensive strategy review.[64] It quickly became apparent that Britain had insufficient forces, especially ships, to meet conditions in Europe, the Mediterranean, and the Far East simultaneously. Anticipated German, Italian, and Japanese rearmament, especially naval construction, meant that the strategic calculus would worsen over time.[65] Because Chamberlain and his Cabinet did not believe that they could devote more funding to the navy, British strategy would need to change. As a result, Chamberlain implemented a two-pronged strategy: better relations with the revisionist powers, an approach now known as appeasement, and limited rearmament.[66]

Alternatively, Britain could have sought alliances to create a balance against the dictators. However, according to historian David Reynolds, Chamberlain, "believed that allies could be liabilities as well as assets" and that "alliances against Hitler would entail concessions and greater dependence."[67] From a British perspective, moreover, France was unstable, and Britain was at odds with many French policies, particularly over France's treatment of Germany, a pillar of appeasement. Central Europe was too weak, and Russia was not a realistic option. The United States was isolated and withdrawn from world affairs.[68] Reducing the number of adversaries via appeasement, therefore, remained the logical option.

Successful appeasement depended on rearmament; however, time would work against the British, especially if Germany or Japan chose not to be appeased. In particular, considerable time would elapse before new ships began arriving in the fleet in sufficient numbers. In the interim, therefore, the British recast their priorities and the disposition of the fleet. The initial recommendation of the Chiefs of Staff to continue the long-standing British policy of sending a fleet to the Far East in the event of hostilities failed to take into account deep British entanglement in the Mediterranean, the empire's most vital sea line of communication.[69] Given that Italy and Germany were de facto and then de jure allies and that Europe and the Mediterranean were much closer to the home islands, neither stationing more ships in the Far East nor dispatching an adequate fleet to the Pacific in the event of hostilities was a viable option. It also was becoming increasingly apparent to the British that they could accommodate either Japan or the United States, but not both. Although Chamberlain argued for appeasing Japan, the Cabinet ultimately concluded that the only viable, if unpalatable, alternative was to seek closer cooperation with the United States.[70]

At this point, however, the United States did not have much to offer. On the diplomatic front, the Baldwin government and the Hoover administration split over how to respond to the Japanese seizure of Manchuria in 1931, causing Baldwin to complain, "You will get nothing out of Washington but words, big words, but only words."[71] The U.S. policy of nonrecognition of Japanese actions further complicated British efforts to negotiate some form of settlement. Moreover, strong isolationist sentiment constrained Hoover from pursuing a multilateral settlement; therefore, U.S. diplomacy proceeded unilaterally, further irritating British leaders.[72] Nor would matters quickly improve. Roosevelt's collapsing of the World Economic Conference, congressional and public concerns over war debts, Secretary of State Cordell Hull's drumbeat about Imperial Preference and free trade, economic competition, passage of the Neutrality Act of 1935, the feeble U.S. response to the remilitarization of the Rhineland, and fuzzy rhetoric from Roosevelt about a "peace conference" only deepened already substantial British distrust of the United States as a viable international partner.[73] Indeed, Robert Vansittart, Britain's senior career diplomat from 1928 to 1938, who happened to be married to an American and had long favored courting the United States, lamented, "We have been too tender, not to say subservient with the US for a long time past. It is we who have made all the advances, and received nothing in return. It is still necessary, and I desire as much as ever, that we should get on with this untrustworthy race. But we shall never get far; they will always let us down."[74]

On the military front, the United States had less to offer. At this time, its army was little more than a constabulary force. The Army Air Corps was small and mostly outmoded. The navy, the most ready of the services, was still starved for personnel and training, and growing increasingly obsolescent. Moreover, caught in the throes of the Great Depression, the United States remained focused on redressing its severe economic problems. Nor was Franklin Roosevelt then the powerful figure that history remembers. Focused on internal problems, he had little time or inclination to deal in foreign affairs. Even if he had such a proclivity, public reactions in the wake of the publication of the book *Merchants of Death*—an indictment of arms manufactures and financiers for dragging the United States into World War I—the Nye Committee hearings in Congress on the role of munitions manufacturers and financiers entangling the United States with Britain in World War I, and a strong isolationist sentiment inside the United States would have thwarted any military initiatives.[75] As a result of these twin threads, Britain ignored the United States as a potential security partner through the mid-1930s.

Nonetheless, the increasing spiral of international tensions and shared national interests later in the decade gradually drew the two powers closer. Already strained U.S.-Japanese relations reached new depths with the Sino-Japanese clash at the Marco Polo Bridge in Beijing on 7 July 1937 that triggered "the China Incident," a euphemism for the Japanese invasion of central China accompanied by widespread and large-scale Japanese atrocities, epitomized by the rape of Nanking.[76] The British, too, had become increasingly alarmed over events in the Far East, and Japanese provocations against British shipping and personnel in late 1937 heightened these anxieties.[77] Indeed, on four separate occasions in July and August, Chamberlain extended feelers to U.S. ambassador Robert Bingham about potential cooperation to rein in Tokyo. Chamberlain received no positive responses. Worse yet, in September Roosevelt inexplicably canceled a proposed visit by Chamberlain to Washington that the president himself had initiated the previous May.[78] For Roosevelt to renege on his invitation must have reinforced Chamberlain's views of feckless American policy and of an equally hopeless Franklin Roosevelt.

Events in early October could only have reinforced Chamberlain's perceptions. On 7 October 1937, Roosevelt delivered what has become known as his Quarantine Speech in Chicago, the heartland of isolationism and the home of Robert McCormick, newspaper and radio mogul, strident isolationist, and rabid FDR foe. Troubled for some time by German, Italian, and especially Japanese actions, Roosevelt likened aggressor actions to a disease and noted:

> When an epidemic of physical disease starts to spread, the community approves and joins in a quarantine of the patients in order to protect the health of the community against the spread of the disease. . . . War is a contagion. . . . We are determined to keep out of war . . . but we cannot have complete protection in a world of disorder in which confidence and security have broken down. . . . Most important of all, the will for peace on the part of all peace-loving nations must express itself to the end that nations that may be tempted to violate their agreements and the rights of others will desist from such a course. There must be positive endeavors to preserve the peace. America hates war. America hopes for peace. Therefore, America actively engages in the search for peace.[79]

Reactions to the speech varied. In Britain, Foreign Secretary Anthony Eden and others in the Foreign Office took it as a positive sign that Anglo-American cooperation might be possible. Conversely, "Chamberlain thought the President 'had rather embarrassed the situation' and was worried by the possibility that he might take action without first having agreed to meet, with Britain, all the consequences of the Japanese retaliation."[80] Within the United States, the isolationist press reacted violently, and public opinion expressed mixed responses.[81] Regardless, Roosevelt immediately backpedaled from any commitments via both media and diplomatic channels. As historian Richard Overy notes, "He had tested the water and found it too hot."[82] Roosevelt quickly added insult to injury. Chamberlain had called for convening an international conference in Brussels to begin on 3 November 1937 to coordinate international options for resolving the war in China. Roosevelt informed Chamberlain that the United States, rather than taking any leadership, would pursue a policy of "independent cooperation" and urged the British to do the same.[83]

A further blow came when Secretary of State Hull formally declined to enter into staff talks with the British over the Far East, an initiative Roosevelt himself had first floated in January and again in March. To be fair to Roosevelt, the British dithered over his initiative until November, when the Cabinet finally directed Ambassador Ronald Lindsay to offer staff talks. In light of the British announcement that His Majesty's Government could not release a large element of the fleet for service in the Far East, Secretary of State Hull ultimately rejected the offer on 27 November.[84] No wonder an exasperated Chamberlain remarked to his Cabinet, "The main lesson to be drawn [is] the difficulty of securing effective cooperation from the United States of America."[85]

Regardless of who bore what responsibility for the failed initiative, the frustration and accumulated damage went well beyond the Brussels Conference. As historian David Kennedy concludes,

> And, if one remembers how often the American hand had been proffered, only to be withdrawn, as at London in June 1933, or Chicago in 1937—or how often it had not been extended at all, as in Ethiopia in 1935 or in Spain in 1936, or in the Pacific in late 1937—one's breath returns and with a measure of sympathy for Chamberlain's predicament. Judging Roosevelt to be "a dangerous and unreliable horse in any team," and keenly aware of how inadequately armed and politically isolated Britain was, Chamberlain concluded, not unreasonably, that he had little choice but to seek some kind of accommodation with the dictators.[86]

Throughout the 1920s and 1930s, the United States and Britain remained distant from each other. Economically, the two countries were keen business competitors. Their different and frequently conflicting responses to the Great Depression heightened the economic stakes. The (non)repayment of war debts and mutual resentment over each other's trade policies further irritated political elites. Both countries eschewed foreign commitments and remained aloof diplomatically, especially the United States. Although the two countries had largely laid their naval rivalry to rest after 1930, and neither side believed an Anglo-American military conflict possible, residual hard feelings remained. For mainly U.S. domestic political reasons, the two nations found it difficult to identify common interests and shared approaches for dealing with the rising threats from the dictators, whether in Europe or in the Pacific.

Personalities exacerbated these problems. A succession of British prime ministers saw the United States as an unreliable or incapable political, economic, diplomatic, or military partner. It is difficult not to see their point. This view became predominant under Neville Chamberlain, whose innate distrust of the United States generally and of Franklin Roosevelt specifically impeded collaborative efforts. In Chamberlain's defense, Roosevelt's own oft-stated distaste for British imperialism, dramatic policy swings, and flights of military fancy did not help matters.

By November 1937, the two nations were largely estranged, and for good reasons. After nearly two decades of economic competition, diplomatic dysfunction, weak militaries, and dystopian personalities, it appeared to many on both sides of the Atlantic that too many obstacles stood in the way of the United States and Britain finding sufficient common cause and interests. There simply was not sufficient impetus to impel the two countries, neither friend nor foe, to common action. International events, however, would soon conspire to draw them more closely together.

3

Groping in the Dark

U.S.-British Coalition Encounters, 1936–1939

In broad daylight on 12 December 1937, Japanese aircraft sank the gunboat U.S.S. *Panay* and three Standard Oil tankers anchored in the Yangtze River off Nanjing, China. All vessels were clearly marked with large, painted American flags. The attack killed three sailors and wounded forty-eight sailors and civilians. Japanese artillery units also fired on the British gunboat H.M.S. *Ladybird* as well as on commercial oil tankers anchored on the Yangtze River but well away from ongoing fighting.[1] In response, Roosevelt wanted to apply economic sanctions against Japan. However, because sanctions alone had proved futile after the Japanese occupation of Manchuria in 1931, he believed it would be necessary to employ naval forces in a long-range quarantine to deny Japanese access to foreign markets. Because neither Britain nor the United States had sufficient naval strength to control the vast reaches of the Pacific Ocean, implementation of a distant blockade raised the issue of cooperation between the British and U.S. navies. Thus, despite having declined an offer of naval staff talks only two weeks earlier, Roosevelt reconsidered the possibility of naval conversations.[2]

At a diplomatic reception on 16 December, Roosevelt met secretly with Ambassador Ronald Lindsay, whom Chamberlain had authorized to offer a fleet of eight or nine capital ships for a demonstration against Japan if the United States would do likewise. Roosevelt called for direct staff talks between the two navies, and, "as Lindsay put it, Roosevelt then plunged into 'his worst "inspirational" mode.' The object of the staff talks would be for a blockade or 'quarantine' of Japan, the occasion of which must be the 'next grave outrage by the Japanese.'"[3] Roosevelt proposed a distant blockade and opined that U.S. ships would not base out of Singapore. He did offer a visit to Singapore by U.S. cruisers currently at Sydney, Australia, but rejected mobilizing the U.S. Fleet and declined to engage U.S. and British fleets in combined operations.[4]

Roosevelt decided in late December to send Captain Royal E. Ingersoll, the director of the U.S. Navy's WPD, to London to engage in exploratory talks with the British. Ingersoll was the natural selection for such a mission. The son of a rear admiral, Ingersoll was born in Washington, D.C., on 20 June 1883. Graduating second in his class from Annapolis in 1905, he served in the communications section of the Office of the CNO during World War I. Staff duty in the Office of the CNO from 1930 to 1933 and selection as chief of the WPD in 1935 marked him as one of the navy's best.[5] On 23 December 1937, Ingersoll, accompanied by the CNO, Admiral William D. Leahy, reported to Roosevelt for his instructions. Regarding his meeting with the president, Ingersoll later recalled receiving vague guidance "to arrange for parallel action in the Far East."[6] Otherwise, Ingersoll later noted that he left Washington with no real idea of the desired results of his mission beyond exploring what could be done and how far the British were willing to go.[7]

On New Year's Day 1938, Ingersoll met with Foreign Secretary Anthony Eden and Permanent Under Secretary Alexander Cadogan. At the beginning of the meeting, Eden noted that he had no information on the purpose of Ingersoll's mission and inquired about conversations between Hull and Lindsay. Equally in the dark, Ingersoll replied that he had no idea about the discussions, but apparently as a result of those discussions Leahy had ordered him to London "to obtain naval information on which to plan and to base decisions, if necessary, as to future action."[8] Eden expressed dismay with this explanation, and Cadogan noted in his diary that Ingersoll "seems nice and his instructions are helpful, but even he seems not clear on his objective."[9] Eden nonetheless arranged for Ingersoll to meet with the Admiralty staff.[10]

Ingersoll, accompanied by U.S. naval attaché Captain Russell Willson, met two days later with Lord Ernle Chatfield, the first sea lord. Each officer noted that neither had any instruction from his government except to seek information. Chatfield commented that where possible the two nations should act in concert and synchronize political and military efforts. At this point, Ingersoll noted that the U.S. Fleet had been brought up to 80 percent of strength but that it could not be mobilized further without calling up the reserves, which would require the president to declare a state of national emergency—an unlikely event. Finally, he indicated that initial U.S. deployments would cover the U.S. West Coast and Hawaiian Islands and that the fleet would not advance beyond that position until all ships were prepared for operations against the Japanese.[11]

Chatfield, in turn, informed Ingersoll that he had resisted all government attempts to reinforce the Far East in driblets and that he hoped not to move naval forces until he had a fleet capable of meeting the Japanese on equal terms. He then raised the question of unity of command for the two fleets, remarking "that as a principle he believed that since the two fleets would be widely separated at first and probably for some time, there could not be unity of command in a tactical or strategical [sic] sense and that strategic cooperation would be all that was possible."[12] He stressed, however, that it was imperative that the two fleets arrange for proper means of communication, including cyphers, as well as for the mutual exchange of intelligence should the two fleets ever act together.[13]

After his meeting with Chatfield, Ingersoll met with Captain Thomas V. Phillips, director of plans at the Admiralty, and other key staff members. In their initial meeting, Phillips outlined Royal Naval plans for the Far East in the event of an emergency and detailed the forces currently available. Due to rising tensions with Italy and Germany, there was a substantial gap in available versus required forces. Phillips, however, gave no indication of how the British planned to make up the deficit. Ingersoll then briefly outlined U.S. plans, noting that all ships in commission would move to Hawaii within twelve to fifteen days of mobilization. He once again emphasized that mobilizing reserves and pulling ships out of mothballs would require the president to declare a state of national emergency.[14] The discussions turned next to the question of combined action in a distant blockade or quarantine. After prolonged consideration, the two officers failed to reach an understanding on combined action of the two navies but generally agreed loosely to coordinate actions between the two geographically distant and distinct fleets.[15] Their final topic of the day concerned arrangements for liaison between the two fleets. Phillips proposed sending a British signals expert to Washington to confer with U.S. communications personnel to determine what combined facilities would be required. Ingersoll remained noncommittal but mentioned that his superiors hoped that the Admiralty could post to Washington an additional assistant naval attaché who was well versed in current British plans.[16]

Ingersoll and Willson met with their British counterparts over the next several days. A British-U.S. working group drafted a nonbinding Record of Conversation, an agreed version of agreements that reflected the results of the talks. Chatfield would be the approval authority for the British. Ingersoll noted that although he could make no commitments, he was certain that Admiral Leahy would approve the document.[17] The Record of Conversation addressed five general categories: (1) the planned composition, state of readiness, and initial movements of fleets; (2) general policy (including political); (3) current forces; (4) intercommunications arrangements; and (5) strategic policy.[18] Under the first topic, the British detailed the composition of the substantial fleet that they planned to base at Singapore—eight battleships, one battle cruiser, three aircraft carriers, twenty-one cruisers, seven destroyer flotillas, and twenty-five submarines. The British added a caveat that the exact composition of an eventual fleet would depend on the situation in the Atlantic and the Mediterranean, thus opening up the fissure through which H.M.S. *Prince of Wales,* H.M.S. *Repulse,* and Singapore would eventually be lost to the Japanese.[19]

The outline of tentative American options also began with a considerable caution: the United States could take no action unless the U.S. Fleet was at 100 percent complement, which would require President Roosevelt to declare a national emergency. Although such a declaration was unlikely, prudent planning dictated that the working group consider this assumption. If the U.S. Fleet did participate, the Advanced Force and a majority of the fleet would deploy to Honolulu, advance gradually across the Pacific through the Japanese mandated islands, and establish an advance base at Truk in the Caroline Islands.[20]

The general policy portion of the record outlined the political aspects of cooperation. Although both sides agreed that the synchronization of political action and naval movements would be ideal, such action was unlikely. At best, the planners hoped to coordinate the arrival of the U.S. Fleet at Honolulu with the British Fleet at Singapore. The two parties also agreed on full, reciprocal use of each other's territorial waters, although the British were unable to commit the dominions at the time. In the segment on current forces, the British noted that in the event of an emergency they would withdraw forces from China to either Hong Kong or Singapore, while concentrating their fleet at Singapore. The United States also would withdraw its forces from China to the Philippines and base the U.S. Asiatic Fleet at Manila.[21]

The Record of Conversation also addressed liaison measures as well as the agreed provisions for codes, cyphers, calls, and signals procedures between the two fleets in the event of combined operations. The report addressed arrangements for distributing the Allied Code Book (1919 version), which would be issued immediately to the Royal Navy, and if the Foreign Office approved, five hundred copies would be sent to the British embassy in Washington for distribution to the U.S. Navy should that become necessary. In addition, British representatives in Singapore would directly supply the U.S. Asiatic Fleet.[22] In terms of liaison mechanisms, per British requests, the U.S. Navy would assign a signal officer and enlisted sailor to each flagship of the CINC, Far East, Singapore, and Hong Kong. In turn, the British would assign liaison personnel with the CINC, U.S. Fleet; the CINC, U.S. Asiatic Fleet; and the Communications Office, Washington, D.C.[23] Outside the record, both sides agreed that the current interchange of information between Captain Willson and the Admiralty was sufficient and that an additional exchange of officers between headquarters in Washington and London was neither necessary nor desirable. If future events dictated, there could be an exchange of officers conversant with the two navies' respective war plans.[24]

The final element of the document assigned areas of strategic responsibility should the two governments institute a distant blockade. The British would assume authority for the area bounded roughly by Singapore, Netherlands East Indies, New Guinea, and New Zealand. The United States would take responsibility for a line extending from Cape Horn to the west coast of South America, Panama Canal Zone, U.S. and Canadian Pacific coasts, and Alaska. The planners did not establish firm lines of demarcation between the two spheres, left a void in the central Pacific, and specifically excluded Hawaii from the area under consideration.[25]

Upon completing the revised Record of Conversation, Ingersoll attended his final meeting with the Admiralty staff. Chatfield noted that the "conversations had been most helpful to them in obtaining a better understanding of what the mutual problem would be if it developed."[26] He added that the situation had not yet reached the point where it would be necessary to dispatch the British Fleet to the Far East and that if that requirement arose, additional coordination would be necessary. He also pointedly remarked that, for the moment, the time was not ripe for such discussions. The meeting closed with Chatfield's admonition that the two nations had to impress upon the Japanese that their present course risked a new arms race, which they would lose. Ingersoll replied only that he would convey Chatfield's views to Admiral Leahy.[27]

In retrospect, Ingersoll's mission produced mixed results. From a broad perspective, how Britain or the United States might convey such a message to Japan was unclear. Ingersoll and Phillips had agreed on only the most tentative plans based on wishful thinking that each nation could depend on the other to take up its partner's respective slack. In addition, the plans were contingent upon the most optimum of circumstances. Finally, Chatfield's notice that further talks would not be necessary eliminated the realistic possibility of cooperation in the near future.

In the short term, no combined action of the two fleets emerged from the talks. Neither nation nor its navy dramatically altered its strategic thinking or plans. Nevertheless, according to historian Lawrence Pratt, the talks allowed each side to "[explore] the foundations of the two powers' naval strategies."[28] In perhaps the most interesting twist, in the midst of Ingersoll's conversations Roosevelt offered that if the British agreed to take similar steps, he would announce that the U.S. Fleet was scraping its bottoms—a key preparation for extended deployment, that U.S. cruisers would visit Singapore, and that the Pacific Fleet maneuvers would be moved up to February 1938.[29] The British declined. As Pratt notes, "For once the British had to assess their own, rather than an American willingness to act."[30] In the end, the British decided that it was not a good time to deplete their forces in either the Atlantic or the Mediterranean, and His Majesty's Government decided to do nothing more than protest to Tokyo.[31] Roosevelt was apparently not the only one who could back pedal.

In the longer term, Ingersoll's mission represented an important first step in Anglo-American cooperation. Granted, an absence of clear political, policy, or strategic guidance hampered the discussions, as did significant caveats from both sides. However, the fact that the conversations occurred at all was a major accomplishment. Ingersoll's mission established a precedent. For the first time in twenty years, the two navies were engaged in coalition planning. A dialogue between them and, hence, between their political leaders and nations had begun. Each side gained insights into the other's strategic thinking and plans. Moreover, the parties shared some of their greatest secrets, demonstrating an increasing level of trust in each other.[32]

After Ingersoll returned to Washington, he notified Willson on 2 February 1938 that Admiral Leahy had approved the Record of Conversation and that Willson was to inform Chatfield.[33] On the same day, Leahy informed his major subordinates of the substance of the conversations and warned his commanders that they might have to modify current strategic and operational plans to reflect the Record of Conversation. Leahy also noted that in the event of combined British and American action in the Pacific commanders would receive appropriate signals instructions.[34] These instructions were soon forthcoming, as Willson forwarded on 10 February the implementing instructions outlined in the Record of Conversation.[35] Thus, within a month of Ingersoll's return to Washington, the "simple" Record of Conversation was influencing American naval planning.

For a variety of reasons, largely political, a hiatus in such conversations ensued. Chamberlain was reluctant to proceed too quickly because of the worsening situation in Europe and because he had been let down too frequently by massive swings in U.S. policy. As a result, Britain delayed a planned reciprocal visit of Ingersoll's Admiralty counterpart to Washington.[36] This delay did not dismay the Americans. Writing to Ingersoll on 4 March 1938, Willson noted that he had not raised the issue of such a visit out of concern that the British would read more into the invitation than was merited. Moreover, he pointed out that his current role as a conduit between Leahy and Chatfield was satisfactory. Ingersoll concurred with Willson's recommendation, especially in the wake of subsequent publicity surrounding his own trip to London. Ingersoll noted that he felt the British should not send a representative until after Congress had adjourned. At that time, he would remind Leahy and "then let him take it up with the 'big boss' to remind him of what he said."[37]

The two officers' cautious approach was well advised. As indicated earlier, American revulsion to World War I had spawned a loose but broadly encompassing anti-interventionist or noninterventionist movement that included pacifists, isolationists, socialists, internationalists, disarmament proponents, nationalists, xenophobes of many stripes, and unilateralists. These groups gained strength throughout the 1920s, and anti-interventionism was in full tide by late 1937.[38] Together these loosely allied factions enjoyed broad public support and wielded considerable power in Congress, especially the U.S. Senate.[39] The House of Representatives also contained a strong strain of anti-interventionism, best exemplified, perhaps, by the so-called Ludlow amendment to the U.S. Constitution. First introduced by Representative Louis Ludlow (D–Ind.) in 1935, the initiative sought to require a national referendum on a declaration of war. The proposal enjoyed considerable public support: respondents in public-opinion polls in September 1935, 1936, and 1937 overwhelmingly supported the idea. Although delaying tactics initially allowed the Roosevelt administration to block progress on the bill, the *Panay* incident allowed Ludlow to bring the bill to the floor of the House on 10 January 1938. Only intense administration efforts narrowly defeated the bill 209 to 188.[40]

Nor did Roosevelt have much room for political maneuver against the noninterventionists. The New Deal remained under assault, and because Roosevelt needed all of the congressional support he could muster, he could not risk alienating key progressive but strongly isolationist senators from the Midwest and West. Roosevelt's efforts to "pack" the Supreme Court in response to several court decisions overturning critical New Deal legislation also created a firestorm that left him politically weakened. In addition, he was about to launch what would prove to be an abortive and politically costly effort to purge Democratic leaders opposed to his legislative agenda. In addition, the country was in the midst of the "minidepression" that had begun in 1937.[41] Thus, by March 1938 the combination of global turmoil, widespread anti-interventionist sentiment, and domestic political difficulties meant that Roosevelt and his principal agent, the U.S. Navy, had to exercise great caution in their overtures to the British during this period. For the moment at least, cooperation would remain at the attaché level, and the exchanges between Willson and his contacts in the Admiralty continued, though on a limited basis, throughout 1938 and early 1939.[42]

Ingersoll's discussions with the Royal Navy were not the only efforts at cooperation with the British, however. Even before the naval exchanges, Lieutenant Colonel Raymond E. Lee, the U.S. military attaché in London, established and maintained informal contacts with the British army. Lee's important role in Anglo-American collaboration over the next three years deserves some elaboration of who he was. A Missouri native, Lee graduated from the University of Missouri with a degree in civil engineering and was commissioned into the Coast Artillery Corps in 1909. After duty as an instructor at West Point from 1913 to 1917, he served in the field artillery in France during World War I. After routine assignments, he was in the War Department General Staff from 1928 to 1932. Most important for this story, he was the U.S. military attaché in Britain from 1935 to 1939 and again from 1940 to 1941, when, in the words of former secretary of state Dean Acheson, he "became the indispensable guide and comforter, smoothing irritations, untangling confusions, interpreting visitors to their hosts, and vice versa, trying to harmonize the flow of information and requests from London and Washington and often the uncoordinated flows that came back."[43]

Lee noted in an April 1938 letter to the assistant chief of staff, G-2 (intelligence), that over the past two years he had established arrangements for periodic private interviews between the U.S. military attaché staff and "various qualified Spokesmen [sic] of the [British] War Office."[44] He continued that there was no written record, which allowed for a freer flow of information.[45] Contrary to Roosevelt's sanction of the naval talks, however, it appears that Lee made these overtures on his own initiative, perhaps an indication of the low level of importance Roosevelt placed on army-to-army contacts.

The tentative nature of these exchanges and the importance of personalities in these contacts was aptly demonstrated when Colonel Bradford G. Chynoweth replaced Lee. In a letter to Colonel J. A. Crone, G-2, War Department, Chynoweth noted that he was having a difficult time getting any information out of the British. The flow of information improved only after a polite but pointed letter to Brigadier General Frederick Beaumont-Nesbitt, chief of British Military Intelligence, in which Chynoweth noted the amount of information that the British attaché in Washington was receiving and commented, "Wouldn't it be to the ultimate advantage of both our countries if freedom [of information] could become reciprocal?"[46] Unfortunately, Chynoweth did not have much of an opportunity to develop a close working relationship with his British counterparts. From almost the beginning of his tour, he maintained a running feud with Joseph P. Kennedy Sr., the American ambassador to Great Britain (and father of future U.S. president John F. Kennedy), and he returned home in September 1939.⁴⁷ Lee eventually replaced Chynoweth and resumed his War Office contacts, but not until the fall of France in June 1940. During this critical gap, the flow of information between the two armies was restricted.

Like Lee, Captain Willson used his contacts in the Admiralty to resurrect the idea of further staff talks. Due to rotate back to the United States, Willson suggested to Admiralty authorities a review of the Ingersoll–Phillips Record of Conversation. He accordingly met on 13 January 1939 with Captain J. G. L. Dundas and Commander T. C. Hampton of the Admiralty Plans Section to discuss possible revisions. The British representatives noted the dramatic changes in the European situation and indicated that the increased German and Italian threat necessitated strengthening of the Home Fleet. This reinforcement would come at the expense of the Far East Fleet, which the Royal Navy had intended to dispatch to the western Pacific in the event of an emergency. The officers also warned that "the exact composition of the Far Eastern Fleet is subject to modification with the passage of time."⁴⁸ In short, the British served notice that the Americans could expect limited British aid in the Pacific, and, therefore, "the possibility of tactical cooperation between the United States and British Fleets has acquired added importance."⁴⁹

By April, the British felt the changed naval situation in the Atlantic required further modification of the accord, and the Admiralty pushed for another American representative to come to London. Because the Roosevelt administration was working to appeal or revise the Neutrality Act, neither the State Department nor the Navy Department was receptive to such a mission. After much back-and-forth communication, U.S. officials eventually agreed that Commander Hampton, who had worked with Captain Willson in January on the revised Record of Conversation and would soon depart for the Far East, could include a stopover in Washington when he crossed the United States in early June.⁵⁰

To ensure secrecy, the first discussions took place at Admiral Leahy's private residence on 12 June 1939. Besides Leahy and Hampton, Captain Robert L. Ghormley, Ingersoll's successor as director of plans, and Captain L. C. A. Curzon-Howe, the British naval attaché, also were present. According to a subsequent report, Hampton got straight to the point: the dramatically changed situation in Europe required the British to retain all of their capital ships in the Atlantic. In the event of Japanese aggression, Britain would be unable to send its agreed fleet to the Far East and would rely only on the China Station Detachment and dominion naval forces. If Japan intervened in an ongoing European conflict, Britain would first concentrate on driving Italy from the war and then turn its attention to the Far East. Hampton gave no indication of how long the Admiralty believed it would take to knock out Italy, though he did say that Singapore could withstand a ninety-day siege.[51] In response, Leahy cautioned that he was presenting only his personal views and that he could not go beyond the parallel action Ingersoll had discussed in 1938. He nevertheless outlined the American options as contemplated at the time. If there were an ongoing war in Europe and Japan were to intervene against Britain in the Far East, then the United States, as a neutral nation, would dispatch a major portion of the U.S. Fleet to Hawaii, secure the Caribbean, and safeguard the South American coast. After discussing plans for cooperation in a combined radio direction-finding project and agreeing to review procedures for exchange of communications in the Far East, the parties adjourned.[52]

The same group met two days later, again at Leahy's home. Hampton pointedly asked Leahy about intentions for disposition of the U.S. fleet in the event of a European war. Again, Leahy responded that he was only giving his personal opinion but emphasized that "he believed, however, that so long as the present administration is in power his opinion would probably represent the policy of the administration."[53] Leahy's comment undoubtedly was well founded because he had long been associated with Franklin Roosevelt. After graduating from the U.S. Naval Academy in 1897, Leahy served aboard the U.S.S. *Oregon* in the Spanish-American War, saw service in the Philippines Insurrection, and participated in the multinational repression of the Chinese Boxer Rebellion. In 1915–1916, he skippered the secretary of the navy's dispatch boat, where he began a long friendship with then assistant secretary of the navy Franklin Roosevelt. After World War I, Leahy held a long series of commands, including on destroyers in the Scouting Force (1931–1932), on battleships of the Battle Force (1935–1936), and then on the Battle Force itself from April 1936 to his selection as CNO in January 1937. He also served as chief of the Bureau of Ordnance and chief of the Bureau of Navigation, which actually dealt with personnel. In all of these positions, he worked under the watchful eye of Roosevelt, who treated the navy as his own. Roosevelt appointed Leahy CNO in January 1937, in which position he served until 1 August 1939, when he reached mandatory retirement age. Roosevelt, however, would continue to use Leahy's considerable talents, first as governor of Puerto Rico and then in the highly sensitive position of U.S. ambassador to Vichy France from January 1941 to July 1942, when Roosevelt appointed him chief of staff to the commander in chief of the United States Army and Navy (i.e., the president himself). In this position unique to American annals, Leahy served multiple roles that would include the modern-day versions of chairman of the Joint Chiefs of Staff, chief of staff to the president, and national security adviser to the president.[54]

Continuing the conversation with Hampton, Leahy stressed that the United States would remain neutral, deploy a majority of the fleet to Hawaii as a deterrent to Japan, and augment current forces in the Atlantic to preserve American neutrality.[55] Hampton then asked about U.S. strategy in the event Britain and the United States allied against the Axis Powers or possibly Japan. Leahy and Ghormley outlined a similar strategy, except that the U.S. Navy assisted by British naval forces in the Far East would be responsible for the Pacific, while the Royal Navy, augmented by available U.S. forces, would handle the Atlantic.[56]

From appearances, it seems that the level of collaboration reached an entirely new level at this time. The talks progressed from discussions of parallel action in the Far East to the possibility of active cooperation of naval forces, complete with the division of the world into spheres of responsibility. Even if this view was not conveyed to Commander Hampton, the United States would take British plans into account as the Americans developed their new war plans—the so-called Rainbow series that the United States would develop from June 1939 forward.

One must acknowledge, however, that the two powers were still a long way from full collaboration. First, there were no political agreements. Although Leahy no doubt was accurate in his assessment that his views were representative of the Roosevelt administration, he was not Roosevelt. As later events would show, the president had mixed emotions on how to support the antifascist powers and frequently changed course. At this time, he had not made up his mind about the degree of U.S. support to Britain and France. And, as will play out during 1940–1941, his frequent backtracking calls into question exactly when the president made up his mind and about what. Even if Roosevelt had reached a firm commitment in his mind at this point, which is doubtful, he would still need quite some time to marshal public and congressional support for aid to Britain.

Second, these were general discussions, not the detailed plans necessary for complementary, much less combined, fleet actions. Much further collaboration would be required to convert these generalities into concrete plans for action. Nevertheless, as Hampton concluded, the talks had promoted good will between the two navies, and the British had found out that American plans were fundamentally in agreement with British naval strategy.[57] Indeed, historian Greg Kennedy concludes, "By the end of 1939, the cooperation of the two nations in Far Eastern matters, while still tempered by the need to protect national interests, was very close. A parallel but not joint policy was indeed a reality."[58]

After Hampton left Washington, there were no further face-to-face discussions between naval staff planners in 1939. The level of collaboration reverted to informal exchanges between naval attachés. This limited flow of information would continue even after the outbreak of the war in Europe in September 1939. The level of exchange, however, would not continue as it had in the prewar days, for Britain was now again at war, and both sides, each for its own reasons, proceeded at a cautious pace.[59]

The final element of coalition planning and experience in the interwar period returns to the Anglo-French relationship. In the wake of Mussolini's adventures in Ethiopia, the British in 1935 briefly considered staff talks with the French. However, cognizant that the Anglo-French staff talks begun in 1906 had led, despite disclaimers of "no political commitments," to the bloodbath of 1914–1918 by a seemingly inexorable route, British leaders limited the scope of the conversations to exchanges between military attachés.[60] Even then, the Cabinet insisted that the discussions be limited strictly to British responsibilities under the Treaties of Locarno of 1925. British representatives could discuss technical matters only, and government leaders proscribed them from expanding the talks to include strategy, combined planning, or other such political issues.[61]

If the Cabinet appeared hesitant, the British Chiefs of Staff expressed their strong opposition to any conversations with the French whatsoever. The Chiefs of Staff, too, feared the French would view talks as a moral commitment to intervene on the Continent in the event of a Franco-German war. More importantly, they were painfully aware of Britain's total unpreparedness and feared that circumstances would draw an ill-equipped and vulnerable Britain into war against its national security interests.[62]

Spurred on by German reoccupation of the Rhineland in March 1936, staff talks took place on 15–16 April 1936.[63] The talks focused, however, only on highly technical military matters. The army participants in the talks addressed probable points of debarkation and transportation networks available to move an expeditionary force to its assembly areas. Naval delegates exchanged information on forces in commission, signal communications, and data on French ports. Air force representatives traded data on their respective aircraft strengths and reviewed the location of French airfields. A comment from Field Marshal Sir Cyril Deverell, chief of the Imperial General Staff in 1937, summed up the British military's reticence in engaging in substantive talks: "The French had become embarrassing in their endeavors to acquaint us with their plans although we, on our part, had communicated nothing to them."[64] The British further demonstrated the depth of their commitment to Anglo-French planning when they suspended discussions shortly after the April 1936 conversations.

Throughout 1936 and 1937, the talks remained in limbo, primarily because of internal dissension within the British government.[65] Many in government and the military remained Francophobic, and continued instability in the French government reinforced their distaste. Nor did anyone wish to repeat the entangling alliances that many believed responsible for Britain's bloodletting in World War I. Importantly, the Chiefs of Staff remained adamant in their opposition to staff talks. As Sir Henry Pownall, director of military operations and intelligence in the War Office, recorded in his diary, "We never wanted *formal* Staff Conversations, but we *do* want an interchange of information so that we can settle administrative problems that would occur if British troops landed in France."[66]

Ultimately, the Cabinet authorized resumption of the staff talks.[67] However, even when the British resumed contact in July 1938, the conversations remained restricted to an exchange of largely technical information between attachés. Direct staff talks were forbidden, and planning officers had to submit prepared questionnaires through the attachés when they needed information— a long, tedious process that produced little of value. As Lee, the U.S. Army attaché, noted after a dinner with Pownall, General Albert LeLong—French attaché to London—and Brigadier General Beaumont-Nesbitt in late March, "The important deduction to be drawn from this conversation is that, so far, few staff arrangements and probably none at all, have been made between the British and the French."[68] Only after the Nazi seizure of rump Czechoslovakia in March 1939 forced the realization that appeasement had failed did full-scale conversations between Britain and France resume, and even then the British Chiefs of Staff harbored doubts about French trustworthiness.[69]

The talks took place in three distinct stages: 29 March–4 April, when the Allies formulated their common policy for the conduct of the war; 24 April–3 May, when they discussed possible operations in specific theaters; and the summer of 1939, when they coordinated and polished final details.[70] At the first conference, the British and French planners established that the defense of France would be the focus of combined planning.[71] The planners also agreed that because the French would provide the overwhelming majority of the forces, they would determine the strategic direction for the combined forces to follow.[72] Although superficially encouraging, General John V. Gort (Viscount Gort), commander of the BEF, received detailed instructions little different from his predecessors in World War I, and in terms of coalition planning of operations the partners returned to the failed policies of 1914–1917.[73] Cooperation at the tactical level continued throughout the summer of 1939. By early June, the British and French staffs had completed plans for moving two British corps to assembly areas northwest of Amiens. By 10 July, the British Field Force, later designated the BEF, received its defensive sector on the French left flank facing the Franco-Belgian border. By that date, planners had completed administrative and logistical coordination.[74]

Both sides saw the need for establishing an organization akin to the SWC of World War I. Apparently, in early April, General Maurice Gamelin, CINC of the French army, proposed the establishment of a much more powerful three-tiered set of executive bodies. The first level was a Comité de guerre or Consiel supériéur, consisting of the prime ministers, ministers of defense, and Chiefs of Staff, which would provide overall policy guidance. A Haut comité militaire, consisting of the Chiefs of Staff and CINCs, would determine Allied military strategy and direct military operations. At the final level, four separate subcommittees would handle issues concerning land/army, air, naval, and colonial matters. The British did not respond until mid-July, when Chamberlain proposed a nonexecutive council on the model of World War I: the prime minister and one minister only as well as a permanent staff of military representatives to provide advice.[75] When the British stood firm, the French acquiesced on 3 August. With less than thirty days until the outbreak of war, there was little opportunity to assemble, organize, and develop the processes necessary for successful higher direction of the war effort.[76] With the German invasion of Poland, Anglo-French cooperation moved from the planning to the execution stage.

With the onset of war in Europe, Britain's focus naturally shifted to military cooperation with France, and conversations between the British and American militaries lapsed. They would not resume until after the fall of France nine months later. Nonetheless, by mid-1939, Britain and the United States had forged their first military links, however tenuous. Insufficient political guidance to U.S. military leaders and planners and a British reluctance to face up to the realities of the strategic situation meant that these initial conversations yielded limited results as Anglo-American collaborative efforts tentatively and hesitantly groped toward a modicum of military cooperation. Nonetheless, given the near total mutual ignorance of the other's strategic plans and the absence of any cooperation prior to January 1938, by mid-1939 the respective naval staffs garnered substantial insight into the plans of their counterparts. Recognizing that neither partner could adequately defend both the Atlantic and the Pacific, the level of cooperation had progressed from some vague plans for loosely coordinated parallel action in the Far East to an apportionment of the world into spheres of strategic responsibility and a division of labor between the British and American fleets.

Planning, however, remained in a most rudimentary stage far short of combined cooperation, much less true collaboration. Understanding between the armies of the two countries was extremely limited and being carried out at the lowest level possible. On naval matters, a lack of realism afflicted both sides of the Atlantic. Nascent cooperation had yet to address such fundamental issues as which theater should take precedence or the methods, procedures, and techniques of close cooperation. Nor were there provisions for a permanent organization or processes to coordinate future cooperation, making it likely that any near-term collaboration would be on an ad hoc basis.

More important than any objective achievements, however, were the intangible results of the various informal contacts. The increasing frequency and level of the staff talks drew the United States out of strategic isolation, started the military planners of both countries thinking in terms of Anglo-American cooperation, and convinced staff officers that collaboration was not only desirable but also necessary. At the same time, these initial contacts established a rapport that increased as the conversations continued. While these relationships developed, the staff talks became more and more binding as each nation formulated new plans that took into account what each knew of its counterpart's intentions. Thus, even without formal commitments, the coalition increasingly intertwined as the two military establishments became, even if unconsciously, ever more dependent on one another.

Once war broke out in Europe, neither Britain nor France would seek the United States as a military partner or ally. Each, however, would turn to the United States for badly needed war materiel. The consequences of these interactions would draw the militaries of Britain and the United States closer. To understand how this occurred and why, the narrative next examines how negotiations over the supply of war materiel increasingly bound the two countries together more tightly.

4

Ties That Bind

The Effects of Supply Negotiations on Anglo-American Cooperation, 1938–1940

In the wake of "the war to end all wars" and the Great Depression, the western European democracies eschewed the maintenance of sizeable military forces or the materiel necessary to equip them. This resulted in a general state of military unpreparedness in those democracies. Indeed, despite considerable German and Italian rearmament in the early 1930s, only overt aggression by the revisionist powers sufficiently awakened the democracies to begin their own rearmament programs late in the decade. As a consequence, Britain and France found themselves far behind their potential adversaries. Worse yet, they individually and collectively lacked sufficient raw materials, plant capacity, and, perhaps that most important asset, time to make up the lost ground. In the period 1938–1940, therefore, the issue of rearmament dominated British and French strategic calculus as they sought to remedy their ends, ways, and means mismatch.

Recognizing the limits of their own industrial capacities, Britain and France cast longing glances at the relatively untapped industrial potential of the United States. Securing U.S. materiel assistance, however, was no simple matter. American industrial potential was significantly underdeveloped and for some specialized items of equipment nonexistent. Moreover, having neglected its own armed forces for the previous two decades, the United States had recently embarked on its own, albeit limited, rearmament program, making it likely that any Anglo-French procurement efforts would conflict with American needs.

Underdeveloped U.S. industrial capacity was not the only hurdle. The convergence of diplomatic, economic, political, and security issues led Congress to pass a series of neutrality laws throughout the second half of the 1930s. Principally a result of noninterventionist sentiment, the Nye Committee hearings on munitions as a leading cause of U.S. entry into World War I, rising tensions in the Far East, and an increasingly likelihood of an Italian invasion of Ethiopia, Congress passed the initial Neutrality Act on 31 August 1935. Intended to last six months, the law prohibited the export of "arms, ammunition, and implements of war" to any foreign nation at war. Arms manufacturers had to apply for export licenses. Largely as a consequence of the Italian invasion of Ethiopia the previous October, Congress renewed the act on 29 February 1936, extending the provisions until 1 May 1937. Importantly, the law added a stipulation barring U.S. citizens from extending private loans to any belligerent nation. Although Roosevelt opposed the law, he reluctantly signed the bill because of strong noninterventionist sentiment and heavy domestic pressure on his New Deal agenda.[1]

Continued international turmoil and the Spanish Civil War prompted Congress not only to renew the Neutrality Act in May 1937 but also to strengthen its provisions. U.S. registered ships could no longer transport any arms to a belligerent country, even if the materiel was produced outside the United States. The president could deny belligerent ships access to U.S. ports and territorial waters. Reflecting concerns over the ongoing internal conflict in Spain, the scope of the act included civil wars. When the act passed with only one dissenting vote, Roosevelt voiced no objections, once again conserving his political capital for ongoing and upcoming battles over the New Deal. In deference, however, to public sympathy for nations standing up to the dictators and Roosevelt's protests that the Neutrality Act tied his hands in foreign policy, the act did contain a so-called cash-and-carry provision. At the president's discretion, belligerents could purchase supplies but not arms and only so long as they immediately paid for the supplies in dollars and transported them on non-U.S. ships. Britain and France were the only potential belligerents that would have both the hard currency and the shipping available for transport, so this key provision greatly favored these two countries over Germany and Italy. However, contrary to the remainder of the act, whose provisions were permanent, the cash-and-carry provisions would expire after two years.[2]

There were also considerable issues on the British side of the Atlantic. Even in the wake of Captain Royal Ingersoll's mission, Neville Chamberlain continued his dim view of the United States as a viable partner. For example, in January 1938 he scorned Roosevelt's initiative for a "peace offensive" as "wooly and dangerous."[3] Chamberlain also cemented his hold over foreign policy when Anthony Eden resigned as foreign secretary in February 1938. Eden's departure, coupled with Robert Vansittart's ouster from his long-held position as permanent under secretary at the Foreign Office, left British foreign policy firmly in Chamberlain's hands and no strong advocate of cooperation with the United States in the Cabinet.[4] Indeed, Chamberlain's views of the United States would soon become so poisonous that when it came time to name Sir Ronald Lindsay's replacement as ambassador to the United States, Chamberlain complained "that the Americans are so rotten, it does not matter . . . who we send."[5] His attitude would only harden, and with appeasement holding sway, any substantive Anglo-American collaboration remained unlikely so long as he remained in government.[6]

Chamberlain was not the only one harboring suspicions. Chamberlain's actions and Eden's departure from the government heightened suspicions of British policies in the minds of Roosevelt and key members of his administration. In Roosevelt's case, this did not take much because he bore considerable animus to British policies generally and to Chamberlain particularly. Anti-imperialist to his core, Roosevelt distrusted the British upper class, disliked Britain's foreign policy and tactics, and objected to British trade policies, especially Imperial Preference. Key Roosevelt advisers in the State Department, such as Cordell Hull, Leo Cowley, Adolph Berle, Breckinridge Long, and H. L. Whitney, had one or more of these bones to pick with Britain. Not least, Chamberlain's policy of appeasement continued to eat away at U.S. public support of Britain and France against the dictators.[7]

Nonetheless, by early 1938, given the obvious German and Italian military advantage, Britain and France had little choice but to seek materiel from American sources to supplement their own production. Although the British and French sought a wide range of materiel and equipment, their purchase of U.S. aircraft provides a comprehensive yet concise overview of the entire process. Moreover, from a strategic perspective, aircraft were Britain's most urgent requirement. Britain had staked much on the RAF as both a deterrent and defense force, and domestic production simply could not meet demand.[8]

Interestingly, the French government took the first step toward closing the aircraft gap in January 1938 after Chamberlain criticized his partner in November 1937 for the "lamentable" condition of its air forces.[9] When Edward Daladier became the French minister of defense in January 1938, he and Guy La Chambre, the minister for air, proposed a massive expansion of the French air force. When it rapidly became apparent that the French aircraft industry was incapable of making up lost ground, Premier Camille Chautemps authorized Senator Baron Amoury de La Grange, a longtime friend of President Roosevelt, to undertake a personal mission to the United States to examine the possibility of buying American aircraft. After a weekend with Roosevelt at Hyde Park, La Grange reported that "the President is thus completely in favor of all measures that the French government might believe necessary to reinforce its air formation in time of peace and in time of war."[10] Encouraged by Roosevelt's response, the French quickly dispatched a purchasing mission to the United States to assess the capacity of the American aircraft industry. The mission soon discovered that the U.S. aircraft industry was not that far ahead of their own. U.S. production capacity meant that only 100 Curtiss-Wright P-36 pursuit aircraft would be for sale and not until April 1939. The French were realists, however, and sought to place an order. But then the tumultuous political situation within France and internal French fiscal policies halted negotiations.[11]

Internal French issues were not the only obstacle. Concerned that foreign orders would delay his own plans for expanding the U.S. Army Air Corps, Major General Henry H. "Hap" Arnold, chief of the corps, refused the French permission to examine the aircraft. From Arnold's perspective as someone who had long championed U.S. air power, such resistance made sense. After graduating from West Point in 1907, Arnold quickly established a life-long reputation as a maverick who did not suffer superiors lightly when he protested a commission in the infantry rather than the cavalry. After an initial assignment in the Philippines, Arnold became army aviator 2 in 1911 after taking lessons from the first two army officers taught by the Wright Brothers. Although winning the inaugural Mackay Trophy in 1912, Arnold returned to the infantry after two near-death flying experiences. While on a second tour of the Philippines, he made the acquaintance of First Lieutenant George C. Marshall, who would have a tremendous influence on Arnold's later career. Returning to aviation at the behest of Brigadier General William "Billy" Mitchell, the father of the Army Air Corps, Arnold spent World War I in Washington. One of Mitchell's acolytes, Arnold testified at Mitchell's court-martial despite having been warned off. Nonetheless, in the 1920s and 1930s Arnold won numerous national and international aviation awards and trophies and continued to move up in the hierarchy of the Army Air Corps. By 1936, Arnold was assistant chief of the U.S. Army Air Corps, taking over as chief when Major General Oscar Westover was killed in a plane crash. Throughout this period, Arnold had remained the staunch proponent of a strong air arm. He had justifiable concerns that at this late juncture French or British orders might disrupt his carefully laid plans for expanding the Army Air Corps.[12]

Only after U.S. ambassador to France William C. Bullitt repeatedly interceded with Roosevelt and a direct order from the president did Arnold allow the inspections. Shortly thereafter, the French ordered all 100 aircraft that would be available by April 1939. The French were still not in the clear, however. Continuing internal political divisions and Arnold's delaying tactics stymied the negotiations. Bullitt once again had to throw his personal weight behind the French when he wrote to Roosevelt in early May complaining that the French had been unable to close the deal.[13] Roosevelt confirmed the original contracts signed in April and directed that the French would receive a further 45 aircraft per month in the ten months following April 1939. He added that he had instructed the Navy and War Departments to cooperate fully with future French missions.[14]

Prompted by French orders, the British followed a similar path. However, given the lead time required by American industry, the British decided in late 1937 to expand their own manufacturing potential through the purchase of machine tools instead of directly purchasing aircraft.[15] The British and French would ultimately purchase $100 million ($1.69 billion in 2016 dollars) worth of machine tools and invest another $138 million ($2.33 billion in 2016 dollars) in machine tools in U.S. factories.[16] These purchases were not sufficient to close the gap between them and the Germans, however, and in April 1938 the British dispatched an air mission to the United States to investigate the purchase of modern aircraft for the RAF. J. G. Weir, director of the Bank of England, headed the delegation. Air Commodore Arthur T. Harris accompanied him.[17] After two months of lengthy discussions with major U.S. aircraft companies on facilities, designs, capacities, and availability of aircraft, the British placed contracts for 450 trainer aircraft.[18]

Supply negotiations entered a hiatus until late September 1938, when the Munich Crisis and dismemberment of Czechoslovakia stirred the democracies to action. Convinced that Hitler was "incorrigibly aggressive," Roosevelt concluded that "a Europe dominated by Hitler would eventually pose a grave threat to American security."[19] In Roosevelt's mind, safeguarding U.S. security translated into a military policy of defense of the Western Hemisphere, coupled with a U.S. foreign policy of deterring Germany through military aid to Britain and France. An ardent convert to air power, Roosevelt firmly believed that if Britain and France or even the United States had air power sufficient to match Hitler, then Munich would never have occurred. He therefore decided to expand the capacity of the American aircraft industry by using British and French orders to build up American industrial strength.[20]

The French government shared Roosevelt's assessment of Munich. Jean Monnet, the great French patriot and statesman, noted in his memoirs that Daladier had returned from Munich humiliated, declaring, "If I had had three or four thousand aircraft . . . Munich need have never happened."[21] Eager to purchase aircraft, Daladier immediately dispatched Monnet to the United States, an ideal choice to lead the French mission. Monnet had served on or headed several Allied supply committees during World War I. Dedicated to the Allied cause, he eventually chaired the Anglo-French Purchasing Commission, and after the fall of France he ably served British and U.S. war efforts. In the postwar era, he crusaded for European unity, and the European Union stands as a monument to his efforts.[22]

Wasting no time, Monnet left promptly for New York and upon arrival proceeded directly to Hyde Park, where he met with Roosevelt to discuss various proposals for French acquisition of aircraft. After the weekend, Roosevelt handed Monnet over to Henry Morgenthau, secretary of the Treasury, and Ambassador Bullitt. Together, the three men negotiated means for bolstering the franc, paying for the aircraft, and circumventing the U.S. Neutrality Act. The French were willing to spend upward of $65 million (approximately $1 billion in 2016 dollars) to acquire 1,000 aircraft. The initial whirlwind negotiations climaxed on 21 December, when Roosevelt authorized the French to inspect and purchase up to 1,000 aircraft of the latest American designs, provided they did not conflict with U.S. procurement for the spring of 1939.[23] Monnet quickly discovered, however, that the type of combat aircraft available to the French could not compete with the latest European types and that the most modern models capable of meeting the Germans on an equal basis remained on the War Department secret list.[24]

Worse yet, Monnet's requests ran headlong into full-scale opposition from the War Department, particularly from Secretary of War Henry H. Woodring. A staunch isolationist and opponent of providing any military aid to other countries, Woodring was abetted by Hap Arnold, who was reluctant to release American secrets or take any action that might delay the Army Air Corps' own 10,000-plane program. Despite Morgenthau's active support and the president's tacit approval, only another directive from Roosevelt to Arnold cleared the way for the French to see the latest prototypes.[25] Roosevelt's explicit instructions did not halt foot dragging in the War Department, however. When Monnet attempted to negotiate an option to purchase an additional 1,500 planes in January 1940, the War Department, led by Woodring and Arnold, dug in its collective heels, forcing another impasse.[26] Matters came to a head at a conference on 16 January 1939 when Roosevelt cleared the way for the delivery of the initial orders and authorized Monnet to purchase additional aircraft. Monnet very quickly placed orders that stretched existing U.S. industrial capability to its maximum, and French attention shifted from negotiating contracts to waiting for American industrial capacity to catch up with the orders.[27]

However, *l'affaire* Chemidlin almost derailed the French purchases. Shortly after Roosevelt's stern conference with reluctant War Department officials on 16 January, General Arnold instructed Air Corps officials in California to allow a French team to examine the latest prototype of an experimental Douglas bomber. While demonstrating low-altitude acrobatic skills, the aircraft crashed, killing the American pilot and injuring his passenger, French captain Paul Chemidlin. Local authorities initially tried to cover up Chemidlin's identity, but the story soon leaked, creating a brouhaha not only in the press but also within the noninterventionist faction of the U.S. Senate. After confusing testimony by Morgenthau, Arnold, and General Malin Craig, chief of staff of the army, at hurriedly convened Senate hearings, the noninterventionists smelled blood.[28] Roosevelt ultimately stifled the controversy by openly stating that the government was negotiating aircraft sales to France because it was in the interests of national defense and would aid the ailing American aircraft industry. Once Congress determined that no laws had been broken and that the administration had followed policies for release of information, the controversy waned. The incident was nonetheless a personal embarrassment for Roosevelt as well as for his administration.[29]

Fallout from the controversy had other consequences as well. Trying to tamp down the storm, Roosevelt met privately with the members of the Senate Military Affairs Committee. During their supposedly confidential conversation, he pointed out that countries bordering Germany, in particular France, were in imminent danger, adding, "That is why the safety of the Rhine frontier does necessarily interest us." One senator inaccurately leaked that Roosevelt had said, "America's frontier is on the Rhine," unleashing another torrent of media and congressional attention.[30] At a press conference a few days later, Roosevelt significantly backed away from his initiative to seek revision of the Neutrality Act. As a U.S. diplomat reported to Roosevelt, the reversal, of course, "gave Hitler and Mussolini 'reason to believe now that American public opinion will not tolerate any other than an attitude of the most rigid neutrality. . . . [Your] disavowal has cleared the atmosphere concerning America as far as the dictators are concerned.'"[31]

Shortly thereafter, events in Europe seized public and congressional attention. In mid-March, Hitler completed the dismemberment of Czechoslovakia, established German protectorates over Bohemia and Moravia, and occupied the two regions. At the same time, an "independent" Slovakia sought German "protection." On 21 March 1939, Germany annexed the Baltic port city of Memel—formerly a city in East Prussia and currently designated "Klaipeda, Lithuania"—and began making strong demands on Poland over Danzig and the Pomorze region in German Pomerania, lost in the post–World War I settlement. Just as Munich had been a watershed for Roosevelt, these acts of aggression led to a dramatic British shift away from appeasement. On 31 March, Britain and France offered security guarantees to Poland, followed a week later by a pact of mutual assistance.[32]

The British also began reconsidering their relationship with the United States, which diplomatically had been at low ebb. Chamberlain's disdain for the utility of the United States as a possible partner meant that from the German Anschluss of Austria in March 1938 to the seizure of Prague in March 1939, the United States was of little or no consequence in British policy, thinking, or strategy.[33] After Prague, however, the government's tone and outlook altered. Chamberlain acquiesced to a royal visit to the United States that he had long opposed. Over the objections of many in the Foreign Office and Cabinet, he selected Phillip Kerr, Lord Lothian, as the next ambassador to the United States.[34] Foreign Secretary Edward F. L. Wood, Lord Halifax, at last recognizing the imperative of cooperating with the United States, made sure that Roosevelt received up-to-date intelligence briefings.[35]

The British were concomitantly considering how to establish industrial capacity within the United States that could support the British munitions program.[36] Complicating this initiative were well-founded British concerns that the "cash-and-carry" provision of the Neutrality Act of 1937 would expire in May 1939 and that such an outcome would prevent British purchases from leaving the United States in the event of a European war.[37] As indicated earlier, in the face of intense anti-interventionist pressure and public opposition in the wake of the Chemidlin controversy, Roosevelt had backed off from revising the Neutrality Act.[38] Moreover, a series of domestic political defeats further weakened his ability to engage in a stronger foreign policy. As a result of his attempt to "pack" the Supreme Court and his failed purge of Democrats opposed to the New Deal, he suffered a considerable backlash: in the midterm elections of 1938 Republicans gained thirteen governorships, doubled their numbers in the U.S. House of Representatives, and took eight seats in the U.S. Senate. As a consequence, Roosevelt had to devote his remaining political capital into sustaining the New Deal, leaving little or none to expend on foreign affairs.[39]

During this same period, American attitudes toward Britain hardened. Even in the summer before Munich, "the columnist Dorothy Parker declared bitterly that appeasement had 'brought British stock to an all-time low' in the minds of the American public."[40] Equally troubling for the British ability to obtain war supplies was the fact that "by January 1939, returning English Speaking Union lecturers reported that 'anti-Chamberlain feeling' was intense."[41] By late spring, matters only got worse as these speakers reported "American opinion to be solidly opposed to propaganda, war debt, and Neville

Chamberlain."[42] The situation in Prague only further riled noninterventionist sentiment in the United States.[43] Although spoken in 1940, the words of Senator William E. Borah, the Lion of Idaho, rang true in the aftermath of Munich and Prague: "What in history has been more shameful than England and France conferring with Benes at midnight in Prague while they played Judas to Czechoslovakia? Let England go to the wilderness and perish with her sins. They are guilty; Germany, France, and England. Guilty as dogs."[44]

The combination of these factors led to a resounding Roosevelt defeat when the administration tried to extend the cash-and-carry provisions of the Neutrality Act. The significance of this defeat was not lost on Chamberlain or on Hitler and Mussolini.[45] Nonetheless, the British did not have much of an alternative, and discreet negotiations for the dispatch of an official mission to the United States continued through late July when Roosevelt notified Joseph Kennedy Sr. in London and William C. Bullitt in Paris that he saw no objections to the establishment of foreign purchasing missions in the United States as long as they abided by the Neutrality Act.[46]

The British quickly sent Arthur Balfour, Lord Riverdale, a leading business executive and dedicated public servant, for exploratory talks in the United States. Riverdale soon met with Louis Johnson, assistant secretary of war, informing Johnson that he had come "to visit Washington to get in touch with him and other departments of State with a view to discussing our immediate requirements and our requirements in case of war, and developing a system of close cooperation."[47] Johnson, in turn, notified Riverdale that the French had already sent two missions, whereupon the two men agreed that the British and the French would need to work out some form of quota arrangement.[48]

Johnson's assistant, Colonel James Burns, and Brigadier General Charles T. Harris, assistant chief of ordnance, visited Riverdale at his hotel for further talks. The three men reviewed British requirements and discussed potential conflicts between the British and American programs. Burns made a complete report to Johnson, who bypassed his boss, Secretary of War Woodring, and submitted it directly to Roosevelt. As Johnson told Riverdale, "The President expressed himself as 100% in favor of what we are doing." Johnson stressed the importance of the British sending a strong liaison officer to Washington who could deal with him directly and establish an organization capable of expanding to a full mission in the event of war. Over the next several days, Riverdale and his U.S. counterparts addressed technical points such as the means of payment, intricacies of the Neutrality Act, and Canadian-American business ventures.[49]

In his final report to the British minister of supply, Riverdale made several key points. First, he noted that the Americans were keen on providing assistance. He commented that Johnson, but not Secretary of War Woodring, had observed that "even if they [the Americans] were in the war they would be prepared to share the production of their country with us, giving us something in the proportion of three out of eight units." Second, Riverdale emphasized the imperative of sending a strong individual to control all British arrangements and contacts with the United States. Third, he counseled that a very few orders placed right away could seal a much broader deal with the Americans by convincing them that the British were serious about procuring U.S. manufactures. Finally, Riverdale strongly advised the British government to establish a nucleus-purchasing mission as soon as possible.[50]

Hitler's invasion of Poland on 1 September 1939 added impetus to Riverdale's recommendations. The British government quickly appointed Colonel J. H. Greenly as comptroller general of the British Purchasing Commission for North America. Within a week of the outbreak of the European war, Lord Lothian, Lindsay's replacement as ambassador to the United States, informed the Foreign Office that Roosevelt had granted permission for Greenly to come to the United States, provided he traveled by way of Canada and held official accreditation with the Canadian Purchasing Commission.[51]

At this point, the pace of negotiations slowed as the British realized that until Congress amended the Neutrality Act, early establishment of a purchasing mission would yield no results. British concerns proved well founded. Roosevelt's call on 21 September 1939 for a special session of Congress to revise the Neutrality Act provoked a massive response. In a three-day period, the White House received more than a million letters running one hundred to one against lifting the arms embargo.[52] Despite this opposition, a Gallup Poll on 4 October indicated that 62 percent of respondents favored amending the law to allow Britain and France to purchase material. Although the poll number dropped to 56 percent by 3 November, the amendment passed, and on 4 November Roosevelt signed the revised Neutrality Act of 1939 into law.[53]

The new law was a mixed blessing. On the one hand, it eliminated the arms embargo and restored the cash-and-carry provision, thereby giving Britain and France a tremendous advantage. On the other hand, it sustained the prohibition of Treasury or private loans to belligerents, stipulated that material shipments could go only in foreign holds, and established very broadly defined and geographically large "danger zones" that U.S. ships could not enter. These zones included not only belligerent waters but also many of the primary sea-lanes to nonbelligerents as well.[54]

Historians have mixed views about whether the passage of the amended act in 1939 represented a significant shift in anti-interventionist influence in the United States. Robert Divine sees it as a crucial turning point. David Haglund characterizes the cash-and-carry provision as a step away from absolute isolation but believes that the collective restrictions within the act represented the epitome of isolationist thought. Striking a balance, David Kennedy concludes that "this limited revision of the neutrality law reflected the precarious equilibrium in which American diplomacy was now suspended. Public opinion and official policy alike hung quivering between hope and fear—hope that with American help the Allies could defeat Hitler, and fear that events might yet suck the United States into the conflict."[55]

Even as the debates over the bill were under way, Ambassador Bullitt informed President Roosevelt that the British and French would send purchasing missions as soon as Congress repealed or amended the Neutrality Act.[56] Despite a green light from Roosevelt, the purchasing commissions took some time to gel. Greenly, for example, had traveled to the United States and conducted a detailed investigation of the situation. Upon completing his assessment, he advised establishing two separate bodies, one for Canada and one for the United States. Greenly also recommended that Canadian businessman Arthur Purvis head the British Purchasing Commission in New York and that both missions should be subordinate to a central board located in Ottawa.[57] The Cabinet accepted Greenly's recommendations and created the British Purchasing Commission in late October. However, Anglo-French disagreements over a single, combined mission or two separate national missions and the size and scope of purchases, in particular Chamberlain's concerns that purchases would exacerbate Britain's dollar drain and delay importation of much-needed machine tools, further complicated matters. Ultimately, Greenly received direction to work with Rene Pleven, the newly appointed French representative, although London proscribed Greenly from initiating any new purchases, authorizing him only to survey the capacity of American industry.[58]

Despite the supposed Anglo-French consensus, Pleven found an extremely confused situation when he arrived in the United States in December. The confusion stemmed largely from inadequate coordination within the Anglo-French Purchasing Commission that had resulted in too many missions, too many conflicting orders, and too little information to justify the demands placed on American industry. A purchasing mission under Colonel Paul Jacquin offers but one example of the problems experienced. Immediately after revision of the Neutrality Act, Jacquin placed an order for more than 1,000 combat aircraft, 200 trainers, and 5,000 aircraft engines.[59] The size and scale of the order on top of the existing agreements caught the Americans off guard and resulted in Roosevelt firing off a letter to Bullitt complaining that the British and the French were operating at cross-purposes. Roosevelt told Bullitt that he wanted "one Frenchman and one Britisher in Washington who will have the complete and final say for their Governments. They would have to meet once a day, put all the cards on the table, stop crossing their wires, and give us a chance to know what they want and when they want it."[60] In response, Monnet negotiated a merger of the two separate missions under Arthur Purvis of the British Purchasing Commission that would provide a long-term benefit to Anglo-American collaboration.[61]

The Americans, too, had been rationalizing their organization. On 6 December 1939, Roosevelt formed the President's Liaison Committee, an intragovernmental body that was to represent the U.S. government in all contacts with foreign governments concerning the purchase of war materials in the United States. The committee would meet weekly, handle liaison with foreign governments, and determine availability, priorities, and prices of war materials and supplies.[62] To expedite matters, Roosevelt established the Clearance Committee within the Army-Navy War Munitions Board "to obtain information on all foreign orders and facilitate the placement of orders by 'friendly foreign governments' where they would promote the growth of an American arms industry, at the same time striving to prevent competition with Army and Navy procurement." In his typical divide-and-conquer management style, Roosevelt placed the committee under the authority of Secretary of the Treasury Morgenthau, thereby keeping control in the hands of a close subordinate and, just as importantly, out of the hands of isolationist Secretary of War Woodring.[63]

Collaboration on aircraft purchases seemed to get off to an auspicious start. The French, for example, received first priority on all P-40 fighters, the newest U.S. type, had clearance to examine the latest American prototypes, and could negotiate directly with manufacturers on means to increase U.S. production.[64] All was not as it appeared on the surface, however. Existing orders already had stretched the American aircraft industry to the utmost. For the moment, the French would be able to procure only 8,400 aircraft, and delivery would occur between October 1940 and September 1941. Only new capacity, especially for the production of engines, or diversion of production away from the Army Air Corps could resolve the problem.[65]

If the French were to receive all aircraft they needed then, the only remaining solution was to convince the Army Air Corps to divert its current deliveries to the French. Not surprisingly, Pleven ran head on into Major General Hap Arnold, who was understandably reluctant to see his own armament program delayed.[66] Then suddenly in early February 1940, Arnold did a complete turnabout. After receiving a crushing report from the U.S. air attaché in London that concluded that all current U.S. aircraft were inadequate for modern combat, Arnold apparently realized that the cost of modernizing aircraft ordered in 1939 would never get through an economy-minded Congress. He also recognized that if Congress found out that the aircraft were unsuitable for modern combat, there would be a great deal of explaining to do. It dawned on Arnold and the Air Corps staff that the best single answer to these problems would be to sell the existing and largely inadequate aircraft to the British and French to make room for newer, more capable models.[67] Thus, by 24 February, Purvis and Pleven were able to negotiate an Anglo-French purchase of 7,000 aircraft, the largest peacetime order in U.S. history, and announced that they were willing to spend upward of $1 billion ($17.1 billion in 2016 dollars) for the procurement of American aircraft.[68]

Not all was smooth sailing, however. Secretary of War Woodring still privately opposed any sale of U.S. equipment to foreign governments, and Arnold remained adamant that the British and French not receive the most up-to-date U.S. designs. Matters came to a head at a 12 March meeting at the White House when Roosevelt called the U.S. principals together and announced "that there was to be no more resistance from the War Department, no more leaks from Johnson and Arnold to the Republican and isolationist press. [Looking directly at Arnold, Roosevelt said that] [u]ncooperative officers would find themselves assigned to duty in Guam."[69] Although General George C. Marshall, chief of staff of the army and Arnold's boss, quickly acquiesced, the confrontation did not end resistance from Secretary Woodring. Despite Roosevelt's warning and advice from his subordinates, Woodring steadfastly refused to release designs or prototypes or to sign contracts. Finally, on 10 April the president ordered Woodring to comply or resign. General Arnold would remain banished from the White House for nine months, with all of the attendant consequences for the Army Air Corps.[70]

Roosevelt's breaking of the logjam represents the old case of too little, too late. The day before Roosevelt's confrontation with Woodring, Hitler launched his first assault on the West, seizing Denmark and Norway. A month later the Wehrmacht invaded France and the Low Countries, and by 22 June 1940 the Germans had defeated France and thrown the BEF back across the English Channel.

With the fall of France, the relationship between the United States and Great Britain entered a new phase. This change offers a convenient point to evaluate the course of Anglo-American cooperation in supply matters. Up to the defeat of France, the results of the supply negotiations had little immediate, tangible effect. The limited number of aircraft purchased in the United States that saw action in the battle for France did little to stem the German tide. Over the longer term, however, both Britain and the United States accrued substantial benefits from the supply talks, although the British tended to play down the significance of early American assistance. For example, in his official history *North American Supply*, H. Duncan Hall points out that French orders for aircraft and engines through December 1939 greatly exceeded British orders. In a similar vein, the British Army Staff in Washington noted in the final report of its operations that in March 1940 the British government had signed only 110 contracts, mostly for tanks.[71] What both accounts fail to mention, however, was that on 16 June 1940 the French signed over to the British all of their American contracts, totaling $612 million ($10.5 billion in 2016 dollars). Thus, the British received a considerable share of the U.S. armaments production. In comparison, the entire budget for the U.S. Army in fiscal year 1940 was approximately $850 million, and by 13 June 1940 the army had authorized new contracts of only $257 million.[72]

The United States directly profited from the negotiations as well. In the aircraft industry alone, the British and French spent approximately $61 million ($1 billion in 2016 dollars) for capital construction that resulted in about 6 million square feet of additional plant space. At the same time, capacity for engine production quadrupled, and the total capacity of the aircraft industry rose from approximately 3,500 to 20,000 aircraft per year.[73] By the first half of 1940, British and French orders for aircraft engines were triple the orders for all of 1939 and more than double what the U.S. Army and U.S. Navy were buying: more than 13,000 compared to about 5,000.[74]

The importance of the foreign orders went far beyond numbers. Foreign orders meant new plants, and new plants meant increased employment during a period of deep economic depression. There were also times when existing aircraft facilities on the verge of collapse received a new lease on life or a foreign order kept open an assembly line that later benefited the United States. For example, the Grumman Company could not interest the U.S. Navy in the F4F Wildcat, a carrier-based fighter. Because these planes were available, the French placed an order for 100 of them. When France surrendered, Britain took over the order, keeping the assembly line hot. The F4F eventually would be the front-line U.S. Navy fighter during the naval battles of Coral Sea and Midway and during the Guadalcanal campaign.[75] In addition, the aircraft industry gained critical experience in large-scale planning and methods of expansion that provided long-range advantage not only to the United States but to Britain as well.[76] In no small way, the British and French orders laid the economic and technical foundations for the unparalleled production that would truly allow the United States to become the "Arsenal of Democracy."

Of course, special circumstances contributed to the success of the supply negotiations. First, the U.S. public political climate was more open to discussions on supply matters than they were for military staff talks. Foreign orders put unemployed Americans back to work, which undoubtedly helped increase public acceptance of the discussions. The idea that supplies for Britain and France could keep America out of the war also helped. Finally, because the talks on supplies took place openly, the American public and Congress gradually became accustomed to the idea of Anglo-American cooperation. A second element in the success of the supply discussions was that the British and American representatives dealt in cold facts. In this context, solutions were possible. Even though one or both participants might have been dissatisfied with the results, they usually were able to arrive at a compromise that not only facilitated a distribution of the resource pie but also forged psychological links between the parties. Third, personalities mattered. On the negative side, Chamberlain, Woodring, and to a lesser degree Arnold slowed down the process. On the positive side, Roosevelt, Morgenthau, Marshall, Monnet, and Purvis moved the process forward, breaking logjams at critical moments. Almost continuous discussions fostered the opportunity for the growth of mutual trust and confidence between the two nations. Finally, as American production continued to rise, the British would have still greater opportunity to seek American assistance, paving the way for more discussions and possibly cooperation. At the same time, as the United States granted increased access to American production, the two nations' arms programs inexorably became more and more enmeshed.

Future cooperation, however, depended on whether Britain would survive long enough to make effective use of these supplies. In the summer of 1940, this question preoccupied Franklin Roosevelt and his advisers as they peered through the uncertainties to determine how best to safeguard the United States and its interests.[77] In doing so, they had to decide whether to provide supplies to Britain or to retain them for the ill-equipped U.S. armed forces.

5

The Americans Come to Listen, August–September 1940

The fall of France in June 1940 marked a major watershed in World War II. The crushing defeat of Allied forces in France and the Low Countries demonstrated the ruthless power of the Wehrmacht. The loss of France also left an extremely weak Britain as the last barrier to German hegemony in western Europe. The Royal Navy was at its limit; the RAF had almost no reserves; and although the majority of the BEF had escaped Dunkirk, it lost most of its heavy equipment and small arms. Italy had entered the war, threatening control of the Mediterranean, lifeline of Britain's empire. Ominously, Japan continued to ratchet up tensions in the Far East. These new strategic conditions would drive dramatic changes in the geostrategic environment and open new opportunities for Anglo-American collaboration.

One positive and perhaps most important strategic change occurred on 10 May 1940, when Winston Churchill replaced Neville Chamberlain as prime minister and concurrently assumed the office of minister of defence.[1] For the United States as well, this change seemed a propitious opportunity. Not only were Chamberlain and his strong anti-American biases gone, but Roosevelt already had established a relationship with Churchill. Shortly after Churchill's return as first lord of the Admiralty the previous September, Roosevelt wrote to him, "What I want you and the Prime Minister to know is that I shall at all times welcome it if you will keep me in touch personally with anything you want me to know about."[2] With Chamberlain's permission, Churchill maintained sporadic contact with Roosevelt via letters, messages, and occasional telephone conversations, usually to address steps taken to protect U.S. neutral rights or to pass on tidbits of naval operations, such as the sinking of the German pocket battleship *Graf Spee*.[3]

However, it is important to recall that at this point Churchill's hold on power was tenuous, and many anticipated his rapid fall. He was still the Churchill of Gallipoli, who had championed the failed operation in Norway that had been the proximate cause for Chamberlain's ouster. Many in Parliament remembered that although Churchill had railed against unpreparedness in the late 1930s, he had sowed the seeds of that weakness while serving as chancellor of the Exchequer in the 1920s. Churchill was trying to lead a National government but had once deserted the Conservatives for the Liberal Party and then once more recrossed the aisle to rejoin the Tories. As a result, much of the Conservative Party throughout the 1930s disdained him. Moreover, he was a longtime opponent of the Labour Party. Legitimate questions swirled around Churchill in May 1940. How long might he retain the premiership? Who might replace him? What accommodations might another government have to make with Hitler?[4]

In the end, Churchill would be the man of the hour. His first crucial act was to convince the War Cabinet that Britain would fight on alone if France fell, which was neither as easy nor as unanimous as he later portrayed in his multivolume history of the war, *The Second World War*.[5] To implement this policy, Britain required a new strategy and especially the means to carry it out. If Britain survived the autumn, its only weapons were its traditional reliance on blockade and economic warfare, in this case supplemented by an eventual bomber offensive. The British army would have to grow substantially and be completely reequipped if it was ever to assume the offensive. It was becoming increasingly apparent that Britain's very survival and, certainly, its ultimate victory would depend on large-scale American assistance.[6]

What was the likelihood of such support? Anti-interventionist movements strongly circumscribed American policy. Moreover, even if a dramatic overnight shift in U.S. public opinion would have allowed Roosevelt to extend direct military aid, there was not much assistance to offer. Those who have experienced the United States only as a global superpower may have difficulty recognizing that in the late 1930s the United States truly was a minor military power. Despite the revitalization program started in 1936, the U.S. Navy was still a force in transition, and not until 1942—and then only if the government could sustain the current building program—would it truly become a "navy second to none." The Army Air Corps was almost nonexistent. The bulk of its aircraft were obsolete, and many of its newest models were outmoded the day they rolled off the assembly line. In spring 1940, the army's total active duty authorized strength was 269,023 (including the Army Air Corps), and that was a 40 percent increase over the number in 1939. Granted, the active component could be augmented by 200,000 soldiers from the National Guard and 110,000 (mostly officers) from the Organized Reserves, but these personnel had not yet been called to active duty and were marginally trained at best. Most units had not trained above small-unit levels in decades, and the army had not conducted large-scale maneuvers since the end of World War I. Almost all units completely lacked modern arms and heavy equipment. It would take years to raise, train, and equip an effective fighting force.[7]

Nor did the United States have much to offer in terms of materiel aid. For example, in mid-May 1940, in his first correspondence to Roosevelt after becoming prime minister, Churchill asked for the immediate loan of forty to fifty destroyers as well as the urgent dispatch of all possible antiaircraft artillery and ammunition to England.[8] Roosevelt demurred on the question of destroyers but promised to help as much as possible on the remaining requests.[9] By the end of June, 500,000 rifles, 80,583 machine guns, 25,000 automatic rifles, 316 mortars, and 895 75-mm guns (with one million rounds of ammunition) were on their way to England. Henry Morgenthau, secretary of the Treasury, even pried 50 dive bombers and 750 thousand-pound bombs from the navy.[10] However, this unselfish act nearly emptied the supply cupboard of equipment and supplies badly needed for American rearmament. As Major Walter Bedell Smith, assistant secretary to the army's General Staff worried in a note to Major General Edwin Watson, the president's military aide, "If we were required to mobilize after having released guns necessary for this mobilization and were found to be short in artillery materiel . . . everyone who was a party to the deal might hope to be found hanging from a lamp-post."[11]

Nor were there yet any strategic plans for an army expeditionary force or for cooperation with allies because plans after 1919 assumed the United States would act unilaterally. The war plan schema of the interwar era—the so-called color plans, where each contingency had a specific color code name—reflected these conditions.[12] Because of inadequate military capability, many of these plans were essentially training exercises for staffs or students, with Plan Orange, the U.S. Navy plan for a possible campaign against Japan in the Pacific, being the key exception.[13]

As early as the Munich Crisis, U.S. leaders had recognized that the color plans were largely useless under the changed strategic conditions. The U.S. Joint Planning Committee of the Joint Army–Navy Board began examining military actions that might be required should one or more of the fascist powers violate the Monroe Doctrine, coupled with simultaneous Japanese efforts against the Philippines. Over the next six months, the U.S. Joint Planning Committee examined scenarios that might confront the United States. These reviews evolved into the Rainbow plans, so called to distinguish them from the color plans and because the scenarios assumed multiple opponents or coalition partnerships or both.[14]

- Rainbow 1 assumed that the United States would act unilaterally to prevent a violation of the Monroe Doctrine in the Western Hemisphere, which extended in the east from Greenland south to the Brazilian bulge (10 degrees south latitude) and in the west to Hawaii, Samoa, and Wake Island. The army and navy would protect the continental United States, U.S. overseas possessions, and U.S. trade routes while conducting a strategic defensive in the Pacific along the Alaska–Hawaii–Panama line until the situation in the Atlantic clarified sufficiently to permit the fleet to concentrate on operations in the Pacific.
- Rainbow 2 assumed that the United States would act in concert with Britain and France to perform the mission outlined above, but with the territory in the west extended throughout the Pacific. The plan anticipated limited U.S. action in Europe and the Atlantic, thereby freeing U.S. forces for immediate offensive operations in the Pacific.
- Rainbow 3 assumed that the United States would act alone to defend the territory outlined in Rainbow 1, but immediate operations could commence in the Pacific (essentially an updated and reinforced Plan Orange).
- Rainbow 4 once again assumed the United States would operate alone to prevent a violation of the Monroe Doctrine. In this case, however, the plan included the Western Hemisphere to the tip of South America. As in Rainbow 1, U.S. forces would remain on the strategic defensive in the Pacific along the Alaska–Hawaii–Panama line.
- Rainbow 5 assumed concerted action by the United States, Britain, and France. First priority was hemisphere defense, as assumed in Rainbow 1, but the plan envisaged the rapid projection of U.S. power into the eastern Atlantic and Africa or into Europe or both to defeat Germany and Italy. The partners would assume the strategic defensive in the Pacific until success against Germany and Italy allowed the transfer of major forces necessary for an offensive against Japan.

By June 1940, national leaders had approved Rainbow 1, shelved Rainbow 2, deferred (and ultimately canceled) Rainbow 3, moved an adjusted Rainbow 4 to top priority, and deferred Rainbow 5 until completion of Rainbow 4. The new Rainbow 4 assumed the defeat of France and Britain and Japanese entry into the war. The focus remained on defending the Western Hemisphere, to include the Alaska–Hawaii–Panama line. A key difference between Rainbow 1 and Rainbow 4 was that with Britain and France out of the war, the U.S.

forces required and the materiel to support them were much larger in Rainbow 4.[15]

At this point, U.S. leaders faced two stark strategic choices: accelerate rearmament and (1) retreat to hemisphere defense or (2) extend aid to Britain.[16] Army planners believed it would be many months before they would have the ground and air forces necessary for even a static defense of the continental United States, and an expeditionary force capable of effective employment beyond U.S. borders was even further away.[17] Any aid to Britain would extend those time horizons, perhaps significantly, and looming always was the question of whether Britain would survive. Thus, the army urged the president to contemplate no action outside the Western Hemisphere.

A perceived threat of Axis influence in Latin America was a key reason behind this recommendation. Although in hindsight the situation in Latin America may not look serious, at the time it was a significant concern for U.S. political and military leaders. By 1940, between 1 million and 1.5 million ethnic Germans lived in Latin America, largely concentrated in southern Brazil, Argentina, and Chile, with pockets throughout Central and South America. Axis economic penetration, especially by Germany, accounted for 16 percent of Latin American imports and 10–11 percent of exports in 1938, with the latter proportion rapidly expanding. A growing number of German and Italian military missions were equipping and training key Latin American militaries.[18] By the late 1930s, a combination of inept agitators and spies, fascist victories, British propaganda, amateur American spies, news reporting, and polemics had "stoked the activity into a fevered vision prevalent inside the U.S. government and among the public at large that a Nazi takeover by a 'fifth column' could be imminent. FDR believed it, and his military prepared for it."[19]

In retrospect, these anxieties, although perhaps exaggerated, had a basis in reality. No one had expected Germany to defeat France in a mere six weeks or to stand poised to defeat Britain. Judged in the light of the moment, there were legitimate concerns about Germany using French North Africa as a springboard to Brazil, which would have placed the vital Panama Canal and the continental United States within range of German bombers. Alternatively, Brazil, Central America, or Mexico could serve as a staging area for actions against the Caribbean or the continental United States.[20]

Several quick examples highlight the level of anxiety. As historian Max Friedman points out, "Of the nearly 100 meetings of the joint planning committee [sic] of the State, Navy, and War Departments in 1939 and 1940, all but six had Latin America at the top of the agenda."[21] Concerns went beyond meetings. After discussions with the president on 24 May, General George Marshall and Admiral Harold Stark directed the preparation of concrete plans for the occupation of all French, Dutch, Danish, and British possessions in the Western Hemisphere to prevent them from falling into German hands. On 25 May, Roosevelt ordered to Stark to prepare a plan, Pot of Gold, to airlift 10,000 U.S. troops into northeastern Brazil to prevent any lodgment of a German force. The cruisers U.S.S. *Quincy* and U.S.S. *Wichita* made port calls in Latin America in June after rumors of a fascist-inspired coup in Uruguay.[22]

Although Roosevelt remained concerned about Latin America throughout the summer, the threat to Britain was more immediate.[23] Moreover, if Britain survived, then Germany would find it difficult, if not impossible, to undertake major operations against the Western Hemisphere. Thus, on 13 June 1940 Roosevelt presented a number of strategic hypotheses to the army and navy intelligence chiefs:

1. Time. Fall and winter of 1940.
2. Britain and the British Empire are still intact.
3. France is occupied, but the French Government and the remainder of its forces are still resisting perhaps in North Africa.
4. The surviving forces of the British and French Navies, in conjunction with U.S. Navy, are holding the Persian Gulf, Red Sea, and the Atlantic from Morocco to Greenland. The Allied fleets have probably been driven from the Eastern Mediterranean, and are maintaining a precarious hold on the Western Mediterranean.
5. Allied land forces are maintaining their present hold in the Near East. Turkey maintaining its present political relationship to the Allies.
6. Russia and Japan are inactive, taking no part in the war.
7. The U.S. active in the war, but with naval and air forces only. Plane production is progressing to its maximum. America is providing part of Allied pilots. Morocco and Britain are being used as bases of supplies shipped from the Western Hemisphere. American shipping is transporting supplies to the Allies. The U.S. Navy is providing most of the force for the Allied blockade. (Morocco to Greenland.)[24]

The president's assumptions made his military leaders extremely anxious. They believed that a successful German invasion of the British Isles was likely and doubted that the French would continue resistance in North Africa. The U.S. Joint Planning Committee felt that active U.S. participation would spread too thin America's already overcommitted resources. It also cited the poor state of American readiness and concluded that any action along the president's outline would precipitate German subversive activities in Latin America and might encourage Japan to enter the war. The military advisers also expressed concern that the continued forward presence of the U.S. Fleet in Hawaii might provoke rather than deter Japan. Not least, the planners opined that the United States could do nothing useful by intervening, and U.S. forces needed to retain all equipment and materiel for their own mobilization and training. Although Marshall and Stark were more optimistic than their planners, they were less optimistic than Roosevelt and recommended no more aid to Britain and a U.S. focus on Rainbow 4, defense of the Western Hemisphere.[25]

Roosevelt's explicit assumption about the commitment of air and sea forces is perhaps the most interesting hypothesis. As Mark Lowenthal observes, until the fall of France, U.S. foreign policy and national security issues were "unitary and easily isolated from one another, or inter-connected only in hypothetical scenarios."[26] This configuration allowed Roosevelt to make a series of ad hoc decisions, which gave him maximum flexibility but did not result in a coherent policy. This was an opportunity, if one can call it that, to clarify future policy. However, what was the policy to be? Was this a case of Roosevelt having made up his mind to bring the United States into the war? Was it simply worst-case planning? Was the omission of ground forces an effort to limit liability?

Roosevelt's military chiefs sought clarity on these questions, for they opposed U.S. entry into the war at the time. Marshall, Stark, and their respective planning staffs recommended that the president adopt a policy that involved a defensive position in the Pacific, no further commitments for aid to Britain or France, and immediate mobilization for the defense of the Western Hemisphere. In typical Roosevelt fashion, however, he overruled his advisers on several key points, stepped back from some assumptions, hedged his bets, and retained the utmost flexibility he could. His military advisers returned on June 22 with revised recommendations. Again, in keeping with Roosevelt's modus operandi, there was no signed record of an ultimate approval, but subsequent events indicate that the following revised recommendations became the basis for policy:

1. A defensive position by the United States
2. Nonbelligerent support of the British Commonwealth and China
3. Hemisphere defense, including possible occupation of strategic bases on the soil of Allied nations' western colonies in the case of those nations' defeat
4. Close cooperation with South America

5. Speeding of production and training of manpower, including a draft act and "progressive" [Roosevelt's term] mobilization
6. Preparation of plans for the "almost inevitable conflict" with the totalitarian powers, to ensure concerted action with other nations opposing Germany, Italy, and Japan[27]

Although Roosevelt's guidance appeared to subordinate British materiel requests to U.S. requirements, he soon was directing "that British munitions orders were to be accepted, even though at some cost to American rearmament."[28] His new priorities were due to Britain's dire situation and Churchill's persistent entreaties.[29] In a message to Roosevelt on 15 June, Churchill noted that the Royal Navy had only sixty-eight serviceable destroyers available.[30] Moreover, after the British attack on the French fleet at Mers-el-Kebir on the coast of French Algeria on 3 July in response to the armistice of 22 June between Germany and the Vichy French government, there were concerns that the remainder of the French fleet might fall into German or Italian hands.[31] Should that occur, the overstretched Royal Navy faced ceding the eastern Mediterranean or being unable to control the empire's other sea lifelines. Circumstances in the RAF were not much better. During May and June 1940, the RAF lost 959 aircraft, 477 of them fighters. The government had stripped Fighter Command to the bare minimum during the Battle of France, and by 4 June had only 446 operational aircraft, of which 331 were modern Spitfires or Hurricanes. Worse yet, the RAF had a mere 36 fighters in reserve.[32] The position of the British army was in many ways worse than that of its fellow services. Losses in the evacuation from Dunkirk had been so severe that there were not enough rifles for every soldier, and small-arms ammunition was woefully short. The vast majority of heavy weapons that remained in the United Kingdom were obsolescent. Finally, it would take many months before British industry could begin to make up the losses.[33]

Even before the fall of France reinforced the reality, the British had reached the conclusion that the United States was now their only source of aid. The British government greatly expanded orders for heavy equipment, such as tanks and artillery, as well as for small arms and ammunition.[34] These increased orders, along with Roosevelt's decision to grant all aid short of war, set the stage for the first conflicts that emerged in the early summer between British requirements and America's own rearmament program.[35] Negotiations to resolve these conflicts would continue throughout the remainder of 1940.

As early as May that year, the British had become increasingly anxious about their ability to procure U.S. supplies. These fears, due largely to a dollar drain and the cash-and-carry provision of the Neutrality Act, lessened somewhat when Roosevelt assured Arthur Purvis of the British Purchasing Commission that he would not allow any interference with existing British orders. Nonetheless, even with Roosevelt's assurances, the British worried that as the United States accelerated its own rearmament, the British would get only what did not interfere with American needs or U.S. types of equipment.[36]

Recognizing these realities, in July 1940 the War Office sent its first direct representatives to the United States under Michael B. Dewar, vice president of the British Federation of Industries. This delegation also contained three officers, most notably Brigadier General Douglas H. Pratt. These officers were present not simply to render technical advice but to lobby directly with their American counterparts. This meeting established for the first time face-to-face contacts between military personnel of the British War Office and the U.S. War Department. In these initial negotiations, the British attempted to convince the U.S. military to adopt existing British equipment and designs as a means of quickly replenishing depleted British stocks. For example, Dewar tried to induce the U.S. Army to adopt the British Mark III tank for mass production and use by both armies. By this time, however, the U.S. Army had already settled on the production of the M-3 medium tank, and Dewar failed to persuade the army to convert to the British model.[37]

Despite this initial setback, the British persisted in pressuring the Americans to adopt British types of equipment. In August, the War Office sent a second delegation under Major General Ridley Pakenham-Walsh, who was "to endeavor to persuade U.S. Army Authorities to adopt British types of weapons, more especially the A.12 and A.15 tanks, 25 pounder gun-howitzer and 12-pounder A. T. [antitank] gun." If unsuccessful, Pakenham-Walsh was to convince the Americans to produce British equipment in parallel or at least to secure production of component parts of British equipment.[38] Pakenham-Walsh was no more successful than Dewar. In his official report, he noted multiple meetings with senior U.S. Army officials, who complained that they had spent months getting designs approved only to have the British request new equipment that disrupted those painstakingly laid plans.[39] In short, if the British wanted equipment, they were going to have to take what the United States offered—like it or not.

As British official historian H. Duncan Hall notes, by August 1940 only the United States could undertake new capital expenditures, but "the American Government was not ready to provide them except for the production of types that would be used by the Armed Forces of the United States."[40] Thus was the problem of standardization resolved to American advantage—neither a diplomatic nor an elegant solution, but a solution nonetheless.

Standardization of production types was not the only source of friction. U.S. officials were highly frustrated with the increasing number of competing and frequently contradictory purchasing missions that added to the confusion. In his diary, Pakenham-Walsh recorded that at a meeting of the U.S. Defense Advisory Committee, Major General Charles M. Wesson, chief of ordnance, "blew up," venting that the British did not know what they wanted, and, as a result, their "endless commissions were wasting [the Americans'] time." Wesson added that the Defense Advisory Committee would take no more orders until the British standardized their designs and coordinated their requests.[41] At a later meeting with Secretary of War Henry L. Stimson, Brigadier General George V. Strong, chief of the WPD, admonished the British to establish their priorities: "(a.) those required at once; (b.) those required in three to six months; and (c.) those required later."[42]

In his final report, Pakenham-Walsh acknowledged the confusion stirred by the number and diversity of British missions in the United States but laid blame for these problems squarely at the feet of leaders in London because "inadequate direction and coordination," not numbers, were the source of confusion.[43] He commented in his diary that multiple missions received insufficient and oftentimes conflicting directions, ministries failed to provide timely and accurate information on conditions in Britain, and a lack of coordination existed between the ministries, particularly between the War Office and the Ministry of Supply.[44] His report also faulted the British organization in the United States, where he noted an absence of centralized control and no policy staff or coordination machinery to provide direction. Last, he observed that the service missions were in disarray, largely because of insufficient military staff to provide informed advice to the civilians who had to make decisions on what to buy.[45]

To streamline British procedures, Pakenham-Walsh recommended that all missions in North America be subordinate to a central mission located in Washington. This body would include a headquarters and policy section made up of the head of the British Purchasing Commission (who would hold Cabinet rank), representatives from the dominions, and a permanent policy staff. The policy section would obtain advice from the three service staffs, which would increase in size and responsibilities, as well as from a scientific staff and a materiel staff. A procurement section would be responsible for production, purchase, and financing. Finally, the mission would include an inspection staff to ensure the quality of the materiel purchased.[46] British authorities implemented the obvious suggestions at once, enacted others haphazardly, and never implemented many. However, the organization of the British Purchasing Commission and large elements of the British Joint Staff Mission, which eventually came into being in 1941, ultimately incorporated many of Pakenham-Walsh's recommendations. Hence, although Pakenham-Walsh might not have been fully successful in the short term, his recommendations contributed to the long-term success of British supply operations and Anglo-American military cooperation.

Regardless of conflicts over supply issues, the flow of British requests for materiel assistance increased. When combined with existing contracts and the emergency shipments of June and July, the total British orders represented a substantial portion of American arms production, which rekindled concerns within elements of the U.S. government and military.[47] Even with Roosevelt's decision to provide all aid short of war, U.S. authorities needed assurance that equipment desperately needed for American rearmament would not end up useless or in German hands. The basic issue from a U.S. perspective was whether Britain had the resolve to continue the war and, subsequently, whether it could use the American aid successfully to defend the British Isles. To answer these questions, Roosevelt required better information. To obtain that information, he sent a series of missions to the United Kingdom in late summer of 1940.

The negotiations that preceded the dispatch of these missions began on 11 June 1940, when Lord Lothian approached Secretary of State Cordell Hull with Churchill's proposal for a staff conference between naval representatives to discuss fleet dispositions in the Atlantic and Pacific. Hull gently rebuffed Lothian but promised to forward the request to the president.[48] A week later Lothian made a personal request to Roosevelt during a private meeting. Although Lothian suggested a staff conference, he reported that the "President asked whether these conversations should take place between say, my [British] Naval attaché and Chief of Staff here, or between the United States Naval Attaché in London and somebody in the Admiralty," a far more informal methodology without any attendant complications in larger-scale staff talks.[49] Noting that the British naval attaché would soon return to London, Lothian recommended accepting the president's proposal.[50]

Confusion then set in on both sides of the Atlantic. Hull informed Lothian that each power should determine its own course of action. Because of the strong likelihood that Roosevelt would run for an unprecedented third term, Hull insisted that there should be no direct talks between naval representatives. Because even a whiff of public knowledge might lose Roosevelt the election, Hull wanted only limited contact and then strictly through diplomatic channels. In light of Roosevelt's eager acceptance of the idea just a week earlier, this volte-face understandably confused Lothian, and he requested instructions from the Foreign Office.[51]

The British suffered indecision as well, generating lengthy internal discussions. Ten days after Lothian's message, Lord Halifax, the foreign secretary, urged Churchill to accept Roosevelt's suggestion for naval talks as soon as possible. Halifax noted that, if for no other reason than courtesy, Churchill needed to respond. More importantly, Halifax stressed, in light of Hull's latest discussions with Lothian, the president's enthusiasm might cool. Finally, Halifax pointed out Japan's menacing attitude in the Pacific and his belief that the British Chiefs of Staff favored talks at the earliest opportunity. Churchill remained cool to the idea, fearing talks would devolve into discussions about the disposition of the British Fleet should Britain fall to German invasion.[52]

Despite Churchill's reluctance, Britain's increasingly dire circumstances underscored the need for greater collaboration with the United States. The British Chiefs of Staff, for instance, recently had completed a broad outline of British strategy as well as an analysis of the level of assistance required from the United States. They concluded that American assistance would be required in air, sea, and land forces as well as in materiel and economic aid. The Admiralty went so far as to convene a committee under Admiral Sir Sidney Bailey to investigate in detail the amount of aid required and "to provide for full tactical and strategic cooperation on all forms of naval warfare."[53]

About the same time, the British Joint Planning Staff took the service ministries and the government to task for their confused actions and lack of a prompt reply to Roosevelt's initiative. They criticized the Admiralty for treating the conversations as a private preserve and expressed dismay that the Admiralty created the Bailey Committee without consulting the Air Ministry or War Office. The Joint Planning Staff further chastised the Admiralty for failing to include air and army matters in the basis of the conversations. Although they understood that "it is extremely important not to frighten them [the Americans] off by raising the favourite bogey about the flower of American manhood being slaughtered on the battlefields of Europe, etc.," they felt it critical that all three American services attend any staff talks. They concluded by noting "that the Prime Minister has decided the moment would be premature to have conversations with the United States," an attitude they could not understand. They urged the Chiefs of Staff to "strike while the iron is hot and get down to the conversations at once."[54] These arguments and Halifax's recommendations apparently carried the day, for the Foreign Office informed Lothian that the prime minister had accepted Roosevelt's offer of staff conversations and recommended that the talks be held in London in order to ensure greater security and prevent press leaks. Lothian replied a week later that Roosevelt agreed and that he was conferring with the secretary of state and the U.S. Chiefs of Staff on the best method of conducting the talks.[55]

In preparing for the upcoming discussions, the Joint Planning Staff suggested that the British Chiefs of Staff start the conversations with a general appreciation of the British strategic situation, provide initial guidance for the talks, and then let the various joint committees and services work out specific policies with the American representatives. The committees and services could refer proposed policies back to the respective country's Chiefs of Staff and governments for approval. Importantly, the Joint Planning Staff advised that "while we should not say any more than we find essential, we suggest that we should be authorized to discuss strategic questions with the U.S. representatives as if we were Allies." In addition, they asked that Lothian receive instructions to request adding a full air representative to the delegation. Finally, so as not to frighten off the Americans, they suggested the inclusion of a British army observer, perhaps the attaché, but not a full delegate.[56]

Contrary to these recommendations, the British Chiefs of Staff insisted that the conversations begin strictly as naval talks and then develop at their own pace. The Chiefs of Staff did agree that the talks eventually should include air discussions and perhaps even army talks. Lothian could suggest including an air representative in the American delegation, but he was not to stress the matter. Finally, although the talks could be full and frank, the British Chiefs of Staff would allow the Americans to take the lead and set the pace of the discussions. British representatives were not to press, out of fear of overwhelming the American delegation.[57]

British anxieties over American participation were relieved somewhat when Lothian unexpectedly reported on 20 July 1940 that Under Secretary of State (Benjamin) Sumner Welles had informed him that an admiral and a general would leave shortly for England. Two days later Lothian cabled home that a qualified air representative would be included and that the delegation hoped to leave in about a week.[58] As the British Chiefs of Staff concluded with some relief in a note to the prime minister, "The inclusion of a General and of a representative qualified to discuss Air matters in the American delegation would appear that the President is prepared to discuss Air and Army matters as well as Naval."[59] Lothian even concluded that the strength and composition of the American delegation indicated that the United States was ready to initiate a general exchange of information.[60] Little did the British know.

Bolstered by this new information, the British continued planning for what they assumed would be staff talks during the first weeks of August. The Admiralty's planning staff recommended that officers of equivalent rank should meet with the Americans and that the director of plans of the three services be included. The naval staff further suggested that if the Admiralty envisioned a future delegation to the United States, then the Royal Navy representatives at the current conference should be those officers earmarked for that delegation, thereby providing a degree of continuity to the talks and establishing personal relationships.[61]

Unsure of the extent of the Americans' instructions, the British Chiefs of Staff charged the Joint Planning Staff with formulating the foundations for the talks. The planners assumed that they would have no idea of American instructions or interests until the conference began; the British would be fully frank and would address the strategic situation openly and candidly; they would treat the Americans as if they were active allies; the talks would not commence before 12 August; and absolute security would surround them. As previously recommended, the British Chiefs of Staff would open the talks with a general discussion of the strategic situation, after which the Americans would make a series of day visits to various headquarters to observe British procedures and the general situation. These visits would last for approximately one week, allowing the planning staffs to complete the British strategic appreciation. Upon return from the tour of headquarters and units, the American representatives would meet with the respective directors of plans for detailed discussions, and the substance of the talks would fall to the service ministries.[62]

On 10 August, Colonel Raymond Lee, the U.S. military attaché, notified the War Office that the American delegation was en route to London. In the interests of security, they were traveling under the cover of special observers because there were more than thirty such U.S. officers already present in England as observers. Lee also told the British that the American representatives would first report to the U.S. embassy and would remain at Ambassador Joseph Kennedy's disposal. When ready, the U.S. embassy would initiate the meetings.[63] With Lee's notification, British preparations moved into the final stages. For security purposes, all memoranda, minutes, and agendas issued in conjunction with the talks would be headed "Anglo-American Standardization of Arms Committee."[64]

The final composition of the British delegation offers a clear indication of the importance the British placed on the success of the discussions. Vice Admiral Thomas V. Phillips, vice chief of the Naval Staff, interlocutor with Captain Royal Ingersoll in January 1938, led the delegation. Air Marshal Sir Richard Peirse, vice chief of the Air Staff; Lieutenant General Sir Robert H. Haining, vice chief of the Imperial General Staff; and Major General Hastings Ismay, secretary of the War Cabinet, were the remaining members. This was a very high-powered group, especially when compared to the composition of the American delegation. Granted, the principal British negotiators—Captain C. S. Daniel, Royal Navy, director of plans; Brigadier General I. S. O. Playfair, British army; and Air Commodore J. C. Slessor, RAF—held positions similar to their American counterparts, but this does not diminish the level of attention showered on the U.S. delegation by the highest levels of the British military establishment.[65]

The proposed agenda for the first meeting provides interesting insights into British assumptions about the conference. After brief introductory remarks, the British would invite the Americans to present U.S. views on the scope of the conversations. The British then wished to state that the conversations should be based on mutual security and interests and that "the most satisfactory basis for discussion will be an assumption that the United States are [sic] our active Allies—with a suitable qualification." A final point stipulated that any agreements reached between the British and U.S. planners would be subject to confirmation by authorities of both nations.[66] The first and final items lead to the conclusion that the British hoped to guide the Americans toward full-fledged, freewheeling conversations that would end in concrete agreements. Although it is easy to understand why the British wanted a firm commitment from the Americans, it is equally easy to see why they were unlikely to get one. That the British would make such statements, which were likely to discomfit the Americans, is an indication of just how tone-deaf they were on this issue.

The U.S. delegation included Rear Admiral Robert L. Ghormley, until recently the assistant CNO. When the initial negotiations for the conversations had been focused on naval issues, Stark selected Ghormley to become the special naval observer (SPENAVO) London, and Roosevelt personally briefed Ghormley on 15 July.[67] When the talks expanded to include air and army representatives, General Marshall added Major General Delos C. Emmons, commanding general of the General Headquarters Air Force, and Brigadier General George V. Strong, chief of the WPD, to the delegation.[68] Ghormley's special relationship with Stark and President Roosevelt and the fact that he was to remain in London, whereas the other Americans were to discuss technical matters and then return home, placed Ghormley in a unique position.

The Americans brought an interesting mix of experience to the conversations. Emmons had begun his career as an infantry officer, commissioned from West Point in 1909. After serving with the mission tracking Pancho Villa along the border with Mexico in 1916–1917, he transferred to the Aviation Section of the Signal Corps. After rising through a variety of command and staff assignments, by the summer of 1940 he was the commanding general of the General

Headquarters of the Air Corps. Brigadier General George V. Strong had been commissioned into the cavalry from West Point in 1915 but had commanded an artillery regiment in the St. Mihiel and Meuse-Argonne offensives in World War I. In the interwar years, in addition to normal peacetime assignments, he served as an instructor at the Military Academy from 1919 to 1923 and attended both the Command and General Staff College and the Army War College. He had been assigned to the War Department General Staff since June 1938.[69]

Born in Portland, Oregon, on 15 October 1883, Rear Admiral Ghormley graduated from the University of Idaho in 1902 and then from Annapolis in 1906. Commissioned in 1908, Ghormley rose rapidly through naval ranks. As a lieutenant, he commanded U.S. Naval Forces during the brief Nicaraguan Campaign of 1912. During World War I, he served as flag lieutenant to the commander of Battle Force One based in England before returning to Washington, D.C., where he served in the Navy Department. In the 1920s, Ghormley commanded a destroyer, was the officer in charge of enlisted personnel in the Bureau of Navigation, served as an aide to the assistant secretary of the navy, was executive officer of the battleship *Oklahoma* (BB-37), and, finally, served as secretary to the General Board of the U.S. Navy. His promotion to captain in 1929 was a signal of the navy's respect for his many talents. In the early 1930s, he became the assistant chief of staff and fleet operations officer to the commander of Battle Force, U.S. Fleet, and later CINC, U.S. Fleet. After commanding the battleship U.S.S. *Nevada* for one year, in June 1936 Ghormley returned to duty as assistant chief of staff and fleet operations officer of the U.S. Fleet. After attending the Naval War College and being promoted to rear admiral in October 1938, he became director of the WPD in the Office of the CNO in August 1939 and then assistant CNO.[70]

The two groups met for the first time on 20 August 1940. Ghormley's opening remarks must have unsettled the British, for he immediately informed them that neither he nor any one else was in charge of the U.S. delegation. Moreover, he stressed that the U.S. delegation was not in any way a joint mission. Each member was an individual representative of his service, and they would not and could not act as a corporate body. Ghormley then further upset the British when he added, "It should also be understood that none of these observers have [sic] been authorized to make any commitments on behalf of their Government."[71] Thus, in the first few minutes Ghormley swept away the underpinnings of the British plan for the talks. He equally dashed British hopes for a U.S. commitment to Britain or any idea that the Americans were there to engage in formal staff talks.

After Ghormley's cautionary remarks, Strong steered the discussions toward supply matters, an issue that had been and would continue to be a source of irritation for U.S. authorities. Strong noted that the greatest problem currently confronting Anglo-American cooperation was the conflict between British and American supply programs. He stressed that the Americans wanted the problem addressed immediately. He emphasized that the United States needed accurate data on the British situation and requirements so that it could develop a coordinated plan. For the British, Peirse replied that they were prepared to furnish full and candid information and to cooperate with the American program. Strong, reiterating his comments to Pakenham-Walsh weeks earlier, then added that the U.S. representatives wanted the British to distinguish between their short-term needs for the defense of the United Kingdom and the long-term requirements for when the British shifted over to the offensive. Once British production capacity had been determined, he continued, it would be possible to formulate and evaluate their strategic plans for the future.[72]

Peirse took a conciliatory stand, noting that the two sets of requirements were inextricably linked. From a British perspective, the first priority was an agreed strategy from which they could then deduce production requirements. He quickly added that the Americans would better understand the problems of the war after they had heard the British Chiefs of Staff's views on future strategy. Toward the end of this first meeting, the discussion centered on technical matters, in particular antiaircraft defenses, until Ghormley introduced the topic of the Far East and pointedly inquired if the British Chiefs of Staff were going to discuss this important issue. Phillips agreed on the importance of these matters and assured Ghormley that they would certainly come up for discussion. Shortly thereafter, the meeting adjourned, suspending the formal conference while the Americans visited various installations and headquarters.[73]

While the delegation was away on its inspection tour, Colonel Lee forwarded a questionnaire from the U.S. delegates requesting the views of the British Chiefs of Staff on a wide range of strategic and tactical matters. The Americans were interested in the overall British strategic concept of the war, British plans for operations in the Mediterranean, British ideas on offensive action in western Europe, materiel requirements for both the short and long term, the potential role of Russia and Japan, and steps anticipated for the defense of British interests in the Western Hemisphere.[74] This rather extensive list of particulars, combined with the Americans' declarations about their inability to make commitments and the independent nature of the three officers, confused the British about the true nature of American objectives. The British quickly concluded, nevertheless, that the problem lay not with them, but with the Americans. As the Joint Planning Staff commented in a report to the Chiefs of Staff, "It seems probable that their [the American delegates'] precise functions have not been defined, and that it may well be possible to lead them into the staff conversations proper which the President appeared to have in mind in the first place and which we expected that the American Delegation would be empowered to undertake."[75] To ensure a solid basis for the next round of detailed talks, the Joint Planning Staff urged the Chiefs of Staff quickly to sound out the Americans about the full extent of their authority. Thus, despite American warnings, as far as the British were concerned, the stage was set for full-fledged staff conversations.

The second full meeting of the Anglo-American Standardization of Arms Committee convened on 29 August 1940. The British Chiefs of Staff, Admiral of the Fleet Sir Dudley Pound, Air Chief Marshal Sir Cyril Newall, and Field Marshal Sir John Dill hosted the session. Colonel Raymond Lee and Captain Alan G. Kirk, the U.S. naval attaché, accompanied the U.S. representatives. Newall, as the senior member of the Chiefs of Staff Committee, outlined the procedures for the remainder of the discussions. The Chiefs of Staff would deliver the British view of the current strategic situation, and then in a subsequent meeting the British would present a general outline of future British strategy. The directors of plans would be available to clear up any specific questions and would have full authority to discuss all matters. Newall added the caveat that "any points agreed or conclusions reached during these discussions would of course be subject to confirmation by the Defense Authorities in the United States and England."[76]

Newall then offered an overview of the strategic situation that he described under three broad categories: political, economic, and potential enemy action. After quickly passing over the political situation, he outlined the British economic position, especially their dependence on overseas supply and the need for increased American economic and industrial cooperation. On the Axis side, he emphasized German susceptibility to blockade, in particular their dependence on external oil and food supplies. Regarding German action, Newall posited that to win the war the Germans would have to either successfully invade the United Kingdom or destroy British industrial capacity and morale through air attack or sever Britain's overseas lines of communication. The Chiefs of Staff, therefore, considered the likely areas of German activity to be in the North Atlantic, the Middle East (in particular an attack on Egypt), movement through the Iberian Peninsula to secure French North Africa, and an assault into the Balkans.[77]

Newall next summarized the strategic picture. On the positive side was

British naval supremacy, the power of blockade, and ability to draw on resources from the empire and the rest of the free world. The Germans, however, controlled the Continent and had air and land superiority. For the moment, the Germans held the strategic initiative. Nonetheless, the British were not overly anxious. If they could secure their sea lines of communication and maintain the blockade, then time was on their side. Given that the Germans probably would continue air and naval attacks on the United Kingdom and begin an offensive against Egypt, the British would concentrate on these key theaters of operations.[78]

At the conclusion of his strategic overview, Newall outlined the British production program. He noted problems in establishing a balanced program, especially in terms of manpower allocation and steel production. He added frankly that it was "essential that we should get everything from America that can be supplied," while the British themselves concentrated on ships and "certain aircraft and armaments that cannot be obtained from the United States."[79] The armaments would equip an army of fifty-five divisions (empire total), twenty-one of which would protect overseas interests, while the remaining thirty-four would perform home defense and offensive operations. The British contemplated that they would have twenty to thirty divisions available for offensive action by spring 1942. Contained within these figures was an armored force of five divisions and ten independent brigades. The rearmament program would also provide the RAF with approximately 7,500 aircraft during the same period. Newall emphasized that this program included the maximum British industrial potential and a substantial increment from the United States.[80]

Closing his remarks, Newall opened the floor for general discussion. Strong immediately inquired how the U.S. representatives could get a definitive statement of British production requirements from the United States. Newall replied that the directors of plans could discuss supply and production matters in some detail. A general discussion followed on current execution of their strategic concept, ways of enforcing the blockade, the British targeting strategy for the air offensive against Germany and Italy, and some technical discussions on equipment. Shortly thereafter the meeting adjourned.[81]

The delegations met again two days later when the British Chiefs of Staff delivered their appreciation on (analysis or estimation of) future strategy. Newall again carried the brunt of the discussion and began the meeting with a brief synopsis of the overall strategic situation. Foremost, he noted that Germany was the main point and that all other opponents were subsidiary. Although currently on the strategic defensive, the British "were engaged in a relentless offensive" both economically and physically in the air. However, with the ejection of the BEF from the Continent and the loss of most of its equipment, the British needed significant materiel assistance from the United States. The RAF was still outnumbered and in urgent need of additional aircraft and trained pilots. Naval losses had been considerable, and the British anticipated more.[82]

The key element of the current strategy was defense of the United Kingdom. Although the situation was serious, Newall declared, "we are confident of our ability to withstand any attacks on this country, and our whole policy is based on this assumption."[83] He then outlined the major elements of British strategy for ultimately defeating Germany:

1. To insure [sic] the security of the United Kingdom and our Imperial possessions and interests.
2. [To] [m]aintain command of sea communications in the oceans, the Home waters, and the Eastern Mediterranean and to regain command throughout the Mediterranean.
3. To intensify economic pressure.
4. To intensify our air offensive against both Germany and Italy.
5. To build up our resources to an extent which will enable us to undertake major offensives operations on land as opportunity offers.[84]

Newall then explained in detail how the British intended to implement the strategy. To achieve the first two objectives, they planned to reinforce the Middle East, strengthen their garrisons in West Africa, and establish or reinforce existing naval bases throughout the world. Although Newall stressed the importance of the naval bases at Gibraltar and Alexandria, he focused on Singapore, "on which depends our future ability to maintain a fleet in the Far East in the event of war with Japan."[85] He was less distinct about plans for the latter three points of their strategic outline. On the economic front, the British believed, mistakenly, that the Germans would face a severe shortage of food in the near future and inaccurately concluded that by the summer of 1941 German military operations would be "largely hamstrung through shortage of oil."[86] There was no real discussion of the British air offensive or the means to place a force on the Continent for major land operations, although Newall highlighted the advantages inherent in the Royal Navy's command of the sea. Newall did add that one of their first steps would be the elimination of Italy, which would secure the Mediterranean and release land and naval forces for use elsewhere, in particular the employment of naval assets in the Far East.[87]

The discussion shifted to British views of the situation in the Far East. The

Chiefs of Staff first emphasized that regardless of conditions in the Far East nothing would distract them from their first priority of defeating Germany. The loss of the French Fleet and the Japanese occupation of French Indochina, however, meant that the British no longer would be able to send a battle fleet to the Pacific. Instead, they would anchor their position in the Far East on Singapore, basing a defense on two premises: air power could replace sea power, and the army could hold the Malay Peninsula. The British recognized the difficulty in maintaining their lines of communication to the Far East and the challenges in defending their position there. In this regard, they stressed "the immense value of active American cooperation in the event of war with Japan" and that "the support of the American battle fleet would obviously transform the whole strategic situation in the Far East."[88]

After Newall opened for questions, Ghormley challenged the British assessment. After addressing relatively minor issues, such as the defense of Hong Kong and facilities in Alexandria, he directly asked if future British plans relied on continued economic and industrial aid from the United States "and whether they counted upon the eventual active cooperation of the United States." Newall replied that British plans assumed continued industrial support and assistance from the United States, in an ever-increasing volume. He emphasized that "the economic and industrial cooperation of the United States were [sic] fundamental to our whole strategy" but that active U.S. cooperation was a matter of high political policy and therefore had not been considered. Ghormley then asked if the British "considered that the final issue of the war could only be decided on land." Newall affirmed this point but added that the Chiefs of Staff hoped for a weakening and perhaps a complete internal collapse of the German war effort that would ease the British army's task. Neither Newall nor his peers elaborated, however, on how the British would bring about this debilitated state.[89]

Ghormley then returned his attention to the Far East and inquired what action the British would take should the United States send part of the Pacific Fleet to the Atlantic. Specifically, would the British give priority to the Mediterranean and Mideast or to the defense of Singapore? Pound replied that they would dispatch a small force to Ceylon. He further explained that because they would be unable to send a force of sufficient size to engage the Japanese fleet on equal terms, they felt that it would be better to control the Indian Ocean than to try to force their way through a numerically superior Japanese fleet.[90]

Strong then interjected that the two governments had agreed that a periodic exchange of information would be desirable. He proposed that the time had come to conduct these exchanges on a regular basis and "outlined certain methods by which the sources of information at the disposal of the United States might be placed at the disposal of the British Government."[91] Newall deferred on the matter but promised to take it up with the prime minister.

This interchange concluded this third and final formal meeting between the special observers and the British Chiefs of Staff. At this point, the individual nature of each officer's mission came into play. After brief talks with members of the British War Office, Strong left the United Kingdom during the first week of September to report personally to General George C. Marshall and President Roosevelt. Emmons remained in Britain for an additional time to meet with Air Ministry and aircraft industry officials. Ghormley, in his position as SPENAVO, remained in London for further talks with the Admiralty staff.[92]

Upon Emmons's return from Britain, he and Strong briefed Secretary of War Stimson on the results of their mission.[93] In a distillation of their lengthy report intended for President Roosevelt, the two officers presented their observations and recommendations. The two generals noted that they had talked to everyone in Britain—"the King, the PM [prime minister], the War Cabinet, practically all members of the Government, the Chiefs of Staff, and the personnel of the High Command of the Army, Navy, and Air Forces"—and that they had visited every type of command headquarters, installation, and factory.[94] They commented that British morale was high, perhaps bordering on overconfidence, and that the British were convinced of eventual victory. For the moment, the chief British concerns were the Mediterranean, the Near East, and the Far East. Strong and Emmons pointed out that in matters of production British industry had suffered little material damage but that the Germans had not yet employed the Luftwaffe to full effect. Troublesome was their conclusion that "the British do not know their full combined requirements for munitions, nor did they know their own actual or potential production capabilities. . . . [T]hey desire us to assure at our expense their material requirements."[95]

The report continued that the loss of British shipping represented a serious threat, and with the increasing U-boat menace it would only get worse. They observed that although the Royal Navy lacked sufficient numbers of destroyers and long-range aircraft and even a system for meeting the submarine threat, it was supremely, if not overly, confident that it would ultimately succeed. In a similar vein, the representatives noted that although the RAF was performing yeoman service in the war so far, it had yet to face more than 25 percent of the Luftwaffe. They also expressed concern that the training of pilots and aircrews was a bottleneck that would take some time to work out. Their final observations dealt with the numerous visits to field headquarters and units.

The comments were of a more technical nature, such as the need to increase antitank elements in U.S. units, changes in fighter tactics, and so on—insights that would prove extremely valuable to the American forces if the United States were to enter actual combat.[96]

Prior to offering their conclusions, Strong and Emmons passed on Churchill's most pressing requests for assistance. The prime minister urged Roosevelt to dispatch as quickly and in the greatest quantity possible machine tools, flying boats, torpedo boats, rifles, and airplanes. Churchill went so far as to ask Roosevelt to allow U.S. Army and Navy pilots to volunteer to fly for the RAF while on official leave of absence, wherein they would, according to Churchill, obtain "wonderful training by giving them actual combat experience."[97]

Strong and Emmons were straightforward in their conclusions and recommendations. They concluded that the defense of England would remain a matter of air power, and, based on the current situation, the RAF would probably hold. They were convinced that the British would be able to repel an invasion attempt as long as they did not thin their forces too much through reinforcement of the Middle East. The two officers opined that 15 October was the critical date for an invasion and concluded that after that point the British strategic situation would brighten considerably. Perhaps most important for future Anglo-American collaboration was their final conclusion: "We both have the very definite feeling that sooner or later the United States will be drawn into this war."[98]

The Anglo-American Standardization of Arms Committee talks represented a key transition point in Anglo-American collaboration. Granted, there were no real cooperative efforts or planning because the Americans came simply to listen, to assess Britain's ability to survive, and to report their conclusions to President Roosevelt. The high degree of access to British personnel, policies, and secrets as well as British candor led the Americans to conclude that Britain would survive. Their final report reinforced Roosevelt's decision, at a critical time, to continue all aid short of war. This decision also opened the door to further and increased collaboration between the two countries' militaries.

The talks also opened up new realms of potential collaboration. Roosevelt previously relied solely on conversations between naval officers, and the inclusion of an air officer and a ground officer in the delegation represented a new phase in his thinking. It also indicated a realization that a reliance on naval power alone might not be sufficient to ensure British survival or ultimate triumph over Germany and Italy. With this realization came the potential to expand the scope of any future Anglo-American discussions. Strong and Emmons were greatly impressed with British methods and willingness to share their experiences with the American military. They also noted that such information was extremely valuable. Their conclusion that continued talks were in the best interests of the United States augured well for increasing interaction between the two militaries. Their assessment that the United States would eventually be drawn into the war underscored the need to gather as much information as quickly as possible.

Those decisions and events would lie in the future, however. In the near term, Rear Admiral Ghormley remained in London to continue discussions with the Admiralty staff. Where those discussions might lead remained unknown.

6

Two Steps Forward, One Step Back
Inching toward Collaboration, Autumn 1940

In the wake of the Anglo-American Standardization of Arms Committee talks, cooperative efforts between Great Britain and the United States entered a new phase. The U.S. War Department, true to the recommendation made by Generals Strong and Emmons, dispatched an increasing flow of observers to Britain that provided a further opportunity for collaboration between the land and air forces. Strong and Emmons's conclusion that Britain would continue to fight validated Roosevelt's decision in favor of all aid short of war, therefore paving the way for substantial negotiations between the two nations in the logistics arena. Rear Admiral Ghormley remained in London to continue discussions with the Admiralty staff, thus increasing the likelihood for cooperation between the two powers' naval services.

As indicated earlier, even before the Anglo-American Standardization of Arms Committee talks, Roosevelt and Stark decided in early July to send Ghormley to England for naval conversations. On 15 July 1940, with Admiral Stark present, Roosevelt briefed Ghormley on the purpose and scope of his mission. In typical Roosevelt fashion, the president rambled about the world situation and offered vague hints for guidance. Ghormley received only oral instructions, so the full details of the guidance from Roosevelt remain cloaked to history.[1] That said, subsequent events offer hints regarding the president's intent. At his meeting with Admiralty representatives on 17 August, Ghormley informed the British that he was "to obtain such information as they are willing to impart on such subjects as their future plans and fleet dispositions both present and future and such information of a like nature that they would not usually give to an attaché." The British apparently read more into Ghormley's purpose. As he informed Stark, they were convinced or had convinced themselves that he was in Britain "to begin staff talks immediately leading to our entry into the war and detailed plans for naval help." Ghormley then informed Stark that he would delay any talks with the British until the CNO informed him that Congress was more inclined to favor them.² Two days later Stark notified Ghormley that the president's oral instructions precluded any intimation of imminent U.S. entry into the war but added, "If you desire, however, there would be no objection to personal, theoretical, and unofficial discussions of an informed and entirely personal nature with the view of receiving their suggestions and ideas as to how the United States naval forces might be employed if we ever became involved in the war."³ In short, Ghormley was to operate in the gaps and seams of ambiguous policy and go as far and as fast as he was comfortable so long as there were no "official" commitment.

Not until the conclusion of the Anglo-American Standardization of Arms Committee talks at the end of August was Ghormley able to pursue his independent discussions with the Admiralty. When meeting with First Sea Lord Admiral Sir Dudley Pound on 2 September, Ghormley informed him that on his own responsibility he wanted all Admiralty ideas about the independent role of the U.S. Fleet or about cooperation with the Royal Navy should the United States enter the war. During the course of this initial conversation, Pound let slip the existence of the so-called Bailey Committee Report. Ghormley quickly requested a copy.⁴

Some background on this report is useful in understanding the evolution of Anglo-American cooperation in this period. On 15 June 1940, the Admiralty directed Admiral Sir Sidney Bailey to convene a committee to investigate forms of assistance desired from the U.S. Navy. Specifically, the committee was to examine potential areas of responsibility, the general policy of cooperation between the two navies, and various technical matters, such as the amount of information and when U.S. authorities should receive it as well as appropriate communications arrangements for such exchanges. The Admiralty also enjoined Bailey from divulging the existence of his committee to anyone without a need to know, but especially not to the U.S. naval attaché to Great Britain.⁵ The committee, whose permanent members included Rear Admiral W. S. Chalmers and Captain L. C. A. St. J. Curzon-Howe, the former naval attaché in Washington who had taken part in the Hampton conversations, deliberated over the course of the next six weeks and compiled their findings into a full report submitted on 26 August 1940.⁶

The report initially addressed the expected role of U.S. Fleet elements in the Pacific. The British assumed that for the time being the United States would maintain a strong fleet to deter Japan and protect American and British interests in the Far East. The committee exhibited some confusion concerning operational commands of naval forces, however. On the one hand, the report noted that, for internal Commonwealth reasons, Australian and New Zealand naval forces might receive strategic responsibility for Austral-Asian waters. On the other hand, the committee observed that because neither of those two dominions possessed capital ships, and British battleships and aircraft carriers were likely to remain in the Atlantic and Mediterranean, any such vessels assigned to the southwestern Pacific would have to come from the United States. The British, therefore, should ask the Americans to assume responsibility for both the Pacific and Australian waters.[7]

Confusion also existed within the Bailey Committee over the extent of U.S. naval assistance required in the Atlantic. On the one hand, committee members felt that because of too many unknowns, U.S. strategic responsibility should be limited to the western Atlantic and West Indies from Nova Scotia south, although the area might be expanded later to include the Azores. However, the British also wanted immediate assistance in the Royal Navy's own area of operations in the Atlantic, especially in the antisubmarine campaign in the Western and Northern Approaches to the United Kingdom. Of lesser but still critical importance was the British desire that the Americans reinforce British naval forces in northern waters, augment air-reconnaissance assets throughout the Atlantic, participate in convoy protection, and employ submarines to supplement British assets.[8]

Concerning the always delicate topic of operational control of forces, the committee proposed that the nation tasked with strategic responsibility for an area should also exercise operational command and control over all naval forces in that area. For example, British forces in the Pacific would fall under American direction, and the Royal Navy would control U.S. forces operating in the Northern and Western Approaches or the Northern Patrol. As liaison methods follow naturally from command arrangements, the committee next noted that they had relied on the historical example of U.S. and British naval cooperation in World War I, in particular the Sims mission.[9] Although control and liaison provisions may have echoed the "Sims model" of World War I, the relative size and capabilities of the two navies had changed significantly since 1918, and subsequent events would demonstrate the British assumption invalid.

The report raised the possibility of secret staff talks between the two nations' armed forces. The committee urged that such talks take place in London, though its members were open to conversations in Washington. Admiral Bailey opined that a naval officer should head any joint staff mission because the negotiations would be concerned predominantly with naval matters. Regarding the membership of the British naval mission, the committee proposed that the head of the delegation should already be known and trusted by U.S. naval authorities and should be of sufficient rank to deal directly with the

U.S. CNO and the president. The committee also felt it critical that the head of the mission should have plenty of sea duty behind him and be fully conversant with current Admiralty policies. Finally, it noted that the naval mission should remain independent of the existing naval attaché organization in Washington and that its size should be the minimum necessary to conduct business. The committee likewise proposed the dispatch of an American naval mission to London and outlined similar requirements and policies for the U.S. delegation. An ideal head of mission should be sufficiently senior to deal with the vice chief of the Naval Staff and the first sea lord and preferably would be the man eventually designated as the commander of U.S. naval forces operating in British waters. The committee also recommended that the Americans send a strong staff of specialist officers.[10] Again, the Sims mission of World War I seems to have stood out in British thinking.

The committee singled out intelligence activities for more detailed consideration. They first recommended that the Admiralty and the U.S. Navy Department maintain independent intelligence organizations that would operate in close cooperation with each other as well as with the Canadian Naval Intelligence Headquarters. Each mission would have a liaison officer whose sole function would be to facilitate the flow of information between organizations. They also urged an immediate exchange of information on intelligence centers and areas of operation, the appointment of liaison officers to include all fleets and squadrons, the establishment of a combined U.S.-British cypher and code system for use when America entered the war, and cooperation between U.S. and British radio direction-finding stations, especially in the Pacific.[11]

The Bailey Committee Report represented a great deal of British thought on both their plans and the level of assistance they envisioned from the United States. Originally intended strictly for internal use, the report contained sensitive British data and intentions as well as candid assessments, conclusions, and recommendations affecting both Britain and the United States. It appears Bailey demurred when Ghormley requested a copy, noting that although he had strict instructions to provide the Americans with all information they requested, he felt the report contained information Ghormley might find offensive.[12] Nonetheless, after some quick revisions, Ghormley received a copy—another indication of the lengths to which the British were willing to go to gain Ghormley's trust.

From 17 September to 6 October 1940, Ghormley met almost daily with the Bailey Committee or individual members, "with the idea," he wrote Stark, "that preliminary planning will be reduced to a minimum should the United States become involved in the present hostilities." He also advised Stark that the Admiralty viewed the discussions as groundwork for possible full staff talks that might develop in the near future.[13] Ensuring that the British would not get the wrong perception of his intent, Ghormley reiterated at his first meeting "the views he expressed were merely expression of his own opinion and must not be regarded as the official views of the United States Naval Authorities."[14] With that formality out of the way, the participants got down to business.

British planners exhibited keen interest in the Pacific. Concerned with their position in the Far East, in particular Singapore, Admiralty staff officers pointed out that the movement of the American fleet from its base in Hawaii to Singapore would possibly "keep the Japanese quiet."[15] Ghormley countered that a move to Singapore would leave the U.S. West Coast vulnerable and create long lines of communications vulnerable to a Japanese flank attack. When Ghormley then asked if the British would release dominion naval forces from service in the Mediterranean and Atlantic should war break out with Japan, the British hedged: such a decision would depend on the situation at the time. Ghormley cautioned that the British had not adequately recognized the Japanese threat and urged them to revise the Bailey Report to reflect the actual strategic situation.[16] Ultimately, there was no resolution of this divergence in strategic viewpoints, and the failure to resolve these differences would continue to vex Anglo-American collaborative efforts until February 1942, when the Japanese capture of Singapore and subsequent seizure of Southeast Asia put an end to the debate.

Discussion turned to the Atlantic when the British inquired if the United States would also declare war on Italy if America entered the war against Germany. Ghormley expressed his view that the United States would likely declare war on both nations. Following up, the British then noted that, given the current naval situation in the Mediterranean, they would welcome American assistance in the Atlantic. Taking a lesson from the British, Ghormley responded that the situation in the Pacific would dictate how much aid could go to the Atlantic. He did note, though, that the existing forces in the Atlantic would remain there, with the possible exception of several ships that would undergo modernization. The parties agreed there would be no delimitation of areas of responsibility in the Atlantic because of rapid changes in the international situation.[17]

Ghormley and his British interlocutors turned next to liaison and command-and-control arrangements. Ghormley agreed to London as the venue for any future staff talks. He pointed out that a U.S. mission would be predominantly naval because he doubted the army would attend out of concern for any perception of a U.S. ground commitment. For the moment, the parties deferred the decision on the final composition of any missions. They agreed to evaluate requirements based on circumstances at the time, though they did conclude that joint service missions might prove useful.[18]

The planners further agreed that the Royal Navy would exercise strategic direction and control of the U.S. forces employed in British waters, but administrative control would remain with the senior U.S. Navy officer in the United Kingdom. Ghormley disputed the recommendation that the U.S. naval headquarters should be located within the Admiralty, as it was in World War I. He argued for an independent U.S. naval headquarters, with only liaison officers actually located in the Admiralty. Ghormley conceded that it might ultimately prove necessary to co-locate an element of the American staff with their British counterparts.[19]

On the issue of assigning liaison officers within the two fleets, Ghormley observed that the U.S. Navy already had several officers posted to various British naval commands and that British officers occupied a few positions within the U.S. Fleet. Ghormley acknowledged that the numbers were small and hoped they would increase, but, for the moment, British officers serving on U.S. ships was a political question, and restrictions would probably remain in effect. In the event of a policy change, Ghormley indicated the fleet units that should receive British officers.[20]

With the most important overarching strategic issues out of the way, the conversations moved to more concrete areas of cooperation. Concerning the protection of shipping, Ghormley quickly acceded to a British recommendation that the United States assume responsibility for the Pacific Ocean as well as responsibility for the protection of all shipping and the organization of all convoys there. Agreement was less rapid on arrangements for the Atlantic. Ghormley opined that Ottawa, the proposed convoy coordination center, was too far from U.S. ports and recommended New York or Washington instead. Although he accepted for the moment that the British convoy system and organization would continue in the period immediately after U.S. entry into the war, he laid down the marker that the convoy system eventually would have to absorb U.S. inputs.[21]

The conversations continued to address ever more detailed and technical talks on equipment, procedures, and techniques. The Admiralty passed much information through Ghormley to the U.S. Navy on such topics as communications, minesweeping techniques, gunnery, naval aviation, antisubmarine warfare, and intelligence that would save the lives of many American sailors. British willingness to share their intelligence and tactical experience also fostered mutual confidence and trust.[22] By 11 October 1940, Ghormley had completed his initial conversations with the Bailey Committee and reported to

Stark that he thought the next step should be full-fledged staff conversations, adding that he was "not going to push this, but let the situation develop here for the time being."[23]

Ghormley did not have to wait long because international events began to intensify, prompting the engagement of the highest levels of American and British governments. On 22 September, Japan began occupying French Indo-China (currently Vietnam, Laos, and Cambodia), and on 27 September Germany, Italy, and Japan announced the signing of the Tripartite Pact. Among other provisions, Article 3 of the pact declared, "They further undertake to assist one another with all political, economic and military means if one of the Contracting Powers is attacked by a Power at present not involved in the European War or in the Japanese-Chinese conflict"—a warning clearly directed at Britain and, more importantly, the United States.[24] On 1 October, Lord Lothian, the British ambassador to the United States, notified London that Secretary of State Hull had on the previous day raised the question of "whether it would not be possible for the United States, Australia, and Dutch and ourselves to have private staff discussions immediately on technical problems which would be involved in common action for defense."[25]

For some reason, London delayed responding to Lothian. Granted, there was much on Britain's docket. The Blitz—the German bombing campaign on British cities—was reaching its height. Postmortems over the Dakar fiasco (22–25 September), how to defend Egypt, and whether to reopen the Burma Road, the supply line to China closed in the spring under intense Japanese pressure, consumed the War Cabinet.[26] Having decided to reopen the Burma Road, Churchill contacted Roosevelt on 4 October to notify him of the decision and to propose that the United States send a naval squadron, "the bigger the better," to Singapore as a badly needed show of support that might deter Japan.[27] Based on advice from Stark and Marshall, who recommended such a visit only if the United States were prepared to go to war, Roosevelt apparently did not respond.[28]

On 6 October, the British Chiefs of Staff learned that the Americans continued to press for staff conversations and that they wanted a preliminary round of talks in London, to be followed by principal conversations in Washington. No mention of a meeting in Singapore troubled the Chiefs of Staff, who wanted to press for a conference there even if it meant only British, Dutch, and dominion attendance. Nonetheless, they recommended that London agree to holding talks in Washington as soon as possible. Once the initial talks were complete, then representatives to a conference in Singapore could address specific operational matters.[29]

With the announcement of the Tripartite Pact, it had become apparent that if the signatories adhered to the agreement, the United States would be embroiled in a war against all three powers, not just against Japan. As a result, the British joint planners concluded that two sets of staff conversations would have to take place: one in the United States or the United Kingdom to discuss American participation in the European war and a second conference in Singapore to examine the specific military problems faced in the Pacific. The planners acknowledged that the U.S. government would probably have to make major policy and strategy decisions before the conferences could begin but once more urged that both sets of conversations commence as soon as possible.[30]

At the same time, negotiations at the governmental level also continued. Lothian reported on 8 October that Hull continued to press for an answer to his request for a staff conference to discuss the situation in the Pacific. The ambassador noted that he had informed Hull of London's initial agreement for a conference in Washington, but he was awaiting official confirmation. Finally, Lothian noted that he had raised with the secretary of state the possibility of including the European situation in the talks.[31] By 10 October, the Joint Planning Committee had refined its appreciation of the American request, and the British Chiefs of Staff recommended that a joint mission representing the three services, the minister of economic warfare, and officials from Canada, Australia, New Zealand, and the Netherlands should attend a conference held in Washington or London. They also felt that the conversations should cover the entire world situation and grand strategy. Recognizing that the disposition of the U.S. Fleet would affect both the Atlantic and the Far East, the Chiefs of Staff emphasized that this topic should be a priority in any negotiations.[32]

Discussion on the Far East, as the British saw it, should have the objective of coordinating British, American, and Dutch actions in the event of war with Japan. American participation in any future conference was particularly important because the British had no inkling of U.S. plans for the Pacific. The British Chiefs of Staff also recommended limiting the scope of the talks to the area encompassed by the Far East, the Indian Ocean, and Australasia. A conference would develop plans for the strategic employment of all available Allied forces within these geographic bounds and arrange the technical and administrative details that would permit the effective operation of multinational forces.[33]

Beyond determining an overall strategy, the Chiefs of Staff also hoped staff talks would establish coalition command relationships within the Far East. The British concluded for two reasons that strategic responsibility for the Far East and the Pacific should fall under the strategic direction of an American admiral. First, they believed in an inextricable link between the Pacific and the Far East. Second, the United States would provide the preponderance of power in the Pacific, so the Americans would want and should have responsibility for that region. The British would retain control of the Indian Ocean and would invite the Americans and Dutch to place their forces under British command. The Chiefs of Staff felt the question of control of land forces would not arise because of the distance and geographic separation involved. Because of the mobility inherent in air power, however, the Chiefs of Staff recommended that air units operating outside British territory should fall under the control of the host nation.[34]

On the very day the Chiefs of Staff provided their recommendations, British leaders received a rude shock. In a complete about-face, Hull informed Lothian that due to rising rhetoric surrounding Roosevelt's campaign for an unprecedented third term, Hull was "for the present opposed to anything like a conference either in Washington or London or in Singapore because as he said it could not take place without the press finding out and inflating its significance." Lothian added that Hull still wanted a conference but that he was unsure of the timing, the terms of reference, or the location.[35]

Realizing that a major U.S.-British conference was not in the offing, the British essentially followed a two-track approach: conversations with Ghormley in London and plans for a multilateral conference in Singapore with representatives from national commands in the Far East. In approaching these separate activities, British planners in London developed coordinated negotiating positions that informed events in Washington, London, and Singapore. For ease of understanding the complex series of intertwined events, it is necessary to address one strand at a time. Although the narrative turns first to events in London, it is important to remain cognizant that events there and in the Far East moved forward in parallel. Discussion of the development of overall policy and strategy that affected talks in both areas falls in the London strand. Throughout the discussion that follows, it is also important to understand that although the British developed a common policy for action in the Far East for their distant commanders to pursue, the same apparently was not occurring in Washington. Not only were Ghormley and Admiral Thomas C. Hart, CINC, U.S. Asiatic Fleet, operating without clear guidance from Washington, but each was also largely in the dark about what the other was doing.

On 16 October, Bailey expanded the nature of the talks when he introduced Ghormley to Admiral Roger M. Bellairs, recently selected as the Admiralty delegate to the now postponed conversations in Washington. Bellairs also was the chair of the Anglo-Dutch-American Committee that was "supposed to prepare plans and set priorities for what the British were calling the 'U.S.-U.K.-Dutch Technical Conversations.'"[36] Together, Bailey and Bellairs informed Ghormley of Lord Lothian's recent conversations with Hull, although they may have failed to mention Hull's recent turnabout. They then told Ghormley that Lothian was to invite U.S. participation in a military conference in Singapore between British, Dutch, Australian, and New Zealand representatives. The two British admirals also invited Ghormley to attend a similar conference in London. Noting that he had no specific instructions concerning such a conference, Ghormley declined to attend until he had received formal instructions from his superiors. He did indicate that he was willing to continue informal discussions on the subject of the Far East so long as the British realized that no commitments were involved.[37]

Ghormley notified Stark on 17 October that the Admiralty had made him aware of the Hull–Lothian exchanges and had invited him to a conference in London and that he had declined to attend.[38] Coincidentally, just as Ghormley's message arrived, Stark was writing to Ghormley. Stark confided that he assumed Ghormley was continuing his noncommittal talks with the British. He also informed Ghormley that he would soon send him a copy of Rainbow 3, the latest American war plan for Japan. Stark cautioned that the plan was for Ghormley's use only, though he could show it to the U.S. naval attaché in London, Captain Alan G. Kirk. Under no circumstances could he show it to the British. More importantly, Stark added a penned postscript to the letter that informed Ghormley, "Your dispatch just received. Get in on any and all staff conversations you can—go as far as you like."[39]

Perhaps due to the frequent disruptions in transit of diplomatic mail, it appears that Ghormley did not receive Stark's letter in a timely fashion and let the situation develop at its own pace. For instance, he did not meet again with Bellairs until 25 October, when he informed Bellairs that the United States would intervene to assist the British and the Dutch in the Far East only if they had taken strong action to defend themselves. Even then, he was unsure of eventual U.S. action. More importantly, at this meeting Ghormley gave Bellairs a questionnaire on specific, technical matters designed to elicit the extent of British preparations for the defense of Singapore. Although Bellairs met again with Ghormley on 29 October to clarify items in the questionnaire, he did not respond to Ghormley's questions on Singapore until 2 November because he had to vet his replies through the British Chiefs of Staff.[40] In addressing Ghormley's questions to the Chiefs of Staff, Bellairs noted that the British faced a clear dilemma:

> On the one hand, we shall say to the Americans that the whole safety of the Far East depends upon the arrival of their battle fleet at Singapore. On the other hand, we shall also have to say that we have not placed a garrison in Malaya sufficiently powerful to ensure that the base at Singapore will be intact when the United States fleet arrives. It would be idle to suggest that the deficiency should be made up with United States land and air forces, as these could hardly arrive in Malaya in advance of their fleet which would be required to cover their passage.[41]

Moreover, Bellairs underscored the likelihood that given such a proposition the United States would probably refuse to send a fleet, leaving the British to face the Japanese alone.[42] The British Chiefs of Staff countered that there was no reason at present to assume that Singapore would remain vulnerable to a Japanese attack some time in future or that it would not be able to hold out until U.S. reinforcements arrived. They therefore directed Bellairs to emphasize the difficulties inherent in a Japanese attack on the island.[43] Time and Japanese actions would prove Bellairs's assessment the more accurate.

Equally peculiar were British notions on the size of the U.S. naval force that the British wanted sent to Singapore. To face the Japanese on equal terms, the British called for a battle fleet of eight or nine battleships, three aircraft carriers, and an appropriate escort force and supply train. In short, the British wanted the majority of the U.S. Fleet based in Singapore. The size of such a force would either denude the defense of the U.S. West Coast or abandon reinforcement of the Royal Navy in the Atlantic, neither a palatable option. Recognizing this dilemma, British planners had a ready solution: "A small, fast striking force of cruisers and a carrier is suggested. Such a force could also operate offensively against the coast of Japan if ships of long endurance are provided and thus create distraction to the Japanese and assist in delaying their southward advance. If Manila is hard pressed this force could afford it some temporary relief by raiding the Japanese lines of communication."[44] In sum, this task force, based out of Singapore, was to carry out offensive and defensive operations across the length and breadth of the Pacific Ocean from Alaska to Mexico—in all, a scenario more befitting a Lewis Carroll novel than a strategic operating plan.[45] That the British realized the contradictions and deficiencies inherent in their own proposals and yet continued to press them on the Americans remains a source of bewilderment.

Ghormley, too, seemed somewhat at sea in his thinking. On 6 November 1940, he wrote Stark that he was somewhat at odds with himself and his instructions. He noted that the British were pleased with Roosevelt's reelection but that he was unsure of what this really meant, for the president had explicitly stated in his campaign that the United States would not enter the war. Ghormley felt himself in a policy vacuum, uncertain of what guidance he should follow. As rapidly as policies were changing, he felt rather out of touch with Washington. The only way out of this dilemma, he remarked, was for staff talks in Washington as soon as possible.[46] Ghormley's doubts must have been short-lived, for two days later he launched into discussions with the British delegates designated for the future Anglo-American staff conversations. The talks covered respective British and American strategies for the Pacific and the Far East and proved to be quite fruitful. The British concluded that U.S. and British grand strategies were quite similar: both rested on the premise of a defensive in the Pacific while concentrating first on Germany. Both sides also agreed on the paramount importance of the security of the United Kingdom and the maintenance of the lines of communication to the British Isles.[47]

Areas of disagreement did surface, however, most of which centered on what type of defensive strategy an eventual coalition should adopt for the Pacific. British planners concluded that although the U.S. authorities might be willing to accept the loss of the Philippines, Borneo, the Netherlands East Indies, and Singapore, Britain could not accept the loss of Singapore. To protect this supposed keystone of the empire and the means of preventing a Japanese breakout into the Indian Ocean, the British wanted the United States to base substantial elements of the U.S. Pacific Fleet in Singapore. Failing that, Britain would have to strip its Atlantic and Mediterranean fleets to send a force to the Far East. Under current conditions, however, forces available would be insufficient to meet the Japanese threat; thus, for the British the second choice was no option at all. Although Ghormley acknowledged the importance of the British position and that Americans might have to be educated on this point, he did not believe that U.S. military authorities would agree to such a plan.[48] For the moment, the planners suspended further discussion on the issue pending Ghormley's receipt of additional guidance from Washington.

Shortly thereafter, Ghormley received a letter from Stark dated 16 November. In contrast to the guidance from the previous month to "get in on any and all staff conversations you can—go as far as you like," the CNO noted in this letter that he could provide Ghormley with no more guidance than what Roosevelt had given at the White House. Stark continued, though, that any practical plan, even though officially noncommittal on the part of the United States, was better than no plan at all. The CNO also informed Ghormley that he had just completed a detailed estimate of the current situation (the so-called Plan Dog Memorandum) and that he was "endeavoring to get hold of the British ideas as soon as I possibly can. In fact I would like to have staff talks looking to just what to do in case we should suddenly get into this war."[49]

Keeping with the spirit of Stark's instructions, Ghormley approached Pound on 19 November, specifically asking whether U.S. naval planners could count on Britain to secure all mutual Anglo-American interests in the Atlantic, leaving the U.S. Fleet free to concentrate on the Japanese. Instead of answering the question, Pound launched into a discourse on British strategy. He noted that of the Atlantic and Far East theaters, the first interest was to contain the Japanese so that the British could concentrate on delivering a knockout blow to Germany. However, to hold the Japanese it would be necessary to secure Singapore. Pound opined once more that the best way to defend the fortress would be to base a substantial portion of the U.S. Fleet at Singapore, where it could contain the Japanese Fleet north of the Malay Barrier, freeing the remainder of the U.S. Pacific Fleet to join the British in eliminating the German and Italian naval forces. He conceded that this plan might expose the American West Coast to hit-and-run carrier raids but believed that their effect would be marginal. When pressed on the original question, he admitted that even though the United States would be responsible for the entire Pacific, the British would still require large-scale assistance in the Atlantic, mostly in the form of destroyers and long-range patrol aircraft.[50]

In the days that followed, the Admiralty responded to Ghormley's questions from several weeks earlier. These documents included a detailed elaboration of the British order of battle for both current and future operations.[51] The significance of providing Ghormley with these documents cannot be overstated. An order of battle is among the most closely guarded of national secrets, and the fact that the British had given such sensitive data to the United States was a clear indication of how far the British were willing to go to secure American cooperation. Despite this show of cooperation, however, not all issues moved forward. In subsequent discussions on the Far East, the fundamental differences over Singapore continued to defy resolution. At an impasse, Ghormley and his British interlocutors agreed to disagree, proverbially kicking the can down the road to any subsequent staff talks. Fortunately, about this time Lothian notified the Admiralty that President Roosevelt had agreed to hold full staff talks in Washington.[52] At that point, talks in London between Ghormley and Admiralty representatives shifted to preparations for the long-awaited staff conversations.

The proposed meetings in Washington nearly derailed even before they started. After his discussions with Admiral Pound, Ghormley forwarded British views on Singapore as well as their uncompromising attitude about it to

Admiral Stark, who shared them with General Marshall. After review by both army and navy war plans staffs, Washington responded through naval and diplomatic channels. The message was clear: British plans were not in U.S. interests. If the British insisted on this strategy as a basis for the upcoming talks, there was no need for conversations.[53] The very next day, Admiral Pound sent Ghormley an extremely conciliatory letter, informing him that the U.S. Navy Department "had formed an inaccurate impression" of British strategy and "the spirit in which the British Naval Staff intend to enter the forthcoming staff discussions." He conceded that the British strategic view might not have taken into account all of the factors that affected the American decision-making process. Pound agreed the talks would serve no purpose if the delegates had to adhere to a rigid, preconceived position. The British delegates, therefore, had instructions that would "leave them free to discuss the whole strategical field in a spirit of realistic cooperation with the U.S. authorities in order to arrive at that joint plan which will best fulfill the common interests of the United States and ourselves."[54] Pound's initiative temporarily smoothed the Navy Department's ruffled feathers, although, as later events reveal, the British seemed incapable of not raising U.S. ire over defense of the Far East.

Planning for the staff conference moved ahead regardless of this stumbling block. Seeking insights into British intentions, policy, strategy, and plans to help American planners prepare for the upcoming talks, Lee and Ghormley on behalf of Marshall and Stark submitted separate questionnaires to the War Office and the Admiralty in the first week of December.[55] The British, however, considered their answers so sensitive that they refused to hand them over to the Americans until the delegation was at sea en route for the United States.[56] This also meant that planners in Washington would not have access until after the British arrived—another source of U.S. irritation at British methods that only added to American suspicions.[57]

As little further planning or negotiations could take place without the British responses, a brief hiatus in London ensued. Lord Lothian's sudden death in Washington on 12 December unexpectedly extended this interlude. The British government did not want its delegation to sail until a new ambassador could accompany the representatives. Unfortunately, internal British political machinations precluded the rapid selection of Lothian's successor, and the Cabinet did not confirm Lord Halifax's appointment until early January 1941. Thus, the delegation, including Ghormley and Lee, did not leave England until 15 January 1941, arriving in the United States on 23 January 1941.[58]

Although the talks in London may have gone into brief hiatus, efforts in the Far East maintained a steady pace in early autumn 1940. Parallel with their discussions with Ghormley, the British arranged a conference in Singapore for late October. Although the talks were to be "without prejudice or any political commitment," participants were to operate under the assumption that the British, Dutch, and Americans were at war with Japan. The intent of the conference was to coordinate British, Dutch, and American plans for the strategic employment of all forces as well as all technical and administrative arrangements that would allow close, effective cooperation. The discussions would be limited to the Indian Ocean, the Far East, and Australasia. More specifically, British representatives were to determine whether the U.S. Fleet would take the place of the British Fleet in the Far East. They also needed to ascertain whether the Americans could defend both the Pacific and the Far East simultaneously, and whether the U.S. Navy would establish an advanced fleet base at Hong Kong, Manila, Guam, or Honolulu. The guidance for command and control supposed that the United States would assume command throughout the Pacific and Far East, with British and Dutch naval forces operating under American strategic direction. The Indian Ocean would remain under British command. Air units operating outside their own national territory would fall under the direction of the host nation.[59]

The conference convened in Singapore on 25 October. After persistent pressure from the Foreign Office and Ghormley, the U.S. Navy Department on 25 October belatedly approved the attendance of Commander A. C. Thomas, the U.S. naval attaché in Bangkok.[60] Due to the late notification, Thomas did not attend any meetings until 28 October. Moreover, to British chagrin, Thomas arrived with "no orders except that he is not to commit [the] U.S.A. Government in any way," and he appears to have been more an observer than a participant.[61]

A number of items from Thomas's report of the conference merit attention, nonetheless. The British envisaged that the defense of the Far East would consist of two phases: the security of existing Allied bases and maintenance of current lines of communication while exerting the maximum possible economic pressure on Japan. During the initial period, the British assumed that available naval forces would include the U.S. Asiatic Fleet, the British China Station Flotilla, the Australian and New Zealand squadrons—both currently performing missions outside the Far East—and the Royal Netherlands East Indies Fleet, though, oddly, given the intent of the conference, the Dutch did not attend. Throughout this phase, each force would operate under its own CINCs, would remain within its own sphere of responsibility, and would defend strictly its own national territories.[62]

Details of forces available in the second phase were much hazier. The British declined to speculate on the composition of a British Far Eastern Fleet, noting that it would depend on the world situation and the amount of time available during the first phase. They did recommend that during the first phase all Allied naval forces present in the Pacific and the Far East, including the waters of the Netherlands East Indies, Malaya, Australia, and New Zealand, would operate under unified strategic command. The British informed Thomas that they desired an American naval officer as commander.[63]

Operational-level naval plans during the second phase called for direct attacks against Japanese lines of communication and mandated islands, both of which would "be almost entirely a United States responsibility."[64] The British did not rule out attacks against the Japanese home islands but once again proposed that they would be a U.S. responsibility. British and dominion forces predominantly would safeguard lines of communication in the Indian Ocean and adjacent waters, although the British expressed willingness to assist in defending the Netherlands East Indies. In his report, Thomas observed that any courses of action proposed for the second phase were either quite limited or relied on rapid U.S. involvement. Concerning the question of where the United States might establish an advanced base for the Pacific Fleet, he noted that the British considered Guam an excellent option for operations against the Japanese mandated islands. At the same time, they offered to make Singapore available to U.S. naval forces but noted that the United States would have to assist in the construction of additional port facilities. The British also urged the establishment of an Allied operational headquarters at Singapore once war broke out.[65]

Regarding potential Japanese actions and possible Allied counteractions, the British opined that the Japanese would not attack Australia, that Hong Kong was liable to attack, and that seaborne attacks against Malaya, Borneo, and the Netherlands East Indies were unlikely, though land and air attacks against Malaya were probable. They also believed that the Japanese would concentrate their attacks on the lines of communication in the Pacific and Indian Oceans, that they would attack the Philippines and Guam, and that they would execute small raids against targets outside the main theater of operations. The British limited their comments on potential Allied courses of action to a statement that all Allied bases provided suitable sites to launch attacks against Japanese lines of communication.[66] Overall, these views provide an excellent example of the gross underestimation of Japanese power and overexaggeration of the potential of Allied power that pervaded Western military thinking about the Pacific and Far East prior to Pearl Harbor and Japanese operations in 1942 that swept over the Pacific and the Far East.

Thomas apparently clung strongly to his role as strictly an observer at this first Singapore conference, for authorities in London immediately began preparing for a second, fuller conference. The initial planning document outlined an extensive set of questions concerning American plans for the defense of U.S. possessions in the Pacific: capabilities of possible U.S. Fleet bases; U.S. military bases in Alaska and the Pacific islands; strengths, dispositions, and plans for army and air forces; communications networks and procedures; air defense; and chemical weapons capabilities. Most importantly, the British wanted to know "how far would [the] U.S.A. be willing or able to make up our deficiencies in troops and air defenses in Malaya, and those of the Dutch in the Netherlands East Indies."[67] British delegates received instructions to establish the size of an American fleet to be based at Singapore, the means to ensure its safe arrival, and its projected time of passage. They also were to identify possible naval operations before the arrival of the main fleet. In addition, they would prepare detailed operational plans, study options for economic warfare, and identify problems of air, land, and sea forces in both the Pacific and Far East.[68]

The second conference in Singapore ran 9–14 November 1940. This time Admiral Thomas C. Hart, CINC, U.S. Asiatic Fleet, dispatched his chief of staff, Captain William R. Purnell, to the conference. These two officers merit a brief aside. Hart was born in Michigan in 1877 and graduated from the U.S. Naval Academy in 1897. Commissioned 1899, he commanded a force of seven submarines in Ireland in World War I. Made rear admiral in September 1929, he was commander of Submarines, U.S. Pacific and Atlantic Fleets, in 1929–1931. From 1931 to 1934, Hart served as the superintendent of the U.S. Naval Academy, which was followed by another command stint as commander of the Cruiser Division of the Scouting Force from 1934 to 1936. He served as a member of the General Board of the Navy in 1936 until his assignment as CINC, U.S. Asiatic Fleet, from June 1939 to June 1942.[69]

Purnell, chief of staff of the U.S. Asiatic Fleet, was born on 6 September 1886 in Bowling Green, Missouri. He graduated from the U.S. Naval Academy in 1908 and was commissioned in 1910. During World War I, Purnell captained a series of destroyers and won the Navy Cross for action against German U-boats. Alternating sea and shore duty in the interwar era, he served as secretary to the General Board of the Navy from April 1936 to December 1938. After serving as the commanding officer of the cruiser U.S.S. *New Orleans* from January to December 1939, Purnell assumed duties as chief of staff and aide to Admiral Hart. Purnell would be promoted to rear admiral in November 1941.[70]

Purnell's report of the second conference in Singapore indicated that despite repeated calls for U.S. attendance, the conference addressed only British strategic plans and assistance desired from the Dutch. As a result, Purnell reviewed an agenda for proposed British and Dutch discussions and received a briefing on British plans for cooperation with Dutch forces. He concluded that the British had little confidence in the Dutch ability to defend themselves, yet, strangely, the British planned on Dutch forces defending the Singapore–Netherlands East Indies area to free British forces to protect imperial lines of communication in the Indian Ocean.[71] When Purnell opined that the British might find this a tough sell to the Dutch, British admiral Geoffrey Layton, CINC, China Station, replied, "I know it. I don't expect to, but I'll try it and not bother over final details because I believe that all that is needed to stop a Japanese Southward [sic] advance is the notice of a joint Anglo-Dutch–United States agreement."[72] Even at the time this outlook seemed naive.

When Purnell returned to Manila, there was little to show in the way of increased Anglo-American cooperation—no strategy, no operational plans, and no arrangements for command. It would seem, especially given British pressure for American attendance at the conference, that British leaders in Singapore squandered an opportunity. Perhaps searching for a positive outcome, Admiral Hart noted in his diary, "The visit serves to put Ad. Leighton [sic, a misspelling of "Layton"] and me in much better touch, we should understand each other if anything happened, and we shall henceforth have a better picture of what my British friends really have at Singapore."[73] Shortly after Purnell's visit, authorities in London—probably because of the impasse in the conversations with Admiral Ghormley—asked to postpone further talks in the Far East until higher-level talks had decided the major issues, allowing local talks to develop detailed combined operational plans.[74]

Discussions shifted back to Singapore in early February 1941, when the British once more pressed for comprehensive talks between representatives of Britain, the Netherlands East Indies, Australia, New Zealand, and the United States. Even though the British tried to convince the U.S. authorities to send an official representative from Washington, the ubiquitous Captain Purnell arrived in Singapore "with powers to agree to a joint plan of operations of United States, British, and Dutch forces but without making political commitments."[75] Paradoxically, Stark directed Hart's representative to impress upon the British and the Dutch that realistic planning was critical and that any plan based on U.S. involvement was unsound.[76]

Given this contradictory guidance, it is hardly surprising that few concrete results in coalition cooperation emerged from the talks. The conferees essentially established national spheres of responsibility for the British, Dutch, and Australians, confirmed that naval forces would operate under national command within those spheres, and agreed that air forces would operate under the command of the host nation but were subject to recall. The representatives reaffirmed the need to strengthen bases within the theater and that the defense of sea communications would be concentrated in the Indian Ocean.[77] Upon Purnell's return to Manila, Hart complained to Stark that the delegates had barely gotten through the preliminaries and that a great deal of coordination remained. In addition, he expressed concern that the British were too defensively minded and fixated on protecting their trade routes. Hart concluded that, though he saw some progress, "what Napoleon or some other Old Guy said about the unwieldiness and low collective efficiency of Allies does come to mind."[78] Certainly, friction oftentimes happens when potential allies deal with each other, especially given the constraints under which Hart operated. However, as Hart acknowledged, the potential allies were talking to each other, had more than a passing knowledge of each other's respective plans, and had set the stage for more comprehensive talks.

The success of those future talks depended on the British and Americans reaching an agreement on overarching policy and strategy issues for possible actions in the Far East. To this point, such agreement did not seem likely. Whether in London or in Singapore, the British had been resolutely tone-deaf to the messages they were sending and receiving. Although continually stressing the importance of Singapore, they did not appear interested in actually defending the supposed keystone of the empire—a task they assigned to the Dutch and predominantly the Americans. Moreover, the British approach, "We want your help so much that we will let you pay for the privilege of taking up our 'generous' offer to base in Singapore," did not help matters. The British also blithely ignored the fact that basing large elements of the U.S. Fleet at Singapore exposed U.S. possessions in the Pacific and the entire U.S. West Coast to Japanese attacks. Perhaps such an option might seem acceptable to a country already at war and suffering considerable air and sea attack, but it seems inconceivable that the British expected the United States to expose its fleet and population to such risks. Not least, British plans envisaged British and dominion forces focusing on trade-route protection while the U.S. Navy undertook the most difficult and dangerous missions against the main units of the Imperial Japanese Navy. This division of responsibilities gave the impression, certainly to authorities in Washington, that Britain once more was scheming to get the United States to pull its imperial chestnuts out of the fire. As the reader will discover, these perceptions would dog the conduct of the upcoming staff talks in Washington and beyond.

In 1940, American and British representatives achieved greater, albeit still limited, success in their efforts to resolve conflicts in materiel matters. The events of the summer of 1940 convinced the British government that strictly commercial dealings were no longer feasible and that direct negotiations between agencies of the two governments would be necessary. At the same time, Jean Monnet and Arthur Purvis of the British Purchasing Commission recognized that the Americans would launch major new arms programs only if they received large and well-coordinated requests. Purvis therefore requested that the British government send a single emissary to the United States to negotiate a broad range of British orders.[79]

In response, Sir Walter Layton arrived in Washington on 22 September 1940 with rather wide discretionary authority to conduct negotiations, though final approval for purchases of weapons of foreign design remained in London.[80] By mid-October, Layton had completed an initial assessment and submitted a full list of British army ordnance requirements, complete with rationale for their justification.[81] Although American authorities quickly acknowledged this request, because of the Neutrality Act the U.S. government was able to provide financial credits only for materiel that U.S. forces also could use.[82] This latter restriction left the British caught between the proverbial rock and a hard place. American equipment, though eventually plentiful, would be of little immediate use to British units. Desperately needing their own types of equipment for their 55-Division Program, they could not afford to buy it.[83] At this point, U.S. War Department representatives, perhaps reversing a lesson from World War I, suggested that the British fully equip ten of their divisions with American materiel, a proposal known as the "A" program. This would expand U.S. industrial capacity while reducing British supply problems for the remaining forty-five divisions, or the "B" program. Although not particularly enamored with this solution, the British recognized that it offered not only equipment but also a possible means of drawing the United States a little closer to actual involvement in the war. It also offered continued access to a fair portion of American war production. The War Cabinet, therefore, instructed Layton to accept the arrangement, and on 20 November 1940 the United States and Britain announced they had agreed to partial standardization of arms and equipment.[84]

Layton also helped reform the British supply organizations operating within the United States. Although the streamlined organization helped, problems remained. Once again aircraft purchases offer an illustrative case. The growing partnership had created the Joint Aircraft Committee in September 1940 to ensure maximum standardization of Anglo-American aircraft and equipment, develop schedules of production, and establish procedures for allocating aircraft between Britain and the United States. Success of the Joint Aircraft Committee, however, depended on timely and accurate information from both parties.⁸⁵ Unfortunately, the British did not always fulfill either of those requirements. For example, at a meeting between Purvis and Henry Morgenthau, the U.S. Treasury secretary, the latter complained of reports from U.S. Army Air Corps representatives that American aircraft sent to Britain were sitting in shipping crates because of a lack of trained pilots. To address the matter, Purvis informed the Foreign Office that if Britain expected to continue to receive aircraft, it would have to provide accurate and up-to-date information on the current aircraft and pilot production in the United Kingdom as well as a nine-month projection of both categories. Although acknowledging the sensitive nature of the information, he added that dissemination would be restricted to President Roosevelt, Secretary Morgenthau, Secretary of War Henry Stimson, and Secretary of the Navy William Franklin Knox.⁸⁶

Despite eventually receiving the requested information, the Americans wanted a better understanding of overall British thinking regarding air matters, and Morgenthau pressed the British to send Air Marshal Charles Portal, chief of the Air Staff, to Washington to explain the current air situation in the United Kingdom, the RAF's strategy, and current and future operations. Unwilling to send Portal, who was fully engaged in fighting the Battle of Britain, the British government dispatched Air Commodore John C. Slessor, the director of plans, who despite his relatively junior rank—but not intellect or abilities, as the U.S. staffs would soon find out—would prove to be a critical figure in building the evolving coalition.⁸⁷ Slessor was born in India in June 1897, the son of an army major. Despite contracting childhood polio that left him disabled in both legs, he gained by means of family connections an appointment to the RAF on his eighteenth birthday. Initially serving in Britain to combat German Zeppelin raids, he later flew in the Sinai and Sudan until he was wounded in 1916. Having received the Military Cross, Slessor returned to flying in 1918, seeing action over France. Briefly leaving the RAF in 1919, he quickly returned in 1920 and built a strong reputation as a flyer and advanced thinker. During the 1920s, he alternated flying assignments, mostly in India, with staff postings. In 1931, he attended the Staff College, Camberley, remaining on the Directing Staff until 1935, when he returned to flying duties and command once more in India. In 1936, he published *Air Power and Armies,* which advocated close support of ground operations and air interdiction immediately behind the battle lines. On 17 May 1937, he was appointed deputy director of plans at the Air Ministry. He assumed the duties of director of plans on 22 December 1938, remaining in this key position until his assignment to the British Purchasing Commission to procure aircraft and supplies in the United States in the autumn of 1940.⁸⁸

Comfortable with his mission "to inform U.S. administrators as to the U.K. air strategy and other operational particulars, all with a view to an effort on the part of the U.S. administrators to bring about a concerted drive so as to meet promptly U.K. needs," Slessor nonetheless asked for Portal's approval of his negotiating tactics. Foremost, he requested permission to talk openly and freely with the Americans and asked for authority to provide any information they might request. Second, he wanted to expand his contacts beyond the upper levels of civil government, for, as he cogently pointed out, Cabinet members lacked the requisite technical expertise and would have to consult their staffs anyway, so the intermediaries should be eliminated to reduce confusion. Third, Slessor emphasized that the most critical element of his mission was to convince the Americans that the British were not making exorbitant demands but were requesting only what they actually needed. He stressed that he could do all this only if he received timely and accurate information.[89]

Slessor recognized that because the British had not previously imparted such information outside their own government, the broad range of information Morgenthau sought would likely be a sticking point. Slessor therefore asked Portal to obtain permission from William A. "Max" Aiken, Lord Beaverbrook, the minister of aircraft production, to pass on the information needed by the Americans on a regular basis. He received a personal briefing from Beaverbrook that proved quite an eye-opener. As Slessor informed Portal and Archibald Sinclair, secretary of state for air, Beaverbrook totally distrusted Americans and was convinced that they could not keep secret British pilot and production information. Worse still, according to Slessor, Beaverbrook remarked that "Americans were purely material and would only help if they thought we were strong and going to win. If they thought we were going to lose they wouldn't stir a finger to help us but would concentrate on their own defense." Slessor indicated that, for this reason, Beaverbrook "had constantly made statements making out that we [British] were better off than we are and said he would only tell them [the Americans] what suited him and what he wanted them to think." Slessor then informed Sinclair and Portal that he could not agree to these premises as a basis for his negotiations and requested additional instructions.[90] Slessor's dilemma was somehow resolved, for ten days later, on 29 October 1940, Churchill himself reported that Slessor had received a frank and detailed briefing on expected British requirements for aircraft and pilots through June 1941, including explicit figures on distribution of aircraft and the pilot training program that he could share in meetings with the Americans. Armed with this information, Slessor departed England in early November.[91]

Two key decisions, one American and one British, greatly affected Slessor's initial negotiations. On 8 November 1940, Roosevelt, three days after his reelection to a third term, announced that henceforth 50 percent of all U.S. aircraft and other war production would go to Britain. Although on the surface this decision should have made Slessor's job easier, it also generated resistance from the U.S. Army and Army Air Corps, which correctly believed that the arrangement would slow their own programs. For example, the War Department General Staff estimated that the new allocation formula would delay the heavy-bomber program by nine months and the hemisphere defense plan by seven to eight months. Although an internal War Department report concluded that if the aircraft allowed Britain to hold out against the Germans, then it was in the best U.S. interests to share the aircraft equally, this opinion was not universally shared within the War Department.[92] As Colonel Orlando Ward, assistant secretary of the War Department General Staff, noted in his diary, "The 50–50 deal is working with 33 planes for the U.S. and 409 for the foreigners. A 50–50 deal like one horse for them, one rabbit for us. . . . We are like a pointer pup. If someone with a red moustache, a swagger stick, and a British accent speaks to us, we lie down on the ground and wiggle."[93]

Even with Roosevelt's decision, Slessor would still have to produce figures to support British requests. Here was the second decision that would affect Slessor's mission. Despite Churchill's earlier pronouncement that Slessor could share information freely, the prime minister decided that information available to U.S. personnel, both in Britain and in the United States, "should be steadily damped down, and its circulation restricted as far as possible."[94] Slessor, apparently unaware of this decision, continued to petition his superiors for previously promised but now denied information. Beyond Churchill's embargo was the added complication that the War Cabinet had authorized giving the Americans only published casualty counts for aircraft and pilots, and there were substantial differences between actual and published counts, by as much as two hundred aircraft per month.[95]

Slessor's frustration at being unable to satisfy American demands reached such depths that he once again cabled Portal, pleading for information. Because he had seen no information on British production since September, he noted he could not comply with President Roosevelt's request for a balance sheet of British forces and potential. He added plaintively, "I do not mind being made to look a fool, though the Americans cannot be expected to understand and I cannot explain to them why the Director of Plans who has been sent to America to discuss this sort of thing with them is kept in ignorance of so vital a factor as British production and the effect on it of Enemy [sic] bombing." He further emphasized that if the British were really interested in obtaining increased

American assistance, as the prime minister had just communicated to Roosevelt, then "we must take them into our confidence and tell them the facts even if unpalatable."[96] The logjam of information finally broke on 6 January 1941, when Beaverbrook authorized Purvis of the British Purchasing Commission, who had the information all along, to pass it to Slessor.[97] Even so, the information arrived too late to be of much immediate value because, with the staff talks about to begin in Washington, both sides realized that major decisions were unlikely.

With the break in supply negotiations and further staff discussions postponed until the arrival of the British delegation in Washington for the American-British Conversations, a brief pause ensued in Anglo-American cooperative efforts. The course of events since September 1940, when U.S. leaders decided that supporting Britain was worth the risk, had been a remarkable roller-coaster ride. The United States stood poised to enter into full-fledged staff conversations, notwithstanding the caveat "no political commitments." The emerging partners made strides in rationalizing and standardizing war materiel, but largely because of American industrial strength and British need. Initially intended to take six weeks, Ghormley's mission lasted four and a half months, and after mid-October Ghormley and the Bailey Committee exchanged strategic ideas and contingencies, even if these discussions were not collaboration in a strict sense. After Roosevelt's acceptance of the British suggestion for full staff talks, the discussions between Admiral Ghormley and the Admiralty staff evolved into true collaboration.

The tactical and technical information passed from the Bailey Committee to Ghormley was priceless and undoubtedly saved hundreds, if not thousands, of American lives in the initial period after American intervention. Concerning cooperation in the Atlantic, Ghormley and the Admiralty achieved substantial progress on delimiting command relationships, liaison arrangements, the amount of U.S. assistance required, and the means for protecting shipping as well on as numerous technical matters, such as codes, cypher systems, and recognition signals. The failure to demarcate areas of strategic responsibility begged resolution. In the Pacific, a fundamental and deeply rooted conflict of national interests blocked any significant progress. Because neither side would alter its position, no solution emerged.

The seeming inability to arrive at a strategic plan for the defense of the Pacific, unresolved issues in the Atlantic, and continuing frictions over the allocation of materiel all underscored the difficulties of conducting negotiations at great distance and through intermediaries. These differences also highlighted the necessity for full staff conversations between Britain and the United States. For all their fits and starts, however, the various conversations in the autumn of 1940 set the stage to take Anglo-American collaboration to the next level, and the actors were about to enter.

7

Full-Dress Talks

The American-British Conversations-1 Conference, January–March 1941

On 23 January 1941, Britain's newest battleship, H.M.S. *King George V,* sailed into the mouth of the Potomac River bearing Edward F. L. Wood, Lord Halifax, the new ambassador to the United States. Attached to his party and traveling incognito as civilian advisers to the technical staff of the British Purchasing Commission were the British representatives to the upcoming military conversations between the British and American planning staffs. These officers would meet with their American counterparts over the course of the next two months to forge a comprehensive agreement on combined British and American action should the United States enter the war against the Axis Powers. The success or failure of the wide-ranging negotiations would determine the future course of Anglo-American collaboration and probably the outcome of the war.[1]

The British military delegation traveled in secret for good reasons. Following his fireside chat of 29 December 1940, where he called upon the United States to become the "arsenal of democracy," Roosevelt had introduced his "Lend-Lease" legislation on 6 January 1941. Although popular response to his radio broadcast was quite positive, anti-interventionist tendencies still ran high in many places, especially the U.S. Senate. Thus, although the bill's passage was likely, it was not assured. Moreover, the Johnson Debt Default Act of 1934 prohibiting private or public loans to countries that owed the United States debts from World War I remained in effect, as was the cash-and-carry provision of the Neutrality Act of 1939. Britain was suffering a dollar drain, and as Lord Lothian purportedly announced upon returning to the United States from Britain on 23 November 1940, "Well, boys, Britain's broke. It's your money we want."[2] Churchill confirmed Britain's rapidly dwindling dollar reserves and warned Roosevelt that the effectiveness of the German U-boat campaign was placing the British ability to carry materiel in dire jeopardy.[3] In short, this was not a propitious moment for the American public to discover that its military was engaged in high-level staff talks with the British on how the two countries might cooperate should the United States, in Roosevelt's directed language, "be compelled" to enter the conflict.[4]

Because of the importance of the talks and the high levels of talent that each side brought to the negotiations, it is worth examining the major participants in some detail. Although Churchill initially wanted a civilian head of the delegation, his advisers dissuaded him because of the need to avoid any hint of political connotation to the talks.[5] As a result, Rear Admiral Roger M. Bellairs, former Admiralty director of plans, led the British delegation. Bellairs's delegation included Rear Admiral Victor H. Danckwerts, current director of plans; Major General Edwin L. Morris, former War Office director of staff duties; and Air Commodore John C. Slessor, director of plans, Air Staff.[6] As Raymond Lee noted in his diary, "It is a strong team, for these two with the airmen [sic], Slessor, who is now in Washington, were all together on the Joint Planning Committee two or three years ago, and should know what they are about."[7] Indeed, Bellairs had been the naval assistant to the first sea lord from 1919 to 1925 and Admiralty director of plans from 1928 to 1930, where he also attended the London Naval Conference. Although officially retired upon promotion to rear admiral in 1932, Bellairs was almost immediately appointed as the British naval representative to the League of Nations Permanent Advisory Committee, a post he held until the start of World War II. Once the war commenced, Bellairs worked on sensitive projects for the Admiralty, such as the recent Bailey Committee, which had explored areas of cooperation with the U.S. Navy, as well as the recently established U.S.-U.K.-Dutch Technical Conversations. Similarly, Danckwerts had been not only the director of plans for the past two years but also a planner and deputy director of plans from 1932 to 1936. Morris also had considerable experience in the War Office, serving as a General Staff officer in 1931–1932, deputy director of military operations in 1936–1938, and director of staff duties from April 1939 to October 1940.[8] (Slessor's extensive qualifications were elaborated in chapter 6.)

On the U.S. side of the table, Major General Stanley D. Embick was the senior representative of the U.S. Staff Committee. Embick had served on the American delegation to the SWC in World War I and as a delegate to the Paris Peace Conference in 1918–1919. He was an instructor at the Army War College in 1921–1923 and joined the War Department General Staff from 1926 to 1930. Promoted to brigadier general in 1930, Embick served as the assistant chief of staff and then deputy chief of staff in 1935–1938. A major general in 1936, he commanded IV Corps Area and then Third Army from 1938 to 1940. Embick served as a member of the Joint Army–Navy Board in 1940–1941. As a result, Embick was perhaps the U.S. military's most experienced strategic planner. Army chief of staff George Marshall so esteemed Embick that he recalled Embick to active duty after a short retirement so that he could lead the U.S. delegation to the American-British Conversations-1 (ABC-1).[9]

The Army Section at the talks also included Brigadier General Leonard T. Gerow, current head of the War Department's WPD; Brigadier General Sherman Miles, the acting assistant chief of staff, G-2; and Colonel Joseph T. McNarney, a planning officer conversant with Army Air Corps war plans. Gerow had attended the Virginia Military Institute and was commissioned in 1911. He saw action in the Vera Cruz expedition in 1914 and served in the Signal Corps in France during World War I. In the interwar era, he was closely associated with Omar Bradley and Dwight Eisenhower. Gerow had been with the WPD since 1935 and had been named its head in December 1940.[10] Miles was the son of Lieutenant General Nelson Miles, who had led the U.S. Army in Cuba during the Spanish-American War and later served as commanding general of the U.S. Army. Sherman Miles graduated from West Point in 1905 and was commissioned in the cavalry. Prior to U.S. entry into World War I, he served as military attaché to Bucharest (1912–1914) and Russia (1914–1916). During the Great War, he served first with I Corps in the St. Mihiel and Meuse-Argonne offensives and then as assistant chief of staff of Military Intelligence with IX Corps, AEF from 1918 to 1919. He was U.S. military attaché to Turkey from 1922 to 1925 and served in the WPD of the War Department General Staff from July 1934 to October 1938. After a short time as the military attaché in London, 1939–1940, he rejoined the War Department General Staff as the assistant chief of staff of Military Intelligence in April 1940.[11]

McNarney graduated with the U.S. Military Academy Class of 1915, "the class the stars fell on," was "a dour, taciturn, ruthless, and brilliant administrator, . . . [and] rose to the rank of full general on 7 March 1945 while remaining almost unknown outside his profession." An army aviator in World War I, he served in France as commander of the First Observer Group, head of air service III Corps, and staff officer in the Chief Air Service, First Army. McNarney graduated from the Staff College in 1926 and from the Army War College in 1930. He returned to the Army War College as an instructor from 1933 to 1935 and joined the WPD in 1939.[12]

Rear Admiral Robert Ghormley led the Navy Section, assisted by Rear Admiral Richmond Kelly Turner, director of the Naval WPD; Captain Alan G. Kirk, the U.S. naval attaché to Great Britain; Captain Charles M. "Savvy" Cooke Jr. and Captain DeWitt C. Ramsey, both of the Naval WPD; and Lieutenant Colonel Omar T. Pfeiffer, U.S. Marine Corps.[13] Rear Admiral Turner, nicknamed "Terrible," was renowned for his hot temper and heavy drinking. A graduate of Annapolis and commissioned in 1908, Turner made his early mark as a gunnery specialist serving on several battleships in World War I. He earned his naval aviator wings in 1927 at the age of forty-two. Turner headed the Strategy Section of the Naval War College from 1935 to 1938 before commanding the U.S.S. *Astoria* from 1938 to 1940. He served as director of the WPD in the Office of the CNO starting in 1940.[14]

Kirk, Cooke, Ramsey, and Pfeiffer played lesser roles in ABC-1. Kirk at the time was serving as the U.S. naval attaché in London. Like most naval officers of his day, he was a graduate of Annapolis in 1909 and was commissioned in 1911. He served stateside in World War I. In the early 1920s, he was a White House aide and executive officer of the presidential yacht *Mayflower*. An instructor at the Naval War College from 1929 to 1931, he later served as a staff officer of the Battle Force and then the U.S. Fleet from 1937 to 1939. He served as the U.S. naval attaché in London from 1939 to 1941.[15] Captain Charles "Savvy" Cooke graduated from the University of Arkansas in 1905 before graduating from the U.S. Naval Academy in 1910. Primarily a submarine officer through 1933, he was the war plans officer for the U.S. Fleet from 1936 to 1938. From 1938 until the end of ABC-1, he was on the war plans staff of the CNO.[16] Captain DeWitt Ramsey was a naval aviator serving in the Bureau of Aeronautics as head of the Plans Division from 1939 to 1941. With a long background in aircraft carrier aviation, Ramsey would go on to command multiple carrier battle groups during the war. He would eventually become a full admiral after the war, serving as the vice CNO and CINC of the Pacific Fleet.[17] At the time of ABC-1, Lieutenant Colonel Omar T. Pfeiffer was serving in the war plans section of the Marine Barracks, Quantico.[18]

Although the American delegation had been preparing for the staff talks, it suffered from a number of shortfalls. Unlike its corporate British counterpart, it consisted of two independent sections—army and navy. At this time, although the Joint Army–Navy Board existed, it was in no way comparable to the British staff system that developed corporate, interservice positions. As a result, the British noted not only an absence of coordinated U.S. positions but also an oftentimes intense U.S. interservice rivalry that impeded the overall progress of the negotiations.[19] Moreover, although Ghormley had covered considerable ground in the previous three months, much work in Anglo-American collaboration remained. Ghormley had been sincere when he stated that he was providing only his personal views. Certainly, many of these ideas conformed to U.S. government positions, but they lacked official imprimatur. Not least, during his stay in London Ghormley had been out of touch from mainstream planning in Washington, and new issues had emerged. Ghormley and his British counterparts had been unable to settle the question of Singapore and a strategy for the Far East, and, finally, discussions thus far had not addressed land or air issues in any substantive way.

On the British side, the Chiefs of Staff Committee had charged the members of the British delegation with establishing the broad lines of employment of Allied forces of the United States and the British Empire against Germany, Italy, and Japan. More specifically, they were to persuade the Americans to accept the fundamental premise that Germany constituted the greater danger and therefore had to be the first priority, even if this dictated a defensive strategy in the Pacific. To implement this grand strategy, the British required American help. The delegation hoped to convince the Americans to reinforce the British position in the Atlantic, Middle East, and Far East, to accept Singapore as the keystone of the defense of the Pacific, to assume responsibility for the occupation of North Africa, and to forgo their own aircraft-expansion program in order to build up the RAF instead.[20]

American priorities contrasted considerably with the British goals. Although the U.S. planners agreed that Germany posed the principal threat, they were most concerned with the defense of the Western Hemisphere. They concluded "that we cannot afford, nor do we need, to entrust our national future to British direction, because the United States can safeguard the North American Continent, and probably the Western Hemisphere, whether allied with Britain or not."[21] The U.S. delegates agreed that Britain would need direct American assistance to defeat Germany, but they approached British requests for assistance with a great deal of suspicion. In the words of a document from the Joint Army–Navy Board written in preparation for the talks, "It is to be expected that proposals of the British representatives will have been drawn up with chief regard for the support of the British Commonwealth. Never absent from British minds are their post-war interests, commercial and military. We should likewise safeguard our own eventual interests."[22]

In this light, the U.S. Chiefs of Staff provided guidelines for the American negotiators. They expressed their willingness, once the United States became an active belligerent, to reinforce British naval assets in the Atlantic, to assume responsibility for British possessions in the Western Hemisphere (except for the Falkland Islands), and under certain conditions to occupy the Azores, Canary Islands, Cape Verde Islands, and Iceland to free British forces for deployment to more critical theaters. They were even disposed to send token air and land forces to the United Kingdom.[23] Various other American authorities added a number of key caveats. Although open to the occupation of French North

Africa, the United States would do so only if Germany invaded Spain and then only on the condition that Vichy France requested U.S. intervention. War Department planners also wanted to avoid any commitment of U.S. Army forces to the Mediterranean, Middle East, or Far East. In addition, the U.S. Navy had not changed its ideas on the strategy for defending the Pacific, especially the issue of Singapore and the defense of the Malay Barrier. Finally, the Army Air Corps staff wanted no interference in the establishment of its fifty-four-group armament program and was adamant that the United States would not provide air units as piecemeal reinforcement of the RAF.[24]

Against this general background, the conference convened on 29 January 1941. After a brief welcome, Admiral Harold Stark opened the conversations with a joint statement from him and General George Marshall outlining the U.S. negotiating position. Stark indicated that from a U.S. perspective, the objective of the conversations was "to determine the best methods by which the armed forces of the United States and the British Commonwealth can defeat Germany and the powers allied with her, should the United States be compelled to resort to war."[25]

Roosevelt had directed that "be compelled" replace "decide" in the original draft of this statement.[26] For those with a conspiratorial bent, this edit was a classic example of Roosevelt covering his tracks. Conversely, he could have been trying to avoid war for as long as possible and so used this language to preserve his options. In any case, Stark also observed that at the moment the American public wanted to stay out of the war and favored only materiel and economic aid to Britain. The U.S. military was bound to respect this attitude and therefore could not enter into any specific commitments. For the time being, American national policy sought to secure the Western Hemisphere from outside intervention, continue materiel assistance to the British Commonwealth, and use diplomatic efforts to deter Japanese expansion.[27]

Stark then outlined U.S. policy should the United States enter the war. The major objective would be the defeat of Germany, but Stark tempered this statement by underscoring once more that defense of the Western Hemisphere would remain the paramount American interest. The two U.S. chiefs of staff opined that the best way to attain this objective would be for the U.S. military to concentrate its principal effort in the Atlantic and reinforce the British naval position in the Mediterranean. They added that the United States would continue major efforts to keep Japan out of the war, but, failing that, the United States would conduct operations in a manner to ensure that the primary focus was on the Atlantic. Turning to strategic planning, Stark noted that the conversations should examine the measures needed to defeat Germany, such as geographic areas of responsibility, major lines of effort, forces to be committed, unity of strategic effort, and command arrangements—for both supreme command and coalition command of operations. He added, in shades of Pershing in World War I, "as a general rule, United States forces should operate in their own areas of responsibility, under their own commanders, and in accordance with plans derived from the United States–British joint [combined] plans."[28]

Stark then proposed a broad agenda for the conversations that initially called for opening statements and a discussion of each power's military position. A detailed discussion of combined strategy in the Atlantic and the Pacific would follow. Once the two sides had agreed on the basic strategy, they would move to operational concerns. The British agreed to the agenda but requested adding the Mediterranean and Middle East to the strategic-level discussions. They then requested a short recess to prepare a statement on their position, and the meeting adjourned.[29]

When the delegations reconvened, the British first pointed out that the U.K. delegation was a corporate body representing the British Chiefs of Staff in a collective capacity and affirmed that they had absolute freedom of negotiation, subject of course to government approval. Like the U.S. delegation, they reinforced that the objective of the talks was to plan for the employment of the forces of the British Empire and its allies with the forces of the United States in a war against Germany, Italy, and Japan. They, too, emphasized that the conversations could incur no political commitments.[30] Like their American counterparts, the British believed that Europe was the decisive theater and that Germany and Italy should be defeated before the coalition commenced offensive operations against Japan. The British emphasized, however, that the cohesion of the British Commonwealth and the maintenance of the British war effort depended on the security of the Far East and declared, "Singapore is the key to the defense of these interests and its retention must be assured."[31]

At this point, the British laid out the assistance they anticipated would be required from the United States. They foresaw a major U.S. effort in the Atlantic area, with additional naval aid in the Mediterranean. More important, though, was the need for American support of the British bomber offensive. Here, the British required a substantial and immediate reinforcement of heavy bombers as well as a smaller increment of bombers and fighters in the Middle East. The delegates also acknowledged that in the interim they would require massive amounts of materiel aid. Although they understood the American military's rising need for equipment to build up its own forces, they were convinced that Britain should receive a large share of the available production and cogently pointed out that they were actively engaged in fighting and could put the supplies to immediate use, a lever they would effectively use for months to come.[32]

In their closing remarks, the British representatives noted that they generally agreed with the U.S. position on command arrangements but cautioned that a future coalition might at times require a more flexible approach. They advocated that small-scale forces should fall under the operational control of the predominant power, noting, for instance, that a U.S. admiral should command all naval forces in the Pacific and that the RAF would control U.S. Army Air Corps units in Britain. Finally, they added that the employment of these forces would undoubtedly be subject to further discussions.[33]

The preliminary statements indicated general agreement on the major issue of grand strategy—that is, the defeat of Germany first and a strategic defensive in the Pacific—but the two delegations diverged considerably on the ways to defend the Pacific. Indeed, the depth of disagreement quickly led the delegations to skip over the Atlantic and first address the problems posed by cooperation in the Far East. So at odds were their views that they could not agree even on when active cooperation might commence. American planners believed that the U.S. entry into the ongoing war in Europe would precede Japanese aggression in the Far East. The British conversely believed Japan would be an active belligerent prior to U.S. intervention in the conflict. The U.S. planners eventually saw little difference between the two possibilities and offered that either scenario would not alter the disposition of U.S. forces. That said, if the United States were to intervene in Europe prior to Japanese aggression in the Pacific, it would be important to define a suitable Japanese casus belli. The British pushed the U.S delegation to accept that a direct Japanese attack on Dutch or British possessions would constitute a casus belli, but the U.S. representatives insisted that the U.S. government was at that time willing to exert only diplomatic and economic pressure on the Japanese.[34]

After the delegations agreed to disagree, the discussions turned to the specifics of the defense of the Far East and, in particular, the role of Singapore. The British emphasized that the security of Singapore and the Far East were crucial to their overall war effort and to the defeat of Germany. Admiral Turner countered that given the current Japanese position in Indochina, any Japanese expansion into Thailand or the Netherlands East Indies would render Singapore untenable. The Americans also pointed out that should Singapore fall, the Japanese still would be unable to threaten the British position in Australia or in the Middle East; thus, Singapore was not that important. Taking great exception to this view, the British remained adamant that Singapore was vital. They argued that the occupation of Malaya would give the Japanese access to the vital lifelines of the empire running through the Indian Ocean. Faced with a seeming impasse, Admiral Bellairs asked the U.S. delegation to present its views on the defense of the Far East.[35]

At the third meeting, Admiral Turner presented the American position. In general, he laid out that the United States would assume responsibility for all British possessions east of the coast of Australia (exclusive) and that the U.S. Asiatic Fleet would defend the Philippine Islands for as long as possible before withdrawing south to Surabaya in the Netherlands East Indies or Singapore. The U.S. Pacific Fleet would attack Japanese lines of communications through the Marshall Islands, thus diverting Japanese efforts away from the Malay Barrier. Nowhere did Turner address U.S. support of the defense of Singapore, much less indicate that elements of the U.S. Pacific Fleet might reinforce the island bastion. Turner added that for the time being the United States would maintain a fleet in the Pacific as a deterrent force, but at minimum levels that would allow the transfer of fleet elements to augment British forces in the Atlantic. In return for the transfer of U.S. forces to the Atlantic, the United States expected Britain to dispatch sizeable reinforcements from its Atlantic and Mediterranean fleets to the Far East. Turner concluded his remarks by insisting that any reinforcements for the Far East would have to come from British assets because the United States would not reinforce the U.S. Asiatic Fleet.[36]

In response, Admiral Danckwerts noted that even with the transfer of American ships to the Atlantic, the Royal Navy would not be able to release any ships for service with the Eastern Fleet. Danckwerts then asserted that the crux of the issue in the Pacific was not the British Eastern Fleet, but the U.S. Pacific Fleet. He argued that the Pacific and Far Eastern theaters were interrelated entities. The two areas must fall under a single, unified command, which would then employ the U.S. Pacific Fleet to threaten Japanese flanks. He opined that if the U.S. Pacific Fleet were to operate aggressively against the Japanese lines of communications, perhaps even attacking the home islands, the Japanese would be compelled to divert substantial resources to meet the threat. If, however, U.S. naval forces were to remain passive, the Japanese would be able to exert tremendous pressure on the British. Such pressure might force the British to withdraw ships from the Atlantic, thus denuding their already weak forces in what was supposed to be the main theater of operations.[37]

The debate continued over the course of the next week and reached a new peak on 10 February when the U.K. delegation reintroduced the question of the United States reinforcing its Asiatic Fleet. This question evoked an emphatic response from Turner, which Gerow quickly seconded, that there would be no new naval forces sent to the Far East and that the U.S. representatives were not going to alter their position. The meeting ended with the rather discordant conclusion that "for Britain it was fundamental that Singapore be held. For the United States it was fundamental that the Pacific Fleet be held intact and not become firmly committed to the Far East."[38]

Faced with the U.S. delegation's entrenched stance, the British produced an appreciation on the defense of the Far East designed to bring the Americans around to their position. In the initial portion of the paper, the British noted that since 1918 the retention of Singapore had been a cardinal point in British strategy, second only to the defense of the United Kingdom. The British cited that it had always been British policy to dispatch a fleet to the Far East in the event of a war in the Pacific, but that at this time it appeared impossible for them to do so because of the Royal Navy's tenuous hold on the Atlantic and the Mediterranean. The British representatives also reaffirmed that only U.S. action could prevent a Japanese invasion of Australia and New Zealand. If the United States were not actively engaged in the war, Britain might have to give up the Mediterranean and Middle East to protect its position in the Far East. Although they conceded that they were painting a rather bleak picture, they underscored their belief that the loss of Singapore would be a disaster of the first magnitude with severe political, economic, and psychological ramifications far beyond what the Allied forces could withstand and still maintain pressure on Germany. The British negotiators concluded by adding that should they ultimately be able to defeat the Germans, they were unsure if they would have sufficient residual strength to recapture Singapore, much less defeat Japan.[39]

Following this gloomy appraisal, the British turned to the problem of securing Singapore and the degree of U.S. assistance desired. They acknowledged that British forces currently in Malaya were insufficient to repulse a Japanese attack. Contradicting American views on the strength of the Malay Barrier, the British believed that even a minor Japanese assault might overwhelm the British and Dutch defenders. The only way to defend Singapore, therefore, was to base a substantial number of capital ships at Singapore. The logical conclusion to this argument, at least from the British point of view, was that due to the weakness of the British and Dutch fleets, these reinforcements would have to come from the U.S. Pacific Fleet.[40]

Anticipating American reactions to the paper, the British pointed out that, contrary to U.S. fears that such a dispersal of forces would invite piecemeal destruction of the U.S. Pacific Fleet, the plan placed the potential partners in a stronger position vis-à-vis the Japanese. The British staff argued that the Japanese would find themselves caught between two strong coalition bases and fleets. According to British logic, the possibility of a flank attack from either Singapore or Hawaii against lengthy and vulnerable lines of communications would deter the Japanese from attacking either base.[41] Having completed their arguments, the British delegation called upon the U.S. Staff Committee to accept His Majesty's Government's contention that "the security of the Far Eastern position, including Australia and New Zealand, is essential to the maintenance of the war effort of the Associated Powers. Singapore is the key to the defense of these interests and its retention must be assured." Assuming that the force of their argument would carry the day, the British then suggested that the staffs begin identifying specific elements of the U.S. Pacific Fleet for transfer to the U.S. Asiatic Fleet. They also proposed developing the general concepts for operations in the Far East when the delegations next met.[42]

The British proposition took the U.S. representatives aback. The British had failed completely to grasp the depth of the American opposition toward such a plan and had ignored repeated statements from their American interlocutors that the U.S. Pacific Fleet would remain in Hawaii. Major General Embick told General Marshall that the U.S. Staff Committee unanimously opposed the British proposals. Embick also forecast that if the U.S. delegation were to acquiesce, the United States would become fully committed to a war in the Pacific. This commitment would require America to curtail, if not halt, aid to Britain, and the United Kingdom might fall, leaving the United States exposed. He recommended that the Americans adhere to the position of the primacy of the Atlantic theater and that the U.S. Pacific Fleet remain a deterrent and containment force until the coalition had forced a decision in the Atlantic.[43]

In an internal meeting of the U.S. Staff Committee, Admiral Turner noted that the British had been pressing for a U.S. fleet in Singapore since Ingersoll's mission in January 1938. He complained that the British, unable now to meet their commitments, wanted the bulk of the U.S. Navy and a large American army force to salvage their position. He demanded a formal response from Stark and Marshall. In the discussion that followed, it became obvious that the entire U.S. delegation was upset that the British had pressed the issue in the face of repeated American opposition. Embick suggested that the time had come for the committee to present the president with their evaluation of the situation in the Far East and recommend a course of action. At this point, Brigadier General Miles interjected that the main purpose of the conference was to determine how best to secure the British Isles, a topic not yet addressed. He urged that the conference first resolve the issues of cooperation in the Atlantic and then turn to the more troublesome problems of the Pacific. The committee agreed to Miles's suggestion, thereby giving Turner a short breathing space to prepare the official U.S. response on the Far East.[44] This agenda also would permit the two delegations to discuss issues that all believed would be more easily resolved, building, it was hoped, a sense of mutual trust and an air of success.

For the next several days, the two negotiating teams made great strides in resolving the details of cooperation in the Atlantic. On 18 February, however, a new storm of controversy erupted over the Far East that nearly caused the conference to founder. At the height of the disagreements over the British position on the Far East, the British military representatives had given Lord Halifax a copy of their appreciation of the Far Eastern situation. Halifax in turn had taken the matter up with Secretary of State Hull. When the latter discussion surfaced on 17 February, an incensed U.S. delegation reacted intensely to what they perceived as a British attempt to put through their views on a political plane where they had failed at the military level, a direct contravention of the conference rules. As Embick put it to Marshall, "If this procedure continues, it would have the effect of the British dictating the course of the conversations."[45]

The matter occupied the next meeting of the U.S. Staff Committee, where the reaction was unanimously critical. The committee decided to suspend the staff conversations pending receipt and evaluation of a British response. In a stern letter to the British delegation, the U.S. representatives reiterated the injunction that the talks remain on a strictly military level. They admonished the British delegation for violating the terms of reference and warned, "The [U.S.] Committee is of the opinion that political intervention at this stage will retard, rather than advance the work of the Conference," a thinly veiled threat about the future of the conversations if the British persisted in such political maneuvers.[46]

Nor were the Americans the only ones upset. Churchill was furious. The level of his anger and insights into this incident merit a lengthy quotation. On 17 February, in a note to A. V. Alexander, first lord of the Admiralty, and Admiral Pound, Churchill exploded:

> I very much deplore Admiral Bellairs spreading himself in this way, and using such extreme arguments as those contained in the last sentence in paragraph 6. I trust the appreciation has not been sent in. . . .
> What has been the use of all this battling? Anyone could have seen that the United States would not base a battle-fleet on Singapore and divide their naval forces, enabling the Japanese to fight an action on even terms with either one of them. They said so weeks ago, and I particularly deprecated the raising of this controversy. Our object is to get

the Americans into the war, and the proper strategic dispositions will soon emerge when they are up against reality. . . .

The first thing is to get the United States into the war. We can then best settle how to fight it afterwards. Admiral Bellairs is making such heavy weather over all of this that he may easily turn the United States Navy Board into a hindrance and not a help to the main object, namely the entry of the United States.[47]

The combination of Churchill's wrath and the Americans' thinly veiled threat led Bellairs immediately to dispatch a conciliatory reply to the U.S. Staff Committee. In the note, he attempted to explain the close civil–military relationship that existed within the British system of government. He pointed out that it was only natural for the British representatives, as a delegation far removed from the seat of government, to discuss matters with Lord Halifax, who remained a member of the War Cabinet, and for Halifax to use their advice in his discussions with the State Department. This point notwithstanding, Bellairs acknowledged that the British took the American warning to heart and informed the U.S. delegation that they could "rest assured that no further Delegation papers will be communicated to the State Department."[48] The Americans accepted the apology, despite two complaints from Turner that Bellairs had not excluded oral communication as well as a warning that political interference could continue.[49] The ever-candid Air Commodore Slessor later made the point that "some Americans are curiously liable to suspect that they are going to be 'outsmarted' by the subtle British—perhaps because we sometimes do such stupid things that they cannot take them at their face value but suspect them of being part of some dark design."[50]

In any event, the U.S. team let the matter drop, returned to the negotiations, and communicated its report on the U.S. military position in the Far East. In part a response to the British appreciation on their strategy in the Far East, in no small part a reaction to the British faux pas with the State Department, and in part a desire to clarify the American representatives' own views, the report addressed the range of problems facing British and American planners over the Far East.[51]

At the next full meeting of the conference, the Americans essentially repudiated the British strategic appreciation of the previous week. After cautioning once more that any decision on U.S. entry into the war would be a political one, they added that even a direct Japanese attack against British or Dutch possessions might not bring the United States into the war. Therefore, it would be a tremendous mistake for the British to base their plans and strategy on

U.S. involvement. They also reminded the British that defense of the Western Hemisphere remained the principal U.S. concern and that American forces would have to be husbanded carefully to ensure adequate protection should Britain be knocked out of the war. All parties must accept those facts in drawing up their plans.[52]

The American delegation also reaffirmed that the major U.S. effort would be in the Atlantic and that the United States would retain only minimum forces in the Pacific. The United States would not reinforce the Philippines, with the possible exception of some air assets. In addition, the British and Dutch should not predicate a defense of the Malay Barrier upon any American assistance. Although acknowledging the importance of Singapore, the U.S. authorities remained adamant that they would not jeopardize the main Allied effort in the Atlantic by diverting forces to defend the island. An analysis of possible Japanese actions led the Americans to conclude that Hong Kong, Guam, Malaya, Singapore, the Netherlands East Indies, and the Philippine Islands would probably be lost. Less pessimistic about the importance of the losses, the U.S. delegation contended that the significance would be more psychological than substantive. Even with the losses, the Americans felt that the Japanese would neither invade Australia, New Zealand, or India nor present a major threat to British lines of communication in the Indian Ocean. The American proposals were no doubt unpalatable to the U.K. delegation, but the latter realized they were in no position to continue the argument. They passively accepted that all plans for operations in the Pacific would stem from the premise that the U.S. Pacific Fleet would remain in Hawaii and that there would be no U.S. reinforcement of Singapore.[53]

This is a case where U.S. strategic planners were much more clear-eyed in their analysis than were their British counterparts. The Americans recognized that there were more requirements than resources to meet those demands and that hard choices were therefore necessary. The British, despite their own statements that they were stretched to the breaking point, could not bring themselves to make a similar hard choice and continued to cling to the belief that Japan could be deterred or contained by minimal forces. As a result, the British ultimately would suffer damaging defeats throughout the Far East with tremendous loss of life and prestige. This failure to alter their plans to fit geostrategic realities also runs counter to the standard portrayal that the British were more sophisticated strategic thinkers than were their American cousins. In this case, at least, the British come off in a worse light.

Based on the reluctant British agreement to accept American intentions, the two negotiating teams met on 26 February to discuss operational-level plans for the Pacific, in particular how to keep the Japanese from penetrating the supposed Malay Barrier. Apparently unable to let go, the British acknowledged the U.S. decision to maintain the U.S. Pacific Fleet at Pearl Harbor, but nonetheless noted that they disagreed with the decision as well as the strategic premises upon which it rested. However, given U.S. and British interests and existing strategic conditions, they reluctantly accepted that these were the best possible plans that could emerge from the conversations. However, in a parting shot, the British delegation complained that these plans were not the best possible military solutions. Instead, the British proposed sending a fleet of six capital ships to reinforce Singapore. The timing of the departure of this force would depend on the strategic conditions extant at the time. The British would have to draw these reinforcements from British units in the Atlantic and Mediterranean. The British argued further that American ships would have to replace any Royal Navy forces transferred from the Atlantic to the Far East if the coalition did not wish to worsen the already precarious position in the Atlantic. They also hinted that the speed of British reinforcement of Singapore hinged on how quickly the United States shifted assets to the Atlantic. Thus, the British deftly maneuvered the Americans into a corner: simultaneously ensuring the defense of Singapore while tying the Americans ever more closely to the British in the Atlantic. This tack took the Americans by surprise, and they fell back on the answer that the decision would have to be a political one based on the situation at the time.[54]

The British then observed that, with a fleet of six Royal Navy capital ships in Singapore, the Japanese fleet of ten major warships would be caught between the pincers of fifteen U.S. and British capital ships. Of course, the British omitted mention that 6,700 miles separated these fifteen ships and that the Japanese could attack the separate fleets piecemeal, with a decided numerical advantage at either point. Nor, in keeping with British and U.S. arrogance, did they take into account the formidable, if not yet fully known, capabilities of the Imperial Japanese Navy, especially its carrier-based aviation. Regardless, they remarked that the coalition was devoting too much effort to the Pacific, intimating that the United States should use the U.S. Pacific Fleet to strengthen the Royal Navy in the Atlantic.[55] The Americans countered that to effectively deter Japan from war required a fleet of considerable strength. Moreover, should war break out in the Pacific, the U.S. Fleet would then attack through the Marshall Islands, luring the Japanese Fleet into decisive action. The British delegation agreed that such a tactic might work but considered a direct attack on the Japanese home islands a more effective means of bringing the Japanese Fleet to bay. Such an attack also might relieve any pressure on the Netherlands East Indies.[56] Later events would reveal that both parties at this time suffered from different but equally unreal pipe dreams.

Discussion then shifted to how the U.S. Asiatic Fleet might assist in the defense of the southwestern Pacific. The Americans simply noted that because of the distance, both physical and cerebral, it was ill advised for the conferees to discuss the issues. Rather, direct talks should take place among Admiral Hart and British and Dutch representatives in the Far East.[57] In light of Churchill's stinging rebuke and admonition on 17 February to "loyally accept the United States Navy dispositions for the Pacific," the British accepted this modus vivendi.[58] Avoiding further acrimonious debate over the Far East proved an effective short-term expedient for improving relations within the conference. It also established a much-needed level of harmony that calmed tempers as the conferees drafted their final report. Unfortunately, in tabling that discussion, the senior planners not only kicked the can of coalition cooperation down the road once more but also kicked it into the lap of local commanders, who would be operating without an agreed overarching strategy or operational plan—a situation not likely to produce a successful outcome.

The delegations wrapped up the remaining issues in the Pacific when the naval delegates met on 6 March to discuss convoy responsibilities in the Pacific. After much wrangling over how to meet too many requirements with too few forces, the staffs agreed that U.S. responsibility would end at the 180-degree meridian, where the British and Dominion forces would assume accountability. Not pleased with the arrangements, the British reluctantly accepted that these were the best conditions they could get. On this less than triumphant note, the last formal session on the Pacific ended.[59]

In sharp contrast to the tangled negotiations and sharp conflicts that characterized discussions over the strategy in the Pacific, amicable discussion and agreement on the main issues marked the talks concerning cooperation in the Atlantic. Addressed briefly in the initial meetings, the Atlantic was discussed in detail starting with the fourth meeting. The Americans generally had been aware of British positions since the arrival of the British delegation, when Lee and Ghormley finally were able to provide the U.S. delegation with the responses to the questions the Americans had submitted in early December.[60]

The British noted that the threat to their sea lines of communications posed a serious danger. They acknowledged that shipping losses were approaching those of the worst year of the Great War and that annual British imports were already running 6 million tons below minimum requirements. The British candidly admitted that they needed considerable American assistance, including U.S. Navy escorts to cover Iceland, the Northwest Approaches to the United

Kingdom, and the Home Waters. In addition, they wanted the U.S. Navy to establish hunter groups based in Bermuda, the West Indies, and Halifax, Nova Scotia, to counter German surface raiders. Finally, they asked an American squadron to replace the Royal Navy's Force "H" at Gibraltar.[61]

The British responses included requests for help in the air as well. With the demands upon the Royal Navy for convoy protection, the RAF now served as the United Kingdom's first line of defense. The British noted that the RAF was stretched too thin both to defend the home islands and to carry out the air offensive over Germany. The British asked, as a matter of urgency, that the United States deploy a minimum of four squadrons of heavy bombers, ninety-six aircraft, to Britain, complete with supporting materiel and an appropriate allocation of fighters within the first three months of American entry into the war. Thereafter, the British wanted the United States to commit, to the greatest extent possible, all its fighters and bombers to Great Britain. Bombers would attack Germany, and fighters would perform escort duty and support air defense of the United Kingdom. The British also called for substantial reinforcement of their air effort in the Middle East. Paradoxically, the British cautioned that the expansion of the U.S. Air Corps necessary to affect these reinforcements should not disrupt Britain's current allocation of aircraft.[62]

Final British requests concerned assistance from U.S. land forces. Careful not to frighten off the Americans with the specter of a large-scale continental commitment, the British asked that deployment of U.S. land forces be limited to forces in Northern Ireland and British islands in the Atlantic, with a token force in the United Kingdom. The British further requested that the token force be no larger than a brigade group because a large-scale American deployment would only exacerbate already critical supply problems in Britain.[63] This request also reflected British faith in the power of economic strangulation brought about by naval blockade and bombing, which they believed would result in an internal collapse of Germany and thus allow for a coup de grace by small numbers of—British—mechanized forces. The British, abetted by the equal conviction among U.S. air enthusiasts, would cling to this hope despite the contrary British experience until well into 1943.

At a 5 February meeting, the British essentially reiterated these arguments and responded to questions from the American delegation. Turner in particular expressed interest in how and when the British planned to move from defensive to offensive operations in the Atlantic region. The British replied that the two were intertwined and depended on production capabilities, and they began outlining their current materiel priorities. Heretofore, the RAF held first priority, especially fighter production necessary to win the Battle of Britain. Now that the RAF had beaten back the Luftwaffe, aircraft production had shifted to heavy bombers to carry the war to Germany. Similarly, the British army was in the midst of transforming from a purely defensive organization to a strike force capable of offensive operations on the Continent. The British concluded the discussion by noting that the Royal Navy had also shifted from invasion defense to convoy protection.[64]

The discussion continued the next day when Danckwerts raised the possibility of the U.S. Navy positioning a squadron at Gibraltar. Taking this proposal a step further than the day before, he inquired whether the United States could assume responsibility not only for the Atlantic approaches to Gibraltar but also for the western basin of the Mediterranean. Turner replied that this might be possible and used the question as a springboard to address the role of the U.S. Navy once America entered the war. He noted that the United States would accept responsibility for the Atlantic west of 30 degrees West— that is, west of the Azores or approximately 60 percent of the North Atlantic and as far south as Rio de Janeiro. The United States also was prepared to dispatch destroyers and long-range reconnaissance aircraft for escort duties in the Northwest Approaches to the United Kingdom. For the moment, however, Turner asked that the group defer the issue of command arrangements.[65]

When the delegations next discussed Atlantic issues on 10 February, the focus shifted to air and land forces. Embick noted that because of mobilization problems, the U.S. Army would have only four infantry and two armored divisions ready for deployment by 1 September 1941. Nevertheless, the Americans planned to employ their land and air forces in the Atlantic regions and progressively take up British army commitments in the Atlantic, save defense of the British Isles. The only disappointment for the British was that the U.S. Army Air Corps gave first priority to the deployment of fighter aircraft rather than heavy bombers to protect U.S. Navy bases in the eastern Atlantic.[66] Nonetheless, the Americans had without argument fulfilled nearly all British goals for the Atlantic.

The British were less successful in the continuing discussions of naval issues that resumed at the seventh meeting. In response to a British proposal on protection of convoys, Turner argued that the best course of action would be for the U.S. Navy to take responsibility for convoy protection with priority to the Northwest Approaches or North Atlantic Approaches. Turner then addressed the second portion of the British proposal concerning the allocation of U.S. naval forces in the Atlantic. He stated directly, "It is not the intention of the United States to agree to any breaking up and scattering of United States forces into small groups to be absorbed by British commands. . . . [T]he United States proposes to accept full responsibility for operations in certain definite areas, or for executing specific tasks in areas of British responsibility. . . . In brief, United States' forces are to be under United States' command, with each assigned an area or task for which one or the other will have full responsibility." He then "invited" the British delegation to reconsider their position on the type and number of forces needed for a particular area so that the negotiators could reach "proper" decisions on the employment of all naval forces in the Atlantic.[67]

The British delegation obviously got the message, for they acceded to Turner's demands the next day. The conversations then turned to an evaluation of the new British fleet dispositions, which Turner tentatively accepted. Although these new arrangements greatly increased Allied naval power, the British observed that the minimum requirements for the security of the United Kingdom remained unmet. This observation evoked a sharp response from General Miles, who asked the British for a full and definitive statement of their actual requirements. Unfortunately, the British gave only an evasive answer, and the meeting ended on a less than positive note.[68]

The delegations made further progress at the next meeting. U.S. Army representatives agreed to place forces near Freetown, Sierra Leone, to safeguard naval and air bases as well as to bolster the defense of northeastern Brazil. The army members also accepted full responsibility for the defense of Iceland, although they remarked that an occupation before 1 April would delay the dispatch of forces to defend U.S. bases in England until 1 September 1941. Gerow then suggested the deployment of a reinforced regimental group to serve as a token force and questioned whether the British had determined other missions for U.S. land forces in the United Kingdom. Major General Morris acknowledged that such a force would be most welcome but did not respond to Gerow's query.[69]

Colonel McNarney next outlined the proposed deployment of U.S. Army aviation assets. He first noted that the United States would take over the air defense of Iceland, but that would mean that the U.S. Army Air Corps would have no other fighter aircraft available until autumn. When the British recommended including bombers for Iceland, McNarney replied that such a deployment would come at the expense of units currently destined for the United Kingdom. McNarney added that when the United States sent fighters and bombers to the United Kingdom, the fighters would protect U.S. bases and installations, while the bombers would work in close cooperation with the British Bomber Command. McNarney was not prepared, however, to address British proposals for the employment of U.S. air forces assigned to the United Kingdom, and the group deferred the matter.[70]

With these agreements, the delegations had resolved the major issues concerning cooperation in the Atlantic. The remaining talks dealt mainly with the technical aspects of implementing the agreed upon strategy and presented little or no controversy. One exception to this rule occurred when the two naval staffs met to iron out the remaining details of convoy protection. Danckwerts noted that at the present time the U.S. Navy did not have a sufficient number of ships in the Atlantic to meet their existing commitments and that this situation would only worsen when the United States entered the war and expanded its zone of responsibility. Turner acknowledged that the U.S. Navy had too few ships for too many missions. He added that any increase in American escorts would require commensurate reductions from other commitments, such as stripping the southern Atlantic of armed merchant cruisers or withdrawal from the Gibraltar force or another strike force. Not wanting to see such drastic action, the British called for future arrangements based on close, mutual collaboration, thus papering over another problem in order to avoid further controversy.[71]

The 17 February 1941 session was the last formal meeting for nearly a month. The two parties would not convene again until the end of March to review the final report of the conference. On 24 February, the staffs named a steering committee—Bellairs, Ghormley, and Gerow—approved the general format of the report, and agreed that British representatives with guidance from the steering committee would prepare a draft final report that would serve as the basis of a combined paper from the two delegations.[72] The steering committee had the final draft ready for approval on 27 March. When the two delegations met, they went over the text paragraph by paragraph, with some disagreement, mostly from Turner, on several points. When at this late date McNarney suggested the addition of a special report on the allocation of air materiel, Turner exploded and refused to sign anything. The next day Slessor and Turner engaged in a verbal donnybrook, where Slessor described Turner's behavior as "extraordinary" even for the always-cantankerous sailor. Stark apparently prevailed on Turner, and the U.S. Army Air Corps accepted the inclusion of the special report as a supplement, eventually known as ABC-2, to the overall ABC-1 Report.[73]

In view of the foregoing, a detailed discussion of the final report need not detain us at this point. Nonetheless, the absolute critical importance of this document, both as a mark of what had been achieved since 1938 and as a blueprint for future Anglo-American cooperation, requires the outline of its more salient features.[74] The main report fell into two sections. The first comprised those portions of the agreement that the delegations believed would remain relatively unchanged, such as agreed principles of grand strategy, general strategy to implement those principles, and command arrangements. The second portion dealt with subjects that might later be amended; therefore, each subject occupied a separate annex that could be changed without altering the hard-won conclusions given in the main body of the report.[75] In addition, the delegations submitted the "ABC-2 Report on Air Collaboration," which was as much a supplement to the main body as it was an independent report.

The main report established that "the broad strategic objective (object) of the Associated Powers will be the defeat of Germany and her Allies." The report also laid out the major elements of the grand strategy to guide the Anglo-American coalition once the United States entered the war. Because Germany constituted the most dangerous threat, the report deemed the Atlantic and European theaters the most decisive, and the Anglo-American coalition would direct its major effort toward the defeat of Germany. Japanese entry into the war would not alter the grand strategy. The coalition would assume a strategic defensive in the Pacific until after Germany's defeat. Out of deference to the British position in the Mediterranean, the report recognized the importance of that theater to the two powers' overall grand strategy.[76]

The report also outlined the elements of grand strategy necessary to ensure defeat of the Axis Powers. The two military staffs realized that the coalition would remain on the strategic defensive until it had gathered sufficient strength to go on the offensive. A divergence of opinion existed, however, over the fundamental objective of this defense, most particularly the importance of the Far East. Quite naturally, each power sought to safeguard its most crucial national interest—survival. For the United States, this meant safeguarding the Western Hemisphere from political or military penetration by the Axis Powers. In a similar vein, the British were concerned that "the security of the United Kingdom must be maintained in all circumstances," but, as befit their worldwide empire, their interests were more extensive. Security of the United Kingdom also included the successful defense of the British Commonwealth of Nations, of which "a cardinal feature of British strategic policy is the retention of a position in the Far East such as will ensure the cohesion and security of the British Commonwealth and the maintenance of its war effort."[77] In this manner, the two staffs glossed over the fundamental differences that had plagued the conference.

Although recognizing the necessity of an initial period of strategic defensive, the Anglo-American planners intended to take the offensive at the earliest opportunity. They planned for the use of naval, land, and air forces to apply economic pressure by denying critical resources to the enemy; a sustained air offensive against Germany; the early elimination of Italy; use of raids and minor offensives; support of internal resistance within occupied Europe; the buildup of forces; and the capture of key areas to serve as springboards for an eventual offensive on the Continent.[78]

To assist national planners in their efforts to implement the strategic concept, the report outlined broad guidelines for operational planning. The major U.S. effort in the Atlantic theater would be to assist the British in the protection of Allied shipping, with emphasis on the Northwest Approaches. The Mediterranean would assume a secondary role, although the future partners vowed to maintain the current British position in the Mediterranean and to prevent any Axis expansion in North Africa. The first priority of U.S. ground and air forces would be the security of the Western Hemisphere. Any remaining forces would support operations in the Atlantic and European region.[79]

Concerning the defense of the Far East should Japan enter the war, the report reflected the conflicts that existed throughout the conference. The report indicated, "Military Strategy in the Far East will be defensive."[80] It noted that the United States would not reinforce the Far East but would use the U.S. Pacific Fleet to weaken Japanese economic power and divert the Japanese from the Malay Barrier through offensive action directed at the Marshall Islands. The U.S. Navy also would augment British Commonwealth forces in the Atlantic and Mediterranean areas to allow the Royal Navy to shift ships to the Far East. As a means of camouflaging the fundamental disagreements between the two staffs, the report included the critical caveat that the deployment of such forces would depend on the existing situation.[81] Given the current circumstances in the Atlantic and the Mediterranean in addition to British strategic thinking, the probability of such a move seemed low.

The report also stipulated that all planning, regardless of level, would occur on a collaborative basis, including coalition and national operations. To facilitate this process, the report called for establishing a U.S. Military Mission in London and a British Military Mission in Washington. Each would "represent jointly, as a corporate body, their own Chiefs of Staff . . . vis-à-vis the group of Chiefs of Staff to which they are accredited, for the purpose of collaboration in the formulation of Military Policies and plans governing the conduct of the war in areas in which that Power assumes responsibility for strategic direction." In addition, the missions would also represent their respective service in any direct contacts with the other power's appropriate counterparts.[82] The U.S. Mission in London would consist of one flag officer from the army and one from the navy, a joint planning staff composed of equal numbers of army and navy officers, plus a small secretariat (see figure 1). The British Mission in Washington

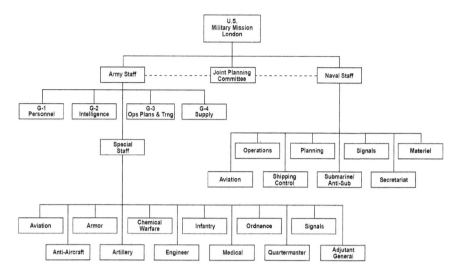

Figure 1. U.S. Military Mission under American-British Conversations-1 (*Source:* U.S. Congress, *PHAH,* 15:1497–1498. See list of abbreviations in the notes.)

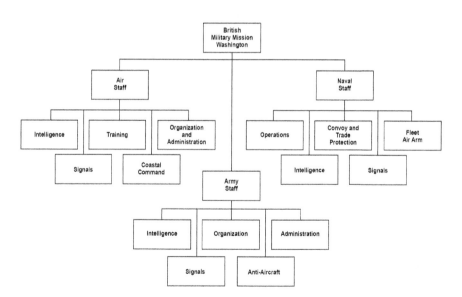

Figure 2. British Military Mission under American-British Conversations-1 (*Source:* U.S. Congress, *PHAH,* 15:1499–1500)

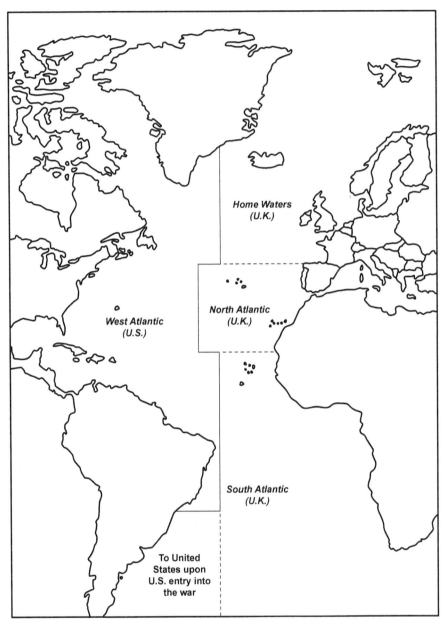

Map 1. Areas of Strategic Responsibility in the Atlantic under ABC-1

would follow similar organizational lines, except it would have three members, one flag officer each from the Royal Navy, British army, and RAF (see figure 2). A joint planning staff composed of officers from all three services would advise the senior members of the mission as well as collaborate with the U.S. staffs in Washington.[83]

Matters of command generally conformed to American desires. Although each power would exercise strategic direction within its assigned areas of responsibility (see maps 1 and 2), forces would operate under their own commanders, and units would be organized for specific tasks. Commanders could neither subdivide forces nor attach them to units of another power. In areas where units of the two nations operated together, the senior officer present would assume command.[84] These decisions hearken back to the U.S.-British experiences during World War I. The British would have preferred "leadership by committee," which was more suited to their command style and offered greater opportunities for them to influence matters within all theaters, but the U.S. view of unity of command prevailed. Although this was not a perfect solution, with it the delegations resolved quickly a once contentious issue, and the partners would not have to flog their way through multiple crises before arriving at a workable solution.

The ABC-2 Report concerning air policy composed the final component of the conference report. Interestingly, little or no disagreement existed between Air Staff officers on grand strategy or strategy. As was frequently the case in the ABC-1 talks as well as in collaboration after December 1941, like services held similar views and often banded together across the table to argue a common cause against the other arms of service. In this case, the representatives of the two air staffs agreed that the bomber offensive represented a critical element of Allied plans and that the United States would support the RAF as quickly and strongly as possible. The major concern was over the allocation of American production between the British and American air forces.[85] The planning staffs apparently reached an amicable settlement. The United States agreed to defer its own Fifty-Four Group Program in favor of supplying the British. Indeed, the British would receive all of their own production, the entire output of the commonwealth, 12,000 aircraft from current U.S. orders, and any production beyond the 12,000 airplanes that manufacturers could squeeze from existing U.S. industrial capacity. In addition, the British would acquire 100 percent of all new production until American entry into the war, and even then there would be a fifty–fifty split.[86]

The delegations met for the final time on 29 March 1941 to review and approve the final versions of the two reports. Contrary to recent meetings,

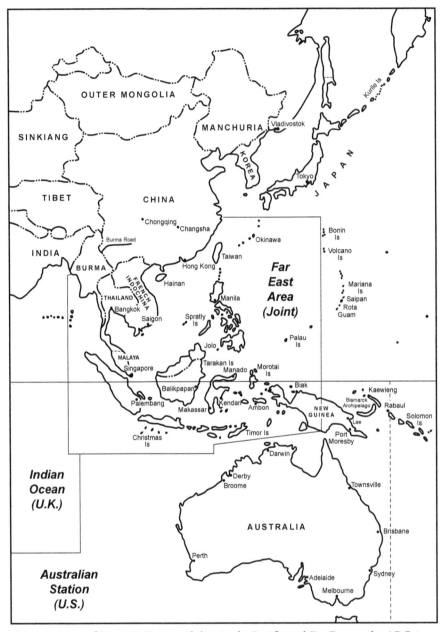

Map 2. Areas of Strategic Responsibility in the Pacific and Far East under ABC-1

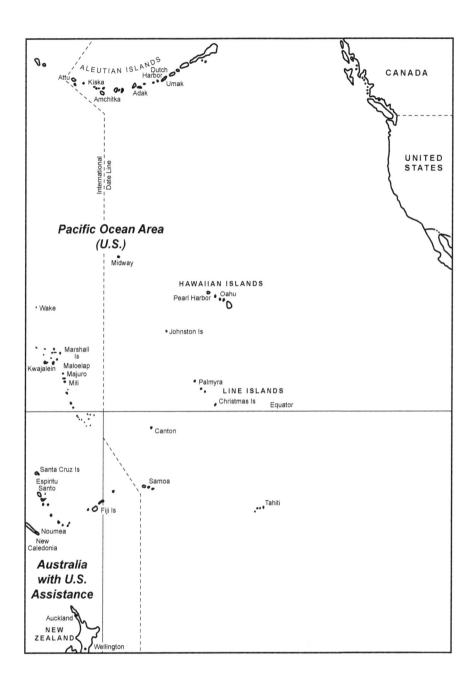

a much more amiable atmosphere prevailed, and the delegations quickly approved both reports. After the officials affixed their signatures to the documents, each delegation gave a closing statement, and the representatives bade their individual and collective farewells.

The two delegations could part with a sense of satisfaction, for they had accomplished much. The planners had established the fundamental principles of a combined grand strategy, delimited and assigned responsibility for strategic areas of operation, and laid down the basis for coalition strategies for the Atlantic and European regions, the Mediterranean, and the Middle East. They agreed upon a common war plan that provided for the detailed implementation of that coalition strategy. They also hammered out key procedures for command, reached agreement on the sticky question of aircraft allocation, and created the liaison machinery that would serve as the conduit for future Anglo-American cooperation.

The talks were not a total success, however. Although the American delegation fulfilled most of the major U.S. objectives of the talks, this was oftentimes the result of British resignation in the face of American inflexibility or as an expedient not to delay U.S. involvement in the war. Other times, U.S. views prevailed because of American power and British need, a combination certain to contribute to future friction within the coalition. The inability to fashion a coherent coalition strategy for the defense of the Far East was the most significant shortcoming. Granted, each nation staked out its position, and respective local commanders in the Far East would soon meet. However, this effort simply papered over the cracks within the coalition, and problems were bound to resurface eventually. However, if we take a long view, the course of events would validate the success of the conference and the outcomes that followed from it. Certainly, strategic circumstances and oftentimes fierce arguments would strain the coalition, but the elemental grand strategy and the implementing strategic principles crafted eight months before the United States entered the war would endure through to victory almost four years later. No small accomplishment.

A brief postscript to the ABC-1 Report offers some insights into the difficulties that would later affect efforts to implement the report's provisions. General Marshall and Admiral Stark tentatively approved the report on 5 April 1941, and it became the basis for the new war plan, Rainbow 5. The British Chiefs of Staff recommended approval of the ABC-1 Report to the prime minister on 1 May. The U.S. Joint Army–Navy Board approved both the ABC-1 Report and Rainbow 5 on 14 May and forwarded both documents to Secretary of War

Stimson and Secretary of the Navy Knox, who approved the documents on 28 May and 2 June, respectively. Knox and Stimson then submitted the report and the war plan to President Roosevelt, who pointedly did not approve either document. On 7 June, Major General Edwin M. Watson, military aide to the president, provided the following explanation for the president's lack of action: "The President has familiarized himself with the two papers; but since the report of the United States–British Staff Conversations, ABC-1, had not been approved by the British Government, he would not approve the report at this time; neither would he now give approval to Joint Army and Navy War Plan RAINBOW-5, which is based upon the report ABC-1. However, in case of war the papers would be returned to the President for his approval."[87]

However, according to official historian Tracy B. Kittredge, Rear Admiral Ghormley informed the Admiralty on 26 April 1941 that President Roosevelt had approved the arrangements made at ABC-1.[88] From Kittredge's comments, it is not possible to determine the level of detail of Roosevelt's approval. Regardless, given Major General Watson's comments more than a month after ABC-1, there may have been more than a little room for confusion among Roosevelt's military subordinates. At the very least, as Mark Lowenthal points out, Roosevelt's response of 7 June was open to wide interpretation.[89] Clearly, Marshall and Stark took the positive view that because Roosevelt had not disapproved the documents, they were valid for planning, and so the two directed their staffs and commanders accordingly.[90]

Roosevelt's lack of a definitive decision also lays open his intent to multiple interpretations. If his inaction is viewed from a negative perspective, one could conclude that it was a political ploy to avoid responsibility or, in more modern parlance, to invoke plausible deniability. That Marshall and Stark chose to implement the documents in the absence of formal approval lends credence to this opinion. Conversely, Roosevelt's inaction could have been a typical ploy to keep all of his options open and not prejudice future decisions by opting to approve the documents. Viewing the president's inaction from the most positive light, one might conclude that the president had yet to make up his mind about ultimate U.S. involvement and did not approve the documents to avoid raising British expectations. Given Roosevelt's penchant for retaining all possible room for maneuver, the most likely interpretation takes the middle road: Roosevelt wanted to preserve all options and not raise British expectations, while allowing his subordinates to plan for a worst-case scenario.

8

Easier Said Than Done

Implementing the American-British Conversations-1 Report, April–July 1941

With the conclusion of ABC-1 at the end of March 1941, coalition efforts entered a new phase. Planning shifted from the largely theoretical plane of grand strategy and broad strategic lines of effort to the formulation of plans necessary to execute decisions reached during ABC-1. Understanding these efforts requires placing them in their appropriate context. It is important to note that although the continued maturation of the coalition was vitally important, it was not the only activity engaging the attention and limited resources of the staffs charged with turning the principles and concepts of the ABC-1 Report into practical realities. The Americans remained focused on developing, mobilizing, and training their rapidly expanding armed forces as well as developing the defense industrial base necessary to equip and sustain those forces. The British remained in a desperate struggle for survival as they continued to wage the Battle of Britain and the Battle of the Atlantic. Moreover, events in North Africa, East Africa, and the Mediterranean increasingly occupied British attention and forces

As time did not stand still during the ABC-1 Conference, the turn of the year offers an appropriate start point for establishing the contemporary context within which the staffs began planning for implementing the accords. The year 1941 began well enough. By 7 February, a British offensive in North Africa cleared the Italians out of Egypt and eastern Libya; the British captured more than 130,000 prisoners and seemed poised to drive Italy from North Africa.[1] Another British offensive launched in mid-February defeated the Italians throughout East Africa, cleared Kenya, liberated Ethiopia, Somalia, and Eritrea, and bagged another 400,000 prisoners.[2] On 28 March, a British naval force under the command of Admiral Andrew B. Cunningham battered the Italian Fleet off Cape Matapan, Greece, sinking three cruisers and two destroyers at the loss of a single torpedo bomber and crew.[3] Greek forces not only halted an Italian invasion that began on 28 October 1940 but also counterattacked and seized the southern third of Italian-occupied Albania.[4]

Then came the Germans. By late January, German aircraft based in Sicily dominated the central Mediterranean, pounding Malta almost daily. On 24 March, General Erwin Rommel, the "Desert Fox," launched his first offensive in Libya. By 29 March, the German Afrika Corps and its Italian allies pushed the British back to the borders of Egypt and invested Tobruk. Rommel was poised to invade Egypt and perhaps seize the Suez Canal, raising the specter that he might drive beyond the Suez into the oil-rich Arabian Peninsula to link up with pro-Axis forces that had staged a coup in Iraq or with other Axis sympathizers fomenting unrest in Syria, Lebanon, and Palestine.[5]

On 6 April, the Wehrmacht invaded both Yugoslavia and Greece to secure the southern flank of their upcoming invasion of the Soviet Union. Yugoslavia capitulated on 17 April, Greece surrendered on 23 April, and the Germans drove the British from Greece and onto Crete with considerable losses. Three weeks later the Germans invaded Crete, forcing the British to evacuate, once again having to abandon their heavy equipment as well as more than 12,000 British prisoners and thousands of Greek prisoners. The Royal Navy suffered grievously while taking off the remnants of the fighting force—1,828 dead; three cruisers and six destroyers sunk; one aircraft carrier, three battleships, six cruisers, and seven destroyers damaged.[6] On the other end of the Mediterranean, rumors abounded about possible German assaults on Gibraltar from either Spain or French Morocco. By June, Britain held only the two ends of the Mediterranean, and that hold was tenuous.

With the advent of better weather, the Battle of Britain resumed, and by May strong raids wreaked havoc on London and other key industrial and port cities.[7] The Battle of the Atlantic was reaching one of its crisis points. In the first six months of 1941, the British lost 2.8 million tons of shipping. This figure was on top of more than 1.25 million tons already lost since the war began as well as 1.7 million tons out of action awaiting repairs. The pace of sinkings made it starkly clear that Britain could lose the Battle of the Atlantic and face starvation or surrender.[8] Adding to the anxieties, in the midst of the crisis on Crete the great German battleship *Bismarck* and its escorts broke out into the Atlantic, sinking the H.M.S. *Hood,* pride of the Royal Navy, and generating tremendous fears for five days until the British sank the *Bismarck* on 27 May.[9]

Although the United States was certainly not in as bleak a position as Great Britain, it faced considerable challenges. The U.S. Army struggled with the mobilization of almost 1.6 million men, a quintupling of the army in less than a year. The number was impressive, but most of these men had been in the army for only a few months, and they lacked equipment for individual training, much less the heavy equipment needed for unit maneuvers. By early summer, the army could muster only a single division capable of extended operations outside the continental United States. Moreover, the army had to cobble this unit together because the conscription law forbade the use of draftees outside the Western Hemisphere. By May 1941, the WPD concluded that not until 1942 could the army conduct hemispheric defense, to include occupying the Azores, and provide forces to the United Kingdom in accordance with ABC-1.[10]

The U.S. Army and the Army Air Corps remained consumed with hemisphere defense. New bases in the Atlantic and Caribbean acquired under the destroyers-for-bases deal in September 1940 had to be reconnoitered and built. Strong rumors of German activities in Latin America, especially Brazil, absorbed considerable attention from Roosevelt and, hence, his military leaders. It is also worth pointing out that throughout much of this period the WPD of the Army Staff had less than twenty-five officers, including the chief and his executive officer, spread across seven staff sections.[11] Implementing the provisions of the ABC-1 Report and all these projects represented only a portion of their duties. As the situation worsened in North Africa and the Atlantic, these planners leaped from one project to another as the tyranny of the urgent dominated.[12]

The U.S. Navy was finding it difficult to maintain a deterrent force in the Pacific while simultaneously attempting to transfer forces to the Atlantic as required under ABC-1. On 9 April, by agreement with the Danish government, Greenland came under U.S. protection. On 25 April, Roosevelt extended the U.S. security zone to 26 degrees west longitude, not quite the mid-Atlantic but including Greenland and Iceland. Although the president was unwilling to begin escorting convoys, the U.S. Navy extended its Neutrality Patrol to these waters.[13] All this occurred in the midst of dramatically expanding the fleet, mobilizing and training new sailors, and developing new bases whether in the United States or under leases recently acquired from Britain.

All of these events culminated in the so-called crisis of May 1941. Losses continued to accelerate in the Battle of the Atlantic. The British seemed on the verge of losing the Mediterranean and the Middle East. On 4 May, Churchill made his most direct plea for the United States to enter the war.[14] On 15 May, Marshal Henri-Philippe Pétain announced an agreement on substantial cooperation between Vichy France and Germany, generating tremendous anxiety in Washington that the Germans would advance from northwestern Africa into northeastern Brazil. General Marshall quickly dispatched Lieutenant Colonel Matthew B. Ridgway to Rio de Janeiro to seek immediate permission for U.S. forces to deploy for defense of northeastern Brazil. Pétain's announcement also resurrected concerns about German submarines gaining access to refueling facilities in Martinique. Rumors at the time, now known to be true, about France granting Germany submarine access to Dakar and German designs on the Azores heightened concerns.[15] Everywhere, it seemed, disaster loomed. As Kenneth Davis eloquently concludes, "In retrospect, no season of all the years of the stupendous global conflict, not even the furiously flaming spring of 1940, would appear to British and American leaders more fruitful with fatal danger to freedom's cause, more crowded with insoluble anxiety producing problems and less lighted for a belief in ultimate victory, than the black spring of 1941."[16]

On 19 May, General Marshall called in his key planners to determine what recommendation he should offer if the president asked about entering the war. Throughout the spring, Roosevelt had seemed unwilling to decide on a way ahead. When the German battleship *Bismarck* took to sea on 22 May, however, it seemed to prod the president into action. On 27 May, Roosevelt gave one of his periodic fireside chats via international radio broadcast. Delivered at the White House before a live audience composed of the Governing Board of the Pan-American Union, the Canadian minister, and their families, Roosevelt offered the American public an unsparing description of the dire British military position, threats to the Western Hemisphere, and peril to United States should Nazi tyranny defeat Britain. As he tried to educate the American public about the need to secure all of the Atlantic Ocean, not just the Western Hemisphere, he closed his remarks with the statement, "Therefore, with profound consciousness of my responsibilities to my countrymen and to my country's cause, I have tonight issued a proclamation that an unlimited national emergency exists and requires the strengthening of our defense to the extreme limit of our national power and authority."[17]

Then, in typical Roosevelt fashion, he did nothing of substance to follow up on this announcement of a dire national emergency. Indeed, at a press conference the next day he denied that the announcement made any difference, remarked that he was not seeking changes to neutrality legislation, and dismissed the idea of escorting convoys.[18] Roosevelt's inexplicable about-face infuriated members of his cabinet, such as Secretary of War Stimson and Secretary of the Interior Harold Ickes, who favored early intervention. Even Roosevelt's closest aid and alter ego, Harry Hopkins, was perplexed.[19] Perhaps Roosevelt was reluctant to take concrete steps toward war, or, as Gloria Barron posits, he sought to avoid alienating the last noninterventionists, "whose support he and the country would ultimately need at the time of American entrance into the war."[20]

Noninterventionist sentiment had been ramping up in response to Roosevelt's introduction of the Lend-Lease legislation. Although he may have airily described the Lend-Lease bill as a way to "get rid of the silly, foolish old dollar sign," on a more practical level the legislation begged the question of how Lend-Lease materiel was to get to Britain, unleashing a blast of anti-interventionist sentiment.[21] Roosevelt publicly took a hands-off approach to the legislation, but it took two months of hard, behind-the-scenes work to secure passage. The debates turned out to be the last gasp of the anti-interventionist movement, but it was a bitter contest nonetheless. The vicious attacks, much of it directed personally at Roosevelt, bothered the normally thick-skinned president. Nonetheless, the debates educated public opinion, generating strong public and congressional support as the bill passed by wide margins of 60–31 in the Senate and 317–71 in the House.[22] Although passage solved the problem of the dollar sign, the problem of how to get the materiel across the oceans had not gone away.

At the same time, the spring of 1941 was a period of significant personal turmoil for Roosevelt. He suffered multiple bouts of flu, and, in the days before antibiotics, recurring sinus, upper respiratory, and throat infections sapped his strength. Hemorrhoids, a by-product of being confined to his wheel chair due to polio, left him anemic. Eleanor, his wife, continually pressured him on economic and social issues. In early June, Marguerite "Missy" LeHand, Roosevelt's longtime secretary, factotum, and organizing force within the White House, suffered two severe strokes, removing the administrative disciple that Roosevelt so desperately needed.[23]

All the while, Roosevelt's key advisers—Morgenthau, Stimson, Knox, Hopkins, and others—prodded him to do more to assist Britain, including escorting convoys. Churchill continued a steady diet of information that allowed Roosevelt to draw his own inferences about the need for more active American involvement.[24] However, FDR remained reluctant to act. Because of his secretive ways, reliance on oral communications that often left advisers wondering what he had really said, and an absence of documentation, one is unlikely to know with certainty why he was so unwilling. Was Roosevelt serious about all means short of war and no more? Would measures include naval and air but not ground forces? Had his previous initiatives been prudent but ad hoc planning, or had he chosen a path? Was he intent on intervening, but only after ensuring that he had overwhelming public support, thereby avoiding problems similar to those Woodrow Wilson suffered after World War I? Was he torn and simply not ready to decide? Roosevelt's comment "When I don't know how to move, I sit" may offer the best insight historians can find.[25] Regardless of why, it is clear that Roosevelt was not leading in the spring and early summer of 1941.

Although the provisions of the ABC-1 Report were to take effect only after U.S. entry into the war, and neither government had approved the report, British and U.S. militaries wasted little time implementing key aspects of the document. Creating conduits for information flow between the two militaries was a logical priority for ensuring effective future planning. The report specified the ultimate size, organization, and tasks of the Military Missions once the United States entered the war, but it contained no provisions for any liaison body to coordinate the two national staffs' activities until that time. To bridge this gap, the ABC-1 conferees recommended the institution of Nucleus Military Missions as quickly as possible "in order that certain details of policies and plans that have been agreed to may be settled in advance and that the change over from peace to war may be effected rapidly and smoothly when the time comes."[26]

Both partners began organizing their respective missions. Rear Admiral Ghormley received his appointment as the special naval observer (SPENAVO) of the Nucleus Mission along with his initial instructions on 5 April 1941. Responsible only to the CNO, Ghormley was to cooperate with the U.S. ambassador to Britain, the U.S. naval attaché, and army representatives. Admiral Stark empowered Ghormley to enter into military discussions, but with no political commitments, to "expedite the preparation of surface, air, and submarine bases for United States naval forces in Europe."[27] Stark also charged Ghormley with establishing the close cooperation necessary to ensure the security of the sea lines of communication to the British Isles. Hearkening back to Admiral William Sims's position in World War I, Ghormley would command all naval forces in northern Europe if the United States entered the war.[28] Ghormley arrived in England on or about 20 April.

Planning for the army portion of the mission was more prolonged because the army had not been as deeply engaged in conversations. In early April, the WPD recommended to General Marshall the early establishment of an army mission under a major general who would be qualified to become the commanding general of all U.S. Army forces in the United Kingdom if and when the United States entered the war.[29] Marshall selected Major General James E. Chaney, an interesting choice for the chief of the Special Army Observer Group (SPOBS) in London who would eventually serve as the initial commander of all U.S. Army and Army Air Force units in the British Isles. Born in Chaney, Maryland, on 16 March 1885, Chaney attended Baltimore City College from 1900 to 1904 before graduating from West Point in 1908 and accepting a commission in the infantry. He served in the Office of the Chief of the Air Service, AEF, during World War I. Transferring to the Air Service in 1920, Chaney eventually served in the Office of the Chief of the Air Corps from 1931 to 1934 and as assistant chief of the Air Corps from 1934 to 1938. After a short reversion to colonel, he was once again a brigadier general in January 1940 when he assumed command of the Air Defense Command. A major general in October 1940, he served as an air observer in the United Kingdom during 1940–1941. After leading SPOBS, he was the initial commanding general of the U.S. Army Forces British Isles from January to June 1942 and subsequently commander of the First Air Force in 1942–1943. After commanding the Army Air Force Basic Training Center in 1943–1944, he served sequentially as the chief of the U.S. delegation of the Anglo-American Delegation to Portugal, commanding general for U.S. Army forces in the Battle for Iwo Jima; commander of U.S. Forces Iwo Jima; commanding general of Western Pacific Base Command; and finally, in October 1945, a member and later president of the secretary of war's Personnel Board in Washington, D.C. Chaney retired in 1947.[30]

Marshall directed Chaney, in conjunction with Ghormley, to engage in negotiations with the British Chiefs of Staff on any military affairs common to U.S. and British interests. Chaney's subordinate special army observers were to consolidate all information and requests and serve as the sole clearinghouse for the exchange of military information on the British side of the Atlantic. Marshall also informed Chaney that he eventually would command all U.S. Army forces sent to Britain. Of interest is the fact that Chaney was an Army Air Corps officer. He ultimately would command all U.S. Army forces in the United Kingdom, so the choice of him for that position may indicate that U.S. leaders were thinking predominantly in terms of employing naval and air forces, with any eventual ground forces a distant third. Arriving in London on 19 May, Chaney quickly formed SPOBS.[31]

Together, the SPENAVO and SPOBS constituted the U.S. Special Observer Group (USSOG) (see figure 3). The name caused some confusion within British and even U.S. ranks—first, because of its similarity to the Strong–Emmons–Ghormley mission of the previous autumn and because large numbers of individual service representatives already in Britain were designated "special observers." Second, despite the encompassing title, USSOG was in no way a corporate body. Chaney and Ghormley had been selected separately and had been given different instructions, had distinct reporting chains, and would

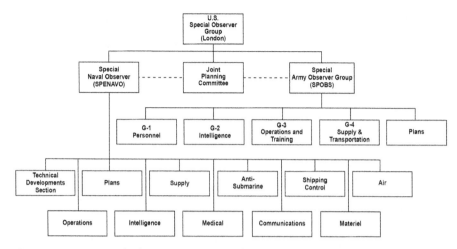

Figure 3. U.S. Special Observer Group, London, May 1941 (*Sources:* AL [41] First Meeting, 29 May 1941, COMNAVEU, Series II, File 190, RG 38.2.4, NACP; Tracy B. Kittredge, "Administrative History, U.S. Naval Forces, Europe," 10, 12, 14, and 19, Tracy B. Kittredge Papers, OAB, NHHC)

only loosely coordinate between each other. That each element of USSOG operated autonomously and frequently without coordinating with each other only further perplexed their British counterparts, who were used to the much more coordinated operating style of the British Chiefs of Staff system.[32]

The importance that the U.S. military placed on USSOG is evident in the quality of the personnel assigned to the missions. For example, within SPOBS, of the initial ten staff officers assigned, seven became general officers: Charles L. Bolte, Homer Case, John W. Coffey, John E. Dahlquist, George W. Griner Jr., Jerry V. Matejka, and Harold M. McClelland. Three—Bolte, Dahlquist, and Griner—went on to be division commanders. Matejka and McClelland became chief of their respective army and army air force signal branches. Bolte, Dahlquist, and McNarney eventually served as four-star generals.[33]

The British also had been hard at the work of fielding their own Nucleus Missions. As early as 4 April, they notified the U.S. Navy and War Departments that Rear Admiral Victor H. Danckwerts, Major General Sir Frederick Beaumont-Nesbitt, and Air Commodore George W. Pirie would head their initial contingent.[34] These arrangements, however, were a stopgap until the British created a British Nucleus Mission in Washington. By late April, the British outlined the major functions of the British Joint Staff Mission (BJSM): first, to represent as a corporate body the British Chiefs of Staff vis-à-vis the U.S.

Easier Said Than Done   169

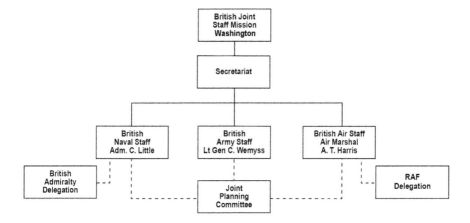

Figure 4. British Joint Staff Mission, Washington, D.C., May 1941 (*Source:* "History of the BAS: The Story of the J.S.M.," Washington, D.C., 1941–1945, CAB 122/1579, TNA: PRO)

Chiefs of Staff and, second, for each head of service to represent in an individual capacity his respective branch of arms vis-à-vis the appropriate service of the U.S. military.[35] Admiral Sir Charles Little, previously the second sea lord; Lieutenant General Henry C. B. Wemyss, late adjutant general of the army; and Air Vice Marshal Arthur T. Harris, formerly the deputy chief of the Air Staff formed the corporate leadership of the British Nucleus Mission.[36] These senior officers constituted a very high-powered delegation, reflecting the importance attached to the mission's efforts, and the broad range of responsibilities and authority that the British government assigned to the mission offers a further indication of the BJSM's significance.[37]

The British organized the BJSM into three main sections to carry out its extensive duties—the British Naval Staff, the British Army Staff, and the British Air Staff. In addition, the British Admiralty Delegation, which controlled all British naval missions in North America, and the RAF Delegation, which controlled all air force missions, retained a semi-independent role within the BJSM.[38] (See figure 4.) Each subordinate organization mirrored the lines of its respective service headquarters in London and contributed to the general corporate responsibilities of the BJSM as a whole (see figures 5 and 6).[39]

The difficulties encountered in creating coherent and efficient channels of communication between the British Chiefs of Staff and the U.S. Chiefs of Staff illustrate the types of problems confronting the Anglo-American coalition as the British and Americans implemented the ABC-1 agreements. For example,

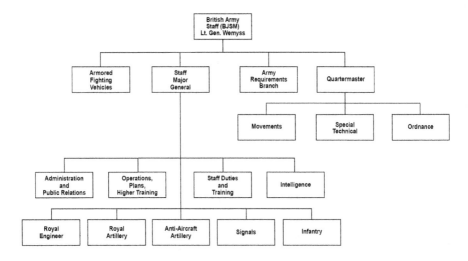

Figure 5. British Army Staff, British Joint Staff Mission, May 1941 (*Source:* Memo, Maj. Gen. Sir Frederick Beaumont-Nesbitt to Brig. Gen. Leonard T. Gerow, 8 Aug. 1941, Army Air Force 334.8, RG 18/293, NACP)

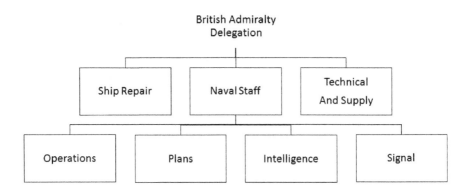

Figure 6. British Admiralty Delegation, British Joint Staff Mission, June 1941 (*Sources:* Lord Halifax to Anthony Eden, message, 17 May 1941, CAB 122/12, TNA: PRO; Rear Adm. Victor Danckwerts to CNO, 4 June 1941, in Tracy Kittredge, "Anglo-American Naval Cooperation, 1939–1945," 332, Tracy B. Kittredge Papers, OAB, NHHC)

the U.S. military at all levels lacked an effective organization for formulating joint U.S. plans. At the highest level, as Captain Arthur W. Clarke, the assistant naval attaché who doubled as British special naval liaison officer to President Roosevelt, noted, "the President acts alone (or at least only with Hopkins and one or two others). He takes decisions without prior consultation with his Chiefs of Staff, and based entirely on the appreciations and knowledge that come to him through all sorts of regular and irregular channels." Clark went on to add that this confused situation could be used to British advantage: "If he [Roosevelt] can be led to understand that he has an authoritative British source in Washington at his elbow, who will always tell him the truth and give him considered military opinion, he is more likely to act along lines commensurate with our views."[40]

Opaqueness at the top of the American planning process exacerbated a lack of coordination at subordinate levels. In a report to their Chiefs of Staff on ABC-1, the British delegation noted, for example, that although the Americans possessed the mechanisms for internal consultation—such as the Defense Advisory Committee, the Joint Army–Navy Board, and the Joint Planning Committee—they seemed incapable of reaching a coordinated or compromise position on any given issue. Instead, they depended on "individual and sporadic personal contacts." As a result, the British "were confronted on several occasions by a U.S. Committee which had made no attempt to resolve its own internal differences of opinion, and failed to appreciate the desirability of meeting us with a carefully considered inter-Service opinion."[41]

The British made their American interlocutors aware of their concerns during a 25 March meeting between Secretary of the Navy Knox, Secretary of War Stimson, Marshall, Stark, and the British delegation to ABC-1. They detailed their misgivings about the American planning machinery and urged U.S. leaders to adopt the more salient features of the British system, such as making members of the Joint Planning Committee direct representatives of the U.S. Chiefs of Staff and creating a permanent joint secretariat.[42] Neither short-term nor long-term evidence indicates that the U.S. authorities accepted this advice, and the lack of an effective joint planning organization at the higher levels of U.S. military decision making would continue to plague the Anglo-American coalition.[43]

This begs the obvious question: Why did the Americans fail to appreciate these shortcomings and take no action to alleviate them? From the available evidence, it is difficult to discern an obvious answer. A plausible reason is that the mobilization of a massive war machine, incorporating new technologies and developing the myriad plans necessary to wage modern warfare, absorbed the full energies of the U.S. services. Although striving to achieve a more efficient and coherent working relationship, the U.S. Chiefs of Staff had not yet been able to institutionalize the solutions, and it would take time before the Americans could birth a successful joint organization. Equally plausible is that interservice rivalries, combined with Roosevelt's divide-and-rule methods of leadership, may have obstructed greater compromise and cooperation.

The absence of a joint U.S. planning system also contributed to problems at lower levels of cooperation. In USSOG, it appears that the SPENAVO and his assistants set up a separate planning system with their British counterparts and then kept SPOBS personnel in the dark. As Colonel Charles L. Bolte, initially plans officer and later chief of staff at SPOBS, noted, "It seemed to me that my primary task was to try and find out from our Navy what they knew and what was going on."[44] Colonel John Dahlquist, SPOBS G-1 (personnel), noted in his diary that he had to set up a conference to work out problems in exchanging information with the U.S. Navy.[45]

Concomitant with the problems within the U.S. planning system was confusion within the British political and military leadership over the amount of information the Americans could receive. Although this issue surfaced periodically throughout the growing relationship, the dispatch of the BJSM to Washington and the arrival of USSOG in London dramatically increased the need for American access to sensitive information.[46] The process by which the British reached an eventual decision on the extent of information available to the U.S. representatives and the machinery required for its dissemination offers insights into the difficulties involved in coalition collaboration.[47]

The British Joint Planning Committee initially recommended that the Americans receive full access to all information, including daily operational reports, intelligence evaluations, and periodic strategic appreciations. Air Chief Marshal Charles Portal and Major General Sir John Kennedy argued that to give the Americans such information before they became active allies would involve U.S. staffs in the formulation of British policy, to the possible detriment of British interests. From Washington, Lord Halifax and Admiral Bellairs pointed out that if the British wanted the United States to continue providing significant aid to Great Britain under Lend-Lease, President Roosevelt would need complete and accurate information. Halifax and Bellairs also noted that the U.S. Chiefs of Staff continued to provide substantial amounts of data to British representatives in Washington. Under such circumstances, they believed, the British had little choice but to grant U.S. representatives full access.[48] Unable to resolve their differences, the British Chiefs of Staff referred the subject back to the Joint Planning Committee, which reaffirmed their original recommendation and added that USSOG personnel should work directly with their British counterparts. They even recommended that Chaney and Ghormley sit with the British Chiefs of Staff Committee when that body addressed matters of coalition interest and that American planners should associate with the British Joint Planning Committee, though the Americans would not be actual members of either group.[49]

The British Chiefs of Staff ultimately accepted the Joint Planning Committee's advice with one key exception: instead of implementing the communications channels contained in the ABC-1 agreement, they proposed what they considered a more streamlined system for the exchange of information.[50] The British Chiefs of Staff essentially felt that the originator of any correspondence should determine the specific channel of transmission—that is, either London to BJSM to U.S. Chiefs of Staff or London to USSOG to U.S. Chiefs of Staff. These procedures would replace the more cumbersome channels specified in the ABC-1 Report, which stipulated that the capital of the nation tasked with strategic responsibility for the area in question would originate any communications. American planners in London readily agreed to the British ideas, but their superiors in Washington rejected the proposals out of hand, refusing to consider any alteration of the ABC-1 Report. As a result, the two military establishments carried out a spirited debate over the channels of communication during the next six weeks. Finally, in mid-August, the two parties agreed that they would in fact utilize the provisions of ABC-1.[51] Although this may seem a trivial example of the difficulties encountered in implementing the ABC-1 accords, establishing the essential channels of communication between the British and U.S. Chiefs of Staff was a prerequisite for resolving any other item on the agenda of Anglo-American collaboration.

The differing aspects of operational planning carried out by the BJSM and USSOG provides another example of the difficulties encountered during early implementation of the ABC-1 Report. Despite the broad scope of responsibilities and missions assigned, it does not appear from the available material that the BJSM developed plans to implement the agreed coalition strategy. Instead, it seems that most planning took place in London between USSOG and the British Chiefs of Staff. The BJSM served simply as an information conduit between London and Washington that became increasingly more concerned with coordinating supply matters and less with strategic planning.[52]

Coalition planning in London proceeded at two different levels. At the upper echelon, USSOG met with the representatives of the British Chiefs of Staff. American staff officers concurrently developed the U.S. plans necessary to implement the decisions reached at the combined level. For example, shortly after Ghormley's return to Britain as the SPENAVO, he and his assistants began working with the British to fulfill the naval provisions of the ABC-1 Report for the Atlantic region. For the most part, the report required little more than close coordination between the two fleets. By the end of May, Ghormley and his Admiralty counterparts finished the initial exchange of convoy data, coordinated proposed naval dispositions in the western Atlantic and the British Home Waters, partially completed the plans for U.S.-British naval cooperation in the Western Hemisphere, reached an accord on the construction and equipping of U.S. naval bases in the United Kingdom, and concluded an agreement for the repair and refitting of a substantial portion of the British Fleet in U.S. shipyards.[53]

Not all efforts were equally successful. Difficulties arose, mostly from British attempts to alter provisions of the ABC-1 Report. For example, because of cruiser losses, the Royal Navy requested that the U.S. Navy assume greater responsibility for cruiser patrol in the Atlantic and the Northwest Approaches to the home isles. They added that redistribution of U.S. cruisers also would require transferring a suitable number of supporting destroyers. They did so, of course, without mentioning that this meant the U.S. Navy would take up operational responsibilities from the Royal Navy. Only in this manner, the British argued, could they reinforce their fleet in the Far East.[54] Ghormley cautioned against such a request, but the British pressed the issue. A week later Ghormley conveyed a stern response from Admiral Stark that "the situation now confronting me does not permit me to recommend that additional destroyers or escort vessels be loaned or transferred to the British."[55]

A second example of rigid U.S. adherence to the report concerns British efforts to alter command arrangements. Shortly after his return to London, Ghormley negotiated an agreement for command of American naval forces in the Western Approaches Command. Unfortunately, the provisions did not conform to ABC-1, and even though Ghormley proposed the changes, officials in the U.S. Navy Department adamantly refused to consider the new measures. They insisted that all U.S. naval forces operate only under American command and British strategic direction, though the CNO might grant case-by-case exceptions for extremely serious situations, such as an invasion of Iceland or Great Britain. Even under those circumstances, British command would have to flow through the U.S. flag officer in Londonderry.[56]

The U.S. Army took more time to get SPOBS up and running. As a result, the first meetings between the full USSOG and British authorities did not take place until 27 May 1941. Colonel Oliver Stanley, chairman of the British Joint Planning Committee, opened the discussions with the British view that "the main object in . . . establishing nucleus missions . . . was to ensure that the machinery would be ready so that the change-over from peace to war could be effected rapidly and smoothly if the United States decided to come into the war."[57] He then noted that the Chiefs of Staff Committee had designated the Joint Planning Staff as the liaison element between USSOG and the British Chiefs of Staff and suggested that a briefing on the British Chiefs of Staff organization and its procedures, practices, and methods might prove useful to the Americans.[58]

After the British explication of their planning and decision-making system, Brigadier General Joseph McNarney, SPOBS chief of staff, described the functions of USSOG. He noted that the first priority was "to coordinate all details in connection with the transportation, reception, location, accommodation, etc., of U.S. Army and Air Corps Forces which it was proposed should be employed in British areas under the Joint [Combined] United States–British basic war plan."[59] McNarney added that USSOG would coordinate British requests for U.S. equipment and materiel. He emphasized that SPOBS could reduce what had been a major impediment in Anglo-American cooperation if the British coordinated their materiel requirements before formally submitting requests to Washington. He then informed the British that Major General Chaney also had responsibility for advising the U.S. Chiefs of Staff on the best means of employing U.S. forces in British areas and that Chaney could fulfill this mission only if the British kept the U.S. mission closely abreast of the British strategic situation, including the conditions not only in the United Kingdom but also in the Middle East and Far East. McNarney concluded by carefully pointing out that "at the present stage, however, while the United States were [sic] not in the war, there was little joint [combined] planning that could be done other than might arise over modifications to the 'Joint Basic War Plan' agreed in Washington."[60] Thus, although substantial collaboration was still possible, planners remained limited by the conservative outlook that still bound the U.S. Chiefs of Staff.

The first meeting dealing with substantive issues of implementing the provisions of the ABC-1 Report convened on 3 June. During this wide-ranging meeting, the staffs addressed plans for the U.S. relief of British ground and air units in Iceland, the movement of U.S. Army Air Corps and antiaircraft artillery elements to relieve British units in Northern Ireland, and the movement of a token U.S. Army force to the United Kingdom. The bulk of the discussion focused on the detailed American answers to more than one hundred questions from the British that covered almost every aspect of the proposed deployment of American forces, such as ration plans, troop billets, ammunition storage, number of vehicles by type, as well as such major issues as airdrome locations and the location of the token regimental force. The detailed nature of the written questions and answers allowed the representatives quickly to pass over the numerous issues, noting many agreements and few disagreements.[61]

After reviewing the questions and answers, the planners identified a number of major points not yet addressed. In particular, Chaney emphasized that all decisions, but in particular those concerned with the relief of Iceland, required rapid resolution. To coordinate details still outstanding, the British recommended establishing several combined working committees broken down into four major functional areas: (1) personnel, discipline, welfare, and medical; (2) accommodations, bases, maintenance, and movements; (3) communications; and (4) air defense and coastal defense of Iceland.[62] From this point, as Colonel Dahlquist later noted, "the bulk of the work . . . was generally done by direct communications between the interested staff officer of SPOBS and the pertinent British staff officer or agency."[63] Over the course of the next several weeks, the various committees addressed and usually resolved lesser but vital details necessary for the efficient implementation of the ABC-1 accords.[64]

Perhaps the most important of these early deliberations concerned the arrangements for American relief of British forces in Iceland. As early as 4 June, the two groups met to discuss the requirements for the antiaircraft defenses of the island. The next day, Colonel George W. Griner, SPOBS G-4 (supply), met to discuss the living accommodations, transport arrangements, and port facilities that would be available to U.S. forces, all of which he described as inadequate. A meeting between McNarney and British Air Ministry representatives on 6 June established a War Office–Admiralty–Air Ministry committee to work with SPOBS staff officers on the movement of U.S. forces to Iceland and their subsequent relief of British forces.[65] The success of their discussions allowed SPOBS to dispatch a reconnaissance party to Iceland on 11 June. Based on the need to construct adequate facilities before the full blast of winter, Chaney recommended to the War Department that the first U.S. convoy arrive in Iceland before 31 July 1941. Thus, if American forces were to relieve British forces before the summer of 1942, the War Department would have to decide quickly and well before U.S. entry into the war.[66]

As part of planning for the relief of the British forces in the United Kingdom, USSOG carried out extensive reconnaissance in Northern Ireland and Scotland for prospective sites of U.S. naval and air bases as well as inspections of potential locations for the token ground force in central and southeastern England.[67] Indeed, even before the formal establishment of USSOG, Captain Louis Denfield, U.S. Navy, accompanied by two assistants, conducted a reconnaissance of potential naval bases in Northern Ireland and Scotland. He suggested establishing naval installations at Londonderry and Rosneath on the Clyde and seaplane facilities at Loch Erne in Northern Ireland and Loch Ryan in Scotland. President Roosevelt released $50 million from Lend-Lease funds, and construction on the sites began in late May.[68]

In addition to its efforts to implement the ABC-1 Report, USSOG oftentimes had to address problems not anticipated in the agreement. For instance, although the final report stipulated the command arrangements between the highest levels of British and American units, it did not anticipate the difficulties encountered at lower echelons of British and American cooperation. One illuminating example of such a problem that Bolte later cited concerned the commander of a U.S. antiaircraft unit in Northern Ireland who found himself responsible to three separate chains of command. Although an army officer, he was under the operational control of the RAF because of British organizational policies, yet he was directly responsible to the U.S. naval officer commanding the base, and he reported to SPOBS in London for all administrative, logistical, and command matters.[69]

In early August, General Chaney submitted a report to the War Department that summarized SPOBS's accomplishments, provided an assessment of the current strategic situation, and offered his recommendations for future action. Although immediate events might appear grim, Chaney remained optimistic about the eventual outcome. He noted that so long as Russian resistance continued, there was little chance of a German invasion of Britain. In addition, he pointed out that although the British had suffered reverses in the Middle East, they would hold on.[70] Chaney's recommendations for future action covered a wide range of topics. He advocated increasing the fighter strength in Northern Ireland to four day and two night squadrons, although most of the materials and construction workers necessary to build bases for these aircraft would have to come from the United States. Chaney also addressed ongoing SPOBS reconnaissance in Scotland, underscoring that he made no commitments to take over any British site or installation. He noted that SPOBS continually emphasized it was not authorized to make any commitments and that any new construction would be contingent upon U.S. entry into the war. Finally, if the United States dispatched larger numbers of troops to the United Kingdom than currently anticipated, he recommended establishing a headquarters for the European Theater of Operations as soon as possible after American entry into the war.[71]

British and U.S. planners also were at work in the Pacific as they sought to devise a viable strategy for the Far East, which had eluded the negotiators of the ABC-1 Report. Both British and U.S. military establishments responded quickly to the recommendation of the ABC-1 planners, who had urged that "the Chiefs of Staff of the United States and United Kingdom should convene a Conference of these Commanders [of Associated and Allied Forces] in the Far East as soon as possible."[72] As a result, the British called for a conference in Singapore on 21–27 April 1941.

In the first week of April, Stark and Marshall notified their respective commanders, Admiral Hart and Major General George Grunert, commanding general of the Philippines, of the upcoming talks. The chiefs of service authorized each commander to send a representative. Local preparations in Manila were hit or miss. Only Grunert received a complete copy of the ABC-1 Report for review as well as instructions from Marshall to begin planning immediately based on the report. Inexplicably, Grunert did not immediately share the report with Hart, who had only a few hours to review the document before his representative, Captain William Purnell, had to depart for Singapore.[73]

The British, in contrast, engaged in their customary detailed preparatory work. Air Chief Marshal Sir H. Robert Brooke-Popham, CINC, Far East, and designated chair of the conference, received a lengthy summary of the ABC-1 Report and his instructions for the discussions on 10 April. The talks would occur in two stages: a first conference between American, Dutch, and British representatives, then a follow-up meeting between British and Dutch officers. Brooke-Popham was to ensure that the talks were devoid of any political commitments, which were subject to governmental approval, and conducted with complete frankness. Delegates were "to prepare plans for the conduct of Military [sic] operations in the Far East on the basis of [the] report of [the] Washington Conference [ABC-1]." Finally, Brooke-Popham also was to seek agreement on the employment and disposition of all forces before and after the arrival of the British Far East Fleet and determine the details of continued cooperation, such as liaison, communications, exchanges, and the like.[74]

The American-Dutch-British (ADB) Conference convened on 21 April 1941 with twenty-six delegates in attendance, representing five nations and fifteen separate headquarters. Captain Purnell and Colonel A. C. McBride, assistant chief of staff to Major General Grunert, were the principal U.S. representatives, although Captain A. Allen and Lieutenant Colonel Frank Brink, the U.S. naval and army observers in Singapore, also attended. Air Chief Marshal Brooke-Popham had requested Hart and Grunert and later expressed disappointment because he felt the U.S. attendees were too junior in rank and seemed apprehensive of their superiors in Washington.[75]

Over the course of the next six days, the representatives hammered out an agreement on the strategic concept of operations that would have far-reaching implications both for the defense of Allied interests in the Far East and on continued Anglo-American cooperation.[76] The report initially outlined probable Japanese and friendly courses of action, concluding that the Japanese could advance only incrementally and that the presence of the U.S. Pacific and Asiatic Fleets would deter Japan from a major move south unless "the Japanese accept great risks."[77] Future events would prove these conclusions largely inaccurate because the planners seriously misjudged Japanese capabilities. Given the long history of Japanese bold action, the delegates should have examined the possibility that the Japanese might pursue a more daring course of action.

An optimistic appreciation of coalition offensive capabilities tipped the opposite end of the scale. Within the report, the attendees outlined the importance of air operations against Japanese-occupied territories and home islands, the use of Luzon as a deterrent to Japanese action in Southeast Asia, the support of Chinese regular forces, the establishment of Chinese irregular forces, the organization of subversive activities in Japan, and the immediate institution of an economic blockade.[78] Nowhere, however, did the planners elaborate on the forces or plans necessary for such operations; thus, their forecasts represented wishful thinking at best.

Given the wide range of potential Japanese operations and the limited ability of the Associated Powers to respond, the delegates underscored the necessity for collective action. Their recommendations, however, concerning the circumstances under which such action should occur undoubtedly exceeded their instructions against political commitments. The delegates proposed that their governments consider Japanese movements into Thailand, Portuguese Timor, or New Caledonia as a direct act of war and that home governments authorize immediate military counteraction without referral to political decision makers. In addition, they recommended that the movement of large bodies of Japanese warships or convoys toward the Philippines or Malaya or movements that crossed the 6-degree north parallel should constitute an immediate casus belli. In short, the delegates wanted to make an automatic military response contingent on vague, prearranged political commitments. Hart later told Stark that Purnell objected to these provisions, but the remainder of the delegates overruled him.[79]

The planners also failed to follow the overarching guidance contained in the ABC-1 Report. Strategic planning at the conference paid lip service to the primacy of the Atlantic theater and the subsequent need to conduct a strategic defensive in the Far East. The planners instead adopted a very aggressive strategy for responding to Japanese attack. Moreover, the ADB Report based the defense of the Far East not only on protection of the sea-lanes but also on the security of Singapore. They also designated retention of Luzon as important to the security of the Far East even though U.S. planners had long ago announced that they would not reinforce the Philippines, essentially writing off the islands.[80]

Subordinate plans to support this strategy were rather hazy. The representatives primarily foresaw the use of independent naval forces operating to secure their respective national territories. Air and land forces, with the exception of British units guarding the Burma and Malaya frontiers, would defend air and sea bases from enemy attack. Air forces would seek out and attack raiders, naval forces, and expeditions.[81] Hearkening back to previous conferences at Singapore, the delegates divided the employment of the naval forces into two phases: before and after the arrival of the British Far Eastern Fleet. In the initial period, Dutch naval elements would ensure the local defense of their territories. Royal Navy and dominion squadrons would defend local bases and the empire's sea lines of communication. The U.S. Asiatic Fleet would first support the defense of Luzon and then withdraw to Singapore to operate under the strategic direction of the British CINC, China. The report offered little guidance on how to carry out these missions.[82]

Plans for executing phase two were even less precise. Upon its arrival, the Far Eastern Fleet would operate from Singapore. Even though the combined naval forces of the Associated Powers would be inferior in size and capabilities to the Japanese main fleet, the delegates proposed "to seize the initiative, launch powerful counterattacks against such Japanese forces as may have established their position in territories of Associated Powers, and intensify the attack on Japanese forces, territories, and sea communications."[83] This optimism notwithstanding, the report contained the all-important caveat that "so many developments must precede the arrival of the British Far Eastern Fleet that it is not profitable to examine in greater detail the operations that would then be possible."[84] In other words, more than a little doubt existed about whether the partners would be able to retain their position until the fleet reached Singapore or that the British Fleet would even arrive. Regardless, the net result remained that no strategic plan existed for the second phase.

The report dealt more firmly with matters of command. Planners confirmed, as specified in the ABC-1 Report, that the United States would exercise unified command in the Pacific. Within the Far East, the CINC of the British China Station would command all naval forces except those elements of the U.S. Asiatic Fleet defending the Philippines. The delegates also called for the unified command of all air assets under the CINC, Far East, to ensure maximum effectiveness. All land forces would remain under national command.[85] Finally, the report confirmed the adequacy of existing liaison arrangements, outlined current communication procedures, and called for a conference at the end of May to coordinate communications, codes, and cyphers.[86] The negotiations ended on 27 April, when the various representatives signed the approved report and departed for their respective headquarters.

The conference report received mixed reviews. The American view was largely negative. In a letter to the War Department, General Grunert noted that the air and land forces currently at hand were insufficient to fulfill the missions assigned in the report. Worse still from an American perspective was that "the naval cooperation envisaged by the conference appears to favor defense of Singapore, trade lanes, and sea communications and leaves the support of the Philippine land and air defense more or less incidental to the former."[87] In his report to the CNO, Admiral Hart echoed Grunert's complaints and provided an even more detailed criticism. Hart strongly disagreed with the conclusions that the Japanese could not attack more than one objective at a time and believed that the Japanese could simultaneously attack the Netherlands East Indies, Australia, and New Zealand. The defensive nature of the report, the absence of any operational planning, and the lack of attention paid to the defense of the Malay Barrier all greatly bothered Hart. Finally, Hart opposed British attempts to tie home governments to a political decision to "delegate authority to Far East Commanders to commence hostilities in the event of certain Japanese actions."[88]

The British Chiefs of Staff, in contrast, were generally satisfied with the conference results. Granted, planners in London had only a summarized report to work from as they questioned several key findings, such as the political commitments and the importance of Luzon. Any misgivings they had, however, stemmed more from the fact that these issues depended on American attitudes and not that they varied from British strategic thinking. Thus, after offering a few minor criticisms, the Joint Planning Committee concurred with the major recommendations of the conference.[89]

The British eventually would find out that the Americans did not share their views, but unforeseen circumstances delayed the U.S. response. One striking example sums up how things went wrong and then cascaded. American authorities in Washington did not receive a complete copy of the ADB Report until nearly two months elapsed. Although Grunert forwarded a copy via Pan American Air Clipper on 8 May, representatives of the commandant of the Twelfth Naval District in San Francisco intercepted the report. Instead of forwarding the report by airmail, they sent it literally on a slow boat to Norfolk,

Virginia, which was not due there until 16 June.[90] As a result, U.S. authorities had to rely initially on a summarized version of the report obtained from the BJSM. The initial U.S. review of this abbreviated report resulted in a lukewarm verdict. Both Stark and Marshall informed the British that although the summary provided the general gist of the conclusions reached at the conference, they would give no final approval or disapproval until they had an opportunity to examine the full text.[91]

In addition to the summarized report, the British included a proposal for revising their command structure in the Far East. The attachment also described a British recommendation for new liaison arrangements between the British and American naval commanders.[92] The U.S. response to these proposals was harsh and emphatic. Commander L. R. McDowall, secretary to the Joint Army–Navy Board, in a letter to the BJSM noted that the CNO and CSA "regret they must reject this paper in its entirety, as either being contrary to the commitments of ABC-1, or as relating to matters which are the sole concern of the British Government. They see no present need for a paper of this character, but will consider new proposals if the British Chiefs of Staff are of an opinion that such are necessary."[93] The tenor of the response was due in part to long-standing American objections to the British command structures in the Far East, which U.S. authorities believed were unduly complex and significantly complicated liaison matters. The British previously felt unable to comply with U.S. requests to simplify those command arrangements because of problems involved in coordinating with dominion naval forces.[94] As a result, long-standing friction over command and liaison arrangements in the Far East provided the spark for already primed tinder.

The vehemence of the American response took the British aback. As far as they were concerned, they had simply kept the U.S. authorities informed of changes within the internal British command structure, which in no way conflicted with ABC-1. Indeed, the British believed that the entire matter lay beyond American purview. They had provided the American CNO and army chief of staff a copy of the proposals out of simple courtesy. In a pointed rebuke, Admiral Danckwerts informed the prickly Turner that "I suggest that if, in the future, you receive a paper from us whose purpose you do not clearly understand, it would assist the process of cooperation if you were to send for me and ask me to explain it before the Chief of Naval Operations writes an official letter rejecting a paper which is only sent for his information."[95]

Danckwerts's written admonition apparently did not end the matter. Turner provided a picayune critique of the British arrangements that accentuated how the Americans, or at least Turner and presumably his superiors, saw the provisions of ABC-1 in an almost contractual manner.⁹⁶ As Mark Lowenthal describes the different views of ABC-1, "for Britain ABC-1 was an ad hoc compromise . . . another step towards actual war; . . . for the United States it was the holy writ of grand strategy . . . a precise definition of roles should war eventuate."⁹⁷ Lowenthal opines that an absence of clear political guidance was largely responsible for this rigid adherence to the ABC-1 Report. Because Roosevelt had neither approved nor disapproved the report, any changes to ABC-1 might require new negotiations, which the American military very much wanted to avoid. In addition, Lowenthal concludes that, "given the lurking American suspicions of British methods and motives, adherence to ABC-1 became a test of faith between the prospective allies when viewed from Washington."⁹⁸ Shortly thereafter, Danckwerts met with Turner, and "after a somewhat acid discussion" they decided to defer the matter until the two staffs could discuss the entire ADB Report.⁹⁹ However, the matter clearly left a bitter aftertaste. In a letter to the vice chief of the British Naval Staff, Admiral Thomas Phillips, Danckwerts commented that the Americans had reacted badly and "have almost accused me of having pulled the wool over their eyes and concealing these arrangements during the process of the Joint Staff Conversations [ABC-1]. It produced from them a somewhat tasteless letter [from the CNO and chief of staff of the army]."¹⁰⁰

In the midst of this brouhaha, the Americans finally obtained a copy of the full ADB Report and began dissecting its contents. By 3 July, the U.S. authorities had found the conference recommendations wanting in almost every instance. Foremost, the Americans noted that, despite the disclaimer in the introduction, the report contained explicit political commitments with which U.S. authorities simply could not agree. The U.S. Chiefs of Staff expressed willingness, nonetheless, to refer these points to respective governments for decision. Should national leaders resolve the political questions, then the militaries could return to the issues.¹⁰¹

The U.S. Chiefs of Staff next reiterated their objections to the new British command arrangements. Under ABC-1, the United States had agreed to place the U.S. Asiatic Fleet under British strategic direction. With the new command arrangements, U.S. authorities had concerns that the British might employ the U.S. Asiatic Fleet in the Indian Ocean, outside the Far East, and in defense of solely British interests. The U.S. Chiefs of Staff also questioned the purpose of coordinating with an existing command structure only to replace it with a new, inexperienced organization once war broke out.¹⁰² As a result, the U.S. Chiefs of Staff eventually withdrew American naval forces in the Far East from British strategic control.¹⁰³

On a more fundamental level, the American authorities, echoing Hart, expressed doubt that the representatives at Singapore had formulated viable operational plans for the defense of the Far East. They pointed out that although the staff officers had been "assembled in Singapore for the purpose of drawing up a practical operating plan for the Far East in accordance with the ABC agreements[, the] report of the ADB conversations cannot be considered as a practical operating plan. . . . [T]here is no strategic operating plan set forth for operations in common by the three Powers involved."[104] In particular, the Americans conveyed their displeasure at the significant failure of the report and therefore of the British to grasp the importance of defending the Netherlands East Indies, the so-called Malay Barrier. U.S. authorities underscored that, at British insistence, the ABC-1 Report had included a statement on the importance of the Far East to the commonwealth war effort. Yet, out of forty-eight British naval vessels available for deployment in the eastern theater, the ADB Report assigned only three ships to operate anywhere near the vicinity of the Malay Barrier. Radiating suspicion, the U.S. Chiefs of Staff bluntly observed, "All British naval forces are assigned to escort and patrol work, most of them at great distances from the position which the British Chiefs of Staff have asserted to be 'vital.' It may be pointed out that the naval defense of this position is entrusted, by the ADB report, solely to the United States and Dutch forces."[105]

The U.S. authorities also voiced dissatisfaction with several lesser but still important aspects of the report. They disagreed with the need to establish a combined staff headquartered in Singapore because they foresaw little necessity for a supreme commander. With no commander, there would be no need for a staff. Second, they noted that although the United States might strengthen the defense of the Philippines, the current strategic situation severely restricted American action. They were extremely hesitant, therefore, about sections of the report identifying Luzon as a base for offensive operations.[106] In their concluding paragraph, Stark and Marshall recommended that any future deliberations held in Singapore hold closely to a detailed agenda approved in advance by home governments. Finally, "the Chief of Naval Operations and the Chief of Staff will be pleased to entertain suggestions which [the British Chiefs of Staff] may have to offer with respect to such an agenda," clearly suggesting another conference to address shortcomings in the ADB Report.[107]

Despite the validity of the U.S. objections, it is worth pointing out that American authorities bore a fair share of responsibility for the flaws in the ADB Report—starting from the top down. As indicated earlier, President Roosevelt had neither approved the ABC-1 Report nor offered specific guidance. The U.S. military did not have an effective organization, mechanism, or process that would have helped create such an agenda. Hart and Grunert, therefore, operated under extremely vague guidance, and Hart had yet to receive a copy of the complete ABC-1 document. Moreover, Washington vetoed either Hart's or Grunert's attendance at the conference. As a result, the lower-ranked U.S. attendees were not as seasoned at the political-military interface as were the other delegates. In addition, all parties, including Washington, were trying to accomplish too much in too little time. The ADB Conference ran for less than a week in comparison to the nearly two months for ABC-1. Finally, and not least, the deep disagreements and deferred decisions on the Far East from ABC-1 did not get better with age. Differences continued to fester, increasing already high levels of frustration that took little to set off.

After USSOG presented these views, the British Chiefs of Staff turned American objections over to the Joint Planning Committee for evaluation. By 1 August, the Joint Planning Committee completed its work, which combined an analysis of the ADB Report and the U.S. reaction. For the most part, the staff planners' observations coincided with the Americans, though the conclusions drawn from their analysis differed substantially. The Joint Planning Committee judged that the main fault of the report stemmed from the delegates' failure to adhere to the conference's terms of reference. They also agreed with the American contention that the report contained overt political commitments.[108] On the matter of the proposed changes to British command structures in the Far East, however, the Joint Planning Committee rejected U.S. criticisms. They saw the issue as solely an internal British affair and remained convinced that either party could make any command arrangements it desired within its own areas of strategic responsibility. As far as British control of the U.S. Asiatic Fleet was concerned, the British felt certain that this would occur only after the U.S. position in the Philippines had become untenable. Unable to retire to Hawaii, the U.S. Asiatic Fleet would have to move to Singapore, where it was only logical for the fleet to fall under British operational control. If, however, the Americans continued to press on this last issue, then the planners favored amending that particular section of the ADB Report to meet any U.S. objections.[109]

The British Joint Planning Committee also expressed dismay at American criticism that the ADB conference failed to produce a practical plan for operations. Indeed, they somewhat plaintively remarked, "This is not understood. There is a complete outline plan for the initial employment of all naval forces; thereafter we must be guided by events."[110] Although this statement is true, it does reflect the British failure to understand what the U.S. authorities meant by the term *practical*. Yes, a plan existed, and plans may go only as far as the opening battle, but the Americans believed that the probable coalition had insufficient forces available in the Far East to accomplish the myriad tasks outlined even in phase one of the report. Thus, in American eyes, the "detailed" British plans were little more than wishful thinking.

At the same time, the British staff remained perplexed about the Americans' inability to grasp the realities of the British two-phase defensive strategy in the Far East. For the British, it was obvious that before the arrival of substantial reinforcements, local naval forces would be too weak to accomplish much more than limited defense, convoy, and escort duties. With this reality, the staff planners could not understand how the Americans could expect the British in phase one to deploy their understrength fleet in defense of the Malay Barrier.[111] Conversely, one can easily see how the American planners remained suspicious of actual British intent. The British clearly had failed to provide adequate means for the defense of Singapore, which they had declared be the keystone of the British Empire.

Finally, unlike their American counterparts, the British planners did not view these conflicts as serious. They believed that the coalition staffs could easily resolve any differences by addressing the specific points at issue. This, in the British view, required achieving agreement on the broad issues and then taking the time necessary to iron out minor conflicts. Given the deteriorating situation in the Far East, the Joint Planning Committee urged that the British and American staffs reach these general agreements as quickly as possible. Because the majority of the outstanding issues fell within the naval arena, the planners recommended a conference between the respective naval commanders in the Far East at the earliest opportunity.[112]

Although on the surface the British and U.S. staffs appeared to have agreed on the need for another conference to resolve differences in the Far East, strong undercurrents threatened resolution of the outstanding issues. For U.S. military authorities, the ADB Report was filled with illusions, fraught with danger, and loaded with conflicts. Worse, the report only increased their suspicions of British motives and exacerbated tensions within the coalition. To be fair to the conference participants in the Far East, their inability to resolve the larger issue was not entirely their fault. Only the highest levels of political and military leadership in London and Washington could resolve the basic problems of strategy. Unfortunately, those leaders had shifted the responsibility to local commanders in hopes that they might somehow cut through the Gordian knot that London and Washington had tied.

Fortunately for the growing partnership, a stronger community of trans-

Atlantic interests had allowed collaborative efforts in London to proceed quickly. Nevertheless, the critical question facing the emerging coalition was whether planners could continue that progress while bridging the wide divergence of strategic views of the Far East, overcoming wishful British thinking, reducing American suspicions of British motives, and devising strategies better aligned with the realities of the resources available. Moreover, coalition planners needed to accomplish all of this in the midst of a dynamic and rapidly changing strategic environment that was calling into question key elements of the coalition's agreed strategy.

Rear Admiral William S. Sims upon his return to the United States from the European theater, February 1919. Photo NH 2839, Naval History and Heritage Command.

General of the Armies John J. Pershing as chief of staff, U.S. Army. Personality Collection, Pep-Pete, RG827s, Temp Box 232, U.S. Army Military History Institute.

Captain Royal E. Ingersoll, ca. 1930s. Photo NH 90919, Naval History and Heritage Command.

Admiral William D. Leahy as chief of naval operations, ca. 1939. Photo NH 50873, Naval History and Heritage Command.

Major General Henry H. "Hap" Arnold, chief of the U.S. Army Air Corps, 1941. U.S. Army Signal Corps Photo 127185, Personality Collection, Arno-Arw, RG827s, Temp Box 10, Folder Henry H. Arnold, U.S. Army Military History Institute.

General George C. Marshall, chief of staff of the army, with Secretary of War Henry H. Woodring, August 1940. Signal Corps Photo 115869, George C. Marshall Collection, RG690sm, box of photos from 1881 to 1957, Folder 1920 to 1940, U.S. Army Military History Institute.

Vice Admiral Robert L. Ghormley, 1942. Photo NH80-G-12864-A, Naval History and Heritage Command.

Admiral Thomas C. Hart, commander in chief, U.S. Asiatic Fleet, 1939. Photo NH 492271-KN, Naval History and Heritage Command

Rear Admiral Richmond Kelly Turner, February 1944. Photo 80-G-216636, Naval History and Heritage Command.

President Franklin D. Roosevelt signing the Lend-Lease bill, March 11, 1941. U.S. Army Signal Corps Photograph 119174, Franklin D. Roosevelt Collection, RG393S, Box 1941, Folder 3, U.S. Army Military History Institute.

Major General James E. Chaney (right) and Brigadier Charles L. Bolte (left), London, 1942. Charles L. Bolte Collection, 1897–1968, Box 1, Folder 26, U.S. Army Military History Institute.

Staff of the Special Army Observer Group (SPOBS), London, 1941. Seated from left to right are the primary staff: Homer Case, Dale D. Hinman, Harold M. McClelland, Donald A. Davison, Joseph T. McNarney, James E. Chaney, Owen (?) Summers, Alfred J. Lyon, Charles L. Bolte, George W. Griner Jr., John E. Dahlquist. Charles L. Bolte Collection, 1897–1968, Box 1, Folder 23, U.S. Army Military History Institute.

President Franklin D. Roosevelt and Prime Minister Winston S. Churchill on board the H.M.S. *Prince of Wales* during the Atlantic Conference, August 1941. Standing immediately behind the president and the prime minister, from left to right, are General George C. Marshall, Admiral Ernest J. King, Admiral Harold R. Stark, and General Sir John Dill. U.S. Army Signal Corps Photograph 125855, Franklin D Roosevelt Collection, RG939s, Box 1, F117319–126976, U.S. Army Military History Institute.

Admiral Ernest J. King, ca. 1942. Photo 80-G-23712, Naval History and Heritage Command.

Senior U.S.-British military leaders on board the H.M.S. *Prince of Wales* during the Atlantic Conference, August 1941. *Left to right:* Air Chief Marshal Wilfrid Freeman, Major General Henry H. Arnold, Admiral Harold R. Stark, Admiral Sir Dudley Pound, Admiral Ernest J. King, General George C. Marshall, General Sir John Dill, Rear Admiral Richmond Kelly Turner. Photo GCM07086, George C. Marshall Foundation, Lexington, Va.

General George C. Marshall and the heads of the War Department General Staff, November 1941. *Left to right:* Brigadier General Leonard T. Gerow, War Plans Division; Brigadier General Raymond A. Wheeler, supply; Brigadier General Sherman Miles, intelligence; Major General Henry H. Arnold, U.S. Army Air Force; General George C. Marshall *(seated);* Brigadier Wade H. Haislip, personnel; Brigadier General Henry L. Twaddle, plans and training; Major General William Bryden *(seated),* general administration. U.S. Army Signal Corps Photo 125898, George C. Marshall Collection, RG690s, Box 1881 to 1957, Folder 1941, U.S. Army Military History Institute.

First picture ever taken at a U.S. Joint Army–Navy Board meeting, November 1941. *Seated left to right:* Brigadier General H. F. Loomis, Major General Henry H. Arnold, Major General William Bryden, General George C. Marshall, Admiral Harold R. Stark, Rear Admiral Royal E. Ingersoll, Rear Admiral John H. Towers, and Rear Admiral Richmond Kelly Turner. U.S. Army Signal Corps Photo 125899, George C. Marshall Collection, RG 690s, Box 1881 to 1957, Folder 1941, U.S. Army Military History Institute.

9

Muddy Waters

Reexamining the Coalition's Grand Strategy,
June–October 1941

The coalition's failure to agree on a strategic approach to the Far East was not the only thread left hanging from ABC-1. American negotiators never fully bought into the British policies and strategies for the Mediterranean and Middle East, but they were willing to gloss over these differences to move forward with the more pressing and more easily agreed upon provisions for the Atlantic region. However, with the debacles of spring and early summer 1941, U.S. military leaders could no longer overlook these differences. U.S. planners were especially concerned that British efforts in the Middle East were undermining the defense of the Far East, despite the British giving the latter priority above the Mediterranean. Worse, the Americans worried that the Mediterranean campaign was jeopardizing the defense of Britain, the coalition's top priority. In addition, the British were asking the United States to underwrite their position in the Mediterranean with massive infusions of materiel sorely needed for the U.S. Army and Army Air Force.[1]

Rapidly changing strategic conditions also called into question other issues agreed at ABC-1. As U.S. planners delved into the British strategy, questions arose over the heavy bomber offensive: Was the British targeting doctrine appropriate? Could bombing produce suitable results? And was production of heavy bombers the most effective use of scarce resources?[2] Although U.S. escort of convoys was to occur only after U.S. entry into the war, German successes in the Battle of the Atlantic caused the partners to examine whether U.S. escort of convoys would have to begin before formal U.S. belligerency.[3] The allocation of war materiel necessary to implement the provisions of the ABC-1 Report, in particular the limited means available to meet an exponential rise in U.S. requirements, continued to nettle planners. Ever-changing priorities also generated considerable friction within the coalition. Rising Japanese bellicosity raised concerns about a two-ocean war before the partners were ready.

Throughout this period, Churchill carried on low-key but persistent efforts to bring the United States into the war, while Roosevelt tacked to the winds of public opinion.[4]

The greatest geostrategic shift stemmed from the German invasion of Russia on 22 June 1941. Although the British welcomed a respite from the threat of a German invasion, it was not immediately apparent whether Russia would survive. In the first month, the Russians took almost a million casualties, lost more than 5,000 tanks, and suffered thousands of aircraft destroyed as the Germans penetrated 200–500 miles into the Soviet Union. By 26 September, when the Germans sealed off the "Kiev pocket," capturing more than 660,000 prisoners here alone, they held a line from Leningrad in the north to the Crimea in the south. The Russians lost approximately 2.5 million men, hundreds of thousands of square miles of territory, and enormous quantities of equipment. Several American and British observers forecast that the Germans would defeat the Russians within six to eight weeks, leaving the Germans free to turn their full attention to Britain.[5]

Even if Russia withstood the German onslaught, Soviet participation in the war created massive problems for the Anglo-American coalition. Political, diplomatic, and strategic issues would dog the new partners, but the most pressing challenge was that Russian entry complicated an already complex and confused allocation of Allied war material because Joseph Stalin immediately and increasingly demanded Russia's fair share of U.S. and British war production.[6] Because of these upheavals, throughout the late summer and fall of 1941 national and coalition leaders and military planners reexamined major elements of Anglo-American strategy.

General Sir John Dill opened the debate on 6 May 1941 when he forwarded to Churchill a paper on the relationship between the defense of North Africa and the defense of the United Kingdom. Dill argued that although "the loss of Egypt would be a calamity . . . it would not end the war. A successful invasion alone spells our final defeat."[7] Thus, Dill argued, defense of the United Kingdom and even the security of the Far East should take precedence over the Middle East. To ensure defense of the home islands, Dill recommended that Britain should send no new reinforcements to Egypt, save normal maintenance requirements, for three months.[8] Churchill later recorded that he "was astonished to receive this document," and he sharply repudiated Dill's contentions, reaffirming the current strategy.[9]

Churchill's view carried the day, and the flow of men and materiel to the Middle East continued uninterrupted, but his decision did not halt the reevaluation of British strategy. Indeed, Churchill's running roughshod over Dill may have spurred the military to further action, for within a month the Joint Planning Committee completed a comprehensive review of British strategy. The report concluded that even with American materiel help the British currently were too weak to defeat Germany. The staff planners also reaffirmed Dill's view that Germany could not win unless the Germans successfully invaded Britain, which the planners considered unlikely. They concluded, therefore, that the conflict would devolve into a war of attrition where an opponent's economy and morale became the principal targets. In line with these conclusions, the Joint Planning Committee recommended that the British follow a strategy of naval blockade, assault on the periphery, and air offensive to prepare the way for a final land campaign to ensure a total German defeat. They optimistically—overly so, as time would tell—concluded that this strategy could lead to a German collapse without an all-out land assault.[10]

By early July, the effects of Soviet entry into the war on the allocation of materiel under Lend-Lease and concerns over the British position in the Middle East led President Roosevelt to dispatch Harry Hopkins, his alter ego, to Britain to evaluate the situation. Although gravely ill from stomach issues that continually ravaged his body, Hopkins immediately plunged into discussions with U.S. and British authorities. In his usual direct manner, Hopkins, whom Churchill previously had dubbed "lord root of the matter," broadly questioned aspects of British strategy, in particular Lend-Lease and allocation of materiel.[11] Concerned by this scrutiny, the British queried Chaney and Lee about why the U.S. Chiefs of Staff were challenging British strategy. Both men indicated that they were unsure if Hopkins's views accurately reflected the attitudes of the U.S. Chiefs of Staff. Chaney nonetheless pointed out that the American military leadership wanted to ensure that the British did nothing to jeopardize the security of the United Kingdom. Although both agreed that the British should fight for every inch of the Middle East, they argued that the British should not prejudice the security of truly vital areas for one of marginal strategic value.[12] The British concluded that they would have to provide the U.S. Chiefs of Staff with a fresh appreciation of the strategic rationale for retaining the Middle East and assure the Americans of the security of the United Kingdom. If necessary, they would send "an officer specially qualified to speak or a very full brief" to Washington to convince the Americans of the validity of British strategy.[13]

To further clear the strategic air, Churchill chaired a conference two days later, on 24 July, that included the British Chiefs of Staff and an American contingent composed of Hopkins, Averell Harriman (Roosevelt's Lend-Lease "expediter" in Britain), Ghormley, Chaney, and Lee. Hopkins led off the meeting by pointing out the level of U.S. aid pouring into the Middle East. He advised the British that if they expected continued American assistance, they would have to develop a coherent strategy for the region. He added that they needed to include a more structured process for allocating materiel that did not rely on the opportunism that had thus far characterized their efforts. Hopkins also cautioned Churchill and his military leaders that key members of the U.S. defense establishment—including the Chiefs of Staff—believed that Britain's current tenuous hold on the Mediterranean and the Middle East could quickly deteriorate. Given the risks, Hopkins noted, might it not be better to divert scarce resources to the defense of the home islands and to the Battle of the Atlantic? Hopkins added a final warning that the British grasped neither the depth of U.S. anxieties over the military situation in the Mediterranean nor the fact that the United States did not share Britain's interests there.[14]

Chaney echoed Hopkins and pointed out that Britain had four major objectives: (1) defense of the United Kingdom and its sea lines of communications; (2) defense of Singapore and the trade routes to Australia and New Zealand; (3) defense of sea commerce in general; and (4) defense of the Middle East. Although all were important, Chaney emphasized that the British could not meet all of these missions. They needed, therefore, to establish priorities and hold to them. He bluntly informed the British that the Middle East was neither essential to the survival of the empire nor a suitable position from which to launch a decisive offensive against Germany. Chaney also expressed concern that the British continued to strip the defenses of the United Kingdom, the most critical theater, to reinforce the Middle East. He agreed that Hitler's Russian adventure had granted Britain a temporary reprieve from invasion, but he did not believe the Russians would last more than six to eight weeks, when the Germans then could turn their full attention on a denuded Britain.[15]

Admiral Ghormley and, to a lesser extent, Lee took another tack. They pointed out that the defense of the Western Hemisphere remained the principal concern of the United States. The Middle East was important, therefore, only if it kept the Germans off the west coast of Africa. Moreover, any major reinforcement of the Middle East would siphon off escort vessels desperately needed to keep open the sea-lanes to Britain and would negate this minor benefit. Again, it was a matter of priorities, and the Americans remained convinced that the Middle East should not take precedence over more critical theaters.[16]

The prime minister, in turn, launched into a vigorous defense of British policies. He noted that the Royal Navy was turning the tide of the U-boat campaign. Patrolling by the U.S. Navy in the western Atlantic would free up British escorts to protect the routes to the Middle East. Churchill emphasized that Britain stood better prepared to withstand an invasion attempt than ever before. The RAF was half again stronger than in September 1940, and the army was immeasurably superior to the bedraggled force that had barely survived Dunkirk. Britain, Churchill concluded, could defeat a German invasion. The British Chiefs of Staff supported Churchill on all points. In addition, they pointed out that for the moment the Mediterranean and Middle East remained the only places where the British could engage Axis forces with any chance of success. Similarly, only in this region could the British divert German troops and supplies from the hard-pressed Russians.[17]

Churchill then fired his final defensive salvo. He emphasized the prestige and psychological value of the Middle East, observing that a voluntary British withdrawal from North Africa could have a catastrophic effect on the Muslim world and the Far East. Second, he slyly pointed out that gaining control of the Mediterranean would free the Mediterranean Fleet for service in the Far East—a point bound to appeal to the Americans. Finally, he underscored that the British had invested too much in the Middle East to withdraw. They simply did not have enough ships to move the 600,000 men and mountains of supplies amassed in the region. They would have to stay and fight.[18]

Although the British rationale only partially placated Hopkins, further major conversations halted while Hopkins took a no-notice trip to meet with Stalin to convince the Soviet leader of U.S. willingness to provide all possible aid and assess whether the Soviets could hold out. Upon his return from Moscow, Hopkins immediately embarked on an ocean voyage to the first wartime meeting between Churchill and Roosevelt.[19]

The meeting, code-named Riviera, took place at Placentia Bay, off Argentia, Newfoundland.[20] Perhaps best remembered because of the iconic photo of Churchill and Roosevelt during Sunday services on board the *Prince of Wales,* the meeting was also the source of the Atlantic Charter, the proposed peace aims of the eventual Anglo-American coalition. Of more importance, the conference provided a unique opportunity to resolve some of the outstanding issues surrounding coalition grand strategy, for key military leaders accompanied the two statesmen.[21] Thus, Riviera allowed the highest military authorities of each nation to meet individually and collectively for the first time, establish some personal rapport, and discuss firsthand the military issues facing the coalition.

Not surprisingly, the partners approached the conference from differing perspectives. As the proposed British agenda reveals, the British hoped to discuss a wide variety of strategic issues.[22] The Americans, in contrast, remained preoccupied with defense of the Western Hemisphere and the problems associated with mobilizing and equipping their rapidly expanding armed forces. Russian entry into the war and increasing Soviet demands for a share of Anglo-

American production had further disjointed these efforts.[23] These divergent objectives resulted in neither side being prepared to address the issues that its counterpart considered most crucial.

The Americans came less prepared for in-depth conversations than did their British peers. This was due in no small part to Roosevelt's penchant for secrecy, no doubt heightened by security concerns and potential political fallout from the meeting. The president gave Marshall and Stark only three days' notice of their departure and forbade them from telling their bosses or subordinates. Arnold had only a day's notice, and his preparatory instructions were limited to advice to pack enough heavy clothes for ten days.[24] During the sea journey to Argentia, Roosevelt refused to address policy or strategy issues, focusing solely on his personal meetings with Churchill. Only after arriving at Argentia would he meet with his military advisers, when he once more avoided substantive discussion of the most pressing policy and strategy matters.[25]

The British, in contrast, came fully prepared for detailed discussions of grand strategy. During their voyage, Churchill and his military chiefs completed the final revision of their paper on future strategy. Based on lengthy self-examination and comments from Hopkins and USSOG, the appreciation outlined the current situation as well as present and future strategy. Foremost, the British had to ensure the security of the United Kingdom from invasion. Only slightly less important was the safeguarding of the sea communications in the Atlantic. As far as the Middle East was concerned, the British intended "to make the Germans fight for every inch of the way" and believed they could maintain their position even if Russia collapsed. The defense of Singapore posed a more difficult problem, but the British noted that they had been strengthening the base and that those efforts would continue.[26]

The appreciation noted that although the Soviet Union's survival remained in doubt, its resistance would have little or no effect on fundamental British strategy. Nonetheless, even in the short term, continued Soviet opposition would profoundly affect German options: postponement of an invasion of the United Kingdom, a respite in the Middle East, and the greatly reduced likelihood of a move into Iberia and French Northwest Africa. More critical for the British was U.S. entry into the war. Indeed, the British optimistically opined that "the intervention of the United States would revolutionize the whole situation" and "would not only make victory certain, but might also make it swift."[27]

In the meantime, the British would base their present and future strategy on blockade, subversion, and bombing. The Chiefs of Staff conceded that blockade was the weakest link in the chain at the moment but stressed that action in Russia and the Mediterranean would tighten the ring. They also noted that although subversive activities and propaganda existed only on a small scale, the operations had achieved some success and planned to expand such efforts. The British considered strategic bombing to be the key element of British offensive action. Only security of the United Kingdom would have higher priority. The British intended to produce a massive heavy-bomber force for use primarily against the German rail network and civilian morale, with the aim of precipitating an internal German collapse that would obviate the need for anything more than an army of occupation.[28]

Should Germany not collapse, the British were "prepared to accelerate victory by landing forces on the Continent to destroy any elements of the Germans which still resist, and strike into Germany itself."[29] The Chiefs of Staff carefully pointed out that they did not envision a massive land campaign á la 1914–1918. Instead, they foresaw highly mechanized and armored forces that would slash through the German positions in occupied Europe, turn over conquered territory to armed resistance groups, and then strike, if necessary, to the heart of Germany.[30] From the British viewpoint, at least, they were ready to present a well-developed, well-thought-out, and thoroughly coordinated strategic appreciation at the upcoming conference.

High drama loomed on the Anglo-American horizon when on 9 August 1941 H.M.S. *Prince of Wales,* carrying the prime minister and his party, cut through the early-morning mists of Placentia Bay. Roosevelt could hardly have chosen a more symbolic location. A combination of British territory and the New World, Argentia also contained one of the U.S. leased bases granted in the destroyer-for-bases deal the previous September. As the British entered the bay, they found a flotilla of U.S. warships, including the heavy cruisers U.S.S. *Augusta* and U.S.S. *Tuscaloosa,* which had borne President Roosevelt and his aides to the conference site two days earlier.

For the military representatives, the Riviera Conference, also referred to as the Atlantic Conference, was a hodge-podge of formal and informal meetings, casual discussions in wardrooms, and chance encounters in companionways spread across multiple ships. There was no mutually agreed agenda for either individual meetings or the conference as a whole. All subjects could and did come up for discussion. Given their modus operandi, Roosevelt and Churchill may have intentionally promoted this chaos when they agreed that all meetings would be functional, vice plenary—that is, air–air, army–army, navy–navy, diplomat–diplomat, and president–prime minister—thereby ensuring that the two leaders were the sole conduits through which all information and, more importantly, all decisions moved.[31] These arrangements would lead a frustrated

Lieutenant Colonel E. I. C. Jacob, military assistant to the War Cabinet, to record in his diary: "This day has been almost entirely wasted from the point of view of joint [combined] discussion. We have been here two days and not yet succeeded in getting the opposite sets of Chiefs of Staff around a table. . . . We have played into [American] hands by allowing discussions to proceed in separate compartments."[32]

Although several of the major military actors present at the Atlantic Conference had already entered the stage, the meeting at Placentia Bay saw the first direct, personal contact between key members of the respective Chiefs of Staff. Thus, the conference offers an opportune point to introduce several of them more formally. On the American side, the senior member (by one month) was Admiral Harold R. Stark, CNO. Born in Wilkes-Barre, Pennsylvania, on 12 October 1880, Stark graduated from the Naval Academy in 1903 and was commissioned in 1905. As captain of the destroyer U.S.S. *Patterson* in 1914, he became acquainted with then assistant secretary of the navy Franklin Roosevelt while transiting the tricky waters of Maine en route to Roosevelt's family retreat at Campobello. In 1917, Stark led a squadron of destroyers from the Philippines to European waters, for which he received the Distinguished Service Medal and assignment to London, where he served as an aide to Admiral William Sims. He also served as aide to the secretary of the navy from 1930 to 1933. After promotion to rear admiral in 1934, he assumed the duties of the chief of the Bureau of Ordnance from 1934 to 1937. After Stark did a stint as commander of Cruiser Division Three in the Battle Force from 1937 to 1938 and then of all cruisers in the Battle Force in 1938–1939, Roosevelt vaulted him over the heads of fifty more senior officers to the position of CNO on 1 August 1939.[33]

Accompanying Stark was Admiral Ernest J. King, CINC, U.S. Atlantic Fleet. Born on 23 November 1878 in Lorain, Ohio, King attended the U.S. Naval Academy, served as the commander of the brigade of midshipman, and graduated fourth academically in 1901. Commissioned in 1903, he excelled in sea duty and commanded a small ship, the U.S.S. *Terry*, during the U.S. occupation of Vera Cruz in 1914. From 1915 to 1919, King served on the staff of Admiral Henry T. Mayo, CINC, U.S. Atlantic Fleet. A versatile officer, King became submarine qualified in 1922 and a naval aviator in 1927. He commanded the U.S.S. *Lexington*, one of the first U.S. aircraft carriers, from 1930 to 1932. After graduating from the Naval War College in 1933, he had a three-year assignment as the chief of the Bureau of Aeronautics. An innovative naval tactician, King used seaplanes and aircraft carriers in ways that included successful attacks on Pearl Harbor and Mare Island, California, in fleet exercises in 1938. Despite these successes, King's volcanic temper, rudeness, routine verbal abuse of subordinates, clashes with seniors and subordinates, womanizing, and heavy drinking no doubt contributed to his being passed over for promotion, reassigned to the General Board of the Navy, reduced in rank to rear admiral, and set for retirement in June 1939. Resurrected by CNO Harold Stark, Secretary of the Navy Frank Knox, and Franklin Roosevelt in January 1941, King became CINC, Patrol Force, and was promoted once more to vice admiral. On 1 February 1941, the Patrol Force was redesignated the Atlantic Fleet, and King received a promotion to full admiral. Although legend has it that King declared on his return to command, "When they get in trouble, they send for the sonsabitches," King denied that he ever made such a statement but noted that "he would have if he had thought of it."[34]

General Henry H. "Hap" Arnold was chronicled in an earlier chapter, which leaves only General George C. Marshall, chief of staff of the army. This limited space cannot do justice to a man who has generated numerous biographies, articles, and accolades. Courtly, competent, self-disciplined, possessed of a white-hot temper that he learned (mostly) to master, reserved to the point of icy, draconian, compassionate, demanding but empowering, and supremely trusted by all he encountered—Roosevelt, Congress, foreign leaders be they civilian or military, subordinates, and soldiers—are but a few of George Marshall's many attributes. Born on 31 December 1880 in Uniontown, Pennsylvania, Marshall graduated from the Virginia Military Institute in 1902 and accepted a commission in the infantry. After initial service in the postinsurrection Philippines, he was the top graduate of the Staff College, qualified for second year, and then stayed on as an instructor for two years. A brilliant staff officer, during World War I he served initially with the First Infantry Division, the first American division to deploy to France in 1917. Marshall's performance led to his assignment as the G-3 (operations) officer of First Army, where he planned the reduction of the St. Mihiel salient and the transfer of the entire AEF across the battlefield in time to launch the Meuse–Argonne offensive. Marshall served as General John Pershing's aide from 1919 to 1924, when Pershing was the chief of staff of the army. Progressive assignments as a battalion commander in Tianjin, China, from 1924 to 1927 and then assistant commandant of the Infantry School from 1927 to 1932 led to his command of the Eighth Infantry Regiment in 1932–1933. Duty as senior instructor with the Illinois National Guard from 1933 to 1936, duty supervising large-scale Civilian Conservation Corps camps and activities, and Pershing's intervention with Roosevelt led to Marshall's promotion to brigadier general in 1936. Service on the War Department General Staff and then as deputy chief of staff in 1938–

1939 followed. Roosevelt selected Marshall over thirty-five officers his senior to serve as chief of staff of the army from 1 September 1939 to November 1945.[35]

The lead members of the British military delegation to the conference included Admiral Sir Dudley Pound, first sea lord; General Sir John Dill, chief of the Imperial General Staff; and Air Vice Marshal Wilfrid Freeman, vice chief of the Air Staff. As the senior member of the British Chiefs of Staff, Pound led the British military delegation. Born to an English father and an American mother on the Isle of Wight, Pound entered the Royal Navy as a cadet in 1891 at the age of fourteen. During World War I, he initially served at sea for a short period before joining the Admiralty staff as naval assistant to the first sea lord. As flag captain on the battleship H.M.S. *Colossus*, he sank two cruisers and fended off two destroyers during the Battle of Jutland in July 1916. Upon leaving *Colossus* in July 1917, Pound served in a series of appointments in the Operations and Plans Divisions of the Admiralty. After two short stints, one on H.M.S. *Hood* and one as commander of H.M.S. *Repulse,* he returned to the Admiralty in 1922, ultimately serving as the head of the Plans Division until 1925. From 1927 to 1929, Pound held the position of assistant to the chief of the Naval Staff before commanding a cruiser squadron. A vice admiral in 1930, he became the second sea lord and chief of personnel in 1932. In 1936, he succeeded to the position of CINC, Mediterranean. Appointed first sea lord on 31 July 1939, despite evidence of a brain tumor that the fleet medical officer withheld from him, Pound had led the Royal Navy from the start of the war.[36]

General Sir John Dill was the senior army representative to the talks. Born in Belfast on 25 December 1881, Dill was commissioned from Sandhurst in 1901 and saw major action during the Boer War. He also saw extensive combat in France throughout World War I, was wounded, earned the Distinguished Service Order, and reached the rank of brigadier general. From 1919 to 1922, he served on the directing staff of the Staff College, Camberley. After two brigade-level commands, Dill joined the Imperial Defence College in London from 1926 to 1928. After nearly two years as the brigadier of the General Staff of the India Army, he returned to Camberley as the commandant of the Staff College from 1931 to 1934. He then served as the director of military operations and intelligence in the War Office for two years. In August 1936, the War Office sent Dill, a lieutenant general by now, to restore order to Palestine and Transjordan as the general officer commanding British forces there. From 1937 to 1939, Dill was the general officer commanding of Aldershot Command, which was designated as the headquarters for First Corps of the BEF in the event of war. Dill took the First Corps to France but was recalled in April 1940 to be the vice chief of the Imperial General Staff for General Edmund Ironside.

In the midst of the disasters in France and Belgium, Dill became the chief of the Imperial General Staff on 26 May 1940.[37] It is important to note that at this point in the narrative relations between Dill and Churchill had become increasingly strained as Dill tried to buffer Churchill's personality. As historian Alex Danchev notes, the relationship between the two was "throughout . . . an association strikingly lacking in empathy or understanding, etched in fundamental disagreement, and scarred by mutual dissatisfaction welling up at times to personal distaste."[38]

Air Vice Marshal Sir Wilfrid Freeman rounded out the British military leadership at the Riviera Conference. Freeman's attendance resulted from Churchill's decision to have Air Marshal Sir Charles Portal, chief of the Air Staff, remain in London to "mind the store," so to speak, in the absence of the other two key members of the Chiefs of Staff. Nonetheless, Freeman was highly qualified for the upcoming discussions. Initially commissioned as an infantry officer in 1908, he became a pilot in 1914 and alternated between combat and training assignments throughout World War I. In 1918, he attended the Royal Navy Staff College, and in 1922 he joined the directing staff of the RAF Staff College, remaining there until 1925. In January 1927, he was deputy director of operations and intelligence on the Air Staff. From 1928 to 1933, Freeman held a number of key command and staff positions in Britain and the Middle East before becoming commandant of the RAF Staff College in December 1933. Most importantly, from 1936 to 1940 Freeman served as the air member for Research and Development, later renamed Development and Production in 1938. In this role, he was responsible for many critical decisions concerning aircraft development and production, including heavy bombers such as the Stirling, Halifax, and Lancaster, perhaps the best heavy bomber of World War II. He also championed development of the Hurricane and Spitfire fighters, radar, and the jet engine. Freeman became vice chief of the Air Staff on 5 November 1940.[39]

Shortly after the British arrival at Placentia Bay, the military representatives quickly linked up with their counterparts for a few minutes of informal conversation before attending an introductory lunch in Admiral King's mess. The military staffs dispersed afterward for their first round of more formal conversations. The talks between the naval leaders took place on the U.S.S. *Augusta*, Admiral King's flagship, where Admiral Pound opened the discussions by providing a copy of the British Review of Grand Strategy and a paragraph-by-paragraph discussion ensued. There was little time for more than a cursory discussion if the group was to discuss all points, and no decisions emerged.[40] Nevertheless, even this short, rambling discussion exposed several rifts. Rear Admiral Turner, for instance, expressed severe doubts about the viability of British plans for the occupation of the Canary Islands, which Pound quickly countered.[41] Turner commented that the British need not retain their place in Egypt to safeguard the oil supplies in the Middle East and even suggested that the British could give up Palestine and Syria as well without overly jeopardizing the oilfields in Iran. Stark quickly corrected his subordinate and assured the British that the United States recognized the importance of holding the region.[42]

At the same time, Stark noted that he differed with the British on the point of precedence between the Middle East and the Far East. Because the United States did not depend on the Far East for natural resources, it "placed the importance . . . of the Middle East before that of Singapore." Stark said he understood that the British, in contrast, were prepared to sacrifice the Middle East for the sake of Singapore, a point that he considered dubious. He urged the British to reconsider whether the commodities of Malaya were truly vital to their war effort.[43]

Finally, Stark raised the issue of the heavy-bomber program and asked if the British really intended to give production of heavy bombers absolute first priority. If so, this program would interfere with the production of all other aircraft, including several that the British already had deemed essential to their war effort. Worse still, Stark added, making heavy bombers the top priority would severely affect the repair and construction of British naval vessels, including escorts, in the United States. Stark therefore urged the British to reconsider their decision in light of the conflicts within the supply and allocation system.[44]

To the British attendees' disappointment, initial discussions between army and army air force representatives also revolved around supply issues. Although Dill and Freeman gave a brief exposition on the war situation and British policy for the home isles, Middle East, and Far East and asked for the Americans' comments, Marshall skirted the issue and elaborated on the materiel problems facing American planners resulting from the massive expansion and rearmament program under way. Marshall pointed out that the U.S. Army faced tremendous shortages of aircraft, tanks, artillery, and ammunition. Recent public knowledge of these shortfalls would make it more difficult to continue supplying Britain at the expense of the American training program.[45] Training equipment was not the only issue, as many tactical units lacked their full complement of equipment. Marshall noted, for example, that the Philippines currently had no tanks, and "if a crisis arose in the Far East the military authorities would be called to account if there was a grave lack of equipment." Similarly, pilots had to wait up to eight months after completing initial flight training before airplanes arrived at their units.[46]

Finally, Marshall raised the issue of priorities. There simply were not enough resources to meet all requirements, and the partners would have to make some tough choices. Only recently had the U.S. Army and Navy resolved their own conflicts and then only after hard decisions. Complicating the already difficult allocation of supplies between the United States and Britain was the addition of Soviet needs. The British propensity to add new requirements and shift priorities without warning, Marshall further criticized, continually disrupted American plans. For example, he said, the recent British shift to heavy bombers as number-one priority would adversely affect all army programs, the tank program in particular. Politely but firmly, Marshall was telling the British to get their priorities in line, a point to which he would return repeatedly throughout the conference.[47]

After the general meeting broke up, Arnold and Freeman retired for further conversations on air matters. Again, heavy bombers were the prime topic. Although both agreed to the production figures for all other aircraft, the British noted, "The figures for heavy bombers quoted by Major-General Arnold were considerably lower than those supplied to the British Air Commission."[48] Freeman hammered on the importance of the heavy bomber, and Arnold agreed to investigate possible avenues for an increase in heavy-bomber production. But, as Arnold recorded later in his journal, the British requests for 1,000 heavy bombers and 2,000 pilots a month were "wishful" thinking and noted, "We can't do it as easily as that. . . . Where will they come from?"[49]

From the records, it appears that preparation for and participation in the president's dinner for the British delegation occupied the remainder of Saturday. The brief initial discussions had set the tone for the conference: the British would press for discussion of grand strategy, whereas the Americans would emphasize their concerns about materiel, equipment, and supplies. The two sides would spend considerable time talking past each other because the British wanted to drag the Americans into conversations about strategy, especially ends and ways, but the Americans were fixated on priorities for allocating scarce means.

Discussions on Sunday, 10 August, followed a similar pattern, although an early agreement on arrangements for escorting convoys proved an exception to the rule. At ABC-1, negotiators had agreed that the U.S. Navy would assume escort responsibilities once the United States entered the war, and navy planners had been studying the issue since that time. However, German successes in the Battle of the Atlantic and changes in geostrategic conditions caused coalition leaders to examine whether to accelerate the timetable. As a number of historians have pointed out, it made little sense to appropriate $7 billion dollars for Lend-Lease equipment if it ended up on the bottom of the ocean.[50] The plan that emerged, designated Navy Hemisphere Plan 4, called for escort of all U.S. and Icelandic ships to and from Iceland. Most importantly, the plan included a clause stipulating that "shipping of any nationality . . . may join such United States or Iceland flag convoys, between United States ports and bases and Iceland."[51] In other words, the U.S. Navy would escort British and Allied shipping, thus raising the likelihood of a U.S. confrontation with Germany.

This course of action was not without political or military risks. Although increasingly marginalized, anti-interventionist sentiment remained strong in the United States. On 31 March 1941, Senator Charles W. Tobey (R–N.H.) introduced a resolution prohibiting American escort of ships to Britain. At the time, public-opinion polls indicated that the majority of Americans opposed using the U.S. Navy to escort supplies to Britain. At the end of June, influential isolationist Senator Burton Wheeler (D–Mont.) introduced a resolution calling for an investigation of whether the U.S. Navy already was escorting British ships.[52] Moreover, an amendment of the conscription law extending service beyond twelve months and increasing the number of draftees was pending in Congress. Roosevelt, hesitant to take strong action that might jeopardize the bill, ordered issue of Navy Hemisphere Plan 4 in mid-July, minus the clause on escorting all ships. The conscription amendment passed the House by one vote (203–202) at the time the Atlantic Conference ended, so Roosevelt's concerns seem well placed.[53]

In the wake of the dispatch of U.S. troops to Iceland on 5 July 1941, a shift in public opinion offered Roosevelt more political maneuvering room. By the end of the negotiations at Argentia, the British and Americans reached full agreement on convoy responsibilities, and Navy Hemisphere Plan 4 went to the fleet on 13 August with an effective date of 13 September.[54] The first eastbound transatlantic convoy to receive full U.S. escort, HX 150, sailed from Halifax on 16 September 1941. American escorts picked up the first westbound convoy, ON 18, south of Iceland on 24 September 1941. From that point forward, the U.S. Navy was an integral part of the defense of the sea-lanes and on a virtual war footing in the Atlantic.[55] Sir Alexander Cadogan later called this achievement the high point of the conference.[56]

The British and U.S. Chiefs of Staff achieved less success when they finally met at their first full conference aboard the *Prince of Wales* on Monday, 11 August, to discuss the coalition's future strategy. As host, Admiral Pound presided over this meeting and offered the British Review of Grand Strategy as the basis for a detailed point-by-point discussion. Stark quickly interjected that "this meeting was for discussion only and that considered comments would be sent later after thorough study."[57] Only at that time, Stark averred, would the Americans submit a formal reply, especially since the Review of Grand Strategy appeared to stray from ABC-1. In light of this rebuff, Pound recommended that the group review the document paragraph by paragraph to clear up any confusion.[58]

The overall tenor of the conversations did not differ significantly from the informal talks that had taken place two days earlier, with the Americans concentrating on the supply matters rather than on the planning aspects of the strategy. Once more Marshall pointed out that the current consumption of materiel and combat losses in the Middle East were not commensurate with the relative low priority of that theater, especially vis-à-vis the extensive materiel requirements of the U.S. Army and Army Air Force. Moreover, new Russian and Chinese demands undoubtedly would arise, and there simply were not enough U.S. supplies to meet current, much less anticipated, demands. In Marshall's view, the British needed to make tough choices about priorities and stick to them. Stark reinforced the army chief of staff's view by noting that the British seemed to have two "first" priorities: (1) security of the United Kingdom and its sea communications and (2) the heavy-bomber offensive. Again, he pointed out the conflicts between construction programs for naval escorts and heavy bombers and urged the British to reconcile themselves to one or the other as the top priority. As far as which should have precedence, Stark commented that the United States would not feel comfortable about the security of the sea-lanes until the rate of ship construction exceeded the rate of destruction.[59]

In the midst of the deliberations over the security of the North Atlantic sea-lanes, Admiral Pound guided the discourse to potential operations against the Atlantic islands (Azores, Canaries, Cape Verdes), noting that the British stood prepared to secure the Canary Islands and that he understood the United States was willing to occupy the Azores. After some initial disagreement between Marshall and King, Marshall agreed to the proposition but emphasized the critical necessity for speed in the execution of these missions. In addition, Marshall elaborated the constraints imposed by the large number of draftees who were limited to one year of service and no employment outside the Western Hemisphere, small numbers of regular soldiers with only three-year enlistments, and the havoc wrought on mobilization and training plans by the recent deployment of 10,000 personnel to relieve Iceland. Marshall bluntly concluded that at the moment the U.S. Army did not have sufficient forces available to fulfill all the missions the British wanted, and the partners would have to decide whether to use U.S. Army forces for the Azores operation or to augment the U.S. Marine Corps in Iceland with another 5,000 soldiers to relieve all British forces there. Even if he found enough troops to carry out both operations, the army would be unable to perform any other missions for at least six months.[60]

As it became obvious that the group would not have sufficient time to discuss the remaining two-thirds of the British paper, Turner drew "attention to the fact that in some points the paper was at variance with ABC-1." He emphasized that ABC-1 "had been drawn up as a guide to action, not only after the U.S. came into the war, but as a guide to British action before that." Pound countered that the British Chiefs of Staff "regarded ABC-1 as generally sound, but that it must be subject to modification from time to time, as the situation developed."[61] This exchange revealed a significant difference of opinion. As historian Theodore Wilson observes, for the Americans "the 'Review of Grand Strategy' did represent the coming back to life of many notions assumed dead and buried," a retrogression, whereas for the British it was simply another step forward in the evolutionary process.[62] These differing perspectives, a product of differing national and military service cultures, would afflict the coalition for months to come.

After the combined meeting, the two staffs adjourned for individual service talks. Little of importance surfaced in the discussions between the army delegations. Marshall reiterated his misgivings. On the positive side, he noted that the recent and anticipated reinforcements of the Philippines presented a substantial threat to a Japanese move toward the south and would therefore serve as a deterrent to Japanese aggression. Finally, Marshall expressed strong U.S. concerns about Axis penetration into South America, especially Brazil. Dill then quickly sketched out British plans for defending the Middle East, including the Western Desert as well as northern Syria and eastern Anatolia, should the Germans advance through the Caucasus. After desultory discussion of Russian supply demands, Dill departed.[63]

Discussions between the naval chiefs of staff proved more substantial and appear to represent the core of military issues covered at the conference. Contrary to Turner's earlier assertion that the ABC-1 Report was the guideline for all action, Stark informed the British that the United States no longer planned to send surface forces to the United Kingdom. Similarly, naval patrol planes would remain stationed on the western side of the Atlantic. The Americans would still send a force to Gibraltar, although it might be smaller than stipulated in ABC-1.[64] Turning to the Pacific, both sides agreed to suspend the political elements of the ADB Report. The Americans apparently acquiesced to the new British command arrangements in the Far East that had proved so nettlesome throughout the spring and early summer. They confirmed that the CINC of the U.S. Asiatic Fleet would operate under the strategic direction of a British CINC of the Eastern Fleet, with the caveat that Hart would retain full operational control over U.S. naval forces. The negotiators agreed to defer several issues until the U.S. representatives could fully review the report. Turner, about whom Jacob noted, "you could never imagine him taking anyone's advice on any point," criticized the British plan to cover their trade routes rather than defend the Malay Barrier.[65] Despite the Americans' expressed reservations, the British concluded, "These amendments would, it is thought, go far to remove U.S. objections to the original form of the [ADB] Report."[66]

A second full conference met the next day, Tuesday, 12 August 1941. Once again, the major topic was the all-too-familiar issue of supply allocation. Pound began the discussions by boldly opining that it was evident that the coalition could alleviate its supply situation only if the United States converted a large segment of its civil economy to military production. Although the Americans did not openly disagree, Turner laid blame for supply difficulties on the BJSM. He complained that all three British services submitted requirements without any indication of priorities either for items within lists, between lists, or between theaters. U.S. planners could only guess what the British wanted and where they wanted it to go. After admonishing the British to establish the appropriate machinery and procedures called for under ABC-1, Turner bluntly told the British that they could not get more of one thing without getting less of another.[67]

Dill then shifted the conversation to a discussion of U.S. operational planning in the event of U.S. entry into the war. He asked if the British could offer any assistance. Turner dodged the question and answered that respective army and navy war plans conformed to the provisions of ABC-1. When pressed, Marshall stated that the Americans had given considerable attention to the defense of the Western Hemisphere, but aside from some preliminary studies of operations in French Northwest Africa, there had been no planning for action in the Eastern Hemisphere. For the moment, the United States would concentrate on mobilizing and equipping the forces necessary to accomplish whatever tasks might be required.[68] At that point, the meeting adjourned, and the British prepared for their imminent departure.

Before sailing, the air representatives held a hasty, final meeting. Besides the continued litany of complaints about confusion within the British procurement system, two major issues surfaced. First, Arnold notified the British that if they continued to receive 50 percent of all U.S. production in heavy bombers, they would get 2,300 such aircraft by June 1943. He quickly added, however, that he was not acknowledging any specific commitment. Second, Arnold and Freeman confirmed the portions of the ABC-1 Report outlining employment of American air forces in the United Kingdom. Ironically, during this last discussion, Arnold discovered that Hopkins and Harriman had failed to forward information to the military authorities in Washington, demonstrating that inadequate internal coordination was not solely a British problem.[69] With this last coordination, the Atlantic Conference closed, and shortly thereafter the British sailed home.

At the policy level, the conference yielded mixed results. On the one hand, the mere existence of the conference and publication of the Atlantic Charter clearly aligned the two countries more closely than heretofore, certainly in public eyes, fulfilling a key British policy objective.[70] However, that exposure was a mixed blessing because anti-interventionists quickly took Roosevelt to task. Boake Carter, a popular news commentator of the 1930s and arch New Deal critic, opined that the conference "smacks of the sort of secret Hitler–Mussolini meetings at the Brenner Pass, where the two dictators blandly decided how many lives should be carved up to accomplish their aggressive purposes."[71] Congressman George Tinkham (R–Mass.), another staunch Roosevelt foe, considered charging the president with treason for having made "a declaration of war without Congress, on a British battleship."[72] Nor were Carter and Tinkham lone voices, as newspapers in the Midwest, in particular those part of the McCormick empire, excoriated the president.[73]

Moreover, despite the meetings and promulgation of the Atlantic Charter, the British did not get what they wanted most: a U.S. commitment to full-scale belligerency. This failure was a tremendous disappointment. Churchill, at least, had built up tremendous expectations for the meeting. He had even written Queen Elizabeth, later Queen Mother, on the eve of his departure, "I must say I do not think our friend would have asked me to go so far for what must be a meeting of world-wide notice unless he had in mind some further step; in fact, the meeting will be a step forward in itself."[74] Little did he know how small that step would be.

Granted, Roosevelt offered a few positive, if unannounced, steps. The British could draw solace from his commitment to allow any ship to join U.S. convoys escorted to Iceland, even though he delayed public announcement of the policy. Most importantly, as Churchill informed the War Cabinet upon his return, "The President had said that he would wage war, but not declare it, and that he would become more and more provocative. If the Germans did not like it, they could attack American forces."[75] Or was this another example of Roosevelt dissembling? As David Reynolds observes, "Historians disagree about Roosevelt's candour on this point: perhaps he was anxious to get into the conflict, or perhaps he was just telling the British what they wanted to hear."[76] One can conclude with certainty that the statement was not an example of Churchill hearing what he wanted to hear and conveying it to a war-weary Cabinet. John Martin, one of Churchill's private secretaries, separately confirmed that he heard Roosevelt make the remark.[77] But Roosevelt could have meant exactly what he said but within *his* context of waging war: an undeclared naval war may have been as far as he was willing to go. More likely, he was simply keeping his options open.

Even if Roosevelt had been sincere when he made this statement, how much faith could the British put into those words? As the prime minister informed the Cabinet, Roosevelt believed "he was skating on pretty thin ice in his relations with Congress. . . . If he were to put the issue of peace and war to Congress, they would debate it for three months."[78] Moreover, the British had ample evidence of Roosevelt later publicly repudiating far less daring statements. Indeed, almost immediately upon his return from Argentia, when asked by a reporter whether his meeting with Churchill "had brought the United States closer to war[,]" FDR replied flatly that, no, it had not."[79] The British, conditioned by years of Roosevelt's startling turnabouts, would have been justified in fearing another. Even British foreign secretary Anthony Eden, among the strongest proponents of close Anglo-American relations, feared in August 1941 that "FDR means to keep out of war and dictate the peace if he can."[80] The narrow extension of the U.S. conscription law on 12 August also cast a pall over the British delegation. Through their political lens, the British interpreted the close outcome as Roosevelt on the verge of a no-confidence vote that would have toppled the government.[81]

From a military perspective, the Riviera Conference produced mixed results as well. There had been a good exchange of views even if the two sides frequently talked past each other. Each side had a much better understanding of the factors driving the other's approach to strategy. Although not happy with the British position on the Middle East, U.S. authorities had been unwilling to let the issue derail the conference. The British now had a much clearer understanding of the obstacles facing the mobilization of the U.S. Army and Army Air Force. The coalition's military leaders reached agreement on escorting convoys, which the United States would implement on 1 September. The two militaries had agreed to fundamental changes in BJSM procedures for requesting materiel and designating priorities. Both agreed that Russian entry into the war would affect future allocation of war materiel, but it would take time to understand the full consequences.⁸² Regrettably, the military leaders failed to resolve their differences over the Far East, which essentially got lost in the shuffle of other pressing issues. Granted, they agreed that the ADB Report required revision, but the leaders did not address the underlying conflict over strategy that was the core of the problems between them. By continuing to defer these larger issues to local commanders, they added to the complexity, ambiguity, and friction, ensuring that the Far East would continue to cause tensions within the coalition.

During their enforced isolation on the return trip from Argentia, the British Chiefs of Staff recorded their major conclusions about the conference. The British had long recognized American concerns over defense of the continental United States, but they apparently realized for the first time the depth of U.S. anxiety over Axis penetration of Latin America, which had translated into possible U.S. operations in South America as well as the securing of key Atlantic islands at the expense of other operations. To their dismay, the British had learned that American planning to date had focused almost totally on defense of the Western Hemisphere.⁸³

The British Chiefs of Staff also came away with a much better understanding of the U.S. Army and Army Air Force expansion programs and the problems each raised. Although "the American Chiefs of Staff are naturally obsessed with the shortage of equipment of their new forces" and "are much exercised to arrive at a correct order of priority for our requirements and a fair allocation of new production," the British conceded that Britain was largely responsible for the problems and vowed to take positive steps to simplify and centralize their system.⁸⁴ At the same time, the British were not pleased with U.S. expansion plans. As one influential British staff officer later noted, the U.S. Army program called for an army of 4 million men—an estimate that would prove to be 50 percent too low—but the British considered it far too large a force that would only waste natural resources, factory production, and manpower.⁸⁵ The British expressed even less satisfaction with Arnold's plans for the U.S. Army Air Force. Despite his assurances about Britain's share of the heavy-bomber production, the British concluded, "It became evident, although they did not state this officially, that the Americans do not intend to ratify [ABC-2], under which the major part of American heavy bomber production was to be allocated to the United Kingdom."⁸⁶

Despite these issues, the British Chiefs of Staff remained optimistic about the overall results of the conference. Granted, American insistence on the ABC-1 Report as their "bible," except, of course, when the American military wanted to act unilaterally, bothered the British. British military leaders were nonetheless pleased with confirmation of U.S. air forces in Britain, satisfied with the division of responsibilities for occupying the Atlantic islands, and certain that they had convinced the Americans of the importance of the Middle East. They also believed that the ADB agreement needed only minor amendments, thus ensuring another victory for British strategic planning. Aside from some anxieties that the Americans might criticize British bombing policies, the British believed that the U.S. Chiefs of Staff had accepted the British outlines of future strategy. As Brigadier General Vivian Dykes, director of War Plans, concluded in his summary of the conference for Dill, the Americans essentially accepted the British strategy for winning the war—that is, first, weakening Germany by air attack, blockade, and propaganda and subversive activities and then landing forces on the Continent to administer a coup de grace.[87] Although Dykes's assessments were generally correct, little did he know how badly he misjudged American acceptance of the British-designed ways and means to implement them.

On the other side of the Atlantic, upon return from Riviera the U.S. Chiefs of Staff prepared their formal reply to the British Review of Grand Strategy. Contrary to British expectation, the Americans forwarded through Chaney and Ghormley a highly critical assessment of the British strategic appreciation. The comments began with a quotation of the strategic concept contained in the ABC-1 agreement and an accompanying admonishment that these principles were sound not only after American entry but also for current British conduct of the war. In general, the Americans quarreled with the vague wording of the British concepts. For instance, the Americans did not believe that "destruction of morale" constituted an appropriate objective for the bombing campaign and argued that the British should attack only targets with a direct effect on German military power.[88] As an interesting aside, this stand did not disappoint all segments of the British military establishment. As Sir John Kennedy later told Brigadier General Lee, the War Office had argued along similar lines but lost the debate within the British Chiefs of Staff Committee.[89]

The U.S. Chiefs of Staff also disagreed with proposed British strategy for the offensive employment of land forces. The U.S. authorities noted the lack of thought devoted to the employment of sufficient land forces to bring about German defeat. They pointed out that although "naval and air power may prevent wars from being lost, and by weakening enemy strength, may greatly contribute to victory[,] . . . [i]t should be recognized as an almost invariable rule that wars cannot be finally won without the use of land armies."[90] In short, the idea of a using small army to deliver a coup de grace to a Germany on the verge of collapse was another example of wishful thinking at its worst.

Other criticisms of the strategy review illuminated how badly the British misperceived U.S. acceptance of the document. Although recognizing the importance of the Middle East, the Americans believed that the British overstated their case. The British could give up Egypt, fall back on Sudan or Iraq, and still safeguard their oil supplies. In a similar vein, U.S. leaders agreed that Singapore was important but noted that its retention was not a paramount concern. They also concluded that if the Philippines or Netherlands East Indies were to fall, Singapore would become untenable. Thus, the Americans urged the British to consider diverting supplies to the Dutch or Chinese.[91]

Perhaps most disappointing to the British were the Americans' cautions against overestimating the effect of U.S. entry into the war. Ghormley and Chaney informed the British Chiefs of Staff that "while participation by United States naval forces will bring an important accession of strength against Germany, the potential combat strength of land and air elements has not yet been sufficiently developed to provide much more than moral effect. . . . Involvement of United States military forces in the near future would at best involve a piecemeal and indecisive commitment of forces against a superior enemy under unfavorable logistic conditions."[92] For the moment, as far as the U.S. military leaders were concerned, America could make its greatest contribution by remaining neutral and continuing to act as the "Arsenal of Democracy," a conclusion that could have hardly comforted the beleaguered British.

In retrospect, from a long-term coalition aspect, two of the most important accomplishments achieved at Riviera may have been the most intangible. The first concerned the fact that the military leaders and key subordinate staff officers established personal contacts, found common cause, and developed empathy and understanding of their counterparts.[93] The relationship established between Dill and Marshall, in particular, would be the most important military relationship for the long-term success of the coalition. On the day after his return from Riviera, Dill uncharacteristically wrote Marshall, "I sincerely hope that we shall meet again before long. In the meantime, we must keep each other in touch in the frank manner upon which we agreed."[94] A few days later Marshall responded in kind, and as Alex Danchev remarks, "This exchange inaugurated a regular correspondence in itself an important channel of the flourishing but still illicit common-law alliance."[95]

The importance of the relationship between Dill and Marshall cannot be overstated. When Dill arrived in Washington in December 1941, eventually to become the head of the BJSM and Churchill's personal representative as minister of defence, his professionalism would foster a close friendship with Marshall—uncharacteristic for both—that would allow Dill to translate between

London and Washington, smooth ruffled feathers and egos on both sides of the Atlantic, and serve as an exemplar of what a coalition partner should be. So close and so important would this personal and professional relationship become that Marshall received congressional permission to bury Dill in Arlington National Cemetery upon the field marshal's untimely death in November 1944.[96]

Nor was this admiration of Dill restricted to the U.S. side of the Atlantic. No one less than Alan Francis Brooke, Lord Alanbrooke, Dill's successor as chief of the Imperial General Staff for the remainder of the war, later remarked on the importance of Dill's assignment. An extensive and hypercritical diarist, Alanbrooke, after Churchill, was possibly most responsible for British victory in World War II. In an annotation to his diary entry recounting the meeting with Churchill to convince the prime minister to make Dill the U.K. military representative in the United States, Alanbrooke observed, "I look upon that half hour's discussion with Winston at 10 Downing Street on December 11th as one of my most important accomplishments during the war, or at any rate amongst those that bore fruit."[97]

The Riviera meeting also cemented a bond between Roosevelt and Churchill. They had finally met and taken the other's measure, and each was satisfied that he had a partner with whom he could work. This was no small accomplishment, for as Harry Hopkins's biographer, Christopher D. O'Sullivan, reminds us, "historians and the public have come to see the Churchill–Roosevelt relationship as inevitable, but meetings between great personages do not always go smoothly."[98] It is doubtful that this was a true friendship—at this point in his life, Roosevelt may have been beyond that capacity—but there was mutual respect. Certainly, absent the mutual respect that began at the Atlantic Conference, the coalition would not have withstood the stresses and strains of the next four years as well as it did.

Neither side left the Atlantic Conference unsure of the need to address materiel issues and of the importance of developing feasible solutions. As early as April 1941, the U.S. War Department had begun to consider armaments problems on a comprehensive basis.[99] The German invasion of the Soviet Union added impetus to these efforts, and on 9 July President Roosevelt tasked the U.S. services to prepare a comprehensive estimate of "the overall production requirements required to defeat our potential enemies."[100] As the army and the navy worked on their respective programs, the two services diverged. Whether for reasons of strategy or perhaps for perceived bureaucratic and budgetary imperatives, the navy saw only a limited role for ground forces. Interestingly, this view aligned the navy with the British strategy. The army, in contrast, argued for forces sufficient to invade Europe and defeat Germany.[101] By the time of the Atlantic Conference, the War Department had nearly completed its portion of the review, known as the Victory Program.[102]

During the same period, the British compiled and prioritized their supply requirements. Prompted by a letter from Secretary of War Stimson, Arthur Purvis, head of the British Purchasing Commission, who unfortunately was killed in an airplane accident en route to the Atlantic Conference, gave his "whole-hearted concurrence" to Stimson's call for an overall coalition production plan. Churchill reinforced this view and toward the end of July called for combined coordination of requirements and the means to fulfill them. By 29 July, Sir Edward Bridges, civil secretary of the War Cabinet, began funneling a substantial list of British requirements and requests to Harriman in London.[103]

The Atlantic Conference and Hopkins's mission to meet with Stalin convinced Roosevelt that the Anglo-American coalition would have to make substantial materiel commitments to the Russians. Roosevelt also realized that the supplies would have to come out of existing stocks; therefore, the United States and Britain would have to accept reductions. He consequently charged Knox and Stimson to develop a plan for equitable distribution of war supplies among Great Britain, the Soviet Union, the United States, and the other anti-Axis powers. The president added that this plan must be complete before 1 October, the scheduled date of a conference in Moscow between British, Russian, and U.S. supply authorities. Once the coalition more fully understood Russian requirements, Roosevelt intended to call another conference between ranking British and U.S. military leaders to apportion supplies.[104] Shortly thereafter, however, the British Chiefs of Staff urged that Britain and the United States prepare a list of critical items needed to meet requirements in their respective areas of responsibility. Once national staffs compiled the information, a combined British-U.S. committee would meet in Washington to produce an overall production agreement.[105]

When the initial U.S. estimates reached London, British authorities were deeply disappointed to learn that U.S. production by the end of 1942 would barely equal that of the United Kingdom and Canada. Moreover, U.S. production of items that the British considered most critical, such as heavy bombers and medium tanks, would be substantially less than commonwealth output. This assessment caused great consternation in London, and the British immediately called for a conference to convene in late August. Harriman and Beaverbrook eventually arranged for a combined conference in London on 15 September as a preliminary before the British-U.S. mission traveled to Moscow.[106]

The American delegation arrived in London on 15 September.[107] Despite a lengthy and tedious trip, two hours after arrival the British whisked the U.S. delegation to the first meeting. Beaverbrook tried but failed to dominate the meeting and railroad the Americans into quick decisions. He proposed that the group should first determine the total materiel available from U.S. sources. The parties could then consider British requirements and decide on the total British allotment. Only then would the conference decide the Russian allotment of equipment.[108] Beaverbrook's shrewd but transparent approach would have allowed the British to get their full share from the United States without revealing British or commonwealth industrial capacity. It also might allow the British to avoid contributing their fair share to the Russians. Unsurprisingly, Harriman, a business titan, saw through Beaverbrook's machinations and called for subcommittees divided into functional areas that would determine the total production available from the combined Anglo-American capacity. Once the working groups determined their production figures, the full committee could determine an equitable distribution among the United States, Britain, and the Soviet Union. Beaverbrook objected strenuously until Harriman intimated that Beaverbrook might go on to Moscow alone, at which point Beaverbrook capitulated.[109]

The subcommittees quickly hammered out agreements with two key exceptions—production of merchant shipping and aircraft allocations. The first instance was not so much a conflict as recognition of fact. The British estimated that by 1942 they would be losing ships at a rate of 5.5 million gross tons per year, but the entire British Empire could replace only 1 million tons. The British acknowledged that some form of assistance, yet unknown, would be required from the United States.[110] Aircraft posed a more controversial problem. Under the new agreement, Britain would receive approximately 1,000 fewer aircraft than under the ABC-2 accord. The American recantation understandably upset the British, particularly given the rigid U.S. adherence to ABC-1 in other matters. The British delegates countered that instead of the numbers of aircraft specified in ABC-2, they should receive their original Lend-Lease allocations. Any aircraft for the Russians would come from orders for the U.S. Army Air Force. Under this plan, Britain would receive less aircraft than ABC-2 allowed but considerably more than proposed under the new agreement. Chaney and Harriman rebuffed this request, and after Beaverbrook tabled another unacceptable plan, Harriman adjourned the meeting to allow the British time to reconsider the alternatives.[111]

Upon reconvening, the British vigorously pressed still another option, arguing for an increased portion of heavy-bomber production. Harriman categorically stated that there would be no change in the number of aircraft available to the British. Faced with the American resolve, Beaverbrook conceded to the original U.S. proposal. As he did so, he noted, "The British representatives were actuated by their anxiety to serve their country, but they also had a great desire to meet the wishes of the Americans to whom they did not want to appear ungrateful. They did not agree with them, but nevertheless they accepted them."[112]

Once all subcommittees determined their requirements, the work of the conference proceeded quickly. By 19 September, the Planning Committee had determined the final figures for the British services. The next day, at a meeting of the full committee, Admiral Bellairs pointed out that the combined requirements of the United States and the United Kingdom would undoubtedly exceed the American production capacity. He therefore recommended approval of the Planning Committee's proposal, but with the key provision that merchant shipping, heavy bombers, and tanks receive a higher priority.[113]

With the agreement, the combined Beaverbrook–Harriman Mission traveled from Scapa Flow to Murmansk on the cruiser H.M.S. *London* and then flew to Moscow, arriving there on 28 September. After the heated discussion in London, the Moscow Conference was almost anticlimactic. The Russians gave the delegation little information beyond their demands for equipment. After three days of somewhat icy negotiations, the delegates signed a supply protocol on 1 October.[114] Once negotiators completed the agreements in London and Moscow, there were no further high-level substantive discussions on allocation of materiel until after the United States entered the war. As coalition planners struggled to find the resources necessary to implement the agreements, the logistical elements of the coalition's reexamination of grand strategy lay dormant.

With the end of the Moscow Conference, the reexamination of the coalition's grand strategy in light of the dynamic changes in the geostrategic circumstances came to mixed ends. The militaries achieved considerable success in planning for operations in the Atlantic region, most notably convoy escorts, division of responsibility of occupation of the major Atlantic island groups, and the deployment of U.S. air forces to the United Kingdom. Unfortunately, the reexamination also ripped open old wounds, and solutions to the many difficulties still facing the coalition would be problematic. In some cases, the coalition planners' efforts, though well intentioned, reinforced old suspicions, created confusion, and muddied the strategic waters. In other cases, decisions resulted from the United States flexing its growing muscles—rigid adherence to the ABC-1 Report, veto of the ABD Report, the incorporation of Roosevelt's preferred language into the Atlantic Charter, and ultimatums over allocation of materiel—all of which created additional strains.

Worse yet, critical differences over developments of the coalition's grand strategy remained unresolved. The rhetoric of supply allocation masked underlying U.S. concerns about elements of British strategy: defense of the Far East, the efficacy of heavy bombing, the Middle East and Mediterranean as a distraction from the main effort, and the amount of land forces necessary for the defeat of Germany on the Continent. Individually and collectively, these differences complicated strategic planning and presaged arguments over strategy that would occupy the coalition for the remainder of the war. Although the partners had accomplished a great deal during this period, much remained to be done. Would they have enough time?

10

Racing an Unseen Clock
More Problems Than Solutions

While Anglo-American collaboration during late summer and early fall of 1941 concentrated on the issues of the higher direction of the war, during the latter days of 1941 planners in Washington, London, and the Far East strove to convert theoretical plans into operational reality. As a result, the period immediately preceding Pearl Harbor saw intense activity by British and American staff officers. For the most part, however, they did not devote their energies to the issues of Anglo-American collaboration. The British army and RAF concentrated on building up forces in the Mediterranean and Middle East for the next offensive against Rommel. The Royal Navy focused on the Battle of the Atlantic and operations in the Mediterranean. U.S. naval staffs toiled over planning and carrying out their part of the war in the Atlantic. The U.S. Army and Army Air Force struggled with the challenges of mobilizing, equipping, and training forces on a new and massive scale. Moreover, the principal focus of U.S. Army and U.S. Navy planning concerned the defense of the United States, its island outposts, and the Western Hemisphere.

Within the Atlantic theater, coalition cooperation between planning staffs naturally increased as the U.S. Navy assumed greater responsibility for convoy protection of not only American but also British and Allied shipping in the North Atlantic. Likewise, planning continued between British and American army and air staffs for the deployment of U.S. forces to the United Kingdom. The level of British and American cooperation expanded as the BJSM sorted out its organization and became a central clearinghouse for procurement issues. Closer collaboration also emerged in London as USSOG absorbed more responsibility for administering Lend-Lease activities in the United Kingdom. At the same time, the Far East gathered a growing share of the coalition's attention as each partner, in its own way, attempted to deter Japan's entry into the war. American and British staffs in the Far East labored to create a viable plan for a coalition defense of the southwestern Pacific in the event deterrence failed.

The majority of coalition planning and coordination took place in London. This made sense because most actual coalition operations would involve the employment of U.S. forces in areas of British responsibility. Moreover, because the British were fully engaged in fighting Germany and Italy, they had little time or interest in regions under American strategic direction. In addition, as one staff officer with the BJSM pointed out, the current political environment in Washington prevented any substantive discussions of combined war plans there, and the U.S. government did not appear inclined toward further negotiations.[1] For example, although there was close coordination between the Navy Department and the British Naval Staff, most of this concerned convoy operations and the exchange of technical data. There was no planning for combined naval combat operations. From a ground-force perspective, there was even less cooperation. As Lieutenant Colonel Frank Vogel, director of plans of the British Army Staff, pointed out to his superiors in London in late October, "There is no disguising the fact that at present the [U.S.] War Dept. is not forthcoming so far as planning is concerned, they avoid consulting us if they can and never invite us to any of their meetings."[2]

To a large degree, the absence of U.S. interaction with the BJSM outside of procurement matters is understandable. The demands on an army and air force that had more than quintupled in size in the space of eighteen months and were expected to grow further from 1.5 to 4 million soldiers and airmen consumed army planners. Moreover, the staffs of the U.S. War Department and the Army General Staff were suffering their own growing pains. In the planning arena, continental defense and defense of Latin America absorbed the time and energy of the small WPD. Any "spare" time away from these activities focused on the Philippines, where the army leadership was reexamining the feasibility of reinforcing the islands as a deterrent to Japan. There was simply too much to do and too few people and too little time available.[3]

Although most of coalition planning occurred in London, matters occasionally arose that had to be coordinated through both missions. Establishment of a combined communications committee in London and Washington provides an illuminating case of how the two parties worked through initiatives, the time required to do so, and the difficulties inherent in achieving consensus in negotiations before Internet, email, and video teleconferencing. Although this example may seem a minor matter when compared to the major issues facing the coalition, establishing clear and effective lines of communication between the partners was a prerequisite for progress in other areas.

In the midst of the ABC-1 Conference, the U.S. delegation requested establishment of an Associated Communications Committee in London should the

United States enter the war. The British Chiefs of Staff approved the proposal, and the drafting committee incorporated the concept into the Communications Annex (IV) of the main ABC-1 Report.[4] Events in the summer and fall of 1941 swiftly demonstrated that the coalition would need the committee even before U.S. entry into the war. Moreover, it quickly became apparent to both sides that the real requirements inherent in cooperation rapidly had outstripped the original concepts outlined in the ABC-1 Report because more organizations and personnel would be necessary to ensure effective cooperation. On 25 August 1941, Major General Hap Arnold raised with Air Marshal Arthur Harris the question of whether to establish a Joint Air Communications Board to standardize air communications procedures, methods, and equipment. Harris agreed to Arnold's proposal but inquired of his superiors in the Air Ministry if the board would be a subcommittee of the London Communications Committee specified in the ABC-1 Report.[5] A month later the U.S. Joint Army–Navy Board met to consider the matter of establishing the London Communications Committee specified in the ABC-1 Report and concluded that conditions required two separate committees: a London Communications Committee with responsibilities as outlined in ABC-1 and an Inter-Service Communications Board in Washington to handle similar responsibilities in the Western Hemisphere.[6]

In the same week, members of USSOG met in London with the British Inter-Service Security Board to discuss a common code list and system for the two powers. They observed that the ABC-1 Report failed to address the problems of combined army or air force communications and proposed an amendment to the Communications Annex to provide for communications planning. Brigadier General McNarney of the USSOG drafted the revised annex, which he submitted to the authorities in Washington on 8 October.[6] After consulting with the Chiefs of Staff in London, the BJSM forwarded a series of recommendations to the U.S. Chiefs of Staff a week later. They urged revision of the Communications Annex of the ABC-1 Report to reflect formation of the two recommended committees and proposed additional subcommittees for coordination of air and land communications. The British also recommended that the two bodies perform only advisory functions with no executive authority. Finally, the British commented that although they did not expect the London Communications Committee to be the supreme authority, they did hope "that it will be agreed that it will have the final say in any matter which requires coordination between the two committees."[8] Nearly a month later the U.S. Chiefs of Staff agreed to establish the two committees as advisory bodies. However, U.S. authorities wanted each body to have equal standing, all recommendations to be reviewed by both committees, and final approval vested in both the British and the U.S. Chiefs of Staff. Like the British, they also called for a similar revision of the communications portion of the ABC-1 Report and recommended establishing more than a dozen subcommittees to handle the burgeoning requirements for communications coordination.[9]

The London Communications Committee held its first meeting two days later, on 12 November 1941, nearly three months after Arnold had raised the issue and almost eight months after ABC-1. As the first order of business, the committee began revising the Communications Annex to the ABC-1 Report. An immediate impasse ensued because each delegation received conflicting instructions. Although the differences may seem trivial, the impasse illuminates much of the friction inherent in the relations between the two partners. The U.S. committee members were under instructions to completely revise the annex and add paragraphs on air and land communications similar to those existing for naval communications. The British preferred to let the existing annex stand unchanged and instead draft an independent air–ground agreement that would not be part of ABC-1. The British argued that substantive amendment and approval through channels by both sets of Chiefs of Staff would take more time than the coalition might have. The chief U.S. representative, Lieutenant Colonel Jerry Matejka, finally stated that the Americans would adhere to their instructions until Washington changed them.[10]

The delegates could accomplish nothing more on this issue, so they switched to a discussion of the respective roles of the London committee and Washington board. The British advanced the premise that the Washington board was "an integral part of the Associated Communications Committee [London]" and implied that the London committee was the superior body. The Americans countered that each committee was but one part of a whole and had equal standing. Once again a deadlock ensued; the London committee made no progress, and the meeting eventually adjourned without result.[11] Neither conflict would be resolved until the de facto allies formed the Combined Communications Committee well after Pearl Harbor.

Cooperation between USSOG and the British authorities in London provides a more favorable example of the collaborative efforts during the fall of 1941. The navies, in particular, operated at a high level of collaboration. For instance, the SPENAVO and his personnel oversaw the construction of U.S. naval bases at Londonderry, Northern Ireland, and three bases in Scotland—Loch Earne, Rosneath, and Loch Ryan.[12] The two navies carried out the convoy escort program agreed upon at the Atlantic Conference. Moreover, with President Roosevelt's "shoot on sight" order of 11 September in the wake of the "*Greer* Incident," the U.S. Navy moved from the planning to the execution phase of Anglo-American cooperation when the U.S. Navy provided its first escort of other than U.S. or Icelandic vessels for an eastbound convoy on 16 September. The U.S. Navy essentially waged limited war from that point forward.[13]

General Chaney and his staff officers in the army section of USSOG also enjoyed considerable success in developing the plans necessary to implement their respective portions of the ABC-1 Report. By mid-August, SPOBS personnel had reconnoitered all potential base sites in Northern Ireland, finished preliminary inspections of pursuit aircraft bases in the United Kingdom, and decided that the token brigade-size ground force would be stationed in the vicinity of Wrothem, Kent, southwest of London. Chaney also indicated his satisfaction with airdromes for the U.S. bomber force.[14]

On 20 September, Chaney submitted a comprehensive report to the War Department outlining SPOBS's recommendations for the employment of U.S. Army and Army Air Force units in the United Kingdom after the United States entered the war. All units, totaling approximately 107,000 men, would operate under British strategic direction, and all, save the bomber force, would operate under British tactical command as well. Chaney urged the early establishment of a supreme American headquarters in England to exercise the command functions delimited under ABC-1 and to ensure the employment of U.S. forces strictly in accordance with the provisions of ABC-1 and U.S. policy.[15] The War Department apparently took no action on Chaney's recommendations, which is not surprising because his plans were contingent upon U.S. entry into the war. After U.S. entry into the war, however, these recommendations, even though the U.S. Army did not implement all of them, provided the basis for the initial movement of forces to the United Kingdom in early 1942. More importantly, they served as the initial plans and blueprint for Operation Bolero, the buildup of supplies and forces for the eventual cross-channel invasion at Normandy in June 1944.

In addition to coalition planning under ABC-1, Chaney and SPOBS also became responsible for coordinating the technical aspects of all logistics and materiel cooperation with the British, in particular Lend-Lease. In light of the growth of Lend-Lease activities in Britain and the complications added by the increasing aid given to Russia, in late August Chaney strongly recommended to the War Department that it revise SPOBS's duties. He urged immediate establishment of "a technical section of air, ordnance, and signal specialists to plan and coordinate with British, the exchange of information concerning research, development, methods of manufacture, military characteristics, and modernization to supervise the activities of U.S. service teams, technical observers, and test of U.S. equipment in campaign. This section also would be available to advise on Lend-Lease and administer details delegated to military authorities."[16] A month later a surprised Chaney received word that the War Department had not accepted his recommendations. His thinly stretched and overworked staff would instead assume the additional functions he had outlined in his letter. To exacerbate the problem, on 19 November the War Department informed him that SPOBs would also take on responsibility for overseeing all military aspects of the Lend-Lease program for Russia.[17]

These new responsibilities placed SPOBS in an unenviable position. Individually, either formulating the plans to implement the ABC-1 accords or administering Lend-Lease for either Britain or Russia was more than enough to occupy fully the limited SPOBS staff. The combination of the three missions nearly overwhelmed them. At the very least, the demands sowed a great deal of confusion within the American ranks, which stemmed largely from too few people trying to accomplish too many disparate tasks in too little time. This internal confusion naturally carried over into their relations with the British.[18] This small illustration points out the daily handicaps under which the SPOBS staff and their British counterparts labored in the days leading up to Pearl Harbor and partially explains the slow progress of coalition planning efforts.

Beyond these demands, USSOG eventually became embroiled in the continuing debate over the British Review of Grand Strategy introduced at the Atlantic Conference and later harshly criticized by the U.S. Chiefs of Staff. Remarkably, the British took nearly six weeks to digest and reply to the American comments on the strategic review. By mid-November, the British Joint Planning Committee had reassessed the document and found its original conclusions quite satisfactory. Indeed, in an internal memorandum, the planners expressed dismay that the U.S. Chiefs of Staff failed to grasp the innate correctness of the proposed British grand strategy.[19] Without doubt, the British were almost totally tone-deaf on this issue and remained unaware of how seriously upset the Americans were with British strategy.

The British Joint Planning Committee organized their critique under four major points. First, they believed that the U.S. Chiefs of Staff failed to comprehend the full effect of American entrance into the war. Although the British planners appreciated that substantial time would be required to realize the full potential of American mobilization, they fervently held that the moral effect on the allied peoples would be a large and rapid contribution. Moreover, like a drowning man seeing a life preserver, they convinced themselves that this moral effect might immediately tilt the scales against Germany.[20] Second, despite U.S. reluctance and inability to undertake operations outside the Western Hemisphere anytime soon, the British staff officers wanted to continue contingency planning for operations in French Northwest Africa. They agreed that the current situation did not favor such an operation, but they felt that circumstances seldom remained static, and a sudden strategic shift, such as U.S. entry into the war, might make such an operation possible. Nor did the British recognize that the limited number of U.S. planners had no time for such a remote contingency.[21]

Points three and four of the British Joint Planning Committee report addressed the issue of an air versus land offensive to defeat the Germans. On this issue, once again, the British believed that the American military leaders had missed the point. For the British, the heavy bomber constituted the only major offensive weapon Britain could wield at the time. Contrary to American perceptions, the British believed they were concentrating their efforts on military targets, thus simultaneously weakening the German military machine while eroding civilian morale. Granted, the current scale of operations was small, but the British remained convinced that sufficient numbers of heavy bombers provided largely by the United States, of course, would bring Germany to its knees. Only then, according to the Joint Planning Committee, would the British undertake significant land operations on the Continent. However, undertake them they would. Finally, the planners observed that the Americans had failed to grasp the complementary nature of the heavy-bomber offensive and the use of land forces.[22]

The content and tone of the Joint Planning Committee's remarks conveyed two key impressions. First, the British believed their strategy to be sound. Second, the British felt they needed to educate the U.S. Chiefs of Staff before the neophyte Americans did permanent damage to the British procurement program in the United States. In other words, the British determined that they simply needed to talk louder and slower. That the British still clung, after six weeks of deliberation, to their ideas in the face of strong and sustained U.S. resistance to the strategy review is remarkable. For example, the thought that U.S. entry into the war would suddenly alter Hitler's strategic calculus seems a conclusion born of desperation, particularly considering that Germany controlled almost all of Europe and the Wehrmacht was approaching Moscow. In addition, Britain's own experience in withstanding the Blitz should have given the planners pause about the efficacy of bombing. Simply because the bomber was the only offensive weapon available did not make it an effective option. Granted, the British were trying to make a virtue of necessity, but their misplaced faith in aerial bombardment did not stand up to the test. This failure did not stop the British, however, from concluding that they had to make the Americans see the error of their ways.

While the British debated the best means to convince the Americans of the validity of the strategic-bombing concept, USSOG was carrying out its own evaluation of the British bombing campaign and bomber program. The Americans' conclusions were largely negative. In a cable to Washington, Rear Admiral Ghormley commented on a recent mass night raid in which the British incurred very high losses for little concrete result. Ghormley noted that, to make matters worse, the losses were due more to bad weather than to German action. He added that daylight bombing was impractical, if not prohibitive, even though most of the Luftwaffe was serving on the Russian front. Based on his appraisal and, no doubt, on some parochial service interest, Ghormley recommended that the United States move from production of heavy bombers to ground support and naval aircraft.[23]

Shortly thereafter, members of USSOG met with the British Joint Planning Committee to discuss the British reaction to the U.S. criticism of the Review of Grand Strategy. Brigadier General Dykes noted that the original paper was prepared as a brief statement of British intentions, and he could readily expand on any points where the U.S. Chiefs of Staff had questions. He added that, perhaps, the paper had been too brief in parts, thus leading to misunderstandings. To resolve these issues, the British would now offer a more detailed explication of their points.[24] After quickly passing over such secondary issues as the importance of U.S. entry into the war and operations in French Northwest Africa, the British representatives focused the discussion on the role of the heavy-bomber offensive in British strategic thinking.[25] They agreed that only a land offensive could bring about the total defeat of Germany. However, the British pointed out that at the moment they could not undertake such operations and would not be able to do so until after their strategy of wearing away at German superiority through air power, blockade, propaganda, and subversion had time to take effect. Only then, they emphasized, could the British military invade the Continent with any assurance of success.[26] As far as the British were concerned, the heavy bomber offered the best means of weakening Germany. Dykes also reassured the Americans that the British would concentrate on military targets. Their analysis, however, had concluded that the most lucrative military target was the German transportation network, which would also strike at civilian morale. Thus, they would get a double return on their investment. In conclusion, according to Brigadier General Lee, "Dykes said that they had examined it [the bombing strategy] from every point of view and would be very glad if we could give them the solution."[27] The debate then ranged off on the validity of the British targeting strategy and the effectiveness of their bombing effort. The meeting ended inconclusively and led Lee to conclude that "the whole impression left on my mind by two hours and a half discussion is there is a wide abyss still existing between Great Britain and the United States in terms of time and thought."[28]

An abyss also existed within the American mission as well. Several key members of USSOG—Ghormley, Chaney, and McNarney—had been unable to reach an internal consensus on the efficacy of British bombing strategy. All agreed that at the moment the bomber remained Britain's only offensive weapon. However, the real issues were, first, a matter of effectiveness and, second, what production priority the heavy bomber should have. Here, Chaney and McNarney, both air officers, disagreed with Ghormley, who urged a cut in bomber production to free up raw materials for other programs, most likely with ship building in mind.[29] Thus, the divided Americans in London could offer no reasoned alternative to the British strategy. Before USSOG could transmit the new British rationales to Washington for assessment there, the Japanese attacked Pearl Harbor on 7 December, and events overtook any future analysis as the tyranny of the urgent temporarily deferred arguments over issues of strategy in Europe.

Concurrent with these discussions were near continuous debates over strategy and plans for the Far East. That the Anglo-American military planners had to focus almost solely on the Far East was due in no small part to their inability to develop a viable defense plan for the region before the Japanese opened their initial offensives. At the Atlantic Conference, the U.S. and British Chiefs of Staff aired their differences over the ADB Report. After sometimes bitter discussion, the two sides agreed, or so at least the British thought, that the British Chiefs of Staff would draft a revised report. By the end of August, the British had completed their new version, entitled ADB-2. Few substantive differences existed between the original ADB Report and the ADB-2 Report. For example, although the British removed all elements with a political connotation from the main body of the report, they simply moved them to an annex, with the blithe caveat, "The following matters of a political nature, and hence unsuitable for inclusion in a Military Agreement, were included in the Report of the American-Dutch-British Conversations. It is recommended that these matters be discussed between respective Governments of the Associated Powers."[30]

Nor did the amended version contain any substantive changes in the strategic and operational terms. The British stressed that their commitments to the dominions demanded that the Far East area of responsibility had to include the Netherlands East Indies, Australia, and New Zealand. To meet U.S. objections, they added a caveat that this provision in no way implied that national forces—that is, the U.S. Asiatic Fleet—would have to serve outside their respective national areas. In addition, again out of deference to the Americans, the revised report underscored the importance of the defense of the Netherlands East Indies to the security of Singapore and emphasized that the coalition would defend the northern line of the Malay Barrier with all naval and air forces that they could make available.[31]

The British did not, however, elaborate on what forces would be available for this important mission. In fact, they removed the initial disposition of naval forces originally contained in the ADB Report. Instead, following U.S. recommendations at ABC-1 in Washington, the British planners suggested deferring such details to local commanders, who could develop comprehensive operational plans once the respective governments approved the main report. Finally, the report stipulated that the U.S. Asiatic Fleet would come under the strategic direction of the British CINC of the China Station only at the discretion of Admiral Hart, the CINC of the U.S. Asiatic Fleet—another point yielded to the Americans.[32]

If the British believed that this new version of the report would placate the Americans, they were sadly mistaken. Reaction from the U.S. military authorities was almost universally negative. In letters to Stark, Ghormley criticized the British for failing to eliminate the political connotations of the agreement. He noted the report did not resolve U.S. objections to the British command structure in the Far East. Nor did the report provide for British naval forces to "take a predominant part in the defense of the British position in the Far East area until the problematical arrival of British reinforcements."[33] He concluded that as matters stood, the report did not present an effective plan for the defense of the Far East and that "personally, I think the only way to do that job is to start from scratch and do it all over again, not take a finished draft and try to correct it to meet new suggestions."[34]

For the moment, the British remained blissfully unaware of the American reaction. Indeed, an Admiralty message to the British Admiralty Delegation in Washington assumed imminent American approval of the revised ABD-2 Report, revealing the depth of that ignorance. The message also laid out the potential agenda items for another conference in Singapore. This meeting would include representatives from all affected nations, who would flesh out the operational details for the defense of the Far East, identify initial forces likely to be available, prepare detailed operational plans, and outline a potential distribution of forces.[35] In the first week of October, however, "Terrible"

Turner informed Admiral Danckwerts of the BJSM that "while the American Chiefs of Staff had not completed their full examination of ADB-2 and while the proposals have met some of our objections, we do not feel that the fundamental defects have been eliminated. In fact, I am inclined to think that the ADB agreement not only is not an advance on the ABC-1 Report but that it actually represents a retrograde step."[36]

Continuing his lecture, Turner added that the U.S. Chiefs of Staff remained convinced that the defense of the Malay Barrier was a British-Dutch responsibility and urged "that the British Chiefs of Staff in London give this matter their earnest attention, and endeavor to prepare an effective campaign plan that will have real teeth in it." Turner noted that the U.S. Army and Navy staffs would continue a detailed examination of the report and that for the time being it would be better to continue coordination through cooperation than to attempt to put together a new agreement. In other words, for the Americans, at least, doing nothing was better than implementing the current British proposal. Finally, Turner informed Danckwerts that due to "interests of security" he was unable to provide the British with any information on the new U.S. joint (combined) war plan Rainbow 5. In a gratuitous dig, Turner added that this was "a view which the British Chiefs of Staff apparently share, as we are never informed concerning the details of projected British operations."[37]

The matter remained in limbo until the end of October, when Ghormley notified the Admiralty that the U.S. military authorities considered the ADB-2 Report a dead letter. He recommended drafting a new plan, preferably by the local commanders in the Far East, based on the ABC-1 Report.[38] The British finally took the less-than-subtle hint. The Admiralty instructed its delegation in Washington to inform the U.S. Chiefs of Staff that because of the issuance of the U.S. war plan Rainbow 5, the changed situation in the Far East, and the American reluctance to accept ADB-1 or ADB-2, the British were willing to start anew with another conference based on the ABC-1 Report. The British also informed the U.S. authorities that, per American requests, they would consolidate the British command structure in the Far East under the CINC of the Far Eastern Fleet and that they were readying a capital ship task force for dispatch to the southwestern Pacific.[39]

In an immediate reply, Admiral Stark expressed satisfaction with the British action, especially the decision to streamline their command structure. However, Stark intimated that the British had not gone far enough. He urged the British to consolidate all commonwealth naval forces in the Far East in this new command. He also informed Admiral Pound that he was still disturbed that the British had not allocated adequate forces to execute their portion of the strategy. Worse, Stark believed the British continued to disperse those limited forces.[40] He also criticized Pound's call for another ADB conference. He pointed out that the ABC-1 Report contained sufficient detail to cover the existing situation. Stark agreed to the need for detailed operational planning, but he bluntly pointed out that although Admiral Layton and Admiral Hart had agreed on various plans for combined action, these plans were entirely unrealistic because the British did not have the forces to hold up their end of the bargain. Ironically, given the American fixation on unity of command, Stark concluded, "Due to the intricacies of the problem it seems preferable for the US and UK forces and the three air elements in the Far East to coordinate operations by the method of cooperation and not by unity of command."[41]

Less than a week later Admiral Stark and General Marshall reiterated these views in a formal letter to the BJSM. The U.S. Chiefs of Staff commended the British for their decision to send naval reinforcements to Singapore. However, they pointed out that with the decreased likelihood of a German invasion of the British Isles, the British also could afford to release air elements for service in the Far East. Moreover, although the U.S. Chiefs of Staff again confirmed that the ADB and ADB-2 Reports were unacceptable, they nevertheless declined Pound's call for another conference. They proposed instead that the naval portions of the ABC-1 Report remain in effect and recommended amending the air and land portions of the Washington accords to reflect current forces and future reinforcements destined for the Far East. Above all, U.S. authorities wanted to avoid another "large conference of so many diverse elements as were represented at the ADB Conference." They advocated keeping future collaborative efforts on the broadest possible plane, preferably at the levels of the Chiefs of Staff. Once the Chiefs of Staff reached a major decision, then the local commanders would be free to develop detailed operational plans. These plans would not be combined plans, however, for again, the Americans affirmed, "coordination of operations would be by method of cooperation" only.[42]

To this end, the U.S. Chiefs of Staff recommended that the individual national staffs develop their own plans and that representatives of the respective national services could then meet to coordinate their efforts. To set the wheels in motion, the Americans invited Admiral Sir Tom Phillips, CINC of the newly established British Far Eastern Fleet, to Manila as soon as he reached Singapore and established his command. In Manila, Phillips would confer with Admiral Hart and General Douglas MacArthur, who had been recalled to active duty by Roosevelt in July 1941 as commander of the U.S. Army Forces in the Far East.[43]

The dispatch of Phillips and his small force to Singapore represents a belated British recognition after nearly four years that the United States was not going to "pull the British chestnuts out of the fire" in the Pacific. The British would have to assume responsibility for defense of Singapore and the Far East. To be fair, circumstances in the Atlantic had changed decidedly in the previous several months. The sinking of the *Bismarck* and active U.S. escort of convoys had freed up Royal Navy assets for employment in the Far East. Moreover, Phillips's initial force was the vanguard for what would be a much larger capital fleet, even if it lacked adequate land or naval aviation support.[44]

The upcoming conference between Phillips, Hart, and MacArthur would not be the first efforts in collaboration at the local level since the ADB Conference in April that year. Despite ambiguous guidance and limited information from Washington, Admiral Hart had maintained almost continuous contact with his British and Dutch counterparts. Unfortunately for the soon-to-be allies, these talks had not been very productive. In the first place, it appears that the Navy Department had failed to keep Hart adequately informed about U.S. strategy and plans or the status of Anglo-American cooperation. As a result, Hart was never sure how much information he could give to the British and Dutch; therefore, he gave them either only general information or nothing at all until such time that the Navy Department belatedly authorized him to do so.[45]

At the same time, lack of timely information from Washington may not have had a severely deleterious effect on Anglo-American cooperation in the Far East because local planning proceeded at a painfully slow pace. For instance, Admiral Layton did not forward the British plans based on the ADB proceedings until 18 July, a full two months after the conference. Even with this delay, Layton noted that the plans lacked sufficient detail. Hart's response time was not much better—he did not acknowledge receipt of the plans for two weeks and failed to provide more than general information and comments.[46]

Another major problem lay in the British plans, which relied on the provisions of the ADB Report. The United States had rejected the arrangements, so the British plans for combined operations were virtually worthless. Worse still from Hart's standpoint, the British based their defensive schemes largely on air power, which they did not possess in the Far East, at the expense of the other facets of modern warfare. Hart blamed the latter problem on Air Chief Marshal Sir Robert Brooke-Popham, CINC, Far East, of whom Hart held a very low opinion.[47] The net result of the efforts between the local commanders from April to November 1941 meant that when Phillips, Hart, and MacArthur met in Manila in December they would still be struggling with basic issues of collaboration. More importantly, they lacked an overarching coalition grand strategy as well as an agreed coalition theater strategy to guide their deliberations. That this state of affairs existed nearly a year after ABC-1 and almost four years since Ingersoll's visit to London in January 1938 augured poorly for the upcoming talks.

Admiral Phillips arrived in Manila on 5 December, and discussions commenced the next day. Hart began with a comment that all agreed the meeting was a preliminary conference "from which it is hoped that he [Phillips] and I can agree upon everything that is basic for Joint Plans; after which he will bring into consultation the New Zealand, Australian, and other British Empire forces and those of the N.E.I. [Netherlands East Indies]."[48] From the notes on the conference, it appears that two major issues surfaced during the discussions. The first concerned the technical aspects of cooperation. MacArthur stated that army and navy forces would operate independently of each other, though the army would supply air cover for any naval offensives. A good portion of the conversations dealt, therefore, with the practical aspects of army–navy coordination, such as means of controlling aircraft over water, recognition signals, communications, procedures, antiaircraft control, and the like. From the general tone of the report, it seems that Hart and Phillips were more concerned with the intricacies of army–navy coordination than with cooperation between the two navies.[49]

The other major issue concerned the use of Manila as an advance base for offensive operations. At the start of his remarks, Admiral Phillips informed the two American commanders that at present he had only two capital ships, H.M.S. *Prince of Wales* and H.M.S. *Repulse,* because the aircraft carrier H.M.S. *Indomitable,* slated as the third member of the original task force, had run aground off Jamaica and was unavailable. However, he expected two more capital ships by Christmas, and an additional two, perhaps three, battleships could leave England at any moment. Thus, within six weeks Phillips hoped to have seven capital ships to carry out operations against the Japanese Fleet.[50]

Although Phillips acknowledged Singapore's utility as a defensive base, he noted its unsuitability for offensive operations. He inquired about the feasibility of using Manila as an Allied advanced base. A lengthy interchange ensued that covered all aspects of the defense of the Philippines, the state of the defenses of Manila Bay, and port facilities. At the conclusion of these discussions, Phillips urged the establishment of Manila as a forward operating base as soon as possible. Because of the strategic situation, the state of the current defenses, and the remote possibility of major reinforcements, Hart remained skeptical of the idea. He only promised to take up the matter with his superiors.[51]

Despite his reservations on the question of Manila, Hart noted his satisfaction with the results of the first day's meeting. As he commented in a message to the Navy Department, the three officers made plans for the initial disposition of all surface forces—the British Battle Fleet at Singapore and a U.S. cruiser strike force in the vicinity of Borneo. They also completed arrangements for the use of naval air and submarine assets, established command relationships, and made provisions for the exchange of liaison officers. True to his word, Hart also raised the issue of developing Manila into an advance base.[52]

The three commanders agreed to a second day of meetings. Unfortunately, an intelligence report indicating a major Japanese movement toward Malaya intervened, and Phillips hastily returned to Singapore on the evening of 6 December.[53] Two days later (Far East time), the Japanese struck Pearl Harbor and throughout the Far East. By 10 December, U.S. naval and air forces on Oahu had suffered grievous losses, MacArthur's air force was largely destroyed on the ground, and Hart's tiny fleet was withdrawing south, soon to be crushed alongside its Dutch ally defending the Malay Barrier. Phillips, who had been integral to Anglo-American naval cooperation since 1938, lay with the *Prince of Wales* and *Repulse* at the bottom of the South China Sea.[54]

Historian Ian Cowman blames the United States for the loss of these two great ships. He argues that ultimately the two ships were lost not because of tactical events but "rather more [because of] US intransigence in February 1941 [at ABC-1]. This forced a resurrection of the defunct Eastern Fleet strategy."[55] Cowman overstates his case. The British did not have to resurrect such a strategy. Strategy is about hard choices, and they could have taken a page from the American approach to the Philippines, recognized that Britain had more commitments than resources, established priorities, focused on defending the sea lines of communication to Australia and New Zealand across the Indian Ocean, and not reinforced Singapore. This appears to be the decision they made concerning ground forces at least, for in early December 1941 Field Marshal Dill told General Alan Brooke (later Lord Alanbrooke), incoming chief of the Imperial General Staff, that "he had done practically nothing to meet [the Japanese] threat . . . we were already so weak on all fronts that it was impossible to denude them further to meet a possible threat."[56] However, Churchill and the War Cabinet chose to reinforce Singapore and the Far East with ships.

Churchill could have followed Admiral Pound's advice and waited until the Royal Navy gathered sufficient ships to provide a balanced fleet. Granted, such a fleet would have required Britain to assume greater risk in the Atlantic and the Mediterranean and would have needed significantly more power and resources, including most of Britain's aircraft carriers, if it were to stand any chance against the Japanese. However, according to official historian Stephen

Roskill, the British intended to send only a single aircraft carrier. Moreover, Phillips did not mention an aircraft carrier in his conversations with Hart and MacArthur.[57]

A force such as Phillips described—even at full strength—could have been a recipe for an even bigger disaster that likely would have led to even greater losses of ships and lives. This is not an argument from hindsight with knowledge of the great carrier battles that soon dominated the war in the Pacific. The Royal Navy had launched the first successful carrier-based aviation attack against the Italian Fleet at Taranto in November 1940. A Swordfish torpedo bomber had crippled the *Bismarck* sufficiently to allow the home fleet to catch up to and sink the battleship. British carrier aviation soundly defeated the Italians at Cape Matapan. The Royal Navy suffered grievously from land-based aircraft during campaigns in Norway, Greece, and Crete. Thus, the British had more than sufficient advance warning about what was likely to occur, even if they, like others, had not grossly underestimated the proficiency of the Imperial Japanese Navy.

Churchill instead chose to send the two ships to Singapore. However, as Christopher Bell ably argues in a very balanced analysis of the episode, "These movements were part of the attempt to create an impression of growing British strength and resolve in the Far East, but it is important to understand that they were conceived as part of a broader strategy of deterrence."[58] Churchill was trying to persuade the Japanese that Britain was acting in concert with the United States, which also was reinforcing the Philippines at this time. The hope was that the appearance of what seemed to be coordinated Anglo-American actions might convince the Japanese that an attack on British possessions would bring the United States into the conflict, thereby reinforcing the deterrent effect of the deployment of the small detachment.[59] Unfortunately, the Japanese were not impressed, deterrence failed, and Churchill, who grossly overestimated the deterrent power of the Allied force, must bear a considerable share of the responsibility for the disasters that followed.

Substantial blame for the loss of the two ships has to fall on their commander, Admiral Tom Phillips. As Bell points out, positioning the ships at Singapore as a deterrent did not have to lead inevitably to their loss. Phillips sailed the ships forward from Singapore without air cover even though aware of Japanese air resources and without knowledge of Japanese fleet dispositions. This movement was either a calculated risk or reckless gamble, depending on one's perspective. However, as Bell notes, "the recently promoted Phillips lacked first-hand war experience and was well known for underestimating the vulnerability of capital ships to aircraft."[60]

Regardless of the assignment of blame, the Japanese crippled coalition naval power in the Pacific and set the stage for a multipronged offensive that by April 1942 effectively ejected the British, Americans, and Dutch from the Far East and the Pacific west of Hawaii. With the British pushed back into the Indian Ocean and the loss of all British and U.S. possessions in the western Pacific and Southeast Asia, there was no longer much need for Anglo-American collaboration in the war against Japan. Indeed, until the summer of 1945 the Pacific largely would remain an American lake.

In many ways, the final, intense efforts in Anglo-American collaboration during the last months of 1941 represent both a culmination of the labors of the coalition and a continuation of the dichotomy in U.S.-British cooperation that had existed since the beginning of the military conversations in 1938. The partners, the Americans especially, were still finding their feet and working through new organizations and unfamiliar policies and processes, many of which were cumbersome and time consuming. These conditions offered considerable opportunity for confusion, misapprehension, and friction. Strict U.S. adherence to the letter of ABC-1 did not help, nor did British efforts to ensure London's dominance of many aspects of the coalition. As the parties ironed out issues, streamlined processes, sanded down some friction points and oiled others, cooperation would improve in terms of both timeliness and effectiveness.

As time consuming and frustrating as all meetings and conferences may have been, it was better to take these necessary steps so that negotiations, procedures, and processes were in place before the tidal wave of crises that swept over the coalition after Pearl Harbor. In the Atlantic, either much of the ABC-1 Report was in force, or the staffs had completed detailed planning and were awaiting American entry into the war. Unfortunately, on the other side of the globe, there was no commensurate success story. When Japanese bombs fell on the Philippines, Hong Kong, Malaya, and Singapore, no comprehensive strategy existed for a coalition defense of the southwestern Pacific, and the now de facto allies had only cursorily addressed the most fundamental areas of cooperation.

The reasons for these differences run like thread throughout the course of Anglo-American collaboration over the previous four years as well as the last three months of 1941. Neither collectively nor individually did the partners possess sufficient resources to handle both regions simultaneously. Anglo-American planners recognized this fact and agreed early on to concentrate their efforts in the Atlantic while remaining on the defensive in the Pacific. The coalition could not agree, however, on what such a strategic defensive would entail. Therein lay the rub. That said, the projected buildup of a substantial capital fleet at Singapore indicates ultimate British acceptance of U.S. arguments for the defense of the Malay Barrier and the Far East. Had the Japanese allowed the British time to establish a fleet in the Far East, the British and Americans could have resolved their differences, perhaps, and opened a way for full cooperation in the Pacific. Regrettably, the Japanese refused to cooperate, and the coalition's unseen clock expired.

Conclusion

By the time the Japanese bombed Pearl Harbor, Britain and the United States had been engaged in collaborative military efforts for nearly four years. Granted, much of the early collaboration was hesitant and rudimentary. However, the pace of cooperation accelerated in the summer and fall of 1940. Moreover, from January 1941 on, Anglo-American military staffs were deeply engaged in planning for what most recognized would be eventual U.S. entry into the war. It is reasonable to ask, therefore, how well these efforts prepared the now allies for the trials of global war. Given the complexities of the collaboration and the number and scope of subsidiary themes in the narrative, it is appropriate first to address those subordinate topics before turning to overarching conclusions and observations.

The Special Relationship

Franklin Roosevelt reached out to Winston Churchill shortly after Churchill returned to government as first lord of the Admiralty in September 1939. No doubt, Roosevelt's innate curiosity, penchant for personal diplomacy, and desire for insider information motivated the president to develop a relationship with His Majesty's Government during this time of crisis. Given his history with then prime minister Neville Chamberlain, however, Roosevelt could not be sure that Chamberlain would enter into such an arrangement. Churchill's long opposition to appeasement made him more likely to accept Roosevelt's proffer, and Roosevelt's sub-rosa relationship with the Admiralty during World War I when he served as the assistant secretary of the navy offered a suitable point of entry to the first lord. With Chamberlain's full knowledge, Roosevelt and Churchill initially maintained a desultory correspondence. Upon Chamberlain's resignation, Churchill's ascension to the premiership, and the fall of France, however, the Churchill–Roosevelt relationship moved to an entirely different level.[1]

Churchill later translated this new affiliation into two great peoples bound together in common cause. The cause may have been common, and the bond may have existed, but it is clear now that Churchill dramatically overstated his case.[2] First, the two leaders' roles and responsibilities were quite different. Roosevelt was head of state, whereas Churchill was the king's first minister, an important distinction. Although the dominant personality within His Majesty's Government, Churchill still had to take the War Cabinet and full Cabinet into account during his decision making. A vote of no confidence could turn him out of office overnight. Short of impeachment, Franklin Roosevelt would serve the remainder of his four-year term and if reelected in November 1940 would enjoy another four years in office. Although Roosevelt had to deal with Congress and may have been susceptible to public opinion, he was still the chief executive of the U.S. government and as commander in chief directly commanded the U.S. Armed Forces. As a result, each leader enjoyed advantages or suffered circumscribed authority different from the other.

Second, Churchill was leading an active belligerent, engaged in a daily struggle for national survival. Conversely, Roosevelt led a nation not yet at war, whose populace generally had no desire to become embroiled in another European conflict within a generation. Churchill's priorities were national survival, defense of the home islands, and security of the links to the British Empire. Roosevelt's primary duty was securing the United States and its overseas possessions. British and U.S. national interests converged because Roosevelt saw an independent Britain as key to the security of the Western Hemisphere and the United States. So long as Britain and the Royal Navy existed, Hitler was unlikely to launch a successful assault across the Atlantic. After June 1940, therefore, as historian B. J. C. McKercher notes, "On both sides of the Atlantic, the cold calculation of national interests brought Britain and the United States—and Churchill and Roosevelt—closer together."[3] Nonetheless, as Calvin Christman points out, "Mutual interests are not the same as mutual trust."[4]

This is not to say that Churchill and Roosevelt did not enjoy a special relationship. There was mutual trust and even mutual admiration between them.[5] They appeared to enjoy each other's company. However, national interest, not some idea of a close personal bond that translated into a bond between the two nations, formed the basis of that relationship.[6] As the war continued, the United States assumed the role of dominant partner. Moreover, as the two nations' interests diverged, the personal relationship between the two leaders also began to fray. Only Roosevelt's untimely death and Churchill's magisterial version of history, *The Second World War,* allowed Churchill to shape and at times to manipulate the historical narrative of the wartime relationship—whether personal or national—for his own purposes in the Cold War.[7]

Even assuming that the relationship was necessary for Anglo-American success, it was still insufficient to guarantee victory. Stated more boldly, a close relationship between Roosevelt and Churchill was helpful, indeed fortuitous, but ultimately not essential. Neither Churchill nor Roosevelt enjoyed a close relationship with Stalin, yet all three and their nations managed to cooperate sufficiently to defeat Germany.

Conversely, a functioning collaboration between British and U.S. militaries was the sine qua non for success in the Atlantic, North Africa, the Mediterranean, and western Europe. Although the two leaders might set policy, others below them in rank had to turn that policy first into strategy and then into actions to achieve those strategies and policies. As Mark Lowenthal observes, "The pattern of unofficial contacts between the two governments was of great significance."[8] Nowhere was this truer than in the military arena. In a war of global proportions, this meant balancing military ends, ways, and means to achieve success. It also meant putting together a military coalition, in the words of a postwar report from British army staff in Washington, that "had not been attempted in history as between Allies."[9] That condition meant, eventually, a solid organization with thousands of military and civilian staff and refined policies and procedures to turn the leaders' vision into reality. Anglo-American military collaboration prior to Pearl Harbor was the basis for the coalition's success.

Roosevelt's Intent

Few issues surrounding Franklin Roosevelt's leadership are more controversial than the question of how the United States became involved in World War II. Opinions of contemporaries and historians alike run a broad range. Characterizations of Roosevelt as duplicitous manipulator dragging the United States into an unnecessary war against public will or as "reluctant belligerent" outline the extremes of the argument. The middle ground offers equally divergent opinions. On the one hand, Roosevelt was a timid leader whose haphazard decisions and inadequate guidance and oversight caused the United States to stumble into war with Japan and then Germany and Italy. On the other hand, he was a wise leader who foresaw eventual U.S. involvement and slowly but steadily educated his fellow citizens into grasping the need for American participation.[10]

Each of these arguments contains an element of truth. Viewed in hindsight, it is easy to construct an almost linear progression of events that supports the conclusion that from the very beginning of the conflict in 1939 Roosevelt was intent on entering the war but bided his time: amendment of the Neutrality Act of 1939 with its "cash-and-carry" provision; communications with Churchill; arms and ammunition as well as various missions to the United Kingdom during the summer and fall 1940; the destroyer–bases deal of September 1940; the Arsenal of Democracy Speech (December 1940); Lend-Lease and ABC-1 from January to March 1941; extension of Neutrality Patrols in the

Atlantic; occupation of Iceland in July 1941; the Atlantic Charter; the "shoot on sight" order in September 1941; and a shooting war in the Atlantic offer a compelling narrative to those who view Roosevelt's actions in a jaundiced light.

Hindsight, however, may present a much clearer picture than events did at the time. Roosevelt was a consummate politician and a considerable strategist. Politics and strategy are not static activities; each requires iterative assessments, calculations, and decisions, oftentimes in highly dynamic environments where an opponent's decisions add to the complexity. Because of the volatile, uncertain, and ambiguous nature of their work, politicians and strategists like to keep as many options open for as long as possible and close options only when circumstances force them to do so. That was certainly the case with Franklin Roosevelt, an iterative thinker, who loathed closing any options. Thus, as the situation evolved, so, too, did Roosevelt's thinking. Thus, what can appear in hindsight as an almost linear connection of events was anything but linear at the time as Roosevelt continuously scanned the strategic environment and evolved his positions as conditions dictated. And as numerous examples indicate, Roosevelt frequently chose not to act.

Up to ABC-1, at least, Roosevelt's actions resulted from ad hoc decision making, not some concerted plan. For example, Roosevelt only reluctantly challenged neutrality laws throughout 1938–1941. Whether he did so out of personal conviction or concern for isolationist public opinion will likely remain an open question. Although he made decisions in the summer of 1940 that caused the United States to provide an increasing flow of aid to Britain, Britain's survival underwrote U.S. national security. The president authorized Rear Admiral Ghormley to pursue unofficial talks with the Admiralty in the fall of 1940, but Ghormley in London and Stark in Washington struggled to place those conversations in a coherent geostrategic context because of an absence of policy guidance. Historians are unlikely to know with any assurance how much guidance Stark received from the president. What we do know is that if Stark received guidance from Roosevelt, he did not transmit it to Ghormley, who tried to give the British the impression that he had no guidance from the president. In the end, one must take Ghormley's laments of inadequate guidance at face value and conclude that he was operating on his own in a policy vacuum that Roosevelt created.

To complicate matters, Roosevelt was prone to launching trial balloons that he himself popped because he tended to follow sweeping rhetoric with little or no action. If he took a step forward, he frequently took another step back or to the side. Throughout 1940 and much of 1941, Roosevelt justified his actions, which the American public largely accepted, as a means to keep first

France and Britain and later Britain in the war. Alternatively, these actions plausibly supported the defense of the Western Hemisphere and the United States. Indeed, one could view Roosevelt's actions in the fall of 1940 and summer of 1941 as establishing an outpost line—lease of British bases from Newfoundland to the Caribbean, occupation of Iceland, U.S. Navy patrols, and defense of the Caribbean and South America—that protected the Western Hemisphere and the United States as much as it assisted the United Kingdom. Although a conspiratorial reading of events also is plausible, the evidence indicates that Roosevelt was hedging his bets. He saw British survival as a keystone to U.S. defense and any benefit to Britain was secondary to protecting U.S. interests.

With the completion of ABC-1, there was little doubt that the United States was drawing closer to war. This does not mean that Roosevelt was intent on speeding up that process. One must recall that Roosevelt himself had the phrase "compelled to resort to war" inserted into the report. To the chagrin of his key civilian advisers, he seemed in no hurry to create such conditions. Despite subsequent planning under the provisions of ABC-1 and the many disasters of April–May 1941, Roosevelt took no major action. Even after the passage of Lend-Lease, he was reluctant to begin escorting convoys and instead expanded the scope of ongoing Neutrality Patrols. His military leaders likewise suffered from an absence of clear and direct guidance against which to develop their plans. It is clear that Roosevelt provided neither strong leadership nor definitive guidance, a condition that led J. G. Utley to conclude, "The failure to coordinate diplomatic ends and military means was typical of the chaos that plagued foreign policy management in Washington during 1940–1941."[11] These conditions hardly seem those of a man intent on bringing the United States into the war.

Those individuals of a more skeptical persuasion may simply conclude that Roosevelt's policy zigzags and vague guidance were intentional, simply part of a deception that, in modern parlance, offered the president plausible deniability. Alternatively, these hesitations and retreats could have been the result of not yet making up his mind and wanting to keep as many options open as he could, for as long as possible. This latter conclusion certainly is in keeping with Roosevelt's overall modus operandi, whether in political or policy realms. Thus, it can be concluded that throughout 1940–1941 Roosevelt would do only what was needed at a particular moment and no more, thereby ensuring the greatest flexibility for future initiatives.[12]

Geostrategic conditions eventually compelled Roosevelt to step closer to war. However, this outcome had as much to do with threats to U.S. national interests posed by German successes in the Atlantic, Europe, and the Mediterranean and aggressive Japanese acts in the Pacific as it did with any desire to support Britain. Although Russian resistance exceeded early expectations, the Germans were on the outskirts of Moscow, and the first Russian counteroffensive had yet to strike. British losses in the Battle of the Atlantic looked to be spiraling out of control, and attacks on U.S. ships were rising. Nonetheless, only after several sinkings of U.S. ships did Roosevelt finally act. Even then, the U.S. Navy was his chosen instrument, and active naval operations did not have to translate necessarily into formal U.S. entry into the war.

Nor would U.S. entry in the war inevitably have led to commitment of air or land forces. Naval operations may have been sufficient in the president's mind. Indeed, Roosevelt's actions in the summer of 1941 lend credence to other plausible outcomes. For example, his lackadaisical approach to renewal of conscription legislation caused many to wonder at the time, as well as later, about the president's ultimate intent.[13] Similarly, Roosevelt's guidance in the late summer and early fall of 1941 to send home Army National Guard units and reduce the projected size of the army and the army air force indicate that even if the United States entered the war, the president may have intended to restrict U.S. intervention to naval forces. Even with naval and limited air force participation in the war, absent Japanese entry into the war, army forces may have provided only for hemispheric defense.[14]

Given Roosevelt's penchant for secrecy, misrepresentations, and diversionary tactics as well as the absence of written records, history likely will never know with certainty his true intent.[15] This might have been part of his ploy. As John Charmley notes, the president may have gotten the last laugh on this matter: "The story is told of how, on the evening of the inauguration of the Roosevelt Library, the President was in high, good humour, and when asked why, he responded: 'I'm thinking of all the historians that will come here thinking they'll find the answers to their questions.'"[16] Perhaps author Lynne Olson's judgment best sums up the controversy:

> That image of the president as a sinister "super-Machiavelli," intent on ramrodding America into conflict in insidious and unlawful means doesn't hold up. But neither does the more beneficent idea, put forward by many historians, that Roosevelt, knowing full well that America must enter the war but hamstrung by strong isolationist public opinion before Pearl Harbor, had no alternative but to edge the country toward intervention by indirect and often devious methods. . . . And it's far from clear that Roosevelt himself, while certainly determined

to help Britain, ever intended that America go to war, at least in the sense of sending troops.[17]

In the end, Roosevelt's ultimate intent may not really matter. Nazi or Japanese aggression or a combination of the two likely would eventually have impinged sufficiently on U.S. national interests to draw the United States into war with one or both powers. Clearly, Japanese actions soon would have crossed an American red line, and there was no other power that could have met the challenge. Britain, preoccupied with Germany and Italy, certainly could not. Nor could the French, who already had acquiesced to Japanese occupation of Indochina. The Dutch were incapable of meeting the Japanese without outside support. In Europe, perhaps an Anglo-Russian coalition might have been able to halt Nazi and Fascist aggression without U.S. intervention. Conversely, such a coalition may only have been able to secure a tenuous peace, with a strong Germany dominating western and central Europe. To avoid straying too far into conjecture, suffice it to say that regardless of Franklin Roosevelt's motivations, German and Japanese actions were likely ultimately to have drawn even a reluctant belligerent into World War II.

Churchill as Grand Strategist

The flood of assessments of Winston Churchill as strategist shows no sign of abating, but the importance of his role as grand strategist in the establishment of the Grand Alliance and, especially, of Anglo-American collaboration is not in doubt. During 1940–1941, Churchill held a weak geostrategic hand, which he played with considerable skill. First, he convinced his own government and then the British people that Britain could and would fight on after Dunkirk. Second, he persuaded Franklin Roosevelt not only that would Britain survive but also that it could put to good use any war supplies the United States might provide. He even convinced the American people to help pay for the bulk of those supplies. Finally, stiff resistance during the Battle of Britain convinced Adolf Hitler to turn on the Soviet Union, granting Britain respite and ultimately sowing the seeds of Germany's destruction.

After France collapsed and Britain stood alone, Churchill's overriding priority was to bring the United States into the war at Britain's side.[18] Throughout 1940–1941, Churchill assiduously cultivated Franklin Roosevelt to that end. As John Colville, one of Churchill's trusted private secretaries recorded in his diary in 1948, "Winston said: 'No lover ever studied every whim of his mistress as I did those of President Roosevelt.'"[19] By carefully feeding Roosevelt select bits of critical or interesting information, Churchill fostered the relationship while simultaneously playing on Roosevelt's concerns over U.S. national interests. For example, in the summer of 1940 Churchill hinted not so subtly that unless the United States provided materiel support, Britain might suffer defeat. He foreshadowed the consequences of a new government or peace conditions that might mean that the Royal Navy no longer buffered the United States. Churchill also used this tactic as leverage during the negotiations over the destroyer–bases deal to spur Roosevelt to an agreement. Although some have concluded that Roosevelt may have gotten the better end of the "hard bargain," Churchill got the United States to align with Britain, a most unneutral act that was far more important than fifty obsolescent destroyers.[20]

In a similar fashion, Churchill also deftly stroked U.S. public opinion. His magnificent oratory not only bolstered British morale but also seized the moral high ground that helped convince the American public that Britain was worth helping. Similarly, Churchill's statement in his speech in support of Lend-Lease, "Give us the tools and we will finish the job," played well to the American public.[21] It also played well to Roosevelt's desire that America be the "Arsenal of Democracy" and possibly to avoid its becoming an active belligerent.

Churchill also was one of the strongest proponents for staff talks with the United States. Beginning with the Anglo-American Standardization of Arms Committee discussion in August 1940, he made sure that Americans had remarkable access to key British policymakers, military leaders, and planning staffs as well as to the latest British plans and assessments. Although the amount and level of information going to U.S. military authorities were tightened up, the flow of intelligence was extraordinary, particularly since the Anglo-American relationship had no formal status, and there were no guarantees that the United States would enter the war as an active belligerent. Building slowly upon the limited naval talks in 1938–1939 and cooperation in materiel and allocation issues going back to 1938, the staff talks progressed from primarily naval conversations in fall 1940 to full-fledged staff talks (ABC-1) in Washington in spring 1941. Churchill's initiatives reaped tremendous strategic advantages. Although not yet a de facto ally, the United States had gone well beyond neutrality or even nonbelligerency to planning for combined, coalition operations should the United States enter the war, which was an increasing likelihood.

With the Japanese attack on Pearl Harbor, Churchill at long last achieved his ultimate goal of bringing the United States into the war at Britain's side. Granted, even had Churchill not been prime minister, U.S. national interests may eventually have drawn the United States into the conflict. However, "possible" does not equal "guarantee." This certainly might not have been the case, for example, if Neville Chamberlain had remained in power. Moreover, absent Churchill's tireless efforts to educate U.S. leaders and gradually but inextricably to weave U.S. and British policy, grand strategy, and strategy, the United States might have focused on the Pacific in the wake of Pearl Harbor. Certainly, strong public sentiment and key leaders in the U.S. Navy were pulling in that direction. That in the end the United States adhered to the grand strategy of dealing with Germany first is to Churchill's great credit. As Sir Michael Howard, for example, notes, "Churchill's greatest achievement lay not so much in the leadership he provided for his own countrymen as in the clarity with which he saw, from the very beginning of his Administration, that Britain was now dependent on the United States for her continued survival, and in the patience, the skill, the tenacity and the charm with which he coaxed the American people and their President in underwriting British independence."[22] Churchill's own account in *The Second World War* offers the most poignant assessment of his significant accomplishment:

> No American will think wrong of me if I proclaim that to have the United States at our side was to me the greatest joy.... So, we had won after all! Yes, after Dunkirk; after the fall of France; after the horrible episode of Oran; after the threat of invasion, when apart from the Air and our Navy, we were almost an unarmed people; after the deadly struggle of the U-boat war—the first Battle of the Atlantic, gained by hand's breath; after seventeen months of lonely fighting and nineteen months of my responsibility in dire stress. We had won the war. England would live; Britain would live; the Commonwealth of Nations and the Empire would live. We should not be wiped out. Our history would not come to an end. I went to bed and slept the sleep of the saved and thankful.[23]

Evolution and Iteration Lead to Victory

Despite Churchill's reported optimism on 7 December 1941, he had no inkling at the time of how long the war would last or of its eventual outcome. Nor when the bombs fell on Pearl Harbor was the Anglo-American coalition prepared for the audacity, ferocity, and proficiency of Imperial Japanese forces as they swept the Indian and Pacific Oceans from Ceylon to Australia to Hawaii to the Aleutians. Moreover, in the spring of 1942 German general Erwin Rommel resumed the offensive. By June, he seized Tobruk—rendering Churchill and the British public a considerable shock—and drove the British army back behind the Egyptian border. On the Russian front, the Wehrmacht launched a massive offensive. In the Southeast, the Germans reached Stalingrad and were on the verge of breaking through into the Caucasus. Months would be necessary before U.S. mobilization and the training, equipping, and employing of U.S. forces would hit its full stride.[24]

Given the seemingly endless series of disasters that befell the Anglo-American armed forces in the months following Pearl Harbor, it would have been hard to convince the average man on the street, be it Broadway or Piccadilly, that the military staffs of the two powers had ever talked to each other, much less engaged in nearly continuous staff conversations for the better part of two years. The lack of initial success against the Axis Powers was not, however, an accurate indicator of either the quantity or quality of work accomplished by the U.S. and British military establishments.

Despite the many faults in the coalition and the material unpreparedness of the United States, the partners were prepared mentally for the conduct of war on a global scale. Although largely ignorant of each other's plans, procedures, and intentions when they first made contact in January 1938, the military staffs had by December 1941 skillfully crafted the coalition's war aims and grand strategy. The partners integrated their national strategies and plans to support that grand strategy, developed operational plans necessary to achieve those ends, and constructed a coherent command structure to execute the entire program. As important, the two nations coordinated plans for producing and allocating war materiel. Finally, the Anglo-American military planners continually sought new and better methods to increase the operational efficiency of their individual and collective forces.

The coalition planners' greatest tangible achievement was the development of the grand strategy for the defeat of the Axis Powers. Long before the entry of the United States into the war, Anglo-American military staffs set the defeat of Germany as the coalition's top priority, recognized the importance of maintaining the British position in the Mediterranean and the Middle East, and agreed to stand on the strategic defensive in the Far East should Japan enter the war. To secure these objectives, the militaries agreed to use economic warfare to wear down the Axis Powers, carry out a strategic bombing offensive against Germany, strive quickly to eliminate Italy from the war, support resistance movements within occupied territories, and seize positions from which to launch a final offensive against Germany.

The fact that these now allied nations implemented these elements of grand strategy in toto and followed them throughout the war underscores the vital importance of the early informal negotiations. Granted, the coalition partners debated these issues, quite hotly at times, during the course of the war. There were many twists and turns along the journey, but the fact remains that the Anglo-American coalition followed the path of grand strategy that American and British planners had charted prior to December 1941. Moreover, no plan is perfect. As author Edward Miller reminds us, "Strategists are not clairvoyants."[25] Nor do minor divergences from a base plan invalidate the overall plan. Absent the extensive prior preparations, the Anglo-American coalition would have required considerably more time to react effectively, thereby substantially prolonging the war.

The development of the military strategy and the operational plans necessary to support the coalition's grand strategy also proved a significant achievement. Because the coalition had accepted the principle of "Germany first" nearly a year earlier, the staffs were able to complete a significant amount of collaboration prior to U.S. entry into the war. Despite sometimes diverging interests, differing views on strategy and operational approach—for example, with respect to the Mediterranean, the Far East, and the role of the heavy bomber—and competing materiel requirements, the respective staffs had completed considerable planning for employment of U.S. forces if the United States entered the war.

The importance of this planning is difficult to overstate. On the one hand, the amount of planning and the scope of those plans, especially for operations against Germany and Italy, made it difficult to walk away from those decisions. In the wake of Pearl Harbor, especially if Germany had not declared war on the United States, public outrage over the attack could have diverted the United States to greater activity in the Pacific at the expense of the Atlantic and Germany first. Moreover, even though Admiral Stark was an Atlanticist, other key U.S. Navy personnel, such as King and Turner, might have turned the United States more toward the Pacific.

At the same time, the planning that preceded the U.S. entry into the war served as the basis for the initial Allied efforts. By Pearl Harbor, the respective national planners had begun implementing a combined war plan for the Atlantic region. The U.S. Navy was cooperating closely with the Royal Navy in convoy operations in the northern Atlantic. Indeed, the U.S. Navy engaged in a virtual shooting war with the German navy from September 1941 on. Similarly, the deployment of U.S. Army Air Force planes and personnel laid the foundations for the deployment and employment of the Eighth U.S. Army Air Force in the short term and ultimately the U.S. Strategic Air Forces Europe, which first wrested air control from the Luftwaffe and then unremittingly pounded Germany from early 1944 until the end of the war in Europe. The staffs also developed the plans for the initial movement of U.S. Army units to the United Kingdom for employment against Germany. As a result, once the United States entered the war, deployments commenced quickly, allowing U.S. forces to engage much sooner and probably shaving six to twelve months off the war in Europe.

Equally important was the fact that many of the plans, even those not fully executed in the short term, later served as the basis for other Allied operations. For instance, the Bolero Plan for the buildup of supplies and men for the eventual invasion of France had its roots in the planning conducted before December 1941. In the shorter term, the buildup of supplies for Bolero helped support the invasion of North Africa in November 1942. Over the longer term, from January 1943 to July 1944 alone, almost 16 million tons of cargo and 1.7 million troops were transported to the United Kingdom in anticipation of the D-Day invasion of Normandy on 6 June 1944.[26]

These Anglo-American successes were all the more remarkable because the U.S. military had not yet mastered the intricacies of joint, much less coalition planning. Granted, the Joint Army–Navy Board had existed since 1903, but this body largely deconflicted plans independently developed by army and navy staffs. Trying to carry out coalition planning with a partner not effectively organized or practiced in joint planning added a considerable degree of difficulty. That British and U.S. staffs could effectively plan on such an ad hoc basis is to their lasting credit.

Coalition planners did not achieve total success in their efforts at strategic and operational planning. Whereas planning for the Atlantic and Mediterranean regions made considerable headway, the sailing in the Pacific and Far East was much less smooth. In fairness, however, neither independently nor collectively did the United States and Great Britain initially possess the military forces necessary to face Germany and Japan simultaneously. Forced at the time into a zero-sum game, the coalition chose to concentrate the majority of its forces against Germany, thus leaving insufficient forces to face the Japanese threat.

The near total failure of the Anglo-American staffs to fashion a functional plan for the defense of the Far East compounded the problem of inadequate forces. Here the coalition foundered on the rocky shoals of the Singapore issue. For a variety of imperial reasons and perceived military imperatives, the British remained wedded to Singapore. However, due to inadequate thought, poor planning, and, especially, insufficient resources, the British could not provide an adequate defense for what they repeatedly emphasized was the keystone of the empire. Although one may empathize with their plight, one should spare little sympathy for the British position. They could have made some hard choices about priorities, such as American recognition that the United States would not be able to hold the Philippines, and modified their ends and ways commensurate with their limited means. They instead consciously decided to hold fast to Singapore and convince the Americans to take up responsibility for defending British interests. U.S. planners, in contrast, adamantly refused to reinforce Singapore at the expense of broader U.S. interests in the Pacific. To make matters worse, some U.S. planners, in particular those in the navy, resented what they viewed as duplicitous British efforts to draw the United States into defending imperial interests that the British themselves were unwilling or unable to defend. The U.S. Chiefs of Staff essentially forced the British to secure their own interests at Singapore.

In the end, strategic conditions proved wrong the British assumptions about Singapore and the Far East. The loss of the bastion was not irretrievable. Indeed, had the British written it off sooner, they likely would have been spared the loss of more than 130,000 killed or captured in Malaya and Singapore as well as the loss of key ships off Malaya and in the Indian Ocean. No one celebrates this fact, but it adds weight to the contention that American planners and leaders were much more clear-eyed than their British counterparts about the nature of a strategic defensive in the Far East.

Without agreement at the highest echelons of command, it was unrealistic to expect local commanders in the Far East to conceive and implement a comprehensive plan for the defense of the region. This does not mean that local planners did not try to work out solutions. To the contrary, as the ADB Report indicates, planners in the Far East found common cause. However, their efforts failed to satisfy the leadership in Washington, who simply vetoed the report. Worse still, neither coalition partner subsequently provided clear guidance to the local commanders that would allow them to develop coherent plans that nested within national and coalition strategies. As a result, despite many months of effort, commanders in Manila and Singapore had little to show beyond a loosely worded agreement to continue coordination through cooperation—a thin paper stretched over a large crack in the coalition. Last-minute British concessions and efforts to dispatch a fleet to Singapore offered hope of eventually reaching a compromise. Japanese successes across the Pacific, however, eliminated the naval forces that would have served as the vehicle for such close collaboration, and with them went the last possibility for a successful combined Anglo-American defense of the Far East until much later in the war.

In hindsight, it is easy to criticize leaders and planners for not establishing clear strategic priorities and guidance in the summer and fall 1941. However, at the time they were beset by a broad variety and number of strategic challenges.

As a result, there were more strategic requirements than resources available to address them. Because the ends–means mismatch was so severe, it would have been difficult to resolve these challenges simply by changing ways. Moreover, such a conclusion presumes that the coalition partners could agree on those ways, which they did not. Last, only U.S. entry into the war could resolve these critical points of contention.

The military staffs enjoyed greater success in their efforts to establish a coherent command structure for the execution of the coalition's military strategy. The U.S. and British Chiefs of Staff divided the world into areas of strategic responsibility that ensured unity of strategic direction within those theaters and allowed for the efficient use of the coalition's military power. (See map 3.) This practice allowed the partners to focus their efforts and resources in their respective areas of responsibility. There were two key exceptions to this policy. In the Atlantic region, the planners subdivided the area and assigned strategic responsibility to one of the coalition partners. In the southwestern Pacific, however, Anglo-American planners were unable to construct a rational command structure in the Far East, largely because of their inability to fashion a coherent strategy for the defense of the area. Unfortunately, last-minute British attempts to accommodate American objections to their command structure proved too small, too fragmented, and too late to provide any substantive assistance.

Staff planners also created functional liaison machinery for the coalition. By December 1941, the liaison system had progressed through successive stages from the occasional exchange of individual staff officers to the establishment of large-scale military missions in both London and Washington. Although the lines of communication between the respective Chiefs of Staff were cumbersome at first, the coalition planners rapidly streamlined them. The relationship between USSOG in London and the British Chiefs of Staff was particularly exemplary. Although the affiliation between the BJSM in Washington and the U.S. Chiefs of Staff was less close, this state of affairs stemmed as much from poor joint U.S. Army–U.S. Navy coordination as it did from coalition problems. In any event, the system, although not perfect, provided flexibility, facilitated improved communications, and allowed for the transfer of vital information between the respective Chiefs of Staff. Despite its growing pains, the liaison machinery matured into an organization that rapidly emerged as one of the major strengths of the wartime coalition. At the local level, liaison organizations produced mixed results. In the Western Hemisphere, the Atlantic region, and the Mediterranean, liaison systems functioned quite ably. In the Pacific, the liaison structure never progressed beyond the rudimentary phase of the periodic exchange of individual staff officers or commanders.

Conclusion 249

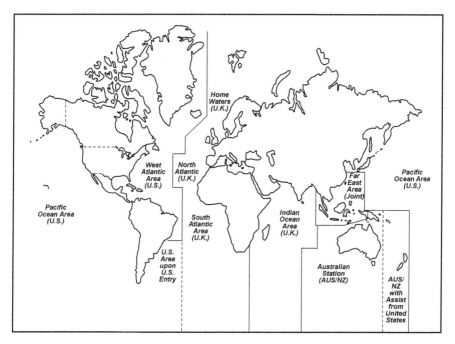

Map 3. Areas of Strategic Responsibility, 1 December 1941

Although the events of December 1941–January 1942 rapidly overwhelmed the provisions for coordination laid out in the ABC-1 Report, the report provided the basis for the Combined Chiefs of Staff organization and procedures that emerged from Arcadia, the first wartime conference of the official Allies held in Washington from 24 December 1941 to 14 January 1942.[27] The organization would take time to evolve and would experience growing pains. However, the time required to evolve the new structure and processes for high-level strategic direction undoubtedly was shorter than if the coalition had to start from zero.

A similar mixture of success and failure accompanied Anglo-American efforts to allocate war materiel efficiently. The foremost problem facing the coalition in this regard was the lack of sufficient manufacturing capacity to provide the quantities of war materiel that each partner required. Although the problem was not entirely resolvable, coalition members could have alleviated it had they quickly established a comprehensive structure for the distribution of raw resources, a priority of manufacture, a system for the allocation of finished goods, and a priority of shipment. From the outset, however, the British and Americans approached the problem from opposite directions. On the one hand, British planners first developed their military strategy and then allocated resources in accordance with the priorities inherent in their strategic objectives—that is, an approach in which ends drive means. On the other hand, U.S. planners first sought to determine the ultimate capacity of U.S. and British industry and then to fashion a strategy that made maximum use of industrial potential—an approach in which means drives ways. As a result, each side considered that the other had put the cart before the horse, and the coalition consumed a great deal of time sorting out production priorities.

British failure to coordinate their purchasing missions further complicated the situation. Throughout 1938–1941, British efforts to procure supplies from the United States too often operated at cross purposes and created much confusion, which thoroughly exasperated American political and military leaders. Anglo-American planners and leaders could have ameliorated some of these difficulties had the coalition agreed on a broadly based program of standardized arms and equipment. Each nation, however, approached the problem from its own national perspective, and so, in spite of the tremendous effort, the coalition achieved only limited success in this arena. More often than not, compromise resulted from dire British need and American ability to force through a solution, which created friction within the coalition.

Despite these issues, the partners resolved many of the core problems in allocating war supplies by December 1941. The British organized and streamlined the British Purchasing Commission; the partners settled priorities of manufacture, achieved a modest level of standardization, and agreed to numerous accords for allocating materiel. These achievements resulted in a nascent logistics structure that allowed for the coherent allocation of supplies, provided for flexibility in the execution of policy, and permitted growth. By the time of Pearl Harbor, the coalition had completed much of the all-important preliminary work concerning the manufacture and distribution of materiel, and so, with minor refinements, the Anglo-American logistics organization stood ready for the test of war.

Just as important, the negotiations first with the French and then with the British gave U.S. manufacturers a three-year head start on capitalization, design, development, and manufacturing. The sale of equipment and use by Britain and France also allowed the United States to battle-test and revise designs or in some cases time to develop entirely new equipment, such as aircraft and tanks. It also allowed the United States to take advantage of British developments and to pool resources, such as radar, sonar, and microwave technology. Not least, agreements on grand strategy and strategy established the capabilities needed for the United States to develop its own force structure, industrial mobilization, and fielding, equipping, and training of units. This saved much time and avoided at the very least a one- to two-year delay in the fielding and deployment of U.S. forces.

Although these accomplishments are significant, other less tangible but crucial factors contributed to the development of the coalition. Beyond gaining an understanding of national interests and objectives as a result of the early, informal contacts, the individuals involved in the negotiations came to understand one another and to garner insights into the personal idiosyncrasies, traits, and perceptions of their counterparts. These insights, in turn, allowed for increased understanding of national objectives and predispositions and provided potential solutions to problems facing the coalition.

More importantly, the lengthy negotiations that preceded the entry of the United States into the war allowed the participants at all levels to establish professional and personal relationships based on mutual trust, confidence, and respect. One cannot overemphasize the significance of this point. Only after forging such affiliations could the coalition begin to resolve its major conflicts. In the case of the Anglo-American staff discussions of 1938–1941, these relationships allowed for the continuous flow and exchange of information between military establishments. This information flow fostered reciprocal trust and respect and generated an ever-increasing spiral of cooperation. The high level of mutual confidence served to bond the British and American staffs and produced a symbiotic relationship far out of proportion to the sum of the partners' individual capabilities. Most significantly, the mutual trust and respect between the staffs generated perhaps the most critical ingredient of any coalition—the ability to meld divergent national perspectives into a coherent agreement when issues of significant national importance were at stake. Although the U.S. and British staff planners were not always successful in achieving agreement, more often than not they were able to compromise their individual service or national position for the common good.

Finally, several matters of accepted lore surrounding Anglo-American collaboration in this period require dispelling. In the first instance, the idea that British led the strategic dance or, worse still, duped their less-sophisticated or naive American cousins does not stand up to scrutiny. In reality, the Americans drove the development of grand strategy in this period. The U.S. military, beginning with Admiral Stark's Plan Dog in November 1940, guided the coalition to the dominant grand-strategy principle of "Germany first" as a growing convergence of American and British interests in the Atlantic region contributed to this decision. Moreover, the U.S. view that substantial U.S. forces would be necessary to defeat Germany prevailed over British desires for American forces to safeguard mutual interests in the Far East while Britain took responsibility for the Atlantic. As subsequent events would amply demonstrate, the idea that Britain could prevail over Germany absent considerable U.S. assistance seems implausible. In a similar vein, the U.S. refusal to reinforce Singapore compelled the British to revise their plans to defend the Far East. Thus, rather than hewing to the British grand-strategic line, U.S. planners led their British counterparts. The Americans also got their way on such divergent issues as unity of strategic direction, unity of command within areas of responsibility and theaters of operation, levels of U.S. support for operations in the Mediterranean, standardization of arms and equipment, and the allocation of materiel.

The Americans also routinely prevailed at the political level. Clearly, the United States drove a hard bargain on the destroyers-for-bases deal. Equally, the United States leveraged dire British straits to demand cash payments prior to the passage of Lend-Lease as evidence that Britain truly had reached its limits. For example, Roosevelt demanded payment of $50 million in gold transported by a U.S. war ship from South Africa, seized some British assets in the United States, and coerced the sale of others as proof of British fiscal exhaustion.[28] All of this caused Churchill publicly to support Lend-Lease while privately lamenting that the bill would mean, "as far as I can make out[, that] we are not only to be skinned, but flayed to the bone."[29] The United States also used Lend-Lease as quid pro quo for ending Imperial Preference.[30] In addition, the allocation of Lend-Lease materiel among China, Russia, and Britain followed U.S. guidance. At the highest policy levels, Roosevelt's language, not Churchill's, dominated the Atlantic Charter. Not least, Roosevelt made decisions at his pace, not Churchill's.

The characterization of the military coalition as competitive also has been overstated. This is not to say that competition did not exist. It clearly did. However, the military element of the coalition may have been the least-competitive aspect of the partnership. Certainly, there were those within the U.S. Navy—a group represented especially, perhaps, by Turner and King—who undoubtedly were biased. However, both Turner and King were naturally parochial, abrasive, and belligerent. Turner had earned his nickname "Terrible" long before he engaged with the British. And as one of King's daughters once remarked about her father, "He is the most even tempered man in the Navy. He is always in a rage."[31] Their competitive nature may have stemmed more from their innate personalities than from Anglo-American rivalry. At the same time, the other services were much less competitive. Certainly, U.S. and British army leaders differed over how to defeat the Wehrmacht, but Marshall and Dill were not competitive. Relations between planners on the War Department General Staff and the BJSM generally were amicable. The U.S. Army Air Force and the RAF were perhaps the least competitive of all. Certainly, they quarreled over allocation of aircraft, but leaders of both air forces fervently believed in the power of the heavy bomber and frequently united to defend their beliefs against their naval and army rivals.

Although the Anglo-American coalition was perhaps the most collaborative, interdependent military coalition then known, this does not argue that personal relations or altruism provided the basis of the relationship. Both militaries entered into this coalition with their eyes open and a strong understanding of the national interests at stake. However, they also faced the common challenge of solving real problems in the real world and under tremendous pressure. In that, they succeeded. They took vague, ambiguous policy guidance and turned it into grand strategy, which they then used to derive strategic ways to achieve grand-strategic ends. They established relationships, created the initial links and conduits of information, groped toward consensus, exchanged ever-more sophisticated levels of information—some among the most carefully guarded national secrets—and built the foundations of the relationship between the two militaries and, as a result, between the two nations. These relationships were sufficiently strong to withstand the stresses and strains of four years of war as well as the setbacks and the victories that naturally occur during war.

Although certainly not preparing the Allies for the exact circumstances they encountered upon American entry into the ongoing war, the sum of Anglo-American collaborative efforts before Pearl Harbor prepared the two nations' military staffs to cope with and adapt to evolving strategic conditions. No doubt, there was friction, sometimes quite serious, within the emerging coalition, as well as perceived and real competing national interests; differences over policies, strategies, and plans to protect those interests; and personal antipathies. Although such stresses within the coalition and postwar or contemporary criticisms of those tensions cannot be ignored, there also can be no doubt that the military members of the coalition managed to overcome these hurdles and helped lay the foundation for the most successful military coalition in history. British and U.S. political and military leaders as well as the planners who toiled daily to make cooperation a reality deserve great credit for their accomplishments.

This fuller picture of Anglo-American collaboration prior to Pearl Harbor puts the military contribution into its proper context. The success, then, of the wartime coalition from Pearl Harbor to V-J Day did not stem alone from common language, heritage, and political systems or the personal sympathies of the two heads of state. Rather, in large measure success was the product of an evolutionary process that took place between the military staffs before the entrance of the United States into the war. In short, the success of the military negotiations established a precedent and paved the way for discussions between the two powers across a broad spectrum of issues. These military deliberations led to close cooperation in political, diplomatic, and economic arenas and further cemented the relations between the two powers. Accomplishments in these other areas could not guarantee military success, but the achievement of the early, informal military collaboration served as the keystone upon which the coalition built later victory. Put simply, between December 1937 and December 1941 British and American staff planners forged the foundations of the Grand Alliance.

Reflections for the Future

The United States is unlikely to enter into a major conflict in the future without allies or coalition partners, so it may be useful to elucidate some general insights about planning for coalition warfare that might prove useful to future military planners and political leaders. Some of these observations may seem apparent or little more than common sense, but the fact that the United States has continued to stumble over these problems for the past seventy-five years gives one pause to reconsider them nonetheless.

Coalition planning revolves around national interests, which will always be the driving factor influencing the development and conduct of coalition planning and execution. Therefore, identifying relevant national interests of all major parties as quickly as possible, determining where mutual interests exist or overlap, and recognizing any conflicts will be crucial. Partners also must identify the priority of interests, so that if conflicts emerge, they can quickly establish precedent. Although national interests usually are enduring, the ways and means to achieve those respective interests can be quite dynamic and thus require continual management. The key to that management will be ensuring that the coalition recognizes respective national interests, remains alert to ongoing changes in interests or conditions, and resolves conflicts at the earliest opportunity.

A natural tendency exists for partners to gloss over differences in order to achieve consensus. However, coalitions do so at their peril. As the example of Anglo-American coalition differences over the Far East amply illustrates, deferring resolution of tough problems only exacerbates the problem. Later resolution may prove costly or impossible. As a corollary, national leaders and their senior military advisers should not push high-level conflicts down to subordinate commanders for resolution. If there is no agreement at the top, subordinates are unlikely to be able to devise solutions, especially if conflicting national interests are at stake. Indeed, as the example of the Far East in World War II once more illustrates, subordinate commanders are more likely to intensify than to solve problems.

Strategic challenges and requirements will likely exceed the resources available to address these issues. Nowhere is this truer than in the number, type, and quality of personnel who deal with coalition efforts. This admonishment applies especially to the highest leaders, their key civilian and military advisers, and their staffs. There is only so much time in the day, and the stamina of human beings, although variable, is finite. As a result, a coalition—regardless of the level within the parties to the coalition—can effectively handle only a certain number of major issues at any given time. This limitation requires coalitions to establish priorities as quickly as possible, make hard choices, and adapt them as conditions require. None of this is easy, particularly in dynamic geostrategic and national political environments.

To accomplish these difficult tasks means agreeing on a grand strategy as early as possible in the life of the coalition; monitoring the dynamic equilibrium of ends, ways, and means; and adjusting coalition strategy and objectives on a nearly continuous basis. These things, in turn, require an organization and processes to manage the monitoring and evolution of the coalition. After determining national interests and their priorities, establishing command-and-control and liaison mechanisms should be the next order of coalition business. Indeed, these activities may have to proceed in parallel because organizations and processes may need to be in place to adjudicate differences in national interests and approaches.

A successful coalition also depends on the careful selection of the personnel who will interact within the coalition. In short, people and personalities matter, especially in the upper echelons of the coalition. The relationship between Roosevelt and Churchill, for example, was vastly different from a likely one between Roosevelt and Chamberlain had Chamberlain remained prime minister. What might have happened during 1940–1941 had Admiral King been the U.S. chief of naval operations rather than Admiral Stark? At a lower level, how might Anglo-American collaboration evolved if Turner, not Ghormley, had been the special naval observer in London? If any one of these different elements had been in place, the overall coalition relationship undoubtedly would have been much rockier. If all three had occurred, Anglo-American collaboration would have been much more halting. Granted, national interests would likely have brought the two nations into partnership, but victory would have come at a much higher cost in lives and treasure.

Only the naive would presume that national pride and jealousies or personal egos and prejudices will not emerge in any future coalition. Sometimes individuals may cloak these issues in terms of professional disagreements, such as U.S.-British differences early in Operation Iraqi Freedom, when the two militaries quarreled over the best approach to deal with the growing insurgency.[32] The best a future coalition can do is structure organizations and decision-making processes to reduce friction as much as possible. Leaders must continually monitor for conflicts and friction points and quash these problems quickly, as they arise, removing and reassigning individuals if necessary.

Individuals selected for such coalition duties require a number of qualities if they are to be successful. Although always remaining cognizant of their national interests, they must be open-minded when identifying, evaluating, and comparing those national interests with respect to the partner nation's interests. They must be empathetic but not necessarily sympathetic with their partners and be able to see competing points of view. They must be skilled at achieving consensus without surrendering their national interests. At times, they must be able to perform the incredibly delicate task of balancing the achievement of overall coalition objectives with individual national interests.

Fulfilling these conditions is not an absolute guarantee of success, but the Anglo-American collaboration from 1937 to 1941 offers an example of what a future coalition can achieve if its members heed these insights. The Anglo-American coalition also offers an illustration of the difficulties inherent in fulfilling these general principles even when national interests closely align. Finally, this incredibly potent partnership provides a caution that even strong coalitions can develop fissures that require monitoring and tending to over time.

Chronology

1937

1 May	Roosevelt signs Neutrality Act (enlarged statutes of August 1935 and February 1936)
28 May	Chamberlain becomes British prime minister
7 July	Marco Polo Bridge Incident, start of Japanese invasion of central China
6 November	Italy joins Anti-Comintern Pact
11 December	Italy withdraws from League of Nations
12 December	Panay Incident

1938

1 January	Ingersoll mission to Great Britain
January	French begin materiel discussions with the United States
12–13 February	German Anschluss (occupation of Austria)
20 February	Eden resigns as foreign secretary
13 April	Britain begins materiel discussions with the United States
7–29 September	Czech Crisis
29 September	Munich Agreement
12–25 October	Japanese invest Hong Kong, capture Canton and Hankow
19–20 October	Monnet visits Roosevelt at Hyde Park
9 November	Kristallnacht (nationwide German pogrom)

1939

15 March	German occupation of rump Czechoslovakia
21 March	Germans occupy Memel
31 March	France and Britain pledge military support to Poland
7 April	Italy occupies Albania

29 April	Germany, Italy, Spain sign Anti-Comintern Pact
22 May	Formal German-Italian Alliance, Pact of Steel
8–11 June	King George VI and Queen Elizabeth visit United States
12–14 June	British commander T. C. Hampton visits Washington and meets with Admiral William Leahy and other Americans
14 June	Japanese blockade British concession at Tientsin
29 June	Start of Lord Riverdale's visit to the United States to address war materiel
30 June	U.S. Joint Army–Navy Board directed to create war plans Rainbow 1–5
20 August	Danzig Crisis begins
23 August	Nazi-Soviet Non-Aggression Pact
1 September	German invasion of Poland
3 September	France and Great Britain declare war on Germany and Churchill becomes First Lord of the Admiralty
11 September	Roosevelt writes Winston Churchill, inviting correspondence between them
17 September	Soviets invade Poland
5 October	Churchill responds to Roosevelt's first letter (11 September)
4 November	U.S. Neutrality Act amended, repealing embargo on arms and placing exports to belligerents on a cash-and-carry basis.
30 November	Start of Russo-Finnish War (through 12 March 1940)

1940

1 January–31 December	Battle of the Atlantic
9 April	Germany invades Norway and Denmark
10 May	Germany invades Netherlands, Belgium, Luxemburg, and France
10 May	Churchill becomes prime minister
15 May	Churchill's first message to Roosevelt as prime minister, later requests destroyers
27 May	U.S. Fleet to remain in Hawaii and not return to West Coast
28 May–4 June	Dunkirk evacuation
8–9 June	Evacuation of Narvik

Chronology 259

10 June	Italy declares war on France and Britain, invades France
13 June	Roosevelt meets with advisers on U.S. strategic options
22 June	France surrenders
2 July	U.S. export controls against Japan instituted
3 July	British Fleet attacks Vichy French ships at Mers-el-Kebir
10 July	Battle of Britain begins
15 July–3 August	"Wild Bill" Donovon in Britain on special mission for Roosevelt
18 July	British close Burma Road under Japanese pressure
20 July	Congress passes "Two-Ocean Navy" bill
20 August	Anglo-American Standardization of Arms Committee talks commence in London
2 September	U.S.-British destroyers-for-bases deal
7 September	London Blitz begins
13 September	Italy invades Egypt
16 September	Passage of first U.S. peacetime draft
22 September	Japanese troops enter Indochina
26 September	United States bans iron ore exports to Japan
27 September	German-Italian-Japanese Tri-Partite Pact
8 October	Churchill announces reopening of Burma Road
18 October	Japanese bomb Burma Road
28 October	Italians invade Greece
4 November	Admiral Stark's Plan Dog Memo
5 November	Roosevelt reelected to third term
15 November	U.S. flying boats begin patrols from Bermuda
20 November	Stimson–Layton Agreement (standardizes military equipment)

1941

29 January–29 March	ABC-1, Washington, D.C.
11 March	Roosevelt signs Lend-Lease Act
30 March	U.S. Navy begins patrolling western Atlantic
10 April	Roosevelt announces Greenland (Denmark) under U.S. protection
11 April	U.S. Navy extends naval patrol coverage to 26 degrees west; Great Britain covers to 35 degrees west
10 May	Climax of London Blitz

18 May	BJSM nucleus established in Washington, D.C.
19 May	SPOBS established in London
20–31 May	Germans capture Crete
27 May	Roosevelt declares unlimited state of national emergency
27 May	*Bismarck* sunk
22 June	Germany invades the Soviet Union
27 June	Japan declares Greater East Asia Co-Prosperity Sphere
1 July	U.S. Navy aircraft begin antisubmarine patrols from Newfoundland
7 July	U.S. forces assume defense of Iceland
19 July	U.S. Navy begins convoying to Iceland
5 August	U.S.-U.K. embargo on raw materials to Japan
9–12 August	Atlantic Conference
14 August	Atlantic Charter announced
18 August	Extension of Selective Service passes by one vote
4 September	Destroyer U.S.S. *Greer* attacked by U-boat
11 September	Roosevelt issues "shoot on sight" order to U.S. Navy
16 September	United States begins convoy operations in northern Atlantic
1 October	Protocol (in Moscow) among Soviet Union, United Kingdom, and United States on distribution of war materials for the next nine months
17 October	Destroyer U.S.S. *Kearny* struck by German torpedo (11 killed)
31 October	Destroyer U.S.S. *Reuben James* sunk (115 killed)
17 November	Amended Neutrality Act to permit U.S. merchant ships to be armed and to carry cargoes to belligerent ports.
25 November	U.S. Navy begins compulsory convoys
6 December	Germans stopped short of Moscow
7 December	Japanese attack Pearl Harbor

Notes

For detailed information about documents and primary material gathered from archives and repositories located in the United Kingdom and the United States, please see the author's note at the beginning of the bibliography.

Abbreviations

AASAC	Anglo-American Standardization of Arms Committee
ABC	American-British Conversations
ABDA	American-British-Dutch-Australian
ADB	American-Dutch-British
ADM	Admiralty Records
AEF	American Expeditionary Force
AGWAR	Adjutant General, War Department
AIR	Air Ministry Records
AL	American liaison
ALUSNA	U.S. naval attaché, London
ANZAC	Australia–New Zealand Army Corps.
AVIA	Ministry of Aircraft Production Records
BC (J)	Bailey Committee (Joint)
BH	Beaverbrook–Harriman Committee
BJSM	British Joint Staff Mission, Washington, D.C.
BUS	British-U.S.
BUS (J)	British-U.S. (Joint)
CAB	Cabinet Office/War Cabinet Records (War Cabinet as of September 1939)
CAS	chief of the Air Staff
CCS	Combined Chiefs of Staff
CID	Committee of Imperial Defense
CIGS	chief of the Imperial General Staff
CINC	commander in chief
CINCAF	commander in chief, U.S. Asiatic Fleet
CNO	chief of naval operations
COMNAVEU	commander, U.S. Naval Forces, Europe
COS	Chiefs of Staff (British or U.S.) or chief of staff
Encl.	enclosure
FDR	Franklin Delano Roosevelt
FDRL	Franklin D. Roosevelt Library
FO	U.K. Foreign Office

G-2	Intelligence
HMSO	His or Her Majesty's Stationery Office
JB	U.S. Joint Army–Navy Board
MID	Military Intelligence Division
MM	Military Mission
MM (J)	Military Mission (Joint)
NACP	National Archives and Record Administration, College Park, Md.
NHHC	Naval History and Heritage Command (formerly Naval History Division and Naval Historical Center), Washington, D.C.
OAB	Operational Archives Branch, Naval History and Heritage Command, Washington, D.C.
OPD	Operations and Plans Division, Office of the Director of Plans and Operations
OPNAV	Office of Naval Operations
PHAH	*Pearl Harbor Attack Hearings*
PREM	Prime Minister's Office
RAF	Royal Air Force
RG	Record Group
SPD	Strategic Plans Division
SPENAVO	special naval observer
SPOBS	Special Army Observer Group in London
SSA	secretary of state for air
SWC	Supreme War Council
TNA: PRO	The National Archives, United Kingdom, Public Records Office, Kew, London
USAMHI	U.S. Army Military History Institute, Carlisle Barracks, Pa.
USAWWI	*U.S. Army in the World War*
USAWWII	*U.S. Army in World War II*
U.S. GPO	U.S. Government Printing Office
USSOG	U.S. Special Observer Group
WCB	Washington, D.C., Communications Board
WO	War Office
WPD	War Plans Division

Prologue

1. For details of the surrender at Reims, see Forrest C. Pogue, *The Supreme Command*, in *U.S. Army in World War II: European Theater of Operations* (1954; reprint, Washington, D.C.: Office of the Chief of Military History, 1978), 486–490.

2. For background leading up to the ceremony and its conduct, see ibid., 490–493.

3. For details after 15 August 1941 leading up to the surrender ceremony, see *The Reports of General MacArthur*, vol. 1: *The Campaigns of MacArthur in the Pacific*, prepared by his staff (1966; reprint, Washington, D.C.: U.S. Army Center of Military History, 1994), 446–458. For details of the ceremony on 2 September 1941, see ibid., 1:454–458.

Introduction

1. The most useful account is Robert Strassler, ed., *The Landmark Thucydides: A Comprehensive Guide to the Peloponnesian Wars* (New York: Free Press, 1996).

2. U.S. wars in the twentieth century: World War I, World War II, Korea, the Cold War, Vietnam, Operation Desert Shield/Storm (the first Iraq War, 1990–1991), and Kosovo. U.S. wars in the twenty-first century: Afghanistan, Iraq, and Libya thus far.

3. Gordon A. Craig, "Problems of Coalition Warfare: The Military Alliance against Napoleon, 1813–1814," Harmon Memorial Lectures in Military History no. 7, U.S. Air Force Academy, 1965, 1.

4. Jehuda Wallach, *Uneasy Coalition: The Entente Experience in World War I* (Westport, Conn.: Greenwood Press, 1993), 1; U.S. Department of Defense, Joint Chiefs of Staff, *Department of Defense Dictionary of Military and Associated Terms,* JCS Publication 1-02 (Washington, D.C.: Joint Staff , 8 Nov. 2010), as amended through 15 Nov. 2015, at http://www.dtic.mil/doctrine/new_pubs/jp1_02.pdf (accessed 23 Jan. 2016).

5. U.S. Department of Defense, *Department of Defense Dictionary,* 57, and *Oxford Dictionary of US Military Terms,* at http://www.answers.com/topic/coalition-warfare (accessed 5 Nov. 2012).

6. Karl von Clausewitz, *On War,* trans. and ed. Michael Howard and Peter Paret (Princeton, N.J.: Princeton University Press, 1976), 119.

7. For particular aspects of these concerns, see David M. Kennedy, *Freedom from Fear: The American People in Depression and War, 1929–1945* (New York: Oxford University Press, 1999); Robert Dallek, *Franklin D. Roosevelt and American Foreign Policy, 1932–1945* (New York: Oxford University Press, 1979); Waldo Heinrichs, *Threshold of War: Franklin D. Roosevelt and American Entry into World War II* (New York: Oxford University Press, 1988); William L. Langer and S. Everett Gleason, *The Undeclared War, 1940–1941* (New York: Harper and Brothers, 1953); and any one of the many single- and multiple-volume biographies of Franklin D. Roosevelt and Winston Churchill.

8. Maurice Matloff and Edwin M. Snell, *Strategic Planning for Coalition Warfare, 1941–1942,* in *United States Army in World War II: The War Department* (hereafter *USAWWII* plus the specific volume subtitle) (Washington, D.C.: U.S. Government Printing Office [GPO], 1953); James Leutze, *Bargaining for Supremacy: Anglo-American Naval Collaboration, 1937–1941* (Chapel Hill: University of North Carolina Press, 1977); Christopher Thorne, *Allies of a Kind: The United States, Britain, and the War against Japan, 1941–1945* (New York: Oxford University Press, 1978); David Reynolds, *The Creation of the Anglo-American Alliance: A Study in Competitive Cooperation* (Chapel Hill: University of North Carolina Press, 1982); Malcolm Murfett, *Fool-Proof Relations: The Search for Anglo-American Naval Cooperation during the Chamberlain Years, 1937–1940* (Singapore: University of Singapore Press, 1984); and Mark Lowenthal, *Leadership and Indecision: American War Planning and Policy Process,*

1937–1942, 2 vols. (New York: Garland, 1988), are the most notable examples. More specialized accounts that touch on Anglo-American collaboration include Ian Cowman, *Dominion or Decline: Anglo-American Naval Relations in the Pacific, 1937–1941* (Oxford: Berg, 1996); Greg Kennedy, *Anglo-American Strategic Relations and the Far East, 1933–1939* (Portland, Ore.: Frank Cass, 2002); Mark M. Lowenthal, "Roosevelt and the Coming of the War: The Search for United States Policy, 1937–1942," *Journal of Contemporary History* 16 (1981): 413–444; B. J. C. McKercher and Roch Legault, eds., *Military Planning and the Origins of the Second World War in Europe* (Westport, Conn.: Praeger, 2000); Malcolm H. Murfett, "Are We Ready? The Development of American and British Naval Strategy," in John B. Hattendorf and Robert S. Jordan, eds., *Maritime Strategy and the Balance of Power: Britain and America in the Twentieth Century* (New York: St. Martin's Press, 1989); and G. Kurt Piehler and Sidney Pash, eds., *The United States and the Second World War: New Perspectives on Diplomacy, War, and the Home Front* (Bronx, N.Y.: Fordham University Press, 2010).

9. Kennedy, *Anglo-American Strategic Relations and the Far East*, 2. Kennedy argues that the period 1933–1939 is more appropriate and that the analysis should end with the start of the war in Europe in September 1939. Although there may be some logic to his assertions, I believe them to be overstated.

10. Alex Danchev, "On Specialness: Anglo-American Apocrypha," in *On Specialness: Essays in Anglo-American Relations* (New York: St Martin's Press, 1998), 2–4. For a variety of views on the "special relationship" and its importance, see, for instance, Joseph Lash, *Roosevelt and Churchill, 1939–1941: The Partnership That Saved the World* (New York: Norton, 1976); David Reynolds, "Roosevelt, Churchill, and the Wartime Anglo-American Alliance, 1939–1945: Toward a New Synthesis," in William Roger Louis and Hedley Bull, eds., *The Special Relationship: Anglo-American Relations since 1945* (Oxford: Clarendon Press, 1986), 17–41; Keith Sainsbury, *Churchill and Roosevelt at War: The War They Fought and the Peace They Hoped to Make* (New York: New York University Press, 1994); Warren F. Kimball, "Fighting with Allies: The Hand-Care and Feeding of the Anglo-American Special Relationship," U.S. Air Force Academy, Harmon Lecture in Military History no. 41, 1998, at http://www.usafa.edu/df/dfh/harmomemorial/docs/Harmon41.pdf (accessed 10 Aug. 2012); Robert Skidelsky, "Imbalance of Power," *Foreign Policy* (March–April 2002): 46–55; Kennedy, *Anglo-American Strategic Relations and the Far East;* and Andrew Roberts, *Masters and Commanders: How Four Titans Won the War in the West, 1941–1945* (New York: Harper Collins, 2009).

11. Winston S. Churchill, *The Second World War*, 6 vols. (Boston: Houghton Mifflin Press, 1948–1953).

12. Danchev, "On Specialness," 2.

13. For a deconstruction of *The Second World War*, an analysis of its strengths and flaws, and an overall assessment of Churchill and his history, see David Reynolds, *In Command of History: Churchill Fighting and Writing the Second World War* (New York: Random House, 2005). For a description of "sentimentality" and an overview of initial historiography of the special relationship, see Reynolds, *The Creation of the Anglo-American Alliance*, 1–3.

14. Thorne, *Allies of a Kind*, and Reynolds, *The Creation of the Anglo-American Alliance*, are excellent examples.

15. Danchev, "On Specialness," 3–4. For examples of how assessments of the Churchill–Roosevelt relationship have continued to evolve, see John Charmley, *Churchill's Grand Alliance: The Anglo-American Special Relationship, 1940–1957* (New York: Harcourt Brace, 1995), and Jon Meachem, *Franklin and Winston: An Intimate Portrait of an Epic Friendship* (New York: Random House, 2003).

16. For examples of these views of Roosevelt, see Joseph E. Persico, *Roosevelt's Secret War: FDR and World War II Espionage* (New York: Random House, 2001); Dallek, *Franklin Roosevelt and American Foreign Policy*; Lowenthal, *Leadership and Indecision*; and Robert A. Divine, *The Reluctant Belligerent: American Entry into World War II* (New York: Wiley, 1965). For the latest poles in the debates, see Lynne Olson, *Those Angry Days: Roosevelt, Lindbergh, and America's Fight over World War II, 1939–1941* (New York: Random House, 2013), and Jeffrey W. Taliaferro, "Strategy of Innocence or Provocation? The Roosevelt Administration's Road to World War II," in Jeffrey W. Taliaferro, Norrin M. Ripsman, and Steven E. Lobell, eds., *The Challenge of Grand Strategy: The Great Powers and the Broken Balance between the World Wars* (Cambridge: Cambridge University Press, 2012), 193–223.

17. Quoted in Reynolds, *In Command of History*, xix. For only a few of the more recent examples, see, for example, Ian Kershaw, *Fateful Choices: Ten Decisions That Changed the World, 1940–1941* (New York: Penguin, 2007); Carlo D'Este, *Warlord: The Life of Winston Churchill at War, 1874–1945* (New York: Harper Collins, 2008); Max Hastings, *Winston's War: Churchill, 1940–1945* (New York: Knopf, 2010); and William Manchester and Paul Reid, *The Last Lion: Winston Spencer Churchill*, vol. 3: *Defender of the Realm, 1940–1965* (New York: Little, Brown, 2012).

18. David Hackett Fischer, *Paul Revere's Ride* (Oxford: Oxford University Press, 1994), xv.

19. Craig, "Problems of Coalition Warfare," 1–2.

20. For discussions of what might constitute grand strategy, see Robert O'Neill, "An Introduction to Strategic Thinking," in Desmond Ball, ed., *Strategy and Defence: Australian Essays* (Boston: Allen and Unwin, 1982), 27; Basil H. Liddell Hart, *Strategy* (New York: Signet Classics, 1967), 319–322; Paul M. Kennedy, ed., *Grand Strategies in War and Peace* (New Haven, Conn.: Yale University Press, 1991), 5; and Williamson Murray, "Thoughts on Grand Strategy," in Williamson Murray, Richard Hart Sinnreich, and James Lacey, eds., *The Shaping of Grand Strategy: Policy, Diplomacy, and War* (Cambridge: Cambridge University Press, 2011), 1–33. General Albert C. Wedemeyer describes grand strategy as an art and a science, "an art because it deals with many imponderables, intangibles, and human emotions; and . . . a science because many factors in strategy demand a concern with accuracy of measurements and computations which can be determined with scientific exactitude—for example distances, space, speed, etc." (*Wedemeyer Reports!* [New York: Henry Holt, 1958], 82).

21. Some official but not necessarily useful definitions (from U.S. Department of Defense, *Department of Defense Dictionary*, pages indicated parenthetically):

"National Security Strategy—A document approved by the President of the United States for developing, applying, and coordinating the instruments of national power to achieve objectives that contribute to national security" (216); "National Defense Strategy—A document approved by the Secretary of Defense for applying the Armed Forces of the United States in coordination with Department of Defense agencies and other instruments of national power to achieve national security strategy objectives" (214); "National Military Strategy—a document approved by the Chairman of the Joint Chiefs of Staff for distributing and applying military power to attain national security strategy and national defense strategy objectives" (215); "Theater strategy—An overarching construct outlining a combatant commander's vision for integrating and synchronizing military activities and operations with the other instruments of national power in order to achieve national strategic objectives" (315). For examples of the documents, see *National Security Strategy of the United States*, at http://www.whitehouse.gov/sites/default/files/rss_viewer/national_security_strategy.pdf; *National Defense Strategy*, at http://www.defense.gov/pubs/2008NationalDefenseStrategy.pdf; and *National Military Strategy*, at http://www.jcs.mil//content/files/2011-02/020811084800_2011_NMS_-_08_FEB_2011.pdf (all accessed 5 Nov. 2012). Most theater strategies are classified.

22. The *Department of Defense Dictionary* defines operational art thus: "The cognitive approach by commanders and staffs—supported by their skill, knowledge, experience, creativity, and judgment—to develop strategies, campaigns, and operations to organize and employ military forces by integrating ends, ways, and means" (230). It defines tactics as "the employment and ordered arrangement of forces in relation to each other" (306).

23. As Jonathan Utley notes, "Beyond principles and policies it is necessary to examine the execution of policy" (*Going to War with Japan, 1937–1941*, reprint with a new introduction [Bronx, N.Y.: Fordham University Press, 2005], xiv).

24. Conrad H. Lanza, *Napoleon's Maxims* (Harrisburg, Pa.: Stackpole Press, 1940), 85.

25. U.S. Joint Army–Navy Board (JB), 27 July 1938, minutes, Joint Board General Correspondence, 1903–1938, Series 1, Records of Joint Army and Navy Boards, entry NM43 1, Record Group (RG) 225, National Archives, College Park, Md. (NACP). See also the National Security Act of 1947, as amended, and the Goldwater–Nichols Act of 1986.

26. Harry L. Sievers, "Evolution of Combined Action in Warfare," thesis, U.S. Army War College, 1950–1951, no. 82, U.S. Army Military History Institute (USAMHI), Carlisle Barracks, Pa., 17–18, and Francis Hill, "Command Problems in a Multi-national Force," thesis, U.S. Army War College, 1954, no. 494, USAMHI, 34. Historian David Trask notes, "Cooperation among allies is difficult to achieve and sustain because the nations who compose given coalitions rarely fight for exactly the same purpose" (*The United States in the Supreme War Council: American War Aims and Inter-Allied Strategy, 1917–1918* [Middleton, Conn.: Wesleyan University Press, 1961], 3).

27. As a close student of coalition warfare, R. W. Crossley, points out, "There is no

basis for statutory [command] authority, and regulatory authority has not in the past included explicit power to compel compliance. The coalition commander must rely on his ability to persuade" ("Principles of Coalition Warfare: A Preliminary Study," Research Directorate, National Defense University, 1979, photocopy, 90).

28. Vernon Davis, *The History of the Joint Chiefs of Staff of World War II: Organization and Development,* vol. 1: *Origin of the Joint and Combined Chiefs of Staff* (Washington, D.C.: Historical Division, U.S. Joint Chiefs of Staff, 1972), 165.

29. For a detailed history of the origins of the Joint Chiefs of Staff, see ibid., chaps. 1–9. A concise overview is Steven L. Rearden, *Council of War: History of the Joint Chiefs of Staff, 1942–1991* (Washington, D.C.: National Defense University Press, 2012), 1–5, at http://www.ndu.edu/press/lib/pdf/books/council-of-war/council-of-war.pdf.

30. Rearden, *Council of War,* xi.

31. The British Chiefs of Staff (COS) Committee became a formal organization subordinate to the Committee of Imperial Defence in 1923 (ibid., 1).

1. Lessons Lived, Learned, Lost

1. A standard diplomatic treatment is given in George F. Kennan, *American Foreign Policy, 1900–1950* (Chicago: University of Chicago Press, 1951), 14–15, and Daniel M. Smith, *The American Diplomatic Experience* (Boston: Houghton Mifflin, 1972), 203–274. For an explanation of how the Open Door Policy resulted in U.S. involvement with European powers, see Kennan, *American Foreign Policy,* 21–37. Russell Weigley addresses the military aspects in *History of the United States Army* (1967; reprint, Bloomington: Indiana University Press, 1984), 313. For a more recent interpretation, see Fareed Zakaria, *From Wealth to Power: The Unusual Origins of America's World Role* (Princeton, N.J.: Princeton University Press, 1998), 128–180. For a description of the importance of the Spanish-American War, see Walter Millis, *Arms and Men: A Study in American Military History* (New York: Mentor Books, 1956), 167–181.

2. See, for example, George C. Herring, *From Colony to Superpower: U.S. Foreign Relations since 1776* (New York: Oxford University Press, 2008), 38–42, and Henry Kissinger, *Diplomacy* (New York: Simon and Shuster, 1994), 38–42.

3. These conclusions were drawn from Weigley, *History of the United States Army,* chaps. 14 and 15; Maurice Matloff, "The American Approach to War, 1919–1945," in Michael Howard, ed., *The Theory and Practice of War* (1965; reprint, Bloomington: Indiana University Press, 1967), 215; Davis, *Origin of the Joint and Combined Chiefs of Staff,* 7–12; and Tracy B. Kittredge, "United States Defense Policies and Global Strategy, 1900–1941," Historical Section, Office of the Joint Chiefs of Staff, Washington, D.C., 1946–1953, approx. 1200 II, sec. B., 14.

4. Frederick Palmer, *Newton D. Baker: America at War,* 2 vols. (New York: Dodd and Mead, 1931), 1:40.

5. Quoted in ibid., 1:41.

6. A brief summary of the Boer War and its effect on the British military is given in Corelli Barnett, *Britain and Her Army, 1509–1970* (New York: Morrow, 1970),

337–349. For a more detailed and comprehensive treatment, see Thomas Pakenham, *The Boer War* (New York: Random House, 1979).
   7. Robert E. Jenner, *FDR's Republicans: Domestic Political Realignment and American Foreign Policy* (Lanham, Md.: Lexington Books, 2010), 6–7.
   8. For a detailed analysis of rising Anglo-German tensions, see Paul M. Kennedy, *The Rise of Anglo-German Antagonism, 1860–1914* (London: Allen and Unwin, 1980). For Britain's return to continental affairs, concern for the maintenance of the European balance of power, and the origins of the Anglo-French entente, see A. J. P. Taylor, *The Struggle for the Mastery of Europe, 1848–1918* (Oxford: Oxford University Press, 1954), 403–426. A concise review of the internal political events that resulted in the transition from isolation to continental involvement is in Paul Guinn, *British Strategy and Politics, 1914–1918* (Oxford: Clarendon Press, 1965), 3–11. See also Thomas Otte, "The Elusive Balance: British Foreign Policy and the French Entente before the First World War," in Alan Sharp and Glynn Stone, eds., *Anglo-French Relations in the Twentieth Century: Rivalry and Cooperation* (New York: Routledge, 2000), 12–16.
   9. Samuel R. Williamson Jr., *The Politics of Grand Strategy: Britain and France Prepare for War, 1904–1914* (Cambridge, Mass.: Harvard University Press, 1969), 64–65, and Brig. Gen. G. N. Nicolson, "Action Taken by General Staff since 1906 in Preparing a Plan for Rendering Military Assistance to France in the Event of an Unprovoked Attack on That Power by Germany, 6 Nov 1911," memo, in U.K. Foreign Office, *British Documents on the Origin of the War, 1898–1914*, 11 vols., ed. George Gooch and Harold Temperly (London: His Majesty's Stationery Office [HMSO], 1926–1938), 3:186–187.
   10. Nicolson, "Action Taken," 6 Nov. 1911, 3:186–187; Charles à Court Repington, *The First World War, 1914–1918*, 2 vols. (Boston: Houghton Mifflin, 1920), 1:1–14; Williamson, *Politics of Grand Strategy*, 67–71.
   11. Nicolson, "Action Taken," 6 Nov. 1911, 3:186–187; Victor Huguet, *Britain and the War: A French Indictment*, trans. Capt. H. Cotton Minchen (London: Cassell, 1928), 9; Williamson, *Politics of Grand Strategy*, 84–85, 113–114. Given the disparity in the size of the French and British contingents (seventy-two versus six divisions, respectively), it should come as no surprise that the French dominated land-planning issues (Roy A. Prete, *Strategy and Command: The Anglo-French Coalition on the Western Front, 1914* [Montreal: McGill-Queen's University Press, 2009], 30).
   12. Prete, *Strategy and Command*, 32; see also Wilson's diary entries for 9, 10, 11, and 20 January 1911, in C. E. Callwell, ed., *Field Marshal Sir Henry Wilson*, 2 vols. (London: Cassell, 1927), 1:91–92, including Callwell's commentary.
   13. Wilson, diary entry for 9 Sept. 1911, in Callwell, *Field Marshal Sir Henry Wilson*, 1:103. The terms of the agreement are in Meeting between Y. E. Dubail and Sir H. Wilson at the War Office (WO), 20 July 1911, memo, 21 Aug. 1911, in U.K. Foreign Office, *British Documents, 1898–1914*, 7:629–632. See also Williamson, *Politics of Grand Strategy*, 180–182, and Prete, *Strategy and Command*, 1–12, for brief descriptions of the diplomatic-military context of grand-strategy issues, and Prete, *Strategy and Command*, 12–21, for specific British views.

14. Prete, *Strategy and Command*, 30–34.

15. For examples of Wilson's personal negotiations, see Callwell's commentary in *Field Marshal Sir Henry Wilson*, 1:116–117.

16. Prete, *Strategy and Command*, 30–34, 90–91, and William J. Philpott, *Anglo-French Relations and Strategy on the Western Front, 1914–1918* (London: Macmillan; New York: St. Martin's Press, 1996), 8–10, 17.

17. Joffre quoted in Elizabeth Greenhalgh, *Victory through Coalition: Britain and France during the First World War* (New York: Cambridge University Press, 2005), 16. See also, ibid. 10; Prete, *Strategy and Command*, 41–42; and Robert A. Doughty, "France," in Richard F. Hamilton and Holger H. Herwig, eds., *War Planning, 1914* (New York: Cambridge University Press, 2009), 158.

18. Williamson, *Politics of Grand Strategy*, 69, 243.

19. Ibid., 244. Williamson notes that on one Admiralty source there was a marginal note that stated, "On the wish of the British authorities, in order to maintain absolute secrecy, nothing was committed to writing on the subject." The British were so faithful in maintaining secrecy that in July 1912 the French had to supply the Admiralty with a record of the 1908 and 1911 talks (ibid., 244 n.). Williamson was able to overcome this problem by using French archival sources. I have relied on his account.

20. For an account of the Second Moroccan Crisis, see Taylor, *Struggle for the Mastery of Europe*, 465–476.

21. Williamson, *Politics of Grand Strategy*, 321–322. This agreement was an extension of preliminary division of responsibility in 1911, described in ibid., 245–246. The initial terms are in Draft Agreement between the French Naval Attaché and Adm. Sir Francis Bridgeman, 3 July 1912, Admiralty Records (ADM), Archives Case 0091, in U.K. Foreign Office, *British Documents, 1898–1914*, 10:part 2, 602. The final version of the agreement is in *Documents Diplomatique Francais (1871–1914)*, Serial no. 3, 5:485–487. For a brief discussion of the course of the negotiations, see Williamson, *Politics of Grand Strategy*, 288–299. For the evolution of British naval policy and programs up to World War I, see Phillips Payson O'Brien, *British and American Naval Power: Politics and Policy, 1900–1936* (Westport, Conn.: Praeger, 1998), 25–44, 73–94.

22. Williamson, *Politics of Grand Strategy*, 208–209.

23. Meeting between Dubail and Wilson at the WO, 20 July 1911, memo, 21 Aug. 1911, in U.K. Foreign Office, *British Documents, 1898–1914*, 7:629–632, is the most comprehensive document between the two military services, but it does not touch upon unified command or direction. Neither does a similar document containing the final terms of the naval negotiations. Published documents, memoirs, diaries, histories, and so on do not mention unity of command as a subject of discussion. The actual instructions given to the British commanders at the outbreak of the war support the contention that the British Expeditionary Force was to remain an independent army and that there was to be close cooperation with the French, but no unity of command. See, for example, Douglas Haig, *The Private Papers of Douglas Haig, 1914–*

1919, ed. Robert Blake (London: Eyre and Spottiswoode, 1952), 120–121; Sir William Robertson, *Soldiers and Statesmen, 1914–1918*, 2 vols. (London: Cassell, 1926), 1:56–57; and Sir Edward Spears, *Liaison, 1914* (London: Heinemann, 1940), 539–540. For more recent scholarly examinations, see Greenhalgh, *Victory through Coalition*, 12; Roy A. Prete, "The War of Movement on the Western Front, August–November 1914: A Study in Coalition Warfare," Ph.D. diss., University of Alberta, 1979, 71, 145; and Prete, *Strategy and Command*, 36–40.

24. Crossley, "Principles of Coalition Warfare," 92. Nor is there any reason that they should have.

25. Benjamin Franklin Cooling and Lt. Col. Jack Hixson, *The Interoperability of Allied Forces in Europe at the Field Army Level* (Carlisle Barracks, Pa.: USAMHI, 1978). The authors attribute this independent operation to the situation forced upon the Allies by the German offensive of 1914.

26. Philpott, *Anglo-French Relations and Strategy*, 24–30, 31–46. See also Prete, *Strategy and Command*, 95–108, for details of Anglo-French frictions.

27. Philpott, *Anglo-French Relations and Strategy*, 69–76, 76–77, 53–59, 104–106.

28. Ibid., 82–83.

29. For an account of Anglo-French strategic planning for offensive operations on the Western Front in 1916, see ibid., 112–128.

30. Ibid., 86–91. Two excellent general histories of World War I that address these campaigns are John Keegan, *The First World War* (New York: Knopf, 1999), and Hew Strachan, *The First World War* (New York: Viking Press, 2003). For the background on the reverses, see Sir Frederick B. Maurice, *Lessons of Allied Cooperation: Naval, Military, and Air, 1914–1918* (London: Oxford University Press, 1942), 103–111, and Trask, *The United States in the Supreme War Council*, 21–23. For a discussion of Lloyd George's plot to subordinate Haig to Nivelle or cause Haig's resignation and of the discord it sowed between the two commanders, see Greenhalgh, *Victory through Coalition*, 139–145.

31. Philpott, *Anglo-French Relations and Strategy*, 86–91, 150–151. See also David Woodward, *Trial by Friendship: Anglo-American Relations, 1917–1918* (Lexington: University Press of Kentucky, 1993), 113–114.

32. Georges Suarez, *Soixante annèes d' histoire français, Clemenceau*, vol. 1: *Dans la mêlée* (Paris: Tallandier, 1932).

33. Conference of the British, French, and Italian governments, New Casino Hotel, Rapollo, 7 Nov. 1917, minutes, in U.S. War Department, Historical Division, *United States Army in the World War, 1917–1919* (hereafter *USAWWI*), 17 vols. (Washington, D.C.: U.S. GPO, 1948), 2:71–72; Tasker Bliss, "The Evolution of the Unified Command," *Foreign Affairs* 1 (15 Dec. 1922): 6. The United States became a member of the Supreme War Council (SWC) on 17 November 1917 (Ulysses S. Grant III, "America's Part in the Supreme War Council," *Records of the Columbia Historical Society* 29 [1928]: 311). For the negotiations behind the founding of the SWC, see Trask, *The United States in the Supreme War Council*, 24–30. A more recent overview can be found in David Dutton, "Britain and France at War, 1914–1918," in Sharp and Stone, *Anglo-French Relations in the Twentieth Century*, 77–82.

34. Greenhalgh, *Victory through Coalition,* 173–174; pages 180–181 contain a description of the subelements of the SWC and the permanent military representatives.
35. Ibid.; Philpott, *Anglo-French Relations and Strategy,* 151.
36. Philpott, *Anglo-French Relations and Strategy,* 151.
37. Greenhalgh, *Victory through Coalition,* 179.
38. Ibid., 177.
39. Philpott, *Anglo-French Relations and Strategy,* 13–14.
40. Quoted in Maurice, *Lessons of Allied Cooperation,* 7, also in Greenhalgh, *Victory through Coalition,* 17, and James E. Edmonds, *Military Operations in France and Belgium, 1914–1918,* 14 vols. (London: MacMillan, 1922–1940; London: HMSO, 1922–1949), 1:app. 8.
41. Philpott, *Anglo-French Relations and Strategy,* 16. For the tribulations wrought by these instructions on Anglo-French unity of command from the Battle of the Frontiers to the Battle of the Marne, see Prete, *Strategy and Command,* 95–118.
42. Haig, *Private Papers of Douglas Haig,* 121.
43. Maurice, *Lessons of Allied Cooperation,* 5–71, passim. For a detailed description of the ups and mostly downs of British and French unity command issues, see Greenhalgh, *Victory through Coalition,* 12–41, and Prete, *Strategy and Command,* 146–147.
44. Information in this paragraph is from Trask, *The United States in the Supreme War Council,* 20–21, and Maurice, *Lessons of Allied Cooperation,* 75. For a discussion of Lloyd George's efforts to subordinate Haig or force his resignation, see Greenhalgh, *Victory through Coalition,* 139–145, 163–172.
45. Spears, *Liaison,* 527–536, 542–557, 563–578; Haig, *Private Papers of Douglas Haig,* 198–216.
46. Maurice, *Lessons of Allied Cooperation,* 75–86. Several participants confirm Maurice's conclusions: see, for example, Haig, *Private Papers of Douglas Haig,* 188–220; John Charteris, *At G. H. Q.* (London: Cassell, 1931), 185–206; and Maurice Hankey, *The Supreme Command, 1914–1918,* 2 vols. (London: Allen and Unwin, 1961), 2:613–627.
47. Question of Inter-Allied Reserve and a Single Commander, French Military Report to the SWC, 22 Jan. 1918, in U.S. War Department, *USAWWI,* 2:172–173. The first formal request for such a command is in Joint Note no. 14, Military Representatives to the SWC, 25 Jan. 1918, in U.S. War Department, *USAWWI,* 2:182. See also Trask, *United States in the Supreme War Council,* 55–56, and Bliss, "Evolution of the Unified Command," 9.
48. Bliss, "Evolution of the Unified Command," 9, 11, 18–22.
49. Resolution no. 13, SWC, Establishment of the Inter-Allied General Reserve, 2 Feb. 1918, in U.S. War Department, *USAWWI,* 2:189–191; David Trask, *The AEF and Coalition Warmaking, 1917–1918* (Lawrence: University Press of Kansas, 1993), 35–36.
50. Bliss, "Evolution of the Unified Command," 18–20; Philpott, *Anglo-French Relations and Strategy,* 153–154.

51. Bliss, "Evolution of the Unified Command," 20–24; Greenhalgh, *Victory through Coalition*, 181–187; Trask, *AEF and Coalition Warmaking*, 37.

52. Haig, *Private Papers of Douglas Haig*, 295–297; Bliss, "Evolution of the Unified Command," 27.

53. Haig, *Private Papers of Douglas Haig*, 298, emphasis in the original. For Elizabeth Greenhalgh's convincing argument that Haig does not deserve credit for this action, based on an ex post facto reconstruction of his diary, see *Victory through Coalition*, 196–197.

54. A summary of the Doullens Conference and a text of the accord is located in Record of Third Conference, Doullens, 26 Mar. 1918, in U.S. War Department, *USAWWI*, 2:253–254. For a brief description of the conference, see Philpott, *Anglo-French Relations and Strategy*, 155–156.

55. General Headquarters, American Expeditionary Force (AEF), War Diary, Book II, 446, extract in U.S. War Department, *USAWWI*, 2:262. Pershing notified the War Department of the agreement in AEF to Adjutant General, War Department (AGWAR), for COS, Message 801-S, 28 Mar. 1918, in U.S. War Department, *USAWWI*, 2:262

56. Newton D. Baker to General John J. Pershing, letter, 26 May 1917, extracted in Woodward, *Trial by Friendship*, 57–58. Baker's letter also appears in entirety in John J. Pershing, *My Experiences in the World War*, 2 vols., Military Classics series (1931; reprint, Blue Ridge Summit, Pa.: TAB Books, 1989), 1:38–40.

57. Thomas Fleming, "Pershing," in Robert Cowley and Geoffrey Parker, eds., *The Reader's Companion to Military History* (Boston: Houghton Mifflin Harcourt, 1996), 360. See also Pershing's obituary in the *New York Times*, 16 July 1948, at http://www.nytimes.com/learning/general/onthisday/bday/0913.html (accessed 21 Aug. 2015). For definitive biographies, see Frank E. Vandiver, *Black Jack: The Life and Times of John J. Pershing* (College Station: Texas A&M Press, 1977), and Donald Smythe, *Pershing: General of the Armies* (Bloomington: Indiana University Press, 1986). Pershing's own account can be found in Pershing, *My Experiences in the World War*.

58. Conference at Beauvais, 3 Apr. 1918, minutes, SWC 376-1, in U.S. War Department, *USAWWI*, 2:277.

59. SWC to AGWAR, Message 76-S, American Section, 3 Apr. 1918, in U.S. War Department, *USAWWI*, 2:278, informing the War Department of Foch's appointment as commander in chief (CINC) of the Allied Armies in France. For background information on this decision, see Gen. Ferdinand Foch to Minister of War, 14 Apr. 1918; Georges Clemenceau to Foch, Message 149/H.R., 14 Apr. 1918; AEF to AGWAR, message, General Headquarters, 15 Apr. 1918; and AGWAR's Office to Pershing, message, 16 Apr. 1918: all in U.S. War Department, *USAWWI*, 2:323–327.

60. Bliss, "Evolution of the Unified Command," 28.

61. Philpott, *Anglo-French Relations and Strategy*, 157–159.

62. Bliss, "Evolution of the Unified Command," 30. There is an absolute wealth of information on the evolution of unity of command in World War I. The best primary sources are U.S. War Department, *USAWWI*, especially volumes 2, 3, and 12; Mau-

rice, *Lessons of Allied Cooperation*, 72–170; Hankey, *The Supreme Command*, 2:711–813; Grant, "America's Part in the Supreme War Council"; and Peter E. Wright, *At the Supreme War Council* (New York: Putnam, 1921). Bliss's essay "Evolution of the Unified Command" is particularly valuable because of its concise presentation. All of the authors named here were members of or participants in SWC activities. The best secondary source is Trask, *United States in the Supreme War Council*, 53–69. Some interesting views are also given in Philpott, *Anglo-French Relations and Strategy*, and James B. Agnew, "Coalition Warfare: A Successful Experiment in Combined Command," *Parameters*, Spring 1971, 50–64. For a very unflattering commentary on the veracity of Peter Wright's account, see Priscilla Roberts, "Tasker H. Bliss and the Evolution of the Allied Unified Command, 1918: A Note on Old Battles Revisited," *Journal of Military History* 65, no. 3 (July 2001): 671–695.

63. Conversation between Prime Minister Lloyd George, Sir William Robertson, and Gen. John Pershing, 29 Jan. 1918, Versailles, notes, in U.S. War Department, *USAWWI*, 3:32–33.

64. Adm. William S. Sims, with Burton J. Hendrick, *The Victory at Sea*, with an introduction by David F. Trask (1920; reprint, Annapolis, Md.: Naval Institute Press, 1984), 3.

65. David F. Trask, introduction to Sims, *Victory at Sea*, x.

66. Quoted in Josephus Daniels, *The Wilson Era: Years of War and After, 1917–1923* (Westport, Conn.: Greenwood Press, 1974), 67, cited in William N. Still Jr., *Crisis at Sea: The United States Navy in European Waters in World War I* (Gainesville: University of Florida Press, 2007), 21. The same quote is in Rear Adm. William S. Sims to Secretary of the Navy, letter, 7 Jan. 1920, Subj: Certain Naval Lessons of the Great War, in Tracy B. Kittredge, *Naval Lessons of the Great War* (Garden City, N.Y.: Doubleday, Page, 1921), 82. The remainder of the information in the paragraph is from David F. Trask, "William Snowden Sims: The Victory Ashore," in James C. Bradford, ed., *Admirals of the New Steel Navy: Makers of American Naval Tradition, 1880–1930* (Annapolis, Md.: Naval Institute Press, 1990), 282–286, and Mary Klachko, "William Sheperd Benson," in Bradford, *Admirals of the New Steel Navy*, 313.

67. Bradley F. Smith, *The Ultra–Magic Deals and the Most Secret Special Relationship, 1940–1946* (Novato, Calif.: Presidio Press, 1993), 1–3.

68. Trask, introduction to Sims, *Victory at Sea*, xv.

69. Sims, *Victory at Sea*, 11. Sims had known Admiral John Jellicoe, the first sea lord, since 1901 and had maintained a regular and considerable correspondence with him over the years, thereby facilitating cooperation (ibid., 7). The remainder of the material in this paragraph comes from Sims to Josephus Daniels, 19 Apr. 1917, and Graham Greene (permanent secretary of the Admiralty), memo, 20 Apr. 1917, both in Michael Simpson, ed., *Anglo-American Naval Relations, 1917–1919* (Brookfield, Vt.: Gower, 1991), 38, 43.

70. Trask, introduction to Sims, *Victory at Sea*, xviii, and Trask, "William Snowden Sims," 286–287.

71. For Sims's views on the urgency of the antisubmarine campaign, see Sims to

Daniels, 14 Apr. 1917; Sims to Daniels, 18 Apr. 1917; and Sims to Secretary of the Navy (Operations), 11 May 1917, messages, in Simpson, *Anglo-American Naval Relations*, 206–208, 209–210, and 220–223.

72. Sims, *Victory at Sea*, 50; Admiral Wilson Brown, "Four Presidents: As I Saw Them," Adm. Wilson Brown Papers, Franklin D. Roosevelt Library (FDRL), Hyde Park, N.Y., 106–107; and James C. Bradford, "Henry T. Mayo: Last of the Independent Naval Diplomats," in Bradford, *Admirals of the New Steel Navy*, 268. For details of tactical- and operational-level cooperation, including convoy operations, see Still, *Crisis at Sea*, 332–356, 427–443. For British views, see Vice Admiral Sir Montague Browning to Secretary of the Admiralty, "Report of Proceedings since Arrival in the United States," 13 Apr. 1917, in Simpson, *Anglo-American Naval Relations*, 34–37.

73. Simpson, *Anglo-American Naval Relations*, 57–65 (commentary by Simpson); Klachko, "William Sheperd Benson," 316–318; Trask, introduction to Sims, *Victory at Sea*, xvi–xix; Bradford, "Henry T. Mayo," 269.

74. Simpson, *Anglo-American Naval Relations*, 57–65 (commentary by Simpson); Klachko, "William Sheperd Benson," 316–318; Trask, introduction to Sims, *Victory at Sea*, xvi–xix; Bradford, "Henry T. Mayo," 269.

75. Bradford, "Henry T. Mayo," 269; Trask, "William Snowden Sims," 290–291; David F. Trask, "The American Navy in a World at War, 1914–1918," in Kenneth J. Hagan, ed., *In Peace and War: Interpretations of American Naval History, 1775–1978*, 2nd ed. (Westport, Conn.: Greenwood Press, 1984), 208–211.

76. William R. Braisted, *The United States Navy in the Pacific, 1909–1922* (Austin: University of Texas Press, 1971), 289–309, 430; Still, *Crisis at Sea*, 73–76. Examples of Sims's sensitivity to these perceptions can be found in Lieut. R. R. M. Emmet, U.S. Navy, to Sims, 22 June 1917; Sims to President Woodrow Wilson, 4 July 1917; and Sims to Daniels, 16 July 1917: all in Simpson, *Anglo-American Naval Relations*, 68–69, 82, and 89.

77. Trask, introduction to Sims, *Victory at Sea*, xvii.

78. Sims, *Victory at Sea*, 75, 248–249.

79. Cooperation with British Plans Division, Memo no. 71, 30 Dec. 1918, in Simpson, *Anglo-American Naval Relations*, 183–184. For a contrary view, see Still, *Crisis at Sea*, 45. A detailed compilation of records from the American Naval Planning Section is included in U.S. Navy Department, Office of the Naval Records and Library, Historical Section, *The American Planning Section, London* (Washington, D.C.: U.S. GPO, 1923).

80. Diary of Franklin Delano Roosevelt (FDR), entry for 26 July 1918, President's Personal Files, Assistant Secretary of the Navy, 1913–1920, FDR Papers, FDRL, and Still, *Crisis at Sea*, 64.

81. Sims, *Victory at Sea*, 82; Vice Adm. Walter S. Delany, *Bayly's Navy* (Washington, D.C.: Naval Historical Foundation, 1980), 8–9.

82. Quoted in Still, *Crisis at Sea*, 77.

83. Woodward, *Trial by Friendship*, 65. See also H. G. Nicholas, *The United States and Britain* (Chicago: University of Chicago Press, 1975), 67, and Simpson, *Anglo-American Naval Relations*, 66 (Simpson's commentary).

84. Sims to William Pratt (assistant chief of naval operations [CNO]), 7 June 1917, in Simpson, *Anglo-American Naval Relations,* 68. See also Still, *Crisis at Sea,* 46. For further investigation of Anglo-American naval collaboration in 1917–1918, see Dean C. Allard, "Admiral William S. Sims and United States Naval Policy in World War I," *American Neptune,* April 1975, 97–110; Dean C. Allard, "Anglo-American Naval Differences during World War I," *Military Affairs,* April 1980, 75–81; David F. Trask, *Captains and Cabinets: Anglo-American Naval Relations, 1917–1918* (Columbia: University of Missouri Press, 1972); and Braisted, *United States Navy in the Pacific.* For Sims's account of Anglo-American naval cooperation in the war at sea during World War I, see his book *Victory at Sea,* for which he won the Pulitzer Prize in history in 1920. The standard scholarly biography, written by Sims's son-in-law, is Elting E. Morison, *Admiral Sims and the Modern American Navy* (Boston: Houghton Mifflin, 1942).

85. A very few (of many) examples of why amalgamation of land forces was and is exponentially more difficult than amalgamation of naval forces can be given here. As indicated earlier, naval fleets, squadrons, and even ships are self-contained entities and tend to operate independently while at sea. The same is not true of land forces, which, even when operating in units have to collaborate more frequently and in greater depth than must their naval counterparts. At the same time, although the command and control of naval forces are complex, they are relatively simple compared to controlling land forces in a battle. When a helmsman turns the wheel, the ship usually goes where intended, and so, too, does the entire ship's complement—whether 50 or 5,000. The remainder of the ships in the formation conform their movements to the lead vessel. Not so for tens of thousands of soldiers on the battlefield, who have many more places to go and oftentimes have very good reasons for not wanting to go there. The scale of chaos and confusion is exponentially higher on a land battlefield. There was also the difference in the scale of the forces. The U.S. Navy would grow, but not on a scale commensurate with the growth of the AEF. Finally, naval forces did not live under the continuous existential threat that land forces faced.

86. Trask, *AEF and Coalition Warmaking,* 5–6.

87. Ibid., 6.

88. Woodward, *Trial by Friendship,* 48, 53–54; Trask, *United States in the Supreme War Council,* 9–11.

89. Robert B. Bruce, *Fraternity of Arms: America and France in the Great War* (Lawrence: University Press of Kansas, 2003), 38–39, 43, 48, 50–57.

90. Trask, *AEF and Coalition Warmaking,* 6.

91. Woodward, *Trial by Friendship,* 54. For details of the French role in arming, equipping, and training the AEF, see Bruce, *Fraternity of Arms,* 97–143. *Fraternity of Arms* is also an excellent overall battle narrative of U.S.-French collaboration at the operational, tactical, and individual levels.

92. Bruce, *Fraternity of Arms,* 67.

93. Ferdinand Foch, *The Memoirs of Marshal Foch,* trans. Col. T. Bentley Mott (Garden City, N.Y.: Doubleday, Doran, 1931), 233–234. For a description of the pressures on Pershing, see Smythe, *Pershing,* 69–72.

94. See Résumé of [Pétain–Pershing] Interview, 23 Dec. 1917, in U.S. War Department, *USAWWI*, 2:105–106. The British held similar views. See Robertson to Pershing, letter, 30 Jan. 1918, extract in U.S. War Department, *USAWWI*, 3:37–38. For a detailed discussion of the issues swirling around amalgamation at this time, see Bruce, *Fraternity of Arms*, 146–154.

95. For the origins and evolution of the 150-battalion plan, see Pershing, Robertson, and Maclay meeting, 9 Jan. 1918, notes; Robertson to Pershing, letter, 10 Jan. 1918; Pershing, Robertson, and Maclay second meeting, notes, 10 Jan. 1918; and Robertson for War Cabinet, Memo 0.1/135/388, no. 39, American Battalions for British Divisions, 12 Jan. 1918: all in U.S. War Department, *USAWWI*, 3:9–16. For a brief synopsis of the rapid rise and fall of the 150-battalion plan, see Woodward, *Trial by Friendship*, 131–137. For a succinct overview of British pressure for amalgamation, Pershing's pushback, and the eventual assignment of the Twenty-Seventh and Thirtieth Infantry Divisions and II Corps, see Mitchell Yockelson, *Borrowed Soldiers: Americans under British Command, 1918* (Norman: University of Oklahoma Press, 2008), 9–20. At least one American officer concluded that the British were interested only in using the American forces as individual fillers for the depleted British units. See Brig. Gen. George S. Simonds, "Problems of Service with Allies," lecture, 4 Dec. 1931, File 382-A-8, G-2 (Intelligence), no. 8, USAMHI.

96. Pershing, *My Experiences in the World War*, 1:268–269 (Haig's proposal) and 304 (quote).

97. Wilson to Baker, letter, 4 Feb. 1918, quoted in Woodward, *Trial by Friendship*, 137–138. A summary of the move from the 150-battalion plan is given in Conference at Versailles, 29 Jan. 18, notes, in U.S. War Department, *USAWWI*, 3:29–34. For the genesis of the six-division plan and its development, see the documents in U.S. War Department, *USAWWI*, 3:28–39. For its implementation, see the documents in U.S. War Department, *USAWWI*, 3:39–112. The French also actively sought to integrate U.S. forces into their army (see U.S. War Department, *USAWWI*, 3:250–345 and passim).

98. Pershing's decision is in Pershing to AGWAR, 28 Mar. 1918, in U.S. War Department, *USAWWI*, 2:262. For a discussion of the controversy over amalgamation in midst of the crisis, especially Pershing's intent, see Smythe, *Pershing*, 100–104.

99. Lt. Col. Calvin H. Goddard, "A Study of Anglo-American and Franco-American Relations during World War I," 2 parts, Army War College Historical Study no. 5, USAMHI, part 1:2 and part 2:1. There are numerous documents, after-action reports, messages, and so on concerning the service of U.S. units with British and French forces in U.S. War Department, *USAWWI*, 3:112–237, 345–743. For an excellent discussion of the amalgamation issue at this time, see Bruce, *Fraternity of Arms*, chap. 5. Details of U.S. divisional fights under French command are in Bruce, *Fraternity of Arms*, 206–212. For accounts of the U.S. Twenty-Seventh and Thirtieth Infantry Divisions and eventually II Corps under the British, see Yockelson, *Borrowed Soldiers*, 98–212. A firsthand account of service under British command replete with interesting and humorous anecdotes is Ewen Cameron MacVeagh and Lee D. Brown, *The Yankees in*

the British Zone (New York: Putnam, 1920). It is worth noting that a U.S. division had a little more than 28,000 men and was roughly twice the size of a British or French division. For details, see U.S. War Department, *Order of Battle of the United States Land Forces in the World War,* 3 vols., CD-ROM version, CMH EM 0023 (Washington, D.C.: U.S. Army Center of Military History, 1998), disk 3, 2:446–447.

100. Lloyd George to Rufus Isaacs, Marquess of Reading, 14 Apr. 1918, 47:338, cited in Woodward, *Trial by Friendship,* 159.

101. Quoted in Woodward, *Trial by Friendship,* 159.

102. WC 397, 23 Apr. 1918, Cabinet/War Cabinet Records (CAB) 23/6, the National Archives, United Kingdom, Public Records Office (TNA: PRO), London, cited in Woodward, *Trial by Friendship,* 160.

103. As given in Smythe, *Pershing,* 135; see also Trask, *AEF and Coalition Warmaking,* 74–75. In his memoirs, Pershing recounts a much less emotional response: "Foch resorted to his often-repeated question as to whether I was ready to take the risk, to which I replied very positively that I was ready to assume any responsibility that my proposal might entail" (*My Experiences in the World War,* 2:73).

104. For a more complete description of these events, see Trask, *AEF and Coalition Warmaking,* 75–81, and Pershing, *My Experiences in the World War,* 2:60–65, 99–101, 218–220, 243–254.

105. For example, see the operations reports for the French II Colonial Corps at St. Mihiel in U.S. War Department, *USAWWI,* 8:255–288.

106. British troops served with the U.S. Army's Gas Regiment and as the Chemical Section of the U.S. Second Army (U.S. War Department, *Order of Battle of the United States Land Forces in the World War,* disk 3, 2:82, 151). At lower levels, integration was minimal; for example, the U.S. Twenty-Seventh Infantry Division received intermittent attachments of ambulance detachments and artillery units from 24 September to 22 October 1918 (ibid., 3:131). For British refusal, see Bruce, *Fraternity of Arms,* 225.

107. Quoted in Ruth Henig, *Versailles and After, 1919–1933,* rev. ed. (London: Routledge, 1995), 52.

108. Harry Kessler, *Berlin Lights: The Diaries of Count Harry Kessler,* trans. and ed. Charles Kessler (New York: Grove Press, 2000), diary entry for 10 Jan. 1920, quoted in Henry G. Gole, *The Road to Rainbow: Army Planning for Global War, 1934–1940* (Annapolis, Md.: Naval Institute Press, 2003), 3.

109. Clausewitz, *On War,* 87.

110. Major General Fox Conner, "The Allied High Command and Allied Unity of Direction," U.S. Army War College, Washington, D.C., 12 Feb. 1940, File 406-A-32, USAMHI, 29. Conner delivered essentially the same speech each year.

111. Ibid., 28–29.

2. Neither Friend nor Foe

1. Norman Gibbs, *Grand Strategy,* vol. 1: *Rearmament Policy,* in *History of the Second World War: United Kingdom Military Series* (Edinburgh: HMSO, 1976), xxv.

2. Michael Howard, *War in European History* (Oxford: Oxford University Press,

1976), 129. See also Norman Gibbs, "British Strategic Doctrine, 1918–1939," in Howard, *Theory and Practice of War*, 210.

3. Michael Howard, *The Continental Commitment: The Dilemma of British Defence Policy in the Era of the Two World Wars* (London: Temple, Smith, 1972), 93.

4. Quoted in Raymond Sontag, *A Broken World, 1919–1939* (New York: Harper Torchbooks, 1971), 250–251. Sontag adds that this was by no means an isolated incident and that similar events swept England. Even as late as December 1936, politicians such as Stanley Baldwin and Neville Chamberlain were convinced that public opinion would not countenance any commitment to France or the peacetime establishment of an expeditionary force. See Howard, *Continental Commitment*, 114–115.

5. Anne Orde, *The Eclipse of Great Britain: The United States and British Imperial Decline, 1895–1956* (New York: St. Martin's Press, 1996), 41–42.

6. Ibid., 70–72. See also Bernard Porter, *Britain, Europe, and the World, 1850–1986*, 2nd ed. (London: Allen and Unwin, 1987), 91, 102.

7. Porter, *Britain, Europe, and the World*, 85–87.

8. Herring, *From Colony to Superpower*, 436.

9. Akira Iriye, *The Cambridge History of American Foreign Relations*, vol. 3: *The Globalizing of America, 1913–1945* (New York: Cambridge University Press, 1993), 91; Herring, *From Colony to Superpower*, 439, 450–451, 453–456, 458–459. Herbert Feis, State Department economic adviser to Hoover and Roosevelt as well as historian, coined the phrase "diplomacy of the dollar."

10. Ralph B. Levering, *The Public and American Foreign Policy, 1918–1978* (New York: Morrow, 1979), 37.

11. Matloff, "The American Approach to War," 217–218.

12. David Dimbleby and David Reynolds, *An Ocean Apart: The Relationship between Britain and America in the Twentieth Century* (New York: Random House, 1988), 52. This was out of a population of around 105 million.

13. John E. Moser, *Twisting the Lion's Tail: American Anglophobia between the World Wars* (New York: New York University Press, 1998), 9–13, 19–23. See also Skidelsky, "Imbalance of Power," 51, and Stephen W. Roskill, *Naval Policy between the Wars*, 2 vols. (New York: Walker, 1969, 1976), 2:157–159.

14. Moser, *Twisting the Lion's Tail*, 76, 44–45, 38–41.

15. Alan P. Dobson, *Anglo-American Relations in the Twentieth Century: Of Friendship, Conflict, and the Rise and Decline of Superpowers* (London: Routledge, 1995), 10. Dobson provides an encompassing but concise overview of Anglo-American political, economic, and diplomatic issues (1–71). For brief recaps of the major frictions and frustration in British-U.S. relations from 1917 to 1937, see William R. Rock, *Chamberlain and Roosevelt: British Foreign Policy and the United States, 1937–1940* (Columbus: Ohio University Press, 1988), 2–5, 12–14, and Reynolds, *Creation of the Anglo-American Alliance*, 15–16.

16. Reynolds, *Creation of the Anglo-American Alliance*, 11–13.

17. Nicholas, *The United States and Britain*, 74.

18. Dimbleby and Reynolds, *An Ocean Apart*, 100–125.

19. Moser, *Twisting the Lion's Tail*, 45–48, for details of the rubber controversy.
20. Dimbleby and Reynolds, *An Ocean Apart*, 129.
21. J. Pierpont Moffat to Norman Davies, letter, 7 Oct. 1936, Norman Davies Papers, Box 41, Library of Congress, Washington, D.C., quoted in Dimbleby and Reynolds, *An Ocean Apart*, 129.
22. Justus D. Doenecke and John E. Wilz, *From Isolation to War, 1931–1941*, 3rd ed., American History series (Wheeling, Ill.: Harlan Davidson, 2003), 51–52; Kennedy, *Freedom from Fear*, 154–158; B. J. C. McKercher, *Transition of Power: Britain's Loss of Pre-eminence to the United States, 1930–1945* (Cambridge: Cambridge University Press, 1999), 169–172.
23. Richard A. Harrison, "The United States and Great Britain: Presidential Diplomacy and Alternatives to Appeasement in the 1930s," in Donald F. Schmitz and Richard Challener, eds., *Appeasement in Europe: A Reassessment of U.S. Policies* (Westport, Conn.: Greenwood Press, 1990), 103–113.
24. Mark M. Boatner III, *The Biographical Dictionary of World War II* (Novato, Calif.: Presidio Press, 1996), 82–83. For a biography of Chamberlain, see Robert Self, *Neville Chamberlain: A Biography* (Burlington, Vt.: Ashgate, 2006).
25. Greg Kennedy, "Neville Chamberlain and Strategic Relations with the US during His Chancellorship," *Diplomacy and Statecraft* 13, no. 1 (Mar. 2002): 109.
26. Kennedy, "Neville Chamberlain," 108.
27. McKercher, *Transition of Power*, 153.
28. Doenecke and Wilz, *From Isolation to War*, 54; Moser, *Twisting the Lion's Tail*, 88–89; Reynolds, *Creation of the Anglo-American Alliance*, 15. Roosevelt later lamented signing the bill (Smith, *American Diplomatic Experience*, 345). For a brief overview of the range of economic issues dividing the two countries, see Justus D. Doenecke, "The Roosevelt Foreign Policy: An Ambiguous Legacy," in Justus D. Doenecke and Mark A. Stoler, *Debating Franklin D. Roosevelt's Foreign Policies, 1933–1945* (Lanham, Md.: Rowman and Littlefield, 2005), 15–28.
29. O'Brien, *British and American Naval Power*, 132–136; Trask, "The American Navy in a World at War," 212–214.
30. Trask, "The American Navy in a World at War," 215–218; Roskill, *Naval Policy between the Wars*, 77–82.
31. Christopher Hall, *Britain, America, and Arms Control, 1921–1937* (New York: St. Martin's Press, 1987), 4–5. For a description of Churchill's efforts to rein in spending while at the War Office in 1919–1921 and Admiralty spending while he was chancellor of the Exchequer, see Christopher Bell, *Churchill and Sea Power* (Oxford: Oxford University Press, 2013), 85–94 and 103–134.
32. If interested in such details about the Washington Naval Conference, see, for example, Thomas L. Buckley, *The United States and the Washington Naval Conference, 1921–1922* (Knoxville: University of Tennessee Press, 1970); Roskill, *Naval Policy between the Wars*, 300–329; and O'Brien, *British and American Naval Power*, 149–172.
33. Murfett, *Fool-Proof Relations*, 3; B. J. C. McKercher, "No Eternal Friends or Enemies: British Defence Policy and the Problem of the United States, 1919–1939,"

Canadian Journal of History/Annals canadiennes d' histoire 28 (Apr. 1993): 3–5 (the page numbers cited in the notes refer to the pagination in a copy of this article downloaded from ProQuest at http://search.proquest.com/docview/194334699/fulltext/409054CD41494640PQ/4?accoutnid=$4444 [accessed 19 Jan. 2016]); Doenecke, "The Roosevelt Foreign Policy," 15–18; O'Brien, *British and American Naval Power*, 166–172.

34. Murfett, "Are We Ready?" 214–215; Hall, *Britain, America, and Arms Control*, 35.

35. For brief background behind the origins of the conference and its resultant collapse, see U.S. Department of State, Office of the Historian, *Milestones, 1921–1936: The Geneva Naval Conference, 1927*, at http://history.state.gov/milestones/1921–1936/Geneva (accessed 26 Nov. 2012). For a detailed account of especially British preparations, the conduct of the conference, and analysis of the reasons behind its collapse, see Donald J. Lisio, *British Naval Supremacy and Anglo-American Antagonisms, 1914–1930* (Cambridge: Cambridge University Press, 2014).

36. McKercher, "No Eternal Friends or Enemies," 6–11; Murfett, "Are We Ready?" 214–215. See Roskill, *Naval Policy between the Wars*, for the British position (1:502–503) and for the circumstances leading up to the collapse of the talks (1:507–510).

37. For the British position, see Roskill, *Naval Policy between the Wars*, 1:507–510.

38. Moser, *Twisting the Lion's Tail*, 48–52. For details of the run-up, conduct, and consequences of the Geneva Conference, see Hall, *Britain, America, and Arms Control*, 36–58. For Coolidge's proposal, see O'Brien, *British and American Naval Power*, 194–198, and Moser, *Twisting the Lion's Tail*, 58–67.

39. B. J. C. McKercher, "A Certain Irritation: The White House, the State Department, and the Desire for a Naval Settlement with Great Britain, 1927–1930," *Diplomatic History* 31, no. 5 (Nov. 2007): 829; Roskill concurs in *Naval Policy between the Wars*, 1:23. See also Hall, *Britain, America, and Arms Control*, 54–58.

40. McKercher, "A Certain Irritation," 829.

41. For internal British negotiations and preparatory work by MacDonald, see Roskill, *Naval Policy between the Wars*, 2:45–57; McKercher, *Transition of Power*, 37–62; McKercher, "No Eternal Friends or Enemies," 10–13; B. J. C. McKercher, "National Security and Imperial Defence: British Grand Strategy and Appeasement, 1930–1939," *Diplomacy and Statecraft* 19, no. 3 (Sept. 2008): 406–407; and Hall, *Britain, America, and Arms Control*, 94.

42. As Phillips O'Brien observes, "One of the most striking things about the talks was not just how close the sides were to an agreement but how the whole tone of Anglo-American relations had changed since the departure of Coolidge and Churchill" (*British and American Naval Power*, 211). See also Roskill's assessment of Hoover and MacDonald in *Naval Policy between the Wars*, 2:23, 45–53.

43. Roskill, *Naval Policy between the Wars*, 2:66.

44. For teamwork, see Hall, *Britain, America, and Arms Control*, 94.

45. Key treaty provisions are in U.S. Department of State, Office of the Historian,

Milestones, 1921–1936: The London Naval Conference, 1930, at http://history.state. gove/milestones/1921–1936/LondonNavalConf (accessed 26 Nov. 2012). Because the United States deferred construction of heavy cruisers, the de facto ratio of cruisers became 10:10:7 as well.

46. O'Brien, *British and American Naval Power,* 210–213 (quotes on 211 and 212–213). See also Murfett, "Are We Ready?" 218–219, 229; Roskill, *Naval Policy between the Wars,* 2:63; Nicholas, *United States and Great Britain,* 81.

47. Roskill, *Naval Policy between the Wars,* 2:25.

48. Minutes of War Cabinet Meeting 616A, 15 Aug. 1919, CAB 23/15, TNA: PRO, p. 1, in U.K. Cabinet Office, *Cabinet Minutes and Memoranda, 1916–1939,* microfilm, 256 reels (Millwood, N.Y.: KTO, 1978) (a date is sufficient to retrieve a document in the *Cabinet Minutes and Memoranda* reels).

49. Gibbs, "British Strategic Doctrine," 210. For an in-depth analysis of the Ten-Year Rule and its debilitating effect on British military policy, see Gibbs, *Rearmament Policy,* 3–87. The rule remained in effect until 1932, when it was canceled because of Japanese buildup in the Pacific. See Howard, *Continental Commitment,* 96–98, for a discussion of the termination of the rule. For details of British disavowal of a continental commitment beyond the League of Nations and the Treaty of Locarno, see Andrew Webster, "An Argument without End: Britain, France, and the Disarmament Process, 1925–1934," in Martin S. Alexander and William J. Philpott, eds., *Anglo-French Defence Relations between the Wars* (New York: Palgrave MacMillan, 2002), 49–66.

50. Minutes, 23rd Meeting of the COS, CAB 53/2, COS (26), 73, TNA: PRO, quoted in Brian Bond, *Britain, France, and Belgium, 1939–1940* (1975; reprint, London: Brassey's 1990), 14–15.

51. Gibbs, "British Strategic Doctrine," 210.

52. Ibid., 205. See also Sebastian Cox, "British Military Planning and the Origins of the Second World War," in McKercher and Legault, *Military Planning,* 104.

53. Basil H. Liddell Hart, *The British Way in Warfare* (New York: Macmillan, 1933), 37, 114 (quote). Gibbs points out that strategic discussion during the interwar era was limited to an extremely small circle of civilian writers, of whom Liddell Hart was the most important, but that little evidence exists to show that their discussions affected service ministers or heads of the armed forces ("British Strategic Doctrine," 187). For employment of mechanized forces, see Liddell Hart, *British Way in Warfare,* chaps. 9–14.

54. Howard, *War in European History,* 131.

55. A review of the *Royal United Services Institute Journal* from 1919 to 1940 did not reveal any discussion of problems associated with inter-Allied cooperation. Instead, the focus appears to have been on interservice cooperation. See, for example, E. L. Gossage, "Air Cooperation with the Army," *Royal United Services Institute Journal* 72 (Aug. 1927): 561–578, and T. L. Leigh-Mallory, "Air Cooperation with Mechanized Forces," *Royal United Services Institute Journal* 75 (Aug. 1930): 565–577. Benjamin Franklin Cooling and Lieutenant Colonel John Hixson also note that "yet, as before the Great War, the curriculum of the [British] Staff College again failed to

address the details of allied inter-operability below the planning and supreme headquarters level" ("The Interoperability of Allied Forces in Europe at the Field Army Level," 15 Apr. 1977, USAMHI study, photocopy). A librarian at the British Staff College, Camberley, confirmed the absence of any such instruction (letter to the author, 3 Dec. 1980).

56. Weigley, *History of the U.S. Army*, 402. An excellent account of the spirit of the times and its effect on army planning is given in Mark S. Watson, *Chief of Staff: Prewar Plans and Preparation, USAWWII: The War Department* (Washington, D.C.: U.S. GPO, 1950), 15–56. A more recent account of the depth of unpreparedness is located in J. E. Kaufman and H. W. Kaufman, *The Sleeping Giant: American Armed Forces between the Wars* (Westport, Conn.: Praeger, 1996), 1–21, 53–61, 87–101.

57. Matloff, "American Approach to War," 228–229, 231; Ray S. Cline, *Washington Command Post: The Operations Division, USAWWII: The War Department* (Washington, D.C.: U.S. Center of Military History, 1951), 35–36.

58. Gen. Thomas T. Handy, interview by Lt. Col. Edward M. Kroff Jr., 28 Feb. 1974, Oral History Collection, USAMHI, 4; Matloff, "American Approach to War," 218–219. Weigley points out that the majority of the planning concerned mobilization (*History of the U.S. Army*, 406). See also Steven Ross, "American War Plans," in McKercher and Legault, *Military Planning*, 146–166, for an overview of American war planning from 1919 to 1938 that reinforces Matloff's view. A review of the pertinent JB files confirms Matloff's conclusion (JB, entry number NM43 1, Series 1, RG 225, NACP). In *Road to Rainbow*, Gole takes exception to these conclusions in his detailed examination of the contribution of the U.S. Army War College to the War Plans Division (WPD) and war planning during 1939–1940.

59. McKercher, "No Eternal Friends or Enemies," 17.

60. Greg Kennedy, "What Worth the Americans?" in Greg Kennedy, ed., *British Naval Strategy East of Suez, 1900–2000* (New York: Frank Cass, 2005), 92–98; Cox, "British Military Planning and the Origins of the Second World War," 105–106.

61. McKercher, "National Security and Imperial Defence," 415.

62. For events in the period 1935–1936, see A. J. P. Taylor, *The Origins of the Second World War*, 2nd rev. ed. (New York: Fawcett, 1961), 86–101; Norman Rich, *Hitler's War Aims: Ideology, the Nazi State, and the Course of Expansion* (New York: Norton, 1973), 82–89; and Graham Ross, *The Great Powers and the Decline of the European States System, 1914–1945* (London: Longman, 1983), 86–94.

63. Hall, *Britain, America, and Arms Control*, 143–144.

64. For an impressive *tour d'horizon* of internal British politics, global economic conditions, European and Far Eastern diplomacy of the 1930s, and the rise of fascism and totalitarian regimes, see McKercher, "National Security and Imperial Defence," 392–404.

65. Murfett, *Fool-Proof Relations*, 4–8.

66. McKercher, "National Security and Imperial Defence," 392.

67. Reynolds, *Creation of the Anglo-American Alliance*, 9.

68. Rock, *Chamberlain and Roosevelt*, 10–11.

69. COS Review Committee of Imperial Defense (CID), 1305B (Rev), 22 Feb. 37, para. 79–81, CAB 4/25, cited in Murfett, *Fool-Proof Relations*, 18.

70. Hall, *Britain, America, and Arms Control*, 145. By 1933, most key figures in the Admiralty, civilian and especially uniformed, began to see the benefits of collaborating with the United States. The key issue, given isolationist sentiment and recent naval rivalry issues, was whether the United States would actually collaborate (Kennedy, "What Worth the Americans?" 98–101).

71. Quoted in McKercher, *Transition of Power*, 120; also found in Dimbleby and Reynolds, *An Ocean Apart*, 102.

72. McKercher, *Transition of Power*, 121. For the details of the crisis and ensuing difficulties, see ibid., 116–125.

73. Harrison, "United States and Great Britain," passim; Dimbleby and Reynolds, *An Ocean Apart*, 82–104; Reynolds, *Creation of the Anglo-American Alliance*, 10, 75–79; Hall, *Britain, America, and Arms Control*, 116–141; McKercher, *Transition of Power*, 129–131, 186.

74. Quoted in Dimbleby and Reynolds, *An Ocean Apart*, 103.

75. Helmut C. Engelbrecht and Frank C. Hanighen, *Merchants of Death: A Study of the International Armament Industry* (New York: Dodd, Mead, 1934), 9. For an account of the Nye Committee and hearings, see Matthew W. Coulter, *The Senate Munitions Inquiry of the 1930s: Beyond the Merchants of Death* (Westport, Conn.: Greenwood Press, 1997). See also Jenner, *FDR's Republicans*, 57–63, and Manfred Jonas, *Isolationism in America, 1935–1941* (Ithaca, N.Y.: Cornell University Press, 1966), 142–151. A brief overview of the hearings is given in Doenecke and Wilz, *From Isolation to War*, 57–61.

76. Reynolds, *Creation of the Anglo-American Alliance*, 30; Cordell Hull, *The Memoirs of Cordell Hull*, 2 vols. (New York: MacMillan, 1958), 1:531–571; Kennedy, *Freedom from Fear*, 401–402. For the Japanese rampage in Nanking, see Iris Chang, *The Rape of Nanking: The Forgotten Holocaust of World War II* (New York: Penguin Books, 1997).

77. Bradford Lee, *Britain and the Sino-Japanese War, 1937–1939* (Stanford, Calif.: Stanford University Press, 1973), 79–80; James Neidpath, *The Singapore Naval Base and the Defense of Britain's Eastern Empire, 1919–1941* (Oxford: Oxford University Press, 1981), 141. For an inside view of British attitudes toward Japanese action and efforts at fashioning a unified Anglo-American front against Japanese aggression, see Anthony Eden, *The Memoirs of Anthony Eden, Lord Avon*, vol. 2: *Facing the Dictators, 1923–1938* (Boston: Houghton Mifflin, 1962), 593–620.

78. For Chamberlain's overtures, see McKercher, *Transition of Power*, 243–244. For FDR's invitation, see Dallek, *Franklin D. Roosevelt and American Foreign Policy*, 144. The cancellation may have been due to rising isolationist and pacifists sentiment sparked by Japan's invasion of China and bruising debates over the latest and most restrictive Neutrality Act as well as to FDR's domestic problems (e.g., Supreme Court, New Deal legislation, and the minidepression that started that summer) (Dallek, *Franklin D. Roosevelt and American Foreign Policy*, 145–147). Nonetheless, FDR should have better explained the cancellation.

79. FDR, Quarantine Speech, 5 Oct. 1937, in Donald B. Schewe, ed., *Franklin D. Roosevelt and Foreign Affairs*, 16 vols. (New York: Clearwater, 1979), 7:Doc. 524, 10–21; a copy of the speech can also be found at http://millercenter.org/president/speecehs/detail/3310 (accessed 17 July 2012).

80. Murfett, *Fool-Proof Relations*, 63–66; Lawrence Pratt, "Anglo-American Naval Conversations on the Far East of January 1938," *International Affairs* 67 (Oct. 1971): 747 (quote).

81. Divine, *Reluctant Belligerent*, 45; George H. Gallup, *The Gallup Poll, 1935–1971*, 3 vols. (New York: Random House, 1972), 1:71; Richard Overy, with Andrew Wheatcraft, *The Road to War*, rev. ed. (London: Penguin, 1999), 318.

82. Overy, *Road to War*, 318.

83. McKercher, *Transition of Power*, 246.

84. Lowenthal, *Leadership and Indecision*, 1:18–21; Pratt, "Anglo-American Conversations on the Far East," 748–749; Murfett, *Fool-Proof Relations*, 96–97; and Anthony Eden to Ronald Lindsay, 27 Nov. 1937, Message no. 561, F10024/220/10G/F10024/9/10, Foreign Office (FO) 371/20959, Political Departments, General Correspondence, 1906–1966, TNA: PRO, cited in Murfett, *Fool-Proof Relations*, 95; John Major, "The Navy Plans for War, 1937–1942," in Hagan, *In Peace and War*, 239.

85. Quoted in Kennedy, *Freedom from Fear*, 406. See also McKercher, *Transition of Power*, 246.

86. Kennedy, *Freedom from Fear*, 409. See also Murfett, *Fool-Proof Relations*, 70–86, and McKercher, *Transition of Power*, 244–245, for further consequences.

3. Groping in the Dark

1. For a concise description of the Panay crisis, see U.S. Department of State, *Peace and War: United States Foreign Policy, 1931–1941* (Washington, D.C.: U.S. GPO, 1943), 45–53. See also Murfett, *Fool-Proof Relations*, 105–106.

2. Lee, *Britain and the Sino-Japanese War*, 90–91; Reynolds, *Creation of the Anglo-American Alliance*, 30–31; Hull, *Memoirs*, 1:544–545. John McVickar Haight discusses FDR's concept of the quarantine in "Franklin D. Roosevelt and a Naval Quarantine of Japan," *Pacific Historical Review* 40 (May 1971): 203–225.

3. Pratt, "Anglo-American Naval Conversations on the Far East," 750–751, 758; Lindsay to FO, message, 17 Dec. 1937, ADM 116/3922, TNA: PRO.

4. Murfett, *Fool-Proof Relations*, 103–104.

5. Adm. Royal E. Ingersoll, "The Reminiscences of Adm. Royal E. Ingersoll," 1965, Columbia University Oral History Project, Operational Archives Branch (OAB), Naval History Division (now Naval History and Heritage Command [NHHC]), Washington, D.C., 70; Lindsay to FO, 17 Dec. 1937, ADM 116/3922, TNA: PRO. Promoted to rear admiral in 1938, Ingersoll would command Cruiser Division Six. From 1940 to 1942, he served as assistant to the CNO. As part of the post–Pearl Harbor reorganization of the U.S. Navy in January 1942, Ingersoll received command of the U.S. Atlantic Fleet and promotion to vice admiral. A promotion to admiral followed in July 1942. In addition to commanding the Atlantic fleet until May 1943,

Ingersoll also had responsibility for antisubmarine warfare in the Atlantic and defense of the Western Hemisphere. In November 1944, he assumed command of the Western Sea Frontier in the Pacific and responsibilities of deputy CNO until his retirement in August 1946 (Boatner, *Biographical Dictionary of World War II*, 250, and R. Manning Ancell, with Christine M. Miller, *The Biographical Dictionary of World War II Generals and Flag Officers: The U.S. Armed Forces* [Westport, Conn.: Greenwood Press, 1996], 555).

6. Ingersoll, "Reminiscences of Adm. Royal E. Ingersoll," 70; see also U.S. Congress, Joint Committee on the Investigation of the Pearl Harbor Attack, *Hearings of the Joint Committee on the Investigation of the Pearl Harbor Attack*, 79th Cong., 1st sess., 39 vols. (Washington, D.C.: U.S. GPO, 1946), 9:4273 (hereafter cited as U.S. Congress, *PHAH*).

7. Ingersoll, "Reminiscences of Adm. Royal E. Ingersoll," 71.

8. Memo for CNO, 1 Jan. 1938, Correspondence Re: British-U.S. Conversations in London, 1938–1939 (Adm. Ingersoll Mission), Box 116, Series VII, Strategic Plans Division (SPD), Records Relating to U.S. Navy Operations Received from OAB, NHHC, Office of the Chief of Naval Operations, RG 38.2.4, NACP (hereafter cited as item, Ingersoll Mission File, RG 38.2.4, NACP). Eden's version of the meeting is in Eden, *Facing the Dictators*, 619–620. See also Murfett, *Fool-Proof Relations*, 130.

9. Alexander Cadogan, *The Diaries of Sir Alexander Cadogan*, ed. David Dilks (New York: Putnam, 1972), 31, entry for 1 Jan. 1938. Ingersoll noted in his journal that Eden appeared to be more interested in immediate action than in long-range planning (Memo for CNO, 1 Jan. 1938, Ingersoll Mission File, RG 38.2.4, NACP).

10. Memo for CNO, 1 Jan. 1938, Ingersoll Mission File, RG 38.2.4, NACP.
11. Memo for CNO, 3 Jan. 1938, Ingersoll Mission File, RG 38.2.4, NACP.
12. Ibid.
13. Ibid.
14. Ibid.
15. Ibid.
16. Ibid.
17. Memo for CNO, 10 Jan. 1938, Ingersoll Mission File, RG 38.2.4, NACP.
18. Record of Conversation between Captain R. E. Ingersoll (U.S. Navy) and Captain T. V. Phillips (Royal Navy), 13 Jan. 1938, Ingersoll Mission File, RG 38.2.4, NACP. There is no difference in form or substance between this final copy and the original draft contained in the same file. The substantive issues are also contained in Ingersoll for Captain T. V. Phillips, memo, n.d., Ingersoll Mission File, RG 38.2.4, NACP.
19. Record of Conversation between Ingersoll and Phillips, 13 Jan. 1938. It is interesting to note that in the final version of the Record of Conversation the British did not detail the forces that they actually had available in the Far East—that is, one aircraft carrier, ten cruisers, nine destroyers, and fifteen submarines.
20. Ibid.
21. Ibid.

22. Ibid., and Memo for CNO, 5 Jan. 1938, Ingersoll Mission File, RG 38.2.4, NACP. The British had gone so far as to prepare call signs for all U.S. ships.

23. Record of Conversation between Ingersoll and Phillips, 13 Jan. 1938.

24. Memo for CNO, 5 Jan. 1938.

25. Record of Conversation between Ingersoll and Phillips, 13 Jan. 1938.

26. Meeting between Lord Ernle Chatfield, Captain Thomas V. Phillips, Captain Royal E. Ingersoll, and Captain Russell Willson, in Memo for CNO, 13 Jan. 38, Ingersoll Mission File, RG 38.2.4, NACP.

27. Ibid.

28. Pratt, "Anglo-American Naval Conversations on the Far East of January 1938," 745.

29. Ibid., 759; Major, "Navy Plans for War," 240; Doenecke and Wilz, *From Isolation to War*, 78; Reynolds, *Creation of the Anglo-American Alliance*, 33; Cowman, *Dominion or Decline*, 153.

30. Pratt, "Anglo-American Naval Conversations on the Far East," 757–758.

31. Ibid.

32. As Lawrence Pratt observes, if "the exchanges of December 1937 . . . did not exactly herald a new 'hands across the sea' period of Anglo-American relations, it was at least an important beginning. For from these first hesitant contacts would spring the entire technical apparatus of co-operation that supported the Anglo-Saxon revival of the war years" ("Anglo-American Naval Conversations on the Far East," 759; see also Murfett, *Fool-Proof Relations*, 138).

33. Ingersoll to Willson, letter, 2 Feb. 1938, Ingersoll Mission File, RG 38.2.4, NACP.

34. CNO to CINC, U.S. Fleet, and CINC, Asiatic Fleet (CINCAF), letter, 2 Feb. 1938, Subj: Possible Parallel Action by the United States and British Fleets in the Pacific, Serial no. 218, Enclosure (Encl.) A, Ingersoll Mission File, RG 38.2.4, NACP.

35. Willson to Director, Naval Intelligence, letter, 10 Feb. 1938, Ingersoll Mission File, RG 38.2.4, NACP.

36. Cowman, *Dominion or Decline*, 137–138.

37. See Willson to Ingersoll, letter, 4 Mar. 1938, and Ingersoll to Willson, letter, 28 Mar. 1938, Ingersoll Mission File, RG 38.2.4, NACP. See also Lowenthal, *Leadership and Indecision*, 1:121–122, and Murfett, *Fool-Proof Relations*, 184–185.

38. Wayne S. Cole's book *Roosevelt and the Isolationists, 1932–1945* (Lincoln: University of Nebraska Press, 1983), is the classic account by the leading historian of isolationism/noninterventionism. See also Cole's initial but still relevant account *America First: The Battle against Intervention, 1940–1941* (Madison: University of Wisconsin Press, 1953). In *Isolationism in America*, Manfred Jonas was one of the first to highlight the broader aspects of noninterventionism (see especially chapter 2). In *Storm on the Horizon: The Challenge to American Intervention, 1939–1941* (Latham, Md.: Rowman and Littlefield, 2003), Justus D. Doenecke provides an encyclopedic catalog of the broad range of anti-interventionist movements and their views. For a succinct overview of anti-interventionism, see Doenecke and Wilz, *From Isolation to War*, chapter 1.

A very brief survey of the movements and their effects on foreign policy can be found in Overy, *Road to War,* 310–315.

39. In *Senate Munitions Inquiry of the 1930s,* Coulter offers a detailed account and analysis of the groups allied around nonintervention. See also Jenner, *FDR's Republicans,* 57–63, and Jonas, *Isolationism in America,* 142–151. Brief overviews can be found in Doenecke and Wilz, *From Isolation to War,* 57–61, and U.S. Senate, "Merchants of Death," n.d., at http://www.senate.gov/artandhistory/history/minute/merchants_of_death.htm (accessed 16 Jan. 2016). A copy of the Nye Committee report of 1936 can be found at http://www.bpl.org/online/govdocs/nye_committee.htm (accessed 30 Nov. 2012).

40. As indicated in the three polls, public support for the Ludlow amendment was 75, 71, and 73 percent, respectively (Overy, *Road to War,* 317; Ole R. Holsti, *Public Opinion and American Foreign Policy,* rev. ed. [Ann Arbor: University of Michigan Press, 2004], 17–18; Kennedy, *Freedom from Fear,* 403; Divine, *Reluctant Belligerent,* 48–49). Jonas gives a brief summary of the initiative in *Isolationism in America* (158–166).

41. For FDR's need of Senate support, see Kennedy, *Freedom from Fear,* 390–391; Jenner, *FDR's Republicans,* 106–115; and Divine, *Reluctant Belligerent,* 7–10, 15–22, 27–34. Key senators included Robert La Follete (P–Wisc.), Gerald Nye (R–N.D.), George Norris (R–Neb.), Hiram Johnson (R–Calif.), William Borah (R–Idaho), Bronson Cutting (R–N.M.), Key Pittman (D–Nev.), and Burton D. Wheeler (D–Mont.). For details of the Supreme Court "packing" scheme and its consequences, see Conrad Black, *Franklin Delano Roosevelt: Champion of Freedom* (New York: Public Affairs, 2003), 404–418; Jenner, *FDR's Republicans,* 84–85; and Kennedy, *Freedom from Fear,* 325–339. Kennedy diminishes the effects of the court-packing scheme. Overy provides a quick summary of these events in *Road to War* (314–315).

42. Leutze, *Bargaining for Supremacy,* 32–33. In *Anglo-American Strategic Relations and the Far East,* Kennedy outlines the cooperative relationships (15–26). Murfett is less optimistic about the level of information exchange (*Fool-Proof Relations,* 180–182).

43. For the biographical info on Lee, see Dean Acheson, foreword to Raymond E. Lee, *The London Journal of General Raymond E. Lee, 1940–1941,* ed. James R. Leutze (Boston: Little, Brown, 1971), xi–xviii, ix (quote), and Ancell, *Biographical Dictionary of World War II Generals and Flag Officers,* 185.

44. Lt. Col. Raymond E. Lee to Assistant Chief of Staff (COS), G-2, letter, 28 Apr. 1938, Subj: Army Information and War Office Control, Military Intelligence Division (MID) Report no. 9771-249, Security Classified Correspondence and Reports, 1917–1941, Series 65, War Department General and Special Staffs, entry A1 65, RG 165, NACP (hereafter item, RG 165/65, NACP); see also Colonel Bradford G. Chynoweth to Colonel E. R. W. McCabe, letter, 5 May 1939, Bradford G. Chynoweth Papers, Correspondence File, Apr.–Sept. 1939, USAMHI.

45. One example of this method was a meeting in February 1938 between Major General Desmond F. Anderson, deputy director of British Military Intelligence, and

Lieutenant Colonel Hayes A. Kroner, assistant U.S. military attaché, where Anderson intimated that the War Office was willing to show the Americans any and all items of British equipment, including those still in the developmental stages (Memos of Conversations between Anderson and Kroner, 7 Feb. and 12 Feb. 1938, MID Report no. 9971-249, RG 165/65, NACP). There are numerous other examples in this file.

46. Chynoweth to Colonel J. A. Crane, letter, 5 May 1939, and Chynoweth to Brig. Gen. Frederick Beaumont-Nesbitt, letter, 17 July 1939, in Chynoweth Papers, Correspondence File, Apr.–Sept. 1939, USAMHI. Chynoweth commanded the Visayan Force in the Philippines in 1941–1942, was captured by the Japanese in 1942, and held prisoner until 1945.

47. Chynoweth Papers, Correspondence File, Apr.–Sept 1939, USAMHI, passim.

48. Information contained in this passage is from Record of Conversation, London, 13 Jan. 1939, Ingersoll Mission File, RG 38.2.4, NACP, in connection with bringing up to date the Ingersoll conversations in London in January 1938. The changed conditions in Europe included rising German bellicosity and rearmament coupled with the Anschluss of Germany and Austria, the Sudetenland Crisis, the Munich Crisis, and the breakup of Czechoslovakia as well as a closer Berlin–Rome relationship and increasing Italian demands in the Mediterranean.

49. Ibid. Murfett's description in *Fool-Proof Relations* (199–203) conforms to this account.

50. Minute of Meeting, PD 07577/39, 24 Mar. 1939, ADM 116/3922, TNA: PRO. See also Lowenthal, *Leadership and Indecision*, 1:127–128, and Murfett, *Fool-Proof Relations*, 219–221, for additional details.

51. Cdr. T. C. Hampton to Director of Plans, Admiralty, report, 27 June 1939, app. I, and Report of Meeting, 12 June 1939, ADM 116/3922, TNA: PRO. For the U.S. version of the conversation, see Memo of Informal Conference at the Residence of the CNO, 12 June 1939, Ingersoll Mission File, RG 38.2.4, NACP.

52. Cdr. Hampton to Director of Plans, Admiralty, Report of Meeting on 12 June 1939, 27 June 1939, app. I, ADM 116/3922, TNA: PRO.

53. Memo of Informal Conference at the Residence of the CNO, 14 June 1939, Ingersoll Mission File, RG 38.3.4, NACP.

54. Boatner, *The Biographical Dictionary of World War II*, 307–308; Ancell, *Biographical Dictionary of World War II Generals and Flag Officers*, 568–569. Leahy also served as a member of the U.S.-British Combined Chiefs of Staff (CCS). He retained his post under President Harry Truman until his retirement in 1949. For Leahy's personal account, see William D. Leahy, *I Was There: The Memoirs of FDR's Chief of Staff* (New York: Whittlesey House, 1950). The standard scholarly biography of Leahy is Henry H. Adams, *Witness to Power: The Life of Fleet Admiral William D. Leahy* (Annapolis, Md.: Naval Institute Press, 1985).

55. Memo of Informal Conference at the CNO's Residence, 14 June 1939, Ingersoll Mission File, RG 38.2.4, NACP.

56. Ibid.; Cdr. Hampton to director of plans, Admiralty, Report of Meeting on 14 June 1939, app. II, ADM 116/3922, TNA: PRO. Hampton's version differs in that

he noted that Admiral Leahy indicated that in the event of war with Japan the United States could send a fleet of at least ten capital ships to Singapore but that this would depend on the strategic situation and the state of American public opinion. Leahy added that at the moment the U.S. Navy had no existing plans for such a move.

57. Cdr. Hampton, Report of Meeting, 14 June 39, ADM 116/3922, TNA: PRO.

58. Kennedy, *Anglo-American Strategic Relations and the Far East*, 41. Other historians present a less-effusive if still overall positive assessment. See, for example, Lowenthal, *Leadership and Indecision*, 1:135, and Cowman, *Dominion or Decline*, 149.

59. Kittredge, "United States Defense Policies and Global Strategy, 1900–1941," 105; Adm. Alan G. Kirk, "Reminiscences of Vice Adm. Alan G. Kirk," 1962, Columbia University Oral History Project, OAB, Naval History Division/NHHC, 133.

60. For talks following the Ethiopian crisis, see Gibbs, *Rearmament Policy*, 206–209, and Bond, *Britain, France, and Belgium*, 21. Pownall noted in his diary, "[M]ilitarily they were very little good" (Sir Henry Pownall, *Chief of Staff: The Diaries of Lieutenant General Sir Henry Pownall*, 2 vols., ed. Brian Bond [Hamden, Conn.: Archon Books, 1973], 1:142, entry for 21 Mar. 1938).

61. Minutes of Cabinet Meeting 28 (36), 8 Apr. 1936, 7, and app. 1, 1–2, CAB 23/83, TNA: PRO, in U.K. Cabinet Office, *Cabinet Minutes*.

62. Gibbs, *Rearmament Policy*, 610; Minutes of Cabinet Meeting 56 (36), 2 Sept. 1936, CAB 23/85, in U.K. Cabinet Office, *Cabinet Minutes;* Pownall, *Chief of Staff*, 1:142–143, diary entries for 10 and 11 Apr. 1938.

63. Reaction to remilitarization of the Rhineland and the call for staff talks can be followed in U.K. House of Commons, *Text of Proposals Drawn Up by the Representatives of Belgium, France, United Kingdom of Great Britain and Northern Ireland, and Italy,* Command Paper 5134 (London: HMSO, 19 Mar. 1936), 3, and U.K. House of Commons, *Correspondence with the Belgian and French Ambassadors Relating to "Text Proposals Drawn Up by the Representatives of Belgium, France, United Kingdom of Great Britain and Northern Ireland, and Italy." London, 19 March 1936, CMD 5134,* Command Paper 5149, Misc. no. 4 (London: HMSO, 1 Apr. 1936), 1. Both command papers are located in U.K. House of Commons, *Sessional Papers, 1935/1936,* 28:49–56 and 57–62, respectively. See also Minutes of Cabinet Meeting 24 (36), 25 Mar. 1936, CAB 23/83, TNA: PRO, which include the following statement: "There was general agreement that the military conversations provided for in Section III of the proposals are a binding commitment" and Minutes of Cabinet Meeting 25 (36), 1 Apr. 1936, CAB 23/83, TNA: PRO, both in U.K. Cabinet Office, *Cabinet Minutes*.

64. Gibbs, *Rearmament Policy*, 610–611; Deverell quote from Defense Plans (Policy), CID Subcommittee, First Meeting, 19 Apr. 1937, in Gibbs, *Rearmament Policy*, 611n.

65. Gibbs offers a concise discussion of the internal dissension within the British government (*Rearmament Policy*, 622–636). For specific examples, see Minutes of Cabinet Meeting 18 (38), 6 Apr. 1938, CAB 23/93, TNA: PRO; Cabinet Papers 94 (38), 11 Apr. 1938, Annex 1 and Annex 2, CAB 24/276, TNA: PRO; Minutes of Cabinet Meeting 21 (38), 27 Apr. 38, 7, CAB 23/93, TNA: PRO; and Cabinet Papers

122 (38), Staff Conversations with France and Belgium, Encl. 1, report by the CID COS Subcommittee, 20 May 1938, 7, CAB 24/277, TNA: PRO, all in U.K. Cabinet Office, *Cabinet Minutes*.

66. Pownall, *Chief of Staff*, diary entries for April 1938, quoted in Bond, *Britain, France, and Belgium*, 7, emphasis in original. The other material in this paragraph comes from Gordon Martel, "Military Planning and the Origins of the Second World War, " in McKercher and Legault, *Military Planning*, 18–21; Martin S. Alexander and William J. Philpott, "Introduction: Choppy Channel Waters," in Alexander and Philpott, *Anglo-French Defence Relations between the Wars*, 12; Martin S. Alexander and William J. Philpott, "The Entente Cordiale and the Next War: Anglo-French Views on the Future of Military Cooperation, 1928–1939," in Martin S. Alexander, ed., *Knowing Your Friends: Intelligence inside Alliances and Coalitions from 1914 to the Cold War* (London: Taylor and Francis, 1998), 61–62; COS 218th Meeting, CAB 53/8, COS 680, 4 Feb. 1938, CAB 24/274, TNA: PRO, cited in Murfett, *Fool-Proof Relations*, 156; Oliver Harvey, *The Diplomatic Diaries of Oliver Harvey, 1937–1940* (New York: St. Martin's Press, 1970), 87, entry for 8 Feb. 1938. For an overview of the evolution of French and British policy after Munich, see Talbot Imlay, "The Making of the Anglo-French Alliance, 1938–1939," in Alexander and Philpott, *Anglo-French Defence Relations between the Wars*, 93–100 and 100–112, respectively.

67. For a description of splits within the Cabinet and the debate to resume conversations, see Harvey, *Diplomatic Diaries*, 91, entry for 16 Feb. 1938.

68. The Lee quote is from MID Reports, British Isles, vol. 3 (1939), Tab 124, Report no. 400001, 22 Mar. 39, Box 184, Harry L. Hopkins Papers, FDRL. For other material in this paragraph, see Minutes of Cabinet Meeting 26 (38), 25 May 1938, in U.K. Cabinet Office, *Cabinet Minutes*, and L. A. Hawes, "The Story of the 'W' Plan: The Move of Our Forces to France in 1939," *Army Quarterly and Defense Journal* 101 (July 1971): 448–452.

69. Anthony Clayton, "Growing Respect: The Royal Navy and the *Maritime Nationale*, 1918–1939," in Alexander and Philpott, *Anglo-French Defence Relations between the Wars*, 35; Thomas Martin, "Imperial Defence or Diversionary Attack?" in Alexander and Philpott, *Anglo-French Defence Relations between the Wars*, 171; Martin S. Alexander and William J. Philpott, "Anglo-French Views on Co-operation," in Alexander, *Knowing Your Friends*, 61–62, 70–72; and Lord Gort to Cyril Newall, letter, n.d. (c. late Aug. 1938), cited in John Colville, *Man of Valour: The Life of Field Marshal the Viscount Gort, VC, GCB, DSO, MVO, MC* (London: Collins, 1972), 110.

70. Bond, *Britain, France, and Belgium*, 30–31; a memorandum (CP (37) 41, Role of the Army, CAB 24/267, TNA: PRO, in U.K. Cabinet, *Cabinet Minutes* prompted the Cabinet's decision. For the schedule of the talks, see Gibbs, *Rearmament Policy*, 656–657. This schedule was strictly in line with the procedures laid out by the COS in Cabinet Papers 40 (39), CID, COS Subcommittee, and Staff Conversations with France and Belgium, 6 Feb. 1939, CAB 24/283, 4–5, in U.K. Cabinet, *Cabinet Minutes*.

71. Gibbs, *Rearmament Policy*, 668.

72. Lionel F. Ellis, *The War in France and Flanders, 1939–1940,* in *History of the Second World War, United Kingdom Military Series* (London: HMSO, 1953), 5. This is not to intimate that it should have been any different, given the strategic situation.

73. Ibid., 11–12, online version, at http://www.ibiblio.org/hyperwar/UN/UK/UK-NWE-Flanders/UK-NWE-Flanders-1.html (accessed 4 Aug. 2015).

74. Ibid., 6–9; Pownall, *Chief of Staff,* 1:207, 211–213, entries for 5 June and 10 July 1939; Colville, *Man of Valour,* 127, 130. A detailed account of Anglo-French cooperation from September 1939 to June 1940 is contained in James N. Hickock II, "Anglo-French Military Cooperation, 1939–1940," typewritten manuscript, 282 pp., n.d. (c. 1983), Research Office, Office of the Dean, U.S. Military Academy, West Point, N.Y.

75. William J. Philpott, "The Benefit of Experience? The Supreme War Council and the Higher Management of Coalition War, 1939–1940," in Alexander and Philpott, *Anglo-French Defence Relations between the Wars,* 210–216.

76. Ibid., 217; Alexander and Philpott, "Introduction," 14.

4. Ties That Bind

1. U.S. Department of State, *Milestones, 1921–1936: The Neutrality Acts, 1930s,* at http://history.state.gov/milestones/1921–1936/Neutrality_act (accessed 2 Dec. 2012). For background information, details, and consequences of the 1935 act, see Divine, *Reluctant Belligerent,* 15–26; Dallek, *Franklin D. Roosevelt and American Foreign Policy,* 102–121; Levering, *The Public and American Foreign Policy,* 57; and Kennedy, *Freedom from Fear,* 395. For the 1936 act, see Divine, *Reluctant Belligerent,* 26–31, and Dallek, *Franklin D. Roosevelt and American Foreign Policy,* 117–121.

2. U.S. Department of State, *Milestones, 1921–1936: The Neutrality Acts.* For 1937, see Divine, *Reluctant Belligerent,* 34–38; Dallek, *Franklin D. Roosevelt and American Foreign Policy,* 135–140; and Kennedy, *Freedom from Fear,* 398–401.

3. Quoted in Harvey, *Diplomatic Diaries of Oliver Harvey,* 68, entry for 13 Jan. 1938.

4. Although Eden ostensibly left the Cabinet over Chamberlain's appeasement policies, particularly concerning Italy and Ethiopia, in reality his resignation was due as much to Chamberlain's refusal to look upon the United States as a potential partner. For details of Eden's departure, see Eden, *Facing the Dictators,* 666–679.

5. Quoted in Harrison, "United States and Great Britain," 127; Harrison cites Harvey, *Diplomatic Diaries of Oliver Harvey,* 148. See also Richard A. Harrison, "A Presidential Demarche: Franklin D. Roosevelt's Personal Diplomacy and Great Britain, 1936–1937," *Diplomatic History* 5, no. 3 (July 1981): 269–270.

6. McKercher, "No Eternal Friends or Enemies," 19; Murfett, *Fool-Proof Relations,* 165; McKercher, *Transition of Power,* 253; Kennedy, "Neville Chamberlain," 113–114; Overy, *Road to War,* 323.

7. Alan Dobson, *U.S. Wartime Aid to Britain, 1940–1946* (New York: St. Martin's Press, 1986), 7; Kennedy, "Neville Chamberlain," 113; Moser, *Twisting the Lion's Tail,* 84–85, 108–115.

8. Cox, "British Military Planning and the Origins of the Second World War," 111–113.

9. John McVickar Haight, *American Aid to France, 1938–1940* (New York: Atheneum, 1970), 4–7. A quick survey of the French air force confirmed that France had only twenty-seven modern aircraft capable of matching Germany's estimated one thousand first-line aircraft.

10. Ibid., 4–7, quote from Senator Baron Amoury de La Grange to J. C. Cailleux, president of the French Senate, letter, 21 Jan. 1938, on 7.

11. Haight, *American Aid to France*, 8–10.

12. Boatner, *Biographical Dictionary of World War II*, 14–15; Ancell, *Biographical Dictionary of World War II Generals and Flag Officers*, 362–363; Thomas Coffey, *Hap: The Story of the U.S. Air Force and the Man Who Built It, General Henry H. "Hap" Arnold* (New York: Viking Press, 1982), 1–180, passim. See also Henry H. Arnold, *Global Mission* (New York: Harper and Brothers, 1949); Dik Daso, *Hap Arnold and the Evolution of American Airpower* (Washington, D.C.: Smithsonian Institution Press, 2000); and Bill Yenne, *Hap Arnold: The General Who Invented the U.S. Air Force* (Washington, D.C.: Regnery History, 2013).

13. Haight, *American Aid to France*, 10–12; William C. Bullitt to FDR, letter, 11 May 1938, in Orville Bullitt, ed., *For the President: Personal and Secret Correspondence of Roosevelt and William C. Bullitt* (New York: Houghton Mifflin, 1972), 256–257.

14. FDR to Bullitt, letter, n.d., in Bullitt, *For the President*, 260.

15. H. Duncan Hall, *North American Supply*, in *History of the Second World War: United Kingdom Civil Series* (London: HMSO, 1955), 108–109.

16. Arthur Herman, *Freedom's Forge: How American Business Produced Victory in World War II* (New York: Random House, 2012), 87.

17. Group Capt. G. C. Pirie (British air attaché) to Col. John B. Coulter, letter, 13 Apr. 1938, MID Report no. 300-W-540, RG 165/65, NACP. Harris would later become marshal of the Royal Air Force (RAF), lead RAF Bomber Command, and earn the nicknames "Bomber" and "Butcher" Harris.

18. Hall, *North American Supply*, 105–106, and H. H. Arnold for Exec. G-2, memo, 12 May 1938, MID Report no. 300-W-540, RG 165/65, NACP.

19. Barbara Reardon Farnham, *Roosevelt and the Munich Crisis: A Study of Political Decision-Making* (Princeton, N.J.: Princeton University Press, 1997), ix, 14, 147, 137 (quotes).

20. John M. Blum, ed., *From the Morgenthau Diaries*, vol. 2: *Years of Urgency, 1938–1941* (Boston: Houghton Mifflin, 1965), 28, 49, 113–114; Haight, *American Aid to France*, 28–30; Dallek, *Franklin D. Roosevelt and American Foreign Policy*, 172–173; Farnham, *Roosevelt and the Munich Crisis*, 200.

21. Jean Monnet, *Memoirs*, trans. Richard Mayne (New York: Doubleday, 1978), 117–118.

22. For details of Monnet's outstanding life and accomplishments, see François Duchene, *Jean Monnet: The First Statesman of Interdependence* (New York: Norton, 1980). Douglas Brinkley and Clifford Hackett's edited volume *Jean Monnet: The Path*

to European Unity (New York: St. Martin's Press, 1991) contains chapters that address specific aspects of Monnet's life in detail.

23. Monnet, *Memoirs,* 119–121; Blum, *Years of Urgency,* 64–66; Haight, *American Aid to France,* 32–40, 46–47; Farnham, *Roosevelt and the Munich Crisis,*179.

24. Haight, *American Aid to France,* 74.

25. Blum, *Years of Urgency,* 66–71; Monnet, *Memoirs,* 121–122; Haight, *American Aid to France,* 88.

26. Blum, *Years of Urgency,* 70–71; Haight, *American Aid to France,* 77–81, 83–86, 91–93.

27. For the conference and its results, see Haight, *American Aid to France,* 91–93; Eric Hammel, *How America Saved the World: The Untold Story of U.S. Preparedness between the World Wars* (Minneapolis: Zenith Press, 2010), 90–91, and Coffey, *Hap,* 193–194. For the exhaustion of the existing U.S. plant capacity, see Watson, *Chief of Staff,* 299.

28. Irving B. Holley Jr., *Buying Aircraft: Material Procurement for the Army Air Forces,* in *USAWWII: Special Studies* (Washington, D.C.: U.S. GPO, 1964), 199; Coffey, *Hap,* 194–195.

29. Blum, *Years of Urgency,* 71–77; Monnet, *Memoirs,* 122; Holley, *Buying Aircraft,* 199; Coffey, *Hap,* 194–195.

30. Kennedy, *Freedom for Fear,* 421.

31. John Cudahy to FDR, letter, 9 Feb. 1939, quoting Eamon de Valera, in Schewe, *Franklin D. Roosevelt and Foreign Affairs,* 13:273, and cited in Kennedy, *Freedom for Fear,* 421.

32. Christopher Thorne's book *The Approach of War, 1938–1939* (New York: St. Martin's Press, 1967) offers a concise overview of the events of March 1939 (92–110) and outlines the repercussions of March 1939 and the Anglo-French search for security (113–147).

33. McKercher, *Transition to Power,* 265–267; Kennedy, "Neville Chamberlain," 113–115.

34. McKercher, *Transition of Power,* 267–268; Greg Kennedy, "Lord Lothian, the Far East, and Anglo-American Strategic Relations, 1934–1941," in Priscilla Roberts, ed., *Lord Lothian and Anglo-American Relations, 1900–1940* (Dordrecht, Netherlands: Republic of Letters, 2010), 114–117; J. Simon Rofe, "Lord Lothian's Ambassadorship in Washington, August 1939–December," in Roberts, *Lord Lothian and Anglo-American Relations,* 138–140; David Reynolds, *Lord Lothian and Anglo-American Relations, 1939–1940,* Transactions of the American Philosophical Society, vol. 73, part 2 (Philadelphia: American Philosophical Society, 1983), 4, 8–13.

35. Murfett, *Fool-Proof Relations,* 204

36. See, for example, F. Sidney Cotton to F. W. Winterbotham, letter, 12 June 1939, Cabinet Offices and Predecessors, Supplementary Registered Files, CAB 104/158, TNA: PRO.

37. Hall, *North American Supply,* 49–51.

38. Farnham, *Roosevelt and the Munich Crisis,* 205. For an example of public opin-

ion, 66 percent of respondents to a Gallup Poll in April 1939 opposed providing materiel to either side (Overy, *Road to War,* 327).

39. Kennedy, *Freedom from Fear,* 349.

40. Nicholas Cull, "The Munich Crisis and British Propaganda Policy in the United States," in Igor Lukes and Erik Goldstein, eds., "Special Issue on the Munich Crisis," *Diplomacy and Statecraft* 10 (July–Nov. 1999): 217.

41. Quote taken from ibid., 222. Also see Divine, *Reluctant Belligerent,* 55, for more background.

42. Cull, "Munich Crisis and British Propaganda," 229.

43. Divine, *Reluctant Belligerent,* 55.

44. Quote taken from Harold Levine and James Wechsler, *War Propaganda in the United States* (New Haven, Conn.: Yale University Press, 1940), 216, cited in Cull, "Munich Crisis and British Propaganda," 118.

45. Jonas, *Isolationism in America,* 215; Divine, *Reluctant Belligerent,* 61; Kennedy, *Freedom from Fear,* 422–423.

46. Lindsay to FO, Message 290, 29 June 1939, and FDR for Joseph Kennedy and William C. Bullitt, memo, 28 July 1939, CAB 104/159, TNA: PRO, quoted in Bullitt, *For the President,* 359. Roosevelt's decision may have been influenced by a joint memo from the assistant secretary of war and the assistant secretary of the navy, who informed him that "'the judicious distribution of such [Anglo-French] orders to domestic industry can be made to serve a very useful purpose in advancing our own plans for the national defense'" (Assistant Secretary of War and Assistant Secretary of the Navy for the President, memo, 30 June 1939, quoted in Watson, *Chief of Staff,* 302–303).

47. Lord Riverdale, Ministry of Supply Purchasing Commission in the United States and Canada, report, 17 Aug. 1939, CAB 104/160, TNA: PRO. See also Hall, *North American Supply,* 65–68.

48. Riverdale report, 17 Aug. 1939, 3.

49. Ibid., 3 (quote), 4–8.

50. Ibid., 9.

51. Minister of Supply, memo, n.d. (c. Sept. 1939), Subj: Purchasing Commission in the U.S.A., War Cabinet Records, WP(G) (39) 2, and Phillip Kerr, Lord Lothian, to FO, Message 453, 8 Sept. 1939, both in CAB 104/161, TNA: PRO. The latter two conditions were to avoid adverse publicity during FDR's attempts to amend the Neutrality Act.

52. Kennedy, *Freedom from Fear,* 433–434; Overy, *The Road to War,* 329.

53. Gallup, *Gallup Poll,* 1:183, 188.

54. Kennedy, *Freedom from Fear,* 433–434; Divine, *Reluctant Belligerent,* 71.

55. Divine, *Reluctant Belligerent,* 73; David Haglund, *Latin America and the Transformation of U.S. Strategic Thought, 1936–1940* (Albuquerque: University of New Mexico Press, 1984), 96, 131; Kennedy, *Freedom from Fear,* 434.

56. Bullitt to FDR, letter, 4 Oct. 1939, in Bullitt, *For the President,* 377.

57. Lothian to FO, Message 605, 11 Oct. 1939, and Record of Informal Meeting, 25 Oct. 1939, both in CAB 104/161, TNA: PRO.

58. Monnet, *Memoirs*, 131; Haight, *American Aid to France*, 156–163. For the back and forth over separate or combined missions, see, for example, FO to Lothian, Message 704, 31 Oct. 1939; Lothian to Chancellor of the Exchequer, Message 598, 3 Nov. 1939; and Anglo-French Supply Committee (39) 33, Commission for Purchases in Canada and U.S., Progress Report no. 1, 17 Nov. 1939, all in CAB 104/162, TNA: PRO.

59. Monnet, *Memoirs*, 130; Haight, *American Aid to France*, 141–142.

60. FDR to Bullitt, letter, 23 Nov. 1939, in Bullitt, *For the President*, 387.

61. Col. J. H. Greenly to Robinson (first name unknown), Message 765, 3 Dec. 1939, CAB 104/163, TNA: PRO; Monnet, *Memoirs*, 130.

62. FDR to Secretary of War and Secretary of the Navy, letter, 6 Dec. 1939, Lend-Lease Documentary Supplement, Historical Files, 1940–1946, International Division, Series 115, Army Service Forces, entry NM25, RG 160, NACP; Blum, *Years of Urgency*, 110–113. For the creation of the President's Liaison Committee and a discussion of Roosevelt's intentions, see Haight, *American Aid to France*, 163–171. The director of procurement of the Treasury, the quartermaster general of the army, and the paymaster general of the navy composed the committee.

63. Richard M. Leighton and Robert W. Coakley, *Global Logistics and Strategy, 1940–1943*, 2 vols., in *USAWWII: The War Department* (1955, 1968; one-volume reprint, Washington, D.C.: U.S. GPO, 1984), 30–31.

64. Haight, *American Aid to France*, 171–174.

65. Ibid.

66. Ibid., 184.

67. Ibid., 184–185.

68. Hall, *North American Supply*, 120; J. Carlton Ward, "The French Aircraft Industry, 1940," speech to the Army Industrial College, 7 Oct. 1940, MID Report no. 2801-1359, RG 165/65, NACP; "Allies to Spend a Billion in U.S.," *New York Times*, 24 Feb. 1940; Haight, *American Aid to France*, 198.

69. Blum, *Years of Urgency*, 117. Monnet recalls the incident (*Memoirs*, 134–135). For more detailed discussions of it, see Haight, *American Aid to France*, 197–216, and Coffey, *Hap*, 8–10, 210–213.

70. Blum, *Years of Urgency*, 119–120; Coffey, *Hap*, 217–220. Roosevelt eventually relented in December 1940, and Arnold returned to the president's fold.

71. Hall, *North American Supply*, 117; Historical Record of the British Army Staff, Washington, D.C., 1940–1946, Historical Outline, chap. 1, p. 3, British Military Missions in Liaison with Allied Forces, Military Headquarters Papers, Second World War, WO 202/916, TNA: PRO.

72. The documents authorizing the transfer are in Hall, *North American Supply*, app. 2, 498–503. For U.S. Army figures, see Watson, *Chief of Staff*, 164, 169.

73. Haight, *American Aid to France*, 222–231.

74. Herman, *Freedom's Forge*, 88.

75. Ibid., 87.

76. Holley, *Buying Aircraft*, 220; Watson, *Chief of Staff*, 300.

77. For a concise overview of the seismic shift in U.S. strategic conditions in the spring and summer of 1940, see David Kaiser, *No End Save Victory: How FDR Led the Nation into War* (New York: Basic Books, 2014), 14–16.

5. The Americans Come to Listen, August–September 1940

1. For a rich account of Churchill's ascent to the premiership, see Lynne Olson, *Troublesome Young Men: The Rebels Who Brought Churchill to Power and Helped Save England* (New York: Farrar, Straus, and Giroux, 2007). See also Andrew Roberts, *The Holy Fox: A Biography of Lord Halifax* (London: Weidenfeld and Nicolson, 1991), 195–209. More concise accounts include Roy Jenkins, *Churchill: A Biography* (New York: Farrar, Strauss and Giroux, 2001), 577–588; Hastings, *Winston's War*, 11–19; Manchester and Reid, *Defender of the Realm,*, 51–61; and Kershaw, *Fateful Choices*, 22–24.

2. FDR to Winston Churchill, letter, 11 Sept. 1939, in Martin Gilbert, ed., *The Churchill Papers*, vol. 1: *At the Admiralty, September 1939–May 1940* (New York: Norton, 1993), 76.

3. For samples of this correspondence, see Gilbert, *At the Admiralty*, 213, 246–247, 559–560, 615, 703, 704, 818, 1222.

4. Jenkins, *Churchill*, 585–590; Williamson Murray, "Churchill Takes Charge," *Military History*, March–April 2008, 26–33; Manchester and Reid, *Defender of the Realm*, 54–58. In *Eminent Churchillians* (New York: Simon and Schuster, 1994), Andrew Roberts clearly details how it was many months before Churchill could cement his hold on the premiership (137–219). Christopher Bell offers a balanced assessment of Churchill's role in promulgating and enforcing the Ten-Year Rule (*Churchill and Sea Power*, 322–328). For a longer discussion of Churchill as chancellor of the Exchequer, see Bell, *Churchill and Sea Power*, 103–134.

5. Compare Churchill, *Second World War*, 2:177–178, and Reynolds, *In Command of History*, 169–174, for the story of the debate in the War Cabinet. In *19 Weeks: America, Britain, and the Fateful Summer of 1940* (Boston: Houghton Mifflin, 2003), Norman Moss offers a concise summary of the debate (137–145). In *Five Days in London, May 1940* (New Haven, Conn.: Yale University Press, 1999), John Lukacs offers a day-by-day account of Churchill bringing the War Cabinet to his side on the question of Britain continuing the war alone.

6. Draft Aide-Memoire, Staff Conversations with the United States of America, COS (40), [25–28 June?] 1940, and Staff Conversations with the United States of America, COS (40) 496, 28 June 1940, both in Air Ministry Records (AIR) 8/433, Chief of the Air Staff, TNA: PRO; J. R. M. Butler, *Grand Strategy*, vol. 2: *September 1939–June 1941* (London: HMSO, 1957), 210, 242–243. In *The Basis and Making of British Grand Strategy, 1940–1943: Was There a Plan?* (Lewiston, N.Y.: Edwin Mellon Press, 1998), Brian P. Farrell addresses the changes in British grand strategy immediately following the fall of France (26–58). Farrell notes that not all in Whitehall saw reliance on the United States in an entirely positive light (53).

7. For the U.S. Navy in transition, see Hammel, *How America Saved the World*,

67–70, and Samuel E. Morison, *Two-Ocean War: A Short History of the United States Navy in the Second World War* (Boston: Little, Brown, 1963), 20–23. For army issues, see Watson, *Chief of Staff,* 126–182, and Weigley, *History of the United States Army,* 418–437, 569.

8. Churchill to FDR, letter, 15 May 1940, in Francis Lowenheim, Harold D. Langley, and Manfred Jonas, eds., *Roosevelt and Churchill: Their Secret Wartime Correspondence* (New York: Saturday Review Press, 1975), 94–95. The full letter is also contained in Martin Gilbert, ed., *The Churchill War Papers,* vol. 2: *Never Surrender: May 1940 to December 1940* (New York: Norton, 1995), 45–46. See also Churchill, *Second World War,* 2:22–23.

9. FDR to Churchill, message, 17 May 1940, in Gilbert, *Never Surrender,* 69–70.

10. Leighton and Coakley, *Global Logistics and Strategy,* 1:33; Blum, *Years of Urgency,* 151–157.

11. Walter Bedell Smith for COS, memo, 11 June 1940, Office of the Chief of Staff Files (archive unknown), Foreign Sale or Exchange of Munitions, quoted in Matloff and Snell, *Strategic Planning for Coalition Warfare,* 17.

12. Matloff and Snell, *Strategic Planning for Coalition Warfare,* 1–5; Stetson Conn, Rose C. Engelman, and Byron Fairchild, *Guarding the United States and Its Outposts,* in *USAWWII: The Western Hemisphere* (Washington, D.C.: Office of the Chief of Military History, 1964), 8–9, 16; Ross, "American War Plans," 145–148, 161; Edward S. Miller, *War Plan Orange: The U.S. Strategy to Defeat Japan, 1897–1945* (Annapolis, Md.: Naval Institute Press, 1991), passim. For an overview of U.S. national-level planning in the interwar years, see Murfett, "Are We Ready?" Plan Yellow, a reprise of the response to the Boxer Rebellion (1900), was an exception to unilateralism (Ross, "American War Plans," 148). For reproductions of the color plans, see Steven T. Ross, *American War Plans, 1919–1941,* 5 vols. (New York: Garland, 1992).

13. Ross, "American War Plans," 148. For a detailed study of the U.S. Navy's Plan Orange, including the influence of the Naval War College, see Miller, *War Plan Orange.* For the role of the U.S. Army War College in developing war plans in the 1930s, see Gole, *Road to Rainbow.* For a briefer overview, see Cowman, *Dominion or Decline,* 58–98.

14. Information contained in this paragraph as well as the details of the Rainbow plans in the subsequent paragraphs are from Matloff and Snell, *Strategic Planning for Coalition Warfare,* 7–8, and Louis Morton, "Germany First: The Basic Concept of Allied Strategy in World War II," in Kent R. Greenfield, ed., *Command Decisions* (1960; reprint, Washington, D.C.: Office of the Chief of Military History, 1971), 24.

15. Matloff and Snell, *Strategic Planning for Coalition Warfare,* 12–13; Ross, "American War Plans," 155–156.

16. David Reynolds, *From Munich to Pearl Harbor: Roosevelt's America and the Origins of the Second World War,* American Way series (Chicago: Dee, 2001), 174. David Kaiser raises another key question: If Britain fell, would the United States defend only the Western Hemisphere or attempt to fight Axis forces worldwide? (*No End Save Victory,* 17).

17. Stetson Conn and Byron Fairchild, *Framework for Hemisphere Defense,* in

USAWWII: The Western Hemisphere (Washington, D.C.: Office of the Chief of Military History, 1960), 32–33, 82.

18. Mark T. Gilderhus, *The Second Century: U.S.–Latin American Relations since 1889* (Wilmington, Del.: Scholarly Resources, 2000), 95–96; R. A. Humphreys, *Latin America and the Second World War*, vol. 1: *1939–1942* (London: Institute of Latin American Studies, University of London, 1981), 6–7; Lowenthal, *Leadership and Indecision*, 1:269–273; Max Friedman, *Nazis and Good Neighbors: The United States Campaign against the Germans of Latin America in World War II* (Cambridge: Cambridge University Press, 2003), 2–3, 48–59. For contemporary concerns about fascist military missions, see Duncan Aikman, *The All-American Front* (Garden City, N.Y.: Doubleday, Doran, 1941), 289–293.

19. Friedman, *Nazis and Good Neighbors*, 2. This assessment is shared in Farnham, *Roosevelt and the Munich Crisis*, 159; Dallek, *Franklin D. Roosevelt and American Foreign Policy*, 233; Haglund, *Latin America and the Transformation of U.S. Strategic Thought*, 17; Doenecke and Stoler, *Debating Franklin D. Roosevelt's Foreign Policies*. For contemporary accounts of concerns, see Carlton Beals, *The Coming Struggle for Latin America* (Philadelphia: Lippincott, 1938); Livingstone Hartley, *Our Maginot Line: The Defense of the Americas* (New York: Carrick and Evans, 1939); Aikman, *All-American Front*; and J. Fred Rippy, *South America and Hemisphere Defense* (Baton Rouge: Louisiana State University Press, 1941).

20. Farnham, *Roosevelt and the Munich Crisis*, 159–161. For an excellent overview of the anxieties bordering on paranoia after the fall of France, see Olson, *Those Angry Days*, 97–108.

21. Friedman, *Nazis and Good Neighbors*, 2.

22. Conn and Fairchild, *Framework of Hemisphere Defense*, 33–34; Doenecke, *Storm on the Horizon*, 131; Hammel, *How America Saved the World*, 158; Friedman, *Nazis and Good Neighbors*; Humphreys, *Latin America and the Second World War*, 1:67. The president never implemented the Pot of Gold plan, which was prepared over a weekend.

23. Conn, Engelman, and Fairchild, *Guarding the United States and Its Outposts*, 13. Lowenthal argues that had the United States assessed the Nazi threat to Latin America earlier and more realistically against German capabilities, limitations, and geography, it would have deemed that threat much less serious. Nonetheless, he adds the caveat that after the events of spring and summer 1940 almost anything seemed possible (*Leadership and Indecision*, 1:277–283).

24. Quoted from Senior Army and Navy Members, U.S. Joint Planning Committee to COS/CNO, report, 26 June 1940, Subj: Views on Questions Propounded by President on War Situation, WPD 4250-3, War College and War Plans Division, 1920–1942, General Correspondence, Series 281, entry number NM84 281, RG 165 (hereafter RG 165/281), NACP, in Matloff and Snell, *Strategic Planning for Coalition Warfare*, 14.

25. Matloff and Snell, *Strategic Planning for Coalition Warfare*, 14–16; Kaiser, *No End Save Victory*, 68–69.

26. Lowenthal, *Leadership and Indecision,* 1:226.

27. Watson, *Chief of Staff,* 110–113. See also Lowenthal, *Leadership and Indecision,* 1:302, and Matloff and Snell, *Strategic Planning for Coalition Warfare,* 20–21.

28. Leighton and Coakley, *Global Logistics and Strategy,* 1:30.

29. Between 15 May and 27 August 1940, Churchill sent FDR eleven messages concerning destroyers and other armaments. See Gilbert, *Never Surrender,* 45–46, 93, 225, 287–288, 337–338, 482–483, 593–594, 688, 704–705, 722–724, 733–784.

30. Churchill to FDR, letter, 15 June 1940, in Lowenheim, Langley, and Jonas, *Roosevelt and Churchill,* 104–106. For details of the plight of the Royal Navy, see Stephen W. Roskill, *The War at Sea, 1939–1945,* 3 vols., in *The History of the Second World War, United Kingdom Military Series* (London: HMSO, 1954–1956), 1:241, 296–297.

31. According to Williamson Murray, FDR's alter ego Harry Hopkins told Sir John Colville, one of Churchill's private secretaries, "that Mers-el-Kebir persuaded the president that Britain would 'stay in the fight alone, and if necessary for years'" ("Churchill in Charge," 33).

32. Churchill, *Second World War,* 2:130; Denis Richards, *Royal Air Force, 1939–1945,* vol. 1: *The Fight at Odds,* in *History of the Second World War: United Kingdom Military Series* (London: HMSO, 1953), 150–156.

33. Churchill, *Second World War,* 2:125, 128.

34. W. K. Hancock and H. M. Gowing, *British War Economy,* in *History of the Second World War: United Kingdom Civil Series* (London: HMSO, 1949), 99; Monnet, *Memoirs,* 138; North American Supply Records (40) 1, 9 July 1940, and (40) First Meeting, 10 July 1940, Minutes and Papers, Committees on Supply, Production, Priority, and Manpower, CAB 92/27, TNA: PRO.

35. Hall, *North American Supply,* 167. For example, by July 1940 the British had placed orders for 10,000 aircraft versus the U.S. order for 4,500 (Leighton and Coakley, *Global Logistics and Strategy,* 36).

36. Historical Record British Army Staff, Washington, D.C., chap. 2, p. 4, WO 202/916, TNA: PRO.

37. Ibid. Although low-level British officers had been in the United States as early as November 1939, these officers did not engage in direct contacts with U.S. authorities. They were instead technical advisers to the British Purchasing Commission or inspected the equipment before shipment to England. For details of the personnel present, see, for example, Lothian to FO, Message 844, 1 Dec. 1939, and French-British Committee (39) 5, 1 Dec. 1939, Anglo-French Coordinating Committee (British Section), Purchasing Missions in Canada and the United States, CAB 104/163, TNA: PRO.

38. Report of Maj. Gen. Ridley Pakenham-Walsh, c. Oct. 1940, Collation Files, Files Concerning Military Planning, Intelligence, and Statistics, Director of Military Operations and Plans, WO 193/313, TNA: PRO, 1. See also Secretary of War Papers, Appointment Books, 1940–1945, entry for 14 Aug. 1940, USAMHI, which noted that Pakenham-Walsh was "in DC to attempt to standardize armaments of U.S. and Great Britain to facilitate production."

39. Report of Maj. Gen. Pakenham-Walsh, 1–2. Pakenham-Wash received criticism from, for example, Major General George Wesson, chief of ordnance; Brigadier General Richard C. Moore, deputy COS; and Major General John Danforth, chief of artillery.

40. Hall, *North American Supply*, 183. For a brief discussion of the "Battle of the Types," see H. Duncan Hall and C. G. Wrigley, *Studies of Overseas Supply*, in *History of the Second World War: United Kingdom Civil Series* (London: HMSO and Longman, Green, 1952), 91–106.

41. Diary of Maj. Gen. R. Pakenham-Walsh, entry for 28 Aug. 1940, Ridley Pakenham-Walsh Papers, Liddell Hart Centre for Military Archives, Kings College, London. As if to emphasize the incoherence of the numerous British missions, Pakenham-Walsh noted in his diary on 5 September 1940 that he saw or talked about the Lock Mission, Tizard Comte, Bailey Mission, and two Canadians.

42. Report of Maj. Gen. Pakenham-Walsh, 2.

43. Ibid., 12. See also Pakenham-Walsh diary, entry for 5 Sept. 1940.

44. Pakenham-Walsh diary, entry for 5 Sept. 1940.

45. Report of Maj. Gen. Pakenham-Walsh, 12–13; Pakenham-Walsh diary, entries for 21 Aug., 29 Aug., and 8 Oct. 1940.

46. Report of Maj. Gen. Pakenham-Walsh, 13–14.

47. For an example of the concern within the State Department, see Breckenridge Long, *The War Diaries of Breckenridge Long: Selections from the Years 1939–1944*, selected and ed. Fred L. Israel (Lincoln: University of Nebraska Press, 1966), 122–123, entry for 13 Aug. 40. See also Hancock and Gowing, *British War Economy*, 227.

48. Hull, *Memoirs of Cordell Hull*, 1:796–797.

49. Lothian to War Cabinet, Message 1019, 17 June 1940, Chief of the Air Staff (CAS), AIR 8/44, TNA: PRO.

50. Ibid.; Hull, *Memoirs*, 1:797–798; and U.S. naval attaché (ALUSNA) London to CNO, Message 201600, June 1940, Message Files, U.S. Naval Attaché, London, and Special Observer, London, Series I, Commander, U.S. Naval Forces, Europe (COMNAVEU), 1938–1947, Records Relating to U.S. Navy Operations Received from OAB, NHHC, Office of the Chief of Naval Operations (hereafter, item, box and file [as appropriate], COMNAVEU, Series I, RG 38.2.4, NACP).

51. Lothian to FO, Message 1105, 24 June 1940, Prime Minister's Office (PREM) 3/457, Operational Correspondence and Papers, TNA: PRO; Hull, *Memoirs*, 1:797–798.

52. Edward Frederick Lindley Wood, Lord Halifax, for Churchill, memo, 27 June 1940, PREM 3/457, TNA: PRO; Churchill to Halifax, memo, 24 June 1940, PREM 3/457, in Gilbert, *Never Surrender*, 407.

53. Draft Aide-Memoire, Staff Conversation with the United States of America, COS (40), [25–28?] June 1940, AIR 8/443, TNA: PRO; Staff Conversations with the United States of America, COS (40) 496 (JP), 28 June 1940, AIR 8/443, TNA: PRO; and Bailey Committee Report, 11 Sept. 1940, Box 116, Series VII, SPD, RG 38.2.4, NACP. A copy of the Bailey Committee Report is also in War History Cases and

Papers, Second World War, ADM 199/691, TNA: PRO. The Admiralty had recalled Admiral Sir Sidney Bailey, a former director of plans, along with Captain L. C. A. Curzon-Howe, former naval attaché to the United States, to active duty to assist in planning for possible cooperation with the United States (Cowman, *Dominion or Decline,* 171).

54. COS (40) 496 (JP), 28 June 1940, AIR 8/443, TNA: PRO, and Minute, J. C. Slessor to CAS, 7 July 1940, AIR 8/443, TNA: PRO.

55. FO to Lothian, 30 June 40, Message 1331, PREM 3/457, TNA: PRO; Lothian to FO, 7 July 1940, Message 1201, AIR 8/443, TNA: PRO.

56. All from British Joint Planning Staff, Staff Conversations with the U.S.A., memo, 9 July 1940, AIR 8/443, TNA: PRO.

57. Extract from COS (40) 538 (JP), 216th Meeting, 10 July 1940, AIR 8/443, TNA: PRO.

58. Lothian to [?], Message 1444, 20 July 40, AIR 8/443, TNA: PRO; Lothian to [?], Message 1471, 22 July 1940, AIR 8/443, TNA: PRO.

59. Note to Prime Minister from COS, 28 July 1940, WO 193/311, TNA: PRO.

60. Lothian to FO, Message 1609, 4 Aug. 1940, WO 193/311, TNA: PRO.

61. Allied Staff Cooperation, memo, 6 Aug. 1940, ADM 199/161, TNA: PRO.

62. Note on Meeting to Be Held on Friday, COS (40) 604 (JP) (Revise), 9 Aug. 1940, Anglo-American Standardization of Arms Committee (AASAC), WO 193/311, TNA: PRO.

63. Brig. Gen. Sherman Miles to Military Attaché London, Message 1091, 6 Aug. 1940, MID Report no. 2257-ZZ-304, RG 165/65, NACP. Details in Memo by Joint Intelligence Committee, COS (40) 621 (JIC), 10 Aug. 1940, AASAC, WO 193/311, TNA: PRO.

64. Security Measures with Regard to Documents, Memo Q 1141, 14 Aug. 1940, AIR 8/443, TNA: PRO. Lee noted that the committee name, "Anglo-American Standardization of Arms Committee," was chosen "in default of any better title" (Col. Raymond Lee to Assistant Chief of Staff, G-2, Washington, D.C., letter, 20 Aug. 1940, Subj: British Memo for American Observers, MID Report no. 2257-ZZ-304, RG 165/65, NACP).

65. AASAC (Joint) First Meeting, 20 Aug. 1940, WO 193/311, TNA: PRO; AASAC, Note by Secretary to Chief of Staff, 14 Aug. 1940, WO 193/311, TNA: PRO.

66. Proposed Agenda for Meeting with the COS, n.d., AASAC, AIR 8/443, TNA: PRO. Compare the actual results of the first meeting discussed later in the chapter.

67. Meeting, 15 July 1940, White House, File 163, Records of Commander, U.S. Naval Forces Europe, 1938–1947, File 163, Special Naval Observer (SPENAVO) London, Meetings 1940–1942, Subject Files, Series II, RG 38.2.4, NACP (hereafter item, file and box [as appropriate], COMNAVEU, Series II, RG 38.2.4, NACP).

68. Davis, *History of the Joint Chiefs of Staff in World War II,* 1:99.

69. Information on Emmons is from Ancell, *Biographical Dictionary of World War II Generals and Flag Officers,* 386. Emmons would be promoted to lieutenant general in October 1940 and would serve in a number of important geographical commands,

such as the Hawaiian Department, immediately after Pearl Harbor but would not see a combat command position. Information on Strong is from ibid., 310. After this mission, Strong returned to the War Department General Staff until May 1941, when he received a promotion to major general and command of the VII Corps, which he held until June 1942, when he returned to Washington as chief of the MID before retiring in February 1944.

70. The information on Ghormley comes from Collections Guides, East Carolina University Libraries, at https://digital.lib.ecu.edu/special/ead/findingaids/1153/ (accessed 17 Aug. 2015); Ancell, *Biographical Dictionary of World War II Generals and Flag Officers*, 538; and Boatner, *Biographical Dictionary of World War II*, 181–182. After U.S. entry into the war, Ghormley remained in London until April 1942, when he was assigned to be commander of South Pacific Forces from April to October 1942 and was responsible for naval operations in support of the seizure of Guadalcanal and operations in the Solomon Islands. Relieved by Admiral Chester W. Nimitz in October 1942 for excessive pessimism in the wake of naval defeats in the Solomon Islands and the tenuous hold on Guadalcanal, Ghormley later served as commandant of the Fourteenth Naval District and Hawaiian Sea Frontier, 1943–1944, until reassigned to serve on the staff of the COMNAVEU, Admiral Harold Stark, his former mentor from 1944–1945. He became commander of U.S. Naval Forces German Waters from May 1945 until his retirement in August 1946.

71. AASAC (Joint) First Meeting, 20 Aug. 1940, WO 193/311, TNA: PRO; Lee to Assistant Chief of Staff, G-2, Washington, D.C., letter, 20 Aug. 1940, Subj: British Memo for American Observers, MID Report no. 2257-ZZ-304, RG 165/65, NACP.

72. AASAC (Joint) First Meeting, 20 Aug. 1940, WO 193/311, TNA: PRO.

73. Ibid.; Lee to Assistant Chief of Staff, 20 Aug. 1940. The itinerary of the American officers' visits to British installations and headquarters included:

21 Aug.: Headquarters (HQ), Fighter Command and Northholt Airdrome
22 Aug.: HQ, Coastal Command, and HQ, Combined Area
23 Aug.: Armored division
24 Aug.: Plymouth and various naval establishments
25 Aug.: Free, possible visit to Admiralty War Room
26 Aug.: HQ, XII Corps
27 Aug.: HQ, Bomber Command, view origin of night bomber raid
28 Aug.: naval operations at Dover

AASAC (Joint) First Meeting, 20 Aug. 1940, Naval Attaché London (Admiral Robert L. Ghormley) to CNO, letters, Box 117, Records Relating to Anglo-American-Dutch Cooperation, 1938–1939, Series VII, SPD, RG 38.2.4, NACP (hereafter cited as item, box number, Ghormley–CNO Correspondence, RG 38.2.4, NACP).

74. COS (40) 659, 24 Aug. 1940, CAB 80/17, TNA: PRO; Preparation of Aide-Memoire for COS, SA (40) 5, WO 193/311, TNA: PRO.

75. Meeting between COS and American Representatives, COS (40) 667 (JP), 26 Aug. 1940, WO 193/311, TNA: PRO; also in same file under JP (40) 401.

76. AASAC (Joint) Second Meeting, 29 Aug. 1940, minutes, WO 193/311, TNA:

PRO. I was unable to locate any written record of the conversations between the Americans and their respective British directors of plans.
77. Ibid., 4–6.
78. Ibid., 6–7.
79. Ibid., 7.
80. Ibid., 7–8.
81. Ibid., 8–10.
82. AASAC (Joint) Third Meeting, 31 Aug. 1940, minutes, 1, WO 193/311, TNA: PRO.
83. Ibid., 2.
84. Ibid., 3.
85. Ibid.
86. Ibid.
87. Ibid.
88. Ibid., 3–4.
89. Ibid., 4–6.
90. Ibid., 6–7.
91. Ibid., 6.
92. Davis, *History of the Joint Chiefs of Staff in World War II,* 100.
93. Secretary of War Papers, Appointment Books 1940–1945, entry for 23 Sept. 1940, USAMHI.
94. Multiple versions of the report are in Strong–Emmons Report File, WPD 4368, RG 165/281, NACP. Although versions vary in their detail, the substance and the major recommendations are identical. See, for example, Memo for COS, 25 Sept. 1940, Subj: Observations in England, WPD 4368, RG 165/281, NACP, 1. The comprehensive list of British leaders engaged provides evidence of the perceived importance of the U.S. delegation.
95. Memo for the President, [23?] Sept. 1940, Subj: Preliminary Report of Gens. Strong and Emmons, WPD 4368, RG 165/281, NACP, 1–2.
96. Ibid., 2–6.
97. Ibid., 6.
98. Memo for COS, 25 Sept. 1940, Subj: Observations in England, WPD 4368, RG 165/281, NACP, 23.

6. Two Steps Forward, One Step Back

1. On Ghormley's briefing, see Meeting, White House, 15 July 1940, File 163, COMNAVEU, Series II, RG 38.2.4, NACP. Vice Admiral Bernard L. Austin, Ghormley's aide on the mission, noted in 1971, "Admiral Ghormley received his instructions orally from President Roosevelt. To the best of my knowledge they were not reduced to writing" ("The Reminiscences of Vice Adm. Bernard L. Austin," 1971, Oral History Collection, OAB, NHHC, 91). See also Leutze, *Bargaining for Supremacy,* 141–142. Leutze remains an excellent source for tracking the details of the naval side of the collaboration. For an excellent description of Roosevelt's methods of opera-

tion, vague language, ambiguous guidance, propensity for bureaucratic legerdemain, and being the sole focal point of information and decision making, see Calvin L. Christman, "Franklin D. Roosevelt and the Craft of Strategic Assessment," in Williamson Murray and Allan R. Millet, eds., *Calculations: Net Assessment and the Coming of World War II* (New York: Free Press, 1992), 216–257.

2. ALUSNA London to Office of Naval Operations (OPNAV), Message 162130, 17 Aug. 1940, Atlantic Dispatches, Box 122, Series VII, SPD, RG 38.2.4, NACP (hereafter cited by item, date, Atlantic Dispatches, Box 122, RG 38.2.4, NACP).

3. OPNAV to ALUSNA London, Message 192255, 19 Aug. 1940, Atlantic Dispatches, Box 122, RG 38.2.4, NACP.

4. ALUSNA London to OPNAV, Message 021907, 2 Sept. 1940, Atlantic Dispatches, Box 122, RG 38.2.4, NACP. The Bailey Committee Report is officially titled "The Report of the Committee on Naval Cooperation with the United States Navy in the Event of the United States of America Entering the War." Copies can be found in ADM 199/691, TNA: PRO, and in Box 116, Series VII, SPD, RG 38.2.4, NACP (hereafter cited as Bailey Committee Report).

5. Directive to Adm. Bailey, 15 June 1940, ADM 199/1157, TNA: PRO.

6. Captain R. Selby, Commander M. G. Goodenough, Commander F. B. Tours, Commander A. C. Stanford, and Lieutenant Commander G. A. G. Ormsby were part-time members of the Bailey Committee (Bailey Committee Report, 1–2).

7. Bailey Committee Report, 4–5.

8. Ibid., 6.

9. Ibid., 7, 9.

10. Ibid., 9–12.

11. Ibid., 39–40. Because of their technical nature or because information flowed through channels already discussed, I have not discussed the remaining sections of the report. For those interested in the exchange of tactical and technical information between the Royal Navy and the U.S. Navy, this report is an excellent starting point.

12. Austin, "Reminiscences of Vice Adm. Bernard L. Austin," 119; Ghormley to CNO, letter, 18 Sept. 1940, Subj: Discussions with British Admiralty Commencing 9 Sept. 1940, Serial no. 15, Ghormley–CNO Correspondence, RG 38.2.4, NACP.

13. Austin, "Reminiscences of Vice Adm. Bernard L. Austin," 119; Ghormley to CNO, letter, 18 Sept. 1940, Subj: Discussions with British Admiralty Commencing 9 Sept. 1940.

14. Bailey Committee (Joint) First Meeting, 17 Sept. 1940, U.S. Naval Cooperation Meetings, 1940, minutes, File 197, COMNAVEU, Series II, Subject Files, RG 38.2.4, NACP (the joint U.K.-U.S. Bailey Committee meetings are hereafter cited as BC (J), meeting number, date, COMNAVEU, RG 38.2.4, NACP); Ghormley to CNO, letter, 18 Sept. 1940, Serial no. 15, Ghormley–CNO Correspondence, RG 38.2.4, NACP.

15. BC (J) First Meeting, 17 Sept. 1940.

16. Ibid.; BC (J) Second Meeting, 18 Sept. 1940, and BC (J), Fourth Meeting, 19 Sept. 1940, Ghormley–CNO Correspondence, RG 38.2.4, NACP.

17. BC (J) First Meeting, 17 Sept. 1940, and BC (J), Second Meeting, 18 Sept. 1940, Ghormley–CNO Correspondence, RG 38.2.4, NACP.
18. BC (J) Third Meeting, 19 Sept. 1940, Ghormley–CNO Correspondence, RG 38.2.4, NACP.
19. Ibid.
20. BC (J) Sixth Meeting, 23 Sept. 1940, Ghormley–CNO Correspondence, RG 38.2.4, NACP.
21. BC (J) Fourth Meeting, 19 Sept. 1940, Ghormley–CNO Correspondence, RG 38.2.4, NACP.
22. See, for example, BC (J) Meetings 4–9, Ghormley–CNO Correspondence, RG 38.2.4, NACP.
23. Ghormley to CNO, letter, 11 Oct. 1940, Ghormley–CNO Correspondence, RG 38.2.4, NACP.
24. Quoted in U.S. Department of State, *Peace and War,* 571–572.
25. Lothian to FO, Message 2141, 1 Oct. 1940, AIR 8/444, TNA: PRO; Hull, *Memoirs of Cordell Hull,* 1:909–912.
26. For a range of these concerns, see the various papers in Gilbert, *Never Surrender,* 890–931, for the first ten days of October 1940.
27. Churchill to FDR, message, 4 Oct. 1940, PREM 3/468, TNA: PRO, in Gilbert, *Never Surrender,* 901–902, and in Lowenheim, Langley, and Jonas, *Roosevelt and Churchill,* 116.
28. Leutze, *Bargaining for Supremacy,* 166.
29. Far East and Anglo-American-Dutch Conversations, Note by Secretary, COS (40) 804, 6 Oct. 1940, AIR 8/444, TNA: PRO.
30. British-American-Dutch Technical Military Conversations, JP (40) 520 (S) Draft, 6 Oct. 1940, Minutes and Memoranda, War Cabinet Joint Planning Committees (later Joint Planning Staff) and Subcommittees, CAB 84/20, TNA: PRO.
31. Lothian to FO, Message 2220, 8 Oct. 1940, AIR 8/444, TNA: PRO.
32. British-American-Dutch Technical Military Conversations, COS (40) 815 (Revise), 10 Oct. 1940, AIR 8/444, TNA: PRO.
33. Ibid.
34. Ibid.
35. Lothian to FO, Message 2241, 10 Oct. 1940, AIR 8/444, TNA: PRO. For a description of Hull's waxing and waning, see Leutze, *Bargaining for Supremacy,* 163–169, and Reynolds, *Creation of the Anglo-American Alliance,* 140–141. For differing perspectives on the presidential campaign and Willkie's increasingly effective attacks against Roosevelt over American entry into the war, see Lash, *Roosevelt and Churchill,* 228–237; Dallek, *Franklin D. Roosevelt and American Foreign Policy,* 247–251; Kenneth S. Davis, *FDR: Into the Storm, 1937–1940* (New York: Random House, 1993), 614–621; and Black, *Franklin Delano Roosevelt,* 564–575, 586–600.
36. Leutze, *Bargaining for Supremacy,* 172. The Anglo-Dutch-American Committee consisted of Admiral Roger Bellairs, Lord Moyne of the Colonial Office, Air Com-

modore John Slessor from the Air Ministry, Major General John Dewing of the War Office, and Commander J. C. Norfolk, secretary (ibid.).

37. Ibid.; ALUSNA London to OPNAV, Message 171600, 17 Oct. 1940, Box 122, Atlantic Dispatches, RG 38.2.4, NACP.

38. ALUSNA London to OPNAV, Message 171600, 17 Oct. 1940.

39. Admiral Harold Stark to Ghormley, letter, 16 Oct. 1940, Folder 4, Ghormley Correspondence, COMNAVEU, Series II, RG 38.2.4, NACP.

40. Leutze, *Bargaining for Supremacy,* 174–175.

41. Allied Strategy in the Far East, Encl., Note by the Chairman of the U.K. Delegation (Adm. Bellairs), COS (40) 893, 2 Nov. 1940, AIR 8/444, TNA: PRO.

42. Ibid.

43. Butler, *September 1939–June 1941,* 487–488; Leutze, *Bargaining for Supremacy,* 174–175.

44. Allied Strategy in the Far East, draft memo, COS (40) 893, 2 Nov. 1940, AIR 8/444, TNA: PRO.

45. In a letter to Hart, Stark commented that the British plan "shows much evidence of their usual wishful thinking" (Stark to Thomas C. Hart, letter, 12 Nov. 1940, Thomas C. Hart Papers, Stark and Hart, 1939–1944 File, OAB, NHHC).

46. Ghormley to CNO, letter, 6 Nov. 1940, Serial no. 41, Box 117, Ghormley–CNO Correspondence, RG 38.2.4, NACP.

47. Meeting with Lord Lothian, notes on COS (40) 810, 8 Nov. 1940, WO 193/315, TNA: PRO; Appreciation of the Policy of the USA in the Event of America Entering the War, minute, 12 Nov. 1940, ADM 199/691, TNA: PRO; Ghormley to CNO, letter, 14 Nov. 1940, Serial no. 51, Box 117, Ghormley–CNO Correspondence, RG 38.2.4, NACP.

48. Meeting with Lord Lothian, notes on COS (40) 810, 8 Nov. 1940; Appreciation of the Policy of the USA in the Event of America Entering the War, 12 Nov. 1940; and Ghormley to CNO, letter, 14 Nov. 1940.

49. Stark to Ghormley, letter, 16 Nov. 1940, Box 117, Ghormley–CNO Correspondence, RG 38.2.4, NACP.

50. Notes on Conference with the First Sea Lord, 19 Nov. 1940, File 79, Folder 1, Ghormley Correspondence, COMNAVEU, Series II, RG 38.2.4, NACP.

51. Admiral Sidney Bailey to Ghormley, letter, 15 Nov. 1940, Subj: Reply to a Letter from Adm. Ghormley dated 25 Oct. 1940, File 79, Folder 4, Ghormley Correspondence, COMNAVEU, Series II, RG 38.2.4, NACP; Ghormley to CNO, letter, 20 Nov. 1940, Subj: Admiralty Reply to Questionnaire Concerning Forces in Far East, Serial no. 54, Box 117, Ghormley–CNO Correspondence, RG 38.2.4, NACP.

52. Lothian to First Lord of the Admiralty, Message 2851, 29 Nov. 40, Private Office Papers, AIR 19/185, TNA: PRO.

53. Lothian to FO, Message 2952, 6 Dec. 1940, Records, British Joint Staff Mission and British Joint Services Mission, Washington Office, CAB 122/5, TNA: PRO; Ghormley to Bailey, letter, 9 Dec. 1940, Serial no. 70, File 79, Folder 1, Ghormley Correspondence, COMNAVEU, Series II, RG 38.2.4, NACP.

54. Admiral Dudley Pound to Ghormley, letter, 10 Dec. 1940, ADM 199/1232, TNA: PRO, also in File 79, Folder 1, Ghormley Correspondence, COMNAVEU, Series II, RG 38.2.4, NACP.

55. Davis, *History of the Joint Chiefs of Staff in World War II*, 1:107–108. See also Lee, *London Journal*, 156, entry for 4 Dec. 1940.

56. Reply to Brig. Gen. Lee's Questions, Encl., COS (40) 31 (0), 16 Dec. 1940, Misc. Correspondence, Box 118, Series VII, SPD, RG 38.2.4, NACP.

57. Lee to Miles, Message 647, 7 Jan. 1941, WPD 4402-1, RG 165/281, NACP; Lee, *London Journal*, 195–197, entry for 1 Jan. 1941; Leutze, *Bargaining for Supremacy*, 210–213.

58. For the internal negotiations within the British government, see Lord Frederick Birkenhead, *Halifax* (Boston: Houghton Mifflin, 1966), 467–470, and Roberts, *The Holy Fox*, 272–280.

59. FO to U.K. High Commissioner, 18 Oct. 1940, CAB 122/8, TNA: PRO.

60. The COS request for FO pressure is found in COS (40) 831, 14 Oct. 1940, AIR 8/444, TNA: PRO (also found in ADM 199/1232, TNA: PRO). For British pressure on Ghormley and Ghormley's requests to the Navy Department, see Note of Meeting between Bellairs and Ghormley, 24 Oct. 1940, ADM 199/1232, TNA: PRO, and ALUSNA London to OPNAV, Message 251900, 24 Oct. 1940, Box 122, Atlantic Dispatches, RG 38.2.4, NACP. For verification of Thomas's attendance, see OPNAV to ALUSNA London, Message 251900, 25 Oct. 1940, Box 122, Atlantic Dispatches, RG 38.2.4, NACP. The cover story was that Thomas had gone to Singapore for medical treatment.

61. Extract, Telegram 624, 30 Oct. 1940, Anglo-Dutch-Australian (40) 21, 2 Nov. 1940, ADM 199/1232, TNA: PRO.

62. Cdr. Thomas to CNO, message, 30 Oct. 1940, Box 116, Series VII, SPD, RG 38.2.4, NACP. It is interesting to note that the message went through British channels—Singapore to London to Washington—and then given to the Navy Department (Clarke to Anderson, letter, 30 Oct. 1940, Box 116, Series VII, SPD, RG 38.2.4, NACP).

63. Cdr. Thomas to CNO, message, 30 Oct. 1940.

64. Ibid.

65. Ibid.

66. Ibid.

67. Draft Questionnaire to Be Put to USA, Anglo-Dutch-Australian (40) 16, 29 Oct. 1940, ADM 199/1232, TNA: PRO.

68. Allied Strategy for the Far East, draft memo, COS (40) 893, 2 Nov. 1940, AIR 8/444, TNA: PRO.

69. See James Leutze, *A Different Kind of Victory: A Biography of Admiral Thomas C. Hart* (Annapolis, Md.: Naval Institute Press, 1981), for the details of Hart's life and career. On 14 December 1941, Hart would begin withdrawing the tiny U.S. Asiatic Fleet southward toward the Netherlands East Indies, per plans. There, Hart assumed command of Allied naval forces in the short-lived American-British-Dutch-Australian (ABDA) Command until 14 February 1942. Already beyond mandatory retirement

age, Hart retired on 30 June 1942 but was recalled to head the Navy Board for the remainder of the war. He retired in February 1945 to accept the appointment to an unexpired seat in the U.S. Senate, where he served until December 1946 (Boatner, *Biographical Dictionary of World War II*, 207; Ancell, *Biographical Dictionary of World War II Generals and Flag Officers*, 547–548).

70. Ancell, *Biographical Dictionary of World War II Generals and Flag Officers*, 596. After the United States entered the war and the U.S. Asiatic Fleet withdrew from the Philippines, Purnell was the COS commander of Naval Forces Southwest Pacific from January to April 1942. In June 1942, Purnell became the assistant COS and the deputy COS in the Office of the Commander in Chief United States Fleet, serving until October 1943, when he was appointed assistant CNO (materiel), a post he held through 1945.

71. Hart to Stark, letter, 4 Dec. 1940, Encl. A, Chief of Staff's Report on the Far Eastern Conference and Anglo-Dutch Cooperation in the Far East, Hart Papers, Box 4, Stark 1939–1941 File, OAB, NHHC.

72. Layton quoted in ibid.

73. Diary of Admiral Thomas C. Hart, entry for 17 Nov. 1940, Hart Papers, OAB, NHHC.

74. ALUSNA London to OPNAV, message, 18 Nov. 1940, ABDA-ANZAC (Australia–New Zealand Army Corps.) Correspondence, Box 122, Atlantic Dispatches, Series VII, SPD, RG 38.2.4, NACP. This delay was obviously a result of the decision to hold the first American-British Conversations (ABC-1) and a desire to defer operational planning until policy had been determined.

75. CNO to CINCAF, 15 Feb. 1941, Box 117, ABDA-ANZAC Correspondence, Atlantic Dispatches, Series VII, SPD, RG 38.2.4, NACP. For discussions leading to U.S. participation, see Bellairs to Ghormley, letter, 9 Feb. 1941, CAB 122/569, TNA: PRO (also in File 191, U.S.-British Staff Conversations, 1941, COMNAVEU, Series II, RG 38.2.4, NACP); and CINC Far East to COS, London, 14 Feb. 1941, extract of telegram, Box 118, U.S.-U.K.-Dutch Conversations File, Series VII, SPD, RG 38.2.4, NACP.

76. CNO to CINCAF, message, 15 Feb. 1941, Box 117, ANZAC-ABDA Correspondence, Atlantic Dispatches, Series VII, SPD, RG 38.2.4, NACP.

77. CINCAF to CNO, letter, 5 Mar. 1941, Subj: Report of Anglo-Dutch-Australian Conference at Singapore on 22–25 Feb. 41, Box 117, ANZAC-ABDA Correspondence, Atlantic Dispatches, Series VII, SPD, RG 38.2.4, NACP.

78. Hart to Stark, letter, 4 Mar. 1941, Hart Papers, Box 4, Stark 1939–1941 File, OAB, NHHC.

79. Hall, *North American Supply*, 183; Monnet, *Memoirs*, 156.

80. Hall, *North American Supply*, 184.

81. Layton met with Secretary of War Stimson on 11 October 1940. See Secretary of War Papers, Appointment Books, 1940–1945, USAMHI, entry for 11 Oct. 1940. Layton's orders were for 1,800 field guns; 5,250 tank guns; 3,000 antitank guns; 3,400 antiaircraft guns; and one million rifles (Hall, *North American Supply*, 184).

82. Hall, *North American Supply*, 185.

83. British requests for the 55-Division Program included, for example, 25-lb artillery versus the U.S. 105-mm, 2-lb versus U.S. 37-mm antitank gun, 40-mm Bofors antiaircraft guns versus U.S. 37-mm and 90-mm, and, as simple as it sounds, the .303 Enfield versus the .30 Springfield or Garand rifles, plus the literally billions of rounds of ammunition needed for them (Memo, 19 Oct. 1940, Subj: Conference with the British Purchasing Committee Regarding New British Production Program, in Larry I. Bland, Sharon R. Ritenour, and Clarence E. Wunderlin Jr., eds., *The Papers of George Catlett Marshall*, vol. 2: *We Cannot Delay, July 1, 1939–December 6, 1941* [Baltimore: Johns Hopkins University Press, 1986], 334).

84. Hall, *North American Supply*, 187–188; Historical Record British Army Staff, Washington, D.C., 1940–1946, Historical Outline, part I, chap. II, p. 5, WO 202/916, TNA: PRO; Monnet, *Memoirs*, 156–157. It is important to note that this agreement did not resolve the standardization problem. When the United States entered the war, the British dropped the "A" Program, and each army continued to utilize its own type of equipment.

85. A letter from the secretary of war to Brigadier General Richard C. Moore on 13 September 1940 (RG 160/115, NACP) established the Joint Aircraft Committee. For the committee's objectives and policies, see Joint Aircraft Committee, minute, 20 Sept. 1940, File 095.35, app. B., Policy Documentation Files, Series 1, Records of the War Production Board, entry PI 151, RG 179, NACP.

86. Arthur Purvis to FO, Message PURSA no. 128, 4 Oct. 1940, AIR 19/185, TNA: PRO.

87. R. G. Melville, minute, 9 Oct. 1940, attached to ibid.; Lothian to FO, Message 2213, 6 Oct. 1940, AIR 19/185, TNA: PRO; Lothian to FO, Message 2247, 9 Oct. 1940, AIR 19/185, TNA: PRO; Archie [Sinclair] to Lord Beaverbrook, memo, 11 Oct. 1940, AIR 19/185, TNA: PRO; Sinclair to Churchill, letter, 22 Oct. 1940, PREM 3/488/1, TNA: PRO.

88. Slessor would remain in the United States to serve as a member of the British delegation to the upcoming ABC-1 (see chapter 8). He would then take command of Number 5 Group of Bomber Command. Given his planning skills, intellect, and strategic outlook, Slessor would participate in many major Allied conferences. After the Casablanca Conference (1943), he assumed command of Coastal (Air) Command, and many credited him not only for saving Coastal Command for the RAF but also for turning the tide in the Battle of the Atlantic. He assumed command of RAF forces in the Mediterranean in late 1943 until May 1945. He served three years as air member for personnel and then headed the Imperial Defence College until January 1950, when he became marshal of the RAF. He commanded the RAF until his retirement in 1953. For the details on Slessor, see Boatner, *Bibliographic Dictionary of World War II*, 507–508; Vincent Orange, *Bomber Champion: The Life of Marshal of the RAF Sir John Slessor, GCB, DSO, MC* (London: Grub Street, 2006); and Sir John Slessor, *The Central Blue: The Autobiography of Sir John Slessor, Marshal of the RAF* (New York: Praeger, 1957).

89. Slessor to CAS, 17 Oct. 1940, AIR 19/185, TNA: PRO.

90. Slessor for Secretary of State for Air (SSA) and CAS, minute, 19 Oct. 1940, AIR 19/185, TNA: PRO.

91. Churchill to SSA and CAS, minute, 29 Oct. 1940, PREM 3/488/1, TNA: PRO.

92. Hull, *Memoirs*, 1:870; Brig. Gen. L. T. Gerow for COS, memo, 14 Nov. 1940, Subj: Effect of Turning Over to the British Every Other Airplane of the Heavy and Medium Types to Be Delivered, WPD 4323-6, RG 165/281, NACP.

93. Diary of Colonel Orlando Ward, entry for 5 Dec. 1940, Orlando Ward Papers, USAMHI.

94. Churchill to Sir E. E. Bridges, memo, 22 Nov. 1940, PREM 3/475/4, TNA: PRO. Churchill did add that this restriction was implemented not out of a lack of confidence in the Americans "but because the wild scattering of secret information must be curbed."

95. Draft memo for CAS, 6 Dec. 1940, AIR 19/185, TNA: PRO.

96. Slessor to CAS, message, 1 Jan. 1941, AIR 19/185, TNA: PRO; Slessor, *Central Blue*, 321.

97. Ministry of Aircraft Production to British Air Commission, message, 6 Jan. 1941, AIR 19/185, TNA: PRO. It appears that Beaverbrook was the major obstacle and that considerable struggles ensued before he relented (see, for example, Assistant Personal Secretary, SSA, to Personal Secretary, SSA, minute, 23 Nov. 1940; Slessor to CAS, Message Z37 3/12, 4 Dec. 1940; and CAS to Beaverbrook, letter, 2 Jan. 1941, all in AIR 19/185, TNA: PRO).

7. Full-Dress Talks

1. The official designation of the talks was "U.S.-British Staff Conversations," but the discussions are more commonly referred to as the "American-British Conversations," or ABC (and often even the redundant "ABC Conversations" or "ABC Talks"), and the final report of the conference is known by the short title "ABC-1" (Colonel Joseph T. McNarney to Acting Assistant COS, WPD, Staff Conversations, memo, 2 Dec. 1940, WPD 4402, RG 165/281, NACP). The delegations met formally on fourteen separate occasions between 29 January and 29 March 1941. Documents from the conference cited with the abbreviation BUS (British-U.S.) are of British origin, whereas those with a serial number beginning 011512 or 09212 are U.S. documents. Documents intended for use only within the British delegation had the label BUS (41), and those for joint British-U.S. use received the label BUS (J) (41).

2. Quoted in Kennedy, *Freedom from Fear*, 465. For general sources about ongoing events, see ibid., 471–475; Davis, *History of the Joint Chiefs of Staff in World War II*, 1:108; and Dallek, *Franklin D. Roosevelt and American Foreign Policy*, 252–261. For Senate and isolationist reactions to Lend-Lease, see Kennedy, *Freedom from Fear;* Dallek, *Franklin D. Roosevelt and American Foreign Policy;* and Kenneth S. Davis, *FDR: The War President, 1940–1943* (New York: Random House, 2000), 98–100, 103–113.

3. For Churchill's long, somber, and perhaps most important message of the war

to FDR on 8 December 1940 laying out Britain's situation in detail, see Gilbert, *Never Surrender,* 1189–1197.

4. Roosevelt's directed language is in FDR for the Secretary of the Navy, memo, 26 Jan. 1941, President's Secretary's Files, Navy Files, FDRL.

5. Major General Hastings Ismay to Churchill, memo, 11 Oct. 1940, and Ismay to Churchill, memo, 20 Nov. 1940, PREM 3/489/4, TNA: PRO.

6. Also attending the ABC were Captain Arthur W. Clarke, the British assistant naval attaché; Lieutenant Colonel Arthur J. Cornwall-Jones, secretary of the British mission and a member of the British Purchasing Commission; and a Canadian observer, Captain P. B. "Barry" German (L. T. Gerow for COS, memo, 26 Dec. 1940, Subj: Army Representatives for Staff Conversations with Great Britain, WPD 4402, RG 165/281, NACP). The British delegation had been selected because of their "exceptional knowledge of 'Allied' liaison machinery" gained during the British experience with the French during 1939–1940 (COS (41) 53, 23 Jan. 1941, WO 193/305, TNA: PRO). For Canadian participation, see Timothy Wilford, *Canada's Road to the Pacific War: Intelligence, Strategy, and the Far East Crisis* (Vancouver: University of British Columbia Press, 2011), 56.

7. Lee, *London Journal,* 198–199, entry for 2 Jan. 1941.

8. For Bellairs, see Rear Admiral James Goldrick, Royal Australian Navy, "The Founders," in Peter Hore, ed., *From Dreadnought to Daring: 100 Years of Comment, Controversy, and Debate in* The Naval Review (Barnsley, U.K.: Seaforth, 2012), 11–12, and at dreadnoughtproject.org/tfs/index.php/Roger_Mowbray_Bellairs (accessed 23 Aug. 2015). An overview of Danckwerts' career is in "Royal Navy (RN) Officers, 1939–1945," at http://www.unithistories.com/officers/RN_OfficersD.html (accessed 17 Aug. 2015). Danckwerts would be promoted to vice admiral and would die of natural causes in January 1944 while serving as the deputy CINC, Eastern Fleet. Morris would be promoted to general and would serve as the chief of the General Staff, India, and ultimately as general officer CINC, Northern Command in Britain. An outline of Morris's assignments can be found in "British Army Officers, 1939–1945," at http://www.unithistories.com/officers/Army_officers_M02.html (accessed 23 Aug. 2015).

9. Gerow for COS, memo, 26 Dec. 1940, Subj: Army Representatives for Staff Conversation with Great Britain, WPD 4402, RG 165/281, NACP; Matloff and Snell, *Strategic Planning for Coalition Warfare,* 32–33. Marshall retained Embick on active duty throughout World War II. Embick served on the Joint Defense Board in 1941–1942 and was chief of the Joint Strategic Survey Committee (a forerunner to the current Strategic Plans and Policy, Joint Staff). He also concurrently served as the chair of the Inter-American Defense Board, ultimately retiring a second time in 1946. For a brief outline of Embick's career, see Ancell, *Biographical Dictionary of Generals and Flag Officers in World War II,* 97.

10. Gerow would head the WPD until February 1942, when he would command the Twenty-Ninth Infantry Division. Beginning on 15 July 1943, Gerow assumed responsibility for the buildup of army forces in the United Kingdom for the cross-

channel invasion. He commanded V Corps during the Normandy invasion and led that unit across France and into Germany. He would be the first U.S. general to enter Paris. Promoted to lieutenant general in January 1945, Gerow commanded the Fifteenth Army, responsible for all rear-area missions in the European Theater of Operations (Boatner, *Biographical Dictionary of World War II*, 180; Ancell, *Biographical Dictionary of World War II Generals and Flag Officers*, 115).

11. Ancell, *Biographical Dictionary of World War II Generals and Flag Officers*, 226.

12. McNarney would join the Army Special Observer Group in London in May 1941, serving as the group's chief of staff. A brigadier general in April 1941, in January 1942 he became a major general and deputy chief of staff for air. In June 1942, McNarney would become the U.S. Army's youngest lieutenant general. In October 1944, he became deputy supreme Allied commander in the Mediterranean and concurrently commanding general, North African Theater of Operations, serving in this position until 1 November 1944, when he assumed responsibilities as commanding general, Mediterranean Theater of Operations, until December 1945. He eventually succeeded Eisenhower as commander, U.S. Army Forces Europe. In the new U.S. Air Force, he headed the Air Material Command until his retirement in March 1947. For McNarney's bio, see Boatner, *Biographical Dictionary of World War II*, 353, and Ancell, *Biographical Dictionary of World War II Generals and Flag Officers*, 424.

13. Army members participating in ABC-1 are specified in AGWAR to Maj. Gen. Stanley D. Embick, letter, 30 Dec. 1940, Subj: Army Representatives for Staff Conversations with Great Britain, Leonard T. Gerow Papers, Operations and Plans Division (OPD), Exec. File No. 4, Item 11b, Series 422, Office of the Director of Plans and Operations, 1942–1948, Top Secret General Correspondence Relating to the Location and Leasing of Atlantic Bases in British Possessions, Allied Military Conferences of World War II, and Plans for the Strategic Direction of Operations of Military Forces in Theaters of Operations, 1940–1945, War Department General and Special Staffs, entry NM84 422, RG 165, NACP (hereafter cited as item, item number, OPD file number, RG 165/422, NACP). Naval members are outlined in CNO to Ghormley, letter, 29 Jan. 1941, Subj: Appointment of Naval Committee to Conduct Staff Conversations with the British, Serial no. 09212, Item 11, OPD Exec. File 4, RG 165/422, NACP; and Minutes of Meeting, U.S. Navy and Army Members, Meeting 2, 29 Jan. 1941, Serial no. 09212-2, Item 1, OPD Exec. File 4, RG 165/422, NACP, which also added Lieutenant Commander L. R. McDowell and Lieutenant William Scobey as secretaries to the U.S. Staff Committee. A list of the participants is in U.S. Congress, *PHAH*, 15:1487.

14. Turner became a rear admiral in December 1941 and remained in the WPD until July 1942, when he assumed command of U.S. amphibious forces in the South Pacific Area from 1942 to 1943. He served as commander of the Fifth Amphibious Force in the Central Pacific Ocean Area from 1943 to 1945; planned and executed landings at Tarawa, Kwajalein, Guam, Iwo Jima, and Okinawa; was promoted to vice admiral in February 1944; became admiral and commander of Amphibious Forces

Pacific in 1945; and was U.S. naval representative to the United Nations Military Staff Committee from 1945 to 1947. For details of Turner's service, see Boatner, *Biographical Dictionary of World War II*, 577–578; Ancell, *Biographical Dictionary of World War II Generals and Flag Officers*, 624; and George C. Dyer, *The Amphibians Came to Conquer: The Story of Richmond Kelly Turner*, 2 vols. (Washington, D.C.: Department of the Navy, 1969).

15. After Pearl Harbor, Kirk took some heat for the "intelligence failure," and in February 1942 he returned to London as naval attaché, serving until February 1943, when he assumed command of the Amphibious Forces Atlantic Fleet. In that position, he supported the invasion of Sicily. Based on his performance, Kirk was selected to command the Western Task Force for the Normandy invasion. In October 1944, he was promoted to vice admiral and assumed command of U.S. Naval Forces, France. Kirk retired on 1 March 1946 and began a career in diplomacy, serving as the U.S. ambassador to Belgium and minister to Luxembourg from 1946 to 1949, ambassador to Moscow from 1949 to 1952, and finally, after a stint in business, ambassador to Nationalist China from 1962 until shortly before his death in 1963. For Kirk's bio, see Boatner, *Biographical Dictionary of World War II*, 280; Ancell, *Biographical Dictionary of World War II Generals and Flag Officers*, 566; "Alan Goodrich Kirk, Admiral, United States Navy," Arlington Cemetery website, http://www.arlingtoncemetery.net/agkirk.htm (accessed 23 Aug. 2015); David Kohnen, "Alan Goodrich Kirk: U.S. Navy Admiral of Intelligence and Diplomacy," in John Hattendorf and Bruce Elleman, eds., *Nineteen-Gun Salute: Case Studies of Operational, Strategic, and Diplomatic Naval Leadership in the 20th and 21st Centuries* (Newport, R.I.: Naval War College Press, 2010), 75–92.

16. After ABC-1, Cooke would command the battleship U.S.S. *Pennsylvania* from February 1941 to June 1942, including the time of its bombing at Pearl Harbor. As rear admiral, he was assistant COS (Plans) for the CINC of the U.S. Fleet, Ernest King, from 1942 to 1945 and was promoted to vice admiral in September 1943. After the war, he commanded the U.S. Seventh Fleet from December 1945 to February 1948, when he retired. All information about Cooke is from Ancell, *Biographical Dictionary of World War II Generals and Flag Officers*, 519.

17. Ibid., 598.
18. Ibid., 652–653.
19. Lowenthal, *Leadership and Indecision*, 2:465.
20. Notes by COS Submitting Draft Instructions for the U.K. Delegation to Washington, Annex, General Instructions and Encl., Instructions for Naval Delegation, COS (40) 1043, 15 Dec. 1940, AIR 8/445, TNA: PRO; Instructions for British Air Rep., 15 Dec. 1940, AIR 9/155, TNA: PRO; Sir John Dill, chief of the Imperial General Staff (CIGS), memo, 19 Dec. 1940, Subj: Detailed Instructions for Military Representatives, WO 193/305, TNA: PRO; British-U.S. Technical Conversations, Instructions for British Air Representative, 28 Dec. 1940, CAB 122/6, TNA: PRO.
21. JB no. 325 (Serial no. 674), 21 Jan. 1941, RG 225/1, NACP.
22. Ibid.

23. Memo for Assistant Chief of Staff, WPD, [17–20?] Jan. 1941, Subj: Staff Conversations with British, Item 13, OPD Exec. File 4, RG 165/422, NACP.

24. Ibid.

25. Statement by CNO and COS, 27 Jan. 1941, Serial no. 011512-3, Item 11, OPD Exec. File 4, RG 165/422, NACP (hereafter Statement by CNO and COS, 27 Jan. 1941); BUS (J) (41) First Meeting, 29 Jan. 1941, Serial no. 09212-3, File U.S.-U.K. Conversations, Box 119, Series VII, SPD, RG 38.2.4, NACP (hereafter cited as meeting and BUS number, date, U.S. serial number, box number, Series VII, SPD, RG 38.2.4, NACP). The opening statement was written and approved by FDR on 27 January 1941; hence, the 27 January date for the first document cited here is an internal U.S. document. Stark read the statement to the British during the first meeting on 29 January, hence the 29 January date on the second document, which is the British record of the first meeting.

26. Roosevelt's directed changes are located in FDR for the Secretary of the Navy, memo, 26 Jan. 1941, President's Secretary's Files, Navy Files, FDRL, and in FDR for Knox, memo, 26 Jan. 1941, JB no. 325 (Serial no. 674), copy, Security Classified Correspondence of the Joint Army–Navy Board, 1910–1942, Series 284, War Department General and Special Staffs, entry NM84 284, RG 165, NACP (hereafter RG 165/284, NACP).

27. Statement by CNO and COS, 27 Jan. 41, Item 11, OPD Exec. File 4, RG 165/422, NACP; BUS (J) (41) First Meeting, 29 Jan. 1941, Serial no. 09212-3, Box 119, Series VII, SPD, RG 38.2.4, NACP.

28. Statement by CNO and COS, 27 Jan. 41, Item 11, OPD Exec. File 4, RG 165/422, NACP.

29. Agenda for U.S.-British Staff Conversations, BUS (J) (41) 4, 27 Jan. 1941, Serial no. 011512-2, Item 11, OPD Exec. File 4, RG 165/422, NACP.

30. BUS (J) (41) 1, 29 Jan. 1941, Serial no. 011512-5, Item 11, OPD Exec. File 4, RG 165/422, NACP.

31. Statement by the U.K. Delegation, BUS (J) (41) 2, 29 Jan. 1941, Item 11, OPD Exec. File 4, RG 165/422, NACP. The penciled annotation "do not agree," apparently in Gerow's handwriting, is next to the passage concerning Singapore.

32. Ibid.

33. Ibid.

34. BUS (J) (41) Second Meeting, 31 Jan. 1941, Serial no. 09212-6, Item 11, OPD Exec. File 4, RG 165/422, NACP.

35. Ibid. The British delegation noted that "the loss of our position in Malaya would in fact mean the disintegration of the British Commonwealth and a crippling of our war effort" (Note by U.K. delegation, BUS (J) (41) 6, 31 Jan. 1941, Annex I, Item 11, OPD Exec. File 4, RG 165/422, NACP).

36. BUS (J) (41) Third Meeting, 3 Feb. 1941, Serial no. 09212-7, Item 11, OPD Exec. File 4, RG 165/422, NACP; the same document is also in Box 119, Series VII, SPD, RG 38.2.4, NACP.

37. Ibid.

38. BUS (J) (41) Sixth Meeting (Revise), 10 Feb. 1941, Ser. 09212-10, Item 11, OPD Exec. File 4, RG 165/422, NACP.

39. Far East Appreciation by the U.K. Delegation, BUS (J) (41) 13, 11 Feb. 1941, Item 11, OPD Exec. File 4, RG 165/422, NACP.
40. Ibid.
41. Ibid. From hindsight, it is easy to see how the British and Americans grossly underestimated the Japanese military's capabilities, abilities, and audacity.
42. Ibid.
43. Embick et al. to COS, memo, 12 Feb. 1941, Subj: Dispatch of U.S. Forces to Singapore, WPD 4402-89, RG 165/281, NACP.
44. Joint Meeting Army and Navy Sections, U.S. Staff Committee for ABC, 13 Feb. 1941, minutes, Serial no. 09212-11, Item 13, OPD Exec. File 4, RG 165/422, NACP. Turner prepared the U.S. response.
45. Conference in COS Office, 18 Feb. 1941, War Department General and Special Staffs, Notes on Conferences, 1941–1942, Army COS, Secretariat, Series 31, entry NM84 31, RG 165, NACP.
46. Quotation is from Declaration by the U.S. Staff Committee, 19 Feb. 1941, Serial no. 011512-7, Item 11, OPD Exec. File 4, RG 165/422, NACP. Other information is from Joint Army and Navy Sections, U.S.-British Conference, minutes, 19 Feb. 1941, Serial no. 09212-15, Item 11, OPD Exec. File 4, RG 165/422, NACP.
47. Churchill to A. V. Alexander and Admiral Pound, memo, 17 Feb. 1941, PREM 3/489/4, TNA: PRO, also cited in Martin Gilbert, ed., *The Churchill War Papers*, vol. 3: *Ever-Widening War* (New York: Norton, 2001), 234–235.
48. Bellairs to Embick, letter, 19 Feb. 1941, Item 11, OPD Exec. File 4, RG 165/422, NACP.
49. Meeting, Navy Section, U.S. Staff Committee, 20 Feb. 1941, minutes, Serial no. 09212-16, Box 119, Series VII, SPD, RG 38.2.4; Joint Meeting Army and Navy Sections, U.S. Staff Committee, 20 Feb. 1941, minutes, Serial no. 09212-17, Box 119, Series VII, SPD, RG 38.2.4.
50. Slessor, *Central Blue*, 358.
51. The committee's report is "The U.S. Military Position in the Far East," 19 Feb. 1941, Serial no. 011512-8, Item 11, OPD Exec. File 4, RG 165/422, NACP.
52. Ibid.; BUS (J) (41) Tenth Meeting, 24 Feb. 1941, Serial no. 09212-18, Box 119, Series VII, SPD, RG 38.2.4, NACP.
53. BUS (J) (41) Tenth Meeting, 24 Feb. 1941.
54. BUS (J) (41) Eleventh Meeting, 26 Feb. 1941, Serial no. 09212-19, Item 11, OPD Exec. File 4, RG 165/422, NACP.
55. Ibid. It is interesting to note the failure to add land-based aircraft and naval aviation to this equation.
56. Ibid.
57. Ibid.
58. Churchill to Alexander and Admiral Pound, 17 Feb. 1941.
59. BUS (J) (41) Twelfth Meeting, 6 Mar. 1941, Serial no. 09212-20, Box 119, Series VII, SPD, RG 38.2.4, NACP.
60. Reply to Brig. Gen. Lee's Questions, COS (40) 31 (0), Encl., 16 Dec. 1940,

and Replies to Adm. Ghormley's Questions, COS (40) 1044 (Revise), 29 Dec. 1940, Box 118, Series VII, SPD, RG 38.2.4, NACP. The American delegation did not receive this information until 23 January 1941, and the press of events, most notably the discussions on the Far East, precluded earlier discussion of the problems in the Atlantic.

61. Reply to Brig. Gen. Lee's Questions, 16 Dec. 1940, and Replies to Adm. Ghormley's Questions, 29 Dec. 1940.

62. Replies to Adm. Ghormley's Questions, 29 Dec. 1940

63. Ibid.

64. BUS (J) (41) Fourth Meeting, 5 Feb. 1941, Serial no. 09212-8 (Revise), Box 119, Series VII, SPD, RG 38.2.4, NACP.

65. BUS (J) (41) Fifth Meeting (Revise), 6 Feb. 1941, Ser. 09212-9, Box 119, Series VII, SPD, RG 38.2.4, NACP.

66. BUS (J) (41) Sixth Meeting (Revise), 10 Feb. 1941, Serial no. 09212-10, Item 11, OPD Exec. File 4, RG 165/422, NACP, and BUS (41) 11, 10 Feb. 1941, WO 193/305, TNA: PRO.

67. BUS (J) (41), Seventh Meeting, 14 Feb. 1941, Serial no. 09212-12, Item 11, OPD Exec. File 4, RG 165/422, NACP.

68. BUS (J) (41) Eighth Meeting, 15 Feb. 1941, Serial no. 09212-13, Item 11, OPD Exec. File 4, RG 165/422, NACP.

69. BUS (J) (41) Ninth Meeting, 17 Feb. 1941, Serial no. 09212-14, Item 11, OPD Exec. File 4, RG 165/422, NACP.

70. Ibid.

71. BUS (J) (41) Twelfth Meeting, 6 Mar. 1941, Serial no. 09212-20, Box 119, Series VII, SPD, RG 38.2.4, NACP.

72. BUS (J) (41) Tenth Meeting, 24 Feb. 1941, Serial no. 09212-18, Box 119, Series VII, SPD, RG 38.2.4, NACP. Same item in Item 11, OPD Exec. File 4, RG 165/422, NACP.

73. BUS (J) (41) Thirteenth Meeting, 27 Mar. 1941, Serial no. 09212-21, and BUS (J) (41) Fourteenth Meeting, 29 Mar. 1941, Serial no. 09212-22, WPD 4402-89, Part VI, RG 165/281, NACP; Leutze, *Bargaining for Supremacy*, 247–248. The correct date of the ABC-1 Report is 29 March 1941, not 27 March 1941, as given on the report.

74. Identical copies of the final ABC-1 Report are in all the major British and American files. For general ease of access, the version used here is from U.S. Congress, *PHAH*, 15:1485–1550.

75. The five annexes were "I. Organization of Military Missions"; "II. Responsibility for the Strategic Direction of Military Forces"; "III. U.S.-British Commonwealth Joint Basic War Plan"; "IV. Communications"; and "V. Control and Protection of Shipping."

76. ABC-1 Report, in U.S. Congress, *PHAH*, 15:1489, 1491.

77. Ibid., 15:1490.

78. Ibid., 15:1490–1491.

79. Ibid., 15:1491–1493.

Notes to Pages 152–161   317

80. Ibid., 15:1491
81. Ibid., 15:1491–1492.
82. Ibid., 15:1494.
83. Ibid., 15:1497, 1499. The discrepancy between the number of principal U.S. and U.K. Mission members was due to the fact that at the time the United States did not have an independent air force and the army air corps representative was included within the Army Staff.
84. Ibid., 15:1493–1494.
85. See Slessor to CAS, 1 Feb. 1941, AIR 19/185, TNA: PRO; BUS (J) (41) Fourth Meeting (Revise), 5 Feb. 1941, Serial no. 09212-8 (Revise), Item 11, OPD Exec. File 4, RG 165/422, NACP; Basic Discussions Concerning American Aviation, memo, n.d. [25 Feb. 1941], RG 165/31, NACP.
86. U.S. Congress, *PHAH*, 15:1545–1550. For the British representatives' highly favorable response to this accord, see, for example, Slessor to CAS, 30 Mar. 1941, AIR 19/185, TNA: PRO, as well as Secretary of State for Churchill, memo, 4 Apr. 1941, and North to Peck (no first names available), letter, 13 Apr. 1941, PREM 3/488/2, TNA: PRO.
87. See CNO, COS, to SPENAVO London, Special Army Observer Group (SPOBS) in London, letter, 5 Apr. 1941, Subj: Tentative Approval of the Rpt U.S.-British Conversations ABC-1, Folder 2, Ghormley Correspondence, Series II, COMNAVEU, RG 38.2.4, NACP. Penned annotations of approval by the secretary of war and the secretary of navy are found in U.S. Congress, *PHAH*, 15:1485, and in Colonel William P. Scobey for CNO, 9 June 1941, Subj: JB no. 325 (Serial no. 642-5), in Joint Army and Navy Basic War Plan—Rainbow no. 5 and United States–British Staff Conversations—ABC-1, Box 122, Misc (1), Series VII, SPD, RG 38.2.4, NACP. For British COS Committee recommendation, see COS (41) 155th Meeting, extract, 1 May 1941, WO 193/305, TNA: PRO. I could find no record of His Majesty's Government's approving the agreement.
88. Ghormley to Pound, letter, 26 Apr. 1941, Serial no. 0042, cited in Tracy B. Kittredge, Commander U.S. Naval Forces Europe, "Administrative History: United States Naval Forces in Europe, 1940–1946," 7 vols., 2,856 pages, London, n.d., 1:18, Tracy B. Kittredge Papers, OAB, NHHC.
89. Lowenthal, "Roosevelt and the Coming of the War," 427.
90. For Marshall's opinion, see Matloff and Snell, *Strategic Planning for Coalition Warfare*, 47. For Stark's approach to the issue, see B. Mitchell Simpson III, *Admiral Harold R. Stark: Architect of Victory, 1939–1945* (Columbia: University of South Carolina Press, 1989), 80–82.

8. Easier Said Than Done

1. Douglas Porch, *The Path to Victory: The Mediterranean Theater in World War II* (New York: Farrar, Strauss, and Giroux, 2004), 108–128; Correlli Barnett, *The Desert Generals*, 2nd ed. (Bloomington: Indiana University Press, 1982), 37–60. For operational details, see I. S. O. Playfair, *The Mediterranean and the Middle East*, vol. 1: *The*

Early Successes against Italy (to May 1941), in *History of the Second World War: United Kingdom Military Series* (London: HMSO, 1974), 257–298, 351–366.

2. Porch, *Path to Victory*, 128–138. Operational details are in Playfair, *Early Successes against Italy*, 391–450.

3. Porch, *Path to Victory*, 52–56; Roskill, *War at Sea*, 1:427–431; Davis, *FDR: The War President*, 147–148.

4. Playfair, *Early Successes against Italy*, 233–235.

5. For German air control over the central Mediterranean, see Playfair, *Early Successes against Italy*, 328. For Rommel's personal take on the campaign in Libya, see Basil H. Liddell Hart, ed., *The Rommel Papers* (New York: Harcourt, Brace, 1953), 99–140. For the British perspective, see I. S. O. Playfair, *The Mediterranean and the Middle East*, vol. 2: *The Germans Come to the Help of Their Ally (1941)*, in *History of the Second World War: United Kingdom Military Series* (London: HMSO, 1974), 1–42. Barnett, *Desert Generals*, 60–65, and Porch, *Path to Victory*, 219–225, provide balanced but differing views. For unrest in Iraq, Syria, and Lebanon, see Butler, *September 1939–June 1941*, 460–463, 516–523, and Playfair, *Germans Come to the Help of Their Ally*, 177–197.

6. Porch, *Path to Victory*, 150–160, 166–172. Playfair, *Germans Come to the Help of Their Ally*, offers an excellent summary of the campaign in Greece (82–84) and addresses the operational details (84–106). For the battle of Crete and naval losses from the battle, see Playfair, *Germans Come to the Help of Their Ally*, 121–152, 177–197. See also Vincent Esposito, ed., *West Point Atlas of American Wars*, 2 vols. (New York: Praeger, 1959), 2:World War II sec., maps 18–22.

7. Butler, *September 1939–June 1941*, 468; Richards, *The Fight at Odds*, 214–218.

8. Churchill's multivolume work *The Second World War* contains a detailed account of British shipping losses and a broad strategic view of the Battle of the Atlantic (3:98–138). For operational details, see Roskill, *War at Sea*, 1:354–418. See also Conn and Fairchild, *Framework of Hemisphere Defense*, 101–121, and Leighton and Coakley, *Global Logistics and Strategy*, 1:59.

9. For a stirring account of the chase and sinking of the *Bismarck*, see Churchill, *Second World War*, 3: 272–286, and Roskill, *War at Sea*, 1:395–417.

10. For the challenges of recruiting, mobilizing, drafting, equipping, training, and sustaining the rapidly growing U.S. Army, see Weigley, *History of the United States Army*, 424–435; Marvin A. Kreidberg and Merton G. Henry, *History of Military Mobilization in the United States Army, 1775–1945* (Washington, D.C.: U.S. Army Center of Military History, 1989), 541–577 (early mobilization), 581–625 (mobilization activities and problems), 654–681 (logistics and industrial mobilization); and Watson, *Chief of Staff*, 183–240. For deployment dilemmas, see Conn and Fairchild, *Framework of Hemisphere Defense*, 120–121.

11. For the size of the WPD and its functions, see Cline, *Washington Command Post*, 51–54. Nor was this problem limited to the United States. For similar British issues of too many tasks and too few personnel, see Brian Farrell, "Yes, Prime Minister: Barbarossa, Whipcord, and the Basis of British Grand Strategy, Autumn 1941," *Journal of Military History* 57, no. 4 (1993): 599–625.

12. Conn and Fairchild, *Framework of Hemisphere Defense,* 83–88, 99–100, 116–129, 139–142, 280–289.

13. For FDR's tortured decision on whether to provide convoy escorts, see Conn and Fairchild, *Framework of Hemisphere Defense,* 104–108; Davis, *FDR: The War President,* 177; and Kennedy, *Freedom from Fear,* 491. For FDR's press conference making the announcement on the new security zone, see Kennedy, *Freedom from Fear,* 492–493.

14. Churchill to Roosevelt, message, 4 May 1941, in Gilbert, *Ever-Widening War,* 599–600.

15. Conn and Fairchild, *Framework of Hemisphere Defense,* 110–115.

16. Davis, *FDR: The War President,* 147.

17. For the text of FDR's address, see "Address of the President Delivered by Radio from the White House: Proclaiming an Unlimited National Emergency," May 27, 1941, at http://www.mhric.org/fdr/chat17.html (accessed 6 Mar. 2013). Background information is given in Davis, *FDR: The War President,* 184–187; Kennedy, *Freedom from Fear,* 493–494; and Conn and Fairchild, *Framework of Hemisphere Defense,* 114–115.

18. Kennedy, *Freedom from Fear,* 494.

19. Kershaw, *Fateful Choices,* 237–238; Kennedy, *Freedom from Fear,* 494; Davis, *FDR: The War President,* 189–190; Robert E. Sherwood, *Roosevelt and Hopkins: An Intimate History* (New York: Harper and Brothers, 1948), 298–299.

20. Gloria J. Barron, *Leadership in Crisis: FDR and the Path to Intervention* (Port Washington, N.Y.: Kennikat Press, 1973), 97. This view is reinforced in Sherwood, *Roosevelt and Hopkins,* 298–299.

21. Sherwood, *Roosevelt and Hopkins,* 225.

22. Dallek, *Franklin D. Roosevelt and American Foreign Policy,* 258–260; Heinrichs, *Threshold of War,* 11–12; Davis, *FDR: The War President,* 131–138. For a quick overview of anti-interventionist sentiment in early 1941, see Doenecke, *Storm on the Horizon,* 169–171.

23. J. Garry Clifford and Robert H. Ferrell, "Roosevelt at the Rubicon: The Great Convoy Debate of 1941," in Piehler and Pash, *The United States and the Second World War,* 13; Davis, *FDR: The War President,* 153–154, 193–195, 209–212, 417–418. For an extremely interesting look into the inner circle of the unofficial White House family and how it influenced FDR, see Frank Costigliola, "Broken Circle: The Isolation of Franklin D. Roosevelt in World War II," *Diplomatic History* 32, no. 5 (Nov. 2008): 677–718.

24. For messages from Churchill to Roosevelt in 1941, see, for example, Gilbert, *Ever-Widening War,* 11–12 (2 Jan.), 227 (15 Feb.), 335 (10 Mar.), 367–368 (19 Mar.), 385–386 (22 Mar.), 424 (30 Mar.), 455 (6 Apr.), 540–543 (24 Apr.), 543 (25 Apr.), 567 (29 Apr.), and 599–600 (4 May).

25. Quoted in Clifford and Ferrell, "Roosevelt at the Rubicon," 12, citing Langer and Gleason, *The Undeclared War, 1940–1941,* 597.

26. Joint Letter of Transmittal, ABC-1 Report, BUS (J) (41) 30, 27 Mar. 1941, Serial no. 011512-22 (R-LT), Box 116, Series VII, SPD, RG 38.2.4, NACP.

27. CNO to Ghormley, letter, 5 Apr. 1941, Subj: Letter of Instructions, WPD 4402-89, RG 165/281, NACP. See also Tracy B. Kittredge, "U.S.-British Naval Cooperation, 1939–1945," OAB, NHHC, 412–413.

28. CNO to Ghormley, letter, 5 Apr. 1941, Subj: Letter of Instructions. See also Kittredge, "U.S.-British Naval Cooperation, 1939–1945," 412–413.

29. Anderson for COS, memo, [Apr. 1941?], OPD Exec. File 4, Item 4, RG 165/422, NACP; memo for COS, 7 Apr. 1941, Subj: U.S. Military Mission in London, WPD 4402-5, RG 165/281, NACP.

30. Ancell, *Biographical Dictionary of World War II Generals and Flag Officers*, 375; Association of Graduates, U.S. Military Academy, *The Register of Graduates and Former Cadets of the United States Military Academy at West Point, New York, 2010* (West Point, N.Y.: Association of Graduates, U.S. Military Academy, 2010), entry 4678, sec. 4, p. 93; "Major General James E. Chaney," U.S. Air Force, at http://www.af.mil/AboutUs/Biographies/Display/tabid/ 225/Article/107447/major-general-james-e-chaney.aspx (accessed 25 Aug. 2015).

31. Gen. George C. Marshall to Maj. Gen. James E. Chaney, letter, 24 Apr. 1941, Subj: Letter of Instructions, OPD Exec. File 4, Item 4, Conference in the Office of the COS, 28 Apr. 1941, COS Notes on Conferences, RG 165/31, NACP; Maj. Gen. Chaney to War Department, Message 1, 23 May 1941, in Capt. Susie J. Thurman et al. (only first author listed), "SPOBS: The Special Observer Group prior to the Activation of the European Theater of Operations," Oct. 1944, mimeo, 242 pp., Charles L. Bolte Papers, USAMHI, 17. For Chaney as an air officer, see Lowenthal, *Leadership and Indecision*, 2:574.

32. According to Colonel Bolte, the plans officer in SPOBS, Admiral Ernest J. King, CINC, U.S. Fleet, coined the designation "U.S. Special Observer Group (USSOG)" (Gen. Charles L. Bolte, interview by Dr. Maclyn Burg, 17 Oct. 1973, Oral History Collection, USAMHI, 29; Gen. Charles L. Bolte, interview by Mr. Arthur J. Zoebelem, 9 Dec. 1972, Oral History Collection, USAMHI, 74).

33. On Bolte, see Ancell, *Biographical Dictionary of World War II Generals and Flag Officers*, 26–27, and Peter B. Flint, "Gen. Charles Bolte, Ex–Army Vice Chief of Staff, Dies at 93," *New York Times*, 13 Feb. 1989, at http://www.nytimes.com/1989/02/13/obituaries/gen-charles-bolte-ex-army-vice-chief-of-staff-dies-at-93.html (accessed 21 Aug. 2015). On Case, see Ancell, *Biographical Dictionary of World War II Generals and Flag Officers*, 48–49, and "Homer Case; Nation's Oldest General at 101," *Los Angeles Times*, 3 Apr. 1996, at http://articles.latimes.com/1996-04-03/local/me-54431_1_homer-case (accessed 21 Aug. 2015). On Dahlquist, see Ancell, *Biographical Dictionary of World War II Generals and Flag Officers*, 74–75. On Griner, see Ancell, *Biographical Dictionary of World War II Generals and Flag Officers*, 123, and "Griner, George Wesley, Jr. (1895–1975)," *Pacific War Online Encyclopedia* (2011), at http://pwencycl.kgbudge.com/G/r/Griner_George_W.htm (accessed 21 Aug. 2015). On Matejka, see Ancell, *Biographical Dictionary of World War II Generals and Flag Officers*, 208, and "Jerry V. Matejka Dies; Retired Major General Was Chief Signal Officer," *Washington Post*, 26 May 1980. On McClelland, see Ancell, *Biographical Dictionary of World War*

II Generals and Flag Officers, 421. On McNarney, see Boatner, *Biographical Dictionary of World War II,* 353; Ancell, *Biographical Dictionary of World War II Generals and Flag Officers,* 424; and Association of Graduates, *Register of Graduates,* entry 5353, sec. 4, p. 104.

34. Establishment of British Nucleus Mission, BUS (J) (41) 40, 4 Apr. 1941, WPD 4402-94, RG 165/281, NACP. For the internal British discussion of the organization of this early mission see First Sea Lord to Bellairs, Message 1120/19, 17 Mar. 1941, and Bellairs to First Sea Lord, Message 2010/21, 22 Mar. 1941, WO 193/305, TNA: PRO.

35. Memo, 26 Apr. 1941, Subj: Establishment of the Military Mission and Procedures, CAB 122/10, TNA: PRO. Note the British misperception that the U.S. COS operated as a joint, corporate body. This misperception would continue to perplex the British for quite some time. For details leading to the selection and arrival of the British Joint Staff Mission (BJSM), Washington, D.C., see Sally L. Parker, "Attendant Lords: A Study of the British Joint Staff Mission, 1941–1945," Ph.D. diss., University of Maryland, 1984, 49–57.

36. COS (41) 201st Meeting, extract, 5 June 1941, WO 193/305, TNA: PRO.

37. For the broad range of the BJSM's authorities and responsibilities, see COS (41) 312 (Final), COS Directive to Joint Staff Mission, Washington, D.C., 19 May 1941, CAB 122/23, TNA: PRO.

38. COS (41) 218th Meeting, extract, 20 June 1941, WO 193/305, TNA: PRO; Military Mission (MM) (41) 83, 7 July 1941, CAB 122/10, TNA: PRO; and COS (41) 419, 9 July 1941, WO 193/317, TNA: PRO. "British Joint Staff Mission" was the official internal British designation for the mission. To ensure secrecy, the British were technical advisers accredited to the North American Supply Committee.

39. See, for example, Anglo-U.S. Liaison Arrangements, 18 Feb. 1941, CAB 122/10, TNA: PRO, and Note for Sir William Douglas, 13 Oct. 1941, CAB 122/66, TNA: PRO, which pointed out that the British Army Staff was "a very miniature replica of the War Office." For organization and functions of the BJSM, see, for example, Maj. Gen. Sir Frederick Beaumont-Nesbitt to Gerow, letter, 8 Aug. 1941, Army Air Force 334.8, entry NM84 293, Central Decimal Files: Security Classified General Correspondence, RG 18, NACP, and British Army Staff, Organizations and Functions, 8 Aug. 1941, WPD 4402-51, RG 165/281, NACP. For the initial sorting out of the BJSM, see Parker, "Attendant Lords," 65–70.

40. Clarke to Lt. Col. Arthur J. Cornwall-Jones, letter, 24 Apr. 1941, CAB 122/1, TNA: PRO. Clarke's role as liaison to Roosevelt may be traced to FDR's original request in late summer 1940 for an informal Royal Navy conduit to the president along the lines of his liaison with the British while serving as assistant secretary of the navy during World War I.

41. British ABC-1 Delegation Report to British COS, COS (41) 250, 2 Apr. 1941, CAB 80/27, TNA: PRO; "History of the British Army Staff, Chapter 1: History of the JSM, Washington, 1941–1945," CAB 122/1579, TNA: PRO.

42. BUS (41) 32, Minutes of Conference, 25 Mar. 1941, WPD 4402-94, RG 165/281, NACP, cited in Davis, *History of the Joint Chiefs of Staff in World War II,*

1:123. Such a staff would have been a predecessor to the modern-day Joint Staff that supports the Joint Chiefs of Staff and their chairman. An embryo Joint Staff came into being with the National Defense Act of 1947. It did not assume its current guise and level of authority until the Goldwater–Nichols Act of 1986.

43. For the short term, see, for example, the comment by Captain G. D. Owens, Royal Navy, who noted that Admiral Danckwerts "found it difficult to make headway because the Americans had no combined staff representative of each service" ("History of the British Admiralty Delegation, 1941–1946," 219, ADM 199/1236, TNA: PRO).

44. Bolte, Zoebelem interview, 9 Dec. 1972, 75. For similar comments, see Bolte, Burg interview, 17 Oct. 1973, 59.

45. Diary of John E. Dahlquist, entry for 26 June 1941, Gen. John E. Dahlquist Papers, USAMHI.

46. Examples of prior concerns can be found in Churchill to SSA, minute, 11 Dec. 1940; Portal to Beaverbrook, letter, 2 Feb. 1941; Portal to Prime Minister, letter, 3 Feb. 1941; Churchill for CAS, note, 5 Feb. 1941; Prime Minister to CAS, minute, 10 Feb. 1941: all in AIR 19/185, TNA: PRO. Churchill continued to tighten up the flow of information (Churchill to SSA, memo, 31 Mar. 1941, PREM 3/475/4, TNA: PRO).

47. JP (41) Fifty-Eighth Meeting, 30 Apr. 1941, CAB 84/7, TNA: PRO.

48. Information for the U.S., JP (41) 342, 30 Apr. 1941, CAB 122/14, TNA: PRO; COS (41) 155th Meeting, 11 May 1941, extract, WO 193/305, TNA: PRO; Liaison with U.S. Mission in London, JP (41) 341 (S), 2 May 1941, CAB 84/30, TNA: PRO.

49. Liaison with the U.S. Mission in London, JP (41) 356, 7 May 1941, CAB 84/30, TNA: PRO.

50. Information for U.S., COS (41) 313, 17 May 1941, WO 913/315, TNA: PRO. For the evolution of the British procedures, see Minute for M.O. 1 from M.O. 1 (a), 23 May 1941, WO 193/317, TNA: PRO; Minute for M.O. 1/BM 955, M.O. 1 to Director, Military Operations and Plans, Liaison with U.S., 25 May 1941, WO 193/317, TNA: PRO; Minute for M.O. 1/BM 966, 28 May 1941, WO 193/305, TNA: PRO; Channel of Communication between Washington and London, JP (41) 460, 17 June 1941, WO 193/317, TNA: PRO; American Liaison (AL) (41) Second Meeting, 30 May 1941, Commonwealth and International Conferences, CAB 99/9, TNA: PRO; and Channels of Communication between U.S. and British COS and Service Depts., Military Mission (Joint) (MM (J)) (41) 35, 27 June 41, WPD 4402-41, RG 165/281, NACP.

51. For USSOG's reaction, see AL (41) Second Meeting, 30 May 1941, CAB 99/9, TNA: PRO. For the initial reaction of the U.S. COS, see Gerow for COS, memo, 3 July 1941, Subj: Channels of Communication between U.S. and British COS, WPD 4402-41, RG 165/281, NACP. One can follow the debate in BJSM, Correspondence on Communications and Operations, Box 117, Series VII, SPD, RG 38.2.4, NACP. The final resolution is contained in Message to Chaney, 15 Aug. 1941, Subj: Channels of Communication between U.S. and British COS and Service Depts., WPD 4402-41, RG 165/281, NACP.

52. For the evolution of the process within British circles, see MM (41) Third

Meeting, 6 June 1941, CAB 122/30, TNA: PRO; [Brigadier General Donald?] Campion to [Clive] Bailleau, memo, 7 June 1941, Ministry of Aircraft Production Records (AVIA) 38/135, TNA: PRO; [Henry] Hancock to Director-General [of the British Purchasing Commission, Arthur Purvis], memo, 16 June 1941, AVIA 38/135, TNA: PRO; Rear Adm. Richmond Kelly Turner to Hancock, message, 12 June 1941, AVIA 38/135, TNA: PRO; British Purchasing Commission to Minister of Supply, message, 13 June 1941, AVIA 38/135, TNA: PRO; Bailleau and Lt. Gen. Henry C. B. Wemyss to Beaverbrook and CIGS, 12 Aug. 1941, AVIA 38/135, TNA: PRO; and Memo by Prime Minister, WP (41) 211, 11 Sept. 1941, CAB 92/28, TNA: PRO. Harry Hopkins, FDR's Lend-Lease adviser, reached the conclusion in late July that the BJSM was more concerned with equipment than with planning (see Lee, *London Journal*, 353, entry for 25 July 1941).

53. Kittredge, "U.S.-British Naval Cooperation, 1939–1945," 392–397, 418, 471–474. See also Kittredge, "United States Defense Policies and Global Strategy, 1900–1941," 18.

54. C. Daniel, director of plans, memo, 21 May 1941, Subj: Proposed Amendments to ABC-1, Ghormley Correspondence, Folder 2, and Minutes of Meeting in Admiralty, 23 May 1941, SPENAVO London, File 163, both in COMNAVEU, Series II, RG 38.2.4, NACP.

55. Minutes of Meeting, Admiralty, 23 May 1941, SPENAVO London, File 163, and Ghormley to Pound, letter, 29 May 1941, Ghormley Correspondence, both in COMNAVEU, Series II, RG 38.2.4, NACP.

56. Ghormley to Rear Adm. [Sir Arthur?] Power, letter, 24 June 1941, Ghormley Correspondence, Folder 2, COMNAVEU, Series II, RG 38.2.4, NACP.

57. AL (41) First Meeting (revised final edition), 29 May 1941, CAB 99/9, TNA: PRO; also in CAB 122/30, TNA: PRO.

58. Thurman et al., "SPOBS," 23–25, and AL (41) First Meeting (revised final edition), 29 May 1941.

59. AL (41) First Meeting (revised final edition), 29 May 1941; also in No. 190, COMNAVEU, Series II, RG 38.2.4, NACP.

60. Ibid.

61. Meeting with USSOG, Agenda, 3 June 1941, WO 193/305, TNA: PRO; Minutes of Meeting with USSOG at WO, 11 a.m., 3 June 1941, WO 193/325, TNA: PRO; and Minutes, M.O. 1/BM 980, 31 May 1941, WO 193/325, TNA: PRO. Much coordination had apparently occurred before the meeting, and preliminary agreements had been reached on numerous items (see Minutes of Meeting with USSOG, WO Brief for DMOB [Directorate of Mobilisation, War Office], 2 June 1941, WO 193/325, TNA: PRO).

62. Minutes of Meeting with USSOG at WO, 11:00 a.m., 3 June 1941, including annex suggesting procedures for dealing with problems.

63. Brig. Gen. W. H. Middleswort to Maj. Gen. J. E. Dahlquist, letter, 16 July 1945, Dahlquist Papers, World War II File, USAMHI (Middleswort's letter contains a copy of Dahlquist's answers to a questionnaire from Marshall).

64. The fact that there were only eight full-fledged meetings between the SPOBS

and WO staffs by the time of Pearl Harbor supports this conclusion. The majority of the meetings of the full staffs held after 3 June 1941 did not deal with combined planning. See AL (41) Third Meeting, Gen. War Position, 6 June 1941; AL (41) Fourth Meeting, Russo-German Campaign, 5 July 41; and AL (41) Fifth Meeting, General Precis of the War to Date, 11 July 1941: all in CAB 99/9, TNA: PRO.

65. Thurman et al., "SPOBS," 32–34.

66. SPOBS to AGWAR, Message 15, 19 June 1941, and Maj. Gen. Chaney, report, Subj: Reconnaissance in Iceland, AG 319.1, contained in Thurman et al., "SPOBS," 43–47 (no date is given for this report in the source cited). For SPOBS planning, see Thurman et al., "SPOBS," 57–74. Col. G. W. Griner took the finalized plans to the United States on 21 June 1941 (Dahlquist diary, entry for 21 June 1941, Dahlquist Papers, USAMHI). For a detailed discussion of the decision to send U.S. forces to Iceland, see Byron Fairchild, "Decision to Land United States Forces in Iceland," in Greenfield, *Command Decisions,* 73–98.

67. For the reconnaissance trips to Northern Ireland on 16–19 July 41, Scotland on 24–28 September 1941, and Kent in August and September, see the diary of General Charles L. Bolte, entries for 16–19 July and 24–28 Sept. 1941, Bolte Papers, USAMHI; Thurman et al., "SPOBS," 47–49; Notes on Conversation between Col. Harold M. McClelland and Lt. Col. G. B. J. Kellie, Minutes M.O. 2/1735, 1 Aug. 1941, WO 193/305, TNA: PRO.

68. Kittredge, "U.S.-British Naval Cooperation, 1939–1945," 392–398, 408–409. See also Samuel E. Morison, *The History of United States Naval Operations in World War II,* vol. 1: *The Battle of the Atlantic, September 1939–May 1943* (Boston: Little, Brown, 1947), 53–54.

69. Bolte, Burg interview, 17 Oct. 1973, 74–75.

70. Thurman et al., "SPOBS," 51–52.

71. Ibid., 52–55, citing Chaney to COS, n.d., AG 381, Great Britain.

72. Joint Letter of Transmittal, ABC-1 Report, 27 Mar. 1941, BUS (J) (41) 30, Serial no. 011512-12 (R-LT), Box 116, Series VII, SPD, RG 38.2.4, NACP.

73. For the authorizations, see Marshall to Maj. Gen. George Grunert, message, 4 Apr. 1941, and CNO to CINCAF, 5 Apr. 1941, Box 117, ABDA-ANZAC Correspondence, Series VII, SPD, RG 38.2.4, NACP. Marshall's initial transmission of the ABC-1 Report and instructions are in Marshall to C. G. Philippines Dept., letter, 2 Apr. 1941, Subj: U.S.-British Staff Conversations, WPD 4402-8, RG 165/281, NACP. For Hart's reaction to the Navy Department's failure to provide him with a copy of the ABC-1 Report and his use of Grunert's copy, see Hart diary, entry for 17 Apr. 1941, Hart Papers, OAB.

74. The summary of the ABC-1 Report is contained in Halifax to Air Chief Mar. Sir H. Robert Brooke-Popham, message, 10 Apr. 1941, CAB 122/8, TNA: PRO. The instructions to Brooke-Popham for the conference are in Eden to Halifax, message, 12 Apr. 1941, BOXES [*sic*] 31, CAB 122/8, TNA: PRO, and Directive to British Representatives at Singapore Conference, MM (41) 1, 13 Apr. 1941, Box 118, U.S.-U.K.-Dutch Conversations File, Series VII, SPD, RG 38.2.4, NACP.

75. A complete list of attendees is in U.S. Congress, *PHAH*, 15:1554; see also Brooke-Popham to Ismay, letter, 16 May 1941, Air Chief Mar. Sir Robert Brooke-Popham Papers, Liddell Hart Centre for Military Archives, Kings College, London.

76. A review of the available material revealed little or no documentation on the conduct of the daily meetings of the American-Dutch-British (ADB) Conversations in Singapore in April 1941. Therefore, the best information on day-to-day events comes from the participants' immediate reactions, contained in their reports to their superiors, and from the main report of the conference, given in U.S. Congress, *PHAH*, 15:1551–1584.

77. Ibid., 15:1562. For a discussion of the potential courses of action available to the Japanese, see ibid., 15:1559–1563.

78. Ibid., 15:1565.

79. Ibid., 15:1564; CINCAF to CNO, letter, 29 Apr. 1941, Subj: ADB Conversations, Apr. 1941, Box 118, U.S.-U.K.-Dutch Conversations File, Series VII, SPD RG 38.2.4, NACP.

80. U.S. Congress, *PHAH*, 15:1558.

81. Ibid., 15:1567–1568, 1574–1575.

82. Ibid., 15:1568–1572.

83. Ibid., 15:1573.

84. Ibid.

85. Ibid., 15:1566–1567.

86. Ibid., 15:1578–1579.

87. Maj. Gen. Grunert to Assistant COS, letter, 2 May 1941, WPD, Subj: ADB Conversations, 21–27 Apr. 1941, Held at Singapore, WPD 4402-18, RG 165/281, NACP.

88. CINCAF to CNO, letter, 29 Apr. 1941, Subj: ADB Conversations, Apr. 1941, Box 118, U.S.-U.K.-Dutch Conversations File, Series VII, SPD, RG 38.2.4, NACP. Hart voiced similar complaints in a personal letter to Stark (Hart to Stark, letter, 29 Apr. 1941, Hart Papers, Box 4, Stark 1939–1941 File, OAB, NHHC) and in his diary (entries for 27 and 28 Apr. 1941, Hart Papers, OAB). Hart later blamed the failure of the conference on the fact that "there were so many conferees present that difficulties were great, without prior agreements, agenda, etc., it was too hard a task for the presiding officer to handle" ("Admiral Hart's Narrative of Events: Asiatic Fleet Leading up to War and from 8 December 1941 to 15 February 1942," Hart Papers, OAB, NHHC [available on microfilm]).

89. Report by British Joint Planning Committee on ADB Conference at Singapore, Apr. 1941, JP (41) 371, 15 May 1941, CAB 122/8, TNA: PRO; Report of the Singapore Conference, ADB Conversations, Apr. 1941, MM (J) (41) 21, 20 May 1941, Box 118, U.S.-U.K.-Dutch Conversations File, Series VII, SPD, RG 38.2.4, NACP.

90. Gerow for COS, memo, 7 June 1941, Subj: U.S.-Dutch-British Staff Conversations at Singapore, WPD 4402-18, RG 165/281, NACP.

91. Ibid.; Cdr. L. R. McDowell to British Military Mission, letter, Report of Singapore ADB Conversations, Apr. 1941, MM (41) 57, 16 June 1941, CAB 122/8, TNA: PRO.

92. The proposals are found in MM (J) (41) 21, 20 May 1941, CAB 122/8, TNA: PRO.

93. Report of Singapore ADB Conversations, Apr. 1941, MM (41) 57, 16 June 1941, CAB 122/8, TNA: PRO.

94. See Turner to Clarke, letter, 5 June 1941, Subj: Cooperation between U.S. and British Commonwealth in the South Pacific, Serial no. 011212-26, WPD 4402-37, RG 165/281, NACP; COS to BJSM, message, 12 June 1941, CAB 22/5, Box 59, TNA: PRO.

95. Rear Adm. Victor H. Danckwerts to Turner, letter, 17 June 1941, CR 47, Box 118, U.S.-U.K.-Dutch Conversations, Series VII, SPD, RG 38.2.4, NACP; also found in CAB 122/5, TNA: PRO.

96. MM (41) 66, 23 June 1941, extract, CAB 122/94, TNA: PRO; Cowman, *Dominion or Decline*, 226–227, reproduces Turner's critique.

97. Lowenthal, *Leadership and Indecision*, 2:576.

98. Ibid., 2:618, 507.

99. MM (41) 66, 23 June 1941, extract, CAB 122/94, TNA: PRO.

100. Danckwerts to Adm. Thomas V. Phillips, letter, 23 June 1941, CAB 122/5, TNA: PRO.

101. CNO/COS, to SPENAVO, SPOBS, letter, MM (41) 106, Annex, 3 July 1941, Subj: Comment on the Report of the ADB Conversations, Singapore, Apr. 41, Serial no. 075112, CAB 122/8, TNA: PRO (hereafter cited CNO/COS, Comments on ADB, 3 July 1941). A less-detailed version is in U.S. Congress, *PHAH*, 15:1677–1679.

102. CNO/COS, Comments on ADB, 3 July 41.

103. Cowman, *Dominion or Decline*, 228–229; Edwyn Gray, *Operation Pacific: The Royal Navy's War against Japan, 1941–1945* (Annapolis, Md.: Naval Institute Press, 1989), 30.

104. CNO/COS, Comments on ADB, 3 July 1941.

105. Ibid.

106. Ibid.; Gerow for COS, memo, 8 July 1941, Subj: Report of ADB Conversations, WPD 4402-18, RG 165/281, NACP.

107. CNO/COS, Comments on ADB, 3 July 41. However, once the United States declared war, the Americans, led by General Marshall, quickly called for establishing such a command, designating a supreme commander, and building a staff. This resulted in the short-lived American-British-Dutch-Australian Command, the first practical Anglo-American coalition command.

108. Report by Joint Planning Committee, U.S.A. Attitude to Report of ADB Conversations at Singapore, JP (41) 621, 1 Aug. 1941, WO 193/315, TNA: PRO; same item found in CAB 84/33, TNA: PRO.

109. Ibid.
110. Ibid.
111. Ibid.
112. Note on JP (41) 648, memo, 10 Aug. 1941, WO 193/315, TNA: PRO.

9. Muddy Waters

1. Reynolds, *Creation of the Anglo-American Alliance*, 209–210.

2. See, for example, JB to SPENAVO, SPOBS London, letter, approved 25 Sept. 1941, Subj: Comment on "Grand Strategy Review" by the British COS, JB no. 325 (Serial no. 729), ABC 381, Office of the Director of Plans and Operations, 1922–1948, Top Secret "American-British-Canadian" Correspondence Relating to Organization, Planning, and General Combat Operations during World War II and the Early Post-War Period, 1940–1948, Series 421, entry number NM84 421, War Department General and Special Staff, RG 165, NACP.

3. Reynolds, *Creation of the Anglo-American Alliance*, 197–199, 201–202; Cowman, *Dominion or Decline*, 20; Morison, *Battle of the Atlantic*, 69–84.

4. See Leighton and Coakley, *Global Logistics and Strategy*, 1:89–96, for examples of materiel issues at a macrolevel view, and Sherwood, *Roosevelt and Hopkins*, 311–316, for specific examples in July 1941. For descriptions of rising coalition concerns, see Churchill, *Second World War*, 3:379–380; Dallek, *Franklin D. Roosevelt and American Foreign Policy*, 273–275; Davis, *FDR: The War President*, 261–264; and Matloff and Snell, *Strategic Planning for Coalition Warfare*, 63–65. For examples of Churchill's importuning just in June and July 1941, see Gilbert, *Ever-Widening War*, 762, 769, 794, 806–807, 827–828, 859–860, 880–881, 897–898, 905–906, and 979–981.

5. For a brief description of the Russian campaigns, see Esposito, *West Point Atlas of American Wars*, 2:World War II sec., 20–22, 74. For details from a German perspective, see, for example, Heinz Guderian, *Panzer Leader*, trans. Constantine Fitzgibbon (Cambridge, Mass.: Da Capo Press, 1996), 140–202, and Erich von Manstein, *Lost Victories* (St. Paul, Minn.: Zenith Press, 2004), 175–203. In *Operation Barbarossa: Hitler's Invasion of Russia, 1941* (Charleston, S.C.: Tempus, 2001), David Glantz offers an excellent overview. Examples of concerns regarding and opinions of the Russian ability to survive as well as possible German reactions are given in Forrest C. Pogue, *George C. Marshall*, vol. 2: *Ordeal and Hope, 1939–1942* (New York: Viking Press, 1965), 72–75; Matloff and Snell, *Strategic Planning for Coalition Warfare*, 53; and Kittredge, "U.S.-British Naval Cooperation, 1939–1945," 519–520.

6. See, for example, Churchill, *Second World War*, 3:340–347.

7. Dill to Prime Minister, memo, 6 May 1941, Subj: The Relation of the Middle East to the Security of the United Kingdom, quoted in Churchill, *Second World War*, 3:375. Background and outcomes are given in Churchill, *Second World War*, 3:373–376.

8. Churchill, *Second World War*, 3:375.

9. Prime Minister to Dill, 13 May 1941, quoted in Churchill, *Second World War*, 3:376. Churchill's full rejoinder is given in *Second World War*, 3:376–377. For an excellent account of this episode as an example of how Churchill could wear down his key leaders, see Reynolds, *In Command of History*, 246–248. In this same passage, Reynolds also demonstrates how Churchill inappropriately sequenced his narrative in the third volume of *Second World War* to undercut Dill's views and reduce possible criticisms of the prime minster's leadership at this key time.

10. Future Strategy: A Review, JP (41) 444, 14 June 1941, 1, WO 193/326, TNA: PRO. The subject headings of the review provide a clear indication of the detailed nature of the report: "II. Defense of the British Isles," "III. Defense of Our Economy," "IV. Offensive against the Germany Economy," "V. War of Morale," "VI. Air Offensive," "VII. Intervention by U.S. and Japan," "VIII. Deductions of British Military Strategy in the Present Phase and Future," "IX. Distant Future."

11. For the background to Hopkins's dispatch to London, see Kittredge, "U.S.-British Naval Cooperation, 1939–1945," 516–517; Sherwood, *Roosevelt and Hopkins*, 314; and Churchill, *Second World War*, 3:377. For a general account of these meetings, see Sherwood, *Roosevelt and Hopkins*, 311–313. Details can be found, for example, in DC [Defence Committee] (41) (S [Supply]) Sixth Meeting, 22 July 1941 [aircraft], and DC (41) (S) (41) Seventh Meeting, 23 July 1941 [tanks], File Book 4: Hopkins Returns to London (Folder 2), Box 307, Sherwood Collection, Hopkins Papers, FDRL.

12. Note, 22 July 1941, 1–2, WO 193/325, TNA: PRO. For an example of the American anxieties, see Pogue, *Ordeal and Hope*, 131–138.

13. Note, 22 July 1941, WO 193/325, TNA: PRO. Little did the British realize that they would soon have the opportunity to present their arguments in person to the U.S. Chiefs of Staff.

14. Record of Meeting, Prime Minister and COS with USSOG, Hopkins, and Harriman, 24 July 1941, reproduced in Kittredge, "U.S.-British Naval Cooperation, 1939–1945," 518–525; John M. Kennedy, *The Business of War: The War Narrative of Major General Sir John Kennedy*, ed. Bernard Fergusson (London: Hutchinson, 1957), 153. Sherwood gives an account that closely follows the official minutes of the conference (*Roosevelt and Hopkins*, 314–315).

15. Record of Meeting, Prime Minister and COS with USSOG, Hopkins, and Harriman, 24 July 1941, in Kittredge, "U.S.-British Naval Cooperation, 1939–1945," 519–520. See also an account of the meeting in Sherwood, *Roosevelt and Hopkins*, 315.

16. Record of Meeting, Prime Minister and COS with USSOG, Hopkins, and Harriman, 24 July 1941, in Kittredge, "U.S.-British Naval Cooperation, 1939–1945," 521–522; see also Sherwood, *Roosevelt and Hopkins*, 315–316.

17. Record of Meeting, Prime Minister and COS with USSOG, Hopkins, and Harriman, 24 July 1941, in Kittredge, "U.S.-British Naval Cooperation, 1939–1945," 524–525; see also Sherwood, *Roosevelt and Hopkins*, 316–317.

18. Record of Meeting, Prime Minister and COS with USSOG, Hopkins, and Harriman, 24 July 1941, in Kittredge, "U.S.-British Naval Cooperation, 1939–1945," 521–522; Sherwood, *Roosevelt and Hopkins*, 316; Lee, *London Journal*, 350, entry for 24 July 1941.

19. For details of Hopkins's trip to Moscow, see Sherwood, *Roosevelt and Hopkins*, 323–344.

20. For a concise description of the negotiations leading up to the Churchill-Roosevelt conference at Placentia Bay, see Churchill, *Second World War*, 3:380–381. A detailed version is in Theodore Wilson, *The First Summit*, rev. ed. (Lawrence: University Press of Kansas, 1991), 6–55.

21. The British delegation consisted of (1) the prime minister's party—Churchill; Sir Alexander Cadogan, permanent under secretary of the FO; Lord Cherwell, scientific adviser; (2) Admiralty—Adm. Sir Dudley Pound, first sea lord and chief of naval staff; Capt. B. B. Schofield, director of trade responsibility; Cdr. M. G. Goodenough, Plans Division; (3) War Office—Gen. Sir John Dill, CIGS; Brig. Gen. Vivian Dykes, director of plans; (4) Air Ministry—Air Vice Mar. Wilfred Freeman, vice CAS; Group Capt. W. M. Yool, assistant to the CAS; (5) Ministry of Defence—Col. Leslie C. Hollis and Lt. Col. E. I. C. Jacob, both military assistants to the War Cabinet (Provisional Administrative Arrangements, R.I.V. (41) (0) 2, 30 July 1941, PREM 3/485/4, TNA: PRO). The principal U.S. representatives were President Roosevelt; Harry Hopkins; Sumner Welles, under secretary of state; Averell Harriman, special representative of the president; Gen. George C. Marshall, chief of staff of the army; Adm. Harold R. Stark, CNO; Adm. Ernest J. King, CINC, Atlantic Fleet; Maj. Gen. Henry H. Arnold, chief of the army air forces; Maj. Gen. James Burns, executive to the assistant secretary of war; Rear Adm. R. K. Turner, director, WPD; Cdr. Forrest Sherman, Office of the CNO; and Lt. Col. C. W. Bundy, assistant director of the WPD, War Department General Staff.

22. The British proposed to discuss *(a)* the general strategic situation, *(b)* the Far East, *(c)* the Middle East, *(d)* the situation and possible U.S. action in North and West Africa, *(e)* the Atlantic, *(f)* possible U.S. action in Scandinavia, and *(g)* development of an air route from Brazil to Africa (Agenda, R.I.V. (41) (0) 1, 29 July 1941, AIR 8/591, TNA: PRO).

23. For examples of Soviet demands for their share of U.S.-U.K. production, see, for example, Churchill, *Second World War,* 3:340–347.

24. Pogue, *Ordeal and Hope,* 141. See also Wilson, *First Summit,* 56.

25. Wilson, *First Summit,* 59–60, 66–68.

26. Memo, General Strategy: Review by the British COS, 31 July 1941, OPD Exec. File 4, Item 10, RG 165/422, NACP.

27. Ibid., 3, 5.

28. Ibid., 3, 4.

29. Ibid., 5.

30. Ibid.

31. Wilson, *First Summit,* 81. As a result of these arrangements, the minutes of the meetings sometimes border on incoherence, making it difficult to follow the trail of a specific issue through the entire conference.

32. Diary of Col. E. I. C. Jacob, entry for Sunday, 10 Aug. 1941, in Gen. Sir Charles Richardson, *From Churchill's Secret Circle to the BBC: The Biography of Lieutenant General Ian Jacob* (London: Brassey's 1991), 72.

33. Stark served as CNO until March 1942, when he was eased out in the wake of the naval reorganizations following Pearl Harbor and became COMNAVEU from March 1942 to August 1945. Stark retired in April 1946. The information on Stark is from Ancell, *Biographical Dictionary of World War II Generals and Flag Officers,* 617, and Boatner, *Biographical Dictionary of World War II,* 532–534. Additional details on

Stark are given in B. Mitchell Simpson III, "Harold Rainsford Stark," in Robert W. Love Jr., ed., *Chiefs of Naval Operations* (Annapolis, Md.: Naval Institute Press, 1980), 119–135. For a complete biography, see Simpson, *Admiral Harold R. Stark*.

34. The rough outlines of King's career can be found in Boatner, *Biographical Dictionary of World War II*, 276–278, and in Ancell, *Biographical Dictionary of World War II Generals and Flag Officers*, 565. The quote in the text is from Eric Larrabee, *Commander in Chief: Franklin Delano Roosevelt, His Lieutenants, and Their War* (New York: Harper and Row, 1987), 153. King's own account of his career is Ernest J. King, with Walter Muir White, *Fleet Admiral King: A Naval Record* (New York: Norton, 1952). The standard biography is Thomas B. Buell, *Master of Sea Power: A Biography of Fleet Admiral Ernest J. King* (Boston: Little, Brown, 1980).

35. After the war, Marshall served as Truman's personal representative to negotiate a peaceful settlement of the Chinese Civil War in 1946. As secretary of state, 1947–1949, he oversaw the development and initial execution of the Marshall Plan for European recovery as well as the development of the doctrine of containment. He served as secretary of defense in 1950–1951 and received the Nobel Peace Prize in 1953. The outlines of Marshall's career can be found in Boatner, *Biographical Dictionary of World War II*, 345–348, and Ancell, *Biographical Dictionary of World War II Generals and Flag Officers*, 205. The definitive account of Marshall's life and career is given in Forrest Pogue, *George C. Marshall*, 4 vols. (New York: Viking Press, 1963–1987), but see also Ed Cray, *General of the Army George C. Marshall, Soldier and Statesman* (New York: Norton, 1990), and Mark A. Stoler, *George C. Marshall: Soldier-Statesman of the American Century* (Woodbridge, Conn.: Twayne, 1989).

36. By March 1942, the brain tumor and hip disease reduced Pound's capacity to serve, and Lord Alanbrooke assumed the duties of chairing the Chiefs of Staff Committee. Pound resigned as first sea lord shortly after the first Quebec Conference in August 1943. He died, fittingly, on Trafalgar Day (21 October) in 1943 (Boatner, *Biographical Dictionary of World War II*, 437). For details of Pound's career, see World War II Unit Histories and Officers, at http://www.unithistories.com/units_index/default.asp?file=../ officers/ personsx.html (by clicking on the following headings in the sequence given: Officers, British, RN, P, PLAC-PUXL, Pound) (accessed 29 Aug. 2015). See also Robin Brodhurst, *Churchill's Anchor: A Biography of Admiral of the Fleet Sir Dudley Pound* (Barnsley, U.K.: Pen & Sword, 2000), and Malcolm H. Murfett, ed., *The First Sea Lords from Fisher to Mountbatten* (Westport, Conn.: Praeger, 1995).

37. Alex Danchev, "Dill," in John Keegan, ed., *Churchill's Generals* (New York: Grove Weidenfeld, 1991), 53–56; Boatner, *Biographical Dictionary of World War II*, 134–135; and World War II Unit Histories and Officers, at http://www.unithistories.com/units_index/default.asp?file=../officers/personsx.html (by clicking on the following headings in the sequence given: Officers, British, British Army, D, DEAC-DIXO, Dill) (accessed 29 Aug. 2015).

38. Danchev, "Dill," 51. For the deterioration of the relationship between Dill and Churchill, see Danchev, "Dill," 56–60, and Churchill's numerous comments on Dill in the third volume of *Second World War*, passim. Churchill ultimately would

remove Dill in November 1941, which unintentionally would reap a tremendous boon for the Anglo-American coalition throughout the remainder of the war. For details, see Alex Danchev, *A Very Special Relationship: Field Marshal Sir John Dill and the Anglo-American Alliance, 1941–1944* (London: Brassey's, 1986).

39. "Air of Authority—a History of RAF Organisation," Royal Air Force, at http://www.rafweb.org/Biographies/Freeman_WR.htm (accessed 29 Aug. 2015).

40. Wilson, *First Summit,* 113–114, and Summarized Record of Meeting., 9 Aug. 1941, U.S.S. *Augusta,* COS (41) 504, 20 Aug. 1941, Annex I, COS (R) 5, part I, WO 193/326, TNA: PRO (hereafter cited as U.S.S. *Augusta* Meeting, 9 Aug. 1941, Naval Discussions).

41. U.S.S. *Augusta* Meeting, 9 Aug. 1941, Naval Discussions, 2.

42. Ibid.

43. Ibid.

44. Ibid., 2–3.

45. Summarized Record of Meeting, 9 Aug. 1941, U.S.S. *Tuscaloosa,* COS (41) 504, 20 Aug. 1941, Annex I, part II, COS (R) 5, 4, WO 193/326, TNA: PRO.

46. Ibid., 4.

47. Ibid., 5.

48. Informal Discussions between Freeman, Arnold, Burns, and Yool, 9 Aug. 1941, COS (41) 504, 20 Aug. 1941, Annex I, part III, Annex 5, COS (R) 12, 5–6, WO 193/326, TNA: PRO.

49. Journal of Major General Henry H. Arnold, entry for 10 Aug. 1941, quoted in Wilson, *First Summit,* 114.

50. Cowman, *Dominion or Decline,* 290; Kennedy, *Freedom from Fear,* 488; Kershaw, *Fateful Choices,* 302. For Churchill's concerns and advocacy for the United States to start escorting convoys, see, for example, Churchill to FDR, message, 7 July 1941, in Gilbert, *The Ever-Widening War,* 905–906.

51. Morison, *Battle of the Atlantic,* 78.

52. Divine, *Reluctant Belligerent,* 108–109, 126.

53. Ibid., 130–131; Wilson, *First Summit,* 183–187; Doenecke, *Storm on the Horizon,* 231.

54. Divine, *Reluctant Belligerent,* 127; Wilson, *First Summit,* 127; Kittredge, "U.S.-British Naval Cooperation, 1939–1945," 552–553.

55. Kittredge, "U.S.-British Naval Cooperation, 1939–1945," 595–596.

56. Cadogan, *Diaries of Sir Alexander Cadogan,* 397, 399, entries for 9 and 11 Aug. 1941, respectively. Perhaps Cadogan indulged in a bit of classic British understatement, for as Canadian historian Marc Milner observes, "For the moment a major objective of British policy had been achieved in bringing the United States closer to direct belligerency" ("Anglo-American Naval Co-operation, 1939–1945," in Hattendorf and Jordan, *Maritime Strategy and the Balance of Power,* 251).

57. Wilson, *First Summit,* 129, quoting the Sherman Memorandum, in Kittredge, "U.S.-British Naval Cooperation, 1939–1945," part 5, app. B (hereafter cited as Sherman Memo, Meeting, 11 Aug. 1941). The British gave the U.S. COS copies Saturday

evening. Summarized meeting minutes are in Future Strategy, 11 Aug. 1941, COS (41) 504, 20 Aug. 1941, Annex II, COS (R) 7, 9, WO 193/326, TNA: PRO (hereafter cited as COS (R) 7, Meeting, 11 Aug. 1941). See also Memo for COS, n.d., Subj: Notes on Staff Conferences 11–12 Aug. 1941 on Board *Prince of Wales,* OPD Exec. File 4, Item 10, RG 165/422, NACP. The British and American versions of the meeting conform on all major issues, though they differ somewhat on detail. This meeting on 11 August is recounted in Wilson, *First Summit,* 128–132.

58. COS (R) 7, Meeting, 11 Aug. 1941, 9; Sherman Memo, Meeting, 11 Aug. 1941.

59. COS (R) 7, Meeting, 11 Aug. 1941; Notes on Staff Conferences 11–12 Aug. 1941, 9; Sherman Memo, Meeting, 11 Aug. 1941.

60. COS (R) 7, Meeting, 11 Aug. 1941; Notes on Staff Conferences 11–12 Aug. 1941; Sherman Memo, Meeting, 11 Aug. 1941.

61. COS (R) 7, Meeting, 11 Aug. 1941; Notes on Staff Conferences 11–12 Aug. 1941; Sherman Memo, Meeting, 11 Aug. 1941.

62. Wilson, *First Summit,* 138.

63. Informal Discussion between Marshall, Dill, and Dykes, 11 Aug. 1941, COS (41) 504, 20 Aug. 1941, Annex IV, COS (R) 9, part I, WO 193/326, TNA: PRO.

64. Informal Discussion between Adm. Stark and First Sea Lord, 11 Aug. 1941, COS (41) 504, 20 Aug. 1941, Annex IV, COS (R) 9, part II, WO 193/326, TNA: PRO.

65. Jacob, diary entry for 11 Aug. 1941, in Richardson, *From Churchill's Secret Circle to the BBC,* 72.

66. Informal Discussion between Adm. Stark and First Sea Lord, 11 Aug. 1941, COS (41) 504, 20 Aug. 1941, Annex IV, COS (R) 9, part II.

67. Meeting, U.S. and British COS, 12 Aug. 1941, on *Prince of Wales,* COS (41) 504, 20 Aug. 1941, Annex III, COS (R) 10, 10, WO 193/326, TNA: PRO (hereafter cited as *Prince of Wales* Meeting, 12 Aug. 1941); Sherman to CNO, memo, 18 Aug. 1941, Subj: Meetings, Informal 11–12 Aug. 1941, 12 Aug. Meeting, reproduced in Kittredge, "U.S.-British Naval Cooperation, 1939–1945," sec. V, pt. B, A B (hereafter cited as Sherman Memo, Meeting, 12 Aug. 1941).

68. *Prince of Wales* Meeting, 12 Aug. 1941; Sherman Memo, Meeting, 12 Aug. 1941.

69. Informal Discussion on U.S.S. *Tuscaloosa,* 12 Aug. 1941, COS (41) 504, 20 Aug. 1941, Annex V, part I, COS (R) 12, WO 193/326, TNA: PRO.

70. Warren F. Kimball, "Anglo-American War Aims, 1941–1943, the First Review: Eden's Mission to Washington," in Anne Lane and Howard Temperley, eds., *The Rise and Fall of the Grand Alliance, 1941–1945* (New York: St. Martin's Press, 1995), 2–3.

71. Quoted in Doenecke, *Storm on the Horizon,* 239.

72. Quoted in ibid.

73. Wilson, *First Summit,* 199–201.

74. Churchill to Queen Elizabeth, letter, 3 Aug. 1941, in Gilbert, *Ever-Widening War,* 1032.

75. WM (41), 19 Aug. 1941, Annex, Secretary's File Only, CAB 65/19, TNA: PRO, in Gilbert, *Ever-Widening War,* 1081.
76. Reynolds, "Roosevelt, Churchill, and the Wartime Anglo-American Alliance," 22.
77. As noted in John R. Colville, *Fringes of Power: 10 Downing Street Diaries, 1939–1955* (New York: Norton, 1985), 428, diary entry for 19 Aug. 1941.
78. WM (41), 19 Aug. 1941, Annex, Secretary's File Only, CAB 65/19, TNA: PRO, in Gilbert, ed., *Ever-Widening War,* 1081.
79. Wilson, *First Summit,* 202.
80. Quoted in Warren F. Kimball, *The Juggler: Franklin Roosevelt as Wartime Statesman* (Princeton, N.J.: Princeton University Press, 1991), 14.
81. Wilson, *First Summit,* 185–186, 193.
82. Lowenthal, *Leadership and Indecision,* 2:622.
83. Report, British-American COS Discussions, 9–12 Aug. 1941, COS (R) 15, 15 Aug. 1941, 3 and 5, AIR 8/591, TNA: PRO (hereafter cited as COS (R) 15, 15 Aug. 1941).
84. Ibid., 4.
85. Sir Leslie C. Hollis, *One Marine's Tale* (London: Andre Deutsch, 1956), 82.
86. COS (R) 15, 15 Aug. 1941, 6. The British received advanced warning of this trend from the BJSM (see Harris to Portal, letter, 16 Aug. 1941, app. II, RAF Delegation Washington, AIR 45/12, TNA: PRO.
87. COS (R) 15, 15 Aug. 1941, 6, 2–3, 5; Dykes for CIGS, memo, 16 Aug. 1941, 1–2, WO 193/326, TNA: PRO.
88. JB to SPENAVO London, SPOBS London, letter, approved 25 Sept. 1941, Subj: Comment on "General Strategy Review by the British Chiefs of Staff," JB no. 325 (Serial no. 729), WPD 4402-64, RG 165/281, NACP (hereafter cited as Comments on Grand Strategy Review, 25 Sept. 1941, JB no. 325), 2. Also found under the same title in ABC 381 (9-25-41), sec. 1, RG 165/421, NACP. The letter from the JB was a greatly watered-down version of the complaints and criticisms that had surfaced within the War Department. See Gerow for COS, Sept. 1941, memo, Subj: Grand Strategy—Review by the British COS, WPD 4402-64, RG 165/281, NACP.
89. Lee, *London Journal,* entry for 15 Nov. 1941, 450.
90. Comments on Grand Strategy Review, 25 Sept. 1941, JB no. 325, 4.
91. Ibid., 4.
92. Ibid., 5.
93. See, for example, Jacob, diary entry for 12 Aug. 1941, in Richardson, *From Churchill's Secret Circle to the BBC,* 76.
94. Quoted in Alex Danchev, "Good Boy: Field Marshal Sir John Dill," in *On Specialness,* 85.
95. Ibid.
96. For Dill's time in Washington and his influence, see Danchev, *A Very Special Relationship.*
97. Field Marshal Lord Alanbrooke, *War Diaries, 1939–1945,* edited by Alex

Danchev and Daniel Todman (Berkeley: University of California Press, 2001), 210, entry for 11 Dec. 1941.

98. Christopher D. O'Sullivan, *Harry Hopkins: FDR's Envoy to Churchill and Stalin* (Lanham, Md.: Rowman and Littlefield, 2015), 53.

99. Robert P. Patterson for Secretary of War, memo, 18 Apr. 1941, Subj: Ultimate Munitions Production Essential to the Safety of America, WPD 4494, RG165/281, NACP.

100. FDR to Secretary of War, letter, 9 July 1941, WPD 4494-1, RG 165/281, NACP.

101. Leighton and Coakley, *Global Logistics and Strategy*, 1:137–139.

102. For a description of the formulation of the Victory Program, see Watson, *Chief of Staff*, chap. 9, and Matloff and Snell, *Strategic Planning for Coalition Warfare*, 58–62. For a personal account by the army officer tasked with overseeing the compilation of the program, see Wedemeyer, *Wedemeyer Reports!* An assessment of the program is given in Charles E. Kirkpatrick, *An Unknown Future and a Doubtful Present: Writing the Victory Program of 1941* (Washington, D.C.: U.S. Army Center of Military History, 1990). In *Keep from All Thoughtful Men: How U.S. Economists Won World War II* (Annapolis, Md.: Naval Institute Press, 2011), 19–30, James Lacey attempts to debunk Wedemeyer's role.

103. Purvis to Stimson, letter, 14 July 1941, WPD 4494-1, RG 165/281, NACP; Bridges to Averell Harriman, letter, 29 July 1941, copy, WPD 4402-72, RG 165/281, NACP; Hancock and Gowing, *British War Economy*, 387.

104. President for Secretary of War, memo, 30 Aug. 1941, WPD 4557-1, RG 165/281, NACP.

105. Chaney and Ghormley to COS, CNO, letter, 1 Sept. 1941, Subj: Proposal of British COS, re: Determination of Overall Requirements of Critical Items, WPD 4494-5, RG 165/281, NACP; COS (41) 515, 22 Aug. 1941, CAB 80/30, TNA: PRO.

106. Hall, *North American Supply*, 330–332.

107. The U.S. delegation to Moscow consisted of Harriman; Adm. William H. Standley; Gens. Embick, Burns, and Chaney; and Cols. Philip R. Faymonville and Charles W. Bundy. Embick did not continue on to Moscow (Matloff and Snell, *Strategic Planning for Coalition Warfare*, 57).

108. Minutes of Conference in Cabinet Building, London, 15 Sept. 1941, 6:00 p.m., WPD 4557, RG 165/281, NACP; Averell Harriman and Elie Abel, *Special Envoy to Churchill and Stalin, 1941–1946* (New York: Random House, 1976), 78.

109. Minutes of Conference in Cabinet Building, London, 15 Sept. 1941, 6:00 p.m.; Harriman and Abel, *Special Envoy*, 78–79. The minutes of the conference credit Embick with the suggestion to divide the conference into smaller working groups. See also Lee, *London Journal*, 400, entry for 15 Sept. 1941.

110. Overall Production Requirements for Victory, Beaverbrook–Harriman Committee (BH) (41) 2, 14 Sept. 1941, WPD 4557, RG 165/281, NACP. For agreements on army, navy, and raw materials subcommittees, see Conference on British-U.S. Production, Summary of Proceedings, BH (41) 7, 16 Sept. 1941, and Conference on Brit-

ish-U.S. Production, Report of Army Subcommittee, BH (41) 8, 16 Sept. 1941, WPD 4557, RG 165/281, NACP.

111. Conference on British-U.S. Production, Summary of Proceedings, BH (41) 7, 16 Sept. 1941; U.S. Proposals for Allocation of American Production, n.d. [16 Sept. 1941], BH (41) 9; and Conference on U.S.-British Production, Summary of Conference, 17 Sept 1941, BH (41) 11, 5–6: all in WPD 4557, RG 165/281, NACP.

112. Conference on British-U.S. Production, Summary of Conference, BH (41) 11, 17 Sept. 1941, 7–8, WPD 4557, RG 165/281, NACP. See Conference on British-U.S. Production, Victory Requirements, BH (41) 14, 19 Sept. 1941, WPD 4494, RG 165/281, NACP, for details of specific allocations.

113. Second Meeting, Conference on British-U.S. Production, BH (41), 20 Sept. 1941, WPD 4944, RG 165/281, NACP; Conference on British-U.S. Production, Summary of Conference, BH (41) 11, 17 Sept. 1941, 7–8, WPD 4557, RG 165/281, NACP. For details of allocations, see Conference on British-U.S. Production, Victory Requirements, BH (41) 14, 19 Sept. 1941, WPD 4494, RG 165/281, NACP.

114. For background on the Beaverbrook–Harriman Mission, see Churchill, *Second World War*, 3:412–419. For Russian demands, see Col. Bundy for COS, memo, 24 Oct. 1941, Subj: Trip with Harriman Mission, WPD 4557-12, RG 165/281, NACP. The terms of the protocol are in Confidential Protocol of the Conference of the Representatives of the United States of America, Union of Soviet Socialist Republics, and Great Britain, 29 Sept.–1 Oct. 1941, Folder 2, WPD 4557, RG 165/281, NACP. For a personal view, see Lee's description of Chaney's account of the mission in Lee, *London Journal*, 419–422, entry for 11 Oct. 1941.

10. Racing an Unseen Clock

1. Lt. Col. Frank Vogel to Brig. Gen. Vivian Dykes, letter, 29 Oct. 1941, WO 193/319, TNA: PRO.

2. Ibid.

3. For details of these activities, see Matloff and Snell, *Strategic Planning for Coalition Warfare*, 63–78; Watson, *Chief of Staff*, 411–452, 453–493; Conn and Fairchild, *Framework for Hemisphere Defense*, 141–155.

4. The initial U.S. request for the new committee is in GLEAM 22, Bellairs to COS, message, 15 Mar. 1941, WO 193/305, TNA: PRO. The British COS approved the request on 19 Mar 41 (COS (41) 172, 19 Mar. 1941, Annex III, WO 193/305, and COS to Bellairs, 19 Mar. 1941, BOXES [sic] 25, WO 193/305, TNA: PRO.

5. Maj. Gen. H. H. Arnold to Air Mar. Arthur Harris and Wing Cdr. Bryans, letter, 27 Aug. 1941, abstract, CCS 334, Washington, D.C., Communications Board (WCB) (1-6-41), sec. 1, Joint and Combined Chiefs of Staff, entry number NM41, RG 218, NACP (hereafter item, RG 218/41, NACP); MM (41) Twenty-Second Meeting, 5 Sept. 1941, abstract, CAB 122/549, TNA: PRO; and Harris to Portal, letter, 13 Sept. 1941, AIR 45/12, TNA: PRO.

6. JB no. 319 (Serial no. 730), 26 Sept. 1941, CCS 334, WCB (1-6-41), sec. 1, RG 218, NACP.

7. AL (41) Seventh Meeting, 23 Sept. 1941, CAB 99/9, TNA: PRO; McNarney to AGWAR, letter, 8 Oct. 1941, CCS 334, WCB (1-6-41), sec. 1, RG 218, NACP.

8. Commander Richard D. Coleridge to McDowell, letter, CS (47) 39, 14 Oct. 1941, Subj: Proposed Formation of Associated Communications Committee in Washington and London, CCS 334, WCB (1-6-41), sec. 1, RG 218, NACP; also found under same title in WPD 4602-1, RG 165/281, NACP.

9. McDowell to Coleridge, letter, 10 Nov. 1941, Serial no. 011512-102, WPD 4602-1, RG 165/281, NACP.

10. First Meeting, Associated Communications Committee (London), 12 Nov. 1941, minutes, CCS 334 (3-1-42), RG 218, NACP; also found in CCS 334, London Communications Committee (11-12-41), RG 218, NACP.

11. Ibid.

12. "Formulation of U.S. Foreign and Defense Policies," 20–22, File 90, Historical Section, COMNAVEU, Series II, RG 38.2.4.

13. On 4 September, the destroyer U.S.S. *Greer* stalked a German U-boat for several hours after a British patrol aircraft alerted the ship and had dropped depth changes. When the German submarine fired a torpedo at *Greer*, the ship also made several depth-charge passes. Although the Germans would not have been able to identify the *Greer* as an American vessel, Roosevelt used the incident as the rationale for his "shoot on sight" order, which effectively placed the United States in a state of undeclared naval war with Germany. For brief descriptions of the *Greer* incident, see Dallek, *Franklin D. Roosevelt and American Foreign Policy*, 287–289, and Kershaw, *Fateful Choices*, 329–333. For details, see Patrick Abbazia, *Mr. Roosevelt's Navy: The Private War of the U.S. Atlantic Fleet, 1939–1942* (Annapolis, Md.: Naval Institute Press, 1975), 223–231, and Thomas A. Bailey and Paul B. Ryan, *Hitler vs. Roosevelt: The Undeclared Naval War* (New York: Free Press, 1979), 168–180. In addition to Abbazia's work, in *Battle of the Atlantic*, chapters 3–5, Morison describes the conduct of naval operations before the U.S. entry into the war. In *Reluctant Belligerent*, Divine describes FDR's order as "a decisive step toward war" (144). The Germans held a similar view (Rich, *Hitler's War Aims*, 243–245).

14. M.O. 2, Encl. 28/M.O. 2 1733, 12 Aug. 1941, minute, WO 193/325, TNA: PRO.

15. For Chaney's recommendations, see Matloff and Snell, *Strategic Planning for Coalition Warfare*, 47–48. Additional information concerning decisions made by the SPOBS about troop totals, bases, locations, and so on is given in WO to British Military Attaché, Washington, D.C., message, 18 Sept. 1941, WO 193/319, TNA: PRO.

16. SPOBS to AGWAR, Message no. 27, 26 Aug. 1941, quoted in Thurman et al., "SPOBS," 85–86. A summary of the message is contained in Brief of Cable from Gen. Chaney, 26 Aug. 1941, WPD 4402-51, RG 165/281, NACP.

17. Gerow for Maj. Gen. Moore, memo, 17 Nov. 1941, Subj: Letter to Chaney, WPD 4402-95, RG 165/281, NACP. This memo is also included in Thurman et al., "SPOBS," 86. Even before this time, the SPOBS staff had shifted from sole concentration on the planning necessary to implement ABC-1 to the gathering of informa-

tion on Lend-Lease matters for the War Department. See, for example, AGWAR to SPOBS, Message no. 49, 11 Sept. 1941, in Thurman et al., "SPOBS," 83–84, which requested specific information on Lend-Lease matters in the Middle East. The assignment of Russian Lend-Lease activities to SPOBS is contained in War Department to Chaney, message, 19 Nov. 1941, quoted in Thurman, "SPOBS," 88.

18. For the confusion, see, for example, Lee, *London Journal*, 422–423, entry for 12 Oct. 1941.

19. Report by the British Joint Planning Staff, General Strategy—American Comments, JP (41) 951, 11 Nov. 1941, War Cabinet Joint Planning Committees and Subcommittees, CAB 84/36, TNA: PRO. A summarized version is in COS to BJSM, message, n.d., BOXES [sic] 127, CAB 122/30, TNA: PRO. For analysis of British failure to grasp U.S. issues, see Cowman, *Dominion or Decline*, 186–192.

20. Report by the British Joint Planning Staff, General Strategy—American Comments, JP (41) 951, 11 Nov. 1941, CAB 84/36, TNA: PRO.

21. Ibid.

22. Ibid.

23. Ghormley's comments are given in Brig. Gen. Miles for COS, memo, 14 Nov. 1941, Subj: Lessons from British Air Offensive, OPD Exec. File 4, Item 4, RG 165/422, NACP. Of course, service parochialism could have motivated Ghormley's comment.

24. AL (41) Eighth Meeting, 21 Nov. 1941, CAB 99/9, TNA: PRO. Lee provides a more personal account of the meeting in *London Journal*, 458–459, entry for 21 Nov. 1941.

25. The fact that the British devoted six pages of explanation to the heavy-bomber program while allowing only two or three short paragraphs for other areas reflects the importance of this topic for them.

26. AL (41) Eighth Meeting, 21 Nov. 1941, CAB 99/9, TNA: PRO; Lee, *London Journal*, 458–459, entry for 21 Nov. 1941.

27. Lee, *London Journal*, 459, entry for 21 Nov. 1941. The general discussion is taken from ibid., 458–459, and AL (41) Eighth Meeting, 21 Nov. 1941, CAB 99/9, TNA: PRO.

28. Lee, *London Journal*, 459, entry for 21 Nov. 1941.

29. Ibid., 467–468, entry for 28 Nov. 1941.

30. Draft Agreement of the Outline Plan for the Employment of Am-Dutch-Br Forces in the Far East in the Event of War with Japan, ADB-2, n.d. [pencil annotation, Aug. 1941], CAB 122/8, TNA: PRO, quotation from annex, 14.

31. Ibid.

32. Ibid.

33. SPENAVO to CNO, letter, 1 Sept. 1941, Subj: ADB-2, Comments On, Serial no. 281, Folder U.S.-U.K.-Dutch Conversations, Box 118, U.S.-U.K.-Dutch Conversations File, Series VII, SPD, RG 38.2.4, NACP.

34. Ghormley to Turner, letter, 2 Sept. 1941, Serial no. 00288, Folder U.S.-U.K.-Dutch Conversations, Box 118, U.S.-U.K.-Dutch Conversations File, Series VII, SPD, RG 38.2.4, NACP.

35. ADM to British Admiralty Delegation, message, 22 Sept. 1941, CAB 122/580, TNA: PRO; ADM to British Admiralty Delegation, message, 22 Sept. 1941, Box 117, ABDA-ANZAC Correspondence, Series VII, SPD, RG 38.2.4, NACP.
36. Turner to Danckwerts, letter, 3 Oct. 1941, Serial no. 011512-72, CAB 122/8, TNA: PRO.
37. Ibid. A summarized version of Turner's comments is found in ADB Report, U.S. Reaction, MM (41) 181, BJSM, 10 Oct. 1941, CAB 122/8, TNA: PRO.
38. SPENAVO to OPNAV, message, 26 Oct. 1941, Box 117, ABDA-ANZAC Correspondence, Series VII, SPD, RG 38.4.2, NACP.
39. ADM to British Admiralty Delegation, message, 5 Nov. 1941, 2, CAB 122/9, TNA: PRO (also found in WPD 4402-18, RG 165/281, NACP); Matloff and Snell, *Strategic Planning for Coalition Warfare*, 76.
40. Stark's comments are in OPNAV to SPENAVO, message, 6 Nov. 1941, Box 117, ABDA-ANZAC Correspondence, Series VII, SPD, RG 38.2.4, NACP. A copy of the same message is in WPD 4402-112, RG 165/281, NACP, and CAB 122/9, TNA: PRO. The final version is in Ghormley to Pound, letter, 7 Nov. 1941, Serial no. 470, COMNAVEU, Series II, File 8, RG 38.2.4, NACP.
41. OPNAV to SPENAVO, message, 6 Nov. 1941, WPD 4402-112, RG 165/281, NACP.
42. McDowell to Coleridge, letter, 11 Nov. 1941, Subj: U.S.-British Commonwealth Cooperation in the Far East, WPD 4402, RG 165/281, NACP, also found in GLEAM 163, BJSM to COS, message, 13 Nov. 1941, copy of letter from 11 Nov. 1941, U.S. Serial no. 011512-104, CAB 122/5, TNA: PRO.
43. Ibid. Turner, perhaps fearing another fiasco if the meeting occurred in Singapore, provided the impetus for Phillips's invitation to Manila (Chief Staff Officer for Adm. Little, memo, 6 Nov. 1941, CAB 122/9, TNA: PRO). The British Joint Planning Committee recommended approval of the American proposals on 21 November 1941 (Far East Staff Conversations, JP (41) 991, 21 Nov. 1941, CAB 84/37, TNA: PRO). Interesting to note that the U.S. Navy Department notified Hart of the upcoming conference on 20 September 1941! See CINC China Station to ADM, message, 20 Sept. 1941, AIR 8/866, TNA: PRO). MacArthur received notice of the change in procedure on 21 November 1941 (see Deputy COS [Maj. Gen. Bryden] to Commanding General, U.S. Army Forces in the Far East, letter, 21 Nov. 1941, WPD 4402–112, RG 165/281, NACP.
44. Reynolds, *Creation of the Anglo-American Alliance*, 243; Cowman, *Dominion or Decline*, 250–251.
45. On Hart's lack of information, see, for example, Hart to Stark, letters, 7 June, 17 July, and 11 Aug. 1941, all in Hart Papers, Box 4, File Stark, 1939–1941, OAB, NHHC. See also Hart's diary entries for 20 Nov. and 7 Dec. 1941, Hart Papers. For the adverse effect of this lack of information on Hart's negotiations with the British, see Hart to Stark, letters, 31 July and 11 Aug. 1941, Hart Papers, File Stark, 1939–1941.
46. Layton to Hart, letter, 18 July 1941, and Hart to Layton, letter, 30 July 1941, Serial no. 04707/14, Box 118, U.S.-U.K.-Dutch Conversations File, Series VII, SPD, RG 38.2.4, NACP. The absence of detailed comment was due in part to the lack

of timely information from the CNO. See Hart to Stark, letter, 31 July 1941, Hart Papers, File Stark, 1939–1941, OAB, NHHC.

47. Hart to Stark, letter, 11 Aug. 1941, Hart Papers, File Stark, 1939–1941, OAB, NHHC; Adm. Thomas Hart, "Reminisences" (1962), Columbia University Oral History Program, OAB, Naval History Division/NHHC, 143–144.

48. Report of Conference, 6 Dec. 1941, Hart Papers, Box 3, File Java 1941–1942, OAB, NHHC (in general, all information on the conference is taken from this report); Hart diary, entry for 6 Dec. 41, Hart Papers; CINCAF to OPNAV, message, 7 Dec. 1941, CAB 122/9, TNA: PRO; and Gen. Douglas MacArthur to Marshall, message, 7 Dec. 1941, WPD 4622-35, RG 165/281, NACP.

49. Report of Conference, 6 Dec. 1941, Hart Papers, OAB, NHHC; MacArthur to Marshall, message, 7 Dec. 1941, WPD 4622–35, RG 165/281, NACP.

50. Report of Conference, 6 Dec. 1941, Hart Papers, OAB, NHHC.

51. Ibid. See also Gray, *Operation Pacific*, 31–32.

52. Hart indicates his satisfaction in his diary entry for 6 Dec. 1941 (Hart diary, Hart Papers, OAB, NHHC). A summary of accomplishments is in CINCAF to OPNAV, message, 7 Dec. 1941, CAB 122/9, TNA: PRO. See also Gray, *Operation Pacific*, 32–33.

53. Samuel E. Morison, *The History of United States Naval Operations in World War II*, vol. 3: *The Rising Sun in the Pacific, 1931–April 1942* (Boston: Little, Brown, 1948), 157.

54. For the loss of the *Prince of Wales* and the *Repulse*, see Roskill, *War at Sea*, 564–567. For an account of the destruction of the ABDA force during the Battle of the Java Sea, 27–28 February 1942, see Morison, *Two-Ocean War*, 88–98.

55. Cowman, *Dominion or Decline*, 293. For a more balanced appraisal, see Bell, *Churchill and Sea Power*, 240–253.

56. As given in a note preceding the entry for 2 December 1941 in Alanbrooke, *War Diaries, 1939–1945*, 205.

57. Roskill, *War at Sea*, 1:554–559.

58. Bell, *Churchill and Sea Power*, 245–246.

59. Ibid., 246–247.

60. Ibid., 249.

Conclusion

1. David Watt, "Introduction: The Anglo-American Relationship," in Louis and Bull, *Special Relationship*, 3.

2. For the origins of Churchill's relationship with FDR, see Churchill, *Second World War*, 2:22–25. For one of Churchill's first uses of the term *special relationship*, see his speech "The Sinews of Peace," Westminster College, 5 Mar. 1946, at http://history1900s.about.com/od/churchillwinston/a/Iron-Curtain.htm (accessed 4 Apr. 2013), more commonly known as the speech in which Churchill coined the appellation "Iron Curtain." For a description of how Churchill overstated the case, see Reynolds, *In Command of History*, 503–504.

3. McKercher, *Transition of Power*, 280.
4. Christman, "Franklin D. Roosevelt and the Craft of Strategic Assessment," 229.
5. Watt, "Introduction," 5.
6. Smith, *Ultra–Magic Deals*, 13.
7. For examples of Churchill's shaping of the narrative of his relationship with Roosevelt, see Reynolds, *In Command of History*, 102, 132–134, 158, 348–351, 503–508.
8. Lowenthal, *Leadership and Indecision*, 1:370–371.
9. Niall Barr, "The British Army and Anglo-American Relations in the Second World War," in Keith Neilson and Greg Kennedy, eds., *The British Way in Warfare: Power and the International System, 1856–1956* (Burlington, Vt.: Ashgate, 2010), 179, citing Historical Record, British Army Staff, Part II: Operations, Plans, and Intelligence, WO 202/917, TNA: PRO.
10. See Divine, *Reluctant Belligerent*. For a brief overview of the historiography of Roosevelt's leadership on the path to war, see Doenecke and Wilz, *From Isolation to War*, 164–172, 177–186.
11. Utley, *Going to War with Japan*, 119.
12. Farnham, *Roosevelt and the Munich Crisis*, 220.
13. For FDR's lackadaisical approach and the need for General Marshall to carry the burden, see Davis, *FDR: The War President*, 251–253, and Watson, *Chief of Staff*, 220–231.
14. For a discussion of Roosevelt's guidance on the National Guard and the size of the army and air force, see Watson, *Chief of Staff*, 360–366; Mark A. Stoler, *Allies and Adversaries: The Joint Chiefs of Staff, the Grand Alliance, and U.S. Strategy in World War II* (Chapel Hill: University of North Carolina Press, 2000), 28–29; and Doenecke, "The Roosevelt Foreign Policy," 35–36. As Lynne Olson concludes, "The president continued to resist the idea that the United States would have to send an army to Europe again, even if the country were forced to go to war against Hitler" (*Those Angry Days*, 200).
15. See, for example, John Charmley, "Churchill's Roosevelt," in Land and Temperley, *The Rise and Fall of the Grand Alliance*, 94.
16. Charmley, *Churchill's Grand Alliance*, 11.
17. Olson, *Those Angry Days*, xx. See additional support for such an assessment in Lowenthal, *Leadership and Indecision*, 2:628, 641, 687; Barron, *Leadership in Crisis*, 106; and Farnham, *Roosevelt and the Munich Crisis*, 231;
18. Kimball, "Anglo-American War Aims," 3; Theodore A. Wilson et al. (only first author listed), "Coalition: Structure, Strategy, and Statecraft," in David Reynolds, Warren F. Kimball, and A. O. Chubarian, eds., *Allies at War: The Soviet, American, and British Experience, 1939–1945* (London: MacMillan, 1994), 81; James MacGregor Burns, *Roosevelt: Soldier of Freedom* (New York: Harcourt, Brace, Jovanovich, 1970), 11.
19. Colville, *Fringes of Power*, 624, entry for 2 May 1948.
20. See, for example, Robert Shogan, *Hard Bargain: How FDR Twisted Churchill's*

Arm, Evaded the Law, and Changed the Role of the American Presidency (New York: Scribner's, 1995), 193–228.

21. Churchill, radio broadcast, 9 Feb. 1941, in Gilbert, *The Ever-Widening War*, 200.

22. Howard, *Continental Commitment*, 144.

23. Churchill, *Second World War*, 3:539–540.

24. For an overview of the various campaigns, see Esposito, *West Point Atlas of American Wars*, vol. 2, and John Keegan, ed., *The Times Atlas of the Second World War* (New York: Harper and Row, 1989). For the time required for U.S. mobilization to hit full stride, see, for example, Leighton and Coakley, *Global Logistics and Strategy*, 1:137–140, 195–212.

25. Miller, *War Plan Orange*, 347.

26. Leighton and Coakley, *Global Logistics and Strategy*, 2:838. Nor do these figures include the numbers needed to support U.S. Navy and Air Force operations in addition to Operation Overlord.

27. Cline, *Washington Command Post*, 47.

28. Kennedy, *Freedom from Fear*, 473; Reynolds, *Creation of the Anglo-American Alliance*, 159, 163–166. The most prominent liquidation was the American Viscose Company, which sold at a tremendous loss to its British owners.

29. Churchill to Sir Kingsley Wood, minute, 20 Mar. 1941, in Gilbert, *The Ever-Widening War*, 372.

30. Christopher Layne, *The Peace of Illusions: American Grand Strategy from 1940 to the Present* (Ithaca, N.Y.: Cornell University Press, 2006), 48–50. See also Lynne Olson, *Citizens of London: The Americans Who Stood with Britain in Its Darkest, Finest Hour* (New York: Random House, 2010), 299–300. Article 4 of the Atlantic Charter is located at http://avalon.law.yale.edu/wwii/atlantic.asp (accessed 4 Apr. 2013).

31. Quoted in Larrabee, *Commander in Chief*, 155.

32. See, for example, Brigadier Nigel Aylwin-Foster, British Army, "Changing the Army for Counterinsurgency Operations," *Military Review* 85, no. 6 (Nov.–Dec. 2005): 2–15, and David Betz, "Failure of British COIN," Insurgency Research Group, 29 July 2008, at http://insurgencyresearchgroup.wordpress.com/2008/07/29/failure-of-british-coin/ (accessed 16 Apr. 2013).

Selected Bibliography

Note on Sources

This work relies substantially on documents and primary material gathered from archives and repositories located in the United Kingdom and the United States. The majority of such information came from documents contained in the public archives of each country. In addition to the central-government archives, a number of subsidiary official repositories—in particular, the archives of several of the services involved in the negotiations described—provided key elements of information. Finally, the private papers of many of the participants, both major and minor, offered key insights.

Naturally, overlap exists between the information contained in the British and U.S. records. Likewise, duplications exist within the records of each nation's services. However, the events that led up to the meetings—for example, the rationale, objectives, and goals; the perceptions of the participants; and the sometimes differing opinions of the results—can be garnered only by meticulously comparing the various files.

In general, British records and documents did not prove to be as fruitful as anticipated. Although usually better organized than U.S. materials, they oftentimes lack background information that explains how or why individuals arrived at decisions. Conversely, U.S. materials contain considerable background and working papers, but the amount of material can be overwhelming. As a general suggestion, researchers in this subject and era may first wish to examine documents in Record Group (RG) 38.2.4, Office of the Chief of Naval Operations, Records Relating to U.S. Navy Operations, at the U.S. National Archives at College Park, Maryland (NACP), to establish general timelines, develop chronological sequences of events, discover critical decision points, and identify key personnel. A review of documents held in the United Kingdom can flesh out the basic outlines and add to details of later collaboration. After reviewing these locations, a researcher will be better prepared for examining the remaining document collections at NACP to amplify the details and find relevant background material from issues identified in the review of British files.

In the United Kingdom, the National Archives, Public Records Office (TNA: PRO), Kew, London, proved the most profitable source of information. TNA: PRO organizes documents by functional area and has inventoried and indexed the collection in detail. The key exception to this rule is the Admiralty files, which hold a huge mass of information. The latter files are extremely cumbersome to sort through. Researchers must possess some insight into specific items of information required and maintain their patience while searching through the files until identifying relevant documents.

Within TNA: PRO, perhaps most important are the records of the British Joint

Staff Mission, Washington (Cabinet Office/War Cabinet Records [CAB] 122). Next in priority are the files contained in Commonwealth and International Conferences (CAB 99); War History Cases and Papers (Admiralty Records [ADM] 199); and the working papers of the various directors of plans—Air Ministry Director of Plans (AIR 9) and War Office Director of Military Operations Collation Files (WO 193). Finally, the files of the British Chiefs of Staff (CAB 79 and CAB 80) and the Prime Minister's Office (PREM 3 and PREM 4 in particular) also contain a wealth of pertinent information. As one might expect, there is considerable overlap and redundancy among the files. Increasing numbers of documents are becoming available on line, but at present the bulk of the material is still in paper form. Some British files and Cabinet memoranda are designated by code letters that are not really acronyms, such as CR, CS, JP, SA, WM, WP, but that are important parts of the document numbers in the filing system, as any researcher will discover.

Private papers of British participants in the collaborative process are available in TNA: PRO; the Liddell Hart Centre for Military Archives, Kings College, London; and the Royal Air Force Museum, Hendon. Of note are the papers of Ridley Pakenham-Walsh and Sir Henry R. Pownall, both contained in the Liddell Hart Centre.

Despite the difficulties inherent in a massive amount of documents organized under multiple filing and classification systems, the records at NACP contain an absolute wealth of information. To be effective at doing research at NACP, researchers need to be thoroughly familiar with Timothy Mulligan, comp., *Guide to Records Relating to U.S. Military Participation in World War II*, 2 vols. (Washington, D.C: National Archives, 2008). In addition, online finding aids and tools, such as the Archival Research Catalogue, are essential for narrowing search areas prior to arrival at NACP. As one might expect, there is considerable redundancy within and among various record groups.

All major NACP record groups detailed in the bibliography merit review. Where possible, the bibliography provides a record entry number that will facilitate eventual electronic access to materials. Where records are not yet available electronically via the Archival Research Catalogue, the entry number facilitates access to textual materials of the collections in NACP. Given the literal mountains of information, it will be years before materials down to the individual document level will be available online. Until that time, researchers will have to rely on textual records. Gaining access to those materials will require researchers to be familiar with the finding aids held at NACP for each record group.

For this work, the most important records held at NACP fall within RG 38, Office of the Chief of Naval Operations; RG 165, War Department General and Special Staffs; RG 218, Joint and Combined Chiefs of Staff; and RG 225, Records of the Joint Army–Navy Board.

As indicated earlier, any examination of early Anglo-American cooperation, especially naval collaboration, should commence with RG 38 and, especially, subgroup 38.2.4, Office of the Chief of Naval Operations, Records Relating to U.S. Navy Operations Received from the Operational Archives Branch, Naval Historical Center. Of greatest significance are the Records of Commander, U.S. Naval Forces Europe, 1938–1947 (Series II, Subject Files), and the Strategic Plans Division (Series VII, Records Relating to Anglo-American-Dutch Cooperation, 1938–1939). The files are extremely well organized and easy to use.

RG 165 is the next most useful U.S. archival source. It is a massive collection of documents, divided into multiple series and subseries. It spans the modern-army and old-army branches. Although the year 1940 is the general dividing line, this is not a hard-and-fast rule. To complicate matters, the army used several different filing systems during the period under investigation. Within the War Department General Staff prior to 1940, file numbers were assigned in numerical sequence as the files were established, and there is neither rhyme nor reason to the organization of the records. Researchers therefore need to examine the many separate series and subseries of documents. Adoption of the War Department Classification Scheme in 1940 simplified matters somewhat, but researchers must be thoroughly familiar with the system if it is to be of any use. Finally, some organizations within the War Department General and Special Staffs (e.g., the Military Intelligence Division, Attachés, and Joint Army–Navy Board documents in RG 165) utilized their own distinctive filing systems.

The most lucrative files concerning early Anglo-American cooperation in RG 165 are: Series 281, General Correspondence, War College and War Plans Division, 1920–1942; Series 421, Top Secret "American-British-Canadian" Correspondence (commonly known as the ABC Files); and Series 422, which is generally referred to as the Operations Division Executive Files. Series 281 is organized according to the classification system in place prior to 1940. To access Series 281, researchers must utilize Series 280. Within Series 281, the most profitable files are in the 4300–4650 file series, in particular 4402, 4323, 4340, 4351, 4368, 4435, 4470, 4494, 4497, 4557, 4662, and 4639. Series 421 also is organized according to the pre-1940 classification scheme. To access Series 421, researchers must utilize Series 420. The series 300 files are the most rewarding. Within Series 422, Executive no. 4 (Items 4, 7, 10, and 11), no. 8 (Book A and Book 1), and no. 10 (Item 1) are the most useful.

RG 218, Records of the Joint and Combined Chiefs of Staff, is another profitable source of information. It is another massive record group organized according to the War Department Classification Scheme. Although most of the files and much of the information postdates Pearl Harbor, many files contain documents prior to that date. In addition, many of the files are incorrectly dated. Thus, the files require extensive review. The series 300 files, in particular 334 and 381, are the most productive.

RG 225, Records of the Joint Army–Navy Board, although cumbersome, requires review. Subject file series 301, 310, 325, 354, and 355 of Series 1, part II, are the most pertinent. This record group contains information found in several other collections (such as RG 165, Series 282 and Series 284) but is better organized and easier to use.

As indicated earlier, the bulk of the collections reviewed at the Operational Naval Archives are now located at NACP. However, the Operational Archives Branch, Naval History and Heritage Center, contains oral histories and private papers of such key individuals as Harold R. Stark, Robert L. Ghormley, Thomas C. Hart, and Tracy B.

Kittredge. No examination of Anglo-American cooperation before Pearl Harbor can be complete without a thorough review of these collections.

Records and papers held in the U.S. Army Military History Institute at Carlisle Barracks, Pennsylvania, also contain some of the key elements of the story of Anglo-American collaboration. Of greatest importance are the numerous documents contained within the U.S. Army War College Subject Files. More important than the documents, however, are the Oral History Collection and the numerous collections of private papers. The U.S. Army Military History Institute has placed great emphasis on establishing a superior oral history program and on becoming the central repository for the private papers of persons directly or indirectly connected to the U.S. Army. The success of these efforts has resulted in a first-class collection of oral histories and private papers, many of which were critical to my investigation. In particular, the papers of Charles L. Bolte, Raymond E. Lee, and Bradford G. Chynoweth proved to be the most productive, though there were many other additional sources of importance.

The official histories published by both the United Kingdom and the United States were invaluable in identifying possible primary sources and their locations. Overall, they are well written, informative, are generally free of obvious bias, and oftentimes point to key files that allow the researcher more quickly to winnow the wheat from the mountains of documentary chaff.

Primary Sources

Personal Papers

United Kingdom

British Museum, London.
- Cunningham, Admiral of the Fleet Sir Andrew.

Imperial War Museum, London.
- Morris, Major General E. L.

Liddell Hart Centre for Military Archives. Kings College, London.
- Brooke-Popham, Air Chief Marshal Sir Robert.
- Dill, Field Marshal Sir John.
- Ismay, General Lord Hastings.
- Pakenham-Walsh, Major General Ridley.
- Pownall, Lieutenant General Sir Henry R.

The National Archives. Public Records Office, London.
- Cadogan, Sir Alexander. Foreign Office, FO 800/293–294.
- Dill, Field Marshal Sir John G. War Office, WO 282.
- Halifax, Lord. Foreign Office, FO 800.
- Hankey, Sir Maurice. War Cabinet, CAB 63.
- Slessor, Marshal of the Royal Air Force Sir John. Air Ministry and Ministry of Aircraft Production, AVIA 75.

Royal Air Force Museum. Archives Collection, London.
- Dowding, Air Chief Marshal Sir Hugh.

Hill, Air Chief Marshal Roderick M.
Maltby, Air Vice Marshal Sir Paul.
Moore-Brabazon, Baron John T. C.
Newall, Marshal of the Royal Air Force Sir Cyril L. N.
Peirse, Air Chief Marshal Sir Richard.

United States

U.S. Army Military History Institute, Carlisle Barracks, Pa.
  Besson, Frank S.
  Bolte, Charles L.
  Case, Homer.
  Chynoweth, Bradford G.
  Clarke, Bruce C.
  Dahlquist, John.
  Donovan, William J.
  Grunert, George.
  Henry, Guy V., Jr.
  Hull, John E.
  Jaynes, Lawrence C.
  Lee, Raymond E.
  MacMorland, Edward E.
  Maxwell, Russell L.
  Robinett, Paul McD.
  Secretary of War Papers. Appointment Books, 1940–1945.
  Ward, Orlando W.
Franklin D. Roosevelt Library, Hyde Park, N.Y.
  Brown, Vice Admiral Wilson.
  Hopkins, Harry L.
  McCrea, Captain John L.
  Morgenthau, Henry J.
  Roosevelt, Franklin D.
    Map Room Files.
    Official Files.
    Official Papers as Assistant Secretary of the Navy, 1913–1920.
    President's Personal Files.
    President's Secretary's Files (includes Confidential File).
Naval History and Heritage Command (formerly U.S. Naval History Division and Naval Historical Center). Operational Archives Branch, Washington, D.C.
  Hart, Thomas C.
  King, Ernest J.
  Kirk, Alan G.
  Kittredge, Tracy B.
  Leahy, William D.

348 Selected Bibliography

Public Documents

United Kingdom

The National Archives of the United Kingdom. Public Records Office, London.
Admiralty Records. ADM 116. Record Office. Cases.
Admiralty Records. ADM 199. War History Cases and Papers, Second World War.
Air Ministry Records. AIR 8. Chief of the Air Staff.
Air Ministry Records. AIR 9. Director of Operations and Intelligence and Plans.
Air Ministry Records. AIR 19. Private Office Papers.
Air Ministry Records. AIR 45. RAF Delegation Washington.
Cabinet Office. CAB 21. Cabinet Registered Files.
Cabinet Office. CAB 23. War Cabinet and Cabinet. Minutes.
Cabinet Office. CAB 24. War Cabinet and Cabinet. Memoranda (GT, CP, and G War Series).
Cabinet Office. War Cabinet. CAB 44. Committee of Imperial Defence. Historical Section. Official War Histories. Draft Chapters and Narratives (Military).
Cabinet Office. War Cabinet. CAB 65. War Cabinet Minutes, WM and CM Series.
Cabinet Office. War Cabinet. CAB 66. War Cabinet Memoranda, WP and CP Series.
Cabinet Office. War Cabinet. CAB 67. War Cabinet Memoranda, WP (G) Series.
Cabinet Office. War Cabinet. CAB 68. War Cabinet Memoranda, WP (R) Series.
Cabinet Office. War Cabinet. CAB 69. War Cabinet Defense Committee (Operations). Minutes and Papers Series.
Cabinet Office. War Cabinet. CAB 78. Miscellaneous Committees. Minutes and Papers, MISC and GEN Series.
Cabinet Office. War Cabinet. CAB 79. Chiefs of Staff Committee. Minutes.
Cabinet Office. War Cabinet. CAB 80. Chiefs of Staff Committee. Memoranda.
Cabinet Office. War Cabinet. CAB 81. Committees and Sub-Committees of the Chiefs of Staff Committee. Minutes and Papers.
Cabinet Office. War Cabinet. CAB 82. Deputy Chiefs of Staff Committee and Sub-Committees. Minutes and Papers (DCOS and other series).
Cabinet Office. War Cabinet. CAB 83. War Cabinet Ministerial Committee on Military Coordination. Minutes and Papers. (MC Series.)
Cabinet Office. War Cabinet. CAB 84. War Cabinet Joint Planning Committees (later Joint Planning Staff) and Subcommittees. Minutes and Memoranda, JP, JAD, and other series.
Cabinet Office. War Cabinet. CAB 88. Combined Chiefs of Staff Committee and Sub-committees. Minutes and Memoranda, CCS and other series.
Cabinet Office. War Cabinet. CAB 92. Committees on Supply, Production, Priority, and Manpower. Minutes and Papers.
Cabinet Office. War Cabinet. CAB 94. War Cabinet Overseas Defence Committee. Minutes and Papers, ODC Series.
Cabinet Office. War Cabinet. CAB 96. Committees on the Far East, FE and FE (O) Series.
Cabinet Office. War Cabinet. CAB 98. Miscellaneous Committees. Minutes and Papers.

Cabinet Office. War Cabinet. CAB 99. Commonwealth and International Conferences.
Cabinet Office. War Cabinet. CAB 101. Historical Section. War Histories. Second World War (Military).
Cabinet Office. War Cabinet. CAB 104. Cabinet Offices and Predecessors. Supplementary Registered Files.
Cabinet Office. War Cabinet. CAB 105. Telegrams.
Cabinet Office. War Cabinet. CAB 110. Joint American Secretariat. Correspondence and Papers.
Cabinet Office. War Cabinet. CAB 120. Minister of Defence. Secretariat Files.
Cabinet Office. War Cabinet. CAB 122. British Joint Staff Mission and British Joint Services Mission, Washington Office. Records.
Cabinet Office. War Cabinet. CAB 127. Private Collections of Ministers' and Officials' Papers. General Ismay. Letters from Admiral Ghormley, June–August 1941.
Cabinet Office. War Cabinet. CAB 138. British Joint Staff Mission and British Joint Services Mission. Minutes and Memoranda. Air Ministry and Ministry of Aircraft Production. AVIA 10. Miscellaneous Unregistered Papers.
Foreign Office. FO 371. Political Departments. General Correspondence, 1906–1966.
Foreign Office. FO 414. Confidential Print. North America.
Foreign Office. FO 461. Confidential Print. America.
Ministry of Aircraft Production and Ministry of Supply. AVIA 9. Private Office Papers.
Ministry of Supply and Aircraft Production. AVIA 38. North American Supply Missions. Second World War. Files.
Prime Minister's Office. PREM 1. Correspondence and Papers.
Prime Minister's Office. PREM 3. Operational Correspondence and Papers.
Prime Minister's Office. PREM 4. Confidential Correspondence and Papers.
War Office. WO 32. Registered Files.
War Office. WO 33. Reports, Memoranda, and Papers, O and A Series.
War Office. WO 106. Directorate of Military Operations and Military Intelligence. Correspondence and Papers.
War Office. WO 163. War Office Council and Army Council Records. Minutes and Papers.
War Office. WO 178. War of 1939–1945. British Military Missions. War Diaries. Second World War.
War Office. WO 193. Director of Military Operations and Plans. Files Concerning Military Planning, Intelligence, and Statistics. Collation Files.
War Office. WO 202. British Military Missions in Liaison with Allied Forces. Military Headquarters Papers. Second World War.
War Office. WO 208. Director of Military Operations and Intelligence. Director of Intelligence Files.
War Office. WO 216. Office of the Chief of the Imperial General Staff. Papers, January 1941–June 1953.

350   Selected Bibliography

United States

National Archives and Records Administration, College Park, Md.
Record Group 18.
   Entry NM53 293. Central Decimal Files: Security Classified General Correspondence.
Record Group 38.
   Entry NM63. Office of the Chief of Naval Operations. Series 99. Secret Naval Attaché Reports, 1936–1943. Subseries 2. London.
   Record Group 38.2.4. Office of the Chief of Naval Operations. Records Relating to U.S. Navy Operations Received from the Operational Archives Branch, Naval Historical Center (now Naval History and Heritage Command).
   Commander, U.S. Naval Forces Europe, 1938–1947. Series I. Message Files. U.S. Naval Attaché, London, and Special Naval Observer, London.
   Records of Commander, U.S. Naval Forces Europe, 1938–1947. Series II. Subject Files.
   Strategic Plans Division. Series III. Miscellaneous Subject Files, 1917–1947. Canada-U.S. Permanent Joint Board on Defense (1941–1942).
   Strategic Plans Division. Series V. Subject Files, 1936–1947. Canada.
   Strategic Plans Division. Series VII. Records Relating to Anglo-American-Dutch Cooperation, 1938–1939.
   Strategic Plans Division. Series IX. Plans, Strategic Studies, and Related Correspondence, 1939–1946.
   Strategic Plans Division. Series XII. Records of the U.S. Naval Members, Permanent Joint Board on Defense, Canada–United States, 1940–1947.
Record Group 59. Diplomatic Branch. Records of Permanent Joint Board of Defense—U.S. and Canada.
Record Group 160.
   Entry NM25. Army Service Forces. Series 115. International Division. Historical Files, 1940–1946.
Record Group 165. War Department General and Special Staffs.
   Entry A1 65. Series 65. Security Classified Correspondence and Reports, 1917–1941 (Military Intelligence Division).
   Entry NM84 12. Subseries 12. Security Classified General Correspondence, 1920–1942. Chief of Staff.
   Entry NM84 15. Series 15. Top Secret General Correspondence, 1941–1947. Subseries 1, 1941–1943.
   Entry NM84 17. Series 17. Secretariat's Reading File, 1939–1942.
   Entry NM84 20. Series 20. Security Classified Cables and Correspondence with the White House, 1939–1946.
   Entry NM84 30. Series 30. Security Classified Conference Notes of the Secretary of the General Staff, 1938–1945.
   Entry NM84 31. Series 31. Army Chief of Staff. Secretariat. Notes on Conferences, 1941–1942.

Entry NM84 39. Series 39. Minutes of Conferences of Joint Chiefs of Staff and Combined Chiefs of Staff, and Transcripts of War Plans Testimony, 1937–1945.
Entry NM84 78. Series 78. Security Classified Correspondence Relating to Military Attachés, 1938–1948.
Entry NM84 210. Series 210. Security Classified General Correspondence (G-3), 1939–1942.
Entry NM84 281. Series 281. General Correspondence. War College and War Plans Division, 1920–1942.
Entry NM84 282. Series 282. War College and War Plans Division. Top Secret Correspondence Relating to Mobilization Plans, 1922–1942 (Color and Quickfire).
Entry NM84 284. Series 284. Security Classified Correspondence of the Joint Army–Navy Board, 1910–1942.
Entry NM84 310. Series 310. Records of the Historical Section Relating to the History of the War Department, 1900–1941.
Entry NM84 421. Series 421. Office of the Director of Plans and Operations, 1922–1948. Top Secret "American-British-Canadian" Correspondence Relating to Organization, Planning, and General Combat Operations during World War II and the Early Post-War Period, 1940–1948.
Entry NM84 422. Series 422. Office of the Director of Plans and Operations, 1922–1948. Top Secret General Correspondence Relating to the Location and Leasing of Atlantic Bases in British Possessions, Allied Military Conferences of World War II, and Plans for the Strategic Direction of Operations of Military Forces in Theaters of Operation, 1940–1945.
Record Group 179.
Entry PI 151. Records of the War Production Board.
Record Group 218.
Entry NM41. Records of the Joint and Combined Chiefs of Staff.
Record Group 225. Records of the Joint Army–Navy Board.
Entry NM43. Series 1. Joint Board. General Correspondence, 1903–1938.
Entry NM43. Series 5. Executive Committee. Security Classified General Correspondence, 1922–1945.
U.S. Army Military History Institute, Carlisle Barracks, Pa.
Allied Interoperability in the 20th Century Collection.
U.S. Army War College Curricular Files.
U.S. Army War College Name Files.
U.S. Army War College Subject Files.

Published Documents, Papers, and Speeches

Allied and Associated Powers. Military Board of Allied Supply. *Report.* 2 vols. Washington, D.C.: U.S. Government Printing Office, 1924.
Bland, Larry I., Sharon R. Ritenour, and Clarence E. Wunderlin Jr., eds. *The Papers of*

George Catlett Marshall. Vol. 2: *We Cannot Delay, July 1, 1939–December 6, 1941*. Baltimore: Johns Hopkins University Press, 1986.
Brooke-Popham, Air Chief Marshal Sir Robert. "Operations in the Far East from 17 October 1940 to 27 December 1941." *London Gazette*, 22 January 1948, supplement to the issue of 20 January 1948.
Churchill, Winston S. *Blood, Sweat, and Tears*. New York: Putnam's, 1941.
Documents on American Foreign Relations (1938–1941). New York: Council of Foreign Relations, 1939–1942.
French Ministère des affaires étrangères. Commission de publication des documents relatifs aux orignes de la guerre de 1914. *Documents diplomatique français (1871–1914)*. Paris: Imprimerie Nationale, 1931.
Gallup, George H. *The Gallup Poll, 1935–1971*. 3 vols. New York: Random House, 1972.
Gilbert, Martin, ed. *The Churchill War Papers*. Vol. 1: *At the Admiralty, September 1939–May 1940*. New York: Norton, 1993.
———. *The Churchill War Papers*. Vol. 2: *Never Surrender: May 1940 to December 1940*. New York: Norton, 1995.
———. *The Churchill War Papers*. Vol. 3: *Ever-Widening War*. New York: Norton, 2001.
Hachey, T. E., ed. *Confidential Dispatches: Analysis of America by the British Ambassador, 1939–1945*. Chicago: Northwestern University Press, 1974.
Kimball, Warren F. *Churchill and Roosevelt: Their Complete Correspondence*. Vol. 3: *Alliance Emerging: October 1933–November 1942*. Princeton, N.J.: Princeton University Press, 1984.
Lowenheim, Francis, Harold D. Langley, and Manfred Jonas, eds. *Roosevelt and Churchill: Their Secret Wartime Correspondence*. New York: Saturday Review Press, 1975.
Nicholas, H. G. *Washington Dispatches, 1941–1945: Weekly Political Reports from the British Embassy*. With an introduction by Isaiah Berlin. London: Weidenfeld and Nicolson; Chicago: University of Chicago Press, 1981.
The Reports of General MacArthur. Vol. 1: *The Campaigns of MacArthur in the Pacific*. Prepared by his staff. 1966. Reprint. Washington, D.C.: U.S. Army Center of Military History, 1994.
The Reports of General MacArthur. Vol. 2: *Japanese Operations in the Southwest Pacific Area*. Prepared by his staff. 1966. Reprint. Washington, D.C.: U.S. Army Center of Military History, 1994.
Schewe, Donald B., ed. *Franklin D. Roosevelt and Foreign Affairs*. 16 vols. New York: Clearwater, 1979.
Schlesinger, Arthur M., Jr., and Roger Bruns. *Congress Investigates: A Documented History, 1792–1974*. New York: Chelsea House, 1975.
Simpson, Michael, ed. *Anglo-American Naval Relations, 1917–1919*. Brookfield, Vt.: Gower, 1991.
U.K. Cabinet Office. *Cabinet Minutes and Memoranda, 1916–1939*. Microfilm, 256 reels. Millwood, N.Y.: KTO, 1978.

Selected Bibliography   353

———. *Cabinet Office List of War Cabinet Memoranda, September 1939–July 1945.* London: Swift Printers, 1977.
U.K. Foreign Office. *British Documents on the Origins of the War, 1898–1914.* 11 vols. Edited by George P. Gooch and Harold Temperly. London: His Majesty's Stationery Office, 1926–1938.
———. *Documents on British Foreign Policy, 1919–1939.* Edited by Sir E. L. Woodward and Rohan Butler. London: Her Majesty's Stationery Office, 1946–1961.
U.K. House of Commons. *Correspondence with the Belgian and French Ambassadors Relating to "Text of Proposals Drawn Up by the Representatives of Belgium, France, United Kingdom of Britain and Northern Ireland, and Italy." London, 19 March 1936. CMD 5134.* Command Paper 5149, Miscellaneous no. 4. London: His Majesty's Stationery Office, 1 April 1936. In *Sessional Papers, 1935/1936,* 28:57–62.
———. *Text of Proposals Drawn Up by the Representatives of Belgium, France, United Kingdom of Great Britain and Northern Ireland, and Italy.* Command Paper 5134. London: His Majesty's Stationery Office, 19 March 1936. In *Sessional Papers, 1935/1936,* 28:49–56.
U.S. Armed Forces Staff College. *Organizations and Command Relationship during World War II.* Norfolk, Va.: U.S. Armed Forces Staff College, 17 December 1951.
U.S. Civilian Production Administration. *Industrial Mobilization for War: History of the War Production Board and Predecessor Agencies, 1940–1945.* Vol. 1: *Program and Administration.* Washington, D.C.: U.S. Government Printing Office, 1947.
U.S. Congress. Joint Committee on the Investigation of the Pearl Harbor Attack. *Pearl Harbor Attack: Hearings of the Joint Committee on the Investigation of the Pearl Harbor Attack.* 79th Cong., 1st sess. 39 vols. Washington, D.C.: U.S. Government Printing Office, 1946.
U.S. Department of Defense. Joint Chiefs of Staff (JCS). *Department of Defense Dictionary of Military and Associated Terms.* JCS Publication 1-02. Washington, D.C.: JCS, 8 November 2010. At http://www.dtic.mil/doctrine/new_pubs/jp1_02.pdf.
U.S. Department of the Navy. Office of Naval Records and Library, Historical Section. *The American Planning Section, London.* Washington, D.C.: U.S. Government Printing Office, 1923.
U.S. Department of State. *Papers Relating to the Foreign Relations of the United States, 1917–1918.* 9 vols., with supplements. Washington, D.C.: U.S. Government Printing Office, 1926–1933.
———. *Peace and War: United States Foreign Policy, 1931–1941.* Washington, D.C.: U.S. Government Printing Office, 1943.
———. Office of the Historian. *Milestones, 1921–1936: The Geneva Naval Conference, 1927.* At http://history.state.gov/milestones/1921–1936/Geneva.
———. Office of the Historian. *Milestones, 1921–1936: The London Naval Conference, 1930.* At http://history.state.gove/milestones/1921–1936/LondonNavalConf.
———. *Milestones, 1921–1936: The Neutrality Acts, 1930s.* At http://history.state.gov/milestones/1921–1936/Neutrality_act.
U.S. Information Service. Office of Government Reports. *National Defense and Neu-*

trality Documents, 1 July 1939–1 July 1941. Washington, D.C.: U.S. Information Service, 1941.

U.S. War Department. *Final Report of the Commander-in-Chief American Expeditionary Force.* Washington, D.C.: U.S. Government Printing Office, 1919.

———. *Order of Battle of the United States Land Forces in the World War.* 3 vols. Washington, D.C.: U.S. Government Printing Office, 1931–1949. Also available in CD-ROM, CMH EM 0023. Washington, D.C.: U.S. Army Center of Military History, 1998.

———. Historical Division. Department of the Army. *United States Army in the World War, 1917–1919.* 17 vols. Washington, D.C.: U.S. Government Printing Office, 1948. Also available in CD-ROM, CMH EM 0023. Washington, D.C.: U.S. Army Center of Military History, 1998.

The War Reports of General of the Army George C. Marshall, General of the Army H. H. Arnold, and Fleet Admiral Ernest J. King. With a foreword and descriptive notes by Walter Millis. New York: Lippincott, 1947.

Woodward, E. L., and Rohan Butler, eds. *Documents on British Foreign Policy.* London: His Majesty's Stationery Office, 1946.

Oral Histories

Austin, Vice-Admiral Bernard L. "Reminiscences of Vice Admiral Bernard L. Austin." 1971. U.S. Naval Institute Oral History Collection, Operational Archives Branch, U.S. Naval History Division (now Naval History and Heritage Command), Office of the Chief of Naval Operations, Washington, D.C.

Bolte, General Charles L. Interviews by Dr. Maclyn Burg, 1973–1975, and Arthur A. Zoebelem, 1972. Oral History Collection, U.S. Army Military History Institute, Carlisle Barracks, Pa.

Clarke, General Bruce C. Interview by Paul K. Walker, 1977. Oral History Collection. U.S. Army Military History Institute, Carlisle Barracks, Pa.

Eaker, General Ira C. Interviews by Lieutenant Colonel Joe Green, 1972. Oral History Collection, U.S. Army Military History Institute, Carlisle Barracks, Pa.

Handy, General Thomas T. Interviews by Lieutenant Colonel Edward M. Kroff, 1974. Oral History Collection. U.S. Army Military History Institute, Carlisle Barracks, Pa.

Hart, Admiral Thomas C. "Reminiscences." 1962. Columbia University Oral History Project. Operational Archives Branch, Naval History Division (now Naval History and Heritage Command), Office of the Chief of Naval Operations, Washington, D.C.

Hull, General John E. Interviews by Lieutenant Colonel James W. Wurman, 1974. Oral History Collection. U.S. Army Military History Institute, Carlisle Barracks, Pa.

Ingersoll, Admiral Royal E. "The Reminiscences of Adm. Royal E. Ingersoll." 1965. Columbia University Oral History Project. Operational Archives Branch, Naval History Division (now Naval History and Heritage Command), Office of the Chief of Naval Operations, Washington, D.C.

Selected Bibliography   355

Kirk, Admiral Alan G. "Reminiscences of Vice Adm. Alan G. Kirk." 1962. Columbia University Oral History Project. Operational Archives Branch, Naval History Division (now Naval History and Heritage Command), Office of the Chief of Naval Operations, Washington, D.C.

MacMorland, Major General Edward E. Interviews by Lieutenant Colonel Richard F. Plechner, 1977. Oral History Collection. U.S. Army Military History Institute, Carlisle Barracks, Pa.

Quesada, Lieutenant General Elwood R. Interviews by Lieutenant Colonel Steve Long and Lieutenant Colonel Ralph Stevenson, 1975. Oral History Collection, U.S. Army Military History Institute, Carlisle Barracks, Pa.

Wedemeyer, General Albert C. Interviews by Colonel Anthony S. Deskis, 1972. Oral History Collection, U.S. Army Military History Institute, Carlisle Barracks, Pa.

Published Diaries, Memoirs, Personal Accounts

Alanbrooke, Field Marshal Lord. *War Diaries, 1939–1945.* Edited by Alex Danchev and Daniel Todman. Berkeley: University of California Press, 2001.

Arnold, Henry H. *Global Mission.* New York: Harper and Brothers, 1949.

Bliss, Tasker. "The Evolution of the Unified Command." *Foreign Affairs* 1 (15 December 1922): 1–30.

Blum, John M. *From the Morgenthau Diaries.* Vol. 1: *Years of Crisis, 1928–1938.* Boston: Houghton Mifflin, 1959.

———. *From the Morgenthau Diaries.* Vol. 2: *Years of Urgency, 1938–1941.* Boston: Houghton Mifflin, 1965.

Brereton, Lewis H. *The Brereton Diaries: The War in the Air in the Pacific, Middle East, and Europe, 3 October 1941–8 May 1945.* New York: Morrow, 1946.

Bullitt, Orville, ed. *For the President: Personal and Secret Correspondence of Roosevelt and William C. Bullitt.* New York: Houghton Mifflin, 1972.

Cadogan, Alexander. *The Diaries of Sir Alexander Cadogan.* Edited by David Dilks. New York: Putnam's, 1972.

Charteris, John. *At G. H. Q.* London: Cassell, 1931.

Churchill, Winston S. *The Second World War.* 6 vols. Boston: Houghton Mifflin, 1948–1953.

———. *The World Crisis.* 4 vols. New York: Scribner's, 1923–1929.

Chynoweth, Bradford G. *Bellamy Park: Memoirs.* Hicksville, N.Y.: Exposition Press, 1975.

Colville, Sir John. *The Fringes of Power: 10 Downing Street Diaries, 1939–1955.* New York: Norton, 1985.

Danchev, Alex, ed. *Establishing the Anglo-American Alliance: The Second World War Diaries of Brigadier Vivian Dykes.* London: Brassey's, 1990.

Daniels, Josephus. *The Wilson Era: Years of War and After, 1917–1923.* Westport, Conn.: Greenwood Press, 1974.

Eden, Anthony. *The Memoirs of Anthony Eden, Lord Avon.* Vol. 1: *Full Circle.* Boston: Houghton Mifflin, 1960.

———. *The Memoirs of Anthony Eden, Lord Avon*. Vol. 2: *Facing the Dictators, 1923–1938*. Boston: Houghton Mifflin, 1962.

———. *The Memoirs of Anthony Eden, Lord Avon*. Vol. 3: *The Reckoning*. Boston: Houghton Mifflin, 1965.

Foch, Ferdinand. *The Memoirs of Marshal Foch*. Translated by Colonel T. Bentley Mott. Garden City, N.Y.: Doubleday, Doran, 1931.

Grant, Ulysses S., III. "America's Part in the Supreme War Council." *Records of the Columbia Historical Society* 29 (1928): 295–340.

Guderian, Heinz. *Panzer Leader*. Translated by Constantine Fitzgibbon. Cambridge, Mass.: Da Capo Press, 1996.

Haig, Douglas. *The Private Papers of Douglas Haig, 1914–1919*. Edited by Robert Blake. London: Eyre and Spottiswoode, 1952.

Halifax, Lord. *Fullness of Days*. New York: Dodd, Mead, 1957.

Hankey, Maurice. *Diplomacy by Conference*. New York: Putnam's, 1946.

———. "The Origin and Development of the Committee of Imperial Defence." *Army Quarterly*, July 1927, 254–273.

———. *The Supreme Command, 1914–1918*. 2 vols. London: Allen and Unwin, 1961.

Harbord, James G. *The American Army in France, 1917–1919*. Boston: Little, Brown, 1936.

Harriman, Averill, and Elie Abel. *Special Envoy to Churchill and Stalin, 1941–1946*. New York: Random House, 1976.

Harvey, Oliver. *The Diplomatic Diaries of Oliver Harvey, 1937–1940*. New York: St. Martin's Press, 1970.

Hawes, L. A. "The Story of the 'W' Plan: The Move of Our Forces to France in 1939." *Army Quarterly and Defense Journal* 101 (July 1971): 445–456.

Hollis, Leslie. *One Marine's Tale*. London: Andre Deutsch, 1956.

Huguet, Victor. *Britain and the War: A French Indictment*. Translated by Captain H. Cotton Minchin. London: Cassell, 1928.

Hull, Cordell. *The Memoirs of Cordell Hull*. 2 vols. New York: MacMillan, 1958.

Ismay, Lord Hastings. *The Memoirs of General, the Lord, Ismay*. London: William Heinemann, 1960.

Johnson, Hagood. *The Services of Supply: A Memoir of the Great War*. Boston: Houghton Mifflin, 1927.

Kennedy, John M. *The Business of War: The War Narrative of Major General Sir John Kennedy*. Edited by Bernard Fergusson. London: Hutchinson, 1957.

Kessler, Harry. *Berlin Lights: The Diaries of Count Harry Kessler*. Translated and edited by Charles Kessler. New York: Grove Press, 2000.

King, Ernest J., with Walter Muir. *Fleet Admiral King: A Naval Record*. New York: Norton, 1952.

Leahy, William D. *I Was There: The Memoirs of FDR's Chief of Staff*. New York: Whittlesley House, 1950.

Leasor, James. *The Clock with Four Hands: Based on the Experiences of General Sir Leslie Hollis*. New York: Reynal, 1959.

Lee, Raymond E. *The London Journal of General Raymond E. Lee, 1940–1941.* Edited by James R. Leutze. Boston: Little, Brown, 1971.
Lloyd George, David. *War Memoirs.* 6 vols. London: Nicolson and Watson, 1933–1936.
Long, Breckenridge. *The War Diaries of Breckenridge Long: Selections from the Years 1939–1944.* Selected and edited by Fred L. Israel. Lincoln: University of Nebraska Press, 1966.
MacVeagh, Ewen Cameron, and Lee D. Brown. *The Yankees in the British Zone.* New York: Putnam, 1920.
Manstein, Erich von. *Lost Victories.* St. Paul, Minn.: Zenith Press, 2004.
Maurice, Sir Frederick B. *Lessons of Allied Cooperation: Naval, Military, and Air, 1914–1918.* London: Oxford University Press, 1942.
Monnet, Jean. *Memoirs.* Translated by Richard Moyne. New York: Doubleday, 1978.
Murphy, Robert. *Diplomat among Warriors.* Garden City, N.Y.: Doubleday, 1964.
Murray, Arthur W., Lord Elibank. "Franklin Roosevelt: Friend of Britain." *Contemporary Review,* June 1955, 362–368.
Nelson, Donald. *Arsenal of Democracy: The Story of American War Production.* New York: Harcourt, 1946.
Pawle, Gerald. *The War and Colonel Warden: Based on the Recollections of Commander C. R. Thompson, Personal Assistant to the Prime Minister, 1940–1945.* New York: Knopf, 1963.
Pershing, John J. *My Experiences in the World War.* 2 vols. Military Classics series. 1931. Reprint. Blue Ridge Summit, Pa.: TAB Books, 1989.
Pownall, Sir Henry. *Chief of Staff: The Diaries of Lieutenant General Sir Henry Pownall.* 2 vols. Edited by Brian Bond. Hamden, Conn.: Archon Books, 1973.
Repington, Charles à Court. *The First World War, 1914–1918.* 2 vols. Boston: Houghton Mifflin, 1920.
Richardson, Admiral James O. *On the Treadmill to Pearl Harbor: The Memoirs of Admiral J. O. Richardson.* Edited by Admiral George C. Dyer. 2 vols. Washington, D.C.: U.S. Government Printing Office, 1973.
Robertson, Sir William. *From Private to Field Marshal.* London: Constable, 1921.
———. *Soldiers and Statesmen, 1914–1918.* 2 vols. London: Cassel, 1926.
Sims, Admiral William S., with Burton J. Hendrick. *The Victory at Sea.* Introduction by David F. Trask. 1920. Reprint. Annapolis, Md.: Naval Institute Press, 1984.
Slessor, Sir John. *The Central Blue: The Autobiography of Sir John Slessor, Marshal of the RAF.* New York: Praeger, 1957.
Spears, Sir Edward. *Liaison, 1914.* London: Heinemann, 1940.
———. *The Picnic Basket.* London: Seeker and Warburg, 1967.
———. *Prelude to Victory.* London: Cape, 1939.
Stettinius, Edward R., Jr. *Lend-Lease: Weapon for Victory.* New York: MacMillan, 1944.
Still, William N., Jr., ed. *The Queenstown Patrol, 1917: The Diary of Commander Joseph Kneffer Taussig, U.S. Navy.* Newport, R.I.: Naval War College Press, 1996.
Stimson, Henry L., and McGeorge Bundy. *On Active Service in Peace and War.* New York: Octagon Books, 1971.

Wedemeyer, Albert C. *Wedemeyer Reports!* New York: Holt, 1958.
Welles, Sumner. *The Time for Decisions.* New York: Harpers, 1944.
Winant, John G. *Letters from Grosvenor Square.* Boston: Houghton Mifflin, 1947.
Wright, Peter E. *At the Supreme War Council.* New York: Putnam, 1921.

Secondary Sources

Official Histories

Australia

Long, Gavin. *The Six Years War: A Concise History of Australia in the 1939–1945 War.* Canberra: Australian War Memorial, 1973.

New Zealand

Gillespie, Oliver A. *The Pacific Official History of New Zealand in the Second World War.* Wellington: War History Branch, New Zealand Department of Internal Affairs, 1952.

United Kingdom

Butler, James R. M. *Grand Strategy.* Vol. 2: *September 1939–June 1941.* In *History of the Second World War: United Kingdom Military Series.* London: Her Majesty's Stationery Office, 1957.

Butler, James R. M., and J. M. A. Gwyer. *Grand Strategy.* Vol. 3: *June 1941–August 1942.* In *History of the Second World War: United Kingdom Military Series.* London: Her Majesty's Stationery Office, 1964.

Edmonds, Sir John E. *Military Operations in France and Belgium, 1914–1918.* 14 vols. London: MacMillan, 1922–1940; London: His Majesty's Stationery Office, 1922–1949.

Ellis, Lionel F. *The War in France and Flanders, 1939–1940.* In *History of the Second World War: United Kingdom Military Series.* London: Her Majesty's Stationery Office, 1953. Also available at http://www.ibiblio.org/hyperwar/UN/UK/UK-NWE-Flanders/UK-NWE-Flanders-1.html.

Falls, Cyril. *Military Operations: France and Belgium, 1917.* 3 vols. London: His Majesty's Stationery Office, 1948.

Gibbs, Norman H. *Grand Strategy.* Vol. 1: *Rearmament Policy.* In *History of the Second World War: United Kingdom Military Series.* Edinburgh: Her Majesty's Stationery Office, 1976.

Hall, H. Duncan. *North American Supply.* In *History of the Second World War: United Kingdom Civil Series.* London: Her Majesty's Stationery Office, 1955.

Hall, H. Duncan, and C. G. Wrigley. *Studies of Overseas Supply.* In *History of the Second World War: United Kingdom Civil Series.* London: Her Majesty's Stationery Office and Longman's, Green, 1952.

Hancock, William K., and H. M. Gowing. *British War Economy.* In *History of the Second World War: United Kingdom Civil Series.* London: His Majesty's Stationery Office, 1949.

Hinsley, F. H. *British Intelligence in the Second World War: Its Influence on Strategy and Operations.* 4 vols. In *History of the Second World War: United Kingdom Military Series.* New York: Cambridge University Press, 1979–1990.
Kirby, Major General Woodburn. *The War against Japan: The Loss of Singapore.* In *History of the Second World War: United Kingdom Military Series.* London: Her Majesty's Stationery Office, 1957.
Playfair, I. S. O. *The Mediterranean and the Middle East.* Vol. 1: *The Early Successes against Italy (to May 1941).* In *History of the Second World War: United Kingdom Military Series.* London: Her Majesty's Stationery Office, 1974.
———. *The Mediterranean and the Middle East.* Vol. 2: *The Germans Come to the Help of Their Ally (1941).* In *History of the Second World War: United Kingdom Military Series.* London: Her Majesty's Stationery Office, 1974.
Postan, Michael M. *British War Production.* In *History of the Second World War: United Kingdom Civil Series.* London: Her Majesty's Stationery Office, 1952.
Richards, Denis. *Royal Air Force, 1939–1945.* Vol. 1: *The Fight at Odds.* In *History of the Second World War: United Kingdom Military Series.* London: Her Majesty's Stationery Office, 1953.
Roskill, Stephen W. *The War at Sea, 1939–1945.* 3 vols. In *History of the Second World War: United Kingdom Military Series.* London: Her Majesty's Stationery Office, 1954–1956.
Webster, Charles K., and Noble Frankland. *The Strategic Air Offensive against Germany, 1939–1945.* Vol. 1: *The Preparation.* In *History of the Second World War: United Kingdom Military Series.* London: Her Majesty's Stationery Office, 1961.
Woodward, Sir E. L. *British Foreign Policy in the Second World War.* 4 vols. In *History of the Second World War: United Kingdom Civil Series.* London: Her Majesty's Stationery Office, 1962–1970.

United States

Claussen, Martin. *Distribution of Air Material to the Allies, 1939–1944.* Army Air Force Historical Study no. 106. [Washington, D.C.]: Assistant Chief of Air Staff, Intelligence Historical Division, July 1944.
Cline, Ray S. *Washington Command Post: The Operations Division.* In *United States Army in World War II: The War Department.* Washington, D.C.: Office of the Chief of Military History, 1951.
Conn, Stetson, Rose C. Engelman, and Byron Fairchild. *Guarding the United States and Its Outposts.* In *United States Army in World War II: The Western Hemisphere.* Washington, D.C.: Office of the Chief of Military History, 1964.
Conn, Stetson, and Byron Fairchild. *The Framework of Hemisphere Defense.* In *United States Army in World War II: The Western Hemisphere.* Washington, D.C.: Office of the Chief of Military History, 1960.
Craven, Wesley F., and James L. Cate, eds. *The Army Air Forces in World War II.* Vol. 1: *Plans and Early Operations, January 1939 to August 1942.* Chicago: University of Chicago Press, 1948.

Davis, Vernon. *The History of the Joint Chiefs of Staff in World War II: Organization and Development*. Vol. 1: *Origin of the Joint and Combined Chiefs of Staff*. Washington, D.C.: Historical Division, U.S. Joint Chiefs of Staff, 1972.

———. *The History of the Joint Chiefs of Staff in World War II: Organization and Development*. Vol. 2: *Development of the JCS Committee Structure*. Washington, D.C.: Historical Division, U.S. Joint Chiefs of Staff, 1972.

Greenfield, Kent R., ed. *Command Decisions*. 1960. Reprint. Washington, D.C.: U.S. Government Printing Office, 1971.

Hayes, Grace P. *The History of the Joint Chiefs of Staff in World War II: The War against Japan*. Annapolis, Md.: Naval Institute Press, 1981.

Hewes, James E., Jr. *From Root to McNamara: Army Organization and Administration, 1900–1963*. U.S. Army Center of Military History, Special Studies. Washington, D.C.: U.S. Government Printing Office, 1975.

Holley, I. B., Jr. *Buying Aircraft: Material Procurement for the Army Air Forces*. In *United States Army in World War II: Special Studies*. U.S. Army Center of Military History Special Studies. Washington, D.C.: U.S. Government Printing Office, 1964.

Kirkpatrick, Charles E. *An Unknown Future and a Doubtful Present: Writing the Victory Program of 1941*. Washington, D.C.: U.S. Army Center of Military History, 1990.

Kreidberg, Marvin A., and Merton G. Henry. *History of Military Mobilization in the United States Army, 1775–1945*. Washington, D.C.: U.S. Army Center of Military History, 1989.

Leighton, Richard M., and Robert W. Coakley. *Global Logistics and Strategy, 1941–1945*. 2 vols. In *United States Army in World War II: The War Department*. 1955, 1968. Reprint. Washington, D.C.: U.S. Government Printing Office, 1984.

Matloff, Maurice, and Edwin M. Snell. *Strategic Planning for Coalition Warfare, 1941–1942*. In *United States Army in World War II: The War Department*. Washington, D.C.: U.S. Government Printing Office, 1953.

Morison, Samuel E. *The History of United States Naval Operations in World War II*. 15 vols. Boston: Little, Brown, 1947–1962.

———. *The History of United States Naval Operations in World War II*. Vol. 1: *The Battle of the Atlantic, September 1939–May 1943*. Boston: Little, Brown, 1947.

———. *The History of United States Naval Operations in World War II*. Vol. 3: *The Rising Sun in the Pacific, 1931–April 1942*. Boston: Little, Brown, 1948.

Morton, Louis. *Strategy and Command: The First Two Years*. In *United States Army in World War II: The War in the Pacific*. Washington, D.C.: Office of the Chief of Military History, 1962.

Pogue, Forrest C. *The Supreme Command*. In *United States Army in World War II: European Theater of Operations*. 1954. Reprint. Washington, D.C.: Office of the Chief of Military History, 1978.

Ruppenthal, Roland. *Logistical Support of the Armies*. 2 vols. In *United States Army in World War II: The European Theater of Operations*. Washington, D.C.: U.S. Government Printing Office, 1953.

Watson, Mark S. *Chief of Staff: Prewar Plans and Preparation*. In *United States Army in World War II: The War Department*. Washington, D.C.: Historical Division, U.S. Department of the Army, 1950.

Books and Articles

Abbazia, Patrick. *Mr. Roosevelt's Navy: The Private War of the U.S. Atlantic Fleet, 1939–1942*. Annapolis, Md.: Naval Institute Press, 1975.

Adams, Henry H. *Witness to Power: The Life of Fleet Admiral William D. Leahy*. Annapolis, Md.: Naval Institute Press, 1985.

Adler, Selig. *The Uncertain Giant, 1921–1941: American Foreign Policy between the Wars*. New York: MacMillan, 1965.

Agnew, James B. "Coalition Warfare: A Successful Experiment in Combined Command." *Parameters*, Spring 1971, 50–64.

Aikman, Duncan. *The All-American Front*. Garden City, N.Y.: Doubleday, Doran, 1941.

Aldrich, Richard J. *Intelligence and the War against Japan: Britain, America, and the Politics of Secret Service*. Cambridge: Cambridge University Press, 2000.

Alexander, Martin S., ed. *Knowing Your Friends: Intelligence inside Alliances and Coalitions from 1914 to the Cold War*. London: Taylor and Francis, 1998.

Alexander, Martin S., and William J. Philpott, eds. *Anglo-French Defence Relations between the Wars*. New York: Palgrave MacMillan, 2002.

———. "The Entente Cordiale and the Next War: Anglo-French Views on the Future of Military Cooperation, 1928–1939." In Martin S. Alexander, ed., *Knowing Your Friends: Intelligence inside Alliances and Coalitions from 1914 to the Cold War*, 53–84. London: Taylor and Francis, 1998.

———. "Introduction: Choppy Channel Waters." In Martin S. Alexander and William J. Philpott, eds., *Anglo-French Defence Relations between the Wars*, 1–25. New York: Palgrave MacMillan, 2002.

Allard, Dean C. "Admiral William S. Sims and United States Naval Policy in World War I." *American Neptune*, April 1975, 97–110.

———. "Anglo-American Naval Differences during World War I." *Military Affairs*, April 1980, 75–81.

Alldrith, Keith. *The Greatest of Friends: Franklin D. Roosevelt and Winston Churchill, 1941–1945*. New York: St. Martin's Press, 1995.

Ambrose, Stephen. "Applied Strategy of World War II." *Naval War College Review* 22 (May 1970): 62–70.

———. "Grand Strategy in World War II." *Naval War College Review* 22 (April 1970): 20–28.

Ancell, R. Manning, with Christine M. Miller. *The Biographical Dictionary of World War II Generals and Flag Officers: The U.S. Armed Forces*. Westport, Conn.: Greenwood Press, 1996.

Arnold, James, and Robert Hargis. *U.S. Commanders of World War II : Army and USAAF*. Oxford: Osprey, 2002.

Arnold, James, and Starr Sinton. *U.S. Commanders of World War II : Navy and USMC.* Oxford: Osprey, 2002.

Ash, Bernard. *The Lost Dictator: A Biography of Field Marshal Sir Henry Wilson.* London: Cassell, 1968.

Association of Graduates, U.S. Military Academy. *The Register of Graduates and Former Cadets of the United States Military Academy at West Point, New York, 2010.* West Point, N.Y.: Association of Graduates, 2010.

Aylwin-Foster, Brigadier Nigel. "Changing the Army for Counterinsurgency Operations." *Military Review* 85, no. 6 (November–December 2005): 2–15.

Bailey, Thomas A., and Paul B. Ryan. *Hitler vs. Roosevelt: The Undeclared Naval War.* New York: Free Press, 1979.

Ball, Desmond, ed. *Strategy and Defence: Australian Essays.* Boston: Allen and Unwin, 1982.

Baptiste, Fitzroy A. *War, Cooperation, and Conflict: The European Possessions in the Caribbean, 1939–1945.* New York: Greenwood Press, 1988.

Barclay, Glen St. J. "Australia Looks to America: The Wartime Relationship, 1939–1942." *Pacific Historical Review* 46 (1977): 251–277.

———. "Singapore Strategy: The Role of the United States in Imperial Defense." *Military Affairs* 39 (April 1975): 54–59.

Barker, Elizabeth. *Churchill and Eden at War.* New York: St. Martin's Press, 1978.

Barnett, Correlli. *Britain and Her Army, 1509–1970.* New York: Morrow, 1970.

———. *The Desert Generals.* Bloomington: Indiana University Press, 1982.

Barr, Niall. "The British Army and Anglo-American Relations in the Second World War." In Keith Neilson and Greg Kennedy, eds., *The British Way in Warfare: Power and the International System,* 179–196. Burlington, Vt.: Ashgate, 2010.

Barron, Gloria J. *Leadership in Crisis: FDR and the Path to Intervention.* Port Washington, N.Y.: Kennikat Press, 1973.

Bartlett, Merrill, and Robert W. Love. "Anglo-American Naval Diplomacy and the British Pacific Fleet, 1942–1945." *American Neptune,* July 1982, 203–216.

Baylis, John. *Anglo-American Defence Relations, 1939–1984: The Special Relationship.* London: St. Martin's Press, 1984.

Beals, Carlton. *The Coming Struggle for Latin America.* Philadelphia: Lippincott, 1938.

Beard, Charles A. *American Foreign Policy, 1932–1940.* New Haven, Conn.: Yale University Press, 1946.

Beasly, Patrick. *Very Special Intelligence: The Story of the Admiralty's Operational Intelligence Center, 1939–1945.* Garden City, N.Y.: Doubleday, 1978.

Beaver, Daniel R. *Newton D. Baker and the American War Effort, 1917–1919.* Lincoln: University of Nebraska Press, 1966.

Beckett, Ian, and John Gooch, eds. *Politicians and Defence: Studies in the Formulation of British Defence Policy, 1845–1970.* Manchester: Manchester University Press, 1981.

Beitzel, Robert. *The Uneasy Alliance: America, Britain, and Russia, 1941–1943.* New York: Knopf, 1973.

Bell, Christopher M. *Churchill and Sea Power.* Oxford: Oxford University Press, 2013.
Bell, R. J. *Unequal Allies: Australian-American Relations and the Pacific War.* Carlton, Australia: Melbourne University Press, 1977.
Ben-Zvi, Abraham. *Illusion of Deterrence: The Roosevelt Presidency and the Origins of the Pacific War.* Boulder, Colo.: Westview Press, 1987.
Birkenhead, Lord Frederick. *Halifax.* Boston: Houghton Mifflin, 1966.
Black, Conrad. *Franklin Delano Roosevelt: Champion of Freedom.* New York: Public Affairs, 2003.
Blum, J. M. *Roosevelt and Morgenthau.* Boston: Houghton Mifflin, 1970.
Boatner, Mark M., III. *The Biographical Dictionary of World War II.* Novato, Calif.: Presidio Press, 1996.
Boll, Michael M. *National Security Planning: Roosevelt through Reagan.* Lexington: University Press of Kentucky, 1988.
Bond, Brian. *Britain, France, and Belgium, 1939–1940.* 1975. Reprint. London: Brassey's, 1990.
———. *British Military Policy between the Wars.* Oxford: Oxford University Press, 1980.
———. *The Victorian Army and the Staff College, 1854–1914.* London: Methuen, 1972.
Borg, Dorothy. *The United States and the Far Eastern Crisis of 1933–1938.* Cambridge, Mass.: Harvard University Press, 1964.
Borneman, Walter R. *The Admirals: Nimitz, Halsey, Leahy, and King—the Five-Star Admirals Who Won World War II.* New York: Back Bay Books, 2012.
Bradford, James C., ed. *Admirals of the New Steel Navy: Makers of the American Naval Tradition, 1880–1930.* Annapolis, Md.: Naval Institute Press, 1990.
———. "Henry T. Mayo: Last of the Independent Naval Diplomats." In James C. Bradford, ed., *Admirals of the New Steel Navy: Makers of the American Naval Tradition, 1880–1930,* 253–281. Annapolis, Md.: Naval Institute Press, 1990.
Braisted, William R. *The United States Navy in the Pacific, 1909–1922.* Austin: University of Texas Press, 1971.
Bridge, C. "R. G. Casey, Australia's First Washington Legation, and the Origins of the Pacific War, 1940–1942." *Australian Journal of Politics and History* 28 (November 1982): 181–189.
Brinkley, Douglas, and Clifford Hackett, eds. *Jean Monnet: The Path to European Unity.* New York: St. Martin's Press, 1991.
British Security Coordination. *British Security Coordination: The Secret History of British Intelligence in the Americas, 1940–1945.* New York: Fromm International, 1998.
Brodhurst, Robin. *Churchill's Anchor: A Biography of Admiral of the Fleet Sir Dudley Pound.* Barnsley, U.K.: Pen & Sword, 2000.
Bruce, Robert B. *A Fraternity of Arms: America and France in the Great War.* Lawrence: University Press of Kansas, 2003.
Bryant, Sir Arthur. *The Turn of the Tide: A History of the War Years Based on the Diaries of Field Marshal Lord Alanbrooke, Chief of the Imperial General Staff.* Garden City, N.Y.: Doubleday, 1957.

Buchanan, Albert R. *The United States and World War II*. New York: Harper, 1964.
Buckley, Thomas H. *The United States and the Washington Naval Conference, 1921–1922*. Knoxville: University of Tennessee Press, 1970.
Buell, Thomas B. *Master of Seapower: A Biography of Fleet Admiral Ernest J. King*. Boston: Little, Brown, 1980.
Burne, Lieutenant Colonel Alfred H. "Global Strategy and the Pacific War." *Marine Corps Gazette* 32 (April 1948): 20–25.
———. "Japanese and American Strategy in the Pacific." *Royal United Services Institute Journal* 93 (August 1948): 417–420.
Burns, James MacGregor. *Roosevelt: Soldier of Freedom*. New York: Harcourt, Brace, Jovanovich, 1970.
Callwell, C. E., ed. *Field Marshal Sir Henry Wilson*. 2 vols. London: Cassell, 1927.
Carew, Michael. *The Impact of the First World War on U.S. Policymakers: American Strategic and Foreign Policy Formulation, 1938–1942*. Lanham, Md.: Rowman and Littlefield, 2014.
Casey, Steven. *Cautious Crusade: Franklin D. Roosevelt, American Public Opinion, and the War against Nazi Germany*. Oxford: Oxford University Press, 2001.
Cashman, Sean D. *America, Roosevelt, and World War II*. New York: New York University Press, 1989.
Challener, Richard D. *Admirals, Generals, and American Foreign Policy*. Princeton, N.J.: Princeton University Press, 1973.
Chang, Iris. *The Rape of Nanking: The Forgotten Holocaust of World War II*. New York: Penguin Books, 1997.
Charmley, John. *Churchill's Grand Alliance: The Anglo-American Special Relationship, 1940–1957*. New York: Harcourt, Brace, 1995.
———. "Churchill's Roosevelt." In Anne Lane and Howard Temperley, eds., *The Rise and Fall of the Grand Alliance, 1941–1945*, 90–107. New York: St. Martin's Press, 1995.
Charteris, John. *Field Marshal Earl Haig*. London: Cassell, 1929.
Christman, Calvin L. "Franklin D. Roosevelt and the Craft of Strategic Assessment." In Williamson Murray and Allan R. Millet, eds., *Calculations: Net Assessment and the Coming of World War II*, 216–257. New York: Free Press, 1992.
Clark, William. *Less Than Kin: Anglo-American Relations*. London: Hamilton, 1957.
Clausewitz, Karl von. *On War*. Edited and translated by Michael Howard and Peter Paret. Introductory essays by Peter Paret, Michael Howard, and Bernard Brodie; with a commentary by Bernard Brodie. Princeton, N.J.: Princeton University Press, 1976.
Clayton, Anthony. "Growing Respect: The Royal Navy and the *Maritime Nationale*, 1918–1939." In Martin S. Alexander and William J. Philpott, eds., *Anglo-French Defence Relations between the Wars*, 26–48. New York: Palgrave MacMillan, 2002.
Clifford, J. Garry. "Both Ends of the Telescope: New Perspectives on FDR and American Entry into World War II." *Diplomatic History* 13, no. 2 (April 1989): 213–230.
———. "A Connecticut Colonel's Candid Conversation with the Wrong Commander-in-Chief." *Connecticut History* 28 (November 1987): 24–38.

Clifford, J. Garry, and Robert H. Ferrell. "Roosevelt at the Rubicon: The Great Convoy Debate of 1941." In G. Kurt Piehler and Sidney Pash, eds., *The United States and the Second World War: New Perspectives in Diplomacy, War, and the Home Front,* 10–37. Bronx, N.Y.: Fordham University Press, 2010.
Coffey, Thomas M. *Hap: The Story of the U.S. Air Force and the Man Who Built It, General Henry H. "Hap" Arnold.* New York: Viking Press, 1982.
Cohen, Warren I. *The American Revisionists: The Lessons of Intervention in World War I.* Chicago: University of Chicago Press, 1967.
Cole, Wayne S. *America First: The Battle against Intervention, 1940–1941.* Madison: University of Wisconsin Press, 1953.
———. *Roosevelt and the Isolationists, 1932–1945.* Lincoln: University of Nebraska Press, 1983.
Coletta, Paolo E. *Sea Power in the Atlantic and Mediterranean in World War I.* Lanham, Md.: University Press of America, 1989.
Collier, Basil. *The Lion and the Eagle: British and Anglo-American Strategy, 1900–1950.* New York: Putnam, 1972.
Colville, John. *Man of Valour: The Life of Field Marshal the Viscount Gort, VC, GCB, DSO, MVO, MC.* London: Collins, 1972.
Colvin, Ian Goodhope. *None so Blind: A British Diplomatic View of the Origins of World War II.* New York: Harcourt, Brace, and World, 1965.
Conant, Jennet. *Tuxedo Park: A Wall Street Tycoon and the Secret Palace of Science That Changed the Course of World War II.* New York: Simon and Shuster, 2002.
Conn, Stetson. "Changing Concepts of National Defense in the United States, 1937–1941." *Military Affairs* 28 (Spring 1964): 1–7.
Cooling, Benjamin Franklin, and Lieutenant Colonel John Hixson. *Allied Interoperability in Peace and War.* Carlisle Barracks, Pa.: U.S. Army Military History Institute, 1978.
Cooper, Duff. *Old Men Forget.* London: Rupert Hart-Davis, 1953.
Corgan, Michael T. "Franklin D. Roosevelt and the American Occupation of Iceland." *Naval War College Review* 45 (Autumn 1992): 34–54.
Costigliola, Frank. "Broken Circle: The Isolation of Franklin D. Roosevelt in World War II." *Diplomatic History* 32, no. 5 (November 2008): 677–718.
Coulter, Matthew Ware. *The Senate Munitions Inquiry of the 1930s: Beyond the Merchants of Death.* Westport, Conn.: Greenwood Press, 1997.
Cowley, Robert, and Geoffrey Parker, eds. *The Reader's Companion to Military History.* Boston: Houghton Mifflin Harcourt, 1996.
Cowman, Ian. *Dominion or Decline: Anglo-American Naval Relations in the Pacific, 1937–1941.* Oxford: Berg, 1996.
Cox, Sebastian. "British Military Planning and the Origins of the Second World War." In B. J. C. McKercher and Roch Legault, eds., *Military Planning and the Origins of the Second World War,* 103–120. Westport, Conn.: Praeger, 2001.
Craig, Gordon A. *War, Politics, and Diplomacy.* London: Weidenfeld and Nicolson, 1966.

Cray, Ed. *General of the Army George C. Marshall, Soldier and Statesman*. New York: Norton, 1990.
Croswell, D. K. R. *The Chief of Staff: The Military Career of General Walter Bedell Smith*. Westport, Conn.: Greenwood Press, 1991.
Cruttwell, C. R. M. F. *The Role of British Strategy in the Great War*. London: Cambridge University Press, 1936.
Cull, Nicholas J. "The Munich Crisis and British Propaganda Policy in the United States." In Igor Lukes and Erik Goldstein, eds., "Special Issue on the Munich Crisis, 1938," *Diplomacy and Statecraft* 10, nos. 2–3 (July–November 1999): 216–235.
Daggett, Stephen. *Costs of Major U.S. Wars*. Washington, D.C.: U.S. Congressional Research Service, 29 June 2010.
Dallek, Robert. *Franklin D. Roosevelt and American Foreign Policy, 1932–1945*. New York: Oxford University Press, 1979.
Danchev, Alex. "Dill." In John Keegan, ed., *Churchill's Generals*, 53–56. New York: Grove Weidenfeld, 1991.
———. *On Specialness: Essays in Anglo-American Relations*. New York: St. Martin's Press, 1998.
———. *A Very Special Relationship: Field Marshal Sir John Dill and the Anglo-American Alliance, 1941–1944*. London: Brassey's, 1986.
———. "A Very Special Relationship: Field Marshal Sir John Dill and General George Marshall." George C. Marshall Foundation, n.d. At http://marshallfoundation.org/marshall/wp-content/uploads/sites/22/2014/04/Dill+Marshall.pdf.
Daso, Dik. *Hap Arnold and the Evolution of American Airpower*. Washington, D.C.: Smithsonian Institution Press, 2000.
Davis, Harold E., John J. Finan, and Peter F. Taylor. *Latin American Diplomatic History: An Introduction*. Baton Rouge: Louisiana State University Press, 1977.
Davis, Kenneth S. *FDR: Into the Storm, 1937–1940*. New York: Random House, 1993.
———. *FDR: The War President, 1940–1943*. New York: Random House, 2000.
D'Este, Carlo. *Warlord: A Life of Winston Churchill at War, 1874–1945*. New York: Harper Collins, 2008.
DeLany, Vice Admiral Walter S. *Bayly's Navy*. Washington, D.C.: Naval Historical Foundation, 1980.
DeWeerd, Harvey. "The American Adoption of French Artillery, 1917–1918." *Journal of American Military Institute* 3 (Summer 1939): 104–116.
Dilks, David. *Churchill and Company: Allies and Rivals in War and Peace*. London: Taurus, 2012.
Dimbleby, David, and David Reynolds. *An Ocean Apart: The Relationship between Britain and America in the Twentieth Century*. New York: Random House, 1988.
Divine, Robert A. *The Reluctant Belligerent: American Entry into World War II*. New York: Wiley, 1965.
———. *Roosevelt and World War II*. Baltimore: Johns Hopkins University Press, 1969.
Dobson, Alan P. *Anglo-American Relations on the Twentieth Century: Of Friendship, Conflict, and the Rise and Decline of Superpowers*. London: Routledge, 1995.

———. *U.S. Wartime Aid to Britain, 1940–1946.* New York: St. Martin's Press, 1986.

Doenecke, Justus D. "The Roosevelt Foreign Policy: An Ambiguous Legacy." In Justus D. Doenecke and Mark A. Stoler, *Debating Franklin D. Roosevelt's Foreign Policies, 1933–1945*, 5–92. Lanham, Md.: Rowman and Littlefield, 2005.

———. *Storm on the Horizon: The Challenge to American Intervention, 1939–1941.* Lanham, Md.: Rowman and Littlefield, 2003.

———. "U.S. Policy and the European War, 1939–1941." *Diplomatic History* 19, no. 4 (September 1995): 669–698.

Doenecke, Justus D., and Mark A. Stoler. *Debating Franklin D. Roosevelt's Foreign Policies, 1933–1945.* Lanham, Md.: Rowman and Littlefield, 2005.

Doenecke, Justus D., and John E. Wilz. *From Isolation to War, 1931–1941.* 3rd ed. American History series. Wheeling, Ill.: Harlan Davidson, 2003.

Doughty, Robert A. "France." In Richard F. Hamilton and Holger H. Herwig, eds., *War Planning, 1914*, 143–174. New York: Cambridge University Press, 2009.

———. *Pyrrhic Victory: French Strategy and Operations in the Great War.* Cambridge, Mass.: Harvard University Press, 2005.

Douglas, Roy. *New Alliances, 1940–1941.* New York: MacMillan, 1982.

Duchene, François. *Jean Monnet: The First Statesman of Interdependence.* New York: Norton, 1980.

Duffy, James P. *Target: America. Hitler's Plans to Attack the United States.* Westport, Conn.: Praeger, 2004.

Dunlop, John. *The Development of the British Army, 1899–1914.* London: Methuen, 1939.

Dupuy, R. Ernest, and Trevor N. Dupuy. *The Encyclopedia of Military History from 3500 B.C. to the Present.* New York: Harper and Row, 1970.

Dutton, David. "Britain and France at War, 1914–1918." In Alan Sharp and Glynn Stone, eds., *Anglo-French Relations in the Twentieth Century: Rivalry and Cooperation*, 77–82. New York: Routledge, 2000.

Dyer, George C. *The Amphibians Came to Conquer: The Story of Admiral Richmond Kelly Turner.* 2 vols. Washington, D.C.: U.S. Department of the Navy, 1969.

Elphick, Peter. *Far Eastern File: The Intelligence War in the Far East, 1930–1945.* London: Hodden and Stoughton, 1997.

Engelbrecht, Helmut C., and Frank C. Hanighen. *Merchants of Death: A Study of the International Armaments Industry.* New York: Dodd, Mead, 1934.

Esposito, Vincent, ed. *The West Point Atlas of American Wars.* 2 vols. New York: Praeger, 1959.

Fairchild, Byron. "Decision to Land United States Forces in Iceland." In Kent R. Greenfield, ed., *Command Decisions*, 73–98. 1960. Reprint. Washington, D.C.: Office of the Chief of Military History, 1971.

Farnham, Barbara Reardon. *Roosevelt and the Munich Crisis: A Study of Political Decision-Making.* Princeton, N.J.: Princeton University Press, 1997.

Farrell, Brian P. *The Basis and Making of British Grand Strategy, 1940–1943: Was There a Plan?* Lewiston, N.Y.: Edwin Mellon Press, 1998.

———, ed. *Leadership and Responsibility in the Second World War.* Montreal: McGill-Queen's University Press, 2004.

———. "Yes, Prime Minister: Barbarossa, Whipcord, and the Basis of British Grand Strategy, Autumn 1941." *Journal of Military History* 57, no. 4 (1993): 599–625.

Fehrenbach, T. R. *FDR's Undeclared War, 1939–1941.* New York: Mackey, 1967.

Feis, Herbert. *Churchill, Roosevelt, and Stalin.* Princeton, N.J.: Princeton University Press, 1967.

———. *The Road to Pearl Harbor.* Princeton, N.J.: Princeton University Press, 1950.

Finney, Patrick, ed. *The Origins of the Second World War.* London: Arnold, 1997.

Fischer, David Hackett. *Paul Revere's Ride.* Oxford: Oxford University Press, 1994.

Fleming, Thomas. "Pershing." In Robert Cowley and Geoffrey Parker, eds., *The Reader's Companion to Military History,* 360. Boston: Houghton Mifflin Harcourt, 1996.

Flint, Roy K. "The United States Army on the Pacific Frontier, 1899–1939." In Joe E. Dixon, ed., *The American Military and the Far East: Proceedings of the Ninth Military History Symposium,* 139–159. Washington, D.C.: U.S. Air Force Academy and Office of Air Force History, 1980.

Ford, Corey. *Donovan of the OSS.* Boston: Little, Brown, 1970.

Fraser, David. *Alanbrooke.* New York: Atheneum, 1982.

Freedman, Lawrence, Paul Hayes, and Robert O'Neill, eds. *War, Strategy, and International Politics: Essays in Honour of Sir Michael Howard.* Oxford: Clarendon Press, 1992.

Freidel, Frank. *Franklin D. Roosevelt.* 4 vols. Boston: Little, Brown, 1952–1990.

French, E. G. *French Replies to Haig.* London: Hutchinson, 1936.

———. *The Life of Field Marshal Sir John French, Earl of Ypres.* London: Cassell, 1931.

Friedman, Max Paul. *Nazis and Good Neighbors: The United States Campaign against the Germans of Latin America in World War II.* Cambridge: Cambridge University Press, 2003.

Frothingham, Thomas G. *The American Reinforcement in the World War.* Garden City, N.Y.: Doubleday, Page, 1927.

Gibbs, Norman H. "British Strategic Doctrine, 1918–1939." In Michael Howard, ed., *The Theory and Practice of War,* 185–212. Bloomington: Indiana University Press, 1965.

———. "The Naval Conferences of the Interwar Years: A Study of Anglo-American Relations. *Naval War College Review* 30 (1977): 50–63.

Gilderhus, Mark T. *The Second Century: U.S.–Latin American Relations since 1889.* Wilmington, Del.: Scholarly Resources, 2000.

Glantz, David. *Operation Barbarossa: Hitler's Invasion of Russia, 1941.* Charleston, S.C.: Tempus, 2001.

Goda, Norman J. W. *Tomorrow the World: Hitler, Northwest Africa, and the Path toward America.* College Station: Texas A&M University Press, 1998.

Goldrick, Rear Admiral James, Royal Australian Navy. "The Founders." In Peter Hore, ed., *From Dreadnought to Daring: 100 Years of Comment, Controversy, and Debate in* The Naval Review, 1–17. Barnsley, U.K.: Seaforth, 2012. At dreadnoughtproject.org/tfs/index.php/Roger_Mowbray_Bellairs.

Gole, Henry G. *The Road to Rainbow: Army Planning for Global War, 1934–1940.* Annapolis, Md.: Naval Institute Press, 2003.
Goodhart, Philip. *Fifty Ships That Saved the World: The Foundation of the Anglo-American Alliance.* Garden City, N.Y.: Doubleday, 1965.
Gopnik, Adam. "Finest Hours: The Making of Winston Churchill." *New Yorker,* August 30, 2010. At http://www.newyorker.com/arts/critics/atlarge/2010/08/30/10083crat_atlarge_gopnik?.
Gossage, E. L. "Air Cooperation with the Army." *Royal United Services Institute Journal* 72 (August 1927): 561–578.
Graham, Dominick, and Shelford Bidwell. *Coalitions, Politicians, and Generals: Some Aspects of Command in Two World Wars.* London: Brassey's, 1994.
Gray, Edwyn. *Operation Pacific: The Royal Navy's War against Japan, 1941–1945.* Annapolis, Md.: Naval Institute Press, 1989.
Greenfield, Kent R. *American Strategy in World War II: A Reconsideration.* Baltimore: Johns Hopkins University Press, 1963.
Greenhalgh, Elizabeth. *Victory through Coalition: Britain and France during the First World War.* New York: Cambridge University Press, 2005.
Gregory, Ross. *America, 1941: A Nation at the Crossroads.* New York: Free Press, 1989.
Grenville, John A. S. "Diplomacy and War Plans in the United States, 1890–1917." *Royal Historical Society, Transactions* 2, serial 5 (1961): 1–21.
Grenville, John A. S., and George B. Young. *Politics, Strategy, and American Diplomacy: Studies in Foreign Policy, 1873–1917.* New Haven, Conn.: Yale University Press, 1966.
Guinn, Paul. *British Strategy and Politics, 1914–1918.* Oxford: Clarendon Press, 1965.
Hagan, Kenneth J., ed. *In Peace and War: Interpretations of American Naval History, 1775–1978.* 2nd ed. Westport, Conn.: Greenwood Press, 1984.
Haglund, David G. "George C. Marshall and the Question of Military Aid to England, May–June 1940." *Journal of Contemporary History* 15 (1980): 745–760.
———. *Latin America and the Transformation of U.S. Strategic Thought, 1936–1940.* Albuquerque: University of New Mexico Press, 1984.
Haight, John McVickar. *American Aid to France, 1938–1940.* New York: Atheneum, 1970.
———. "France and the Aftermath of Roosevelt's 'Quarantine' Speech." *World Politics* 14 (1962): 282–306.
———. "Franklin D. Roosevelt and a Naval Quarantine of Japan." *Pacific Historical Review* 40 (May 1971): 203–225.
Hall, Christopher. *Britain, America, and Arms Control, 1921–1937.* New York: St. Martin's Press, 1987.
Hamilton, Richard F., and Holger H. Herwig, eds. *War Planning, 1914.* New York: Cambridge University Press, 2009.
Hammel, Eric. *How America Saved the World: The Untold Story of U.S. Preparedness between the World Wars.* Minneapolis: Zenith Press, 2009.
Hanson, Kurt, and Robert L. Beisner, eds. *American Foreign Relations since 1600.* 2nd ed. Santa Barbara, Calif.: ABC-CLIO, 2003.

Harrison, Richard A. "A Presidential Demarche: Franklin D. Roosevelt's Personal Diplomacy and Great Britain, 1936–1937." *Diplomatic History* 5, no. 3 (July 1981): 245–272.

———. "Testing the Water: A Secret Probe towards Anglo-American Military Cooperation in 1936." *International History Review* 7, no. 2 (May 1985): 214–234.

———. "The United States and Great Britain: Presidential Diplomacy and Alternatives to Appeasement in the 1930s." In Donald F. Schmitz and Richard Challener, eds., *Appeasement in Europe: A Reassessment of U.S. Policies*, 103–143. Westport, Conn.: Greenwood Press, 1990.

Hartley, Livingston. *Our Maginot Line: The Defense of the Americas*. New York: Carrick and Evans, 1939.

Hastings, Max. *Winston's War: Churchill, 1940–1945*. New York: Knopf, 2010.

Hattendorf, John B., and Bruce A. Elleman, eds. *Nineteen-Gun Salute: Case Studies in Operational, Strategic, and Diplomatic Naval Leadership during the 20th and Early 21st Centuries*. Newport, R.I.: Naval War College Press, 2010.

Hattendorf, John B., and Robert S. Jordan, eds. *Maritime Strategy and the Balance of Power: Britain and America in the Twentieth Century*. New York: St. Martin's Press, 1989.

Hearden, Patrick J. *Roosevelt Confronts Hitler: America's Entry into World War II*. DeKalb: Northern Illinois University Press, 1987.

Heinrichs, Waldo. "President Franklin D. Roosevelt's Intervention in the Battle of the Atlantic." *Diplomatic History* 10, no. 4 (October 1986): 311–332.

———. *Threshold of War: Franklin D. Roosevelt and American Entry into World War II*. New York: Oxford University Press, 1988.

Henig, Ruth. *Versailles and After, 1919–1933*. Rev. ed. London: Routledge, 1995.

Herman, Arthur. *Freedom's Forge: How American Business Produced Victory in World War II*. New York: Random House, 2012.

Herring, George C. *From Colony to Superpower: U.S. Foreign Relations since 1776*. New York: Oxford University Press, 2008.

Herz, Norman. *Operation Alacrity: The Azores and the War in the Atlantic*. Annapolis, Md.: Naval Institute Press, 2004.

Higham, Robin. *Armed Forces in Peacetime Britain, 1918–1940*. Hamden, Conn.: Archon Books, 1962.

———. *The Military Intellectuals in Britain, 1918–1939*. New Brunswick, N.J.: Rutgers University Press, 1966.

Hixson, Lieutenant Colonel John, and B. Franklin Cooling. *Combined Operations in Peace and War*. Rev. ed. Carlisle Barracks, Pa.: U.S. Army Military History Institute, 1982.

Holsti, Ole. *Public Opinion and American Foreign Policy*. Rev. ed. Ann Arbor: University of Michigan Press, 2004.

Hore, Peter, ed. *From Dreadnought to Daring: 100 Years of Comment, Controversy, and Debate in* The Naval Review. Barnsley, U.K.: Seaforth, 2012.

Howard, Michael. *The Continental Commitment: The Dilemma of British Defence Policy in the Era of the Two World Wars*. London: Temple Smith, 1972.

———, ed. *The Theory and Practice of War*. 1965. Reprint. Bloomington: Indiana University Press, 1967.

———. *War in European History*. Oxford: Oxford University Press, 1976.

Humphreys, R. A. *Latin America and the Second World War*. Vol. 1: *1939–1942*. London: Institute of Latin American Studies, University of London, 1981.

Huston, Major General John W. (USAF, ret.). *American Airpower Comes of Age: General Henry H. "Hap" Arnold's World War II Diaries*. Maxwell Air Force Base, Ala.: Air University Press, 2002.

Hyde, H. Montgomery. *Room 3063: The Story of the British Intelligence Center in New York during World War II*. New York: Farrar, Strauss, 1963.

Imlay, Talbott. "The Making of the Anglo-French Alliance, 1938–1939." In Martin S. Alexander and William J. Philpott, eds., *Anglo-French Defence Relations between the Wars*, 92–120. New York: Palgrave MacMillan, 2002.

Iriye, Akira. *The Cambridge History of American Foreign Relations*. Vol. 3: *The Globalizing of America, 1913–1945*. New York: Cambridge University Press, 1993.

Jacobson, Mark, Robert Levine, and William Schabe. *Contingency Plans for War in Western Europe, 1920–1940*. Santa Monica, Calif.: RAND, 1985.

James, Robert W. *Wartime Economic Cooperation: A Study of Relations between Canada and the United States*. Toronto: Ryerson, Press, 1949.

Jenkins, Roy. *Churchill: A Biography*. New York: Farrar, Strauss and Giroux, 2001.

Jenner, Robert E. *FDR's Republicans: Domestic Political Alignment and American Foreign Policy*. Lanham, Md.: Lexington Books, 2010.

Jonas, Manfred. *Isolationism in America, 1935–1941*. Ithaca, N.Y.: Cornell University Press, 1966.

Johnson, Franklyn. *Defence by Committee*. London: Oxford University Press, 1960.

Kaiser, David. *No End Save Victory: How FDR Led the Nation into War*. New York: Basic Books, 2014.

Kaufman, J. E., and H. W. Kaufman. *The Sleeping Giant: American Armed Forces between the Wars*. Westport, Conn.: Praeger, 1996.

Keegan, John, ed. *Churchill's Generals*. New York: Grove Weidenfeld, 1991.

———. *The First World War*. New York: Knopf, 1999.

———, ed. *The Times Atlas of the Second World War*. New York: Harper and Row, 1989.

Kemp, Peter. "Admiral of the Fleet Sir Dudley Pound." In Stephen Howarth, ed., *Men of War: Great Naval Leaders of World War II*, 17–41. New York: St. Martin's 1993.

Kennan, George F. *American Foreign Policy, 1900–1950*. Chicago: University of Chicago Press, 1951.

Kennedy, David M. *Freedom from Fear: The American People in the Depression and War, 1929–1945*. Oxford: Oxford University Press, 1999.

Kennedy, Greg. *Anglo-American Strategic Relations and the Far East, 1933–1939*. Portland, Ore.: Frank Cass, 2002.

———, ed. *British Naval Strategy East of Suez, 1900–2000*. London: Frank Cass, 2005.

———. "Lord Lothian, the Far East, and Anglo-American Strategic Relations, 1934–

1941." In Priscilla Roberts, ed., *Lord Lothian and Anglo-American Relations, 1900–1940*, 107–132. Dordrecht, Netherlands: Republic of Letters, 2010.

———. "Neville Chamberlain and Strategic Relations with the US during His Chancellorship." *Diplomacy and Statecraft* 13, no. 1 (March 2002): 95–120.

———. "What Worth the Americans?" In Greg Kennedy, ed., *British Naval Strategy East of Suez, 1900–2000*, 90–108. New York: Frank Cass, 2005.

Kennedy, Paul M., ed. *Grand Strategies in War and Peace*. New Haven, Conn.: Yale University Press, 1991.

———. *The Rise and Fall of the Great Powers: Economic Change and Military Conflict, 1500–2000*. New York: Random House, 1987.

———. *The Rise of Anglo-German Antagonism, 1860–1914*. London: Allen and Unwin, 1980.

———, ed. *The War Plans of the Great Powers, 1888–1914*. London: Allen and Unwin, 1979.

Kershaw, Ian. *Fateful Choices: Ten Decisions That Changed the World, 1940–1941*. New York: Penguin, 2007.

Kesaris, Paul, and Dale Reynolds, eds. *U.S. Military Intelligence Reports: Combat Estimates, Western Hemisphere, 1920–1943*. Frederick, Md.: University Publications of America, 1985.

Ketchum, Richard M. *The Borrowed Years, 1938–1941: America on the Way to War*. New York: Random House, 1989.

Kimball, Warren F. "Anglo-American War Aims, 1941–1943, the First Review: Eden's Mission to Washington." In Anne Lane and Howard Temperley, eds., *The Rise and Fall of the Grand Alliance, 1941–1945*, 1–21. New York: St. Martin's Press, 1995.

———. *Forged in War: Roosevelt, Churchill, and the Second World War*. New York: Morrow, 1997.

———, ed. *Franklin D. Roosevelt and the World Crisis, 1937–1945*. London: Heath, 1973.

———. *The Juggler: Franklin Roosevelt as Wartime Statesman*. Princeton, N.J.: Princeton University Press, 1991.

King, Ernest J., with Walter Whitehead. *Fleet Admiral King: A Naval Record*. New York: Norton, 1952.

Kissinger, Henry. *Diplomacy*. New York: Simon and Shuster, 1994.

Kittredge, Tracy B. *Naval Lessons of the Great War*. Garden City, N.Y.: Doubleday, Page, 1921.

———. "United States Defense Policy and Strategy, 1941." *U.S. News and World Report*, 3 December 1954.

Klachko, Mary. "William Sheperd Benson." In James C. Bradford, ed., *Admirals of the New Steel Navy: Makers of American Naval Tradition, 1880–1930*, 300–330. Annapolis, Md.: Naval Institute Press, 1990.

Koburger, Charles W. *Franco-American Naval Relations, 1940–1945*. New York: Praeger (Greenwood), 1993.

Kohnen, David. "Alan Goodrich Kirk: U.S. Navy Admiral of Intelligence and Diplomacy." In John B. Hattendorf and Bruce A. Elleman, eds., *Nineteen-Gun Salute: Case Studies in Operational, Strategic, and Diplomatic Naval Leadership during the 20th and Early 21st Centuries*, 75–91. Newport, R.I.: Naval War College Press, 2010.

Koistinen, Paul A. C. *Arsenal of World War II: The Political Economy of American Warfare, 1940–1945.* Lawrence: University Press of Kansas, 2004.

———. *Planning War, Pursuing Peace: The Political Economy of American Warfare, 1920–1939.* Lawrence: University Press of Kansas, 1998.

Kuehl, Warren F. "Midwestern Newspapers and Isolationist Sentiment." *Diplomatic History* 3, no. 3 (July 1979): 283–306.

Kupfer, Charles. *We Felt the Flames: Hitler's Blitzkrieg, America's Story.* Newville, Pa.: Sgt. Kirkland's Press, 2003.

Lacey, James G. *Keep from All Thoughtful Men: How the U.S. Economists Won World War II.* Annapolis, Md.: Naval Institute Press, 2011.

Lane, Anne, and Howard Temperley, eds. *The Rise and Fall of the Grand Alliance, 1941–1945.* New York: St. Martin's Press, 1995.

Langer, William L., and S. Everett Gleason. *The Challenge to Isolation, 1937–1940.* New York: Harper and Brothers, 1952.

———. *The Undeclared War, 1940–1941.* New York: Harper and Brothers, 1953.

Lanza, Conrad H. *Napoleon's Maxims.* Harrisburg, Pa.: Stackpole Press, 1940.

LaPlante, Lieutenant Commander John B. "The Evolution of Pacific Policy and Strategic Planning: June 1940–July 1941." *Naval War College Review* 25 (May–June 1973): 57–72.

Larrabee, Eric. *Commander in Chief: Franklin Delano Roosevelt, His Lieutenants, and Their War.* New York: Harper and Row, 1987.

Lash, Joseph P. *Roosevelt and Churchill, 1939–1941: The Partnership That Saved the World.* New York: Norton, 1976.

Layne, Christopher. *The Peace of Illusions: American Grand Strategy from 1940 to the Present.* Ithaca, N.Y.: Cornell University Press, 2006.

Lee, Bradford A. *Britain and the Sino-Japanese War, 1937–1939.* Stanford, Calif.: Stanford University Press, 1973.

Lee, J. M. *The Churchill Coalition, 1940–1945.* Hamden, Conn.: Archon Books, Shoestring Press, 1980.

Leighton, Richard M. "Allied Unity of Command." *Political Science Quarterly* 47 (1952): 399–425.

Leonard, Thomas M., and Jon F. Bratzel, eds. *Latin America during World War II.* Lanham, Md.: Rowman and Littlefield, 2006.

Leutze, James R. *Bargaining for Supremacy: Anglo-American Naval Collaboration, 1937–1941.* Chapel Hill: University of North Carolina Press, 1977.

———. *A Different Kind of Victory: A Biography of Admiral Thomas C. Hart.* Annapolis, Md.: Naval Institute Press, 1981.

Levering, Ralph B. *The Public and American Foreign Policy, 1918–1978.* New York: Morrow, 1979.

Levine, Harold, and James Wechsler. *War Propaganda in the United States.* New Haven, Conn.: Yale University Press, 1940.

Levy, James P. *Appeasement and Rearmament, 1936–1939.* Lanham, Md.: Rowman and Littlefield, 2006.

Lewin, Ronald. *Churchill as Warlord.* New York: Stein and Day, 1973.

Liddell Hart, Basil H. *The British Way in Warfare.* New York: Macmillan, 1933.

———. *The Rommel Papers.* New York: Harcourt, Brace, 1953.

———. *Strategy.* New York: Signet Classics, 1967.

Lisio, Donald J. *British Naval Supremacy and Anglo-American Antagonisms, 1914–1930.* Cambridge: Cambridge University Press, 2014.

Louis, William R. *British Strategy in the Far East, 1919–1939.* Oxford: Oxford University Press, 1972.

Louis, William R., and Hedley Bull, eds. *The Special Relationship: Anglo-American Relations since 1945.* Oxford: Clarendon Press, 1986.

Love, Robert W., Jr. *The Chiefs of Naval Operations.* Annapolis, Md.: Naval Institute Press, 1980.

Lowenthal, Mark. *Leadership and Indecision: American War Planning and Policy Process, 1937–1942.* 2 vols. New York: Garland, 1988.

———. "Roosevelt and the Coming of the War: The Search for United States Policy, 1937–1942." *Journal of Contemporary History* 16 (1981): 413–444.

Lukacs, John. *Five Days in London, May 1940.* New Haven, Conn.: Yale University Press, 1999.

Luvaas, Jay. *The Education of an Army: British Military Thought, 1815–1940.* Chicago: University of Chicago Press, 1964.

Lyddon, William G. *British War Missions to the United States, 1914–1918.* New York: Oxford University Press, 1938.

MacCloskey, Munro. *Planning for Victory: World War II.* New York: Richards Rosen Press, 1970.

Mahan, Alfred T. *The Influence of Sea Power upon History, 1660–1793.* Tucson, Ariz.: Fireship Press, 2009.

Mahl, Thomas, E. *Desperate Deception: British Covert Operations in the United States, 1939–1944.* Washington, D.C.: Brassey's 1998.

Major, John. "The Navy Plans for War, 1937–1942." In Kenneth J. Hagan, ed., *In Peace and War: Interpretations of American Naval History, 1775–1978*, 2nd ed., 237–262. Westport, Conn.: Greenwood Press, 1984.

Leigh-Mallory, T. L. "Air Cooperation with Mechanized Forces." *Royal United Services Institute Journal* 75 (August 1930): 565–577.

Manchester, William, and Paul Reid. *The Last Lion: Winston Spencer Churchill.* Vol. 3: *Defender of the Realm, 1940–1965.* New York: Little, Brown, 2012.

Manchette, Robert B., with Anne Eales and others, comps. *Guide to the Federal Records in the National Archives of the United States.* 3 vols. Washington, D.C.: U.S. National Archives and Records Administration, 1995.

Marder, Arthur. *From Dreadnought to Scapa Flow: The Royal Navy in the Fisher Era,*

1904–1919. Vol. 1: *The Road to War, 1904–1914*. London: Oxford University Press, 1961.
Marks, Frederick W. *Wind over Sand: The Diplomacy of Franklin Roosevelt*. Athens: University of Georgia Press, 1988.
Martel, Gordon. "Military Planning and the Origins of the Second World War." In B. J. C. McKercher and Roch Laegault, eds., *Military Planning and the Origins of the Second World War in Europe*, 18–21. Westport, Conn.: Praeger, 2000.
Martin, Thomas. "Imperial Defence or Diversionary Attack?" In Martin S. Alexander and William J. Philpott, eds., *Anglo-French Defence Relations between the Wars*, 157–185. New York: Palgrave MacMillan, 2002.
Masland, John W., and Lawrence I. Radway. *Soldiers and Scholars: Military Education and National Policy*. Princeton, N.J.: Princeton University Press, 1957.
Matloff, Maurice. "The American Approach to War, 1919–1945." In Michael Howard, ed., *The Theory and Practice of War*, 213–243. Bloomington: Indiana University Press, 1965.
———. "Prewar Plans and Preparations, 1939–1941." *United States Naval Institute Proceedings* 79 (July 1953): 741–748.
Maurer, John H., ed. *Churchill and Strategic Dilemmas before the World Wars*. Portland, Ore.: Frank Cass, 2003.
McKercher, B. J. C. "'A Certain Irritation': The White House, the State Department, and the Desire for a Naval Settlement with Great Britain, 1927–1930." *Diplomatic History* 31, no. 5 (November 2007): 829–864.
———. "National Security and Imperial Defence: British Grand Strategy and Appeasement, 1930–1939." *Diplomacy and Statecraft* 19, no. 3 (September 2008): 391–442.
———. "No Eternal Friends or Enemies: British Defence Policy and the Problem of the United States, 1919–1939." *Canadian Journal of History/Annals canadiennes d' histoire* 28 (April 1993): 258–293.
———. *Transition of Power: Britain's Loss of Global Pre-eminence to the United States, 1930–1945*. Cambridge: Cambridge University Press, 1999.
McKercher, B. J. C., and Roch Legault, eds. *Military Planning and the Origins of the Second World War in Europe*. Westport, Conn.: Praeger, 2000.
McLachlen, Donald. *Room 39: A Study in Naval Intelligence*. New York: Atheneum, 1968.
Meachem, Jon. *Franklin and Winston: An Intimate Portrait of an Epic Friendship*. New York: Random House, 2003.
Mead, Richard. *Churchill's Lions: A Biographical Guide to Key British Generals of World War II*. Stroud, U.K.: Oaklands Book Service, 2007.
Miller, Edward S. *War Plan Orange: The U.S. Strategy to Defeat Japan, 1897–1945*. Annapolis, Md.: Naval Institute Press, 1991.
Millis, Walter. *Arms and Men: A Study in American Military History*. New York: Mentor Books, 1956.
———. *The Road to War: America, 1914–1917*. Boston: Houghton Mifflin, 1935.

Milner, Marc. "Anglo-American Naval Co-operation, 1939–1945." In John B. Hattendorf and Robert S. Jordan, eds., *Maritime Strategy and the Balance of Power: Britain and America in the Twentieth Century*, 243–268. New York: St. Martin's Press, 1989.

Morgan, Howard W. *America's Road to Empire: The War with Spain and Overseas Expansion*. New York: Wiley, 1967.

Morison, Elting E. *Admiral Sims and the Modern American Navy*. Boston: Houghton Mifflin, 1942.

Morison, Samuel E. *Strategy and Compromise*. Boston: Little, Brown, 1958.

———. *The Two-Ocean War: A Short History of the United States Navy in the Second World War*. Boston: Little, Brown, 1963.

Morris, James M., and Patricia M. Kearns, eds. *Historical Dictionary of the United States Navy*. Lanham, Md.: Rowman and Littlefield, 2011.

Morton, Louis. "American and Allied Strategy in the Far East." *Military Review* 29 (December 1949): 22–39.

———. "Germany First: The Basic Concept of Allied Strategy in World War II." In Kent R. Greenfield, ed., *Command Decisions*, 11–49. 1960. Reprint. Washington, D.C.: Office of the Chief of Military History, 1971.

———. "War Plan ORANGE: The Evolution of a Strategy." *World Politics* 9 (January 1959): 221–250.

Moser, John E. *Twisting the Lion's Tail: American Anglophobia between the World Wars*. New York: New York University Press, 1998.

Moss, Norman. *19 Weeks: America, Britain, and the Fateful Summer of 1940*. New York: Houghton Mifflin, 2003.

Mulligan, Timothy, comp. *Guide to Records Relating to U.S. Military Participation in World War II*. Washington, D.C.: U.S. National Archives and Records Administration, 1996.

Murfett, Malcolm H. "Are We Ready? The Development of American and British Naval Strategy." In John B. Hattendorf and Robert S. Jordan, eds., *Maritime Strategy and the Balance of Power: Britain and America in the Twentieth Century*, 214–242. New York: St. Martin's Press, 1989.

———, ed. *The First Sea Lords from Fisher to Mountbatten*. Westport, Conn.: Praeger, 1995.

———. *Fool-Proof Relations: The Search for Anglo-American Naval Cooperation during the Chamberlain Years, 1937–1940*. Singapore: University of Singapore Press, 1984.

Murray, Williamson. "Churchill Takes Charge." *Military History*, March–April 2008, 26–33.

Murray, Williamson, MacGregor Knox, and Alvin Bernstein, eds. *The Making of Modern Strategy: Rulers, States, and Wars*. Cambridge: Cambridge University Press, 1994.

Murray, Williamson, and Allan Millett, eds. *Calculations: Net Assessment and the Coming of World War II*. New York: Free Press, 1992.

Murray, Williamson, and Richard Hart Sinnreich, eds. *The Past as Prologue: The*

Importance of History to the Military Profession. New York: Cambridge University Press, 2006.

Murray, Williamson, Richard Hart Sinnreich, and James Lacey, eds. *The Shaping of Grand Strategy: Policy, Diplomacy, and War*. Cambridge: Cambridge University Press, 2011.

Musicant, Ivan. *The Banana Wars: A History of United States Intervention in Latin America from the Spanish-American War to the Invasion of Panama*. New York: MacMillan, 1990.

Neidpath, James. *The Singapore Naval Base and the Defense of Britain's Eastern Empire, 1919–1941*. Oxford: Oxford University Press, 1981.

Neilson, Keith, and Greg Kennedy, eds. *The British Way in Warfare: Power and the International System, 1856–1956*. Burlington, Vt.: Ashgate, 2010.

Neilson, Keith, and Roy A. Prete, eds. *Coalition Warfare: An Uneasy Accord*. Waterloo, Canada: Wilfried Laurier University Press, 1983.

Nenninger, Timothy K. *The Leavenworth Schools and the Old Army: Education, Professionalism, and the Officer Corps of the United States Army, 1881–1918*. Westport, Conn.: Greenwood Press, 1978.

Nicholas, Herbert G. *The United States and Great Britain*. Chicago: University of Chicago Press, 1975.

Nish, Ian, ed. *Anglo-Japanese Alienation, 1919–1952: Papers of the Anglo-Japanese Conference on the Second World War*. New York: Cambridge University Press, 1982.

Nixon, Edgar. *Franklin D. Roosevelt and Foreign Affairs, January 1933–January 1937*. Cambridge, Mass.: Belknap Press of Harvard University Press, 1969.

Northedge, F. G. *The Troubled Giant: Britain among the Great Powers, 1916–1939*. New York: Praeger, 1967.

O'Brien, Phillips Payson. *Britain and American Naval Power: Politics and Policy, 1900–1936*. Westport, Conn.: Praeger, 1998.

———. *How the War Was Won: Air–Sea Power and Allied Victory in World War II*. Cambridge: Cambridge University Press, 2015.

Offner, Arnold, ed. *America and the Origins of World War II, 1933–1941*. New York: Praeger, 1975.

———. *American Appeasement: United States Foreign Policy and Germany, 1933–1938*. Cambridge, Mass.: Harvard University Press, 1969.

Olson, Lynne. *Citizens of London: The Americans Who Stood with Britain in Its Darkest, Finest Hour*. New York: Random House, 2010.

———. *Those Angry Days: Roosevelt, Lindbergh, and America's Fight over World War II, 1939–1941*. New York: Random House, 2013.

———. *Troublesome Young Men: The Rebels Who Brought Churchill to Power and Helped Save England*. New York: Farrar, Strauss, and Giroux, 2007.

O'Neill, Robert. "An Introduction to Strategic Thinking." In Desmond Ball, ed., *Strategy and Defence: Australian Essays*, 27–41. Boston: Allen and Unwin, 1982.

Orange, Vincent. *Bomber Champion: The Life of Marshal of the RAF Sir John Slessor, GCB, DSO, MC*. London: Grub Street, 2006.

Orde, Anne. *The Eclipse of Great Britain: The United States and British Imperial Decline, 1895–1956*. New York: St. Martin's Press, 1996.

O'Sullivan, Christopher D. *Harry Hopkins: FDR's Envoy to Churchill and Stalin*. Lanham, Md.: Rowman and Littlefield, 2015.

Otte, Thomas. "The Elusive Balance: British Foreign Policy and the French Entente before the First World War." In Alan Sharp and Glynn Stone, eds., *Anglo-French Relations in the Twentieth Century: Rivalry and Cooperation*, 11–35. New York: Routledge, 2000.

Overy, Richard, with Andrew Wheatcraft. *The Road to War*. Rev. ed. London: Penguin, 1999.

Pakenham, Thomas. *The Boer War*. New York: Random House, 1979.

Palmer, Frederick. *Bliss, Peacemaker: The Life and Letters of General Tasker Howard Bliss*. New York: Dodd, Mead, 1934.

———. *Newton D. Baker: America at War*. 2 vols. New York: Dodd and Mead, 1931.

Pappas, George S. *Prudens Futuri: The U.S. Army War College, 1901–1967*. Carlisle Barracks, Pa.: Association of the U.S. Army War College, 1967.

Paret, Peter, ed. *Makers of Modern Strategy: From Machiavelli to the Nuclear Age*. Princeton, N.J.: Princeton University Press, 1986.

Parrish, Thomas. *Roosevelt and Marshall: Partners in Politics and War*. New York: Morrow, 1989.

Paz, Maria. *Strategy, Security, and Spies: Mexico and the United States as Allies in World War II*. University Park: Penn State University Press, 1997.

Perras, Galen Rogers. *Franklin Roosevelt and the Origins of the Canadian-American Security Alliance, 1933–1945: Necessary, but Not Necessary Enough*. Westport, Conn.: Praeger, 1998.

Persico, Joseph. *Roosevelt's Secret War: FDR and World War II Espionage*. New York: Random House, 2001.

Philpott, William J. *Anglo-French Relations and Strategy on the Western Front, 1914–1918*. London: MacMillan; New York: St. Martin's Press, 1996.

———. "The Benefit of Experience? The Supreme War Council and the Higher Management of Coalition War, 1939–1940." In Martin S. Alexander and William J. Philpott, eds., *Anglo-French Defence Relations between the Wars*, 92–120. New York: Palgrave MacMillan, 2002.

Piehler, G. Kurt, and Sidney Pash, ed. *The United States and the Second World War: New Perspectives on Diplomacy, War, and the Home Front*. Bronx, N.Y.: Fordham University Press, 2010.

Pogue, Forrest C. *George C. Marshall*. 4 vols. New York: Viking Press, 1963–1987.

———. *George C. Marshall*. Vol. 2: *Ordeal and Hope, 1939–1942*. Foreword by General of the Army Omar N. Bradley. New York: Viking Press, 1965.

Pollock, Fred E. "Roosevelt, the Ogdensburg Agreement, and the British Fleet: All Done with Mirrors." *Diplomatic History* 5, no. 3 (July 1981): 203–219.

Porch, Douglas. *The Path to Victory: The Mediterranean Theater in World War II*. New York: Farrar, Strauss, and Giroux, 2004.

Porter, Bernard. *Britain, Europe, and the World, 1850–1986.* 2nd ed. London: Allen and Unwin, 1987.

Pratt, Lawrence. "Anglo-American Naval Conversations on the Far East of January 1938." *International Affairs* 67 (October 1971): 745–763.

———. *East of Malta, West of Suez: Britain's Mediterranean Crisis, 1936–1939.* London: Cambridge University Press, 1975.

Preston, Adrian W. *General Staffs and Diplomacy before the Second World War.* London: Croom Helm, 1978.

Prete, Roy A. *Strategy and Command: The Anglo-French Coalition on the Western Front, 1914.* Montreal: McGill-Queen's University Press, 2009.

Pritchard, Robert J. *Far Eastern Influences upon British Strategy toward the Great Powers, 1937–1939.* New York: Garland, 1988.

Puleston, Captain William D. *High Command in the World War.* London: Scribner's, 1934.

Reardon, Steven L. *Council of War: A History of the Joint Chiefs of Staff, 1942–1991.* Washington, D.C.: National Defense University Press, 2012. At http://www.ndu.edu/press/lib/pdf/books/council-of-war/council-of-war.pdf.

Reeves, Captain Ira L. *Military Education in the United States.* Burlington, Vt.: Free Press, 1914.

Revol, J. "The Defect of Coalitions." *Military Review* 41 (April 1961): 36–38.

Reynolds, David. "1940: Fulcrum of the Twentieth Century?" *International Affairs* 66 (1990): 325–350.

———. "Competitive Cooperation: Anglo-American Relations in World War II." *Historical Journal* 23 (1980): 233–245.

———. *The Creation of the Anglo-American Alliance, 1937–1941: A Study in Competitive Co-operation.* Chapel Hill: University of North Carolina Press, 1982.

———. *From Munich to Pearl Harbor: Roosevelt's America and the Origins of the Second World War.* American Way series. Chicago: Dee, 2001.

———. *In Command of History: Churchill Fighting and Writing the Second World War.* New York: Random House, 2005.

———. *Lord Lothian and Anglo-American Relations, 1939–1940.* Transactions of the American Philosophical Society, vol. 73, part 2. Philadelphia: American Philosophical Society, 1983.

———. "Roosevelt, Churchill, and the Wartime Anglo-American Alliance." In William Roger Louis and Hedley Bull, eds., *The Special Relationship: Anglo-American Relations since 1945,* 17–41. Oxford: Clarendon Press, 1986.

Reynolds, David, Warren F. Kimball, and A. O. Chubarian, eds. *Allies at War: The Soviet, American, and British Experience, 1939–1945.* London: MacMillan, 1994.

Rich, Norman. *Hitler's War Aims: Ideology, the Nazi State, and the Course of Expansion.* New York: Norton, 1973.

Richards, Denis. *Portal of Hungerford: The Life of Marshal of the Royal Air Force, Viscount Portal of Hungerford.* London: Heinemann, 1977.

Richardson, General Sir Charles. *From Churchill's Secret Circle to the BBC: The Biography of Lieutenant General Sir Ian Jacob.* London: Brassey's, 1991.

Rippy, Fred J. *South America and Hemisphere Defense*. Baton Rouge: Louisiana State University Press, 1941.
Roberts, Andrew. *Eminent Churchillians*. New York: Simon and Schuster, 1994.
———. *The Holy Fox: A Biography of Lord Halifax*. London: Weidenfeld and Nicholson, 1991.
———. *Masters and Commanders: How Four Titans Won the War in the West, 1941–1945*. New York: Harper Collins, 2009.
Roberts, Priscilla. "The Anglo-American Alliance, 1914–1933." *Diplomatic History* 21, no. 3 (July 1997): 333–364.
———, ed. *Lord Lothian and Anglo-American Relations, 1900–1940*. Dordrecht, Netherlands: Republic of Letters, 2010.
———. "Tasker H. Bliss and the Evolution of the Allied Unified Command, 1918: A Note on Old Battles Revisited." *Journal of Military History* 65, no. 3 (July 2001): 671–695.
Rock, William R. *Chamberlain and Roosevelt: British Foreign Policy and the United States, 1937–1940*. Columbus: Ohio University Press, 1988.
Rofe, J. Simon. "Lord Lothian's Ambassadorship in Washington, August 1939–December." In Priscilla Roberts, ed., *Lord Lothian and Anglo-American Relations, 1900–1940*, 133–165. Dordrecht, Netherlands: Republic of Letters, 2010.
Rosen, S. McKee. *The Combined Boards of the Second World War*. New York: Columbia University Press, 1951.
Roskill, Stephen W. *Churchill and the Admirals*. New York: Morrow, 1978.
———. *Hankey: Man of Secrets*. 3 vols. London: Collins, 1970–1974.
———. *Naval Policy between the Wars*. 2 vols. New York: Walker, 1969, 1976.
Ross, Graham. *The Great Powers and the Decline of the European States System, 1914–1945*. London: Longman, 1983.
Ross, Steven T. "American War Plans." In B. J. C. McKercher and Roch Legault, eds., *Military Planning and the Origins of the Second World War in Europe*, 146–166. Westport, Conn.: Praeger, 2000.
———. *American War Plans, 1919–1941*. 5 vols. New York: Garland, 1992.
———. *American War Plans, 1941–1945*. London: Routledge, 1997.
———. *U.S. War Plans, 1938–1945*. Boulder, Colo.: Lynne Rienner, 2002.
Rowe, L. S., Clarence H. Haring, Stephen Duggan, and Dana G. Munro. *Latin America in World Affairs, 1914–1940*. Philadelphia: University of Pennsylvania Press, 1941.
Sainsbury, Keith. *Churchill and Roosevelt at War: The War They Fought and the Peace They Hoped to Make*. New York: New York University Press, 1994.
Sanborn, Frederic R. *Design for War: A Study of Secret Power Politics, 1937–1941*. New York: Deven-Adair, 1951.
Scheina, Robert L. *Latin America: A Naval History, 1810–1967*. Annapolis, Md.: Naval Institute Press, 1988.
Schmitz, David F. *Henry L. Stimson: The First Wise Man*. Wilmington, Del.: SR Books, 2001.
———. *The Triumph of Internationalism: Franklin D. Roosevelt and a World in Crisis, 1933–1941*. Washington, D.C.: Potomac Books, 2007.

Schmitz, David F., and Richard D. Challener, eds. *Appeasement in Europe: A Reassessment of U.S. Policies.* Westport, Conn.: Greenwood Press, 1990.

Schulzinger, Robert D. *U.S. Diplomacy since 1900.* New York: Oxford University Press, 2002.

Schwarz, Urs. *American Strategy: A New Perspective.* Garden City, N.Y.: Doubleday, 1966.

Self, Robert. *Neville Chamberlain: A Biography.* Burlington, Vt.: Ashgate, 2006.

Sharp, Alan, and Glynn Stone, eds. *Anglo-French Relations in the Twentieth Century: Rivalry and Cooperation.* New York: Routledge, 2000.

Sheffield, Gary D. *Leadership and Command: The Anglo-American Experience since 1861.* London: Brassey's, 2002.

Sherry, Michael S. *Preparing for the Next War: American Plans for Postwar Defense, 1941–1945.* New Haven, Conn.: Yale University Press, 1977.

Sherwood, Robert E. *Roosevelt and Hopkins: An Intimate History.* New York: Harper and Brothers, 1948.

Shogan, Robert. *Hard Bargain: How FDR Twisted Churchill's Arm, Evaded the Law, and Changed the Role of the American Presidency.* New York: Scribner's, 1995.

Simpson, B. Mitchell, III. *Admiral Harold R. Stark: Architect of Victory, 1939–1945.* Columbia: University of South Carolina Press, 1989.

———. "Harold Rainsford Stark." In Robert W. Love Jr., ed., *Chiefs of Naval Operations,* 119–135. Annapolis, Md.: Naval Institute Press, 1980.

Skidelsky, Robert. "Imbalance of Power." *Foreign Policy,* March–April 2002, 46–55.

Smith, Bradley F. "Admiral Godfrey's Mission to America, June/July 1941." *Intelligence and National Security* 1, no. 3 (1 September 1986): 441–450.

———. *The Ultra–Magic Deals and the Most Secret Special Relationship, 1940–1946.* Novato, Calif.: Presidio Press, 1993.

Smith, Daniel. *The American Diplomatic Experience.* Boston: Houghton Mifflin, 1972.

Smith, Gaddis. *Britain's Clandestine Submarines, 1914–1915.* New Haven, Conn.: Yale University Press, 1964.

Smythe, Donald. *Pershing: General of the Armies.* Bloomington: Indiana University Press, 1986.

Snell, John L. *Illusion and Necessity: The Diplomacy of Global War, 1939–1945.* Boston: Houghton Mifflin, 1963.

Sontag, Raymond. *A Broken World, 1919–1939.* New York: Harper Torchbooks, 1971.

Soybel, Phyllis L. *A Necessary Partnership: The Development of Anglo-American Cooperation in Naval Intelligence.* Westport, Conn.: Praeger, 2005.

Stafford, David. *Roosevelt and Churchill: Men of Secrets.* New York: Overlook Press, 2000.

Stafford, David, and Rhodri Jeffrey-Jones, ed. *American-British-Canadian Intelligence Relations, 1939–2000.* Portland, Ore.: Frank Cass, 2000.

Stevenson, William. *A Man Called Intrepid.* New York: Ballantine Books, 1976.

Still, William N., Jr. *Crisis at Sea: The United States Navy in European Waters in World War I.* Gainesville: University of Florida Press, 2007.

Stoddard, Brooke C. *World in the Balance: The Perilous Months of June–October 1940.* Sterling, Va.: Potomac Books, 2011.
Stoler, Mark A. *Allies and Adversaries: The Joint Chiefs of Staff, the Grand Alliance, and U.S. Strategy in World War II.* Chapel Hill: University of North Carolina Press, 2000.
———. *Allies in War: Britain and America against the Axis Powers, 1940–1945.* New York: Oxford University Press, 2005.
———. "From Continentalism to Globalism: General Stanley D. Embick, the Joint Strategic Survey Committee, and the Military View of American National Policy during the Second World War." *Diplomatic History* 6, no. 3 (July 1982): 303–321.
———. *George C. Marshall: Soldier-Statesman of the American Century.* Woodbridge, Conn.: Twayne, 1989.
———. *The Politics of the Second Front: American Military Planning and Diplomacy in Coalition Warfare, 1941–1943.* Westport, Conn.: Greenwood Press, 1977.
Stoler, Mark A., and Melanie S. Gustafson, eds. *Major Problems in the History of World War II.* New York: Houghton Mifflin, 2003.
Strachan, Hew. *The First World War.* New York: Viking Press, 2003.
Strassler, Robert, ed., *The Landmark Thucydides: A Comprehensive Guide to the Peloponnesian Wars.* New York: Free Press, 1996.
Suarez, Georges. *Soixante annèes d'histoire français, Clemenceau.* Vol. 1: *Dans la mêlée.* Paris: Tallandier, 1932.
Sumner, Ian. *British Commanders in World War II.* Oxford: Osprey, 2003.
Taliaferro, Jeffrey W.. "Strategy of Innocence or Provocation? The Roosevelt Administration's Road to World War II." In Jeffrey W. Taliaferro, Norrin M. Ripsman, and Steven E. Lobell, eds., *The Challenge of Grand Strategy: The Great Powers and the Broken Balance between the World Wars,* 193–223. Cambridge: Cambridge University Press, 2012.
Taliaferro, Jeffrey W., Norrin M. Ripsman, and Steven E. Lobell, eds. *The Challenge of Grand Strategy: The Great Powers and the Broken Balance between the World Wars.* Cambridge: Cambridge University Press, 2012.
Taylor, A. J. P. *The Origins of the Second World War.* 2nd rev. ed. New York: Fawcett, 1961.
———. *The Struggle for Mastery of Europe, 1848–1918.* Oxford: Oxford University Press, 1954.
Terraine, John, Correlli Barnett, and Air Chief Marshal Sir Alasdair Steadman. "Problems of Coalition War." *Journal of the Royal United Services Institute for Defence Studies* 126 (September 1981): 3–14.
Thorne, Christopher. *Allies of a Kind: The United States, Britain, and the War against Japan, 1941–1945.* New York: Oxford University Press, 1978.
———. *The Approach of War, 1938–1939.* New York: St. Martin's, 1967.
Trask, David F. *The AEF and Coalition Warmaking, 1917–1918.* Lawrence: University Press of Kansas, 1993.
———. "The American Navy in a World at War, 1914–1918." In Kenneth J. Hagan, ed., *In Peace and War: Interpretations of American Naval History, 1775–1978,* 2nd ed., 205–220. Westport, Conn.: Greenwood Press, 1984.

———. *Captains and Cabinets: Anglo-American Naval Relations, 1917–1918*. Columbia: University of Missouri Press, 1972.

———. Introduction to Adm. William S. Sims, with Burton J. Hendrick, *The Victory at Sea*, ix–xxvi. Annapolis, Md.: Naval Institute Press, 1984.

———. *The United States in the Supreme War Council: American War Aims and Inter-Allied Strategy, 1917–1918*. Middleton, Conn.: Wesleyan University Press, 1961.

———. "William Snowden Sims: The Victory Ashore." In James C. Bradford, ed., *Admirals of the New Steel Navy: Makers of American Naval Tradition, 1880–1930*, 282–299. Annapolis, Md.: Naval Institute Press, 1990.

Tuohy, William. *America's Fighting Admirals: Winning the War at Sea in World War II*. St. Paul, Minn.: Zenith Press, 2007.

Tyler, J. E. *The British Army and the Continent, 1904–1914*. London: Edward Arnold, 1938.

Utley, Jonathan. *Going to War with Japan, 1937–1941*. Reprint with a new introduction. Bronx, N.Y.: Fordham University Press, 2005.

Vandiver, Frank E. *Black Jack: The Life and Times of John J. Pershing*. College Station: Texas A&M Press, 1977.

Victor, George. *The Pearl Harbor Myth: Rethinking the Unthinkable*. Dulles, Va.: Potomac Books, 2007.

Vinson, John Chalmers. *William E. Borah and the Outlawry of War*. Athens: University of Georgia Press, 1957.

Vlahos, Michael. *The Blue Sword: The Naval War College and the American Mission, 1919–1941*. Newport, R.I.: Naval War College Press, 1980.

Waites, Neville, ed. *The Troubled Neighbors: Franco-British Relations in the Twentieth Century*. London: Weidenfeld and Nicholson, 1971.

Wallach, Jehuda. *Uneasy Coalition: The Entente Experience in World War I*. Westport, Conn.: Greenwood Press, 1993.

Watt, Alan. *The Evolution of Australian Foreign Policy, 1938–1965*. Cambridge: Cambridge University Press, 1967.

Watt, David. "Introduction: The Anglo-American Relationship." In William R. Louis and Hedley Bull, eds., *The Special Relationship: Anglo-American Relations since 1945*, 1–14. Oxford: Clarendon Press, 1986.

Webster, Andrew. "An Argument without End: Britain, France, and the Disarmament Process, 1925–1934." In Martin S. Alexander and William J. Philpott, Eds., *Anglo-French Defence Relations between the Wars*, 49–72. New York: Palgrave MacMillan, 2002.

Weigley, Russell F. *The American Way of War: A History of United States Military Strategy and Policy*. Bloomington: University of Indiana Press, 1973.

———. *History of the United States Army*. 1967. Reprint. Bloomington: Indiana University Press, 1984.

Weiss, Steve. *Allies in Conflict: Anglo-American Strategic Negotiations, 1938–1944*. New York: St. Martin's Press, 1997.

Wilford, Timothy. *Canada's Road to the Pacific War: Intelligence, Strategy, and the Far East Crisis*. Vancouver: University of British Columbia Press, 2011.

Williamson, Samuel R., Jr. *The Politics of Grand Strategy: Britain and France Prepare for War, 1904–1914.* Cambridge, Mass.: Harvard University Press, 1969.

———. "Theories of Organizational Policies and Foreign Policy Outcomes." In Paul Gordon Lauren, ed., *Diplomacy: New Approaches in History, Theory, and Policy,* 137–161. New York: Free Press, 1979.

Wilmot, H. P. *Empires in the Balance: Japanese and Allied Pacific Strategies to April 1942.* Annapolis, Md.: Naval Institute Press.1982.

Wilson, Theodore A. *The First Summit.* Rev. ed. Lawrence: University Press of Kansas, 1991.

———. *WW2: Readings on Critical Issues.* New York: Scribner's, 1974.

Wilson, Theodore A., et al. (only first author listed). "Coalition: Structure, Strategy, and Statecraft." In David Reynolds, Warren F. Kimball, and A. O. Chubarian, eds., *Allies at War: The Soviet, American, and British Experience, 1939–1945,* 79–112. London: MacMillan, 1994.

Woodward, David R. *America and World War I: A Selected Annotated Bibliography of English Language Sources.* New York: Routledge, 2007.

———. *Trial by Friendship: Anglo-American Relations, 1917–1918.* Lexington: University Press of Kentucky, 1993.

Worth, Roland H. *Secret Allies in the Pacific: Covert Intelligence and Code Breaking Cooperation between the United States, Great Britain, and Other Nations prior to the Attack on Pearl Harbor.* Jefferson, N.C.: McFarland, 2002.

Wylie, Rear Admiral Joseph C. *Military Strategy: A Theory of Power Control.* New Brunswick, N.J.: Rutgers University Press, 1967.

Yenne, Bill. *Hap Arnold: The General Who Invented the U.S. Air Force.* Washington, D.C.: Regnery History, 2013.

Yockelson, Mitchell. *Borrowed Soldiers: Americans under British Command, 1918.* Norman: University of Oklahoma Press, 2008.

Zakaria, Fareed. *From Wealth to Power: The Unusual Origins of America's World Role.* Princeton, N.J.: Princeton University Press, 1998.

Unpublished Material

Bowen, Millard G. "Command Problems in a Multi-national Force." Thesis, U.S. Army War College, 1953–1954. No. 414. U.S. Army Military History Institute, Carlisle Barracks, Pa.

Bunch, Stephen G. "No Middle Way: Franklin D. Roosevelt and Limited War, 1940–1942." Ph.D. diss., University of Illinois at Urbana-Champaign, 1994.

Chamberlin, Thomas C. "Anticipated Operational Difficulties in Combined Commands." Thesis, U.S. Army War College, 1957–1958. No. 1246. U.S. Army Military History Institute, Carlisle Barracks, Pa.

Chapman, Edward S. "Command Problems in a Multi-national Force in War." Thesis, U.S. Army War College, 1955–1956. No. 640. U.S. Army Military History Institute, Carlisle Barracks, Pa.

Conner, Maj. Gen. Fox. "The Allied High Command and Allied Unity of Direction."

Lecture, U.S. Army War College, Washington, D.C., 12 February 1940. File 406-A-32. U.S. Army Military History Institute, Carlisle Barracks, Pa.

Cooling, Benjamin Franklin, and Lieutenant Colonel John Hixson. "The Interoperability of Allied Forces in Europe at the Field Army Level." U.S. Army Military History Institute study, photocopy, 119 pp., 15 April 1977.

Craig, Gordon A. "Problems of Coalition Warfare: The Military Alliance against Napoleon, 1813–1814." Harmon Memorial Lectures in Military History no. 7. U.S. Air Force Academy, 1965.

Crossley, R. W. "Principles of Coalition Warfare: A Preliminary Study." Research directorate, National Defense University, 1979. Photocopy.

Goddard, Lieutenant Colonel Calvin H. "A Study of Anglo-American and Franco-American Relations during World War I." 2 parts. Army War College Historical Study no. 5. U.S. Army Military History Institute, Carlisle Barracks, Pa., June 1942.

Hayes, Lieutenant Grace P. "The History of the Joint Chiefs of Staff in World War II: The War Against Japan." 2 vols. Operational Archives Branch, U.S. Naval History Division (now Naval History and Heritage Command), Office of the Chief of Naval Operations, Washington, D.C., 1954.

Hickock, James N., II. "Anglo-French Military Collaboration, 1939–1940." Typewritten manuscript, 282 pages. Research Office, Office of the Dean, U.S. Military Academy, West Point, N.Y., n.d. (c. 1984).

Hill, Francis. "Command Problems in a Multi-national Force." Thesis, U.S. Army War College, 1954. No. 494. U.S. Army Military History Institute, Carlisle Barracks, Pa.

Kimball, Warren F. "Fighting with Allies: The Hand-Care and Feeding of the Anglo-American Special Relationship." U.S. Air Force Academy, Harmon Lecture in Military History no. 41, 1998. At http://www.usafa.edu/df/dfh/harmomemorial/docs/Harmon41.pdf.

Kittredge, Tracy B., Commander U.S. Naval Forces Europe. "Administrative History: United States Naval Forces in Europe, 1940–1946." 7 vols., 2,856 pages. London, n.d. Tracy B. Kittredge Papers. Operational Archives Branch, Naval Heritage and History Center, Washington, D.C.

———. "United States Defense Policies and Global Strategy, 1900–1941." Historical Section, Office of the Joint Chiefs of Staff, Washington, D.C., 1946–1953.

———. "U.S.-British Naval Cooperation, 1939–1945." Operational Archives Branch, U.S. Naval History Division (now Naval History and Heritage Command), Office of the Chief of Naval Operations, Washington, D.C., n.d.

Mead, Dana G. "United States Peacetime Strategic Planning, 1920–1941: The Color Plans to the Victory Program." Ph.D. diss., MIT, 1967.

Mueller, Paul J., Jr. "George C. Marshall and the Strategy of World War II." Thesis, U.S. Army War College, 1967. No. 67135. U.S. Army Military History Institute, Carlisle Barracks, Pa.

Parker, Sally L. "Attendant Lords: A Study of the British Joint Staff Mission, 1941–1945." Ph.D. diss., University of Maryland, 1984.

Pavey, Kenneth G. "Command Problems in a Multi-national Force in Peace." Thesis, U.S. Army War College, 1955. No. 737. U.S. Army Military History Institute, Carlisle Barracks, Pa.

Powers, Thomas L. "The United States Army and the Washington Conference, 1921–1922." Ph.D. diss., University of Georgia, 1978.

Prete, Roy A. "The War of Movement on the Western Front, August–November 1914: A Study in Coalition Warfare." Ph.D. diss., University of Alberta, 1979.

Reagan, David R. "American-British Strategic Planning for Coalition Warfare prior to the Entrance of the United States in World War II." Ph.D. diss., Fletcher School of Law and Diplomacy, 1965.

Ropp, Theodore. "The Historical Development of Contemporary Strategy." Harmon Memorial Lecture in Military History no. 12. U.S. Air Force Academy, El Paso County, Colo., 1970.

Sievers, Harry L. "Evolution of Combined Action in Warfare." Thesis, U.S. Army War College, 1950–1951. No. 82. U.S. Army Military History Institute, Carlisle Barracks, Pa.

Simonds, Brigadier General George S. "Problems of Service with Allies." Lecture, 4 December 1931. File 382-A-8, G-2, no. 8. U.S. Army Military History Institute, Carlisle Barracks, Pa.

Thurman, Capt. Susie J., et al. (only first author listed). "SPOBS: The Special Observer Group prior to the Activation of the European Theater of Operations." October 1944. Mimeo, 242 pp. Charles L. Bolte Papers. U.S. Army Military History Institute, Carlisle Barracks, Pa.

Vann, Walter. "Command Problems in a Multi-national Force in War." Thesis, U.S. Army War College, 1955–1956. No. 1,000. U.S. Army Military History Institute, Carlisle Barracks, Pa.

Index

ABC-1 Report: areas of strategic responsibility and, 154, 155, 156–57; Atlantic cooperation and, 152, 154, 163, 174, 189, 204, 233; command structure and, 152–57, 174, 177, 180–81, 182–83, 184, 185, 205, 221, 227; Far East plans and, 151, 152, 154, 156–57, 177–81, 182–84, 185–86, 189, 204–5, 226, 227, 228; grand strategy and, 6, 151–55, 189–90, 203, 204, 209, 229–30; lines of communication and, 166, 169, 171–73, 181, 219–20, 249, 322nn43, 46, 335n4; Military Missions and, 152–53, 155, 166, 168–71, 172–75, 317n83; salient features and, 150–55, 316nn73, 75; securing Great Britain and, 151, 189, 190, 191, 239; unity of command and, 155, 166; U.S. air forces in Great Britain and, 167, 175, 206, 209, 214, 221; U.S. Army and, 163, 166–68, 174–77, 221–22, 323n61, 323–24n64, 324n66, 336–37n17; U.S.-British approval and, 158–59, 166, 183; U.S. military and, 152–55, 161, 183, 184–85, 205, 208, 214–15, 233, 239; U.S. naval bases in Great Britain and, 174, 176–77; U.S. war materiel and, 155, 189, 205, 213, 221–22

"ABC-2 Report on Air Collaboration," 150, 151, 155, 208, 213

Acheson, Dean, 56

ADB Report, 208, 209, 225, 226, 247, 326n107, 338–39n46; Far East plans and, 179–80; U.S. response and, 181–82, 183–84, 185, 186–87, 204–5, 215, 227, 228, 229

ADB-2 Report, 225–27, 228

Aiken, William A. "Max." *See* Beaverbrook, Lord

Air Power and Armies (Slessor), 125

Alanbrooke, Lord, 211, 231

Alexander, A. V., 142

Allen, A., 178

Allied Code Book (1919), 52

American-British Conversations (ABC-1), 2, 6, 161, 237, 238, 242, 308n74, 309n88, 310n1; ABC-1 Report approval and, 155, 158–59; American participants and, 132–35, 141, 142, 312n13; arrival of British participants and, 128, 131–32, 311n6; Atlantic cooperation and, 135, 139, 141, 142, 144, 145, 146–47, 148–50, 201, 315–16n60; command structure and, 138, 148, 149, 158; Far East plans and, 137, 138–41, 142–45, 146, 158, 230, 231, 314nn31, 35, 315nn41, 44, 315–16n60; grand strategy and, 135–37, 138, 158, 314n25; lines of communication and, 144, 218–19, 335n4; military vs. political decisions and, 142–43; securing Great Britain and, 141–42, 144, 145, 146–49, 315n55; strategic areas of responsibility and, 139, 158; U.S. war materiel and, 137–38, 147–48, 150. *See also* ABC-1 Report; U.S.-British coalition

American-Dutch-British (ADB) Conference, 178–81, 184, 185, 229, 325nn76, 88. *See also* ADB Report

American Expeditionary Force (AEF): unity of command and, 19, 20; U.S.-British cooperation, World

388   Index

American Expeditionary Force *(cont.)*
  War I and, 26, 27, 28; U.S.-French
  cooperation, World War I and,
  19–21, 27, 28–29, 276–77n99,
  277n103; World War I and, 11,
  26–29, 30, 35, 133, 167, 197,
  275n85, 276nn95, 97, 277n106
American War of Independence, 22, 35
Anglo-American coalition. *See* U.S.-
  British coalition
"Anglo-American Standardization of
  Arms Committee," 94–102, 105,
  106, 242, 301n64; results and,
  102–4
Anglo-Dutch-American Committee,
  114, 305–6n36
Anglo-French Entente Cordiale of 1904,
  12–13
Anglo-French Purchasing Commission,
  70, 75
Anglo-French relations, interwar years,
  60–62, 72, 75, 77, 250
Anglo-German Naval Treaty (1935), 43
Anglo-Russian Entente of 1907, 13
appeasement, 3, 43–44, 61, 67, 71–72,
  235, 291n4
Arcadia Conference (1941–42), 8, 249
Army National Guard of the United
  States, 8, 82, 240
Arnold, Henry H. "Hap," xv, 8, 219,
  220, 295n70; Atlantic Conference
  and, 194, 201, 205–6, 329n21;
  biography and, 197; U.S. aircraft
  and, 68–69, 70, 71, 76–77, 79, 205–
  6, 208
Arsenal of Democracy Speech
  (Roosevelt), 131, 237, 242
Associated Communications
  Committee. *See* London
  Communications Committee
Atlantic Charter, 193, 206, 215, 238,
  252
Atlantic Conference, 193–206,
  329nn21–22, 31, 331n56; Atlantic

cooperation and, 201–2, 220–21,
  237–38; Far East plans and, 208,
  210, 225; grand strategy and, 193,
  194–95, 201, 222; results and, 206–
  12, 214–15; securing Great Britain
  and, 194, 195, 200, 203; U.S. war
  materiel and, 205, 207–8
Australia, 43, 49; American-British
  Conversations (ABC-1) and, 138,
  139, 140, 141, 144; Far East plans,
  command structure and, 106–7, 120,
  139; Far East plans and, 111, 112,
  114, 119, 122, 181, 192, 225–26, 231
Austria, 72
Azores, 107, 135, 148, 163, 164, 203–4

Bailey, Sidney, xiii, 92, 106, 107, 108,
  113–14, 300–301n53
Bailey Committee, 92, 106, 107, 108–9,
  110–11, 128, 132, 304n6
Bailey Committee Report, 106–8, 109,
  304nn4, 11
Baker, Newton D., 12, 19–20
Baldwin, Stanley, 39, 42, 44, 278n4
Balfour, Arthur. *See* Riverdale, Lord
Balfour Mission, 26
Battle of Britain, 125, 147–48, 161, 162,
  241
Battle of Jutland (1916), 23, 198
Battle of the Frontier (August 1914), 15
Battle of the Somme (1916), 16
Bayly, Lewis, 25
Beaumont-Nesbitt, Frederick, xiii, 56,
  61, 168
Beauvais agreement, 20
Beaverbrook, Lord, xiii, 126, 128, 212,
  213, 214, 310n97
Belgium, 13, 15–16, 19, 30, 42, 199
Bellairs, Roger M., xiii, 113–15, 132,
  139, 142, 143, 150, 172, 214,
  305–6n36
Benson, William S., 22
Bingham, Robert, 45
Bismarck, 162, 164, 229, 232

Bismarck, Otto von, 12
Bliss, Tasker H., 17, 20, 21, 26
Blitz, 111, 223
Boer War (1899–1902), 12, 198
Bolshevik Revolution, 16
Bolte, Charles L., 168, 172, 177, 320n32
Borah, William E., 73, 287n41
Borneo, 116, 120, 231
Boxer Rebellion, 58, 297n12
Bradley, Omar, 133
Brazil, 85, 86, 149, 163–64, 204
Breckinridge, Henry S., 12
Briand, Aristide, 34
Bridges, Edward, 212
Bridges, Tom, 26
Brink, Frank, 178
British Admiralty, 81, 142; ABC-1 Report and, 174, 227; Bailey Committee and, 92, 106, 107, 108–9, 110–11, 128, 132, 304n6; Bailey Committee Report and, 106–8, 109, 304nn4, 11; intelligence and, 108, 128; interwar years and, 42, 50, 51, 52–53, 55, 57–58; U.S. relations, after fall of France, World War II and, 93–94, 102, 104, 105, 106, 238; U.S. relations, autumn 1940 and, 108–9, 110, 113–14, 117, 118, 128, 300–301n53; World War I and, 21, 22, 25, 198, 235. *See also* British First Sea Lord
British Admiralty Delegation, 169, 170, 226
British Army, 42, 60, 82, 100, 311n8; British Joint Staff Mission (BJSM) and, 169, 170; U.S. relations, after fall of France, World War II and, 89, 95, 98, 99, 103; U.S. relations, autumn 1940 and, 127; U.S. relations, early 1941 and, 148, 152–55; U.S. relations, interwar years and, 56–57, 61, 62, 63, 287–88n45; U.S. relations, mid-late 1941 and, 200–201, 218; U.S. war materiel and, 78, 88, 124, 309nn83–84; World War II, Dunkirk and, 81, 88, 193; World War II, mid-late 1941 and, 193, 195, 217. *See also* British Expeditionary Force (BEF); Dill, John
British Battle Fleet, 231
British Chiefs of Staff: ABC-1 Report and, 158, 204; ABC-1 Report implementation and, 167, 168–71, 172–73, 175; ADB Report and, 181, 182, 184, 185; American-British Conversations (ABC-1) and, 137; Anglo-French relations, interwar years and, 60, 61, 62; Atlantic Conference and, 196, 198, 202–3, 204, 208–9, 225; Far East plans and, 97, 111, 112–13, 114, 115, 184, 227, 306n45; lines of communication and, 219–20, 248, 249, 335n4; U.S. relations, after fall of France, World War II and, 92–93, 94, 97, 98, 102; U.S. war materiel and, 212; World War II, British strategy and, 98–101, 191–92, 193, 194–95, 209, 210, 328n13
British Chiefs of Staff Committee, 9, 135, 173, 175, 209, 267n31
British Eastern Fleet, 57, 120, 139, 178, 180, 205, 228, 231, 311n8
British Expeditionary Force (BEF): Anglo-French cooperation, interwar years and, 61–62; Anglo-French cooperation, World War I and, 13–14, 15–19, 30, 269–70n23; World War I, amalgamation of land forces and, 26, 27, 28, 29, 276n95, 276–77n99, 277n106; World War I aftermath and, 40–41, 278n4; World War II and, 11, 77, 81, 88, 100, 198
British Far Eastern Fleet. *See* British Eastern Fleet
British First Sea Lord, 9, 14, 25, 50, 108, 132, 142, 273n69; Pound as, 106, 198, 329n21, 330n36

British Fleet, 49, 52, 53, 92, 119, 120, 149, 174, 180
British Home Fleet, 57, 232
British Imperial Preference. *See* Imperial Preference
British Inter-Service Security Board, 219
British Joint Planning Committee, 112, 132, 172–73, 174–75, 181, 185, 186, 214; World War II, British strategy, mid-1941 and, 191, 222–24, 328n10
British Joint Planning Staff, 92, 93, 94, 98, 175
British Joint Staff Mission (BJSM), 173, 210, 219, 248, 253, 333n86; ADB Report and, 182, 227, 228; British Admiralty Delegation and, 169, 170, 226; British Army Staff, 169, 170, 218, 321n39; British Naval Staff, 118, 169, 183, 218; formation and, 90–91, 168–71, 172, 321n38; U.S. war materiel and, 205, 207, 217, 322–23n52
British Military Intelligence, 56, 287–88n45
British Nucleus Mission. *See* British Joint Staff Mission (BJSM)
British Purchasing Commission, 74, 75, 76, 89, 90, 124, 125, 128, 131, 212, 250, 299n37
British Review of Grand Strategy, 199, 202–3, 204, 209, 222, 224–25, 333n88, 337n25
British War Cabinet, 82, 111, 124, 127, 143, 196, 206, 207, 212, 231, 236
British War Office, 14, 92, 118, 132, 176, 198, 209, 323–24n64; U.S. relations, after fall of France, World War II and, 94, 102; U.S. relations, interwar years and, 56, 57, 61, 287–88n45; U.S. war materiel and, 89, 90
Brooke, Alan Francis. *See* Alanbrooke, Lord
Brooke-Popham, H. Robert, xiii, 178, 229

Brussels Conference (1937), 46, 47
Bullitt, William C., 68, 69, 70, 73, 75, 76
Burma, 180
Burma Road, 111
Burns, James, 73, 329n21, 334n107

Cadogan, Alexander, xiii, 50, 202, 329n21, 331n56
Cadorna, Luigi, 17
Canada, 74, 75, 112
Canadian Naval Intelligence Headquarters, 108
Canadian Purchasing Commission, 74
Canary Islands, 135, 200, 203
Caporetto, 16, 17, 18
Caroline Islands, 52
Carter, Boake, 206
Case, Homer, 168
cash-and-carry provision of U.S. Neutrality Acts, 66, 72, 73, 74, 75, 88–89, 131, 237
Chalmers, W. S., 106
Chamberlain, Austin, 37
Chamberlain, Joseph, 37
Chamberlain, Neville, xiii, 42, 54, 62, 81, 243, 278n4; appeasement and, 3, 43, 44, 67, 72, 291n4; Japan and, 44, 45, 49; Roosevelt, Franklin D. and, 37, 45, 46, 47, 66–67, 235, 255; U.S. public opinion and, 72–73; U.S. war materiel and, 75, 79
Chaney, James E., xv, 191–92, 209, 210, 213, 334n107; SPOBS and, 166–68, 175, 176, 177, 221–22, 336–37n17; USSOG in London and, 173, 175, 225
Chatfield, Ernle, xiii, 50–51, 53, 54
Chautemps, Camille, 67
Chemidlin, Paul, 70–71, 72
China, 11, 52, 179, 197, 210; Boxer Rebellion and, 58, 297n12; Japan, war with and, 3, 42, 43, 44, 45, 46, 49, 111, 283n78; U.S. war materiel and, 203, 252

Churchill, Winston S., xiii, 39, 280n42, 318n8, 322n46; British Army and, 199, 327n9, 330–31n38; Far East plans and, 231, 232; as first lord of the Admiralty and, 81, 235; as prime minister and, 9, 81–82, 235, 296nn4–5; Roosevelt meeting (Atlantic Conference) and, 193–99, 206–7, 211, 329nn21, 31; Roosevelt special relationship and, 4–5, 81, 211, 235–37, 241–42, 255, 299n29; U.S.-British coalition and, 2, 4, 5, 210, 211, 242–43, 252; U.S.-British relations, after fall of France, 91, 92, 103, 235, 241–42, 299nn29, 31; U.S.-British relations, autumn, 1940 and, 111, 126, 127, 310n94; U.S.-British relations, early 1941 and, 131, 132, 142–43, 146; U.S.-British relations, mid-1941 and, 163, 165, 190, 212; U.S. war materiel and, 83, 88, 103, 127–28, 212, 241, 242; World War II, British strategy, mid-1941 and, 190–93, 194–95
Chynoweth, Bradford G., 56–57, 288n46
Clarke, Arthur W., 171, 311n6, 321n40
Clemenceau, Georges, 16
coalition warfare: challenges of, 254–56, 266n26; defined, 1; naval vs. land force amalgamation and, 26, 275n85; prewar planning and, 14; United States and, 1, 256, 263n2; unity of command and, 7–8, 266–67n27. *See also* grand strategy; U.S.-British coalition; World War I
Cold War, 4, 236
Conner, Fox, 11, 30, 277n110
Cooke, Charles M. "Savvy," Jr., 133, 134, 313n16
Coolidge, Calvin, 39, 280n42
Craig, Malin, 71
Crimean War, 15
Crone, J. A., 56

Cunningham, Andrew B., 161
Curzon-Howe, L. C. A. St. J., 57, 106, 300–301n53
Czechoslovakia, 61, 69, 71, 72, 73, 288n48

Dahlquist, John E., 168, 172, 176
Daladier, Edward, 67, 69
Danckwerts, Victor H., xiii, 132, 139, 148, 150, 168, 182–83, 227, 311n8, 322n43
Daniel, C. S., 95
Dawes Plan of 1924, 34
de Lostende, Mercier, 14
Denfield, Louis, 176–77
Denmark, 77, 163
Deverell, Cyril, 60
Dewar, Michael B., 89
Dill, John, xiv, 98, 252, 327n9; Atlantic Conference and, 200, 204, 205, 209, 210–11, 329n21; British Army career and, 198–99, 330–31n38; British strategy, mid-1941 and, 190–91, 231
"diplomacy of the dollar," 34, 278n9
disarmament, 34–35, 42, 55
Doullens Conference (March 1918), 19
Dundas, J. G. L., 57
Dunkirk, 81, 88, 193, 241
Dykes, Vivian, xiv, 209, 224, 329n21

Eden, Anthony, xiv, 46, 50, 66, 67, 207, 285n9, 291n4
Egypt, 99, 111, 161, 162, 190, 200, 210
Eisenhower, Dwight D., 133, 312n12
Embick, Stanley D., xv, 132–33, 141, 142, 148, 311n9, 334nn107, 109
Emmons, Delos C., xv, 95–96, 102, 103, 104, 105, 301–2n69
Ethiopia, 42, 43, 60, 66, 161, 291n4
European Union, 70
Executive War Board of SWC, 18–19

Far East plans: ABC-1 Report and, 151, 152, 154, 156–57, 177–81, 182–84,

Far East plans *(cont.)*
185–86, 189, 204–5, 226, 227, 228;
American-British Conversations
(ABC-1) and, 137, 138–41, 142–45,
146, 158, 230, 231, 314nn31, 35,
315nn41, 44, 315–16n60; Atlantic
Conference and, 208, 210, 225;
Great Britain and, 97, 100–101,
109, 111, 114–15, 116, 117–23, 184,
192, 285n19, 306n45; Royal Navy
and, 101, 106–7, 117, 120, 138–41,
180–81, 230, 231–34, 285n19; U.S.
Army and, 227, 228, 229, 230, 231;
U.S.-British coalition and, 112–13,
117, 120, 123, 217, 225–34, 244,
245, 246–47, 248, 252, 254–55,
338n43, 339n52; U.S. Navy and,
113, 119, 135, 136, 139, 227, 243,
307–8n69. *See also* American-Dutch-
British (ADB) Conference; Australia;
Netherlands East Indies; New
Zealand; Singapore
First Battle of Ypres (Oct–Nov. 1914),
16, 21
Fisher, John "Jacky," 14
Five Powers Treaty, 39
Foch, Ferdinand, 13, 16–17, 18–19,
20–21, 28, 29, 30, 277n103
France, 84; Anglo-French cooperation,
pre-World War I and, 12–15,
268n11, 269nn19, 21; Anglo-French
cooperation, World War I and,
13–19, 26, 27, 28, 60, 269–70n23,
270n25; Anglo-French relations,
interwar years and, 60–62, 72, 75,
77, 250; cash-and-carry provision
of U.S. Neutrality Acts and, 66, 74,
75; interwar years and, 36–37, 42,
43, 292n9; U.S.-French cooperation,
World War I and, 19–21, 26,
27, 28–29, 276n97, 276–77n99,
277n103; U.S. war materiel and, 63,
65, 67–71, 73, 74, 75–77, 78–79,
250, 294n46, 295n69; World War I

and, 13–21, 26, 27, 28–29, 30, 35,
60, 69–70, 269–70n23; World War
II, fall of and, 57, 62, 70, 77, 79, 81,
82, 85, 87, 241, 296nn5–6; World
War II Vichy government and, 58,
88, 136, 163–64
Freeman, Wilfrid, xiv, 198, 199, 200,
201, 206, 329n21
French, John, 15, 17–18
French Air Force, 60, 292n9; U.S.
aircraft and, 67–71, 75–77, 78
French Army: Anglo-French
cooperation, World War I and,
13–14, 15–19, 28, 30, 60, 61, 62,
269–70n23, 270n25; U.S.-French
cooperation, World War I and,
19–21, 27, 28–29, 276n97, 276–
77n99, 277n103
French Indochina, 101, 111, 138, 241
French Navy, 14–15, 60, 62, 86, 88, 101,
269n21

Gamelin, Maurice, 62
General Allied Reserve (WWI), 18–19
Geneva Conference (1927), 39, 40
German Air Force (Luftwaffe), 43, 69,
102, 148, 224, 245, 292n9
German High Seas Fleet, 23
German Imperial Navy, 14
German Navy, 117
Germany: American-British
Conversations (ABC-1) and,
135, 136–37, 140, 151, 152; early
twentieth century and, 12–14;
interwar years and, 42, 43, 44,
46, 51, 57, 60, 61, 71–72, 288n48;
rearmament and, 43, 65, 288n48;
war materiel and, 66, 67, 69; World
War I aftermath and, 34, 71; World
War I and, 14, 15, 16, 18, 19, 21, 22,
23, 26, 28, 29, 30, 270n25; World
War II, Battle of the Atlantic and,
163, 189, 201–2; World War II,
British strategic bombing of and, xx,

147, 148, 189, 191, 195, 200, 203, 209, 218, 223–25, 337nn23, 25; World War II, fall of France and, 77, 81, 85, 88; World War II, invasion of Soviet Union and, 162, 190, 191, 192, 193, 194, 211, 224, 240, 241; World War II, Latin America and, 85–86, 87, 163–64, 204, 208, 218, 298n23; World War II, Poland invasion and, xix, 62, 74; World War II, Soviet Union, Stalingrad and, 243–44; World War II, vs. Great Britain and, 86, 98–101, 102–3, 111, 147–48, 164, 177, 191, 192–93, 194, 228, 236, 241; World War II and, xix, 3, 109, 117, 241
Gerow, Leonard T., xv, 133, 139–40, 149, 150, 311–12n10, 314n31
Ghormley, Robert L., xvi, 255; ABC-1 Report and, 159, 166, 227; American-British Conversations (ABC-1) and, 133, 146, 150; biography and, 96, 302n70; British relations, after fall of France, 95, 96, 101, 102, 104, 105–6, 238; British relations, autumn 1940 and, 108–11, 113–18, 119, 122, 128, 134–35; British relations, interwar years and, 57, 59; British relations, mid-1941 and, 191–92, 209, 210; USSOG in London and, 167–68, 173–74, 224, 225, 226, 337n23
Gibraltar, 100, 147, 148, 150, 162, 204
Gort, John V., 61
Graf Spee, 81
grand strategy, 255, 266n23; ABC-1 Report and, 6, 151–55, 189–90, 203, 204, 209, 229–30; American-British Conversations (ABC-1) and, 135–37, 138, 158, 314n25; Atlantic Conference and, 193, 194–95, 201, 222; British Review of Grand Strategy and, 199, 202–3, 204, 209, 222, 224–25, 333n88,

337n25; conversations, World War II, autumn 1940 and, 112–13, 116; defined, 7, 265n20, 265–66n21; military strategy vs., 7, 20, 245; World War I and, 20; World War II implementation and, 215, 243, 244–46, 250–52
Great Britain: Anglo-French cooperation, pre-World War I and, 12–15, 268n11, 269nn19, 21; Anglo-French cooperation, World War I and, 13–19, 26, 27, 28, 60, 61, 62, 269–70n23, 270n25; Anglo-French relations, interwar years and, 60–62, 72, 75, 77, 250; appeasement and, 3, 43–44, 61, 67, 71–72, 235, 291n4; British Review of Grand Strategy and, 199, 202–3, 204, 209, 222, 224–25, 333n88, 337n25; cash-and-carry provision of U.S. Neutrality Acts and, 66, 72, 73, 74, 75, 88–89; Far East plans and, 97, 100–101, 109, 111, 114–15, 116, 117–23, 184, 192, 285n19, 306n45; Japan and, 43, 44, 45, 49, 50, 52, 53, 54, 114–15, 116, 144, 281n49; Moscow Conference and, 214; rearmament and, 42, 44, 65; U.S. bases and, 167, 174, 176–77, 217, 220, 221; U.S. forces and, 135, 147, 149, 163, 175–77, 206, 209, 214, 217, 221, 245–46, 311–12n10; U.S. public opinion and, 72–73, 131–32, 136, 242; U.S. relations, after fall of France, World War II and, 91–104, 105–8, 123–24, 302n73, 303n94; U.S. relations, autumn 1940 and, 108–23, 307nn60, 62, 308n81; U.S. relations, interwar years and, 35–40, 44–48, 49–60, 61, 62–63, 66–67, 278n15, 280n42, 283nn70, 78, 291n4; U.S. relations, mid-1941 and, 168–77, 209–10, 321nn35, 40, 328n13, 336n13; U.S. war materiel, after fall of France, World War II

Great Britain *(cont.)*
and, 77–79, 83, 88–91, 92, 97, 99, 100, 101, 103, 238, 242, 299nn35, 37–38, 300nn39, 41; U.S. war materiel, autumn 1940, World War II and, 123–28, 308n81, 309nn83–84, 310n97; U.S. war materiel, early 1941 and, 136, 137–38, 147–48, 150, 165; U.S. war materiel, interwar years and, 63, 65, 66, 67, 69, 72; U.S. war materiel, late 1930s and, 73–74, 75–76, 294n46; U.S. war materiel, late 1941 and, 217, 218, 221–22, 223, 250, 252; U.S. war materiel, mid-1941 and, 175, 189, 191, 201, 205–6, 207–8, 212–14, 215, 322–23n52, 334nn107, 109; U.S. war plans and, 84, 85; war debts to U.S. and, 37–38, 47, 131; World War I aftermath and, 33–34, 40–41, 278n4, 281n53; World War I and, 13–19, 20, 21–27, 28, 29, 30, 31, 35, 38, 198, 269–70n23; World War II, Battle of Britain and, 125, 147–48, 161, 162, 241; World War II, Battle of the Atlantic and, 107, 109, 117, 139, 140, 162, 163, 189, 192, 201–2, 217, 229, 240; World War II, Blitz and, 111, 223; World War II, British strategy, mid-1941 and, 190–93, 194–95, 209–10, 222–25, 231, 243, 337nn23–24; World War II, Dunkirk and, 81, 88, 193, 241; World War II, fall of France and, 81, 82, 86, 87, 241, 296nn5–6; World War II, Far East and, 52, 109, 144, 231–34; World War II, Germany vs. and, 86, 98–101, 102–3, 111, 147–48, 164, 177, 191, 192–93, 194, 228, 236, 241; World War II, Italy and, 81, 88, 99, 100, 161–62, 218, 232, 241; World War II, Mediterranean theater and, 161, 162, 163, 189, 192, 193, 195, 215,

217, 231, 232, 309n88; World War II, Middle East theater and, 137, 147, 177, 191–92, 193, 194, 209, 210, 217; World War II, North Africa and, 88, 161, 162, 190, 193, 243; World War II, strategic bombing of Germany and, xx, 147, 148, 189, 191, 195, 200, 203, 209, 218, 223–25, 337nn23, 25; World War II outbreak and, 11, 60, 62, 63. *See also* American-British Conversations (ABC-1); American-Dutch-British (ADB) Conference; Atlantic Conference; British Admiralty; British Army; British Chiefs of Staff; British Joint Planning Committee; British Joint Staff Mission (BJSM); British Purchasing Commission; British War Cabinet; British War Office; Royal Navy; Singapore; U.S.-British coalition

Great Depression, 3, 36, 37, 43, 45, 47
Great War. *See* World War I
Great White Fleet, 12
Greece, 161–62
Greenland, 163
Greenly, J. H., 74, 75
Grierson, James, 13
Griner, George W., Jr., 168, 176, 324n66
Grumman Company, 78
Grunert, George, 178, 181, 185
Guam, 119, 120, 144

Haig, Douglas, 17, 18, 19, 27
Haining, Robert H., 94
Halifax, Lord, xv, 72, 92, 118, 131, 142, 143, 172
Hampton, T. C., xiv, 57–58, 59, 60, 106, 288–89n56
Handy, Thomas T., 42
Harriman, Averell, xvi, 191, 206, 212, 213–14, 329n21, 334n107
Harris, Arthur T., xiv, 69, 169, 219, 292n17

Harris, Charles T., 73
Hart, Thomas C., xvi, 146, 307–8n69; British relations, autumn 1940 and, 113, 121, 122, 123, 306n45; British relations, late 1941 and, 226, 228, 229–31, 232, 338n43, 339n52; British relations, mid-1941 and, 178, 179, 181, 184, 185, 205, 325n88
Hawaii, 87, 109, 119, 185, 233, 301–2n69, 302n70; American-British Conversations (ABC-1) and, 141, 144, 145; British-U.S. discussions, late 1930s and, 50, 51, 52, 53, 58, 59; Pearl Harbor attack, 225, 231, 235, 242, 243, 313n16
Herriot, Édouard, 36–37
Hitler, Adolf, 43, 69, 74, 75, 77, 82, 192, 236, 241
H.M.S. *Colossus*, 198
H.M.S. *Hood*, 162, 198
H.M.S. *Indomitable*, 230
H.M.S. *King George V*, 131
H.M.S. *Ladybird*, 49
H.M.S. *London*, 214
H.M.S. *Prince of Wales*, 52, 193, 195, 202, 230, 231
H.M.S. *Repulse*, 52, 198, 230, 231
Holland. *See* Netherlands
Hong Kong, 43, 52, 101, 119, 120, 144, 233
Hoover, Herbert, 36, 37, 39, 44
Hopkins, Harry, xvi, 164, 165, 171, 211, 212, 299n31, 322–23n52; British relations, mid-1941 and, 191–92, 193, 194, 206, 329n21
House, E. M., 28
Huguet, Victor, 13
Hull, Cordell, xvi, 91, 92, 142; British relations, autumn 1940 and, 111, 112, 113, 114; British relations, interwar years and, 44, 46–47, 50, 67

Iceland: British forces and, 135, 176, 203, 204; U.S. Army and, 135, 149, 175, 176, 202, 203, 204, 238, 239; U.S. Navy and, 146, 163, 174, 202, 206, 221
Ickes, Harold, xvi, 164
Imperial General Staff, 13, 94
Imperial General Staff, chief of, 9, 16, 41, 60, 198, 199, 211, 231
Imperial Japanese Navy, 123; Japanese Fleet, 41, 101, 117, 145, 180, 230, 232
Imperial Preference, 36, 44, 67, 252
India, 35, 144
Ingersoll, Royal E., xvi, 284–85n5; British relations, interwar years and, 49–50, 51, 53, 54–55, 56, 57, 58, 66, 94, 141, 230, 285n9
Inter-Service Communications Board, 219
Ireland, 35
Ironside, Edmund, 198
Isaacs, Rufus, 28
Ismay, Hastings, xiv, 94
isolationism, 34, 41, 44, 45–46, 55, 70, 75, 202, 238, 283n78, 286–87n38
Italian Fleet, 161–62, 232
Italian Navy, 117
Italy: American-British Conversations (ABC-1) and, 135, 137, 152; interwar years and, 42, 43, 44, 46, 60, 65, 66, 67, 288n48, 291n4; U.S.-British conversation, late 1930s and, 51, 57–58; World War I and, 16, 17, 18, 19; World War II, U.S.-British coalition and, xix, 3, 244, 245; World War II, vs. Great Britain and, 81, 88, 99, 100, 161–62, 218, 232, 241; World War II and, 85, 103, 109, 111, 117

Jacob, E. I. C., 196, 205, 329n21
Jacquin, Paul, 75
Japan: American-British Conversations (ABC-1) and, 138–39, 140–41, 142–43, 145, 151, 152, 315n41;

Japan *(cont.)*
American-Dutch-British (ADB) Conference and, 179–80, 181; China, war with and, 3, 42, 43, 44, 45, 46, 49, 111, 283n78; French Indochina occupation and, 101, 111, 138, 241; Great Britain and, 43, 44, 45, 49, 50, 52, 53, 54, 114–15, 116, 144, 281n49; Russo-Japanese War, 11–12; threat of war, 1930s and, 42, 43, 44, 45, 46, 49, 50, 52–53, 54, 57, 58, 59, 281n49, 288–89n56; threat of war, autumn 1940 and, 106, 109, 111, 112, 114–15, 116, 117, 119, 120, 122, 123; threat of war, 1941 and, 136, 189, 204, 217, 218, 230, 231, 232, 240, 241; threat of war, mid-1940 and, 81, 83, 84, 87, 88, 92, 97, 100–101; United States and, 45, 46, 49, 50, 53, 86, 111, 112, 114, 138, 283n78, 288n46; World War II, Pacific successes and, 120, 247, 288n46; World War II, Pearl Harbor and, 225, 231, 235, 242, 243, 313n16; World War II, Royal Navy losses and, 52, 231–33, 234; World War II, Singapore and, 109, 247; World War II, U.S.-British coalition and, xix, 3, 243
Japanese Fleet, 41, 101, 117, 145, 180, 230, 232
Joffre, Joseph, 14, 15, 17, 18, 26
Johnson, Hiram, 37, 287n41
Johnson, Louis, xvi, 73, 74, 77
Johnson Debt Default Act of 1934, 37–38, 131, 279n28
Joint Air Communications Board, 219
Joint Aircraft Committee, 124–25, 309n85
Jones, H. P., 40

Kellogg, Frank, 34
Kellogg-Briand Pact, 34
Kennedy, John, 172, 209

Kennedy, Joseph P., Sr., 56, 73, 94
Kerr, Phillip. *See* Lothian, Lord
Kessler, Harry, 29
King, Ernest J., xvi, 8, 196–97, 199, 203, 245, 252, 255, 320n32, 329n21, 330n34
Kirk, Alan G., xvi, 98, 114, 133, 134, 313n15
Kitchener, Horatio, 15, 17–18
Knox, William Franklin, xvi, 125, 159, 165, 171, 197, 212

La Chambre, Guy, 67
La Grange, Amoury de, 67–68
Lanrezac, Charles, 15
Latin America, 35, 85–86, 87, 163–64, 204, 208, 218, 298n23
Layton, Geoffrey, 122
Layton, Walter, 124, 228, 229, 308n81
League of Nations, 34, 35, 42, 132
Leahy, William D., xvi, 50, 51, 53, 54, 55, 57, 58, 59, 288n54, 288–89n56
Lee, Raymond E., xvi–xvii; British relations, after fall of France, 57, 94, 97, 98, 301n64; British relations, early 1941 and, 118, 132, 146; British relations, interwar years and, 56, 61; British relations, late 1941 and, 191–92, 209, 224–25, 337n24
LeHand, Marguerite "Missy," 165
LeLong, Albert, 61
Lend-Lease legislation, 131, 172, 177, 191, 202, 237, 242, 252, 322–23n52, 341n28; late 1941 and, 213, 217, 221–22, 336–37n17; passage of and, 165, 239
Lindsay, Ronald, xiv, 3, 46, 49, 50, 67, 74
Little, Charles, 169
Lloyd George, David, 16, 17, 18, 28, 29
Lodge, Henry Cabot, 35
London Communications Committee, 218–19, 220
London Naval Conference, 39–40, 132, 280n42

Lothian, Lord, xiv, 72, 74, 91, 92–93, 118, 131; U.S. relations, autumn 1940 and, 111, 112, 113, 114, 117
Ludendorff, Erich, 29
Ludlow, Louis, 55
Ludlow amendment, 55, 287n40
Luftwaffe. *See* German Air Force (Luftwaffe)
Luzon, 179, 180, 181, 184. *See also* Philippines

MacArthur, Douglas, xix, 228, 229–30, 231, 232, 338n43
MacDonald, Ramsay, 36, 39, 42
Mahan, Alfred Thayer, 12, 23
Malaya, 101, 115, 120, 121, 179, 180, 200, 231, 233, 247; Far East plans, early 1941, 138–39, 140, 144, 314n35
Malay Barrier, 117, 152, 181, 184, 186, 205, 226, 227, 231, 234; Far East plans, early 1941, 136, 139, 140, 144, 145
Malta, 15, 162
Manila. *See* Philippines
Marder, Arthur, 25
Marshall, George C., xvii, 68, 87, 95, 102, 111, 118, 252, 311n9; ABC-1 Report and, 158, 159, 166; ABC-1 Report implementation and, 167, 171, 178; ADB Report and, 182, 184, 228, 326n107; American-British Conversations (ABC-1) and, 136, 141, 142; Atlantic Conference and, 194, 200–201, 203–4, 205, 210–11, 329n21; biography and, 197–98, 330n35; Latin America, possible German military action and, 85–86, 163–64; as part of U.S. Chiefs of Staff and, 8, 133, 182, 197; U.S. war materiel and, 77, 79
Marshall Islands, 139, 145, 152
Martin, John, 207
Matejka, Jerry V., 168, 220

Mayo, Henry T., 24, 196
McBride, A. C., 178
McClelland, Harold M., 168
McCormick, Robert, 46
McDowall, L. R., 182
McNarney, Joseph T., xvii, 133, 149, 150, 168, 175, 176, 219, 225, 312n12
Mediterranean, 44, 52, 54, 198, 237, 246, 288n48; ABC-1 Report and, 151, 152; American-British Conversations (ABC-1) and, 136, 137, 139, 140, 148, 158; British strategy, 1940 and, 100, 101, 109, 116; World War II and, 161, 162, 163, 189, 192, 193, 195, 215, 217, 231, 232, 240, 244, 245, 309n88
Merchants of Death (Engelbrecht and Hanighen), 45
Mexico, 85, 95
Middle East, 138, 198, 244, 336–37n17; Atlantic Conference and, 200, 203, 204, 207, 209; British strategy and, 189, 190; World War II and, 137, 147, 177, 191–92, 193, 194, 210, 215, 217
Miles, Nelson, 133, 141–42, 149
Miles, Sherman, 133
Military Council of SWC, 16–17, 30
military strategy, 7, 20, 245
Milne, George, 41
Mitchell, William "Billy," 68
Moffat, J. Pierpont, 36
Monnet, Jean, 69–70, 76, 79, 124, 295n69
Monroe Doctrine, 83, 84
Morgenthau, Henry, xvii, 70, 71, 76, 79, 83, 125, 126, 165
Morocco, 13, 14, 162
Morris, Edwin L., xiv, 132, 149, 311n8
Moscow Conference, 214
Munich Crisis, 69, 72, 83, 288n48

National Defense Act of 1947, 9
Naval Act of 1916, 23

Naval Program of 1916, 38
Navy Hemisphere Plan 4, 202
Netherlands, 42, 111, 112, 113, 121–22, 123, 143, 144, 146, 210, 233, 241; American-Dutch-British (ADB) Conference, 178–81, 184, 185, 229, 325nn76, 88; Anglo-Dutch-American Committee, 114, 305–6n36; Royal Netherlands East Indies Fleet, 119, 140, 180, 229, 231; "U.S.-U.K.-Dutch Technical Conversations," 114, 132
Netherlands East Indies, 36, 53, 116, 120, 121, 122, 181, 184; American-British Conversations (ABC-1) and, 138, 139, 144, 145; late 1941 and, 210, 226, 307–8n69
Neutrality Act of 1935, 44, 66
Neutrality Act of 1936, 66
Neutrality Act of 1937, 57, 66, 70, 71, 72, 73, 74, 283n78, 294n51. *See also* cash-and-carry provision of U.S. Neutrality Acts
Neutrality Act of 1939, 74–75, 88–89, 124, 131, 237
Newall, Cyril, 98–100, 101, 102
New Deal, 55, 66, 72
Newfoundland, 193, 239
New Zealand, 43, 53, 181, 192, 226, 231; American-British Conversations (ABC-1) and, 140, 141, 144; Far East plans, autumn 1940 and, 106–7, 112, 114, 119, 120, 122
Nicaragua, 96
Nivelle, Robert, 18
Nivelle Offensive (1917), 27
North Africa, 85, 86, 98, 135–36, 152, 163, 194, 205, 223, 224; World War II, Great Britain and, 88, 161, 162, 190, 193, 243; World War II, U.S.-British coalition and, 237, 246, 312n12. *See also* Mediterranean
Norway, 77, 81

Nucleus Military Missions. *See* ABC-1 Report
Nye Committee, 45, 65

operational art, 7, 266n22
Operation Bolero, 221, 246
Operation Iraqi Freedom, 256
order of battle, 117

Pakenham-Walsh, Ridley, xiv, 89, 90, 91, 97, 299n38, 300nn39, 41
Palmer, Frederick, 12
Panama Canal, 53, 85
Paris Peace Conference, 38, 132
Paschendale, 16
Pearl Harbor attack, 225, 231, 235, 242, 243, 313n16
Peirse, Richard, 94, 97
Pershing, John J., 19–20, 26, 27, 28–29, 137, 197, 277n103
Pétain, Henri-Philippe, 17, 19, 27, 163–64
Pfeiffer, Omar T., 133, 134
Philippines, 20, 58, 68, 178, 196, 197, 288n46; Luzon and, 179, 180, 181, 184; threat by Japan and, 83, 116, 119, 120, 144, 179, 180, 200, 204, 210, 218; U.S. Asiatic Fleet and, 8, 52, 139, 180, 185, 308n70; U.S.-British coalition and, 228, 229–31, 232, 233, 247, 338n43
Phillips, Thomas V., xiv, 51, 57, 94, 97, 183; Far East plans, late 1941 and, 228–30, 231, 232, 338n43
Pirie, George W., 168
Plan Dog Memorandum, 116–17, 251
Plan XVII, 14
Pleven, Rene, 75, 76, 77
Poland, xix, 62, 71–72, 74
Portal, Charles, xv, 125, 126, 127, 172, 199
Pot of Gold war plan, 86, 298n22
Pound, Dudley, xv, 98, 101, 117, 118, 142, 227–28, 231, 330n36; Atlantic

Conference and, 198, 199, 200, 202–3, 204, 205, 329n21; as British First Sea Lord and, 106, 198, 329n21, 330n36
Pownall, Henry, 11, 61
Pratt, Douglas H., 89
Pratt, W. V., 40
President's Liaison Committee, 76, 295n62
Pringle, Joel, 25
Puerto Rico, 58
Purnell, William R., xvii, 121–22, 123, 178, 179, 308n70
Purvis, Arthur, xv, 75, 76, 77, 79, 89, 124, 125, 128, 212

Quarantine Speech (Roosevelt, 1937), 3, 45–46

Rainbow series war plans, 59, 83–85, 87, 114, 158–59, 227, 297n16
Ramsey, DeWitt C., 133, 134
Reading, marquess of. *See* Isaacs, Rufus
Repington, Charles á Court, 13
Rhineland, 43, 44, 60
Ridgway, Matthew B., 163–64
Riverdale, Lord, 73–74
Riviera (Churchill-Roosevelt meeting). *See* Atlantic Conference
Robertson, William, 16, 17, 18
Rome-Berlin Axis formation, 43
Rommel, Erwin, 162, 217, 243
Roosevelt, Eleanor, 165
Roosevelt, Franklin D., 228, 295n70; ABC-1 Report and, 159, 163, 183, 184; as assistant secretary of the navy and, 25, 58, 196, 235, 321n40; Atlantic Conference and, 193, 194, 195, 206–7, 215, 238; British relations, after fall of France and, 79, 82, 88, 91–93, 95, 102, 103–4, 105–6, 235, 238–39, 299n31; British relations, autumn 1940 and, 111, 113, 116, 117, 127; British relations, early 1941 and, 131–32, 136, 141, 159, 314n25; British relations, interwar years and, 3, 36–38, 45–47, 49–50, 53–54, 55, 58, 59, 66, 67, 72, 279n28, 283n78; British relations, late 1941 and, 220–21, 336n13; British relations, mid-1941 and, 171, 172, 177, 190, 191, 202, 237–38, 321n40; Churchill meeting (Atlantic Conference) and, 193–99, 206–7, 211, 329nn21, 31; Churchill special relationship and, 4–5, 81, 211, 235–37, 241–42, 255, 299n29; domestic policies, late 1930s and, 45, 55, 66, 72, 283n78, 287n41; France and, 67–69, 70–71, 76; isolationism and, 55, 77, 238; leadership style and, 9, 76, 87, 165–66, 172, 194, 195, 237, 238–39, 240, 303–4n1; neutrality and, 44, 57, 66, 71, 72, 73, 74, 238, 294n51; third term election and, 91, 113, 115–16, 127, 236; U.S. Army and, 240–41, 340n14; U.S.-British coalition, World War II and, 2, 4–5, 252; U.S. Navy and, 3, 51, 52, 55, 56, 58, 196, 197, 240; U.S. war materiel, after fall of France and, 79, 83, 88–89, 91, 103, 238; U.S. war materiel, autumn 1940 and, 125, 127–28; U.S. war materiel, interwar years and, 67–69, 70–71, 73, 74, 75, 76, 77, 294nn46, 51; U.S. war materiel, 1941 and, 165, 211, 212, 237, 322–23n52; war plans and, 85, 86–88, 159, 298n22; World War II entry possibility and, 4–5, 115–16, 136, 164–66, 190, 206–7, 237–41. *See also* United States; U.S.-British coalition
Roosevelt, Theodore, 11–12, 20, 22, 38
Royal Air Force (RAF): ABC-2 Report and, 150, 151, 155, 208, 213; British aircraft and, 88, 126, 127, 147–48, 199, 200, 201; interwar years and,

Royal Air Force *(cont.)*
41, 42, 60; U.S. aircraft, interwar years and, 67, 69, 77–78; U.S. aircraft, mid-1941 and, 201, 205–6, 208, 213–14; U.S. aircraft and, 97, 99, 100, 124–28, 135, 136, 147, 155, 299n35, 333n86; U.S. relations, after fall of France, World War II and, 94, 95, 98, 99, 100, 103; U.S. relations, autumn 1940 and, 125–28, 309n85; U.S. relations, early 1941 and, 133, 135, 136, 138, 147–48, 155; U.S. relations, mid-late 1941 and, 177, 205–6, 219; World War II, Battle of Britain and, 125, 147–48; World War II, fall of France and, 81, 88, 102, 103; World War II, U.S.-British coalition and, xix–xx, 9, 245, 253; World War II and, 193, 217, 292n17, 309n88

Royal Air Force (RAF) Delegation, 169

Royal Navy: Anglo-French cooperation, pre-World War I and, 14–15, 269n21; Anglo-French cooperation, pre-World War II and, 60, 62; areas of strategic responsibility and, 53, 59, 107, 110, 113, 119, 128, 146, 154; Atlantic Conference and, 199–200, 203, 205, 220; British Eastern Fleet, 57, 120, 139, 178, 180, 205, 228, 231, 311n8; British Fleets, 49, 52, 53, 57, 92, 119, 120, 149, 174, 180, 231, 232; command structure and, 50–51, 107, 110, 138, 166, 182, 205, 227; Far East plans and, 101, 106–7, 117, 120, 138–41, 180–81, 230, 231–34, 285n19; interwar years and, 41, 42, 43, 44, 46; lines of communication and, 52–53; loss of British shipping and, 102, 146, 162, 163, 174, 202, 203, 213, 318n8; protecting British shipping and, 110, 115, 128, 131, 139, 146–47, 148–49, 150, 174, 192; U.S. cooperation, World War I and, 21–27, 107, 108, 110, 166, 273n69; U.S. relations, after fall of France, World War II and, 86, 91–97, 98–102, 103, 104, 105–8, 236, 242, 304nn4, 6, 11; U.S. relations, after outbreak of World War II and, 81, 83; U.S. relations, autumn 1940 and, 108–11, 112–18, 128, 242, 300–301n53; U.S. relations, early 1941 and, 134–35, 137, 138, 139, 145, 146–47, 148–49, 150, 152–55, 163; U.S. relations, interwar years and, 3, 38–40, 47, 49–60, 62–63, 280n42, 280–81n45, 285nn9, 19, 286nn22, 32, 288–89n56; U.S. relations, mid-late 1941 and, 166, 168, 183, 211–12, 217, 218, 220–21, 227–29, 245, 322n43; World War I and, 15, 24–25, 198; World War II, Battle of the Atlantic and, 107, 109, 117, 139, 140, 162, 163, 192, 217, 229, 240; World War II, fall of France and, 81, 86, 88; World War II, losses to Japan and, 52, 231–33, 234; World War II, Mediterranean theater and, 161, 162, 217, 231, 232. *See also* American-British Conversations (ABC-1); British Admiralty; U.S.-British coalition

Royal Netherlands East Indies Fleet, 119, 140, 180, 229, 231

Russia, 16, 18. *See also* Soviet Union

Russo-Japanese War, 11–12

Schlieffen Plan, 14
Scott, Hugh, 26
Second World War, The (Churchill), 4, 82, 236, 243, 318n8, 327n9
Sims, William S., 21–23, 24, 25–26, 107, 108, 166, 196, 273n69, 275n84
Sinclair, Archibald, 126
Singapore: ADB conference and, 178–81, 184, 325n76; conference, 1940 and, 111, 112, 113, 114; Far

East plans, after fall of France, 100, 101; Far East plans, autumn 1940 and, 109, 111, 114, 115, 116, 117–18, 119–23, 307nn60, 62; Far East plans, early 1941 and, 135, 136, 137, 138, 139, 140, 141, 142–44, 145, 314n31; Far East plans, interwar years and, 49, 51–52, 53, 54, 58, 288–89n56; Far East plans, late 1941 and, 226, 228–29, 230, 231, 232, 233–34, 246–47, 252, 338n43; Far East plans, mid-1941 and, 180, 181, 185, 186, 192, 194, 200, 210; second conference, autumn 1940 and, 119–22, 307n60; World War II and, 109, 233, 247
Six Division Plan, 27
Slessor, J. C., xv, 95, 125–28, 132, 143, 150, 305–6n36, 309n88
Smith, Walter Bedell, xix, 83
South Africa, 252
Soviet Union, xix, 3, 43, 86, 97, 237; Moscow Conference and, 214, 334n107; U.S. war materiel, Atlantic Conference and, 201, 203, 207–8, 211, 212; U.S. war materiel and, 190, 191, 193–94, 213, 214, 222, 252, 334n107, 336–37n17; World War II, invasion by Germany and, 162, 190, 191, 192, 193, 194, 211, 224, 240, 241; World War II, Stalingrad and, 243–44. *See also* Russia
Spanish-American War (1898), 11, 12, 20, 58, 133
Spanish Civil War, 43, 66
Stalin, Joseph, 190, 193, 212, 237
Stanley, Oliver, 174–75
Stark, Harold R., xvii, 86, 87, 95, 245, 302n70, 329n21; ABC-1 Report and, 158, 159, 166, 171; ABC-1 Report implementation and, 174, 178, 179; ADB Report and, 179, 182, 184, 226, 227–28; American-British Conversations (ABC-1) and, 136–37, 141, 150, 314n25; Atlantic Conference and, 194, 196, 200, 203, 204; biography and, 196, 329–30n33; British relations, autumn 1940 and, 108–9, 111, 114, 115–17, 118, 251, 306n45; British relations, early 1941 and, 122, 123; British relations, late 1941 and, 226, 227–28, 238; Plan Dog Memorandum and, 116–17, 251; as U.S. Chief of Naval Operations (CNO) and, 8, 105–6, 116–17, 166, 182, 196, 197, 255, 329–30n33
Stevenson Plan of 1922 (UK), 36
Stimson, Henry L., xvii, 37, 90, 102, 125, 158–59, 164, 165, 171, 212, 308n81
Strong, George V., xvii, 90, 95, 96, 97, 99, 101–2, 103, 104, 105, 301–2n69
Suez Canal, 162
Supreme War Council (SWC), 16–17, 18–19, 20, 30, 31, 62, 132

Taft, William Howard, 21–22
tanks, 89, 200, 201, 214
Ten-Year Rule, 41, 281n49, 296n4
Thomas, A. C., 119, 120–21, 307n60
Tinkham, George, 206
Tobey, Charles W., 202
Treaties of Locarno of 1925, 60
Tripartite Pact, 111, 112
Truk, 52
Turner, Richmond Kelly, xvii, 182–83, 226–27, 245, 252, 255, 338n43; American-British Conversations (ABC-1) and, 138, 139–40, 141, 142, 143, 147, 148–49, 150, 315n44; Atlantic Conference and, 200, 204, 205, 329n21; biography and, 133–34, 312–13n14

United States: aircraft industry and, 68, 78–79, 82, 86, 155; anti-interventionism and, 55, 72, 75, 82,

402   Index

United States (cont.)
131, 202, 206, 286–87n38; British relations, after fall of France and, 91–104, 105–8, 123–24, 302n73, 303n94; British relations, autumn 1940 and, 108–23, 307nn60, 62, 308n81; British relations, interwar years and, 35–40, 44–48, 49–60, 61, 62–63, 66–67, 278n15, 283nn70, 78, 291n4; British relations, mid-1941 and, 168–77, 191–92, 209–10, 243, 321nn35, 40, 328n13, 336n13; British war debts and, 37–38, 47, 131; coalition warfare and, 1, 256, 263n2; conscription and, 163, 202, 207, 240; disarmament and, 34–35, 55; isolationism and, 34, 41, 44, 45–46, 55, 70, 75, 77, 202, 238, 283n78, 286–87n38; Japan and, 11–12, 45, 46, 49, 50, 53, 86, 111, 112, 114, 138, 283n78, 288n46; Latin America, possible German military action and, 85–86, 87, 163–64, 204, 208, 218, 298n23; neutrality and, 12, 22, 38, 44, 59, 65–66; noninterventionism and, 55, 65, 71, 73, 164–65, 286–87n38, 293–94n38; rearmament and, 65, 88, 89, 161, 193, 200; war materiel and, 39, 65, 66, 77, 79, 89–90, 97, 123–28, 193–94, 203, 214, 293–94n38; war plans and, 59, 83–85, 86–88, 114, 116–17, 158–59, 227, 297nn12, 16, 298n22; World War I aftermath and, 33–35, 41–42, 55, 282n56; World War I and, 12, 17, 19–20, 21–27, 45, 56, 58, 65, 96, 132, 133, 165, 167, 197, 321n40; World War II and, 78, 167, 221, 231–34, 288n46, 302n70, 308n70, 311–12n10, 312n12, 312–13n14, 313n15. See also American-British Conversations (ABC-1); Atlantic Conference; Roosevelt, Franklin D.;
U.S. Army; U.S. Army Air Corps; U.S. Army Air Force; U.S.-British coalition; U.S. Navy
Uruguay, 86
U.S. Army, 12, 82–83, 127; ABC-1 Report and army mission and, 166–68, 174–76, 323n61, 323–24n64, 324n66, 336–37n17; British relations, after fall of France, 89, 95, 98, 99, 103; British relations, early 1941 and, 132–33, 136, 147, 148, 149; British relations, interwar years and, 56–57, 61, 62, 63, 287–88n45; British relations, mid-late 1941 and, 200–201, 203–4, 218; Far East plans and, 227, 228, 229, 230, 231; forces to Great Britain and, 135, 147, 149, 163, 167, 175–77, 217, 221, 245–46, 311–12n10; Iceland and, 135, 175, 176, 202, 203, 204, 238, 239; interwar years and, 41–42, 45, 197–98, 282nn56, 58; mobilization and, 148, 162–63, 193, 203–4, 205, 207, 208, 211–12, 217, 218, 240, 244; rearmament and, 78, 85, 163, 189, 200, 203; Roosevelt and, 240–41, 340n14; unilateralism and, 83, 84, 297n12; World War II, U.S.-British coalition and, 2, 7, 8, 245–46, 251–52, 311–12n10, 312n12, 341n26. See also American Expeditionary Force (AEF); Marshall, George C.
U.S. Army Air Corps, 8, 95–96; ABC-2 Report and, 150, 151, 155, 208, 213; aircraft and, 68, 70, 71, 76–77, 82, 125, 127, 135, 136, 149, 155, 299n35; British relations, autumn 1940 and, 125–28, 309n85; British relations, early 1941 and, 133, 135, 136, 138, 147–48, 149, 155; interwar years and, 42, 45; mobilization and, 163; rearmament and, 136, 155. See also ABC-1 Report
U.S. Army Air Force: aircraft and, 200–

201, 203, 208, 213; bases in Great Britain and, 206, 209, 214, 217, 221; British relations, mid-late 1941 and, 205–6, 219; mobilization and, 207, 208, 217, 218, 240; World War II, U.S.-British coalition and, xix–xx, 8, 245, 253
U.S. Army Chief of Staff (CSA), 8, 26, 197
U.S. Army-Navy Munitions Board, Clearance Committee, 76
U.S. Army Organized Reserves, 8, 82. *See also* Army National Guard of the United States
U.S. Army War College, 30, 96, 132, 133, 277n110, 282n58
U.S. Army War Plans Division (WPD), 42, 90, 95, 118, 133, 163, 166, 218, 282n58, 311–12n10
U.S. Asiatic Fleet, 121, 307–8n69; American-British Conversations (ABC-1) and, 139–40, 141, 146; Far East plans, autumn 1940 and, 113, 119; Far East plans, mid-1941 and, 179, 180, 183, 185, 205, 226; Philippines and, 8, 52, 139, 180, 185, 308n70
U.S. Atlantic Fleet, 8, 24, 121, 196, 197, 284–85n5
U.S.-British coalition: areas of strategic responsibility and, 112–13, 128, 136–37, 249; chronology and, 257–60; command structure and, 226, 227, 228, 248, 249, 326n107; European outbreak of World War II and, 62, 63, 264n9; fall of France and, 77–78, 79, 82, 91, 92, 103, 296n6; Far East plans and, 112–13, 117, 120, 123, 217, 225–34, 244, 245, 246–47, 248, 252, 254–55, 338n43, 339n52; interwar years and, 44–45, 54–55, 57–58, 62–63, 72–74, 76, 83–85, 281–82n55, 283n70, 286n32; late 1941 and, 217– 18, 221, 222; lines of communication and, 6, 218, 219–20, 248, 251; Operation Iraqi Freedom and, 256; personnel and, xiii–xvii, 2–3, 4–5, 210–11, 235–37, 241–42, 251–53; unity of command and, 7–8, 50–51, 112–13, 120, 251–52; U.S. war materiel and, 212, 215, 244, 245, 249–51; World War I, aftermath and, 29–31, 33–34; World War I, naval cooperation and, 21–27, 107, 108, 110, 166, 273n69; World War I and, 6, 26, 27, 28, 31, 35, 155; World War II, defeat of Italy and, xix, 3, 244, 245; World War II, Germany, strategic bombing and, 244, 245, 251; World War II, successes and, xix–xx, 3, 246, 253–54; World War II, U.S. entry and, 1, 3, 8, 210–11, 235, 237, 243–44, 249; World War II, vs. Japan and, xix, 3, 243. *See also* ABC-1 Report; American-British Conversations (ABC-1); American-Dutch-British (ADB) Conference; *armed forces of US and UK;* Atlantic Conference; Churchill, Winston S.; grand strategy; Great Britain; Roosevelt, Franklin D.; United States
U.S.-British Staff Conversations. *See* American-British Conversations (ABC-1)
U.S. Chief of Naval Operations (CNO), 22, 182; Leahy, William D. as, 50, 58; Stark, Harold R. as, 8, 105–6, 116–17, 166, 182, 196, 197, 255, 329–30n33
U.S. Chiefs of Staff, 8–9, 92–93, 321n35; ABC-1 Report implementation and, 168–71, 172, 173, 175; ADB Report and, 183–84, 247; ADB-2 Report and, 227, 228; American-British Conversations (ABC-1) and, 135, 136; Atlantic Conference and, 196, 202–3, 209,

U.S. Chiefs of Staff *(cont.)*
225; British strategy, mid-1941 and, 191, 192, 209–10, 222–23, 224, 328n13; lines of communication and, 219–20, 248, 249, 335n4
U.S. conscription law, 163, 202, 207, 240
U.S. Constitution, 55
U.S. Department of State, 57, 67, 143
U.S. Department of the Navy, 8, 57, 96, 218, 338n43; Far East plans and, 118, 119, 229, 231; intelligence and, 108; war materiel and, 39, 69
U.S. Fleet, 8, 23, 87, 134; Far East plans, autumn 1940 and, 106, 109, 110, 112, 115, 116, 117, 119, 121, 123; Far East plans, interwar years and, 50, 52, 53–54; interwar years and, 38, 39, 49, 58, 96
U.S. Fleet Battle Force, 8, 58, 96, 134, 196
U.S. Fleet Scouting Force, 8
U.S. Joint Army-Navy Board, 132, 134, 135, 158, 159, 171, 182, 219, 246
U.S. Joint Planning Committee of the Joint Army-Navy Board, 83, 85, 86, 171, 321–22n42
U.S. Marine Corps, 8, 133, 204
U.S. Military Academy, 133
U.S. Naval Academy, 58, 121, 134, 196
U.S. Naval Forces in European Waters, 24, 25
U.S. Naval War College, 21, 96, 134, 196
U.S. Navy, 12; ABC-1 Report and, 163, 174, 176–77; aircraft and, 78, 103; areas of strategic responsibility and, 53, 59, 107, 110, 112–13, 119, 128, 146, 148, 154; Atlantic Conference and, 199–200, 201–2, 203, 205, 220; Atlantic cooperation with Royal Navy and, 107, 109, 117, 145, 201–2, 217, 220–21, 229, 237–38, 240, 245; British cooperation, World War I

and, 21–27, 107, 108, 110; British relations, after European outbreak of World War II and, 81, 83; British relations, after fall of France, 86, 91–97, 98–102, 103, 104, 105–8, 304nn4, 6, 11; British relations, autumn 1940 and, 108–11, 112–18, 128, 132, 242; British relations, early 1941 and, 134–35, 136, 137, 138, 139, 141, 145, 146–47, 148–49, 150, 152–55, 163; British relations, interwar years and, 3, 38–40, 47, 49–60, 62–63, 141, 280n42, 280–81n45, 285nn9, 19, 286nn22, 32, 288–89n56; British relations, mid-late 1941 and, 166, 168, 183, 211–12, 217, 218, 220–21, 227–29, 322n43; command structure and, 7, 50–51, 107, 110, 138, 166, 182, 205, 227; Far East plans and, 113, 119, 135, 136, 139, 227, 243, 307–8n69; Iceland and, 146, 163, 174, 202, 206, 221; interwar years and, 42, 43, 45, 49, 82; lines of communication and, 52–53, 172; protecting British shipping, early 1941 and, 135, 146–47, 150, 163; protecting British shipping, late 1941 and, 214, 217, 218, 220–21, 229, 240, 336n13; protecting British shipping, mid-1941 and, 174, 189, 192, 201–2, 203, 206, 207, 237–38, 239; U.S. Atlantic Fleet, 8, 24, 121, 196, 284–85n5; U.S. naval bases in Great Britain and, 174, 176–77, 220, 221; World War I and, 23–25, 38, 50, 96, 134, 196, 275n85; World War II and, 252, 284–85n5, 302n70, 307–8n69, 308n70, 311n8, 312–13n14, 313nn15–16, 329–30n33. *See also* U.S. Asiatic Fleet; U.S.-British coalition; U.S. Fleet; U.S. Pacific Fleet
U.S. Navy Patrol Force, 197

U.S. Navy Scouting Force, 58, 121
U.S. Navy War Plans Division (WPD), 50, 96, 118, 133, 134, 312–13n14
U.S. Pacific Fleet, 8, 54, 101, 116, 117, 120, 121, 134, 139, 140, 144, 179; American-British Conversations (ABC-1) and, 141, 145, 152
U.S.S. *Astoria*, 134
U.S.S. *Augusta*, 195, 199
U.S.S. *Greer*, 221, 336n13
U.S.S. *Lexington*, 196
U.S.S. *Missouri*, xix
U.S.S. *Nevada*, 96
U.S.S. *New Orleans*, 121
U.S.S. *Oklahoma*, 96
U.S.S. *Oregon*, 58
U.S.S. *Panay*, 49, 55
U.S.S. *Patterson*, 196
U.S. Special Army Observer Group (SPOBS), 166–67, 172, 174–75, 176, 177, 221, 222, 312n12, 320n32, 323–24n64, 324n66, 336–37n17
U.S. special naval observer (SPENAVO), 95, 102, 166, 167, 172, 174, 220
U.S. Special Observer Group (USSOG), 185, 194, 217, 220, 248, 320n32; ABC-1 Report implementation and, 173–75, 176–77, 221; British strategy, mid-1941 and, 222, 224–26, 337nn23–24; lines of communication and, 172, 173, 219; structure and, 167–68
U.S.S. *Quincy*, 86
U.S. Staff Committee, 141, 142, 143
U.S.S. *Terry*, 196
U.S. Strategic Air Forces Europe, 245
U.S.S. *Tuscaloosa*, 195
U.S. Supreme Court, 55, 72, 287n41
U.S.S. *Wichita*, 86
"U.S.-U.K.-Dutch Technical Conversations," 114, 132
U.S. War Department, 8, 27, 42, 56, 96, 105, 133, 136, 212, 336–37n17; ABC-1 Report implementation and, 168, 176, 177, 218, 221; U.S. war materiel and, 69, 70–71, 73, 74, 76, 77, 89, 90, 124, 127, 211, 221–22
U.S. War Department General Staff, 127, 132, 133, 197, 252–53, 301–2n69

Vansittart, Robert, 44–45, 66
Venezuela, 12
Vera Cruz, 133, 196
Verdun, 16
Versailles Peace Conference, 24
Versailles Peace Treaty, 29, 34, 35, 38, 43
Victory Program, 212
Virginia Military Institute, 133, 197
Vogel, Frank, 218

Ward, Orlando, 127
war materiel: China and, 203, 252; France and, 63, 65, 67–71, 73, 74, 75–77, 78–79, 250, 294n46, 295n69; Germany and, 66, 67, 69; U.S.-British coalition and, 212, 215, 244, 245, 249–51. *See also* Great Britain; Roosevelt, Franklin D.; Soviet Union; United States; U.S. War Department
Washington, George, 11
Washington Naval Conference of 1921–1922, 38
Washington Naval Treaty of 1922, 24, 39
Watson, Edwin M., 83, 159
Weir, J. G., 69
Welles, Sumner, xvii, 93, 329n21
Wemyss, Henry C. B., 169
Wemyss, Rosslyn, 25
Wesson, Charles M., 90, 300n39
Westover, Oscar, 68
West Point, 20, 56, 68, 95, 96, 133, 167
Weygand, Maxime, 16–17
Wheeler, Burton, 202, 287n41
Wilhelm II, 12

Willson, Russell, xvii, 50, 51, 52, 54, 55, 57
Wilson, Henry, 13, 14, 17
Wilson, Woodrow, 12, 17, 20, 22, 23–24, 26, 27, 28, 29, 35, 38, 165
Wood, Edward F. L. *See* Halifax, Lord
Woodring, Henry H., xvii, 70, 73, 74, 76, 77, 79
Woodward, David R., 25
World Disarmament Conference (1933), 42
World Economic Conference (1933), 36–37, 44
World War I, 125, 198; amalgamation of land forces and, 21, 26–29, 276nn95, 97, 276–77n99, 277nn103, 106; Anglo-French cooperation and, 13–19, 60, 61, 62, 269–70n23, 270n25; British shipping losses and, 146; coalition warfare and, 11, 15–21, 269–70n23; grand strategy and, 20; Royal Navy and, 15, 24–25, 198; submarine warfare and, 21, 23, 24, 38, 121; United States and, 12, 17, 19–20, 21–27, 45, 56, 58, 65, 96, 132, 133, 165, 167, 197, 321n40; unity of command and, 15–16, 17–21, 24–25, 30, 31, 137, 269–70n23, 270n25, 272–73n62; U.S.-British coalition and, 6, 26, 27, 28, 31, 35, 155; U.S.-British naval cooperation and, 21–27, 107, 108, 110, 166, 273n69; U.S.-French cooperation and, 19–21, 26, 27, 28–29, 276n97, 276–77n99, 277n103; U.S. Navy and, 23–25, 38, 50, 96, 134, 196, 275n85. *See also* Germany
World War II: France, fall of and, 57, 62, 70, 77, 79, 81, 82, 85, 87, 88, 241, 296nn5–6; France, Vichy Government and, 58, 88, 136, 163–64; hindsight and, 5–6, 85, 120, 145–46, 232, 237–38, 247–48, 315n41; Pearl Harbor attack, 225, 231, 235, 242, 243, 313n16; submarine warfare and, 102, 107, 131, 164, 192, 284–85n5, 336n13; United States and, 78, 167, 221, 232–34, 288n46, 302n70, 308n70, 311–12n10, 312n12, 312–13n14, 313n15. *See also* Far East plans; Germany; Great Britain; Italy; Japan; Royal Air Force (RAF); Royal Navy; Soviet Union; U.S.-British coalition; U.S. Navy
Wright, Peter, 31

Young Plan of 1929–1930, 34
Yugoslavia, 162

CPSIA information can be obtained at www.ICGtesting.com
Printed in the USA
BVOW08*2118140716
455607BV00002B/2/P